Unsettling the Great White North

Black Canadian History

EDITED BY MICHELE A. JOHNSON
AND FUNKÉ ALADEJEBI

UNIVERSITY OF TORONTO PRESS
Toronto Buffalo London

© University of Toronto Press 2022
Toronto Buffalo London
utorontopress.com

ISBN 978-1-4875-2916-1 (cloth)   ISBN 978-1-4875-2919-2 (EPUB)
ISBN 978-1-4875-2917-8 (paper)   ISBN 978-1-4875-2918-5 (PDF)

Library and Archives Canada Cataloguing in Publication

Title: Unsettling the Great White North : Black Canadian history / edited by Michele A. Johnson and Funké Aladejebi.
Names: Johnson, Michele A., editor. | Aladejebi, Funké, 1983– editor.
Description: Includes bibliographical references.
Identifiers: Canadiana (print) 20210321628 | Canadiana (ebook) 20210321733 | ISBN 9781487529178 (softcover) | ISBN 9781487529161 (hardcover) | ISBN 9781487529192 (EPUB) | ISBN 9781487529185 (PDF)
Subjects: LCSH: Blacks – Canada – History. | LCSH: Blacks – Canada – Social conditions. | CSH: Black Canadians – History. | CSH: Black Canadians – Social conditions.
Classification: LCC FC106.B6 U57 2022 | DDC 971/.00496–dc23

We wish to acknowledge the land on which the University of Toronto Press operates. This land is the traditional territory of the Wendat, the Anishnaabeg, the Haudenosaunee, the Métis, and the Mississaugas of the Credit First Nation.

University of Toronto Press acknowledges the financial support of the Government of Canada and the Ontario Arts Council, an agency of the Government of Ontario, for its publishing activities.

 Canada Council for the Arts   Conseil des Arts du Canada

 ONTARIO ARTS COUNCIL
CONSEIL DES ARTS DE L'ONTARIO
an Ontario government agency
un organisme du gouvernement de l'Ontario

 Funded by the Government of Canada   Financé par le gouvernement du Canada   Canadä

 Slavery Memory Citizenship

 SPACE — SPOTLIGHTING AND PROMOTING AFRICAN CANADIAN EXPERIENCES

SSHRC ≡ CRSH

Contents

Redacted Text, 2019: *Statement from the Artist* ix
CHANTAL GIBSON

Introduction 3
MICHELE A. JOHNSON AND FUNKÉ ALADEJEBI

BOOKEND I. The Future Has a Past: Canadian History and Black Modernity

1 Critical Histories of Blackness in Canada 31
   BARRINGTON WALKER

Section One. Enslaving Blackness

2 Planting Slavery in Nova Scotia's Promised Land, 1759–1775 53
   KAROLYN SMARDZ FROST

3 Where, Oh Where, Is Bet? Locating Enslaved Black Women on the Ontario Landscape 85
   NATASHA HENRY

Section Two. Constructing Blackness across Borders and Boundaries

4 A Forgotten Generation: African Canadian History between Fugitive Slaves and World War I 115
   ADAM ARENSON

5 Petitioning Power: Canadian Racial Consciousness
   Meets Alabama Injustice, 1958   140
   WENDELL NII LARYEA ADJETEY

**Section Three. Building Black Communities
and Shaping Black Resilience**

6 The Shiloh Baptist Church: The Pillar of Strength
   in Edmonton's African American Community   169
   DAVID ESTE AND JENNA BAILEY

7 Establishing Communities   194
   AMOABA GOODEN

8 Montreal's Black Renaissance   222
   SEAN MILLS

Section Four. Controlling Black (Working) Bodies

9 "Likely to become a public charge": Examining Black
   Migration to Eastern Canada, 1900–1930   257
   CLAUDINE BONNER

10 "... not likely to do well or to be an asset to this country":
   Canadian Restrictions of Black Caribbean Female
   Domestic Workers, 1910–1955   280
   MICHELE A. JOHNSON

Section Five. "Schooling" Black Canadians

11 Stories from *The Little Black School House*   313
   SYLVIA D. HAMILTON

12 Black Education: The Complexity of Segregation in Kent
   County's Nineteenth-Century Schools   333
   DEIRDRE McCORKINDALE

13 "We have to strive for the best": The High Aspirations of Black
   Caribbean Canadian Youth of the 1970s and 1980s   357
   CARL E. JAMES

**Section Six. Creating New Diasporic Communities:
Continental African Experiences**

14 Creating Spaces of Belonging: Building a New African
   Community in Vancouver   383
   GILLIAN CREESE

15 "The part of you that's Rwanda": Creating a Rwandan
   Diaspora Community in the Greater Toronto Area
   in the Early Twenty-First Century   402
   ANNA AINSWORTH

**Section Seven. Locating Historical Black Presences
in Cultural Artefacts**

16 Race, Community, and the Picturing of Identities:
   Photography and the Black Subject in Ontario,
   1860–1900   433
   CHERYL THOMPSON AND JULIE CROOKS

17 Hogan's Alley Remixed: Wayde Compton's *Performance
   Bond* and the New Black Can(aan)Lit   455
   PAUL WATKINS

18 Jazz, Diaspora, and the History and Writing of Black
   Anglophone Montreal   488
   WINFRIED SIEMERLING

Section Eight. Black Women's Orality and Knowings

19 "I don't know if I should say this": Black Women, Oral History,
   and Contesting the Great White North   513
   FUNKÉ ALADEJEBI

20 Re-thinking and Re-framing *RDS*: A Black Woman's
   Perspective   538
   ESMERALDA M.A. THORNHILL

BOOKEND II. The Past Has a Future: Critical Intellectual Histories of Blackness

21 Wrestling with Multicultural Snake Oil: A Newcomer's
   Introduction to Black Canada   585
   DANIEL McNEIL

Contributors   611

Redacted Text, 2019:
Statement from the Artist

The image on the cover is taken from Chantal Gibson's *Redacted Text, 2019* and is part of Gibson's *Historical In(ter)ventions* series, a collection of altered texts she began creating in 2010 that range from small handheld books to large-scale installations.

Statement from the Artist

I am a/Historical In(ter)ventionist in the process of decolonizing my body and mind. Using black braided thread and sticky liquid rubber, my altered book sculptures (2010–21) challenge how we create knowledge and construct nationhood. Presented as methods of communication, rather than containers of fixed truth, these dismantled structures question what is included and what is not. They scratch at ideology, undoing tropes and myths, provoking viewers to consider other ways of knowing: What does it mean to read texture over text? How do we mark the voices, the stories, and the bodies that have been violently, systemically erased, silenced, or excluded from dominant Canadian cultural narratives?

Chantal Gibson is an artist-educator living on the unceded ancestral lands of the Coast Salish Peoples. Working in the overlap between literary and visual art, she confronts colonialism head on, imagining BIPOC voices silenced in the spaces left by systemic cultural and institutional erasure. Her work has been exhibited in galleries across Canada and the United States, most recently in the Senate of Canada. Gibson's debut book of poetry, *How She Read* (2019), uses text and image to address the mis/representation of Black women across the Canadian cultural landscape. It was the winner of the 2020 Pat Lowther Memorial Award and the Dorothy Livesay Poetry Prize and a finalist for the 2020 Griffin Poetry Prize. A 2021 3M National Teaching Fellow, Gibson facilitates decolonizing curriculum workshops in classrooms and institutions across the country. She teaches in the School of Interactive Arts and Technology at Simon Fraser University.

UNSETTLING THE GREAT WHITE NORTH

Black Canadian History

Introduction

MICHELE A. JOHNSON AND FUNKÉ ALADEJEBI

Unsettling the Great White North grows out of a desire to offer a scholarly intervention into the continual construction of Canada as a (geographically and) demographically "White" place and space by confirming and theorizing Blackness/es within the country's historical narratives. By centring persons of African descent within the chronicles of Canada's past, this volume engages with and interrupts the myth of benign Whiteness that has been deeply implanted into the country's imaginary. Through its focus on the individual and shared experiences of Black people in Canada, this collection interrogates the well-worn accounts of peaceful Euro-settlement and state creation in exceptional circumstances of racial and cultural tolerance, equity, liberalism, and multiculturalism within what many Canadians believe to be "an arctic land unsullied by conquest."[1] It argues that Black communities in Canada – similar to other unacknowledged, vilified, and marginalized racialized communities – were (and are) essential in the creation of the nation as well as those national myths that are bent on their exclusion; as Eva Mackey argues, racialized communities were (and are) the "necessary 'others' who reflect back white Canada's self-image of tolerance."[2] By their very *being*, Black people in Canada – whose presence across the centuries has often been framed by racialization, racism, varying levels of hostility, prejudice, and discrimination – have been involved in the project of unsettling that self-image. This volume aims to support those efforts through its attention to the lives and experiences of Black people in Canada, including the extraction of labour from Black bodies, the creation of structures of social and institutional segregation, and the systemic and systematic erasure of Blackness/es from the Canadian narrative.

Since the initial call for and submission of contributions to this volume, conversations around Blackness and belonging have taken centre stage in mainstream Canadian media. While the authors in this collection demonstrate the evolving field and breadth of work on Black Canada, they also contribute to ongoing public debates about what it means to be both Black and Canadian. Over the past decade, global protests, mass mobilization, and digital forms of activism have forced a racial reckoning in Canada, making conversations around racial injustice *visible* to mainstream Canadian audiences. Through such movements as #IdleNoMore and Canadian chapters of #BlackLivesMatter, Indigenous and Black communities have engaged in a series of calls to action that forced a rethinking of the historical past to illuminate its present-day implications. Whether in the creation of organizations like Not Another Black Life or through online resource platforms such as #BlackLivesCanadianSyllabus, Black Canadians have tapped into a transnational movement and utilized their diasporic connections to tell a different story of anti-Blackness in Canada. Perhaps most pointed in these critiques were (and are) the ways in which activists positioned the deaths of Black Canadians – including Jermaine Carby, Andrew Loku, Abdirahman Abdi, Regis Korchinski-Paquet, and others – during encounters with police as Canadian stories, shattering myths and assumptions about Canada as a place of refuge from racial violence and discrimination.[3] As part of this demand for public accountability, activists, community members, and academics have considered the contours of anti-Blackness as not just a global phenomenon but also a Canadian problem. This volume emerges from these contemporary conversations to acknowledge that Black Canadian experiences are grounded in recoverable historical pasts. Even in the midst of this publication, the weight of anti-Black violence at the hands of the police and others remains an ever-present part of public debate and resistance in Canada. This collection considers and engages with some of these conversations and recognizes that in the time it takes to compile, analyse, and write histories of Black Canadian life, these debates continue to evolve. Much has changed since the initial submission of these contributions, and while the works presented here do not seek to tell the entirety of the Black experience in Canada (indeed, no singular work can do this), we do aim to highlight the trajectory of critical scholarship in a growing and changing field, amid challenging and difficult public debate and conversation.

It is within this frame that *Unsettling the Great White North* seeks to contribute to, and engage with, the growing field of African/Black Canadian history, which has developed through distinctive but connected historiographical phases. In the late eighteenth century and the first half of the nineteenth century, persons of African descent published personal histories of struggle, escape/migration, and perseverance, while in other cases, narratives capturing Black experiences during the era of slavery were gathered and published to further the abolitionist cause.⁴ In the late nineteenth and early twentieth centuries through to the 1960s, the histories that were produced offered data about aspects of Black life in Canada: some focused on colonial enslavers, some examined the institution of slavery in Canada, others fixated on the "freedom" that Black people supposedly found in "Canaan land," and still others offered short biographies of Black individuals and examined the presence of marginalized Black settlements and communities.⁵ Despite these contributions, the writing on Black Canada was largely ignored by the field of Canadian history, which on some occasions only acknowledged the Black presence through tropes that celebrated Canada's role as a "terminus" in the Underground Railroad. There was little space in the Canadian historical narrative for discussions about how the Great White North was experienced by the enslaved, oppressed, and marginalized persons of African descent whose inconvenient presence was simply elided from the chronicle of the march of/to Canadian "progress."

Even with the publication of Robin Winks's seminal work *The Blacks in Canada: A History* in 1971, which offered a broad, comprehensive, and detailed assessment of Black Canadian history, the Black experience was not always considered as a field worthy of academic study.⁶ While Winks's contribution and analyses included significant shortcomings, he was able to demonstrate the uneven but pervasive patterns of racial segregation, discrimination, and what can be labelled as anti-Black racism throughout the Canadian provinces.⁷ In 1981, the field was augmented with *The Freedom-Seekers: Blacks in Early Canada*, in which Daniel Hill charted the stories of Black Loyalists and refugees alongside the abolitionist movement in Canada.⁸ Persons interested in the field also benefited from James W. St. G. Walker's *Racial Discrimination in Canada: The Black Experience* and Joseph Mensah's *Black Canadians: History, Experience, Social Conditions*, which includes significant segments on the modern history of Black people in Canada.⁹ While not widely embraced, these contributions disrupted national myths that situated Canada as a "White" nation and instead offered the possibility of critical reviews of the ways in which persons of African descent were part of the Canadian landscape.

In addition to these historical overviews, during the last quarter of the twentieth century and into the twenty-first century scholars of Black Canada have spearheaded the development of the historiography, shaped the field, expanded its conceptual framings, and responded to some of the limitations of earlier work, to offer more expansive and nuanced stories of Black Canadian experiences. While some of these contributions have come in the form of edited collections such as *The Promised*

Land and *The Fluid Frontier*, which focus on southwestern Ontario, others have concentrated on one aspect or another of Canada's Black history.[10] These include scholarship regarding the enslavement of persons of African descent in New France and British North American colonies,[11] as well as analyses of the experiences of Black Loyalists during and after the American Revolution.[12] Some publications have explored the exile of the Jamaican Maroons to Nova Scotia and their repatriation to Sierra Leone at the turn of the nineteenth century,[13] while others have assessed those of African Americans who migrated to British North America as a result of the War of 1812.[14] While some scholars have focused on the histories of African American "fugitives," some of whom participated in the American Civil War,[15] others have examined Black experiences during the nineteenth and early twentieth centuries in the western and Prairie provinces where, as in Ontario, Black individuals and communities were frequently "deemed unsuitable."[16]

In addition to these chronologically curated narratives, a range of thematic histories have indicated the complexity of Black communities in Canada. Some have focused on communities and diasporas of Caribbean or African origin,[17] while others have examined critical moments in Black Canadian history, including Black contributions during World War I and the destruction of Black communities in Africville (Nova Scotia) and Hogan's Alley (British Columbia), as well as the 1969 radical Black student uprising in Montreal and its aftermath.[18] In other instances, scholarship has emerged both within and outside of the discipline of history to interrogate the racialized barriers facing Black people in areas of employment, housing, and education, as well as their encounters with policing and systems of (in)justice.[19] As is the case in the wider historical scholarship, while much of the research – especially in the earlier periods – paid little attention to histories of women, gender, or sexualities, that neglect is being addressed,[20] as is the lacuna around Black participation in sports, Black aesthetics, and Black cultural product(ion)s.[21] And all of these efforts have been greatly assisted by reflections on the construction of Blackness/es in Canada, engagement with critical race theory (CRT), and a willingness to push the boundaries of scholarship.[22]

To say that the field of Black Canadian history/studies has come a long way is an understatement. The historical literature focusing on Blackness/es across Canada has grown steadily as scholars across disciplines, community activists, and local historians have continuously contributed to the growth and public understandings of Black life in Canada. Still, there continues to be critical silencing around questions of race and racism within wider Canadian scholarship and discourses of the nation, resulting in an absented Black presence in Canada. In the twenty-one chapters that follow, scholars of Black Canada seek to engage with these concerns and disrupt the reupholstered and re/articulated mythologies of Whiteness to uncover, understand, and bear witness to the challenges, triumphs, negotiations, resistances, and resilience/s of Black communities as they work to negate the tropes of their erasure/s in this place called Canada.

On Resilience as/and Resistance

As part of the project to unsettle the Great White North, the chapters in this volume speak both to the racialized systems of hindrance and exclusion and to the simultaneous nature of Black resistance and resilience in Canada. The often hidden, uneven, and deeply entrenched nature of racism in Canada can make it challenging for Black Canadians to confront social, institutional, and systemic discrimination and to ensure the endurance of Black communities. As Black Canadians organized and implemented practices of everyday survival that sought to reclaim their selfhood, resilience was (and is) a resistive and adaptive strategy.

Indicative of the variety and experiences of Blackness/es in Canada, the authors in this collection examine a range of subjects that address the complex resistance-resilience dialectic. Expanding on the idea of resistive-resilient strategies beyond the classroom where Janie Victoria Ward locates them, the scholarship in this volume resonates with her analysis of the abilities of Black individuals and communities in hostile environments "to negotiate hard times by resisting effectively" and her argument "that successful negotiation facilitates further resilience."[23] The chapters here examine the means by which Black Canadians engaged with the Eurocentric foundations of the nation's mythologies as well as the historical deletions of their presences, contributions, and challenges to negotiate strategies of individual selfhood and collective power. This collection foregrounds the multiplicity of Black experiences in Canada and challenges any conception of Blackness/es in Canada as linear, unchanging, homogenous, and recent. In its close examination of the contested terrains of Black exclusions and belongings in Canada – where persons of African descent have confronted, resisted, endured, and negotiated processes of colonization, enslavement, exploitation, discrimination, and exclusion – the volume interrogates, unravels, and unsettles the Great White North.

The chapters in this collection engage in the histories of African-descended peoples across historical periods and geographies. Therefore, each chapter utilizes the language of the period in its original form. While we acknowledge their potential to startle, offend, or dismay, words such as "slave," "negro," and even "nigger" have been left as they were produced in the historical record and are meant to be understood within their historical contexts. Indeed, the volume unveils and analyses the ways in which language, understood as a practice and conduit of history, often reveals sociocultural, economic, and political hierarchies, as well as locations of power in Canadian society.

While a variety of terms have been used across historical periods to describe persons of African descent (including "Coloured," "Negro," "African Canadian," and "Black"), this collection prioritizes the ways in which persons of African descent sought to define themselves. As a result, there are moments in the volume where "Black Canadian," "African Canadian," and "Black" are used interchangeably. Ultimately, contributors use and capitalize "Black" and "Blackness" to indicate constructed and identifiable identities within diverse communities of African descent that, though dispersed among multiple diasporas including Canada, are connected through shared and dynamic histories and cultures. Some contributors in this volume also capitalize "White" and "Whiteness" to demystify the use of those labels as being either neutral or normative, situating the terms instead as categories that have undergone their own historical racialization and elevation in relation and opposition to non-White, and specifically Black, peoples. Other contributors have chosen not to capitalize "white" to indicate its emptiness and to signify its relationship to the racialization of Black/Blackness. This is an ongoing debate in the scholarship of Black Canada and, as part of the ideological and cultural impetus of this volume, we welcome differing voices and diverse perspectives.

Chapter Breakdown

Unsettling the Great White North is organized into ten sections that reflect the chronological, thematic, and theoretical frameworks that inform writings on African-descended people in Canada. Utilizing a variety of perspectives, the chapters situate Black experiences in Canada across four centuries, and since Blackness/es have usually been silenced and/or treated with suspicion, skepticism, and varying levels of resentment and hostility, they resonate with the tropes of Black resilience and resistance. The contributors to this volume have challenged the silencing of Black histories and have uncovered and re/visited sources, have engaged in debates and extended historical dialogues in ways that highlight the interconnected nature of cultural and social systems (and scholarship), and have examined their impact on Black individuals and communities in Canada. The chapters therefore employ methodological and theoretical approaches that are shaped by a variety of disciplines such as sociology and cultural studies to speak to a range of themes, including enslavement, borders, migrations, settlement, citizenship, community creation, labour, education, and gender.

In the first bookend of this volume, "The Future Has a Past," Barrington Walker unpacks and analyses "the various issues at stake in thinking about historical scholarship as a critical practice." He asks us to consider "the relationship between 'Blackness' and this settler colony we inhabit ... that we now call 'Canada'" and to focus on "the particular positionality of Blacks within the history of settler colonialism and its ongoing modes of colonial governance vis-à-vis Canada's Indigenous peoples." As the launch into the historical interventions and theoretical framings of this collection, Walker's chapter begins with a close evaluation of the historiography of the field of Black Canadian history and an examination of the turn to, and impact of, questions of theory and method. Walker contends that writing critical Black histories in the future needs to move beyond "simple storytelling, fact gathering, and archival spadework" to consider what we want Black Canadian history to do. He argues that the writing of Black Canadian history can and must include the simultaneous practice of theory and method to give way to what he calls "Black archival futurity, an archive that exceeds the limits of manuscript sources or oral histories" to incorporate the Black body and "digitized, disembodied, and artificially intelligent/algorithmic and cybernetic expressions of Blackness and the Black modern." He sees these paths of scholarship as necessary, while heeding Paul Gilroy's reference (in *The Black Atlantic*) to a "counterculture of modernity," as well as the "principles of intersectionality," the echoes of coloniality and "the 'changing same.'" Using three historical case studies from the mid-nineteenth century – the coloured convention movement, the narratives contained in Benjamin Drew's *The Refugee*, and Mary Ann Shadd's *A Plea for Emigration* – Walker examines the "liminal space between fugivity and colonization that shaped the contours of Blacks' experiences in Canada West" to ask how Black Canadian history might "help to secure the liberation of Black peoples from the terror of the racial state" and whether historians of Black Canada "have the luxury of writing history for history's sake."

In section one, "Enslaving Blackness," both Karolyn Smardz Frost and Natasha Henry argue that enslaved Africans were fundamental to the formation of Canada as a White settler colony and examine the fragile relationships of the enslaved to White colonialists in the eighteenth and nineteenth centuries. Mining historical sources to extend the history and historiography on slavery in Canada, these contributors argue that enslaved Black people had a far greater role to play in the development of Canada than has been previously acknowledged. Undertaking a painstaking review of contemporary documentation, Smardz Frost uncovers new research about the lives and experiences of enslaved Africans imported into Nova Scotia by the New England Planters in the years before the American Revolution (in the so-called Planter period). She offers details of the day-to-day, often dangerous and labour-intensive, working lives of enslaved Black individuals who helped to build and structure settlements in Nova Scotia. Not only did Planters exploit the "unwaged labour" of the enslaved, she argues, but in collaboration with their counterparts in New England they extended existing shipping routes; by doing so, the Planters "facilitated a small but lucrative trade in enslaved men, women, and children," in ways that encouraged "the evolution of an extended traffic in Black bodies in both directions up and down North America's eastern seaboard," including Nova Scotia. In stitching together a narrative of enslavement in Nova Scotia, Smardz Frost also gestures toward areas in which additional sources might be identified and further research might be conducted.

While Smardz Frost's chapter speaks to the institution of slavery in Nova Scotia, with poignant illustrations of individual experiences, Henry's examination of the enslavement of persons of African descent uses the close scrutiny of the life of an enslaved Black woman named Bet – who took flight from her enslaver in Belleville, Upper Canada (Ontario), in 1818 – as a window into Canadian slavery. According to Henry, the sparse details that can be gleaned about Bet's life and her resistance to her enslavement present the means to scrutinize the geophysical, sociopolitical, and cultural landscapes of colonial Upper Canada in the eighteenth and nineteenth centuries. In her questioning refrain about Bet's reasons for escape and her possible destination (which might remain unknown), Henry makes the case for using the available information to pry open the myths pertaining to (the non-existence or benign nature of) slavery in the colony and for creating a comprehensive mapping of the presence of enslaved Black people in early Ontario, as a way to better understand "the scale and nature of the system of slavery and its specific manifestation intended to be used as an apparatus of colonial expansion." Scholarly enterprises such as these represent some of the ways in which the dominant myths of the Great White North that have constructed slavery as inconsequential in the development of the Canadian nation might be unsettled.

In section two, "Constructing Blackness across Borders and Boundaries," Adam Arenson and Wendell Nii Laryea Adjetey discuss the ways in which cross-border movements and imaginings marked Black experiences in the nineteenth and twentieth centuries. Disrupting what it meant (and means) to exist inside and outside of national borders, Arenson and Adjetey discuss the complex relationships between Canada and the United States as a lens through which to understand Black participation in nation-building processes. Arenson's examination reviews the forgotten generation of persons of African descent who resided in Canada in the era between the American Civil War and World War I. Arguing for an expanded vision of the role and importance of African Canadian businesses, scholarship, social groups, and politics within the story of the nation, Arenson asserts that the Confederation generation of African Canadians made significant contributions to Canada that have been largely forgotten. Tracing the gaps in the scholarship and attempts to address them, Arenson speaks to the value of transnational histories and uses the example of Anderson Abbott, "a contract surgeon to the US Army" during the American Civil War, to argue that "African Canadian migration into the United States helped to shape the contours of the Confederation generation as families maintained economic, religious, and fraternal ties that stretched across the US-Canada border." For Arenson, it is in their perseverance that the Confederation generation made their mark, since "continuity and survival can be [their] own form of success, based in community organizing and hard-won relationships." Among many persons of African descent, it was by their resilience (as resistance) that they tenaciously inserted Blackness/es into the national imaginary.

Building on this transnational analysis, Adjetey uses the responses of Canadians to the case of Jimmy Wilson, an African American man in Alabama who was sentenced to death for petty larceny, to examine the strategic display of Canadian liberalism and conceptualizations of "race and racial injustice." After laying out the narratives connected with the Wilson case, Adjetey measures the White Canadian outrage against American racism amidst the backdrop of prevailing stereotypes about marauding Black male sexuality that resulted in the Canadian courts "meting out the harshest forms of punishment to Black defendants accused of sexually assaulting white women." According to Adjetey, as White Canadians took great pains to critique the conditions of Africans Americans, they "absolved [the] Canadian conscience" of its own brand of anti-Black racism, so that "many white Canadians could express sympathy for and empathy with African Americans while disavowing the daily injustices and racial inequities that faced African Canadians and other racialized peoples in Canadian society."

As Black Canadians pushed back against the silencing of their communities in the Great White North, reclaiming the meaning of Blackness through community-led initiatives and organizations became a reflection of the sustained and collective fight against anti-Black racism in historical and contemporary contexts. The contributors in section three, titled "Building Black Communities and Shaping Black Resilience," review community spaces and organizational responses to the social, political, and economic exclusion of persons of African descent throughout the provinces. Challenging the predominant focus on Black Canadian experiences in Ontario, Nova Scotia, and Quebec, David Este and Jenna Bailey report on the lesser-known history of African-descended people in Alberta. Assessing data gleaned from archival sources as well as oral histories of African Americans whose families had settled in the Prairies in the early twentieth century, Este and Bailey explore the reasons for their migrations and their experiences in creating rural settlements (Wildwood, Breton, Campsie, Gibbons, and Amber Valley) and living in urban spaces (Edmonton). In their review of institutions such as the Shiloh Baptist Church, Este and Bailey argue that the church reflected Black community cohesion and survival and created a cooperative network of Black leadership and community support that not only fostered the development of Black social life in the area but also addressed the racial injustices that community members experienced in mainstream society. For Este and Bailey, in their "desire to have their own place of worship" these Black Canadians founded an institution that continues to serve its community, and by doing so, they engaged in "a major act of resistance against the anti-Black racism that Black Canadians experienced."

In her discussion of the creation and importance of Black community organizations in twentieth-century Canada, Amoaba Gooden makes the case for an acknowledgement of deep-seated Canadian anti-Blackness that not only reflected the nation's colonial legacies but also helped to shape the foci and means of "resistance and resilience" for Black Canadian community members. Gooden argues that community hubs and organizations – such as the Home Service Association, the Universal Negro Improvement Association, and the Canadian Negro Women's Association – served as institutional and social spaces that addressed the daily oppression that Black Canadians faced, in locales that were sometimes free from the White Canadian gaze. Recognizing the multifaceted, diverse, and complicated nature of Black communities (including groups she identifies as central Canadians, Maritimers, African Americans, and Caribbeans), Gooden explores the central importance of "churches, schools, and benevolent and fraternal organizations," which were involved in strategies and practices of "intentional citizenship" in order to address the strident anti-Black sentiment that many encountered. While Black communities pondered the prevailing "paradox" of legal freedom and continued oppression, belonging and unbelonging, Gooden points out that the

White supremacist exclusions that hindered Black mobility also inspired some Black individuals and groups to create businesses, social clubs, and self-help organizations to serve their communities. Careful to argue that these organizations were not monolithic and were "full of contradictions," she also makes the point that those tensions helped some organizations to "identify, articulate, and act on the structural basis of oppression," facilitated new ways of thinking, and laid the groundwork for Black community-building and organizing efforts in the twenty-first century.

Similarly, Sean Mills reviews the complex interplay among community development, public protest, Black intellectualism, and political organizing that characterized the lives of Black Montrealers in the late 1960s. Mills affirms that, framed by the ideologies of Black Power, the manifestations of Black activism that emerged in 1960s Montreal reflected not only the global focus on racial injustice but the specificities of Black life and community-building in Montreal. Mills contends that the collective activism demonstrated by Black Montrealers ushered in a cultural renaissance that led to the creation of a range of new organizations and institutions and was reflective of resistive responses to the "racism and segregation they faced on a daily basis." In his analysis of the activities of the Congress of Black Writers and other organizations, with their foci on decolonization, the recuperation of Black history, "Black community building," and "transforming Blackness from a source of shame into a source of pride," Mills presents the period prior to the upheaval of the "Sir George Williams Affair" as having set the stage for that confrontation in 1969. In its aftermath, as Mills argues, while some Canadians continued to treat the violent confrontation as "an event having relevance only to Black Canadians," others recognized its impact on Montreal's atmosphere of protest and as a catalyst in the creation of significant Black community organizations that spoke loudly to concerns about the conjoined forced of colonialism and capitalism as well as the possibilities inherent in pan-Africanism. Although some community members did not support the direct actions of Black radicals, most of whom were students, Black communities across Canada understood all too well the factors that had spurred this occasion of violent political confrontation as well as the activism and political organizing that followed in its wake.

Section four, titled "Controlling Black (Working) Bodies," describes how labour, migration, and access shaped Black life in the Great White North. In her chapter, Claudine Bonner analyses the ways in which Canadian immigration policies and officials perceived and responded to Black migrants, particularly those from the Caribbean in the early twentieth century. She outlines patterns of Caribbean migration, including the place of Canada – particularly

Nova Scotia – as a location of "labour migration possibilities" and settlement. With a close examination of Immigration Branch records, Bonner demonstrates how immigration officers used the legislation and "their discretion" to apply notions of (un)assimilability and to identify (and bar) those potential Black immigrants likely to become "public charges." As the Immigration Branch – an arm of the Canadian state working on behalf of the wider population of White settlers – sought to craft and maintain a racialized social hierarchy dominated by Whites, the processes and practices of "gatekeeping" were applied, where Black individuals were "systematically surveilled and restricted by immigration authorities during their migration." In spite of these limitations, Bonner reveals, Caribbean immigrants – alongside previously settled African American and Black Canadian populations – established vibrant communities that founded churches, lodges, and mutual aid societies in the area. Persons of African descent were intermittently recruited as sources of cheap labour but treated with "ambivalence" and hesitation around their presence as "permanent fixtures within the Canadian populace." Bonner asks what this "uneasy relationship" might mean for Black populations currently residing in Canada.

Where Bonner's discussion speaks to the means by which Canadian officials in the Immigration Branch sought to restrict the immigration of Black people from the Caribbean to Nova Scotia in the early twentieth century, Michele A. Johnson's chapter focuses of the exclusion of Black women who were offered or seeking positions as domestic workers and extends the discussion of labour migration into the 1950s. Examining "legislation, Orders-in-Council, and written and applied immigration policies, as well as official correspondence among and between Canadian and Caribbean officials," Johnson argues that "Canadian immigration and other authorities sustained a deliberate and racist rejection of Black female immigration into the Dominion." With a brief introduction to the first Caribbean domestic labour scheme (1910–11) and concluding on the eve of the launch of the second scheme (1955–67), the chapter focuses on the period between the schemes where, without official instigation, individual Canadian employers, prospective Caribbean workers, and Caribbean governments tried to navigate the barriers erected to exclude Black women, who were labelled as intrinsic problems "for all time to come." Johnson examines the sometimes contradictory and often opaque policies, procedures, and attitudes within which anti-Black racism lurked, to situate the stances taken by Canadian government officials in their determination to exclude Black womanhood, lest Black women should become a means by which to unsettle the Great White North, demographically, materially, and discursively.

Viewing education as an important source for economic, social, and political mobility, section five, "'Schooling' Black Canadians," examines how Black Canadians responded to discriminatory practices and Eurocentric assumptions about Black inferiority within Canadian schools by asserting their own self-worth through academic achievement and community learning models. In her discussions of the deeply held desires of African Canadians to provide formal education to their children, Sylvia Hamilton focuses on the fundamental racism that led to the separation and segregation of Black children and youth in Ontario and Nova Scotia. Through her reflections on the production and reception of her 2007 documentary film, *The Little Black School House*, Hamilton reveals consistent and continual experiences of racial prejudice that connected historical practices of segregating groups of African Canadian students to more contemporary practices of exclusion and denial of access to public services. Tracing centuries of Black presences, Hamilton focuses on the Black schoolhouses that contained the lives and stories of students, teachers, parents, trustees, and communities and points to the vivid memories of legalized segregation in the education of Black pupils in the two provinces, while there is no "*apparent*" memory of these violences in the wider society. For her, where there are "remembered and uncovered acts of resistance," such as those captured in her film, they "stand as sites of memory" and speak to "a legacy of resistance."

As Deirdre McCorkindale argues, while the ideologies and practices related to racial segregation are often associated with Jim Crow in the United States or Apartheid in South Africa, the atmosphere and "social convention" of prejudice, opposition, and racial separation in Canada West, with which Black students and their parents had to contend, greatly affected their experiences and prospects. Using the examples of the British American Institute in Dresden, the Wilberforce Institute in Chatham, and the Buxton Mission School in North Buxton, as well as the Princess Street School in Chatham, McCorkindale complicates the perception of separate schools as often the only sources of education but also potential "hindrance[s]" for Black students. Her analysis makes the story of segregation "more complex than simply one of separation" and she concludes that the multiple and varied efforts to gain access to education in Black communities in Canada West represented critical means by which those communities "responded [to] and resisted" the effects of "White supremacy on Black people."

The overarching concerns about racism and discrimination in the nineteenth century that McCorkindale outlines remained paramount for the Black youth whose experiences were examined by Carl E. James in the last decades of the twentieth century. Relying on data extracted from the censuses, studies, and reports of the 1970s and 1980s, James analyses the racialized circumstances within which Black youth and their parents in Toronto (the majority of whom were Caribbean migrants and descendants) navigated educational expectations and schooling experiences where they were consistently placed in lower educational levels and faced prevalent stereotypes and low expectations. In what James labels as the "paradox" of discrimination, some Black students excelled "because of their determination to 'work harder,'" while others determined that given their unlikely access to postsecondary education and resulting high-level employment, the incredible effort was not worthwhile; in these cases, "racism and discrimination operated to stifle their initiative and ambitions." While these realities affected their school participation, academic performance, and educational attainment, as well as their emotional state and psychological well-being, as James argues, Black youth and their parents continued to look to educational achievement, as determined by individual effort, as the path to improved circumstances and status. The resistive/resilience paradigm that frames this collection is apparent in James's analysis, since those who opted out and those who were determined to "make it" in spite of the odds were responding as best they could to the prevailing anti-Black sentiment in Canadian society.

In section six, "Creating New Diasporic Communities: Continental African Experiences," Gillian Creese and Anna Ainsworth assess change and continuity in Black Canadian institutions and organizing and challenge our understanding of Blackness in their discussions of the ways in which new African migrants navigated belonging in the nation and in the twenty-first century. Charting the long-standing history of Black communities in British Columbia, Creese discusses the small but developing community of immigrants born predominantly in sub-Saharan Africa and their complex community negotiations as they – and their Canadian-born/raised children – traverse life in Vancouver. Although new migrants share similar experiences of racialization and marginalization highlighted by others in this volume, Creese emphasizes the ways in which they created spaces of belonging while undergoing processes of "becoming Black" in Canada. Pushing back against anti-Black racism, and with an awareness of "notions of Africa as a common continental homeland" rather than emphasizing "specific ethnic or national origin," according to Creese, these African migrants are creating a "pan-African community" that is not always in alignment with larger and more historical Black communities. And, as they negotiate their place (and plan for a recognized space) in Vancouver, Creese contends that "the resilience of [community] members is evident in the diverse practices of community building," which includes their engagement in gendered processes and activities that kept connections with their "homelands" in Africa and ways of "homemaking" in Canada.

Similarly, Ainsworth charts the contours and meanings of belonging to and among diasporic communities in Canada. Documenting the lives of members of the Rwandan diaspora in the Greater Toronto Area, Ainsworth discusses the impact of the Rwandan genocide and the ways in which legacies of trauma influence individual and collective identities. She reveals a complex interweaving of Rwandese identity, often rooted in ethnonationalism, that varies based on individuals' presumed status during the genocide, interpersonal relationships, local diasporic organizations, and Rwandan state operatives and institutions. These negotiations stand alongside Canadian national narratives that racialize this (and other) diasporic communities under a singular umbrella of Blackness, an appellation that is negatively perceived and constructed by many Canadians. According to Ainsworth, the creation of a Rwandan diasporic community in Toronto continues to be a contested process, as community members hope for improved circumstances while they confront, with "resistance and resilience," an unrelenting anti-Blackness, often framed within the parameters of Canadian multiculturalism.

Section seven, "Locating Historical Black Presences in Cultural Artefacts," challenges the historical erasure of Blackness by examining sites of memory through cultural production and art. Scholars in this section reimagine artistic and cultural production through a lens that focuses on Black knowledges and cultural praxis and gives way for the significance of meaning-making in Black Canadian communities. In their chapter detailing nineteenth-century photographs of Black subjects, Cheryl Thompson and Julie Crooks ask us to consider the importance of curating and documenting Black life in Canada. Explaining the hostile sociocultural milieu within which Black individuals, families, and communities sought the creation and preservation of their images, Thompson and Crooks centre Black self-representation through the choices Black Ontarians made about their photographs and speak to silences in Canadian visual history. While the dominant Western visual culture of the nineteenth century often constructed Blackness as synonymous with slavery, Thompson and Crooks argue that Black people "acquired the means to self-represent and an ability to create counter-images that challenged scientific racism, blackface minstrelsy, and the image of Blackness in the sentimental novel." Chronicling the ways in which Black Canadians reimagined and reinvented themselves through hairstyle choices, clothing, and the positioning of their bodies, Thompson and Crooks call on us to reconsider the role and importance of photography in documenting Black Canadian identities and agency in the nineteenth century.

Expanding the meaning of the archive and methods of interrogation, and remembering what Hamilton refers to as "sites of memory," Paul Watkins reviews spoken word, poetry, images, and oral histories from Vancouver poet/writer/educator Wayde Compton to reimagine Hogan's Alley, Vancouver's historic Black community. Addressing the Black presence in British Colombia from the 1850s, referencing the community's storied scenes occupied by Black artists (including Jelly Roll Morton and Jimi Hendrix), Watkins examines Compton's "mash-up methodology" and imagines his depictions of Vancouver's Black community as a dynamic space that connects past and present histories. Reviewing the restorative praxis in the ways Compton merges multiple histories, Watkins argues that memory work – even if fractured – represents an important part of knowledge production. For Watkins, the hip-hop aesthetics explored in Compton's work challenges existing discourses and introduces neglected Black histories into Canadian literature. As with communities in Nova Scotia and Ontario, Vancouver's Black community resisted forms of displacement and sought to remember Hogan's Alley as part of the Canadian landscape. Indeed, as Watkins argues, in Vancouver (and elsewhere, including Africville), remembering (demolished) Black spaces is an "act of recovery at the crossroads of erasure"; as he follows Compton's acts of "cultural memorialization" by which he "imaginatively fills [historical] lacunae," Watkins urges us to "read, listen, and act."

Outlining the long and complex historical Black presence in Quebec from the seventeenth through the twentieth century – with references to the experiences of the enslaved, Quebec as a destination among African American fugitives, the contributions of Black residents to transnational railway networks, and the development of a "genuine black community" – Winfried Siemerling examines the foundational development of "Montreal jazz." In a world populated by "home-grown talents like the pianists Steep Wade, Oscar Peterson, Oliver Jones, Joe Sealy, and Milt Sealey," Montreal was hailed as *the* place to be between the 1920s and the 1950s. It is within this context that Siemerling examines the literary contributions that often ignored or erased Blackness from the Montreal geography and focuses on some of the texts that demonstrate the parameters of Black emotional and imaginary geographies during Montreal's jazz age; he demonstrates how jazz music reflected visible and audible signs of community and Black history in Canada. His interventions, as well as those of Thompson and Crooks and Watkins, remind us of the multiple readings of Black diasporas in Canada and the cross-cultural influences that connected Black traditions and histories across time and space. For these scholars, Black cultural representations serve as crucial aspects of Black history and remain integral to keeping Black Canada alive.

While several chapters in this collection make interventions into the scholarship about the intersections of race and gender in the review of Black Canadian lives, section eight, "Black Women's Orality and Knowings," centres a Black feminist framework in understanding Black women's unique placement and relationship to discourses of the Great White North. Funké Aladejebi features the stories of Black Canadian women teachers in her discussion of the challenges and triumphs of conducting historical research on (and in) living communities. Discussing the possibilities for Black women's oral narratives, Aladejebi argues that oral history methodologies can be understood as a form of Black Canadian feminist practice that is both political and restorative in nature. In her analysis of Black women's recollections of their professional lives in the mid-to-late twentieth century, Aladejebi not only analyses the stories women chose to discuss but also interprets "the tones, silences, pauses, laughter, and body language of interview participants to reveal the diverse possibilities of their memories, narratives, and identities." Aladejebi contends that the practice of oral history in Black communities considers research participants not simply as mere subjects of historical analysis but rather as "engaged knowledge producers" and "active agents" who made (and make) deliberate and conscious choices about the stories they chose (and choose) to discuss.

Esmeralda M.A. Thornhill's examination of Canadian legal history highlights the significance of grounding Black women's voices in ways that speak back to the racism inherent in the nation's judicial systems. In a meticulous and comprehensive review of the 1997 Supreme Court of Canada landmark case *R. v. S. (R.D.)* (or *RDS*) – its significance, the varying strands and perspectives of narratives concerning the case, its immediate results and consequences, and its lessons – Thornhill argues that "the notion of 'race' and the '*material reality*' of racism insidiously script outcomes and spawn legacies that continue to shore up Law as buttress, mediator, and regulator of the *Great White North!*" In the particular site of Canadian courtrooms, especially where they appear in positions of authority, Thornhill argues that persons of African descent "traditionally have been and are being construed **still** as *disruptive* of the country's touted founding image: 'a White man's country,'" and "when it comes to Blackness, implicit bias and institutionalized prejudice combine to make Law in Canada much more prone to **create** than to **correct** deficits." Employing "an Afrocentric critical race approach, refracted by the lens of [her] own Black Woman's perspective," Thornhill revisits the *RDS* case as a way to offer counternarratives to the construction of the original case as well as the penalties applied against the Black female judge who heard the case. In her analyses of the operations, articulations, and interplays between power and race, Thornhill situates the Canadian courtroom "as a colonized space of White privilege, White entitlement, and above all, White comfort," where Black people, no matter their roles, are perceived with suspicion and contempt and are liable to experience surveillance, dismissal, and marginalization.

Finally, in the second bookend, "The Past Has A Future," Daniel McNeil focuses on the vital enterprise of pushing the scholarship of Black Canada outward by engaging in critical and concerted debates about the complexity of Black experiences. McNeil interrogates the broad influences of the Canadian multicultural state through an assessment of the scholarship by and about Black Canadians, particularly through Peter James Hudson and Aaron Kamugisha's examination of "a Black liberal tradition and a Black radical tradition." In linking those ideas to Paul Gilroy's highly influential contribution *The Black Atlantic*, McNeil places the "Canadian structure of feeling" within the parameters of the "outernational perspectives and ... concept of diaspora" that inform that work and discusses Gilroy's tendency to treat Canada with oversight or else as "a resting area for great artists before they go across the Atlantic to find the *real* drama, action, and history." In his assessment of Black Canadian intellectual traditions and histories, McNeil engages with Richard Iton's *In Search of the Black Fantastic: Politics and Popular Culture in the Post–Civil Rights Era*, which, McNeil says, "examines the relationship between aesthetics, politics, nation, and diaspora," "confronts the assumption that art and culture have no place in real politics," and "demonstrates how diasporic cultural politics can make legible, audible, and visible a range of discourses and experiences." McNeil calls for more critical conversations that consider "the mutually enabling categories of nation and diaspora" in order to acquire "more powerful tools to contest the rather unconvincing depictions of healthy, self-regulating Canadian citizens that veil the violence of settler colonialism."

The chapters in this volume discuss the intimate, personal, and historical placement of Black people in the Canadian nation. The goal of this collection has been to unsettle our understandings of broader national narratives that tend to position Canada as an uncontested terrain of racial equity and belonging. We argue that space must be given to the powerful and transformative ways in which a critical review of Black experiences can enrich and inform our understandings of the Canadian nation. However, our larger goal has been to offer analyses and avenues that might launch further conversations about the ways in which scholars of Black Canada interpret and understand Black resilience, value, and support. This collection addresses the multiple, contradictory, and overlapping experiences of Black historical writing in Canada to articulate a larger political vision, one rooted in a reclamation and recognition of Black agency and advocacy often silenced by broader national narratives. While assessments of the structural and ideological parameters of Black life in Canada constitute the mandate of the volume, contributors to *Unsettling the Great White North* recognize that the project of reclaiming Black Canadian experiences is an unfinished one; our hope is that this work has made a significant contribution to that effort.

NOTES

1 Sherene Razack, ed., *Race, Space and the Law: Unmapping a White Settler Society* (Toronto: Between the Lines, 2002), 3.
2 Eva Mackey, *The House of Difference: Cultural Politics and National Identity in Canada* (Toronto: University of Toronto Press, 2002), 2.
3 Leanne Betasamosake Simpson, Rinaldo Walcott, and Glen Coulthard, "Idle No More and Black Lives Matter: An Exchange," *Studies in Social Justice* 12, no. 1 (2018): 85.
4 David George, "An Account of the Life of Mr. David George, from Sierra Leone in Africa; given by himself in a conversation with Brother Rippon of London, and Brother Pearce of Birmingham," *Baptist annual reg.* (London), 1 (1790–3), 473–4; Boston King, "Memoirs of the life of Boston King, a black preacher, written by himself during his residence at Kingswood School," *Methodist Magazine* (London), 21 (1798), 105–10, 157–61, 209–13, 261–5; John Marrant, *A narrative of the Lord's wonderful dealings with John Marrant, a black ...*, 2nd ed., ed. Rev. Mr. Aldridge (London, 1785); Josiah Henson, *An autobiography of the Rev. Josiah Henson ("Uncle Tom") from 1789 to 1881 ...*, ed. John Lobb (1881; repr., Reading, MA, 1969); Henry Bibb, *Narrative of the Life and Adventure of Henry Bibb* (1849; repr., New York: Dover, 2005); Mary A. Shadd, *A Plea for Emigration; or, Notes of Canada West, in Its Moral Social and Political Aspect: with Suggestions Respecting Mexico, W. Indies and Vancouver's Island, for the Information of Colored Emigrants* (Detroit: George W. Pattison Printer, 1852); Benjamin Drew, *A North Side View of Slavery: The Refugee: or the Narratives of Fugitive Slaves in Canada. Related by Themselves, with*

an Account of the History and Condition of the Colored Population of Upper Canada (Boston and New York, 1856).

5 The British North American colonies were constructed as "Canaan" for African Americans escaping enslavement and oppression, drawing on the biblical narrative of the Israelite movement from slavery into freedom in the "promised land." This trope became even more heightened with the passage of *An Act to prevent the further introduction of Slaves, and to limit the Term of Contracts for Servitude with this Province* in Upper Canada in 1793. While the act prevented the "further introduction" of enslaved persons, it did not free those enslaved in the province; slavery continued in the provinces until the passage in 1833 of *An Act for the Abolition of Slavery throughout the British Colonies; for promoting the Industry of the manumitted slaves; and for compensating the Persons hitherto entitled to the Service of such Slaves* which took effect on 1 August 1834. See Isaac Allen Jack, *The Loyalists and Slavery in New Brunswick* (Royal Society of Canada, 1898); Thomas Watson Smith, *The Slave in Canada* (Nova Scotia Historical Society, 1899); Thomas W. Casey, "*Early Slavery in Midland District,*" *Lennox and Addington Historical Society, Papers and Records* 4 (1912): 12–21; Hubert Neilson, "Slavery in Old Canada: Before and After the Conquest," Literary and Historical Society of Quebec, *Transactions*, n.s., no. 26. (1905): 19–45; W.R. Riddell, "The Slave in Upper Canada," *Journal of Negro History* 4, no. 4 (1919): 372–95; Riddell, "Slave in Upper Canada," *Journal of Criminal Law and Criminology* 14, no. 2 (1923–4): 249–53; Fred Landon, "The Negro Migration to Canada after the Passing of the Fugitive Slave Act," *Journal of Negro History* 5, no. 1 (1920): 22–36; Roy F. Fleming, "Negro Slaves with the United Empire Loyalists in Upper Canada," *Ontario History* 45 (1953): 27–30; Marcel Trudel, *L'esclavage au Canada français*, ed. Abrégée (Montreal: Horizon, 1963); Trudel, *Dictionnaire des esclaves et de leurs propriétaires au Canada français* (Montreal: Hurtubise HMH, 1990); Trudel and Micheline D'Allaire, *Deux siècles d'esclavage au Québec* (Montreal: Bibliothèque Québécoise, 2009); Trudel, *Canada's Forgotten Slaves: Two Hundred Years of Bondage*, trans. George Tombs (Montreal: Véhicule, 2013).

6 Robin W. Winks, *The Blacks in Canada: A History*, 2nd ed. (1971; Montreal and Kingston: McGill-Queen's University Press, 2000).

7 See David Este, "Black Canadian Historical Writing 1970–2006: An Assessment," *Journal of Black Studies* 38, no. 3 (2008): 392.

8 Daniel Hill's scholarship and role as chair of the Ontario Human Rights Commission solidified the significant place and historical relevance of Black survival in Canada, as did his co-founding of the Ontario Black History Society. See Michele A. Johnson and Frank Luce, eds., *Daniel Grafton Hill III: Proceedings of a Symposium on His Life and Work* (Toronto: Harriet Tubman Institute for Research on Africa and its Diasporas and the Ontario Black History Society, 2010).

9 James W. St. G. Walker, *Racial Discrimination in Canada: The Black Experience*, Historical Booklet No. 41 (Ottawa: Canadian Historical Association, 1985); Joseph Mensah, *Black Canadians: History, Experience, Social Conditions*, 2nd ed. (Halifax and Winnipeg: Fernwood, 2010).

10 See Nina Reid-Maroney, Boulou Ebanda de B'béri, and Handel Kashope Wright, eds., *The Promised Land: History and Historiography of Black Experience in Chatham Kent's Black Settlements and Beyond* (Toronto: University of Toronto Press, 2013); Karolyn Smardz Frost and Veta Smith Tucker, eds., *A Fluid Frontier: Slavery, Resistance, and the Underground Railroad in the Detroit River Borderland* (Detroit: Wayne State University Press, 2016).

11 See Marcel Trudel, *L'esclavage au Canada français: Historie et conditions de l'esclavage* (Quebec: Les Presses Universitaires Laval, 1960); Maureen Elgersman, *Unyielding Spirits: Black Women in Slavery in Early Canada and Jamaica* (New York: Garland, 1999); Afua Cooper, *The Hanging of Angélique: The Untold Story of Canadian Slavery and the Burning of Old Montréal* (Toronto: HarperCollins, 2006); Frank Mackey, *Done with Slavery: The Black Fact in Montreal, 1760–1840* (Montreal and Kingston: McGill-Queen's University Press, 2010); Harvey Amani Whitfield, *North to Bondage: Loyalist Slavery in the Maritimes* (Vancouver: UBC Press, 2016); and Harvey Amani Whitfield, *Black Slavery in the Maritimes: A History in Documents* (Peterborough: Broadview, 2018).

12 James W. St. G. Walker, *The Black Loyalists: The Search for a Promised Land in Nova Scotia and Sierra Leone, 1783–1870* (Toronto: University of Toronto Press, 1992); John W. Pulis, *Moving On: Black Loyalists in the Afro-Atlantic World* (New York: Garland, 1999); Mary Louise Clifford, *From Slavery to Freetown: Black Loyalists after the American Revolution* (Jefferson, NC: McFarland, 1999); Barry Cahill, "The Black Loyalist Myth in Atlantic Canada," *Acadiensis* 29, no. 1 (1999): 76–87; James W. St. G. Walker, "Myth, History and Revisionism: The Black Loyalists Revisited," *Acadiensis* 29, no. 1 (1999): 88–105; Harvey Amani Whitfield, "Black Loyalists and Black Slaves in Maritime Canada," *History Compass* 5, no. 6 (2007): 1980–97; Ruth Holmes Whitehead, *Black Loyalists: Southern Settlers of Nova Scotia's First Free Black Communities* (Halifax: Nimbus, 2013).

13 See Mavis Campbell, *Nova Scotia and the Fighting Maroons: A Documentary History* (Williamsburg, VA: Department of Anthropology, College of William and Mary, 1990); Campbell, *Back to Africa: George Ross and the Maroons: From Nova Scotia to Sierra Leone* (Trenton, NJ: Africa World Press, 1993); Allister Hinds, "'Deportees in Nova Scotia': The Jamaican Maroons, 1796–1800," in *Working Slavery, Pricing Freedom: Perspectives from the Caribbean, Africa and the African Diaspora*, ed. Verene A. Shepherd (Kingston, Jamaica: Ian Randle; Oxford: James Currey, 2002), 206–22; James D. Lockett, "The Deportation of the Maroons of Trelawny Town to Nova Scotia, then Back to Africa," *Journal*

of Black Studies 30, no. 1 (1999): 5–14; Lennox O'Riley Picart, "The Trelawny Maroons and Sir John Wentworth: The Struggle to Maintain Their Culture, 1796–1800," *Royal Nova Scotia Historical Society Journal* 44 (1996): 165–87; John N. Grant, *The Maroons in Nova Scotia* (Halifax: Formac, 2002); Ruma Chopra, *Almost Home: Maroons between Slavery and Freedom in Jamaica, Nova Scotia, and Sierra Leone* (New Haven: Yale University Press, 2018).

14 See W.A. Spray, "The Settlement of the Black Refugees in New Brunswick 1815–1836," *Acadiensis* 6, no. 2 (1977): 64–79; Harvey Amani Whitfield, "'We Can Do As We Like Here': An Analysis of Self Assertion and Agency among Black Refugees in Halifax, Nova Scotia, 1813–1821," *Acadiensis* 32, no. 1 (2002): 29–49; Whitfield, *Blacks on the Border: The Black Refugees in British North America, 1815–1860* (Burlington, VT: University of Vermont Press, 2006); Gareth Newfield, "Upper Canada's Black Defenders? Re-evaluating the War of 1812 Coloured Corps," *Canadian Military History* 18, no. 3 (2009): 31–40.

15 These scholars include persons like Bryan Prince and Adrienne Shadd who are descendants of those "fugitives." Prince, *I Came as a Stranger: The Underground Railroad* (Toronto: Tundra Books, 2004); Prince, *A Shadow on the Household: One Enslaved Family's Incredible Struggle for Freedom* (Toronto: McClelland & Stewart, 2009); Prince, *My Brother's Keeper: African Canadians and the American Civil War* (Toronto: Dundurn, 2015); Shadd, *The Journey from Tollgate to Parkway: African Canadians in Hamilton* (Toronto: Dundurn, 2010); Shadd, Afua Cooper, and Karolyn Smardz Frost, *The Underground Railroad: Next Stop, Toronto!* (Toronto: Natural Heritage Books, 2002); Ged Martin, "British Officials and Their Attitudes to the Negro Community in Canada, 1833–1861," *Ontario History*, 66, no. 2 (1974): 79–88; Jason Silverman, "'We Shall Be Heard!': The Development of the Fugitive Slave Press in Canada," Notes and Comments, *Canadian Historical Review* 65, no. 4 (1984): 54–69; Peter Meyler, ed., *Broken Shackles: Old Man Henson, From Slavery to Freedom* (Toronto: Natural Heritage Books, 2001); Linda Brown-Kubisch, *The Queen's Bush Settlement: Black Pioneers, 1839–1865* (Toronto: Natural Heritage Books, 2004); Donald G. Simpson, *Under the North Star: Back Communities in Upper Canada*, ed. Paul E. Lovejoy (Trenton, NJ: Africa World Press, 2005); Joyce A. Pettigrew, *A Safe Haven: The Story of the Black Settlers of Oxford County* (Aylmer, ON: Aylmer Express Press, 2006); Jacqueline L. Tobin with Hettie Jones, *From Midnight to Dawn: The Last Tracks of the Underground Railroad* (New York: Doubleday, 2007); Karolyn Smardz Frost, *I've Got A Home in Glory Land: A Lost Tale of the Underground Railroad* (Toronto: Thomas Allen, 2007); Smardz Frost, *Steal Away Home: One Woman's Epic Flight to Freedom – and Her Long Road Back to the South* (Toronto: HarperCollins, 2017); see also Richard M. Reid, *African Canadians in Union Blue: Volunteering for the Cause in the Civil War* (Vancouver: UBC Press, 2014);

Natasha L. Henry, *Emancipation Day: Celebrating Freedom in Canada* (Toronto: Dundurn, 2010).

16 Crawford Kilian, *Go Do Some Great Thing: The Black Pioneers of British Columbia* (Vancouver: Douglas & McIntyre, 1978); Harold Troper, "The Creek-Negroes of Oklahoma and Canadian Immigration, 1909–11," *Canadian Historical Review* 53, no. 3 (1972): 272–88; R. Bruce Shepard, *Deemed Unsuitable: Blacks from Oklahoma Move to the Canadian Prairies in Search of Equality in the Early 20th Century Only to Find Racism in Their New Home* (Toronto: Umbrella, 1997).

17 James W. St. G. Walker, *The West Indians in Canada* (Ottawa: Canadian Historical Association, 1984); Frances Henry, *The Caribbean Diaspora in Toronto: Learning to Live with Racism* (Toronto: University of Toronto Press, 1999); Carl E. James and Andrea Davis, eds., *Jamaica in the Canadian Experience: A Multiculturalizing Presence* (Halifax and Winnipeg: Fernwood, 2012); Sean Mills, *A Place in the Sun: Haiti, Haitians, and the Remaking of Quebec* (Montreal and Kingston: McGill-Queen's University Press, 2016); Gillian Creese, *The New African Diaspora in Vancouver: Migration, Exclusion, and Belonging* (Toronto: University of Toronto Press, 2011); Wisdom J. Tettey and Korbla P. Puplampu, eds., *The African Diaspora in Canada: Negotiating Identity and Belonging* (Calgary: University of Calgary Press, 2005).

18 Calvin W. Ruck, *The Black Battalion: Canada's Best Kept Military Secret* (Halifax: Nimbus, 2016); Donald H. Clairmont and Dennis William Magill, *Africville: The Life and Death of a Canadian Black Community*, 3rd ed. (Toronto: Canadian Scholars, 1999); Charles R. Saunders, *The Spirit of Africville* (Halifax: Formac, 1992); Jenifer J. Nelson, *Razing Africville: A Geography of Racism* (Toronto: University of Toronto Press, 2008); Wayde Compton, *After Canaan: Essays on Race, Writing, and Region* (Vancouver: Arsenal Pulp Press, 2010); Dennis Forsythe, ed., *Let the Niggers Burn! The Sir George Williams University Affair and Its Caribbean Aftermath* (Montreal: Our Generation Press, 1971); Dorothy W. Williams, *The Road to Now: A History of Blacks in Montreal* (Montreal: Véhicule, 1997); David Austin, *Fear of a Black Nation: Race, Sex, and Security in Sixties Montreal* (Toronto: Between the Lines, 2013); Austin, ed., *Moving against the System: The 1968 Congress of Black Writers and the Making of Global Consciousness* (Toronto: Between the Lines, 2018).

19 Sarah-Jane Mathieu, *North of the Color Line: Migration and Black Resistance in Canada, 1870–1955* (Chapel Hill: University of North Carolina Press, 2010); Cecil Foster, *They Call Me George: The Untold Story of Black Train Porters and the Birth of Modern Canada* (Windsor, ON: Biblioasis, 2019); Makeda Silvera, *Silenced: Talks with Working Class Caribbean Women about Their Lives and Struggles as Domestic Workers in Canada* (Toronto: Sister Vision, 1989); W.W. Anderson and R.W. Grant, *The New Newcomers: Problems of Adjustment of West Indian Immigrant Children in Metropolitan Toronto Schools* (Toronto: Canadian

Scholars, 1987); Carl E. James, *Making It: Black Youth, Racism and Career Aspiration in a Big City* (Oakville, ON: Mosaic, 1990); Vincent D'Oyley, ed., *Innovations in Black Education in Canada* (Toronto: Umbrella, 1994); Keren S. Brathwaite and Carl E. James, eds., *Educating African Canadians* (Toronto: James Lorimer, 1996); Carol A. Aylward, *Canadian Critical Race Theory: Racism and the Law* (Halifax: Fernwood, 1999); Barrington Walker, *Race on Trial: Black Defendants in Ontario's Criminal Courts, 1858–1958* (Toronto: University of Toronto Press, 2010); Walker, ed., *African Canadian Legal Odyssey: Historical Essays* (Toronto: University of Toronto Press, 2012); Robyn Maynard, *Policing Black Lives: State Violence in Canada from Slavery to the Present* (Winnipeg: Fernwood, 2017).

20 Dionne Brand, *No Burden to Carry: Narratives of Black Working Women in Ontario, 1920s to 1950s* (Toronto: Women's Press, 1991); Peggy Bristow, coord., *"We're Rooted Here and They Can't Pull Us Up": Essays in African Canadian Women's History* (Toronto: University of Toronto Press, 1994); Lawrence Hill, *Women of Vision: The Story of the Canadian Negro Women's Association* (Toronto: Umbrella, 1996); Maureen Elgersman, *Unyielding Spirits: Black Women in Slavery in Early Canada and Jamaica* (New York: Garland, 1999); Yvonne Bobb-Smith, *I Know Who I Am: A Caribbean Woman's Identity in Canada* (Toronto: Women's Press, 2003); Nina Reid-Maroney, Boulou Ebanda de B'béri, and Wanda Thomas Bernard, eds., *Women in the "Promised Land": Essays in African Canadian History* (Toronto: Women's Press, 2018); Notisha Massaquoi and Njoki Nathani Wane, eds., *Theorizing Empowerment: Canadian Perspectives on Black Feminist Thought* (Toronto: Inanna, 2007); Karen Flynn, *Moving beyond Borders: A History of Black Canadian and Caribbean Women in the Diaspora* (Toronto: University of Toronto Press, 2011); Daniel McNeil, *Sex and Race in the Black Atlantic: Mulatto Devils and Multiracial Messiahs* (London: Routledge, 2010); Rinaldo Walcott, *Queer Returns: Essays on Multiculturalism, Diaspora, and Black Studies* (London, ON: Insomniac, 2016).

21 Cecil Harris, *Breaking the Ice: The Black Experience in Professional Hockey* (Toronto: Insomniac, 2003); William Humber, *A Sporting Chance: Achievements of African-Canadian Athletes* (Toronto: Natural Heritage Books, 2004); Robert Ashe, *Halifax Champion: Black Power in Gloves* (Halifax: Formac, 2005); Carl E. James, *Race in Play: Understanding the Socio-Cultural Worlds of Student Athletes* (Toronto: Canadian Scholars, 2005); Rinaldo Walcott, *Black Like Who? Writing Black Canada*, 2nd ed. (1997; London, ON: Insomniac, 2002); Walcott, ed., *Rude: Contemporary Black Canadian Cultural Criticism* (Toronto: Insomniac, 2000); Althea Prince, *The Politics of Black Women's Hair* (London, ON: Insomniac, 2009); Cheryl Thompson, *Beauty in a Box: Detangling the Roots of Canada's Black Beauty Culture* (Waterloo, ON: Wilfrid Laurier University Press, 2019); Charmaine A. Nelson, ed., *Ebony*

Roots, Northern Soil: Perspectives on Blackness in Canada (Newcastle upon Tyne: Cambridge Scholars, 2010); Nelson, ed., *Towards an African Canadian Art History: Art, Memory, and Resistance* (Concord, ON: Captus, 2019); Donna Bailey Nurse, *What's a Black Critic to Do? Interviews, Profiles and Reviews of Black Writers* (Toronto: Insomniac, 2003); Winfried Siemerling, *The Black Atlantic Reconsidered: Black Canadian Writing, Cultural History, and the Presence of the Past* (Montreal and Kingston: McGill-Queen's University Press, 2015); Paul Barrett, *Blackening Canada: Diaspora, Race, Multiculturalism* (Toronto: University of Toronto Press, 2015).

22 Cecil Foster, *A Place Called Heaven: The Meaning of Being Black in Canada* (Toronto: HarperCollins, 1996); Althea Prince, *Being Black: Essays* (Toronto: Insomniac, 2000); Cecil Foster, *Where Race Does Not Matter: The New Spirit of Modernity* (Toronto: Penguin Canada, 2005); Foster, *Blackness and Modernity: The Colour of Humanity and the Quest for Freedom* (Montreal and Kingston: McGill Queen's University Press, 2007); Tamari Kitossa, Erica S. Lawson, and Philip S.S. Howard, eds., *African Canadian Leadership: Continuity, Transition, and Transformation* (Toronto: University of Toronto Press, 2019).

23 Janie Victoria Ward, "Resilience and Resistance," in *Souls Looking Back: Life Stories of Growing Up Black*, ed. Andrew Garrod, Janie Victoria Ward, Tracy L. Robinson, and Robert Kilkenny (New York: Routledge, 1999), 181. See also Dorinda J. Carter Andrews, "Black Achievers' Experiences with Racial Spotlighting and Ignoring in a Predominantly White School," *Teachers College Record* 114, no. 10 (2012): 4.

BOOKEND I

The Future Has a Past: Canadian History and Black Modernity

1
Critical Histories of Blackness in Canada

BARRINGTON WALKER

Introduction

This meditative paper considers how we might continue to go about the difficult task of writing critical histories of Blackness in Canada. I want to highlight the various issues at stake in thinking about historical scholarship as a critical practice by attempting to work through a number of themes in the space provided here. As we write our histories of Blacks in Canada, who, exactly, should we remember and why? If narrative is the process through which nations realize and imagine themselves, where do Blacks fit in with this project? Put another way, what, exactly, is the relationship between "Blackness" and this settler colony we inhabit, this space that has had many different names – including and originally Turtle Island – that we now call "Canada." And more specifically, what is the particular positionality of Blacks within the history of settler colonialism and its ongoing modes of colonial governance vis-à-vis Canada's Indigenous peoples?

In attempting to answer these questions – perhaps not quite in the order that I have presented them here – I will consider the existing historiography, much of which has been written with these sorts of critical questions in mind. In addition, I will consider the possibilities for the historiography that is to come – how we might envision the sorts of critical Black histories we will write in the future.

I argue that the writing of critical Black histories must continue to emphasize the move beyond simple storytelling that is all too prevalent during public historical commemorative events that characterize the typical Black History Month fare and, although it is rarer, can still also function as a kind of strategic retreat for some professional (university trained and/or employed) historians as well as their so-called "amateur" counterparts. Such a retreat tragically and needlessly cedes the ground of Black criticality to newer disciplines whose grasp of the complexity of Black histories in Canada is often superficial, bereft of historical or historiographical nuance.

Part I of this paper deals with questions of historiography and sketches a few of the major approaches that have shaped the field of African Canadian history over the past fifty years. Part II turns to questions of theory and method in the writing of African Canadian history. Part III discusses how we might move toward a critical history of Blacks and the racial state, focusing on three historical case studies from the mid-nineteenth century.

Part I. Historiography

I would like to begin my discussion with two early narrative history texts, both of which are important general surveys of Black Canadian history. These are classic texts, but their importance has certainly not diminished with age. The first is Robin Winks's *The Blacks in Canada: A History*, first penned in the late 1960s and republished in the 1990s by McGill-Queen's University Press. The second is Dan Hill's *The Freedom-Seekers*, a textbook that was written in the 1980s. Winks's book, all five-hundred-plus pages of it, is a work that has inspired mixed reactions. This book, though based on an astounding research effort, seems to have been met with what only can be described as a resounding thud by the Canadian historical profession when it was first published. For a book that essentially formally opened up a "sub-discipline" in Canadian history, the response was rather curious. It did not spark the sort of intellectual ferment or create institutional spaces within the Canadian academy that might have been expected.

This was the case for two reasons. First, Winks was writing into a scholarly void that existed precisely because of the overwhelming Whiteness of the Canadian historical profession and its blindness with regard to a critical engagement with Black histories in Canada. The writing of the history of Blacks in Canada, although it had a relatively long history (I will say a bit more on this later) was simply not deemed important nor worthy of serious study when Winks published his book. I met this sort of attitude head on when in the early 1990s I was on the cusp of completing a master's degree at the University of Toronto. At that time, I was rather generously granted a meeting with a leading historian of Canada in one of the country's most respected departments. In response to my query about the possibility of pursuing a doctorate in his department and writing a dissertation in Black Canadian history in partial fulfilment of that degree, I was politely informed by my well-meaning host that writing such a dissertation would prove difficult because the history of Blacks in Canada was virtually non-existent and, by extension, irrelevant. I was thus encouraged (and it is not the last time I would be met with such advice) to perhaps broaden my research to include other non-Anglo Celtic groups in Canada. Winks's book received a somewhat chilly reception for another reason. When Canadians did think about the history of Blacks in Canada, it was in the vein of the celebratory histories written by an earlier generation of historians, most notably Fred Landon.

Landon was a University of Western Ontario–based historian and librarian who was also a member of the interracial board of London's civil rights organization – the Canadian League for the Advancement of Coloured People – and a prolific historian, having produced some three hundred publications, many of which were on the history of Blacks in Canada. Indeed, Landon is regarded by many as the "founder" of the field of Black Canadian history. Landon's work was foundational in the sense that he was one of the first to professionalize the study of Blacks in Canada by disseminating his research in professional journals. Landon's work on the history of Blacks in Canada (he published widely on the history of Ontario beyond Black history) was solid, and it was based on the systematic and conscientious use of primary sources. One of my main bones of contention with Landon, however, was that much of his work – not all – mirrored some of the worst excesses of ideas about the Underground Railroad that were proffered by White abolitionists. As many readers undoubtedly know, the numerous publications that White abolitionists produced tended to rely on a number of rhetorical strategies with which we are still saddled.[1]

First, there was a tendency to trade in rather graphic accounts of the harsh treatment that was inflicted upon the bodies of slaves in order to generate empathy on the part of the intended (White) audiences of these pamphlets. Sadiya Hartman has argued brilliantly in her work *Scenes of Subjection* that the discourse of empathy, the identification of the observer with the slave, ultimately reinforced White supremacy while it facilitated the erasure of the subjectivity of the slave.[2] Secondly, the abolitionists tended to relegate Blacks to the status of those acted upon rather than the central actors in their story. The agency of Blacks, the role that they took in seizing freedom, was often missing in the work of the abolitionists. Third, their work tended to highlight the notion that Canada was a more or less pure haven from slavery. This work was mobilized to support a foundational historical narrative of White Canadian beneficence. It is the creation of a narrative arc that contributes to the making of the nation, and this process sits at the intersection of knowledge (i.e., the archive) and power. Landon's work did not engage in the voyeuristic excesses of his abolitionist predecessors, but it was quite resonant with it on the last two fronts.

Winks's *The Blacks in Canada* was the first critical response to the tradition that Landon and his White abolitionist antecedents represented.[3] Winks's tome was an archival tour de force. His meticulous research was instructive from the standpoint of doing the important work of excavation for writing critical histories. His work shows us that often the first step in writing good critical history is premised upon the importance of empirical archival research, not as mere recovery and retrieval but as a first step en route to critical practice. For Winks, the key to debunking the long cherished myths of Canada as a haven from slavery and a promised land lay in the manuscript sources – what we historians also call primary research. As many others (including myself) have written elsewhere, stories of benevolence via the Underground Railroad and Canada as a welcoming terminus where Blacks enjoyed freedom under the British flag tell only part of the story. Winks's work smashed those myths with astonishing surgical precision. First, he highlighted the central role of slavery in New France and the Loyalist era (Marcel Trudel had also done this earlier in his seminal study of slavery in New France).[4] After charting the various factors – economic, political, legal, and perhaps even social – that caused slavery to peter out, Winks went on to show us that the "afterlife" of slavery in Canada was far from idyllic. In fact, quite the contrary; the single most important contribution of Winks's work was that it made the case that while Blacks enjoyed formal equality, they were subject to pervasive patterns of social and cultural discrimination. This took the form of residential segregation, separate (and inferior) schools, political and economic marginalization from the mainstream of political life, episodes of mob violence, and a popular culture that made the denigration of Blacks one of its central preoccupations. And these cultural products were both home-grown and imported from the torrent of such images being produced south of the border.

So, while Winks's empirical work freed the study of Blacks in Canada from romantic myths about the nation, in other respects his work failed to live up to critical scrutiny. The Canada that was narrated in Winks's book, which was a bald rebuke of the "promised land" narrative, also served to inscribe a narrative of Black subjection and abjection that denied Black Canadians their humanity. For all of its success in shattering the myth of Canadian racial tolerance, there is an unfortunate undercurrent of White (and liberal) supremacy in that book that makes many of us uneasy. This is why many scholars no longer teach this book and why, even among the handful of students who have made their way to my university to undertake advanced study of race in Canada or Black

Canadian history under my supervision, fewer and fewer seem to have grappled with this book. Winks's portrayal of Black Canadians was at times condescending, even insulting. To cite a famous example, in his chapter on the Black Refugees of Nova Scotia Winks wrote that

> the Refugee Negroes were a disorganized, pathetic, and intimidated body who seemed unable to recover from their previous condition of servitude, their sudden voyage up the Atlantic to Nova Scotian shores, and their persistent lack of leaders. They unwittingly fanned the sparks of a more conscious, more organized, white racism than Nova Scotia had known, just as the last vestiges of slavery were passing. These new arrivals clasped their freedom to them, willed themselves to do well, did not want to leave their new found land – and yet failed utterly.[5]

This is but one example in a tome that is rife with these sorts of statements and sentiments. Winks essentially concluded that Blacks in Canada were unsuccessful because by almost every objective measure they were unable to match the successes of Blacks in the United States. Where US Blacks were led by charismatic figures, Black Canadians seemed leaderless. While these charismatic American Black leaders embarked on a variety of programmatic responses to confront White racism in the United States, ranging from Garveyism to civil rights, Blacks in Canada seemed to lack a coherent organizing philosophy and when these ideological currents did manage to trickle across the border, they failed to take root in the shallow soil of Black Canadian life. It is also evident that Winks's construction of Blackness was deeply rooted in the perspective of his own position as an American and influenced – at least in part – by ideas of American exceptionalism.

A number of scholars crafted critical responses to Winks's work. University of Waterloo historian James Walker criticized Winks for writing the history of Blacks "as an issue in white Canadian life" rather than "the history of Negro life in Canada."[6] I have always only partially agreed with Walker's assessment of Winks's work regarding this issue. I do not think you can disentangle Black history from White supremacy or its connection to the idea of race and the emergence of the racial state, because the history of Blacks in the West is inextricably bound with each of these things. It is a fact, nonetheless, that Winks's history tends to reproduce the logic of racism by positing Blacks as the passive recipients of White racial abuse. Indeed, in his preface to the second edition of *The Blacks in Canada* Winks rather strangely remarked that one of the oblique stylistic interventions of the book was his decision to write the chapter on what he called the "nadir" of the Black experience – essentially his narrative account of what we would now call Canadian anti-Black racism – in the passive voice. Given Winks's dim view of Black life, one doubts whether he was merely being even partially ironic.

I have devoted this much attention to Winks because although it is a text that many in our field would like to see dead and buried (about a decade ago a colleague criticized me for devoting time to a text that was over thirty years old at the time) its influence continues to loom large, although this is often unacknowledged. After Winks, much of what followed in the writing of the history of Blacks in Canada built on his important excavation of White supremacy in Canada while providing a critical response to many of the underlying assumptions in his book around the place of Blacks in shaping their own history – which, Winks claimed, was minimal. James W. St. G. Walker's *The Black Loyalists* was first published shortly after Winks's work appeared. Walker's influential book highlights the role of Blacks in forging their own freedom during the American Revolution. They were neither the "flotsam and jetsam" of imperial contests nor the passive beneficiaries of British colonial policy.[7] Walker argued that Blacks forged their own freedom by seizing the opportunities that emerged during the war. They were not "freed" but rather they exercised their "agency" by freeing themselves.[8] Other works written in the aftermath of Winks's work also endeavoured to place Black Canadians at the centre of their own history. Daniel G. Hill's *The Freedom-Seekers: Blacks in Early Canada* explicitly argued that freedom was not something that was conferred upon Blacks in Canada but something that they actively sought out and forged for themselves. This is most poignantly illustrated in the culminating chapter of his book, "The Freedom-Seekers," which provides sketches of eighteen Black Canadians, central historical figures who were the movers of early Black Canadian history.[9] In a similar vein, C. Peter Ripley's 1986 collection, *The Black Abolitionist Papers*, sought to focus explicitly on the contributions and history of Black abolitionists via an extensive introduction and a rich compendium of primary sources. The work is, in essence, an archive of Black emancipatory thought and practice in the nineteenth century, one that seeks to highlight Black abolitionist thought in Canada as part of a larger movement that spanned Britain and the United States.[10] The emergence of agency as a central theme in the history of Black Canadians has been key in subsequent work that emerged in the 1990s and beyond. During this period, the decentring of Black men in Black Canadian history took hold as scholars such as Afua Cooper, Adrienne Shadd, and Maureen Elgersman (to cite just a few) devoted works to Black Canadian women's history.[11] While much of the work on Black women's history somewhat ironically reproduced the recovery mode of writing that characterized much of the male-centred work they were writing against, there is evidence that the latest generation of Black women's history is moving away from that. It is somewhat more attuned to theory, interdisciplinarity, and "a nuanced and audible and resonant conversation between the past and the present."[12]

Thus, for at least two decades now, much of the scholarly writing of critical Black Canadian history has moved largely beyond the simple story and the mythologizing of Canada as a haven from slavery and discrimination (though some recent publications have seemed to return to it in a noteworthy post-revisionist turn that, though avowedly atheoretical, is in fact heavily imbued with certain theoretical and ideological precepts).[13] What historians have turned to now is centring Blacks as the agents of their own history, but there are other issues that we need to consider when writing critical histories of Blackness in Canada as well. I am thinking of three things here: first, how we move beyond histories of "firsts" and the sorts of celebratory histories that often result; second, how we think about Black peoples' relationships to settler colonialism in Canada; and third, how the methodology of the historian can take up the methodological insights born of Black feminist intersectional theory and praxis and the Black modernist chronotopes that emerge from slavery and its aftermath.

Much of the writing of Blacks in Canada has been preoccupied with excavation of the archives to unearth Black "firsts." This is perfectly understandable given the history of White supremacy and the denigration of Blackness that pervades so much of the lived experiences of Black folks in the past, in the present, and very likely into the future. The focus on heroes in the writing and public dissemination of Black histories is thus a predictable response to White supremacist assaults on Black aesthetics, intelligence, and accomplishments. Thus, boilerplate Black History Month celebrations typically feature stories of Black heroism or Black accomplishment in a range of fields including arts, law, science, literature, and even athletics (though typically in the pre–World War II era, as barriers to Black participation in professional and elite-level sports have been torn down outside of a handful of vanilla sports such as golf and hockey). It is understandable too that these sorts of conventions would have found their way into some of the historical scholarship as well, where there has been an inordinate focus on exceptional elites, in large part as a result of the challenges presented by finding sources that might point the way to lesser-known figures.

While it is true that much of the preoccupation with Black Canadian elites has to do with who has produced and left behind documentary evidence of their lives, there is also more going on in the decision that many historians of Black Canada have made to focus on elites. If Blacks are the agents of history, there is also a belief among many historians – both explicitly stated and not – that Black elites, or those who are otherwise particularly accomplished, are the movers and creators of Black Canadian history. This is essentially the Du Boisian "talented tenth" conception of Black history, a holdover from older ideas of history and historical practice that emerged in the nineteenth century and the whiggish preoccupation with ideas of teleology and historical progress.[14] Writing critical histories of Blackness entails not eschewing the history of elites but thinking more carefully and critically about their role in history. A critical approach to history alerts us to the fact that elites are a product of a given social, cultural, and economic context. Moreover, a critical approach to history demands that we also move away from our preoccupation with exemplary historical figures to look at the lives of everyday Black men and women – most of whom were engaged in various sorts of legal and illicit work – to get a sense of how they shaped the contours of modern Black history. Though we have a few excellent studies of slavery in Canada, very few studies of the Canadian Black working class exist, not to mention the Black underclass or lumpen proletariat. Nor do we have many studies of those Blacks who were enmeshed in the criminal justice system, which, again, is understandable given the historic power of dominant stereotypes of Black criminality and historians' discomfort with and resistance to engaging with them. The few historical studies that do exist (sociologists and criminologists have been more likely to take on these issues) are either met with a stony silence or criticized for reifying or trading in negative stereotypes, responses with which I am familiar.[15] But the criminal justice system and the mass incarceration of the prison industrial complex have played an inordinate role in shaping Black life after slavery. Indeed, we need more work that explores the genealogy of the prison and policing in Canada in the Middle Passage and slavery.

Part II. Theory, Method, and Black Canadian History

Writing Black Canadian history involves careful consideration of theory and method. Several questions arise around, first, how we "do" Black Canadian history and, second, what exactly we want Black Canadian history to "do." How are we going to go about the process of systematically remembering the Black past and what is the nature of the archives from which we can draw? How do we define the Black Canadian archive and what is our relationship to it? How does writing Black history in Canada open new ways of thinking about the relationship between time and space? How should historians of Black Canada address the issue of agency in the future?

Rather than offer definitive answers, I would like to offer some tentative positions from which we might begin to respond to such questions. Writing Black history in Canada is a simultaneous practice of theory and method. Historians of Black Canada must double down on the tried and true counterhegemonic strategies of the historian of the quintessential "Others," the subaltern. They must be attuned to the strategies of "reading against the grain" of the gaps and silences and the routinized, often banal violence of the records of officialdom. At the same time, we must expand the archive beyond traditional manuscript and oral history sources. To be sure, both are crucial to the writing of the histories of people who are steeped in a rich oral tradition. At the same time, however, I am gesturing to the Black archival futurity, an archive that exceeds the limits of manuscript sources or oral histories.

Black archival futurities will need to continue to mine the archive that is the Black body, a body that bears the weight of so much of our histories as Black people during slavery and its aftermath and that is so often the focus of critical scholarship on Black histories, cultures, and experiences. The body's archive is contained not only in the ways in which it has been surveilled, constructed, and interpellated but also in the history of Black looks, gestures, gaits, and how the memory of slavery and displacement is embedded within and among them. Past scholars have read slave notices and their vivid descriptions of the infirmaries of runaway slaves as inventories of the violence their masters inflicted upon their bodies. Future historians may well look to the realms of "bioarchaelogies," for example, and the traumas that are archived within us, quietly ticking away in mitochondrial DNA, literally collapsing the past and the present. But while the materiality of blood, bone, sinew, and mitochondria mark one potential path of archival futurities, historians will also have to grapple with digitized, disembodied, and artificially intelligent/algorithmic and cybernetic expressions of Blackness and the Black modern. These archives can neither be reduced to the old notions of what Frantz Fanon called the "bodily epidermal schema" nor be contained by the national or transnational frameworks upon which our prior work has been rooted.[16] The historian will also have to look to these cybernetic expressions of Blackness as an archive of new sites of resistance and struggle.

Lastly, and relatedly, I would like to say a little more about the question of agency. We must heed Gilroy's observation in *The Black Atlantic* about the new chronotopes that emerged in and through the Middle Passage, slavery, and its resultant Black modernity and what this means for writing Black histories. The roots of the formal academic study of history are firmly embedded in the Enlightenment project of empiricism, positivism, rationality, and possessive individualism. Indeed, it is my view that one of the ironies of the turn to the Black historical agent as the mover of history is that the idea of "agency" (by definition the ability of the individual – the historical agent – to act independently in the context of overarching social, cultural, and political structures) is a product of the Enlightenment project, a project that did not include non-White non-Western peoples. We thus need to embrace a future of new historical methods that heed Gilroy's famous and brilliant injunction that the Black Atlantic constitutes the dark side of the Enlightenment – a "counterculture of modernity" – that long anticipated the conditions of modernity that we now call "postmodern."[17] And these insurgent methods must shape how we can begin to write about not broken people or helpless victims but rather those who had to confront the "crushing objecthood" – to invoke Fanon yet again – that battered bodies and psyches, fracturing the subjectivities of those who survived and resisted the barbarous conditions of Black life that created the Black modern.[18] The "double consciousness" that characterizes Black life under modernity can only be partially contained, captured, and embodied by the positivist and empiricist logistics that structure the conventional historical archive.[19]

Future historians of Black Canada will have to develop an approach to writing history that is informed by the principles of intersectionality – and what form that might take, exactly, is unclear – to deal with the fractured Black subject/object as well as the compression of space and time that occurs under the conditions of slavery and post-slavery and how this affects conventional notions of historical progress. The lived experiences of Black people also embody historically and spatially overlapping colonial projects. The practice of carding, for example, gestures to histories and practices of slavery and surveillance in Canada and the Caribbean, Jim Crow in its older and newer iterations, and the racialized deployment of state power against people who embody the Global South regardless of their geographical location. In other words, newer historians of Blackness in Canada and elsewhere will have to puzzle out how a discipline that is wedded to positivist notions of "change over time" can come to grips with the "changing same" of Black life over swaths of time where new iterations of White supremacy supplant the old to ensure the conditions that expedite Black death.[20]

Part III. Between Fugivity and Colonization: Blacks and Canada's Racial State

David Theo Goldberg has argued that "the history of the modern state and racial definition ... are intimately related."[21] Race has always been central in Canadian state formation. The issue of slavery has been central to Canada's emergence as a modern state. Slavery was widely practised in many parts of pre-Confederation Canada, most notably in Prince Edward Island, Nova Scotia, New Brunswick, Upper Canada, and Lower Canada. Scholarly critical transnational histories of Blackness have moved us beyond the nation-state as the primary lens through which to study Black history. And this makes perfect sense given the intertwined histories of Blackness in the Atlantic World and the circulation of Black peoples through the circuits that made up the Black Atlantic. Nonetheless, we need to think more critically about Black Canadians' relationship to settler colonialism and the foundation of a racial state that has its genesis in the dispossession of First Nations peoples.[22] Sunera Thobani puts it brilliantly in her work, regarding the question of citizenship for non-White settlers, "many of whom had been coerced into migration": "Can a citizenship conceived in, and maintained by, a genocidal violence leave untainted any group which comes to be included in its orbit, no matter how severe the forms of their own previous exclusions or how tenuous their subsequent inclusions?"[23]

In my own work I have challenged the promised land myth (in both its historical and more recent and admittedly more nuanced iterations) in favour of a thinking about the liminal space that Blacks occupied between legal equality and social ostracism. But my work has not fully thought through how even the liminal status of Blacks made them not only not-quite-citizens but also not-quite-settlers. Black people did not create the racial colonial state, but they managed to carve out a tenuous hold within it. The significant commercial successes that some Black men were able to achieve were clearly only possible because of the racial state's criminal theft and appropriation of Indigenous land, evidence of how non-White men benefited from the gendered contours of the colonial project. But in the large scheme of things Blacks were supplicants, getting the crumbs of White British-Canadian imperialism when they did manage to own a piece of stolen land outright (as opposed to being placed on tickets of occupation). The well-documented differential treatment of White and Black Loyalists and the shabby treatment of the Refugees are prime examples. What, then, is to be done with what I have elsewhere called the liminal space between fugivity and colonization, the unsteady ground between the ex-slave and the citizen, the fugitive and the settler?

Three case studies highlight the complexities of thinking critically about Blacks' relationship to the racial state in Canada and this liminal space between fugivity and colonization that shaped the contours of Blacks' experiences in Canada West: the coloured convention movement; the narratives collected by Benjamin Drew, who toured Canada West in the nineteenth century and interviewed ex-slaves; and Mary Ann Shadd's colonization guide, *A Plea for Emigration*.

In the nineteenth century, coloured conventions became a staple of Black life in North America. From the early to the late 1800s, coloured conventions sprang up across North America and largely, but certainly not exclusively, in the United States. During this era, which encompassed both the pre- and post-slavery eras, Blacks met to discuss how best to achieve the elusive goal of freedom. In the years before the Civil War the question of slavery loomed large in these discussions. Should Blacks seek to undermine the system from within through political agitation or by forming strategic alliances with Whites from the (relative) safety of the North? Among free Black populations in the northern states during slavery there remained the question of how best to secure their full citizenship under the yoke of impingements on their freedom via a series of anti-Black laws that portended the ubiquitous Black Codes that would mark Black life after slavery in the South. These northern laws and social customs restricted Blacks' freedom in myriad areas of social and civil life. In the post-slavery period, these organizations found themselves facing the same vexing questions in the Northern US and Canada. What the conventionists learned is a lesson that resonates throughout Black North American history: the end of slavery did not mean the end of racial prejudice.[24]

At ten o'clock on the morning of 11 September 1851, the North American Convention commenced its meeting at St. Lawrence Hall in Toronto. The convention's participants, the vast majority of whom were Black, hailed from Canada and the northern United States; one of the delegates, who was White, came from Jamaica. In attendance were stalwarts of the abolitionist movement such as Thomas W.F. Smallwood, a factory owner in Toronto and a Maryland ex-slave; Henry Bibb, Windsor-based Black abolitionist ex-slave and founder of the abolitionist newspaper *The Voice of the Fugitive*, and Martin Delaney, the well-known author, public intellectual, and activist. Over the course of the next two days the convention addressed a number of issues presented as formal motions and reports by various committees and individual delegates. The second day of the convention included, for example, "reports from several delegates, setting forth the moral, civil, and pecuniary condition of our people, in their respective localities." On the third day of the convention it was resolved that, "slavery being a sin against God, and an outrage upon man, we feel sacredly bound, as a convention and as individuals, to make common cause with the enslaved, and never to cease our efforts against slavery until it is swept from the face of the earth or our vital breath and pulsation cease."[25]

It was the first day of the convention, however, that encapsulated the dilemma of the fugitive slave's settler strivings. During the afternoon session, the business committee made the following resolutions, which are worth quoting at length:

1. Resolved, that the infamous fugitive slave enactment of the American Government – whether constitutional or unconstitutional is an insult to God, and an outrage upon humanity, not to be endured by any people; we therefore earnestly entreat our brethren of the northern and southern states to come out from under the jurisprudence of those wicked laws – from the power of a Government whose tender mercies towards the colored people are cruel.
2. Resolved, that we feel truly grateful, as a people, to her Britanic Majesty's just and powerful Government, for the protection afforded us; and we are fully persuaded from the fertility of the soil, and salubrity of climate of the milder regions of Canada West, that this is, by far, the most desirable place of resort for colored people, to be found on the American continent.
3. Resolved, that we warmly recommend to colored settlers in Canada, to use all diligence in obtaining possession of uncultivated lands, for the purpose of making themselves and their offspring independent tillers of a *free soil*.[26]

These resolutions are striking for a number of reasons. The first resolution was an appeal to universal humanity and a rebuke of a republican government that was, in essence, a Herrenvolk democracy based on White supremacy and built upon a foundation of "wicked laws" that were an "insult to God." The second resolution was a further rebuke of American republicanism, which was unfavourably compared to the "just and powerful" government of "her Britanic Majesty." The third resolution spoke to the in-between position of the "colored settler." This resolution called for Black people coming into the province to obtain "uncultivated lands." These were in essence imagined as "terra nullius," empty lands that needed to be tamed, civilized, and put to proper use. Further, it is through cultivating these uncultivated lands that the refugee would be transformed into a citizen (or at least nearer to that ideal). Once cleared and tilled, the land would be put to "the laudable purpose of making themselves and their offspring independent tillers of *free soil*." This attitude toward land and soil and its relationship to (still elusive) national belonging is the key to understanding the attitudes and outlooks of those who would try to make the journey from slaves to citizens. The act of purchasing and tilling "free soil" was then the conduit through which the slave, who has no sovereign claim under the "vel of slavery" not even to his body, can make life anew.[27] But it was a conception of freedom built upon free land that was not free. (The gendered contours of formal citizenship made this calculus more complicated for

Black women, of course, but their participation in the colonial regimes of property ownership gave them many of the benefits of substantive freedom nonetheless.) Put another way: What are the prospects for and possibilities of freedom for a stolen people who settle upon stolen lands?

Consider too the narrative of Ephraim Casey, a free-born Black man who migrated to Colchester, in Canada West. Abolitionist Benjamin Drew recorded Casey's testimony in *The Refugee: or the Narratives of Fugitive Slaves in Canada*, originally published in 1856. In his narrative, Casey introduces himself as hailing "from the State of Georgia, where I was born free. But the laws were not better about learning for a free man than for a slave." At the age of twenty-three, Casey continued, he "emigrated" to Indiana "carrying no property." Once in Indiana, Casey's fortunes seem to have improved dramatically. From his propertyless status in the cotton belt, Indiana afforded him the opportunity to amass some land, a farm sprawling over some eighteen acres. Casey, nonetheless, decided to leave: "I liked the country very well. The Laws bore hard on me before I came away – I had a case in law, and could not prove my side good by the evidence of colored me which caused me a loss of fifty or sixty dollars. I did not feel disposed to stand this, and emigrated to Canada." Once in Canada, Casey settled in Colchester, where he "bought out a white settler, land and stock, for seven hundred and fifty dollars." After having made vast improvements on his newly purchased land, including a new irrigation system, a well, and even a sawmill, his fortunes improved so much he was able to "hire colored men to work for me whenever I wanted their help, and I have seen them hired by others," Casey continued, "but they prefer, so far as I know, to work for themselves, and to get an independent living."[28]

Casey's narrative, though brief, is quite rich. It tells us about the nature and elasticity of fugivity as an analytical category, and it corroborates Michael Wayne's classic findings that while many Black people fled bondage, in fact, more fled conditions of unfreedom rather than slavery qua slavery.[29] It also gives us a window, albeit limited, on the complex relationship among coloniality, race, land, capitalist accumulation, and citizenship. Casey's ability to convert land to capital and leverage capital for substantive citizenship was compromised in the United States because of the overt nature of White supremacy in the form of unequal justice in the courts. Once in Canada, the alchemies of race, citizenship, and capital accumulation changed, allowing him to exercise his property rights in the purchase of land from a White settler and the protection of the law to conduct business, hire employees, and accumulate capital. Nonetheless, like so many such narratives it is silent on the transfer of the land from Indigenous peoples. Colchester's settler-colonial origins began in the late eighteenth century with a series of land purchases and treaties. In the post-Revolutionary era, William Caldwell, a British captain, secured a "grant" from Indigenous peoples and immediately set about preparing the land for soldiers-cum-settlers (the details about how Caldwell secured the land are unclear). In 1787, a man named Thomas Smith surveyed land near the Caldwell "grant" that was joined with it. A few years later, in 1790, "the Ottawa, Chippewa, Potawatomi and Huron Indians" transferred over 1.3 million acres of land to settlers through a Detroit-based British Indian agent named Alexander McKee. This land was exchanged for "'valuable land and merchandise' including blankets, combs, looking glasses, pen-knives, ribbons, silk handkerchiefs, hats, tobacco and rum" worth 1,200 pounds.[30] The treaty stipulated that the Crown was "to have and to hold the said Lands and Premises hereby given and granted, mentioned or intended to be given and granted until His Majesty George the Third, His Heirs and Successors for Ever."[31] This treaty, like scores of others that came before it and would follow, mark the essence of the contract that converted Indigenous land to lots divided by concessions, lines on a map that made settler space and turned land into fungible alienable property. It was this act of exchange, often conducted under highly dubious circumstances with more than a whiff of the coercive power of the colonial state, that created the conditions under which Black people could escape their unfreedom, achieve elusive citizenship, and try to begin anew.

Lastly, consider Mary Ann Shadd's nineteenth-century tract *A Plea for Emigration*. Early in the *Plea*, Shadd turns to the subject of "Soils-Timber-Clearing Lands." In this section she clearly outlines the vision of freedom that was paramount for prospective emigrants, and it is worth citing at length:

> So far as coloured people are interested in the subject of emigration to any country, their welfare in a pecuniary view, is promoted by attention to the quality of the soil. Lands out of the United States, on this continent, should have no local value, if the question of personal freedom and political rights were left out of the subject but as they are paramount too much may not be said on this point; I mean to be understood that a description of lands in Mexico would probably be as desirable as lands in Canada, if the idea were simply to get lands and settle state, or if a permanent nationality is included in the prospect of becoming purchasers and settlers.[32]

For Shadd, pecuniary considerations alone were not sufficient to make the case for Black emigration to Canada, nor were practical considerations such as the fertility and richness of the soil. These things mattered, to be sure, but only in service of the quest for "permanent nationality" or citizenship. Black migrants to Canada West sought to solve the problem of fugivity by staking their claim to national belonging through embracing the logic and practice of settler colonialism. They would find, however, that this offered them no protection from the insurgent Canadian racial state. Indeed, they were to discover that the colonial state, precisely because it was a White supremacist project, would be the antecedent of the racial state. Hence, the promise of substantive freedom was ultimately illusory. A critical history of Blackness in Canada has to take this trajectory seriously, because it has not only greatly shaped the Black past in Canada but also shaped the contours of the Black present and future in rather profound ways.

Conclusion

This brief essay has attempted, through a study of historiography, method, and practice, to engage in a discussion of writing Black Canadian history that continues to move us beyond simple storytelling, fact gathering, and archival spadework. While all of these elements are important aspects of the historian's craft, we must continue to build upon and go beyond these facets to explore the complex relationships among colonization, Blackness, fugivity, and the modern Canadian racial state. Lastly, in these perilous times what do we want Black history to "do"? How can it help to secure the liberation of Black peoples from the terror of the racial state? Does the historian of Black Canada, in other words, have the luxury of writing history for history's sake?

NOTES

This chapter is based on a keynote address by the author at the Black History Month symposium "The Evolving Meaning of Blackness in Canada," held in February 2017 at York University. I would like to thank Professor Carl James in particular for inviting me and for offering the support of the Jean Augustine Chair in Education, Community and Diaspora. Thanks also go to Dr. Scott Rutherford for his helpful feedback and to York University's Department of Humanities and the Harriet Tubman Institute for Research on Africa and Its Diasporas. Thanks also to fellow panellist and commentator Mark V. Campbell, who pushed me to think about his question about digitized representations or archives or Blackness and how that might affect the discipline of history. Much to his annoyance, I dodged the question at the conference – and here I offer only tentative ideas, but it is a start nonetheless!

1 See, for example, Fred Landon, "The Negro in Canada," *Negro History Bulletin* 12, no. 1 (1948): 5, 19–22; and Landon, "Agriculture among the

Negro Refugees in Upper Canada," *Journal of Negro History* 21, no. 3 (1936): 304–12.
2 Sadiya Hartman, *Scenes of Subjection: Terror, Slavery and Self-Making in Nineteenth-Century America* (New York: Oxford University Press, 1997).
3 Robin W. Winks, *The Blacks in Canada: A History* (Montreal and Kingston: McGill-Queen's University Press, 1997).
4 Marcel Trudel, *Canada's Forgotten Slaves: Two Hundred Years of Bondage*, trans. George Tombs (Montreal: Véhicule, 2013); originally published as *L'esclavage au Canada français: Histoire et conditions de l'esclavage* (Laval: Les Presses Universitaires Laval, 1960).
5 Winks, *Blacks in Canada*, 114.
6 Quoted in Winks, xvii.
7 Winks used the term "flotsam and jetsam" to describe, again, the passive role of the Black Refugees, a view he no doubt held of those Blacks who came to Canada during the Loyalist era. See James W. St. G. Walker, *The Black Loyalists: The Search for a Promised Land in Nova Scotia and Sierra Leone, 1783–1870*, 2nd ed. (Toronto: University of Toronto Press, 1992).
8 See Barry Cahill, "The Black Loyalist Myth in Atlantic Canada," *Acadiensis* 29, no. 1 (1999): 76–87; and James W. St. G. Walker, "Myth, History and Revisionism: The Black Loyalists Revisited," *Acadiensis* 29, no. 1 (1999): 88–105.
9 Daniel Hill, *The Freedom-Seekers: Blacks in Early Canada* (Agincourt, ON: Book Society of Canada, 1981), esp. chap. 12.
10 C. Peter Ripley, *The Black Abolitionist Papers*, vol. 2, *Canada, 1830–1865* (Chapel Hill: University of North Carolina Press, 1986), 3. Ripley does not, however, seem to focus on the racism Blacks experienced to the extent that Winks did in his work, even though these themes virtually leap off the pages of many of the primary documents he has placed in this text.
11 See, for example, Maureen Elgersman, *Unyielding Sprits: Black Women and Slavery in Early Canada and Jamaica* (New York: Garland, 1999); Peggy Bristow, coord., *"We're Rooted Here and They Can't Pull Us Up": Essays in African Canadian Women's History* (Toronto: University of Toronto Press, 1994).
12 Nina Reid-Maroney, Boulou Ebanda de B'béri, and Wanda Thomas Bernard, introduction to *Women in the "Promised Land": Essays in African Canadian History*, ed. Reid-Maroney, de B'béri, and Bernard (Toronto: Women's Press, 2018), 4.
13 Nina Reid-Maroney, *The Reverend Jennie Johnson and African Canadian History, 1869–1967* (Rochester, NY: University of Rochester Press, 2013).
14 W.E.B. Du Bois, *The Souls of Black Folk*, in *Three Negro Classics*, ed. John Hope Franklin (New York: Avon Books, 1965), 207–390.
15 Barrington Walker, *Race on Trial: Black Defendants in Ontario's Criminal Courts, 1858–1958* (Toronto: University of Toronto Press, 2010). See also Walker,

ed., *The African Canadian Legal Odyssey: Historical Essays* (Toronto: University of Toronto Press, 2012).
16 See Frantz Fanon, "The Fact of Blackness," in *Back Skin White Masks* (New York: Grove Press, 1967), chap. 6.
17 Paul Gilroy, *The Black Atlantic: Modernity and Double Consciousness* (Cambridge, MA: Harvard University Press, 1993), chap. 1.
18 Fanon, "Fact of Blackness," 109.
19 The concept of "double consciousness" was first developed by W.E.B. Du Bois in his seminal work, *The Souls of Black Folk*; see chap. 1 ("Of Our Spiritual Strivings") in that text. The concept of double consciousness is a foundational one in Black studies, and Du Bois is the foundational thinker of the field.
20 Katherine McKittrick, "'Their Blood Is There, and They Can't Throw It Out': Honouring Black Canadian Geographies," *Topia: Canadian Journal of Cultural Studies* 7 (2002): 33; William J. Harris, "'How You Sound??' Amiri Baraka Writes Free Jazz," in *Uptown Conversation: The New Jazz Studies*, ed. Robert G. O'Meally, Brent Hayes Edwards, and Farah Jasmine Griffin (New York: Columbia University Press, 2004), 312–25.
21 David Theo Goldberg, *The Racial State* (New York: Blackwell, 2002), 2.
22 Many First Nations peoples also clearly profited from Black racial slavery, but those considerations are beyond the scope of this chapter.
23 Sunera Thobani, *Exalted Subjects: Studies in the Making of Race and Nation in Canada* (Toronto: University of Toronto Press, 2007), 95.
24 For a discussion of the myriad anti-Black laws that were passed to circumscribe the life of free Black people in the antebellum North, see Leon F. Litwack, *North of Slavery: The Negro in the Free States, 1790–1860* (Chicago: University of Chicago Press, 1961).
25 "Proceedings of the North American Convention Convened at St. Lawrence Hall, Toronto Canada West 11–13, September 12, Friday Morning," in Ripley, *Black Abolitionist Papers*, 153, 155.
26 "Proceedings," 152.
27 Jared Sexton, "The Vel of Slavery: Tracking the Figure of the Unsovereign," *Critical Sociology* 42, no. 4–5 (2014): 583–97.
28 Ephraim Casey narrative, in Benjamin Drew, *The Refugee: Or the Narratives of Fugitive Slaves in Canada* (1856; Toronto: Prospero, 2000), 375.
29 Michael Wayne, "The Black Population of Canada West on the Eve of the American Civil War: A Reassessment of the Manuscript Census of 1861," *Histoire Social/Social History* 28, no. 56 (1995): 445–85.
30 See *Colchester 225: 150 Historical Facts* (Essex, ON: Town of Essex, 2018), https://www.essex.ca/en/discover/resources/Colchester-225-Revised-Edition-2018-for-WEB.pdf.

31 Crown-Indigenous Relations and Northern Affairs Canada, "McKee Treaty No. 2," *Treaty Texts – Upper Canada Land Surrenders*, last modified March 7, 2016, https://www.rcaanc-cirnac.gc.ca/eng/1370372152585/1581293792285.
32 Mary Ann Shadd, *A Plea for Emigration; or Notes of Canada West*, ed. Phaneul Antwi (1852; Peterborough, ON: Broadview, 2016), 25.

SECTION ONE
Enslaving Blackness

2
Planting Slavery in Nova Scotia's Promised Land, 1759-1775

KAROLYN SMARDZ FROST

In 1899 a Nova Scotia memoir was published telling the story of an enslaved man of great strength. His name was Mintur. Brought to Nova Scotia in 1761 by the Northup family of North Kingstown, Rhode Island, he had been sold on 24 August 1779 to John Palmer of Windsor Forks. The Palmers soon discovered that Mintur was spending his evenings in a concealed location, building a small boat. When challenged, he confessed that he intended to sail south down the Atlantic coast and return to his former New England home. Mintur was prevented from accomplishing his lonely mission. When manumitted some time later, in return for all his years of unwaged labour he was given only his clothing and the amount of "victuals" he could carry on his back. Unable to return to Rhode Island, Mintur walked through the forest to faraway Queen's County, where he married a free African Nova Scotian woman. In a move emblematic of their love of liberty, Mintur and his bride named their son "Freeman."[1]

Slavery, as noted historian Afua Cooper points out, is one of Canada's best kept secrets.[2] Few Canadians are aware that the institution was practised in this country for more than two hundred years by French and British colonizers, the latter of whom gained hegemony over mainland Nova Scotia in 1710. Still fewer know that in the mid-eighteenth century a wave of New England immigrants brought enslaved people with them to Maritime Canada. These "planters," or farmers, came at the invitation of the Nova Scotia government to take up lands abandoned after the Acadian expulsion of the 1750s. Mintur was just one of an uncounted number of enslaved people who were torn from home and family and carried off to Nova Scotia in the years before the American Revolution.

This chapter showcases the results of new research into the lives and experiences of enslaved Africans imported into Nova Scotia by the New England Planters. This is a neglected period in Canada's history of race and slavery, and initial findings suggest that the role of the enslaved people forcibly migrated to Nova Scotia by the Planters was far more significant than has hitherto been suggested. First of all, eighteenth-century British colonial Nova Scotia was, if not a slave society dependent upon enslaved labour as an essential component of the economy, at least a society with slaves.[3] Secondly, investigations confirm that New England Planters profited from slavery in the years leading up to the Revolutionary War and, indeed, after it. They did so not only through the direct exploitation of unwaged labour but also by working with their counterparts in their former New England homes. Together they extended northwards to Nova Scotia shipping routes linking the sugar islands of the West Indies with ports in Massachusetts, Connecticut, Rhode Island, and New Hampshire. This coastal commerce also facilitated a small but lucrative trade in enslaved men, women, and children. Theirs was a tertiary development of Nova Scotia's Planter period and was the evolution of an extended traffic in Black bodies in both directions up and down North America's eastern seaboard.[4]

New England Planter history, and particularly that of the enslaved African New Englanders they brought with them into Nova Scotia, has long been overshadowed in both academic literature and popular understanding by the much larger migration of Black and White American Loyalists occasioned by the Revolution itself.[5] There is but a single scholarly article focused on slavery in Planter-era Nova Scotia and on the unwaged and unwilling workers whose skills and labour were so essential to Planter resettlement. In it the author suggests there may have been no more than 150 to 200 enslaved African New Englanders carried to the colony at the time of the Planter migrations.[6] Such numbers are impossibly low, for wills survive that show as many as seven enslaved people being bequeathed to Planter heirs. Even for the succeeding Loyalist period, though, the fact that White Loyalists imported their still-enslaved human "property" with them, sometimes on the same ships carrying free Black Loyalists, is hardly common knowledge on the part of Canadian educators, the public, or even academic historians. Indeed, "Black Loyalist historiography has consistently overlooked those who remained enslaved," writes historian Harvey Amani Whitfield.[7]

The matter is complicated by the fact that source material regarding African Nova Scotian history for this seminal period is both scattered and difficult to access.[8] No one is sure exactly how many Planters actually moved to Nova Scotia, which at the time included the mouth of the St. John River in what is now New Brunswick; the number is usually estimated at about two thousand families. However, some migrated to Nova Scotia in their own vessels and so were not counted in the government records, while others became discouraged with conditions upon their arrival and returned to New England.[9]

The number of enslaved "servants" the Planters brought with them remains a mystery as well. The problem is partly a semantic one: North American slaveholders, along with government and military officials, used the term "servant" to describe both those who were free and those enslaved, which profoundly obscures the record. Scholars simply cannot determine exactly how many "slaves for life" came to Canada with the Planters or were imported in the following years for personal reasons or for resale. Records ranging from muster rolls to shipping and victualing lists all employ the term "servant," even where is it clear that some, if not all, of the individuals so described were actually enslaved.[10] It should be noted, too, that the milder terminology in no way mitigated the conditions under which the enslaved suffered. Enslaved African Nova Scotians endured the same deprivation and ongoing threat of corporal punishment or being sold away from their families that were the experience of men, women, and children in bondage everywhere in the Americas.

This scholarship is in its infancy. A wide-ranging and well-funded research program would be needed to tease out the multiple documentary and other resources that speak to the history of slavery in Planter-era Nova Scotia. Some relevant documentation lies in Canadian repositories, but much remains to be discovered in archival and other collections located in Connecticut, Massachusetts, Rhode Island, and other parts of the former Thirteen Colonies. Furthermore, since the New England Planters maintained their long history of seafaring and trade after they migrated northwards, there are pertinent records in both Caribbean and British collections. Much, too, still lies unexamined in the private papers held by New England Planter descendants, both in Maritime Canada and elsewhere.

Archaeological research has generally concentrated on the Acadians, French farmers whose settlement preceded the Planter migration, and on sites related to the Loyalists who came after them. Some work has been done on New England Planter sites, but the contemporary lifeways of African Nova Scotians remain an almost entirely unstudied resource, with multiple relevant mid-to-late eighteenth-century sites crying out for excavation and analysis.[11] Likewise, with a considerable amount of extant Planter-era architecture in both Nova Scotia and New Brunswick, almost no scholarly attention had been paid to contemporary buildings relating to enslaved Africans of the era. At least in the earliest years of Planter settlement, the enslaved seem to have lived within the households of their owners, as was the custom in much of colonial New England. However, there were larger slaveholdings too. At least four purpose-built slave cabins are still standing on former Planter properties in Nova Scotia, and there may well be more. There are also several known or suspected cemetery locations in both Nova Scotia and New Brunswick.[12] Finally, north of Port Williams, on the Cornwallis River in Nova Scotia's King's County, stands a small wooden church building dating to 1770. Built by a known slaveholder, John Burbidge, along with his friend William Best, it was moved to a nearby property to make way for the construction of a new church in about 1804; the old church is currently in use as a shed. The fact that Burbidge and a Gibraltar-born settler named Benjamin Belcher, two major contributors to the construction of the new St. John's Anglican Church that replaced it, were both slaveholders suggests the earlier building may well have been constructed, moved, and repaired by enslaved craftsmen.[13]

Slavery had existed in Nova Scotia long before the Planters came, of course, but the first African person who reportedly arrived on Nova Scotian shores came as a free man and valued member of Samuel de Champlain's 1604 expedition to explore New France. It is believed that fifteen years before the landing of enslaved Africans at Virginia's Jamestown settlement in 1619, Mathieu Da Costa, an Atlantic Creole of mixed African and Portuguese heritage, arrived at Port Royal. He served as a translator for the Mi'kmaq and of other First Nations languages. Historian Hilary Russell traced his history in Europe through a series of court cases attesting to the high demand Da Costa enjoyed for his linguistic skills, although detailed evidence of his activities while in Maritime Canada remains to be discovered.[14]

The French held enslaved "servants" in their households at Port Royal, and when the British took mainland Nova Scotia in 1710 they continued the practice. They settled at Port Royal, re-establishing it as Annapolis Royal. British hegemony was confirmed in the Treaty of Utrecht (1713). From the first, military men, along with members of the government and of the merchant elite, imported enslaved African "servants" to care for their families' needs. As Whitfield writes in his important volume *Blacks on the Border*, "white Nova Scotians' first encounter with people of African descent was forged in a context of racial inequality."[15] To counter the British arrival, the French built Fortress Louisbourg near the northern tip of Île Royale (Cape Breton), of which they retained control. A cod fishery was already established, with the finest product sent to France, while a trade with the French West Indies supplied the sugar islands with cheaper cuts of salted and dried fish as food for enslaved workers. The fort was taken under siege in 1745, mainly by a New England–based force, but was handed back to the French under the Treaty of Aix-la-Chapelle three years later. It would again be besieged in 1758 and then finally destroyed by the victorious British in 1760.[16]

Enslaved Africans also helped to establish the new capital of the French colony at Louisbourg. Retired Parks Canada historian Ken Donovan's groundbreaking work on Île-Royale shows that between 1713 and 1758, there were at least 266 enslaved men, women, and children in a population of about 4,000 people. Some 90 per cent of these were of African descent, working in domestic service, fishing, and farming. Most had arrived by way of the French sugar islands, but a few were born in Africa and at least one in India. A number of them were trained artisans. While Black people did not make up a large proportion of the population in French colonial Nova Scotia, their skills and labour were vital to the life and economy of Louisbourg.[17]

The next wave of enslaved Africans arrived when the new British capital of Nova Scotia was established at Halifax in 1749. The city was strategically located in order to neutralize the threat posed by Louisbourg. Enslaved African people were forcibly migrated to British colonial Nova Scotia, some by British military officers, who had acquired their human "property" while serving in the Caribbean. Others were brought by merchants from the Thirteen Colonies, and a few from Britain. Again, most were skilled workers, including an unnamed shipwright whose presence was documented in 1750. Nova Scotia historian Barry Cahill notes that some 400 enslaved Africans as well as 17 free Black people were in Halifax by that time, out of a total population of nearly 3,000.[18] More bondsmen of African descent were imported over the years as personal and domestic servants or as merchandise to be sold at profit. Advertisements printed in the *Halifax Gazette* demonstrate that there was a brisk trade in enslaved men, women, and children between merchants, politicians, and other well-to-do residents. They served in every possible capacity, and indeed, Halifax merchant Joshua Mauger, who grew rich in the West India Trade, crewed and captained some of his ships entirely with enslaved Black sailors in the 1750s.[19]

Efforts to populate the colony with Protestants who would owe their personal and familial allegiance to the Crown had attracted some 2,000 British settlers to Nova Scotia. Many of them were from better-off families, however, and ill suited to the pioneer phase of colonial life, while others were former military officers and soldiers. Some arrived with Black "servants" who had been enslaved in Great Britain prior to their migration, the ships' logs listing their numbers but no names. However, a significant number of these British immigrants abandoned Maritime Canada for the more genteel society of the Thirteen Colonies.[20] To bolster the population, the "Foreign Protestants," mainly German and Swiss immigrants, were also recruited between 1750 and 1753. Some of the approximately 2,500 newcomers worked off their passage in building Halifax, and the rest settled on lands in the Lunenburg area with the promise of provisions and supplies to tide them over until their farms and fisheries could become productive. Their resettlement was put in the hands of military officer Colonel Charles Lawrence. These Europeans did not arrive with enslaved people to assist with the work of settlement, although some purchased such "servants" later. However, the most prominent British newcomer to Lunenburg was Captain John Creighton, justice of the peace and militia office. He had immigrated to Nova Scotia on the *Charlton*, in the same flotilla bearing Governor Edward Cornwallis in 1749. Creighton, whose elegant marble memorial graces St. John's Anglican Church at Lunenburg to this day, apparently arrived in Nova Scotia with three enslaved "servants" in tow.[21]

The New England Planters came next. To understand the importance of the New England Planter migration to African Nova Scotian history, it is useful to explore the context in which it occurred. Great Britain had only the most tenuous hold on its new Canadian possession. In 1750, Nova Scotia (which until 1784 included the modern New Brunswick) was populated by about 2,000 First Nations peoples and about 10,000 Roman Catholic French Acadians.[22] The Acadians had taken only a modified oath of allegiance in 1729–30, refusing to bear arms against France on behalf of the English king. Believing that the Acadians had irreconcilably divided loyalties, the government of the colony chose a drastic solution, with unspeakably tragic consequences. It was decided that French Catholics should be removed from Nova Scotia altogether. But expelling the Acadians also meant putting the vast majority of the province's farms and fisheries out of production. The Grand Dérangement of the 1750s left fallow thousands of acres of farmland. Dyked salt marshes that had proved so fertile were laid waste. Livestock starved, while the fruit of thriving orchards rotted on the ground.[23]

Appointed governor of Nova Scotia in July 1756, Charles Lawrence consulted with Governor Shirley of Massachusetts and arranged to invite New England farmers, or "Planters," to take up the abandoned Acadian farms and coastal fisheries. As noted at the beginning of this chapter, this would result in dozens of enslaved Africans being forcibly imported from the Thirteen Colonies into what is now Maritime Canada. New Englanders had long familiarity with Nova Scotia and the St. John River region. They had served against the French in the siege of Louisbourg, at Fort Beauséjour near the present site of Sackville, New Brunswick, and in other conflicts. They also were experienced pioneers, having migrated repeatedly within Great Britain's American colonies as more and more land was cleared to support New England's growing population.[24] Just as importantly, New Englanders had been engaged in trade with Maritime Canada for decades, including some clandestine exchanges in goods with the French at Louisbourg, despite British regulations against such trade with England's long-time enemy. Since the seventeenth century, New Englanders had also been harvesting great quantities of fish from Nova Scotian waters.[25]

Governor Lawrence published his first proclamation offering lands formerly occupied by Acadians to potential New Englander settlers in October 1758.[26] Town meetings were called in Massachusetts, Connecticut, and elsewhere to discuss Lawrence's proposition and weigh its attractions. A number of queries were subsequently brought to his attention by his New York and Boston-based representatives, so Governor Lawrence issued another proclamation, on 11 January 1759.[27] This second proclamation offers fascinating insight into Lawrence's own attitudes toward the importation of enslaved Africans into colonial Nova Scotia. There would be 100,000 acres granted in twelve townships; each grant would include dyked marshland, uplands for pasture, and wild lands that could be brought under cultivation.[28] Detailed terms included the following statement regarding the planned division of available acreage: "They are to include the best land, and the rivers of the vicinity, to front on the sea, &c. 100 acres of wild wood land will be given to each head of a family of settlers, and 50 acres added for every person in the family, young or old, male or female, *white or black* [my emphasis], subject to a quitrent of 1s. per 50 acres, to begin ten years after the date of the grant."[29]

Governor Lawrence was surely aware that many of the African New Englanders were trained and skilled craftspeople who would prove invaluable in Planter resettlement. The provision to each householder of an additional fifty acres for each accompanying person of African descent was obviously intended as incentive for incoming settlers to transport enslaved people to serve as domestics, artisans, and farm workers. Lawrence's proclamation went on: "The grantees to cultivate or inclose [*sic*] one third of the land in 10 years – one third more in 20 years, and the residue in 30 years. No quantity beyond 1000 acres to be granted to any one person. On fulfilment of the terms of a first grant, the party will be entitled to another, on similar conditions."[30]

Five New Englanders sent by the would-be settlers arrived at Halifax and met with Governor Lawrence and his council on 18 April 1759. Their interest was to ascertain the value and fecundity of the lands they were being offered, to determine how legal title could be acquired and retained for heirs, and to ensure that the settlers' religious and political rights would be protected. The government offered to transport the

Planters' goods and furniture and to underwrite costs for impoverished families who wished to make the journey. The prospective settlers, in turn, wanted assurance that they would be armed at government expense and could not be impressed into military defence for ten years. Governor Lawrence guaranteed the safety of incoming Planter families by establishing forts garrisoned with British soldiers in each area of settlement.[31] No documentation has yet come to light regarding the number of enslaved African New Englanders whom the would-be-settlers expected to carry into Nova Scotia with them, although research continues.

Then the agents took ship and explored the coastline, disembarking on the shores of the Minas Basin to inspect the lands. Returning to Halifax in mid-May, they promised to bring between 150 and 200 settler families to Cornwallis and Horton Townships, each comprising 100,000 acres. More agents arrived from the other New England colonies and eventually thirteen townships were created, though not all were settled by the Planters. Some were less interested in agriculture than in the deep waters and protected harbours of the south and western shores of the province. Fishing families were offered similar terms – each householder was entitled to up to 1,000 acres, including town and "fish" lots, the latter giving direct access to the waterfront. Some of these newcomers also brought enslaved African New Englanders with them, settling the southern and western shores of the province.[32]

More than 8,000 New England Planters ultimately moved to Nova Scotia. Included in the Planter migration was at least one free Black Planter family by the name of Cuffee: Stephen and his wife, Barbara or Barbary, who was a midwife, along with their adult children, Deborah and Isaac. They took up their promised land grant at the South Shore port town of Liverpool, Nova Scotia. Stephen Cuffee passed away early; his son, Isaac, established his own fishery on an island at the mouth of the Mersey River, and daughter Deborah married a White settler and eventually moved to the Yarmouth area at Nova Scotia's western tip. At the time of the American Revolution, Barbary Cuffee and her son chose to relocate to their original Massachusetts home. Documentation of land sales of Barbary's property and of Isaac's island fishery survives.[33]

While their numbers remain uncertain, by far the majority of African New Englanders who came with the New England Planters were enslaved. Nor does this represent a single migration, for merchants, military, and other comfortably off Planter families continued to import, sell, and trade enslaved Africans throughout the period before the American Revolutionary War.[34] The French at Louisbourg had earlier forged commercial ties with both the West Indies and Europe, but it was between the founding of Halifax in 1749 and the time of the American Revolution that British colonial Canada was transformed into a northern node of the Atlantic World trade routes. Linking with relatives and neighbours left behind in New England, merchants among the New England Planters extended the networks of the West Indian trade northwards from Boston, New Haven, and other harbours of colonial America to include Nova Scotian ports.[35]

Of course, colonial New England already had a long history of importing Caribbean sugar and sugar products. A proportion of the sugar was transformed into the rum so beloved by the British Navy. Transporting it along with corn, tobacco, salted and dried cod from the Grand Banks fisheries, and other foodstuffs across the Atlantic to Europe, New England was an important stop on transatlantic trade routes related to slavery and slave-produced goods that were the lifeblood of Atlantic World economies. From Britain, manufactured goods and textiles sailed south in British vessels to the coasts of Africa, where they were exchanged for uncounted millions of people. These terrified and abused souls were carried off to the plantation societies of the Americas, there to be exchanged for sugar and other slave-produced goods, the cruel trajectory beginning all over again.[36]

New England's West Indian trade was a commerce in which Black sailors, shipwrights, caulkers, and other trades and craftsmen provided essential services, and this continued once the New England Planters reached Nova Scotia. Indeed, African New Englanders had been valued hands in Nova Scotia shipbuilding enterprises even before Planter settlement started. With the founding of Halifax in 1749, Captain Thomas Bloss of the Royal Navy was awarded a land grant on Lawlor Island in Halifax harbour. Bloss was clearly intending to begin a shipbuilding and trading operation there, for in the *Boston Post Boy* of 20 August 1750 he ran an advertisement offering five pounds for the return of two absconding sailmakers named Ned and Phillip, the latter of whom was described as being tall, spare, and a little lame. Ned was nineteen and sprightly. Both men spoke broken English, suggesting they were African born. In a fine example of New World acculturation, neither had shoes or stockings but were wearing "Mogizzeens" (moccasins), but whether of Mi'kmaq or perhaps Native American manufacture cannot be ascertained from available evidence.

Captain Bloss died on a trip to England and the planned shipbuilding operation never came to fruition. Interestingly, in September 1751, the *Boston Evening Post* advertised the following: "Just arrived from Halifax and to be sold, ten strong, hearty Negro men, mostly tradesmen, such as caulkers, carpenters, sailmakers and ropemakers. Any person wishing to purchase may inquire of Benjamin Hallowell of Boston."[37] These were very likely what remained of the Bloss shipbuilding crew, now shipped south to Massachusetts for a profitable resale. It would be very useful to explore further the forced labour of African Nova Scotians in shipbuilding, mining, construction, logging, and other commercial pursuits initiated by New England Planter entrepreneurs, in order to fill out our understanding of occupations undertaken by enslaved workers on Canada's eastern seaboard.

According to historian Julian Gwyn, 62 per cent of all vessels entering Halifax harbour from 1749 until the end of 1753 were from New England.[38] At least some of the ships carried enslaved men, women, and children to British Canada. After their arrival starting in 1760, the Planters in Nova Scotia simply imported both their enslaved workers and their existing mercantile contacts with them, expanding their networks over time and securing a leading role in the coastal commerce between Maritime Canada, the Thirteen Colonies, and the Caribbean that would bolster the fortunes of some Planters and their descendants for generations to come.[39]

Both the New England Planters and the Halifax merchants who had already been established when these newcomers arrived dealt in multiple products, including timber, lumber, wheat and other food products, and the ubiquitous dried and salted fish that had already become so crucial a protein source for the enslaved plantation workers of the West Indies. Raw sugar and molasses now travelled northwards not only to Boston, Providence, and New London, Connecticut, but also to Halifax, Liverpool, Yarmouth, and Saint John. While Newfoundland continued to supply the lion's share of dried and salted fish for the West Indian trade – the iconic Newfoundland alcoholic beverage "screech," a very high-proof rum distilled from sugar received in return for fish, is one legacy of it – the products of West Indian plantations along with New England–produced goods also appeared in ads posted by Nova Scotian merchants. The same Planter-owned ships that carried Canadian trade goods south to the ports of the American eastern seaboard and to the Caribbean sometimes brought back small numbers of enslaved people from West Indian and New England ports to be sold on the streets of Halifax and at the mouth of the St. John River. Deprived of home and family, these exploited and disenfranchised workers helped build Maritime Canada as we know it today.[40]

Planter merchants and shipowners sometimes invested in trading voyages that purchased enslaved people in one Caribbean market and sold them at profit on other islands, as did Samuel Starr of Starr's Point, a landmark on the Minas Basin on Nova Scotia's Fundy Shore.[41] African Nova Scotians were also taken south for sale in West Indian markets, for reasons of both punishment and commerce, and this continued through the Loyalist period. Even the Loyalist Church of England minister at Shelburne would one day take advantage of higher prices in the British Caribbean: "[The Reverend] Mr. Rowland sold his Negress for 30£ of this Currency, and 'Tis said she will fetch 300 dollars at New Providence," according to William Booth of the Royal Corps of Engineers. This pernicious aspect of the commerce continued through the Revolutionary War period and into at least the first decade of the nineteenth century.[42]

A more mundane but crucial trade commodity from the Caribbean was salt. In the absence of refrigeration, salt was essential for the preservation of the fish, beef, and pork that were staples of the eighteenth- and nineteenth-century diet and particularly necessary for the long-term conservation of the products of the Grand Banks fisheries.[43] Nova Scotian vessels joined those of the New Englanders who were their relatives and business partners in exploiting the bounty of Atlantic Canada's teeming waters. Dried with two pounds of salt to one of cod, the best product was transported to British and other European markets. As had been the case at Louisburg, the cheapest form of the preserved fish, stacked like cordwood, went south in Nova Scotian trading vessels as an inexpensive yet nourishing protein source for enslaved workers on West Indian plantations. On islands where land was deemed too valuable to grow food for enslaved Africans, and where the profits accruing from the production of staples for export were high enough to justify this deployment of workers, salt cod from the North Atlantic fisheries supplied indispensable nutrients to a diet otherwise composed largely of plantains, greens, bananas, and other vegetable matter.[44]

To return to the initial period of New England Planter immigration, it is important to understand that slavery, while never inscribed in law, was already a normal and accepted part of both Nova Scotian society and the local economy at the time they arrived. Furthermore, the Planters came from parts of New England where slavery was a fact of everyday life. Enslaved Africans and people of African descent served in every possible capacity, including farmhands and housekeepers, craftspeople and multiply skilled labourers. Slavery was popular in New England; by 1750 one in every four families in Connecticut owned at least one enslaved person. About 11 per cent of Rhode Island's overall population was of African descent, nearly all of them enslaved. New England families made vast fortunes from the African slave trade, and Rhode Island and Massachusetts particularly profited from the commerce in Black bodies. Massachusetts had been importing enslaved Africans directly from the African continent since 1634 and traded with other New England colonies. Ten per cent of Boston's population was of African descent in the 1750s, while about 7.5 per cent of the population in New York City was

Black. Connecticut passed gradual abolition legislation in 1784, but the last enslaved person in the state was not finally freed until 1848.[45]

Nor were these heirs to the Puritans particularly benevolent slaveholders. Logbooks survive in the Connecticut State Library of slave traders plying the waters between New London and the African coast, and the development of the trade is detailed in Wendy Warren's 2016 volume, *New England Bound: Slavery in Early New England*. Connecticut had been forced to pass legislation in 1711 requiring slave owners to care for the elderly members of their own enslaved households, lest helpless men and women be abandoned to fend for themselves after years of productive labour on behalf of those who claimed their service. By the same token, the regulations governing African American behaviour were strictly enforced; for example, "by a 1730 law, any black, Indian, or mulatto slave who uttered or published, about any white person, words which would be actionable if uttered by a free white was, upon conviction before any one assistant or justice of the peace, to be whipped with forty lashes."[46]

For the enslaved, the heartache imposed by the Planter migration to Canada had begun long before they took ship. In common with other such migrations throughout the Atlantic World, New England Planter families would have disposed of their "surplus" enslaved people before they left, particularly those not deemed useful or necessary to their own resettlement in Nova Scotia. African Americans therefore lost much-loved family connections as a result of this enforced emigration. In an exodus in some ways as disruptive as the African slave trade that put them or their forebearers on the auction blocks of the New World in the first place, the emigration of the New England Planters tore apart the Black families under their control. There were certain individuals the would-be emigrants chose not to carry with them to their new homeland; they were entrusted to family members. Others the Planters sold off, just as they did their livestock, shops, and land. The pages of the *Connecticut Gazette* displayed multiple advertisements for the sale of enslaved Africans. Some were placed by New England Planters in preparation for their journeys to Nova Scotia, and a thorough search of its pages is expected to turn up still more evidence in this regard.[47]

It is distressingly easy to imagine how it all transpired: one Planter family might take their cook with them but not her aging husband. Another would carry off the shipwright but not his elderly parents. A third would tell the young kitchen maid to pack her personal belongings but to leave her toddler son behind lest he take up too much time and care. A fourth might offer the dairymaid's baby to a neighbouring household where there lived an enslaved woman to serve as wet nurse. As ships pulled away from the New England ports most of their passengers would never see again, grief for the loss of loved ones must have torn the hearts of African New Englanders bound for Nova Scotia.

The Planters travelled in large extended family groups and, once in Nova Scotia, tended to settle in blocks. This meant that in at least some cases their enslaved "servants" might find friends or even relatives living in proximity to their new homes. For instance, Wolfville is a New England Planter town on the Minas Basin of the Bay of Fundy. That section of the shoreline was mainly settled by Connecticut Planters, while the area to the east around Falmouth was largely the preserve of newcomers from Rhode Island, including the Northups who brought the enslaved Mintur mentioned at the beginning of this chapter. Although not of New England stock, Irish-born Colonel Henry Denny Denson, who was one of the original proprietors of Mount Denson (West Falmouth), held a dozen enslaved people. When he died his executors sold three, named Spruce, John, and Juba, to Halifax buyers to settle the estate.[48] Slaveholders only rarely recorded surnames for enslaved people, which presents a perennial problem in researching the biographies of enslaved African Americans – genealogists in the field call this "the wall of slavery" – but the first names of Spruce and Juba are sufficiently unusual that the potential exists for future discovery of earlier transactions regarding their purchase, and even their original transportation to Nova Scotia.

Nova Scotia's South Shore was partly settled by people from Massachusetts, including one of the original grantees at Chester: a noted Baptist minister named John Seccombe, who claimed ownership of the enslaved Dinah and Caesar.[49] At Argyle, just east of Yarmouth in southwestern Nova Scotia, Ranald MacKinnon, a Scotsman and a military man rather than a Planter grantee, had enough enslaved people with him in the province that his holding was known as a "slave farm."[50]

African New Englanders in Nova Scotia suffered even more than did the Planter families who brought them, for the hardest work was reserved for the enslaved. Before they left their New England homes, the Planters and their enslaved workers had known that settlement in Nova Scotia would be difficult, dangerous, and incredibly labour intensive, despite the promised governmental provisions and supplies. The sheer scale of the work to be accomplished was stunning. Housing was a priority. Along the Fundy Shore nearly all the Acadian buildings had been destroyed. The colony's sawmill, located at Dartmouth on the eastern shore of Halifax harbour, had been burned in a raid a couple of years earlier. In the absence of locally milled lumber, some Planter families had the foresight to dismantle their former New England homes and transport them aboard ship, the beams numbered so they could be reconstructed on the Nova Scotian land grants. Others laboriously cut down trees (or more likely had enslaved Africans do so) on their "wild lands" to provide both immediate shelter for their livestock and housing for their families.[51]

Socially, economically, and politically, too, both the Planters and the enslaved individuals whom they carried with them underwent profound upheaval as a result of their removal to Maritime Canada. Free land and seemingly unlimited prospects could not make up for the loss of village and family life, along with the much more developed societal infrastructure of colonial British America.[52] More critically, enslaved Blacks suffered real hardship owing to the straightened financial circumstances of the White Planters who controlled their lives and fortunes; with a few notable exceptions, members of the first generation of Planters were far from wealthy, as Julian Gwyn demonstrates. Newly arrived Planters usually built modest homes, often in the classic Cape Cod storey-and-a-half style, and only in later years constructed more elaborate two-storey houses, or else added on to the ones they had. As noted earlier, most members of the enslaved workforce resided with their owners.[53] Subjected to "family slavery," they endured endless workdays and were under constant surveillance because of living and working with slaveholders in very close quarters. Their treatment would have ranged from relatively comfortable to execrable, depending on the temper and resources of those who claimed their service. Too, there was the constant threat of physical punishment to ensure their compliance.[54]

This form of "family slavery" had been common on the smaller New England farms. While sources describing Nova Scotian slave conditions in these years are few, they are relatively plentiful for contemporary practices in the parts of the Thirteen Colonies from which the Planter families came.[55] For instance, an important source is the diary kept over an astonishing forty-seven-year period by Joshua Hempstead (1678–1758), a farmer and merchant in New London, Connecticut. The diary provides descriptions of the life and work undertaken by an enslaved man known only as Adam. Even more revelatory of the experience of African New Englanders of the Planter period is the detailed description provided by African-born Venture Smith of his own life in slavery in Rhode Island and Connecticut. Smith's mid-eighteenth-century account sheds much light on the conditions of enslavement under which African New Englanders lived prior to the Planter migration, and very likely also on those endured by newly arrived Africans in Nova Scotia during their first years in Canada.[56]

Still, life was even harder in Nova Scotia than it had been for the enslaved in New England. While government provisions might stave off starvation, ships were irregular on the stormy seas, officials had been known to break their promises, and people both Black and White knew they had to grow and preserve enough food for the winter or they and their children would all go hungry. The perennial problem of having enough fodder to overwinter the livestock was somewhat alleviated by the provision of grasslands in each grant, but for those families and their enslaved workers who arrived later in the year, that which was immediately available was often insufficient. Moreover, the beautifully designed and constructed Acadian dykes that drained the fertile salt marshes had been severely damaged in a 1759 storm. Unfortunate Acadian prisoners from Halifax were conscripted to teach these newcomers how to repair and maintain the dykes. It would be interesting to know what interchanges took place between these bereft and displaced Acadians and the enslaved African New Englanders assigned to assist them with the labour.[57]

There were services, too, that were critical to New England Planter success in their new homes. As stated above, the Planters imported enslaved men and women who possessed the specific skills they needed to help with the process of resettlement. Dockyard facilities and wharves had to be built for loading and unloading ships that brought all the imported goods from New England, the Caribbean, and the British Isles and also for the bulk export of surplus foodstuffs, timber, and other trade goods. Warehousing – constructed at least in part by Black hands – was needed to store goods, and gristmills had to be established very soon lest there be no flour for bread except for that imported at astronomical prices from Boston or New York. Blacksmith forges were set up immediately upon arrival, for the smiths, both Black and White, made vast quantities of nails to fasten all those buildings and ships together. Likewise, coopers were needed to produce the barrels in which meat was preserved and fish shipped for export. All of these tasks would have been carried out by enslaved Africans, working in tandem with Planter family members. Having met their owners' immediate requirements, trained craftspeople would have been hired out to other Planter families lacking such skills. In these early years, slaveholders might be paid for the labour of their hired-out artisans and craftspeople in a length of woven cloth from one household, a barrel of apples from another, or perhaps a day's labour offered in barter.[58]

The day-to-day workload for women, Black and White, in Planter-era Nova Scotia was simply staggering. On 30 May 1752, the same Halifax merchant who manned his ships with enslaved Africans, Joshua Mauger, advertised a Black woman for sale in the Halifax *Royal Gazette*. He made particular mention of her housekeeping skills and cooking, as well as her ability to do laundry. Having been "brought up in a Gentleman's family" she could do "Needle-work of all sorts." Slaveholdings were widely scattered and might consist of only one or two people, meaning most of the enslaved men and women had difficulty forming families of their own. However, European-American women of this era delivered an average of a child every two years, so childcare was an important responsibility of enslaved African women. At the same time, everything from the fabric made from sheep's wool and flax they grew themselves to candles and the wicks that went in them had to be made or purchased or bartered for. There was cheese to be made and stored, butter to be churned, and animals to be milked. Laundry was an unimaginable chore, especially in winter when clothes were boiled in great tubs indoors. Even the soap had to be homemade, using lye produced from dripping water through wood ash and boiled up with animal fat. There were chickens to tend, meals to make, and all sorts of foods to prepare and preserve for the winter months. Fruit and vegetables were canned or dried. In the absence of refrigeration, meat was pickled or salted in barrels. Fish, too, was salted and dried on great racks, both for winter consumption and for trade. African Nova Scotian women undertook all these tasks and more, whether working alongside New England Planter women or alone.[59]

Then there were the clothes themselves. Every piece of clothing that was not imported from elsewhere had to be made entirely by hand, down to the buttons, which were carved of wood or bone unless funds could be found to purchase metal ones from Britain or the American colonies. The fabric from which clothing and bed coverings were made had to be manufactured too. Worn-out work shirts and children's wear too tattered to hand down were cut up and made into quilts, meticulously stitched by candlelight or whale oil lamps in the long winter evenings. Sheep were raised and sheared, the wool carded and spun, and the resulting yarn woven into cloth. Flax had to be grown, rotted, and broken to remove the woody stalks, the soft fibres then spun into thread. Weaving was a skill carried out by enslaved women throughout North America, often during the colder months. Then woollen or linen pants and shirts, jackets, skirts, and ladies' blouses and bodices, as well as undergarments, were cut out and sewn, usually at the end of the working day. Such tasks were carried out by firelight, after the children were in bed, and it was done by hand, for there were no sewing machines yet. Needles and thimbles had to be manufactured and were therefore precious, imported at some cost from Great Britain and New England and handed down through generations.[60]

Continued investigation into the lives and experiences of enslaved African New Englanders forcibly migrated to Nova Scotia by the New England Planters is expected to shed more light on this British colonial "society with slaves." It is evident that enslaved Africans offered vital support to the settlement of Planter-era Nova Scotia, not only for their labour but also because of their talents and skills, creativity, and physical strength. As Planters grew more prosperous, additional enslaved Africans were imported from either the Thirteen Colonies or the West Indies. There were far more enslaved people in Nova Scotia than has been suggested by earlier scholars. A case in point is an 1802 will preserved in the Nova Scotia Archives. Benjamin Belcher, whose home was on the Cornwallis River just north of Wolfville and who contributed generously to the building of St. John's Anglican Church at Port Williams, was able to leave seven enslaved "servants" to his heirs. His friend John Burbidge, the church warden who arranged for the church's construction, freed his enslaved "servants." However multiple wills show numbers similar to those listed in the Belcher bequest. These are beginning to add up to considerably more people than natural increase might provide. Further research will undoubtedly show that pre-Revolutionary War Nova Scotia, because of this practice of ongoing slave importation, had a significantly larger enslaved population than previously suspected.[61]

As noted earlier, the Planters found profit in slavery, directly as exploitative owners and sellers of Black bodies but also through their extension of existing Atlantic World shipping routes to include Nova Scotia and modern New Brunswick. Nova Scotian products, including the ubiquitous dried and salted cod that remains a favoured dish in the Caribbean to this day, was originally transported to the West Indies to help support the plantation economies of the island by proving an inexpensive staple food for the enslaved. Examinations of banking records and marine insurance documents are expected to provide new data regarding the purchase, transport, and sale of enslaved Africans and African-descended people between Atlantic Canada and both American and Caribbean ports throughout the Nova Scotian Planter period, and on through that dominated by the Loyalists.

There are some excellent opportunities for future investigation in respect to resistance. Just as they did everywhere in the Americas, enslaved Africans of the Planter period resisted both the fact and the conditions of their oppression. Some voted with their feet. In Halifax, the *Gazette* newspaper published fugitive slave notices alongside those advertising the availability of newly arriving Africans from the Thirteen Colonies and the West Indies.[62] Court records demonstrate attempts of slaveholders to recover their lost human "property," and shipping logs and account books bear mute witness to the fact that human trafficking in this period worked in both directions up and down the Atlantic coast.

Captain Zebulon Perkins of Liverpool, Nova Scotia, was reprimanded by the courts in 1795 for carrying off an African man who was indentured to him. Perkins had shipped twenty-one-year-old Peter to the West Indies, selling his remaining term of service to a merchant residing in Antigua, which would surely mean the young man's ultimate sale into lifelong bondage. Thanks to legal intervention, Perkins was ordered by a Nova Scotian judge to recover and return Peter to his Canadian home.[63]

A kinsman of Zebulon Perkins was the prominent merchant, judge, and politician Simeon Perkins of Liverpool, Nova Scotia. The single most accessible source of information about the lives and preoccupations of Planter-era Nova Scotians that includes details about slaves and slavery is the diary of Simeon Perkins (1734/5–1812). It was published in a series of volumes by the Champlain Society. Formerly a shopkeeper and merchant from Norwich, Connecticut, Simeon Perkins emigrated from his New England home in 1762 after the death of his young wife in childbirth. The extant diaries span most of the period from 1766 until Perkins died in 1812. A leader in his community, he held a series of offices including being in charge of defending Liverpool, with its excellent harbour at the junction of two major rivers, from American privateer attack during the Revolution.[64]

Simeon's grandson, Reverend Joshua Perkins, donated twenty-seven diaries pertaining to his ancestor's Nova Scotia years to the province in 1900.[65] Simeon Perkins's personal journals offer invaluable evidence regarding the New England Planters' attitudes toward slavery and the slave trade, both prior to their migration to Nova Scotia and in the years after they arrived. Perkins, like many of the New Englanders, operated a shipping business. He did so in cooperation with his father-in-law, Ebenezer Backus, who had remained behind in Norwich, and with his own sons and other relations who followed him into the trade. Together they bought and sold goods up and down the eastern seaboard of the Thirteen Colonies (after the Revolution, the newly created United States) from Nova Scotia to the West Indies. He invested in the shipping ventures of his friends and relations in both Nova Scotia and New England. Perkins was a keen observer of human nature and society. In his diary he named names, including a rare mention of African American Planter Barbara Cuffee and her two children who settled at Liverpool. Although a slaveholder himself, it was Simeon Perkins who on 4 May 1772, in his capacity as a justice of the peace, married Deborah Cuffee to her White fiancé when a local minister refused to preside over the interracial couple's nuptials.[66]

Not only did Perkins identify the enslaved people in his own household, but he also described how people of African ancestry were acquired, sold, and treated by other slave-holding settlers. On 7 March

1777, Perkins recorded his purchase of a "negro boy" along with other goods from a deceased neighbour named Hutchinson. On 12 July of the same year he bought Jacob, a boy ten or eleven years old. He paid £35 and casually renamed the child "Frank." No record survives of how young Jacob felt about the change.[67] Simeon's home is preserved as the centrepiece of the Queen's County Museum at Liverpool on the South Shore. Having recently undergone a much-needed restoration, it is perhaps the only standing building in Nova Scotia where we not only have direct evidence of the names and ages of enslaved Africans who lived there but can even make an educated guess as to where they slept.[68]

Another source of critical importance for studying slavery in the New England Planter period is a new database created at the Centre for the Study of the Legacies of British Slave-Ownership at the University College, London. This lists the names of slaveholders awarded compensation for their capital losses occasioned by the British abolition of slavery in most of the empire, effective 1 August 1834. It has been estimated that fully one-fifth of all elite families in Great Britain derived some or all of their income from slave-produced sugar from the Caribbean.[69] This material is now being mined for data regarding both direct and indirect engagement in West Indian slavery in Planter-era Nova Scotia; British immigrants to Atlantic Canada, including government officials, military officers, and Anglican ministers, both held slaves themselves and also had family interests in West Indian sugar plantations.[70]

In tracing the lives of enslaved African Nova Scotians of the Planter period, letters, personal diaries, travelogues, and other sources located in the widely scattered archives, historical societies, libraries, and personal collections of the former Thirteen Colonies must all be investigated. New England Planters maintained their ties with relatives and friends on America's eastern seaboard and travelled back and forth, sometimes taking with them their enslaved servants. One excellent example is that of the last enslaved woman sold in New Haven, Connecticut. Her name was Lois Tritton and she had been born into slavery in Cornwallis (Kentville), Nova Scotia. She and her mother had been left behind as security against a debt when their Halifax-based owners visited their New England relations. The debt was never redeemed, and so the two women were sold in New Haven Green. Their auction took place in 1825.[71]

Court proceedings, too, offer fascinating details for they show how slavery ultimately became untenable in Nova Scotia, although it was not formally ended until the British government passed the Slavery Abolition Act of 1833. Judicial officials including Thomas Andrew Lumisden Strange, Chief Justice of Nova Scotia, and accomplished Massachusetts-born attorney Sampson Salter Blowers, who succeeded Strange in the post, did a great deal to bring the institution of slavery to a *de facto*, if not a *de jure*, end in the province. Despite slaveholders' protests, these senior jurists consistently refused to support their efforts to recover those individuals who fled their service. A similar pattern also emerged in New Brunswick.[72] The last enslaved person known to have been sold in Nova Scotia was a young girl named Percilla, in a transaction dated 6 October 1804. Five years later, on 16 October 1809, an unnamed woman was advertised in the *New Brunswick Gazette*. Her fate is not recorded.[73]

One aspect of enslaved people's lives and aspirations that the dry documentation of their purchase, sale, and court-recorded protest only rarely illuminates is their personal feelings about their separation from loved ones. This was a daily, pernicious fact of slavery. Planter families such as the erstwhile owners of Lucy and Lois Tritton visited back and forth with relatives and business associates who remained on America's Atlantic seaboard. Yet the African Americans who the Planters forcibly removed to Nova Scotia and what is now New Brunswick longed, too, for the loved ones they had been forced to leave behind. At the beginning of this chapter was recounted the story of Mintur and the small boat he was secretly building so he could make the long and perilous sea voyage back to Rhode Island. It is hard to imagine any impetus besides great love for his lost family members that would be sufficiently powerful to cause this courageous man to risk sailing the North Atlantic in so frail a vessel, all alone.

NOTES

I would like celebrate the editors of *Unsettling the Great White North*, Michele A. Johnson and Funké Aladejebi, for their vision in conceiving this landmark volume, and their hard work in bringing it to fruition. I am honoured to have been asked to contribute. The research program presented here was conceived while I was serving as Visiting Bicentennial Professor for Canadian Studies, generously hosted by Yale's Gilder Lehrman Insititute for the Study of Slavery, Resistance and Abolition and the MacMillan Center for International and Area Studies. Important data and advice were provided by the staff of the Beinicke Library at Yale, and both the Connecticut State Archives and Connecticut History Museum. I also appreciate the help of Dale Plummer, City Historian for Norwich, Connecticut, and the volunteers at the Leffingwell House Museum. At Acadia University in Wolfville, Nova Scotia, I must thank Dr. Paul Doerr, Chair of the Department of History and Classics; the Harrison McCain Foundation; the Department of Research and Graduate Studies; and the Esther Clark Wright Archives, especially Pat Townsend. I am grateful to the Planter Studies Centre that supported the research in multiple ways. I also must thank Director Linda Rafuse at Nova Scotia's Queens County Museum. Discussions with Drs. Afua Cooper, Allegra di Bonaventura, Peter Hinks,

Julian Gwyn, and Barry Moody materially contributed to the ideas presented here. Finally I owe a debt of gratitude to several fine scholars who read over this paper in its early stages. Their insightful comments greatly enhanced both its content and presentation. These include Dr. Stephen Henderson, Director, Planter Studies Centre, Acadia University; Dr. Harvey Amani Whitfield, Professor of North American History at the University of Calgary; and David W. States, formerly of Parks Canada, and an extremely knowledgeable historian and genealogical consultant in the study of African Nova Scotian history.

1 "Sale of slave 'Mintur' by Joseph Northrup to John Palmer in Windsor," 1779, MG 100, vol. 14, no. 113, Nova Scotia Archives (NSA), https://novascotia.ca/archives/Africanns/archives.asp?ID=13; C.W. Vernon, "The Deed of a Sale of a Slave Sold at Windsor, NS, in 1779," *Acadiensis* 3, no. 4 (1903): 253–4.
2 Afua Cooper, quoted in Kyle G. Brown, "Canada's Slavery Secret: The Whitewashing of 200 Years of Enslavement," *Ideas*, CBC Radio, Feb 18, 2019, https://www.cbc.ca/radio/ideas/canada-s-slavery-secret-the-whitewashing-of-200-years-of-enslavement-1.4726313.
3 New Brunswick was not divided from the colony of Nova Scotia until 1784. The term "society with slaves" was coined by Ira Berlin, eminent scholar of race and slavery. Berlin distinguishes between "slave societies," whose economies rested on slavery and the slave trade, and "societies with slaves," where enslaved Africans were exploited for their labour and also held as status symbols but the economy was not dependent on the institution. Berlin, *Many Thousands Gone: The First Two Centuries of Slavery in North America* (Cambridge, MA: Harvard University Press, 1998), 95–6.
4 During the 2012–13 academic year, I had the honour of serving as the Visiting Bicentennial Professor for Canadian Studies at Yale University. Struck by the long-neglected history of African New Englanders during the Planter period in Nova Scotia and New Brunswick, exploring the region's New England heritage became my research focus. I was hosted by the Gilder Lehrman Center for the Study of Slavery, Resistance and Abolition, which gave me both research time and proximity to multiple New England archival collections. It was a unique opportunity to explore the early history of African American families, some of whose members were removed to Nova Scotia with the New England Planter migration. What's more, it provided access to some of the personal and business records of the New England Planter families with whom the African Americans were forcibly migrated to the Canadian Maritimes.
5 James W. St. G. Walker, *The Black Loyalists: The Search for a Promised Land in Nova Scotia and Sierra Leone* (Toronto: University of Toronto Press, 1992); and his excellent synopsis, "African Canadians," in *Encyclopedia of Canada's*

Peoples, ed. Paul R. Magosci (Toronto: University of Toronto Press,1999), 139–76. The Black Loyalists had been freed for their service to the Crown during the American Revolution, and about 3,500 of them came to Nova Scotia as a result of the conflict. Most were cheated out of their promised land and 1,196 left for Sierra Leone in January 1792. The rest, along with the heirs to those people once enslaved to the French, British, New England Planters, and White Loyalists, stayed in Maritime Canada. They went on to build homes, churches, and communities in the face of ongoing and persistent discrimination and are ancestors to thousands of proud descendants. The number who made the exodus to Sierra Leone comes from Walker, *Black Loyalists*, 129.

6 Gary G. Hartlen, "Bound for Nova Scotia; Slaves in the Planter Migration, 1759–1800," in *Making Adjustments: Changes and Continuity in Planter Nova Scotia, 1759–1800*, Planter Studies series, ed. Margaret Conrad (Fredericton: Acadiensis, 1991), 123–8. See also Harvey Amani Whitfield, "The Loyalist Arrival and the Structure of Slavery" (unpublished paper, 2012; shared with the kind permission of the author); and Whitfield, "Slavery in English Nova Scotia, 1750–1810," *Journal of the Royal Nova Scotia Historical Society* 13 (2010): 1–19.

7 Harvey Amani Whitfield, "Black Loyalists and Black Slaves in Maritime Canada," *History Compass* 5 (2007): 1987–8. See also Ken Donovan, "Slavery and Freedom in Atlantic Canada's African Diaspora: Introduction," *Acadiensis* 63, no. 1 (2014): 109–15n5. This relative lack of scholarship on Maritime Canadian slavery is now being remedied, largely by eminent historian Harvey Amani Whitfield; see Whitfield, *Black Slavery in the Maritimes: A History in Documents*, Broadview Sources series (Peterborough ON: Broadview, 2018); and Whitfield, *North to Bondage: Loyalist Slavery in the Maritimes* (Vancouver: UBC Press, 2016).

8 Barry Cahill, formerly of the Nova Scotia Archives, has provided the very useful chapter "New England Planters at the Public Archives of Nova Scotia," in *They Planted Well: New England Planters in Maritime Canada*, Planter Studies series, ed. Margaret Conrad (Fredericton: Acadiensis, 1988): 120–31.

9 Ronald S. Longley, "The Coming of the New England Planters to the Annapolis Valley," *Collections of the Nova Scotia Historical Society* 33 (1961): 81–101, reprinted in Conrad, *They Planted Well*, 14–28; Barry Cahill, "Township Records: New England Planters at the Public Archives of Nova Scotia," accessed August 3, 2019, https://novascotia.ca/archives/townships/planters.asp.

10 On both terminology and the potential numbers of Loyalist slaves brought into Maritime Canada, see T. Watson Smith's early but seminal article, "The Slave in Canada," *Collections of the Royal Nova Scotia Historical Society*

10 (1899): 23–6; Whitfield, *North to Bondage*, 34; and Whitfield, "Slavery in English Nova Scotia," 24.

11 Marc Lavoie, "Archaeological Evidence of Planter Material Culture in New Brunswick and Nova Scotia," in Conrad, *Making Adjustments*, 218–33. More recent discussions of archaeology on French and British colonial-era Nova Scotia are found in a series of papers published in *Acadiensis* 43, no. 1 (2014), the results of a forum described in Donovan, "Slavery and Freedom," 109–15.

12 Mary Louise McCarthy, personal communication, 2017. The Saint Paul's Cemetery, Old Burial Ground records in the Nova Scotian Anglican Archives, Halifax, show seven enslaved African Nova Scotian burials from the Planter period. That enslaved servants lived within the households of New England Planters is characteristic of the type of "family slavery" practised in the Thirteen Colonies before the Planters left for Maritime Canada. William Piersen coined the term in *Black Yankees: The Development of an Afro-American Subculture in Eighteenth-Century New England* (Amherst: University of Massachusetts Press, 1988), chap. 3. See also Joanne Pope Melish, *Disowning Slavery: Gradual Emancipation and "Race" in New England, 1780–1860* (Ithaca: Cornell University Press, 1998), 27–31. On Nova Scotia, see Whitfield, *North to Bondage*, 72–80; and Whitfield, "American Background of Loyalist Slaves," *Left History* 14, no. 1 (2009): 66–7. On the need for more research into the archaeological evidence for Planter-era settlement, see Jonathan Fowler, "From Acadians to Planters in the Grand-Pré Area: An Archaeological Perspective," in *The New England Planters in the Atlantic World, 1760–1830*, ed. T. Stephen Henderson and Wendy G. Robicheau (Fredericton: Acadiensis, 2012), 37–61.

13 Sara Beanlands, "Thibodeau Village: Community Engagement, Archaeology, and the Discovery of an Acadian Past in a Nova Scotia Planter Landscape" (unpublished paper presented at Government House, Halifax, April 21, 2015); Catherine Cottreau-Robins, "A Loyalist Plantation in Nova Scotia, 1784–1800" (PhD diss., Dalhousie University, 2012); and Heather MacLeod-Leslie, "SANKOFA/Return and Get It: An Archaeological Exploration of Black Loyalist Identity and Culture in Nova Scotia" (PhD diss., Memorial University of Newfoundland, 2012). Neither Benjamin Belcher nor John Burbidge was a New England Planter, but both received the same land grants as Planters along the Cornwallis River, all of whom contributed substantially to the construction of Saint John's Anglican Church north of Port Williams. See Arthur Wentworth Hamilton Eaton, *The History of Kings County, Nova Scotia, Heart of the Acadian Land* (Salem, MA: Salem Press, 1910), 77, 83–4, 144, 234.

14 Hilary Russell, "Looking for Mathieu Da Costa" (unpublished manuscript, Parks Canada, n.d.); A.J.B. Johnson, "Mathieu da Costa and Early Canada:

Possibilities and Probabilities" (National Parks and Historic Sites of Canada, n.d.), accessed May 31, 2018, http://parkscanadahistory.com/publications/portroyal/dacosta-e.pdf.

15 Harvey Amani Whitfield, *Blacks on the Border: The Black Refugees in British North America, 1815–1860* (Burlington: University of Vermont Press, 2006), 14; Whitfield, "Slavery in English Nova Scotia," 28.

16 B.A. Balcom, "The Cod Fishery of Isle Royale, 1713–58," in *Aspects of Louisbourg: Essays on the History of an Eighteenth-Century French Community in North America*, eds. Eric Krause, Carol Corbin, and William O'Shea (Sidney, NS: University College of Cape Breton Press, 1995), 171ff. John George Bourinot, *Historical and Descriptive Account of Cape Breton* (Toronto: Copp Clark, 1985), 31–2. The authoritative works on slavery under the French Regime are Marcel Trudel's *Deux siècles d'esclavage au Québec* (Quebec: Laval University, 1960), only recently translated into English; *Canada's Forgotten Slaves: Two Hundred Years of Bondage*, transl. George Tombs (Montreal: Véhicule Press, 2013); Afua Cooper's superlatively researched *The Hanging of Angélique: The Untold Story of Canadian Slavery and the Burning of Old Montréal* (Toronto: HarperCollins, 2006); and Frank Mackey, *Done with Slavery: The Black Fact in Montreal, 1760–1840* (Montreal: McGill-Queens University Press, 2010).

17 Kenneth Donovan, "A Nominal List of Slaves and their Owners in Île Royale, 1713–1760," *Nova Scotia Historical Review* 16, no. 1 (June 1996): 151–62.

18 [Barry Cahill], "African Nova Scotians in the Age of Slavery and Abolition," NSA website, accessed June 1, 2018, https://novascotia.ca/archives/africanns/default.asp; Robin W. Winks, *The Blacks in Canada: A History*, 2nd ed. (Montreal and Kingston: McGill-Queens University Press, 1997), 24–60.

19 Kenneth Donovan, "Slaves and Their Owners in Île Royale, 1713–1760," *Acadiensis* 25, no. 1 (Autumn 1995): 9, 9n23. On the importation of enslaved people as servants for particular families, see Whitfield, *Blacks on the Border*, 16.

20 J. Murray Beck, "Cornwallis, Edward," in *Dictionary of Canadian Biography*, vol. 4 (University of Toronto and Université Laval, 2003–), accessed July 25, 2019, http://www.biographi.ca/en/bio/cornwallis_edward_4E.html.

21 Dominick Graham, "Lawrence, Charles," in *Dictionary of Canadian Biography*, vol. 3, (University of Toronto and Université Laval, 2003–), accessed August 7, 2019, http://www.biographi.ca/en/bio/lawrence_charles_3E.html. Tales regarding John Creighton's slaveholding laud the courage of his enslaved servants. Unfortunately unnamed in the documents, his manservant gave warning of the approach of American privateers on 1 July 1782, and an enslaved elderly woman named Sylvia protected both Creighton's child and Creighton's family silver. Ironically, it was John Creighton who was

commended for his *servants'* courage after the celebrated event. J. Murray Beck, "Creighton, John (1721–1807)," in *Dictionary of Canadian Biography*, vol. 5 (University of Toronto and Université Laval, 2003–), accessed August 7, 2019, http://www.biographi.ca/en/bio/creighton_john_1721_1807_5E.html.

22 The First Nations population of Atlantic Canada had been decimated by disease and hardship since the early seventeenth century. Historians believe there were between 8,000 and 12,000 Mi'kmaq, Maliseet, and Passmaquody people when the French colonizers first arrived. See Geoffrey Plank, *An Unsettled Conquest: The British Campaign against the Peoples of Acadia* (Philadelphia: University of Pennsylvania Press, 2001), 23; Ralph Pastore, "The Sixteenth Century: Aboriginal Peoples and European Contact," in *The Atlantic Region to Confederation: A History*, ed. Phillip Buckner and John G. Reid (Toronto: University of Toronto Press, 1994), 35.

23 There is a great deal of literature, both scholarly and popular, on this topic. See, for instance, John Mack Faragher, *A Great and Noble Scheme: The Tragic Story of the Expulsion of the French Acadians from Their American Homeland* (New York: W.W. Norton, 2006); and also his article on the same topic, "'A Great and Noble Scheme': Thoughts on the Expulsion of the Acadians," *Acadiensis* 36, no. 1 (Autumn 2006): 82–92. On the German and Swiss migration, see Winthrop P. Bell, *Foreign Protestants and the Settlement of Nova Scotia* (Toronto: University of Toronto Press, 1961); and Brian Cuthbertson, *Lunenburg: An Illustrated History* (Halifax: Formac, 1996). For the larger context, see Elizabeth Mancke and John G. Reid, "From Global Processes to Continental Strategies: The Emergence of British North America to 1783," in *Canada and the British Empire*, ed. Phillip Buckner (Oxford: Oxford University Press, 2008): 22–42.

24 The Planter Studies Centre at Acadia University has published several superb volumes of collected works. In addition to two volumes cited earlier – Henderson and Robicheau, *Nova Scotia Planters*; and Conrad, *Making Adjustments* – these include Daniel Corey Goodwin, *A Checklist of Secondary Sources for Planter Studies* (Wolfville, NS: Department of History, Acadia University, 1987); Margaret Conrad, ed., *Intimate Relations: Family and Community in Planter Nova Scotia, 1759–1800* (Fredericton, NB: Acadiensis Press, 1995); Margaret Conrad and Barry Moody, eds., *Planter Links: Community and Culture in Colonial Nova Scotia* (Fredericton: Acadiensis, 2001); and Margaret Conrad, ed., *Making Adjustments: Change and Continuity in Planter Nova Scotia, 1759–1800* (Fredericton: Acadiensis, 1991). See also Judith A. Norton, *New England Planters in the Maritime Provinces of Canada, 1759–1800: A Bibliography of Primary Sources* (Toronto: University of Toronto Press and Planter Studies Centre, 1993).

25 Christopher Moore, "The Other Louisbourg: Trade and Merchant Enterprise in Ile Royale 1713–58," *Histoire sociale/Social History* 12, no. 23 (1979): 79–96; see also Donald F. Chard, "The Price and Profits of Accommodation: Massachusetts-Louisbourg Trade, 1713–1744," in Krause, Corbin, and O'Shea, *Aspects of Louisbourg*, 209–27.

26 "By His Excellency Charles Lawrence, Esq., ... A Proclamation," Oct. 12, 1758, published in the *Boston Gazette*, November 6, 1758; *Boston Evening Post*, November 6, 1758; and *Pennsylvania Gazette*, November 16, 1758. Interested parties were to contact Thomas Hancock, who was Governor Lawrence's agent in Boston, or the firm of DeLancey and Watt in New York with questions regarding the terms of settlement.

27 Longley, "Coming of the New England Planters," 18–19; "By His Excellency, Charles Lawrence Esq., ... A Proclamation," Jan. 11, 1759, Commissioner of Public Records, RG 1 vol. 301 no. 3, NSA, https://novascotia.ca/archives/Assembly/archives.asp?ID=3.

28 The dyked salt marshes developed by the Acadians were a particular attraction because they provided immediate and excellent fodder for livestock. The Massachusetts Bay colonies routinely suffered from a shortage of hay, which owing to the climate had to support livestock all winter and well into the succeeding spring. It was laboriously grown and harvested from fields that were previously cleared of timber and had the stumps, brush, and groundcover removed and were then ploughed and planted. Nonetheless, cattle sometimes starved before spring, particularly in the early years. The Nova Scotia government also promised potential settlers that no quitrent would be charged for the first ten years and that after that it would be limited to a shilling for every fifty acres. Grantees had to complete clearing and plant or turn to pasturage one-third of their land per decade so within thirty years all the lands would be under cultivation. See Richard L. Bushman, *From Puritan to Yankee: Character and the Social Order in Connecticut, 1690–1765* (Boston: Harvard University Press, 1980), 32. Land would be laid out by surveyor Charles Morris, whose papers provide fascinating insight into the first stages of resettlement. Morris reviewed conditions pertaining to each Planter settlement he visited. Charles Morris and Richard Bulkeley, "State and Condition of the Province of Nova Scotia Together with Some Observations &c, 29th October 1763," in *Nova Scotia Archives Report*, 1933, app. B, 21–7; see also Phyllis R. Blakeley, "Morris, Charles (1711–81)," in *Dictionary of Canadian Biography*, vol. 4, http://www.biographi.ca/en/bio/morris_charles_1711_81_4E.html.

29 "By His Excellency, Charles Lawrence Esq., .. A Proclamation," Jan. 11, 1759. For discussion, see Cahill, "New England Planters," 121–3.

30 "By His Excellency, Charles Lawrence Esq., .. A Proclamation," Jan. 11, 1759.

31 F.H. Hicks, "Hicks, John," in *Dictionary of Canadian Biography*, vol. 4, http://www.biographi.ca/en/bio/hicks_john_4E.html; Phyllis R. Blakeley, "Denison, Robert," in *Dictionary of Canadian Biography*, vol. 3, http://www.biographi.ca/en/bio/denison_robert_3E.html.
32 Longley, "Coming of the New England Planters," 20–4.
33 Barbary Cuffee to Robert Stevenson, March 7, 1769, Queens County Deed Registers, vol. 1, 258, NSA; "A list of proprietors of the township of Liverpool with their number in family respectively," 1764, Commissioner of Crown Lands, RG 20 series C vol. 43 no. 1, NSA.
34 Hartlen, "Bound for Nova Scotia," 123–8.
35 A general source regarding engagement of New Englanders in the West India trade and its extension to Canada from the American perspective is John J. McCusker and Russell R. Menard, *The Economy of British America, 1607–1789* (Chapel Hill: University of North Carolina Press, 2014), esp. chap. 5, 91–116. Important to this study in relation to slavery are the articles contained in Henderson and Robicheau, *Nova Scotia Planters*. An early, and still very useful, examination of the institution in Atlantic Canada is T. Watson Smith, "The Slave in Nova Scotia," *Transactions of the Nova Scotia Historical Society* 10 (1896–8): 9–19.
36 Enslaved Africans moved back and forth along these coastal routes as well, as is shown in Karima M. Lewis, "Captives on the Move: Tracing the Transatlantic Movements of Africans from the Caribbean to Colonial New England," *Historical Journal of Massachusetts* 44, no. 2 (Summer 2016): 144–75. The classic work on New England slavery is Lorenzo J. Greene, *The Negro in Colonial New England* (New York: Columbia University Press, 1942). On Nova Scotia and the commodities trade, the authoritative book on the topic is Harold A. Innis, *The Cod Fisheries: The History of an International Economy* (Toronto: University of Toronto Press, 1978); Jerry Bannister, "West Indies Trade," in *Oxford Companion to Canadian History*, ed. Gerald Hallowell (Don Mills, ON: Oxford University Press, 2006), 659–60; and Bannister, "Planter Studies and Atlantic Scholarship: The New History of 18th-Century Nova Scotia," in Henderson and Robicheau, *Nova Scotia Planters*, 32–5; Julian Gwyn, *Excessive Expectations: Maritime Commerce and the Economic Development of Nova Scotia, 1740–1870* (Montreal and Kingston: McGill-Queen's Press, 1998), esp. chaps. 2 and 3; and James Sidbury, *Becoming African in America: Race and Nation in the Early Black Atlantic* (New York: Oxford University Press, 2006). On the Planter role in exploiting the trade, see Alexandra L. Montgomery's excellent MA thesis, "'An Unsettled Plantation': Nova Scotia's New Englanders and the Creation of a British Colony, 1759–1776" (Dalhousie University, 2012); her work on the Perkins family of Liverpool is particularly interesting (pp. 5–53); Robyn Brown, "Contingent and Continuum: Simeon Perkins

and 'Loyalist' Nova Scotia, 1773–1785" (MA thesis, Dalhousie University, 2019).
37 Captain Benjamin Hallowell lived at Jamaica Plain, in Boston. He had taken an active role in the conquest of Canada as commander of a twenty-gun boat called the *King George*. A staunch Loyalist, he was forced to flee to Halifax during the American Revolution and then sought refuge in Britain. See Chaim Rosenburg, *The Loyalist Conscience: Principled Opposition to the American Revolution* (Jefferson, NC: MacFarland, 2018), 35–6. Hallowell received a 1,000-acre land grant in Prince Edward County, Upper Canada, but resided at the Town of York. He died in York (Toronto) in 1799, aged seventy-six. See Henry Scadding, *Toronto of Old: Collections and Recollections Illustrative of the Early Settlement and Social Life of the Capital of Ontario* (Toronto: Willing & Williamson, 1878), 366–7. Hallowell was himself a slaveholder at Boston. See Jared Ross Hardesty, "Slavery, Freedom, and Dependence in Pre-Revolutionary Boston, 1700–1775" (PhD diss., Boston College, 2014), 169n19.
38 Gwyn, *Excessive Expectations*, 18.
39 Stephen J. Hornsby and John Reid, eds., *New England and the Maritime Provinces: Connections and Comparisons* (Montreal and Kingston: McGill-Queen's University Press, 2005); George A. Rawlyk, *Nova Scotia's Massachusetts: A Study of Massachusetts–Nova Scotia Relations, 1630 to 1784* (Montreal and Kingston: McGill-Queen's University Press, 1973), 27–4; Gwyn, *Excessive Expectations*, 27–42.
40 An interesting discussion of dietary requirements and changes over time pertaining to enslaved workers in the British Caribbean is provided by James E. Candow, "A Reassessment of the Provision of Food to Enslaved Persons, with Special Reference to Salted Cod in Barbados," *Journal of Caribbean History* 43, no. 2 (July 2009): 265–81.
41 Samuel Starr's papers are in Acadia University's Esther Clark Wright Archives. My thanks to historian Julian Gwyn and Acadia archivist Pat Townsend for bringing Starr's business accounts to my attention. See entry "Freight of a Black Man," March 6, 1786, in "Major Samuel Starr Acct. Current with Nath. Brown." The facing page of the same record reads "By the [?] Proceeds of a Black man sold at Saint Vincent." The Browns were related to the Starrs of New London, Connecticut, and a Nathan Brown, formerly of Ipswich, Massachusetts, was in 1767 listed as one of the original grantees in Yarmouth, Nova Scotia. John Roy Campbell, *A History of the County of Yarmouth, Nova Scotia* (Yarmouth: J. & A. McMillan, 1876), 56.
42 John Rowland not only sold off a young girl to Barbados but also left several slaves in his will, including "Samuel, a black boy, [valued at] thirty-five pounds; William, a ditto, [valued at] thirty pounds; a girl, twenty-five

pounds." William Booth, *Remarks and Rough Memorandums: Captain William Booth, Corps of Royal Engineers, Shelburne, Nova Scotia 1787, 1789*, ed. Eleanor Robertson Smith (Shelburne, NS: Shelburne County Archives and Genealogical Society, 2008), 90–1. The original journal of William Booth, of Shelburne, NS, is in the Esther Clarke Wright Archives, Acadia University. See also "Will of Reverend John Hamilton Rowland," probated May 9, 1798, Shelburne, Nova Scotia, A-104, reel 20168, NSA. On the connection between New England, slavery, and the West Indian trade, see Daniel B. Rood, *The Reinvention of Atlantic Slavery: Technology, Labor, Race, and Capitalism* (Oxford: Oxford University Press, 2017); and Eric Kimball, "'What have we to do with slavery?' New Englanders and the Slave Economies of the West Indies," and Calvin Schermerhorn, "The Coastwise Slave Trade and a Mercantile Community of Interest," both in *Slavery's Capitalism: A New History of American Economic Development*, ed. Sven Beckert and Seth Rockman (Philadelphia: University of Pennsylvania Press, 2016), 181–94, 209–23.

43 It should be noted that cod had been fished on the Grand Banks for centuries by Basque and French fisherman and that a trade in salt cod in return for sugar and rum had been established by the French on Île Royale, or Cape Breton, by the early eighteenth century. See Donovan, "Slaves and Their Owners," 7ff. Enslaved people were carried to Cape Breton on the same ships that plied the waters between Île Royale and the French West Indian islands (pp. 8–9). Donovan shows that a few, too, were sold to Louisbourg purchasers in return for French goods, by New England merchants such as Boston's Peter Faneuil. Donovan cites Peter Faneuil to Thomas Kilby, Boston, June 2, 1737, Faneuil Letter Book, 21–2, 22n68, Baker Library, Harvard University, Boston.

44 While Newfoundland dominated the fisheries and salt cod trade, Nova Scotia's role in supplying cod to feed the enslaved plantation workers of the West Indies is detailed in a number of sources, including that of Harold Innis, who coined the staples thesis in Canadian historiography; see Innis, *Cod Fisheries*. See also Gwyn, *Excessive Expectations*, 116–18; and Mark Kurlansky, *Cod: A Biography of the Fish That Changed the World* (New York: Walker, 1997).

45 On slavery in colonial New England, see Piersen, *Black Yankees*; Melish, *Disowning Slavery*; Kenneth Lockridge, "Land, Population and the Evolution of New England Society 1630–1790," *Past and Present* 39, no. 1 (April 1968): 62–80; and Catherine Adams and Elizabeth H. Pleck, *Love of Freedom: Black Women in Colonial and Revolutionary New England* (Oxford: Oxford University Press, 2009). Of particular interest is Pulitzer finalist Wendy Warren's volume, *New England Bound: Slavery and Colonization in Early America* (New York: Liveright, 2016). Statistics regarding numbers of enslaved people

in each New England state vary, too. See, for instance, Whitfield, *North to Bondage*, 21.

46 Greene, *Negro in Colonial New England*, 138.

47 A thorough examination of the *Connecticut Gazette*, *Boston Weekly Post-Boy*, and other surviving newspapers is underway, the objective being to identify the assets, including human "property," that Planter families sold off before travelling. On the Atlantic slave trade in general, see Hugh Thomas's authoritative *The Slave Trade: The Story of the Atlantic Slave Trade, 1440–1870* (New York: Simon & Schuster, 1997).

48 William Renwick Riddell, "Slavery in the Maritime Provinces," *Journal of Negro History* 5, no. 3 (July 1920): 359–75; J.M. Bumsted, "Denson, Henry Denny," in *Dictionary of Canadian Biography*, vol. 4, http://www.biographi.ca/en/bio/denson_henry_denny_4E.html.

49 Alexandra L. Montgomery, "To Boston in Order for Chester: The Seccombe Family Diaries and Planter Mobility, 1761–1783," in Henderson and Robicheau, *Nova Scotia Planters*, 144–5; S. Buggey, "Seccombe, John," in *Dictionary of Canadian Biography*, vol. 4, http://www.biographi.ca/en/bio/seccombe_john_4E.html.

50 Jackson Ricker, *Historical Sketches of Glenwood and the Argyles, Yarmouth Co., NS* (1941; repr., Yarmouth, NS: Sentinel, 1994), 25; Sharon Robart-Johnson, *Africa's Children: A History of Blacks in Yarmouth, Nova Scotia* (Toronto: Dundurn, 2009), 39ff.

51 Kent Lodge, the former home of Elisha DeWolf after whose family the town is named, is the oldest home in Wolfville and has numbers still visible on the attic rafters. With thanks to Sonia Hewitt, archaeologist, Acadia University (personal communication, 2014), for this information.

52 John Reid, "Change and Continuity in Nova Scotia, 1758–1775," in Conrad, *Making Adjustments*, 45–59.

53 Julian Gwyn, *Planter Nova Scotia 1760–1815: Falmouth Township* (Wolfville: Kings-Hants Heritage Connection, 2010), 28–35.

54 On conditions of African Canadian life in this period, see Hazel C. Hazen, "The Story of New Brunswick's Black Settlers: 1700–1820," *Journal of the New Brunswick Museum* (1989): 44–53; and William Spray, *The Blacks in New Brunswick* (Fredericton: Brunswick Press, 1972). On Nova Scotia in particular, see Whitfield, *North to Bondage*, 72–80; and Whitfield, "American Background of Loyalist Slaves," 66–7. New England antecedents are described in Melish, *Disowning Slavery*, 27–31.

55 Whitfield, *Black Slavery in the Maritimes*, 8. Demonstrating the close relations between colonial New Englanders and people they held in bondage are the diaries of New London, Connecticut, shipwright, lawyer, farmer, and slaveholder Joshua Hempstead. This is the basis for Allegra de Bonaventura's seminal volume, *For Adam's Sake: A Family Saga in Colonial*

New England (New York: W.W. Norton, 2013). Astonishingly, the house Hempstead built in 1678 and associated outbuildings where he worked are still standing and graphically demonstrate the interrelated daily life and work of enslaved and slaveholder.

56 Joshua Hempstead, *Diary of Joshua Hempstead of New London, Connecticut, Covering a Period of Forty-Seven Years, from September 1711, to November, 1758* (New London, CT: New London County Historical Society, 1901); Venture Smith, *A Narrative of the Life and Adventures of Venture, a Native of Africa: But Resident above Sixty Years in the United States of America. Related by Himself* (New London, CT: C. Holt, 1798).

57 Ronnie-Gilles LeBlanc, "Les Acadiens à Halifax et dans l'île Georges, 1755–1764," *Port Acadie: revue Interdisciplinaire en Études Acadiennes/An Interdisciplinary Review in Acadian Studies*, no. 22–23 (2012–13): 53–5. See also John Bartlet Brebner, *The Neutral Yankees of Nova Scotia: A Marginal Colony during the Revolutionary Years* (New York: Columbia University Press, 1937), 37ff; and N.E.S. Griffiths and G.A. Rawlyk, *Mason Wade, Acadia and Quebec: The Perception of an Outsider* (Ottawa: Carlton University Press, 1991), 114–16.

58 Enslaved coopers were common in colonial New England. For the story of Wonn and other skilled craftsmen, see Warren, *New England Bound*; see also chapter 5 ("Intimate Slavery") for household arrangements regarding slave living conditions that seem to have pertained in Nova Scotia as well.

59 Whitfield, in *North to Bondage*, provides an interesting discussion of skill sets and duties of enslaved Africans in rural and urban New England, as well as in Loyalist Nova Scotia (pp. 20–8). On the propensity of Nova Scotian White Planter women to bear a child every two years, see Gwendolyn Davis, "'Clean Your Teeth and Set Straight': Planter Children in the Early Years and Beyond," in Henderson and Robicheau, *Nova Scotia Planters*, 293.

60 Elizabeth Mancke, "At the Counter of the General Store: Women and the Economy in Eighteenth-Century Horton, Nova Scotia," in Conrad, *Intimate Relations*, 167–81. On women's rights and legal status, see Julian Gwyn, "Female Litigants before the Civil Courts of Nova Scotia, 1749–1801," *Histoire sociale/Social History* 36, no. 72 (2003): 311–46. Relevant information about the lives of women in colonial New England is provided in Adams and Pleck, *Love of Freedom*, and by Laurel Thatcher Ulrich in her important volume, *Good Wives: Image and Reality in the Lives of Women in Northern New England, 1650–1750* (New York: Knopf Doubleday, 2010).

61 Hartlen, "Bound for Nova Scotia"; Will of Benjamin Belcher (1743–1802), Kings County Probate Records Estate Case file B7, NSA.

62 Some of these notices calling for the return of missing bondspeople are reproduced under the heading "Slavery and Freedom" in "African Nova

Scotians in the Age of Slavery and Abolition" Nova Scotia Archives, accessed April 3, 2019, https://novascotia .ca/archives/africanns.

63 "Case of a Black Boy Carried Off to the West Indies," April 22, 1794, Shelburne County Court of General Sessions of the Peace, RG 34–321 J 145, NSA. https://novascotia.ca/archives/Africanns/archives.asp?ID=52.

64 C. Bruce Fergusson, "Perkins, Simeon," in *Dictionary of Canadian Biography*, vol. 5, http://www.biographi.ca/en/bio/perkins_simeon_5E.html.

65 Simeon Perkins, *The Diary of Simeon Perkins, 1780–1789*, ed. Harold A. Innis (Toronto: Champlain Society, 1948). Those diaries dating to a period when he returned to Norwich between 1767 and 1769 remained with his descendants. Their location today is unknown.

66 For Deborah Cuffee's marriage, see Simeon Perkins, *The Diary of Simeon Perkins, 1766–1780*, ed. Harold A. Innis (Toronto: Champlain Society, 1948), 45.

67 Perkins, *Diary of Simeon Perkins, 1766–1780*, 143, 158; see also 164.

68 Allen Penney, "A Planter House: The Simeon Perkins House, 1766–7, Liverpool, Nova Scotia," in Conrad, *They Planted Well*, 218–35, esp. 232.

69 Sanchez Manning, "Britain's Colonial Shame: Slave-Owners Given Huge Payouts after Abolition," *The Independent*, February 24, 2013, http://www.independent.co.uk/news/uk/home-news/britains-colonial-shame-slave-owners-given-huge-payouts-after-abolition-8508358.html.

70 The British government did not compensate British North American slaveholders, for it was believed the practice had died out in Canada long before. There are therefore no listings for Canada per se in the "Legacies of British Slave-Ownership" database on the University of London's website (https://www.ucl.ac.uk/lbs/). See Winks, *Blacks in Canada*, 111.

71 "Auntie Lois Tritton," *New Haven Letter*, reprinted in the *Lawrence Daily Journal* (Lawrence, KS), May 31, 1888, 4. Other sources say she was born in Halifax, Nova Scotia, on Christmas Eve. "Death of the Last Slave Sold at New Haven," *New Haven Courant*, reprinted in the *Steuben Republican* (Angola, IN), July 18, 1894.

72 Winks, *Blacks in Canada*, 107–9.

73 A bill of sale for the last slave sold in Nova Scotia – Percilla, aged eight – survives in the Arthur Wentworth Hamilton Eaton Fonds, 1900.011-EAT/105, Esther Wright Clarke Archives, Acadia University. It is reproduced in Whitfield, *Black Slavery in the Maritimes*, 118. For the New Brunswick case, see Smith, *Slave in Canada*, 71.

3

Where, Oh Where, Is Bet? Locating Enslaved Black Women on the Ontario Landscape

NATASHA HENRY

Figure 3.1. *Kingston Gazette*, 6 October 1818, 3

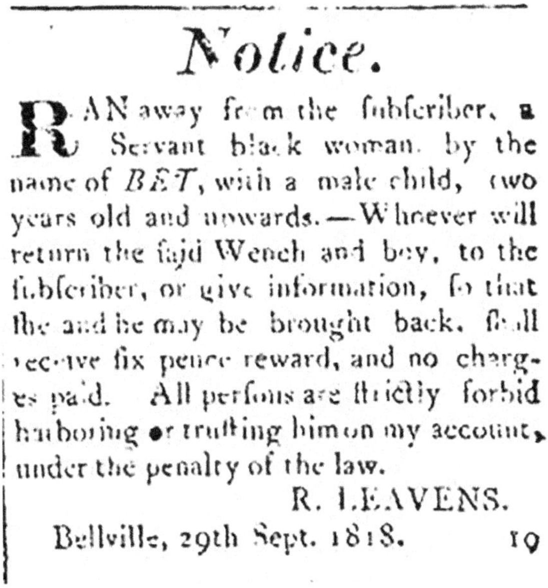

Notice.

RAN away from the subscriber, a Servant black woman, by the name of *BET*, with a male child, two years old and upwards. — Whoever will return the said Wench and boy, to the subscriber, or give information, so that she and he may be brought back, shall receive fix pence reward, and no charges paid. All persons are strictly forbid harboring or trusting him on my account, under the penalty of the law.

R. LEAVENS.

Bellville, 29th Sept. 1818.   19

Ran away from the subscriber, a Servant black woman by the name of *BET*, with a male child, two years old and upwards. – Whoever will return the said Wench and boy, to the subscriber, or give information, so that she and he may be brought back, shall receive six pence reward, and no charges paid. All persons are strictly forbid harboring or trusting him [*sic*] on my account, under the penalty of the law.

R. LEAVENS

Bellville, 29th Sept. 1818.

According to a notice published in the *Kingston Gazette*, an enslaved woman named Bet took flight from her enslaver in Belleville, Upper Canada (now Ontario), in 1818. She was one of hundreds of African and African-descended men, women, and children enslaved in colonial Canada. Considering the intersection of gender and race, this chapter will explore the experiences of enslaved women in southwestern Ontario through the reconstruction of the conditions in which Bet lived and examine what led her to exercise the overt form of resistance of running away twenty-five years after the enactment of the Act to Limit Slavery was passed in Upper Canada in 1793. Secondly, drawing on the research of art historian Charmaine Nelson and on Black studies scholar Katherine McKittrick's work in *Demonic Grounds*, this chapter employs a Black geographies framework to critically examine Bet's life and explore how Bet and other enslaved women negotiated the eighteenth- and nineteenth-century geophysical, sociopolitical, and cultural landscapes of colonial Upper Canada. I will also analyse how the system of slavery in the British colony informed not only economic organization but geographical, social, and political patterns as well.[1] Further, this chapter will interrogate how Bet and other enslaved women have been inscribed on the landscapes of colonial Upper Canada through historical and discursive processes, in texts such as runaway notices and bills of sales, as well as through the act of fleeing. To conclude, this chapter will discuss the need for a comprehensive mapping of the presence of enslaved Blacks in early Ontario to better understand the scale and nature of the system of slavery and its use as a mechanism to develop the colonial communities that came to constitute the nation of Canada. My aim is to recover enslaved Black subjects like Bet from white-authored sources (which are often the only ones available) that documented their subjugation and to (re)write those enslaved in Upper Canada into the collective Canadian memory in order to unsettle the dominant narrative and persistent myth that slavery was inconsequential in Canadian history.[2]

Proof of Her Existence

At the end of September 1818, Bet, an enslaved woman in the town of Belleville, Hastings County, took her infant son and fled to parts unknown. What precipitated her flight? What was she running from? Where was she running to? In this section of the chapter, I will attempt to reconstruct Bet's life, including how she came to be in the new colony of Upper Canada, and examine the broader context of her enslavement. The scant records that provide evidence of Bet's existence and that can be used to piece together her story are archival records that were produced by and for the white men who held her in bondage. In my research to uncover details about Bet's life, I located an instrumental document in the archives, a bill of sale for two slaves, and was able to connect it to the runaway advertisement. The original bill of sale was for Bet and her son:

> Bill of sale of a Negro Woman and Child
> This may certify that I have this day sold for the consideration of forty pounds to me in hand paid by William H. Wallbridge, my Negro woman Bett, of about twenty five years of age, and her infant child, to have and to hold from me or every other person whatever. As witness my hand this 14th day of March 1812.
>
> Joseph Keeler
>
> Witness present
> Elias Wallbridge
> Asa Smith[3]

Records of the sale of slaves contain valuable information with which to trace the footsteps and routes of the enslaved and shed some light on their lives in bondage. The information recorded for each transaction generally included the date of the sale, the number of slaves for sale, the geographical location of the buyer and seller, the sale price, and different characteristics of the slaves for sale such as their age, sex, occupation and skills, and family relationships. This document reveals several things about Bet and her circumstances.

Bet was owned by United Empire Loyalist Joseph Keeler, called "Old Joe" to distinguish him from his son Joseph Abbott Keeler, or "Young Joe." He was a land settlement agent who first travelled to Upper Canada somewhere between 1787 and 1789 with his younger brothers Martin and Eli/Elijah. Keeler made a trip back to Vermont in 1793 and brought with him forty to fifty white families to live as tenants on his land. At the time of Bet's sale, he lived in Cramahe Township in the Newcastle District (later Northumberland County), settling in present-day Colborne, then called Keeler's Creek, where he built a sawmill, flouring mill, carding and woollen mill, and distillery and opened a general store.[4] Keeler legally transferred his ownership of Bet and her infant son to lumber merchant, trader, and farmer William Holloway Wallbridge, who lived in Belleville. Wallbridge and his wife, Mary Everett, were some of the first settlers of Belleville. The transaction was witnessed by Elias Wallbridge, brother of William, and fellow Loyalist Asa Smith. Both witnesses were residents of Ameliasburgh Township, Prince Edward County.[5]

At the time of her sale on 14 March 1812 Bet's age was estimated to be twenty-five, putting her approximate year of birth at 1787. There are no records that indicate how Keeler came to be in possession of Bet, and therefore only speculations can be made. It is possible that Keeler brought Bet with him into the colony on one of his trips to Vermont. Bet also could have been a child of a slave he imported into the province and could have been born in the United States or in Upper Canada. Another possibility is that Keeler purchased Bet as a young girl from another settler or received her from a relative. Joseph's brother Eli/Elijah Keeler, who also lived in Cramahe Township, was a slave owner too.[6]

An assignment of sale dated in March 1824 shows that Eli Keeler owned a young mulatto boy named Tom, who was an apprentice. Keeler sold him to a store owner named Colonel William Bell of Thurlow, Hastings County, the township neighbouring Belleville, for $75 standard currency or £16 5s. 0d.[7] The contract noted that Tom had ten years of service remaining from 29 February 1824, as the child of a woman who was enslaved in the province prior to 1793. This meant Tom was fifteen years of age and was born in 1809.[8] Tom's assignment of sale referenced *An Act to Prevent the further Introduction of Slaves and to limit the Term of Contracts for Servitude* (more commonly known as the 1793 Act to Limit Slavery in Upper Canada). This piece of legislation, passed in the second session of the first parliament of the Legislative Assembly of Upper Canada, stipulated that "enslaved persons who were in the province at the time of its enactment would remain the property of their masters or mistresses for life, unless manumitted (freed) by their enslavers. Children born to enslaved women after 1793 would be freed when they reached twenty-five years of age. Children born to this cohort were free at birth."[9] Since Tom was born after 1793, he was one of the enslaved people who remained held in servitude, reflecting the limitations of the act and the reality that the law did not free any enslaved Blacks when it was enacted. Further, the familial relationship between Joseph and Eli raises speculation about Tom's parentage.

Was Tom the infant son mentioned in Bet's bill of sale? Bet was of child-bearing age in 1812 and Tom's estimated year of birth corresponds to his being an infant in 1812. If Tom was Bet's son, how did he come to be the property of Eli Keeler from William Wallbridge? Tom's assignment of sale stated that he was a mulatto, of Black and white mixed race, and Bet was clearly identified as a "negro" in her bill of sale. The use of the word "negro" indicates the dark hue of her complexion. If Tom was her son, with which white man did Bet have sexual relations and was it likely that it was consensual? Enslaved Black women were often susceptible to sexual exploitation by their white male enslavers, a universal reality that was endemic to the global trade in Black bodies and Canada was no exception.[10] In his in-depth study of slavery in Île Royale (present-day Cape Breton in Nova Scotia), Kenneth Donovan locates archival evidence of enslaved women who worked as domestics in their enslaver's home being impregnated by their enslavers. In one of the most egregious instances of sexual abuse within the Canadian context, Donovan notes that Guinea native Marie Louise, enslaved by merchant Louis Jouet, gave birth to nine illegitimate children while working in the Jouet home. Donovan was also able to identify other examples of male enslavers fathering children with their female slaves in the Canadian colonial archive, which is relatively silent on the sexual violence to which enslaved Black and Indigenous women were subjected.[11]

One week before the arrival of spring in 1812, Bet was forced to relocate fifty-two kilometres east to the harbour town of Belleville, at the Bay of Quinte at the mouth of the Moira River. She had no control over where she or her son were going and had no idea what the future would hold for them both. William Wallbridge's purchase of an enslaved female suggests that he had very particular labour needs he wished to fill. It was common for Black women enslaved in Upper Canada to be engaged in domestic work and they often worked as caregivers to children and performed a myriad of duties in the homes of their enslavers, including washing laundry, sewing, weaving, cooking, cleaning, farming, tending to livestock, and making goods such as soap and candles. This was evidenced in the advertisement that publicized the sale of Peggy and her son Jupiter in 1806, which stated that "the woman is a tolerable cook and washerwoman, and perfectly understands making soap and candles."[12] Bet laboured for a few years for the Wallbridges until she was sold off once again, this time to Roswell Leavens and without her son.

Physician and historian William Canniff wrote that "Leavens, of Belleville, bought a female slave of Wallbridge, for $100. A son of hers was purchased by Captain [John] McIntosh."[13] Canniff was likely referring to Bet as the subject of this sale, given the individuals involved in the sale. Records are unclear as to whether this son was Tom, although one can speculate. It is not known what year Bet's ownership was transferred to Loyalist Roswell Leavens, but she was in his possession in the same locale by 1818, when she made her escape. Leavens, who had arrived prior to 1798, was one of the earliest settlers of Belleville. The town of Thurlow was formed in 1789, and in 1816 Belleville was established as a new village in Thurlow. Leavens lived on a large riverfront lot (present-day southwest corner of Front Street and Bridge Street West), in the core of the growing settlement. He was also a member of the circle of elites who played a key role in developing the infrastructure of the Loyalist settlement.[14] Leavens was one of a number of enslavers in the Thurlow/Belleville area. Between the early 1780s and 1825, records show that eleven Blacks were enslaved in that locale: five were male and six, including Bet, were female (see the appendix to this chapter).

The men named on the bill of sale and the runaway advertisement connected to Bet were some of the earliest Anglo-American Loyalist settlers in Upper Canada.[15] As colonists, they engaged in a range of economic activities and worked to establish their families and settle the colony. Like colonists in other British colonies, they used slave labour to help in these activities and to increase their wealth accumulation and profitability. By utilizing "free labour" instead of hiring white workers, enslavers greatly reduced their labour costs, thus enabling them to generate and access income profits.[16] These businessmen not only traded in household and commercial goods but also traded in slave property within their close circles and with the interested general public. Robin Winks observes that enslaved persons changed hands at a higher rate during Loyalist settlement than they did in New France. Many Loyalists sold their slaves to alleviate the financial difficulties they suffered as they resettled in the new colony.[17]

Bet's Conditions of Labour and Her Flight

Bet, in all likelihood, worked in domestic service for Leavens and his wife, Sarah, to assist their growing family, as was characteristic of the roles performed by many enslaved Black women in Upper Canada.[18] The use of slave labour in upper-class colonial households facilitated the smooth operation of the domestic sphere. Whatever her duties, Bet worked for the Leavens family for some time into 1818. Then, for reasons unknown, as summer gave way to fall, Bet decided to run away. Roswell Leavens placed the advertisement on 29 September, meaning Bet was likely to have run away days before that date. In the advertisement, Bet is referred to as a "servant" – a common euphemism for "slave," and more specifically an enslaved domestic servant, in Canada and other slaveholding territories.[19] Bet is also referred to as a "wench." As it related to enslaved women, "wench" was a loaded word that deserves some dissection, as not only a gendered but also a racialized term.

When this term was used prior to the late eighteenth century to refer to white women, it described a young, unmarried servant of the peasant class who worked for pay.[20] In reference to Black females in the late eighteenth century and into the nineteenth century, the term was almost exclusively employed to describe Black enslaved women of any age in an objectifying and derogatory manner. According to the 1828 edition of the Webster's Dictionary, "in America" *wench* referred to "a black or colored female servant; a negress."[21] A high percentage of "for sale" advertisements and runaway advertisements referring to enslaved Black women in Canada identify the subject as a "wench" or "negro wench." The racialized designation became a universal nomenclature used to identify Black enslaved women. It transcended geographic location and served to delineate racial and class differences between Black and white women. Increasingly in the nineteenth century, the use of the word "wench" in the United States, England, and English-speaking slave societies in the Caribbean expanded to describe women of different races (Black, white, Indigenous), usually on the lower end of the social stratum, as lewd, loose, and promiscuous, based on perceptions of their sexual reputation. The women identified by the term "wench" after the abolition of slavery were of varied races and were viewed as sexualized objects who served the sexual needs of men of all racial backgrounds, by choice or by force.[22]

We also learn that when Bet ran away she was a mother to an infant boy two or three years of age, which means Bet gave birth somewhere around 1815–16. Based on her estimated date of birth from her bill of sale, when Bet ran away she was about thirty-one years old. Leavens offered a reward of six pence for her return, demonstrating that he attributed some financial value to getting her back. Yet the size of the reward offered for Bet and her infant son was not a high sum of money but mere pence on the pound.[23] By 1818 when Bet ran away, the proposed rewards for runaway slaves had drastically declined as slavery was gradually being phased out in the province in accordance with the 1793 Act to Limit Slavery. The notice for Bet ran for three or four weeks in the *Kingston Gazette*.[24]

Returning to the questions that I posed earlier in this chapter, what precipitated her flight? What was she running from? Where was she running to? While it cannot be known for certain, it can be surmised that Bet no longer wanted to remain with the Leavenses because of how she and/or her son were treated or because she wished to agitate for improved circumstances or seek her freedom. In her comparative research, *Unyielding Spirits: Black Women and Slavery in Early Canada and Jamaica*, Maureen Elgersman describes the material conditions in which enslaved Black women lived and how their labour was exploited in Canada under domestic slavery. Elgersman notes that many enslaved women lived under intense scrutiny, likely living in the same quarters with their owners. She observes that "as domestics, Black women in Canada would have spent most of their time within close proximity of their masters and mistresses ... [T]he confines of the domestic sphere may have afforded greater opportunity for chastisement for work undone or done unsatisfactorily, physical abuse, or even sexual assault."[25]

The historiography on the daily lives of enslaved women in Canada is quite thin, but a few texts exist that represent the daily experiences of enslaved women in domestic service in the United States and English-speaking colonies during the early 1800s. These sources help illustrate similar experiences although from different geographical locations. Lucy Delaney, enslaved in Missouri, identifies childminding as her primary duty during her preteen years in her published narrative, *From the Darkness Cometh the Light, or, Struggles for Freedom*.[26] In *Incidents in the Life of a Slave Girl*, Harriet Jacobs also describes how she was used as a nanny beginning in her preadolescent years, labouring as a night nurse and responsible for bringing her young mistress to and from school. Jacobs also notes that she sewed, did a range of household chores including making beds, setting tables, cooking, and baking, waited on guests, and ran errands.[27] Mary Prince's autobiography, *The History of Mary Prince, A West Indian Slave, Related by Herself*, while situated in the West Indies can also be drawn on to glean a better understanding of the conditions under which Bet may have laboured, as both women were born around 1787. In the documentation of her life as a domestic servant on a plantation in Brackish Pond, Bermuda, where she was enslaved, Prince describes working as a young nurse to her owners' newest baby, childminding through the night while her mistress rested. Her list of duties also included washing laundry, baking, picking wool and cotton, washing floors, cleaning, and some cooking. Prince also details the endless chores that her fellow female slave Hetty was expected to do. She recalls,

> She was the most active woman I ever saw, and she was tasked to her utmost. A few minutes after my arrival she came in from milking the cows, and put the sweet-potatoes on for supper. She then fetched home the sheep, and penned them in the fold; drove home the cattle, and staked them about the pond side; fed and rubbed down my master's horse, and gave the hog and the fed cow their suppers; prepared the beds, and undressed the children, and laid them to sleep. I liked to look at her and watch all her doings.[28]

Further, Prince offers insight into her working conditions and treatment. She describes how she and Hetty worked long hours often with little sleep. She lived under constant surveillance and in perpetual fear of physical punishment. Prince explains how she and Hetty were brutally beaten if work was not done to their master's or mistress's liking. Although Bet and Mary lived in different geographic regions, Prince's story provides relevant context to Bet's experience as a servant. Bet and Prince were born around the same time and both women served in domestic capacities for a period of time during their enslavement at the turn of the nineteenth century. It is highly plausible that their experiences paralleled each other and indicated not only the kinds of labour that female domestic slaves were required to do but also the gendered nature of that work.

Elgersman engages in a close study of slave advertisements in newspapers published in the French and British colonies of early Canada to extrapolate detailed information on the labour that enslaved Black women performed. Advertisements of the sale of enslaved Black women marketed a range of domestic capabilities including the ability to perform all kinds of household chores, cooking, washing, making soap, candles, and butter, and hairdressing. Some women were also described as being able to perform farming duties such as taking care of chickens and milking cows.[29] The advertisements are a key source that confirm the largely domestic labour of enslaved Black women and also substantiates the comparison with other colonial contexts.

It is possible that Bet ran away because she was concerned that either she or her son would be sold away from the other. She had already been sold twice before. One familiar feature of slavery was the breakup of enslaved families. Mothers, fathers, and children were violently ripped apart and sold indiscriminately to different buyers. The scholarship of two historians helps to explicate the separation of enslaved families through sales. William Duscinberre surmises that "the threat of being sold away from one's family, or of some family members of one's family being sold away – never to be seen again – was virtually universal."[30] Wilma Dunaway, in her extensive study on the impact of enslavement on Black families, *The African-American Family in Slavery and Emancipation*, writes that enslaved individuals in the Appalachian region articulated that impending separation from family members was a key motivating factor in running away. Whatever concerns enslavers may have had were subsumed under the economic imperative; the feelings of the enslaved or the impact that forced separation would have on enslaved men, women, and children were not factored into the decision. While the operationalization of enslavement was particular to space and time, the processes and impact of selling family members away from one another was likely to be similar wherever slavery was instituted.[31]

For enslaved women like Bet, their enslavers controlled not only their productive labour but their reproductive labour, too. As such, enslaved women provided double value to slave owners. Dionne Brand states that enslaved women giving birth to children represented the "production of a commodity" that provided more bondaged workers for slave owners and their heirs. Jennifer Morgan supports this argument and indicates how slave owners sold the offspring of the females they enslaved who were deemed to be "property," appropriating the reproductive value of enslaved women for personal benefit and, by extension, for the benefit of European colonization.[32] Bet giving birth to a son added property to her enslaver's assets and enhanced her enslaver's wealth. Bet and other enslaved women had limited parental powers and owners could do with their children what they pleased. Enslaved Black women like Bet endured oppressive power dynamics as a result of their social status as slaves paired with their race and gender. Within the hierarchy of power, enslaved Black women were positioned at the bottom of the social pyramid and all those above them in the social hierarchy, including white men and some white women, exercised a tyrannical level of control over their lives. Bet was powerless over whether or when she or her son would be put up for sale. As Morgan remarks, enslavement for a woman was "marked by an enormous degree of uncertainty that was manifested in the bodies of children whose future was out of her control."[33]

While the runaway slave advertisement was, like the bills of sale, produced by white men, its representation of Bet's enslavement is slightly different in that the reader is able to witness Bet exercise some level of agency in her decision to resist her material conditions by fleeing. Bet challenged the system of slavery by stealing herself and her labour from her enslaver as well as her son (which, given her limited legal rights, was quite a statement) and his potential future labour, even if only for a period of time. African Canadian art historian Charmaine Nelson describes slave advertisements and portraits of the enslaved as a rich archive that discloses evidence of the enslaved individual. The text in the advertisements, Nelson explains, creates a mental picture that forces the reader to envisage the subject of the advertisement and to visually identify the runaway, based on the description of their physical characteristics and their dress.[34] Enslaved Black women depicted in runaway advertisements rendered themselves visible, as worthy of some level of recognition, in a system that treated them as invisible because they were deemed to be chattel, not human beings. McKittrick describes this as oppositional geography, whereby the subaltern challenge practices of domination, in this case enslavement, and leave their mark.[35]

Where was Bet's destination? It is not known where Bet intended to flee to or where she was during the time she absented herself. There is historical evidence of some Blacks enslaved in eastern Canada escaping south to the northeastern United States, to New York, Michigan, or other free American territories, and of enslaved runaways fleeing from Upper Canada to Lower Canada (present-day Quebec).[36] What's more, Bet fled with her infant son, so one has to wonder if she had a nearby destination in mind, somewhere where her child would be safe and warm, or if she attempted to brave the Canadian terrain and elements to head south of Lake Ontario to freedom. Elgersman rightly points out that the geography of Canada allowed for a wider range of movement for escaping slaves, albeit within a harsh physical environment.[37] There are several possibilities as to where Bet may have fled to, not necessarily only to the south into the United States.

The Scope of Slavery in Upper Canada

Upon close analysis, the brief information that has been unearthed about Bet in the bill of sale and the runway advertisement explicates aspects of the operation and scope of slavery. Loyalist settlement in Upper Canada after the British defeat in the American Revolution expanded the practice of slavery in the colony.[38] Many Loyalists who immigrated north brought their slave property with them and in fact were encouraged to do so by the government. In 1790, the British colonial government permitted incoming immigrants from the Caribbean and the United States to import "any Negroes, household furniture, Utensils of husbandry and clothing, free from duty."[39] The number of slaves in Upper Canada increased dramatically. Estimates are that approximately three thousand slaves were brought into Canada during the Loyalist migration, with an estimated five hundred to seven hundred going to Upper Canada.[40] Their relocation transplanted aspects of one English slaveholding society to another. Loyalists exiled to British North America forcefully uprooted their enslaved labourers and instituted economic systems, social practices, and laws similar to those in the United States, premised on the same ideas of labour, racial identity and African bondage. However, the difference in the climate, which influenced some of the economic activities in which the colonists were engaged; the size of the settler population; and the limited access to large numbers of slaves resulted in adaptation of the customs and practices of enslavement to make slavery in Upper Canada specific to its geographic location and political context. The trade in enslaved Africans was a core element of slavery wherever it operated and enslaved women like Bet, as well as men and children, were bought and sold in Upper Canada, forced to labour without pay, and dehumanized in their slave status.

The dates of Bet's and Tom's bills of sale and that of Bet's runaway advertisement expose the persistence of slavery in Upper Canada twenty to twenty-five years after the passing of the 1793 Act to Limit Slavery. Bet's status was likely "slave for life" under the 1793 Act to Limit Slavery, because as mentioned earlier, she was approximately thirty-one years old at the time she escaped, meaning she was born around 1787. The second clause of the act stipulated,

> Provided always, That nothing herein contained shall extend, or be construed to extend to liberate any Negro, or other person subjected to such service as aforesaid, or to discharge them or any of them from the possession of the owner thereof, his or her executors, administrators or assigns, who shall have come or been brought into the Province, in conformity to the conditions prescribed by any authority for that purpose exercised, or by any Ordinance or Law of the Province of Quebec, or by Proclamation of any His Majesty's Governors of the said Province for the time being, or of any Act of the Parliament of Great Britain, or shall have otherwise come into the possession of any person, by gift, bequest or bona fide purchase before the passing of this Act, whose property therein is hereby confirmed.[41]

The annotation provided further clarification that "slaves at present within the Province, [are] confirmed in their property therein," meaning that those held in bondage at the time the act took effect would remain enslaved. This clause allowed for the selling of Bet after 1793. McKittrick contends that the laws and legal discourse related to slavery bound enslaved Blacks, and, more broadly, Blackness, to the landscape and at the same time "legally marked Black bodies as objects in that landscape."[42] Legislation objectified enslaved Blacks as the property of their white owners and encoded Black subordination in the white colonial space.[43]

Bet's owners decided to keep her enslaved instead of exercising the benevolence that Canadian enslavers have often been said by historians to possess by manumitting her. Bet's circumstance dispels the erroneous and persistent myth that the 1793 Act to Limit Slavery eradicated slavery in the province. In 1884, historian William Kirby inaccurately stated in a speech that the Loyalist legislators of the first parliament of Upper Canada abolished slavery without any dissent, making Canada the first country in the world to accomplish this feat and "great act of justice to humanity."[44] In another speech at the same event, held to commemorate the one hundredth anniversary of Loyalist settlement in Canada, Lieutenant Governor John Beverley Robinson misinformed the audience that when the first parliament assembled in the town of Niagara, they passed a law that declared there should be no more slavery in Upper Canada, one of the laws that were "of pride to Canadians."[45] And the dissemination of this fallacy continues today. In 2014, a post on the Canadian Museum of Human Rights blog mistakenly noted that "The law freed enslaved people aged 25 and over and made it illegal to bring enslaved people into Upper Canada."[46]

Slavery and the Operation of Race and Gender

Bet's experience reveals details on race and slavery in Upper Canada and the early racial formation of the colony. White propertied (which included slaves) and former military men held the most power, whereas the majority of Blacks in Upper Canada, whom they held in bondage, were property, not legal persons, and had no rights. The men who were establishing the new British colony of Upper Canada saw racial slavery as a necessary tool for its development like other slaveholding jurisdictions. The social construction of race in the British colony of Upper Canada replicated ideas of race in other colonized places in the New World where white superiority was reinforced by racial difference and the subordination of people of African descent.[47]

Runaway advertisements capture the determination of several enslaved Black women in Canada to secure freedom for themselves and their children, which is a corrective to Elgersman's observation that no accounts of enslaved women in colonial Canada escaping slavery with their children were available.[48] In another example of an enslaved woman running away with a child, in 1786 Nancy ran away with a four-year-old boy named Lidge – in all likelihood Nancy's son. They fled with three other slaves. All were enslaved by Caleb Jones in New Brunswick.[49] What their actions speak to is not only their strong will to be free but also the material and other conditions they endured that pushed them to risk their lives and that of their children in the vast, rugged terrain in pursuit of freedom.

An exploration of the relationship between Bet and the landscapes of Upper Canada reveals the embedded racial and gender imbalances within the patterned colonial social and political structures. Nelson offers another critical layer in the employment of landscape as a frame for interpreting the experiences of the enslaved in her discussion on how landscapes undergo racializing processes. She describes how geographic locations become racialized through various human actions, particularly colonization and empire expansion. Through colonization, conquered spaces – in this case, Upper Canada – became constituted and imagined as white but could only be defined as such in juxtaposition to othered First Nations and Blacks. Nelson explains further that geographic places were/are racialized as white because of the presence of a large white population and because of the power exerted by whites in colonizing the Upper Canadian landscape. The coerced construction of white spaces simultaneously excludes and erases racialized Indigenous and Black peoples from the very same landscapes.[50] However, Indigenous people, Black people, and, of particular interest here, enslaved Black women insert themselves in white-constructed spaces in different ways. The runaway advertisements presented in this chapter indicate their oppositional actions of flight and resistance.[51]

The Sociopolitical Landscape of Slavery

Less visible and less measurable, and something that may remain beyond our comprehension, is how the coerced labour of enslaved women like Bet and the five other women held in bondage in the Belleville area contributed to the growth and development of the social and economic landscapes of the colony. Through the domestic duties they fulfilled, enslaved women nurtured, fed, and cared for white settler families and by extension played an important but unrecognized role in supporting and shaping the spatial processes of colonization.[52]

The context of Bet's location in Upper Canada's sociopolitical landscape must be positioned within the transnational system of African enslavement. As an enslaved Black woman, Bet was the chattel of white men, as sanctioned by British colonial rule and custom, and was not legally considered a person.[53] She was denied rights and freedoms afforded to white settlers. This dynamic formed the basis of her relationships with the families of Joseph Keeler and William Wallbridge but was also accepted knowledge among the white population in Belleville and throughout the province. The racially stratified social organization of the relatively young colony of Upper Canada was modelled on other British territories where race-based slavery operated on a much larger scale, especially after the relocation of white colonists from these slave societies to the province.

To be white in Upper Canada automatically designated a person as free, as someone who had the freedom to move around in spaces without restrictions. However, to be a Black person in Upper Canada at the turn of the nineteenth century meant that one could be located in several social categories. A Black individual could be an enslaved person, a freed bondsperson in Canada, a manumitted Black Loyalist, or one of the marginal numbers of freedom seekers who entered the province. Bet's social status dictated her material condition where her labour was exploited, and she had limited control in determining when she worked or what tasks she had to complete, what she ate, what she wore, or where she lived. Within the prevailing conventions of the institution of slavery, Bet would not have had the freedom to travel on her own or without the permission of her white slave owner, although enslaved people were able to exercise varying degrees of permissible movement specific to their enslaver's discretion and to time and place.[54]

In her cartographic dissection of the life of enslaved Black woman Marie-Joseph Angélique in Montreal, McKittrick describes how Angélique's attempted escape and movement after the crime of arson that she allegedly committed challenged the immovability and subordination that she and other enslaved people, including Bet, were subjected to. As McKittrick notes, escape "interrupted the existing landscape and disregarded local slave boundaries" and it resisted the spatial regulation of Blackness.[55] Bet's escape prompted an intra-white collaboration, in what Colleen Walsh has called "a linked landscape of common concern," where fellow enslavers – settlers sympathetic to Leavens's loss, including the newspaper publisher – worked together, in an attempt to secure the recapture of Bet, the fugitive Black body, for her white owner.[56] This racial structuring of the sociopolitical landscape in Upper Canada and slave resistance to it played out in similar ways in many places involved in African enslavement.

The colonial structuring of the Upper Canadian landscape was heavily shaped by race and gender that simultaneously excluded and included Bet and other Black women. It was white men who were issued the majority of the land grants given to new settlers, while white daughters of veterans and widowed wives represented a small percentage of land grant recipients.[57] Many formerly enslaved Black men whose service in the British military was confirmed also qualified for and received parcels of land.[58] I have not located any instances of Black women receiving land grants after the arrival of Loyalists in Upper Canada and before the outbreak of the War of 1812, although records show evidence of one Black woman requesting land from the colonial government.[59] Those who were enslaved, including Bet, were precluded from being land holders, by virtue of their social status. This distribution of Indigenous lands (with and without the permission of First Nations) is at the root of settler colonialism in Ontario, and the coerced labour of enslaved Black and Indigenous peoples that was employed to support the process of settlement through the clearing of land, farming, hunting, fishing, and other economic activities, along with labouring in settler households, resulted in the spatial reformation of the physical landscape that remains today.

Physical Landscapes and Slavery

A reciprocal interaction took place between the physical environment and Bet. The physical geography acted on her and she simultaneously acted upon the physical landscape (through her physical labour and by enacting her escape) in the Bay of Quinte region of Upper Canada. In the beginning of the nineteenth century, at the time of non-Indigenous settlement, the area was surrounded by thick forest. The United Empire Loyalist settlement location of Belleville was originally a Mississauga campsite and afterwards a French missionary village. The town developed on both sides of the Moira River, and the river and forests were central in the economic development of the growing lumber centre.[60] The development of Belleville included other economic activities that relied on the physical landscape. A harbour was built for shipping, for trade with Kingston and Montreal and to export lumber, grain, flour, fur, potash, and farm products.[61] Bet would likely have traversed the physical landscape in eastern Ontario when she was purchased by Wallbridge from Keeler, when her ownership was sold to Leavens, in what might be assumed to be her regular travels with her owners, and when she ran away. Her main mode of transportation for her escape was likely to have been on foot, but she likely travelled by wagon on occasion. She would have encountered all kinds of wildlife and forested land, which Loyalists were working to tame, cultivate, and master.

Physical geographical conditions significantly influenced slavery in Upper Canada. The environment determined the form of enslavement that could and could not exist. The climate determined what kinds of crops enslaved labourers worked to grow and what time of year farming took place, which would have impacted some of the work that Bet was forced to do. As has been referenced in most of the scholarship on slavery in Canada, including the works of Winks, Whitfield, and Elgersman, the cold northern climate was not conducive to the plantation slavery of the southern United States and the Caribbean, where staples such as cotton, rice, sugar cane, indigo, and tobacco were grown. Because of this, slave labour in Canada was employed to farm different crops, including wheat, oats, barley, potatoes, melons, cauliflower, cabbage, parsnips, carrots, beets, spinach, sweet briar, and domestic fruits like pears, raspberries, and apples, mainly for domestic markets.[62] The physical geography also influenced the kinds of domestic tasks that Bet and other enslaved women and men performed.

Bet's Landscaping

As mentioned earlier, just as the landscapes of Upper Canada imposed themselves onto Bet, so did she inscribe herself onto the landscapes, although it may not be explicitly acknowledged by those who were enslavers and by those who document the province's colonial past. She did so through the varied work she performed that contributed to colonial settlement of the white families who held her in bondage and, in turn, to the larger colonizing project. Bet also wrote herself onto the landscape of Belleville and Upper Canada and into the colonial archives through her act of running away, which led to the publication of the text that notified the public of her disappearance. In fact, Bet's very existence and daily living locate her on the early 1800s landscape among other people who were present, including the original Indigenous people who resided in the vicinity (who were largely erased from its narration), as well as the white settlers.

The Obfuscation of the Slavery Archive in Ontario

The bill of sale for Bet and a male child as well as the runaway advertisement that notified the white public of her escape raise the broader question of where Bet and other enslaved women and men are located in the archive. As stories that directly challenge and proscribe the advancement of the dominant narrative of Canadian history, of French and British colonization and white superiority, they are buried, stored away, or dispersed in the archive. McKittrick notes how Blackness and Black enslavement have been carefully landscaped, or erased, out of the national narrative, which has led to the successful intentional concealment and obscuring of their narratives.[63] Some data that could have further illuminated the experiences of the enslaved may have been lost to the archives through misplacement or intentional removal or to disasters like fire. Information on the enslaved is also not easily accessible because many archives with holdings on the early history of Ontario do not have a system specific to locating materials related to slaves and slavery.[64] Interestingly, it was Bet's status as property that created the slim paper trail presented in this chapter. Because she was the legal chattel of white men, some of the transactions related to her ownership were documented, as were those of her escape, which could have led to a financial loss for her enslaver. Further, the historical narratives that recall slave ownership in the Belleville region represent the holding of slaves as a status symbol of the elite. The absence of slave-created documents to gain a sense of who they were as human beings, of their attitudes and perspectives about their material and social conditions, requires scholars of slavery to recuperate enslaved Black subjects from white-authored records that documented their subjugation.

A major gap exists in a contextualized historiography of slavery in Ontario. In her reflection on the state of Indigenous history in Canada, Mary Jane Logan McCallum points to a "broader trend in Canadian history writing to disassociate from its colonial past," as historians tended to separate imperialism from the nation-building of the Canadian state proper instead of treating both projects as a continuum.[65] This sentiment is true for the history of African enslavement, which has not been fully acknowledged by scholars of Canadian history as a mechanism of colonialization. Because this gap persists, we are still at the preliminary recovery stage of Ontario's history of enslavement. Bet is one of an uncalculated number of enslaved persons in Belleville, in Hastings County, in eastern Ontario, and across southern Ontario. However, to date, a robust approximation of exactly how many were enslaved in early Ontario has not been undertaken.

The estimate that more than five hundred Africans were enslaved in Upper Canada has been quoted by all historical works that discuss this subject. One of the earliest sources of this estimate is an article published by William Riddell in the *Journal of Negro History* in 1920, in which he states that the number of slaves "in the province at the time of the Act of 1793 was probably not far from 500." In a note he adds that "this is indicated by a number of facts none of much significance and all together far from conclusive but it is a mere estimate perhaps not much more than a guess and I should not be astonished if it were proved that the estimate was astray by 100 either way."[66] Given Riddell's admission of a "guess," there is a serious need for a comprehensive chronicling of the demographic patterns of African slave ownership in early Ontario both under French rule from the early eighteenth century until 1760 and under British control after 1760. Such an undertaking would establish a more accurate historical knowledge on the scale and nature of the system of slavery and its specific manifestation intended to be used as an apparatus of colonial expansion in the territories that came to make up the nation of Canada. The time has come in Canadian history for a much more critical focus on slavery and for all historical information related to African enslavement in early Ontario to be gathered, collected, and housed together in one easily accessible archival repository, such as a digital database.

Conclusion

This chapter attempted to recount a tiny portion of Bet's life in enslavement in Upper Canada, first, by piecing together limited, fragmentary evidence, likely the only remaining records of Bet's life, and second, by contextualizing her broader history of enslavement both in early Ontario and within the geophysical, historical, cultural, legal, and sociopolitical landscapes of the colony. This brief narrative of Bet's life illustrates some of the challenges of slave genealogy, especially in a province and nation that downplays or disregards its slave past. Slavery was part of the roots of the nation-building project that came to be known as Ontario and, more broadly, Canada. Enslaved persons of African descent, including Bet, were fundamental to the imagined and actual formation of the colony. Colonists of European descent wanted to exploit slave labour to develop Upper Canada on a large scale, but due to political and environmental factors, a specific home-grown, smaller-scale system of slavery formed. Nonetheless, the Canadian brand of slavery was very much part of the transnational system of African enslavement that forcibly imported Africans to the New World where a range of goods and services were produced by the enslaved. In whichever way it operated, slavery and settler colonialism were definitively constitutive of each other in early Canada.

The two archival documents discussed here, the bill of sale and the runaway advertisement, show that Bet was traded between white male Loyalists at least two times. The documents illuminate and raise questions about the complex intersections of race, gender, and enslaved status in Upper Canada. They also encourage an interrogation of how race, gender, and social status shape the writing of Canadian history. This chapter, written two hundred years after her attempted flight, is the first scholarly treatment of Bet's life. There is an archival note that mentions the existence of a transcribed copy of her bill of sale and states that the location of the original (which I have located and cited here) is unknown, and the advertisement of her escape is not referenced in any scholarly writings. The notice of her escape was reprinted in *Historic Hastings* in 1967, accompanied by a caption mentioning that the gradual abolition of slavery in the province was achieved by about 1820. Neither Bet's name nor any other detail about her is included.[67] In an unpublished paper titled "A Settlement at Meyer's Creek," Allan Dempsey reproduces Bet's runaway advertisement and, in a brief paragraph, interprets the 1793 Act to Limit Slavery and its impact on the Loyalist enslavers in the town. Dempsey ends by reporting that the Wallbridges, the Meyers, and the Leavenses freed their slaves, although no evidence is furnished to substantiate this claim. Again, Bet's name is not mentioned, nor is any information about her discussed.[68] Such marginalization and exclusion demonstrate how narratives of Black women in early Ontario are not afforded the same historical interest and attention as those of Anglophone men and women of social standing. Enslaved Black women appear in the archives, as historian Marisa Fuentes points out, through violence, "objectified, disposable, hypersexualized, and silenced."[69]

Although both the bill of sale and the runaway advertisement provide only archival fragments, they remain key historical sources that offer a narrow glimpse into the life of Bet. We are not able to gain an understanding of how Bet perceived her conditions or the world around her. We are merely able to make some observations. The documents allude to a life of oppression and a depraved material culture. Bet and her young son were bought and sold as chattel and her conditions, or some occurrence, precipitated her flight in pursuit of freedom. These historical records also document the oppression and victimization that enslaved Black women endured for posterity and, in that way, historicize details of their experiences. Further, when the traditional gaze of the archives is shifted to the otherwise commodified and silenced enslaved Black women, and refocuses them as historical subjects, these archival documents achieve much more.[70] The advertisement shows how Bet challenged her subjugation by running away. The bill of sale and the runaway advertisement also illustrate complementary processes of how Bet has written herself into the historical archives and inserted herself into specific spaces through documents in which she was recorded and how she inadvertently influenced herself being written into history by her enslavers. Bet wrote herself upon the colonial landscape and was written into colonial text. She forced her enslavers to acknowledge her existence and her humanity when she challenged her status as chattel through escape. Several historians argue that changing the perspectives of documents in the slavery archives from the slave owners to the enslaved develops a new historical method that "makes plausible a new terrain" to tell the stories of the subaltern.[71]

This chapter sought to retrieve one story of an enslaved Black woman in Upper Canada, a woman named Bet. In gathering the known facts of her life together, it centred her as a historical subject in colonial Canada. Additionally, this chapter contextualized Bet's experiences and helped to create a better understanding of the impact of race and gender on enslaved Black women in Canada. The individual life story of Bet and her experiences as an enslaved Black woman and mother encourages a more critical interpretation of the landscapes of Upper Canada that is sorely lacking in the historiography of slavery in the region. A close read of these white-constructed landscapes as they relate to slavery shows how ideologies of race, gender, and legal status have been coded onto them and acknowledges the forced labour that Bet and the other enslaved Africans contributed to the everyday functioning of colonial households, businesses, and economies of Upper Canada. Bet's story and those of other Africans enslaved in early Ontario are deserving of some historical attention. In asking "Where, Oh Where, Is Bet?" this chapter has endeavoured to recover her story from the margins of Canadian history and rightfully insert it into the annals of the past.

Appendix
A Listing of Black People Enslaved in Belleville, Ontario

Slave owner(s)	Enslaved person(s)	Source*	Year documented
William Bell	1 15-year-old boy (Tom)	Assignment of sale	1824
John Richard Bleeker	1 male (Ham)	Canniff, 576	n.d.
Nicholas Lazier	1 female (Sal)	Canniff, 576	n.d.
	1 female (Black Betty)		n.d.
Roswell Leavens	1 female (Bet)	Canniff, 576, *Kingston Gazette*, Oct. 1818	1818
John Walden Meyers	1 female ("Black Betty" Levi)	Rev. John Langhorn Anglican Registers	1796
John McIntosh	1 young boy (Bet's son)	Canniff, 576	n.d.
Samuel Sherwood	1 boy (Ashur/Arthur Hampton)	Sherwood Account Book, 13	1786
		Canniff, 576	1793
		Rev. John Langhorn Anglican Registers	1796
	1 male (Sam)	Sherwood Account Book, 55	1795
John Simpson and Margaret Simpson	1 female	Boyce, 31	n.d.
William Wallbridge	1 female (Bet)	Bill of sale, Canniff, 576	1812

*Sources: "Assignment of a Slave (1824)"; William Canniff, *History of the Settlement of Upper Canada (Ontario)* (Toronto: Dudley & Burns, 1869), 576; *Kingston Gazette*, 9 June 1818, 3; Reverend John Langhorn, *Anglican Registers, 1787–1814* (Kingston, ON: Ontario Anglican Diocese), accessed 10 March 2017, http://my.tbaytel.net/bmartin/langhorn.htm; H.C. Burleigh, ed., *Samuel Sherwood's Account Book 1785–1810* (Kingston, ON: Brown and Martin, 1975); Gerry Boyce, *Belleville: A Popular History* (Toronto: Dundurn, 2008); Bill of Sale of Slaves, Wallbridge Family Papers, 1812.

NOTES

1 Katherine McKittrick, *Demonic Grounds: Black Women and the Cartographies of Struggle* (Minneapolis: University of Minnesota Press, 2006), 107.
2 Throughout this chapter, the term "white" is not capitalized because white and whiteness can be viewed as unmarked, as an ideology that is empty, oppressive, and false, as L.D. Burnett, Richard A. Jones, and David Roediger argue. "Black" and "Indigenous" are capitalized to signify their marked racialization in juxtaposition to whiteness. "Black" is also capitalized to signify its reference to a group of people of the African diaspora. See L.D. Burnett, "To 'B' or Not to 'B': On Capitalizing the Word 'Black,'" *U.S. Intellectual History Blog*, Society for U.S. Intellectual History, April 23, 2016, https://s-usih.org/2016/04/to-b-or-not-to-b-on-capitalizing-the-word-black/; Richard A. Jones, *Postmodern Racial Dialectics: Philosophy beyond the Pale* (Lanham, MD: University Press of America), 225n4; Peter Kolchin, "Whiteness Studies," *Journal de la Société des Américanistes* 95, no. 1 (2009): 117–63.
3 Bill of Sale of Slaves, 1812, Wallbridge Family Papers, MS 93, B253549 – MU8334, Archives of Ontario, Toronto.
4 William Cochrane, *The Canadian Album: Men of Canada: or, Success by Example in Religion, Patriotism, Business, Law, Medicine, Education, and Agriculture*, vol. 5 (Brantford, ON: Bradley, Garretson, 1896), 209; Catharine Anne Wilson, *Tenants in Time: Family Strategies, Land, and Liberalism in Upper Canada, 1799–1871* (Montreal and Kingston: McGill-Queen's University Press, 2009), 91.
5 "Memory Tiles: Elijah Wallbridge," St. Alban the Martyr UEL Memorial Church, accessed March 17, 2017, http://www.uelac.org/St-Alban/biographies/memorial-tiles-Wallbridge-Elijah.php.
6 Several sources discuss enslavement in eastern Ontario and across the province, including William Canniff, *Slavery in Canada, History of the Province of Ontario (Upper Canada)* (Toronto: A.H. Hovey & Co., 1872), 569–79; Thomas W. Casey, *"Early Slavery in Midland District," Lennox and Addington Historical Society, Papers and Records* 4 (1912): 12–21; William Riddell, "The Slave in Upper Canada," *Journal of Negro History* 4, no. 4 (1919): 372–95; William Renick Riddell, "Upper Canada – Early Period," *Journal of Negro History* 5, no. 3 (1920): 316–39; Riddell, "Additional Notes on Slavery: Reciprocity of Slaves between Michigan and Upper Canada," *Journal of Negro History*, 17, no. 3 (1932): 368–77; Isaac Allen Jack, *The Loyalists and Slavery in New Brunswick* ([Ottawa?]: Royal Society of Canada, 1898); Thomas Watson Smith, *The Slave in Canada* (n.p., 1899); Roy F. Fleming, "Negro Slaves with the United Empire Loyalists in Upper Canada," *Ontario History* 45 (1953): 27–30; Michael Power and Nancy Butler, *Slavery and Freedom in Niagara* (Niagara-on-the-Lake: Niagara Historical Society, 1993).

7 William Bell, a former sergeant in the 53rd Regiment of the British Army during the American Revolution, settled in the Belleville area in 1787. He set up a small trading post and operated as a merchant. He introduced apple trees to Belleville in 1791 and taught for a short time at the local Mohawk school. See Gerry Boyce, *Belleville: A Popular History* (Toronto: Dundurn, 2008).
8 "Assignment of a Slave (1824)," *Lennox and Addington Historical Society, Papers and Records* 2 (1910): 41–2.
9 Natasha Henry, "Chloe Cooley and the Act to Limit Slavery," *Canadian Encyclopedia*, last modified January 5, 2016, http://www.thecanadian encyclopedia.ca/en/article/chloe-cooley-and-the-act-to-limit-slavery-in-upper-canada/.
10 Charmaine A. Nelson, *Representing the Black Female Subject in Western Art* (New York: Routledge, 2010), 6.
11 Kenneth Donovan, "Female Slaves as Sexual Victims in Île Royale," *Acadiensis* 43, no. 1 (2014): 153; Donovan, "Slaves and Their Owners in Île Royale, 1713–1760," *Acadiensis* 25, no. 1 (1995): 20–1.
12 *Upper Canada Gazette*, February 10, 1806.
13 William Canniff, *History of the Settlement of Upper Canada (Ontario): with Special Reference to the Bay Quinté* (Toronto: Dudley & Burns, 1869), 576.
14 In 1798, Bet's enslaver was appointed poundkeeper in the town by Thurlow's first council. In this capacity, he was responsible for feeding and taking care of stray livestock, impounding them when necessary. Along with operating a store and blacksmith shop, Leavens was local merchant. He also operated a distillery and a tavern for some time, supplying the town with some of the alcohol it consumed, and was employed as the Thurlow town clerk from 1803 to 1806, 1811 to 1812, and 1813 to 1826. The town clerk took minutes of council meetings and recorded by-laws and registries. Leavens went on to become a lay justice of the peace. He was appointed as one of the original trustees to oversee the establishment of St. Andrew's Presbyterian Church in Belleville. See Gerry Boyce, *Historic Hastings* (Belleville, ON: Hastings County Council, 1967), 35, 258–9; Boyce, *Belleville*, 26, 30, 46; Boyce, *The St. Andrew's Chronicles: An Account of Presbyterianism before 1879 in the Belleville-Hastings County-Quinte Area* (Belleville, ON: St. Andrew's Presbyterian Church, 1978), 4; *Illustrated Historical Atlas of the Counties of Hastings and Prince Edward, Ont.* (Toronto: H. Belden & Co., *1878*), xiv–xv; J.K. Johnson, *In Duty Bound: Men, Women, and the State in Upper Canada, 1783–1841* (Montreal and Kingston: McGill-Queen's University Press, 2014), 80; and Randy William Widdis, *With Scarcely a*

Ripple: Anglo-Canadian Migration into the United States and Western Canada, 1880–1920 (Montreal and Kingston: McGill-Queen's University Press, 1998), 111.

15 Boyce, *Historic Hastings*, 35, 56; Widdis, *With Scarcely a Ripple*, 111; Boyce, *Belleville*, 26, 30, 46.

16 Afua Cooper, *The Hanging of Angélique: The Untold Story of Canadian Slavery and the Burning of Old Montreal* (Athens: University of Georgia Press, 2006), 127–8; Gustavus Myers, *History of Canadian Wealth* (Honolulu: University Press of the Pacific, 2004), 30, 47; Robin W. Winks, *The Blacks in Canada: A History*, 2nd ed. (Montreal and Kingston: McGill-Queen's University Press, 1997), 112.

17 Winks, *Blacks in Canada*, 48; Roy F. Fleming, "Negro Slaves with the United Empire Loyalists in Upper Canada," *Ontario History* 45, no. 1 (1953): 29; Maureen G. Elgersman, *Unyielding Spirits: Black Women and Slavery in Early Canada and Jamaica* (New York: Routledge, 2013), 25, 90.

18 Elgersman, *Unyielding Spirits*, 80.

19 Adrienne Shadd, *The Journey from Tollgate to Parkway: African Canadians in Hamilton* (Toronto: Dundurn, 2010), 42.

20 Tamara Extian-Babiuk, "'To Be Sold: A *Negro Wench*': Slave Ads of the Montreal Gazette 1785–1805" (MA thesis, McGill University, 2006), 31; *World Book Dictionary*, vol. 2 (Chicago: World Book, 2003), s.v. "wench"; Karima K. Jeffrey, "Mother of a New World? Stereotypical Representations of Black Women in Three Postapocalyptic Films," *Journal of Feminist Scholarship* 6 (Spring 2018): 3.

21 Randy J. Sparks, *Where the Negroes Are Masters: An African Port in the Era of the Slave Trade* (Cambridge, MA, Harvard University Press, 2014), 83.

22 For a brief history of the evolution of the meaning of the term "wench," see Sparks, *Negroes are Masters*, 83; Sally L. Kitch, *The Specter of Sex: Gendered Foundations of Racial Formation in the United States* (Albany: State University of New York Press, 2009), 73, 74; Kathleen M. Brown, *Good Wives, Nasty Wenches, and Anxious Patriarchs: Gender, Race, and Power in Colonial Virginia* (Chapel Hill: University of North Carolina Press, 1996), 1–2, 9, 369; and Extian-Babiuk, "To Be Sold," 31.

23 To put the value of the reward into perspective, in the summer of 1818 beef, mutton, and veal averaged 6d/lb. and one head of cabbage cost 6d. See "Price of Provisions," *Kingston Gazette*, June 9, 1818, 3.

24 While the date on the advertisement is 29 September, I have not been able to locate the advertisement in the newspaper printed on that date; it ran in the next week's issue (6 October) and for the two subsequent weeks.

25 Elgersman, *Unyielding Spirits*, 94.

26 Lucy A. Delany, *From the Darkness Cometh the Light; or, Struggles for Freedom* (St. Louis: J.T. Smith, 1891), 19, 24.

27 Harriet Jacobs, *Incidents in the Life of a Slave Girl. Written by Herself* (Boston, 1861), 52, 64, 131–41.
28 Mary Prince, *The History of Mary Prince, a West Indian Slave. Related by Herself. With a Supplement by the Editor. To Which Is Added, the Narrative of Asa-Asa, a Captured African*, 3rd ed. (London: F. Westley & A.H. Davis, 1831), 6–9.
29 Elgersman, *Unyielding Spirits*, 37, 71. An advertisement placed by Catherine Clement, widow of Lewis Clement, stated that the male and female slaves she was selling were "both bred to the business of a farm." *Niagara Herald*, 9 January–13 February 1802.
30 William Dusinberre, *Strategies for Survival: Recollections of Bondage in Antebellum Virginia* (Charlottesville: University of Virginia Press, 2009), 74.
31 A number of historians examine the separation of enslaved families. See Dusinberre, *Strategies for Survival*; Wilma Dunaway, *The African-American Family in Slavery and Emancipation* (New York: Cambridge University Press, 2003), 59; and Heather Andrea Williams, *Help Me to Find My People: The African American Search for Family Lost in Slavery* (Chapel Hill: University of North Carolina Press, 2012).
32 Dionne Brand, "A Working Paper on Black Women in Toronto: Gender, Race and Class," in *Returning the Gaze: Essays on Racism, Feminism and Politics*, ed. Himani Bannerji (Toronto: Sister Vision, 1993), 235; Jennifer L. Morgan, *Laboring Women: Reproduction and Gender in New World Slavery* (Philadelphia: University of Pennsylvania Press, 2004), 1, 100.
33 Morgan, *Laboring Women*, 115.
34 Charmaine Nelson, *Slavery, Geography and Empire in Nineteenth-Century Marine Landscapes of Montreal and Jamaica* (New York: Routledge, 2016).
35 McKittrick, *Demonic Grounds*, xi, xxiv.
36 By 1803 in Montreal, the largest city in British North America at the turn of the nineteenth century, the practice of slavery had become untenable and effectively ended after several high-court rulings placed strict onus on slave owners to prove their ownership. There were no abolition-oriented laws in Lower Canada as in Upper Canada. Frank Mackey also notes that between 1793 and 1803, enslaved Blacks in Lower Canada could have also run away to Upper Canada, as the 1793 Act to Limit Slavery gave freedom to slaves who entered the province; Henry Lewis, enslaved by William Jarvis in Toronto, fled to Schenectady, New York, and sent a letter to his former owner requesting purchase of his freedom. Mackey, *Done with Slavery*, 72–6.
37 Elgersman, *Unyielding Spirits*, 109.
38 Cooper, *Hanging of Angélique*, 83.
39 The Imperial Act Statute 30 Geo. 3, ch. 27, entitled *An Act for Encouraging New Settlers in His Majesty's Colonies and Plantations in America*.

40 James W. St. G. Walker, "African Canadians," in *Encyclopedia of Canada's Peoples*, ed. Paul Magosci (Toronto: University of Toronto Press, 1999), 142, and Anthony Appiah and Henry Louis Gates Jr., eds., *Africana: The Encyclopedia of the African and African American Experience*, vol. 5, 2nd ed. (New York: Oxford University Press, 2005), 722, as cited in Natasha Henry, "Black Enslavement in Upper Canada," *Canadian Encyclopedia*, last modified July 7, 2017, http://www.thecanadianencyclopedia.ca/en/m/article/black-enslavement/.

41 *An Act to Prevent the further Introduction of Slaves and to limit the Term of Contracts for Servitude*, 33 George III C.7., 9 July, 1793 (known as the 1793 Act to Limit Slavery), Statutes of the Province of Upper Canada, 1831, 41–2.

42 McKittrick, *Demonic Grounds*, 111–12.

43 The laws that governed slavery in Upper Canada include the Article 47 of the Articles of Capitulation, 8 September 1760, Montreal, and the subsequent proclamation of George III on 7 October 1763, which affirmed those articles, had all given support to the institution of slavery; The Imperial Act Statute 30 Geo. 3, ch. 27, entitled *An Act for Encouraging New Settlers in His Majesty's Colonies and Plantations in America*; *An Act to Prevent the further Introduction of Slaves and to limit the Term of Contracts for Servitude*, 33 George III C.7., 9 July, 1793 (known as the 1793 Act to Limit Slavery).

44 Mackey, *Done with Slavery*, 442.

45 United Empire Loyalists Centennial Committee, *The Centennial of the Settlement of Upper Canada by the United Empire Loyalists, 1784–1884* (Toronto: Rose Publishing Company, 1885), 84, 114.

46 Matthew McRae, "The Story of Slavery in Canadian History: It Happened Here, Too," Canadian Museum of Human Rights, Winnipeg, accessed August 26, 2019, https://humanrights.ca/story/the-story-of-slavery-in-canadian-history.

47 See, for example, Mervyn C. Alleyne, *The Construction and Representation of Race and Ethnicity in the Caribbean and the World* (Mona, Jamaica: University of the West Indies Press, 2002); and Robin Blackburn, *The Making of New World Slavery: From the Baroque to the Modern, 1492–1800* (London: Verso, 1998).

48 Elgersman, *Unyielding Spirits*, 114.

49 Barrington Walker, *The African Canadian Legal Odyssey: Historical Essays* (Toronto: University of Toronto Press, 2012), 377.

50 Nelson, *Slavery, Geography and Empire*, 9–10.

51 Along with Bet's runaway advertisement as an example, Peter Russell placed the following advertisement in the *Upper Canada Gazette* on 2 September 1803: *"The subscriber's black servant Peggy not having his permission to absent herself from his service, the public are hereby cautioned from employing or harbouring her without the owner's leave. Whoever will do so after this notice may expect to be treated as the law directs."* In 1801, one of William Jarvis's slaves, named Kitty,

was charged with assaulting him and she was brought before the court. In 1811, Jarvis accused an unnamed female slave and a male slave named Prince of theft and running away, according to the court records. Ontario Legislative Assembly, "Minutes of the Court of Quarter Sessions of the Peace for the Home District, 13th March 1800–28th December 1811," *Ontario Sessional Papers*, no. 30, 1933 (Toronto: Herbert H. Ball, Printer to the King's Most Excellent Majesty), 10, 14, 174, accessed April 18, 2017, https://archive.org/details/n06ontariosession65ontauoft .

52 Jennifer L. Morgan and Tiffany King argue that Black female bodies were central to the structuring of lands such as the United States and Canada as colonial settlements. Morgan, *Laboring Women*; King, "In the Clearing: Black Female Bodies, Space and Settler Colonial Landscapes" (PhD diss., University of Maryland, 2013).

53 William A. Link, *North Carolina: Change and Tradition in a Southern State*, 2nd ed. (Hoboken: Wiley-Blackwell, 2018), 45.

54 Most regulations pertaining to the monitoring and control of the movement of slaves were developed locally in the colonies. English common law did not have a statute that defined slavery. John Powell, *Encyclopedia of North American Immigration* (New York: Facts on File, 2005), 272; Caroline Quarrier Spence, "Ameliorating Empire: Slavery and Protection in the British Colonies, 1783–1865" (PhD diss., Harvard University, 2014), 1n21.

55 McKittrick, *Demonic Grounds*, 117.

56 Colleen Walsh, "The Landscape of Slavery," *Harvard Gazette*, December 17, 2010.

57 For more on the issuance of land grants and women and Blacks, see Johnson, *In Duty Bound*.

58 Peter Meyler and David Meyler, *A Stolen Life: Searching for Richard Pierpoint* (Toronto: Dundurn, 1999), 70–6; James W. St. G. Walker, *The Black Loyalists: The Search for a Promised Land in Nova Scotia and Sierra Leone, 1783–1870* (Toronto: University of Toronto Press, 1992), 18, 125.

59 Sarah Long, wife (separated) of Black Loyalist Peter Long, submitted a land grant petition in 1807, but it was denied. Wives were not entitled to land grants. See "Upper Canada Land Petition of Sarah Long," 1807, in Upper Canada Land Petitions (1763–1865), vol. 286, bundle L9, petition 4, microfilm C-2126; Janice Nickerson, *York's Sacrifice: Militia Casualties of the War of 1812* (Toronto: Dundurn, 2012), 18; and Johnson, *In Duty Bound*.

60 Boyce, *Belleville*, 23.

61 Boyce, 30, 40.

62 See Winks, *Blacks in Canada*, 8, 18–19, 112–13; Elgersman, *Unyielding Spirits*, 10–13; Harvey A. Whitfield, *North to Bondage: Loyalist Slavery in the Maritimes* (Vancouver: UBC Press, 2016), 8, 19, 113. Wheat was a main staple in the Bay of Quinté region, as noted in Canniff, *History of the Settlement of Upper*

Canada, 205, 208, 215. Examples of crops grown on the farm of Peter Russell in Toronto with the help of slave labour are found in the diary of Joseph Willcocks, who was employed as the farm manager for a few years. See "The D*iary of Joseph Willcocks* from Dec. 1, 1799, to Feb. 1, 1803," in Appendix B in J.E. Middleton and Fred Landon, *The Province of Ontario: A History, 1615–1927*, vol. 2 (Toronto: Dominion, 1927), 1250–322. Also see description of crops grown on the Toronto estate of William Jarvis, who also used slave labour, in J. Ross Robertson, *Landmarks of Toronto; a collection of historical sketches of the old town of York from 1792 until 1833, and of Toronto from 1834 to 1893*, vol. 1 (Toronto: J.R. Robertson, 1894), 128–9.
63 McKittrick, *Demonic Grounds*, 96.
64 In my research on Bet, I attempted to locate the earliest records of St. Andrew's Presbyterian Church in Belleville (opened 1830) and was informed by the secretary that early records were lost in a fire. Wendy White, email to the author, March 22, 2017.
65 Mary Jane Logan McCallum, *Indigenous Women, Work, and History: 1940–1980* (Winnipeg: University of Manitoba Press, 2014), 10.
66 Riddell, "Upper Canada – Early Period," 326n17.
67 Photocopy of a typewritten document relating to Joseph Keeler's 1812 receipt of sale of an enslaved woman and her child to William H. Wallbridge, Cramahe Township Public Library, accessed March 22, 2017, http://vitacollections.ca/cramahelibrary/2676446/data; Boyce, *Historic Hastings*, 40.
68 Allan Dempsey, "A Settlement at Meyer's Creek" (unpublished paper, c. 1960), 5, Community Archives of Belleville and Hastings County, accessed April 6, 2018, https://discover.cabhc.ca/belleville-early-settlers-meyers-creek.
69 Marisa J. Fuentes, *Dispossessed Lives: Enslaved Women, Violence, and the Archive* (Philadelphia: University of Pennsylvania Press, 2016), 5.
70 Fuentes, 4.
71 Fuentes, 4; McKittrick, *Demonic Grounds*, 119; Sasha Turner, "The Nameless and the Forgotten: Maternal Grief, Sacred Protection, and the Archive of Slavery," *Slavery & Abolition* 38, no. 2 (2017): 234.

SECTION TWO

Constructing Blackness across Borders and Boundaries

4
A Forgotten Generation: African Canadian History between Fugitive Slaves and World War I

ADAM ARENSON

On 2 August 1877, James Douglas died. "The greatest and best British Columbian," as the *British Colonist* newspaper called him, Douglas had been the governor of the colonies of Vancouver Island and British Columbia.[1] "Firemen, Odd-fellows, benevolent societies, marines, Militia, blue jackets from war-ships, the Governor and staff, and the Admiral and staff" were among the nearly five thousand mourners as Douglas's funeral procession wound its way through the streets of Victoria.[2] The local elite, made rich from the gold rushes and from the fisheries that Douglas had helped to establish, paid tribute as well. A steamship was named after Douglas, and a memorial established.[3] Douglas was also venerated by British Columbia's African Canadian community, who counted Douglas as one of their own: Sir James Douglas, Knight Commander of the Order of the Bath, the so-called father of British Columbia, was a man of mixed race, born in Demerara, Guiana, the child of an unmarried Scottish planter and a "free coloured" Barbadian woman.[4]

Douglas and the African Canadians of British Columbia crystallize many of the forgotten realities of African Canadian history in the Confederation generation, the era between the American Civil War and World War I. Though African Canadians with roots in the Caribbean are now the majority, they were extremely rare in British North American colonies between the colonization of Sierra Leone in the late eighteenth century and the altered immigration laws of the twentieth century, moments that shaped the African Caribbean experience in Canada and throughout the global African diaspora. The African Canadian men who honoured Douglas had come as refugees from the United States, but they were not enslaved people escaping along the Underground Railroad. They were free Black men and women who left California after the US Supreme Court's *Dred Scott* decision, which declared that "neither the class of persons who had been imported as slaves nor their descendants, whether they had become free or not, were ... a part of the people" and that those of African descent "had no rights which the white man was bound to respect."[5] These African North Americans – their identity forged, I argue, by experience on both sides of the US-Canada borders – prospered on Vancouver Island, however, as well in the British Columbian mining towns.[6] Unlike hundreds of African Canadians from the Maritime provinces, Quebec, and Ontario, they did not return south during the American Civil War to fight for the Union. Some, however, did take up arms, but in the local militia, the Victoria Pioneer Rifle Company.[7] And, despite their segregated unit, they did not live in Black agricultural settlements. In fact, many lived in the city of Victoria, and some held office and bought real estate – as did some of their most prosperous contemporaries in Toronto and St. Catharines, Ontario.

This chapter describes a generation of African Canadians – including African North Americans, native-born African Canadians, and others of African descent who made their way to the new Dominion of Canada – that has been forgotten in the historical narrative. They are not the African Canadian events and places most often commemorated; this is a history after the imposition of slavery in New France and after Governor John Simcoe's act against slavery. It is a history after the arrival of Black Loyalists and after the Underground Railroad. It is a history that came before the creation of the No. 2 Construction Battalion and the civil rights struggles of Viola Desmond, to name a few better-known events in African Canadian history. Though it was a period of legal, political, and economic striving, the efforts of the Confederation generation of African Canadians are forgotten. This chapter provides a guide to how we can recover the history of the Confederation generation of African Canadians and thereby expand our vision of Canadian history and the role of African Canadian business, scholarship, social groups, and politics within the story of the nation.

My ongoing research is focused on this Confederation generation, seeking to understand how Canadian Confederation – coupled with the general emancipation in the United States and the unfinished rights revolution of US Reconstruction – offered opportunities and alternatives for border-crossing African North Americans and those in both Canada and the United States who stayed put, whether by choice or by necessity. Gathering snippets of information from newspaper accounts and family histories, court records and censuses, church sermons and social-group bulletins, I seek to find how African Canadian, African North American, and African American communities staked out their identities. Working through the existing historiography, however, demonstrates how often the experience of this Confederation generation is absent from the historical narrative. This chapter provides a rereading of the existing literature, both to identify the extent of the gap regarding the Confederation generation in African Canadian history and to provide ideas on how best to recover this history. Throughout, I will argue for the importance of the Confederation generation in helping us build a wider and more complex narrative of experiences of Black life in Canada.

There are several reasons for the absence of scholarship on Black Canadian populations between Canadian Confederation and World War I. The African Canadian population at that time was smaller than in the decades before and after. In these years, African Canadian outmigration was substantial – but in line by percentage with the massive movement of White Canadians into the United States.[8] Though census statistics for African Canadians are not completely accurate, they at least provide a sense of the scale of outmigration: while the peak of the Black population in what is now Canada has been hotly debated, it was likely between 20,000 and 60,000 people in the years 1857 to 1863, or 0.7 to 2.3 per cent of the overall population north of the forty-ninth parallel, and 1 to 3 per cent of the Canada West population.[9] In 1870–1, the combined censuses of Canada and British Columbia report 21,958 African Canadians, about six-tenths of 1 per cent of the overall population of more than 3.7 million. By 1911, the recorded African Canadian population had dropped to its lowest level: 16,877 out of 7.2 million, or under a quarter of 1 per cent.[10] One might see this as explanation enough for the lack of historical scholarship and attention to the African Canadians in these years. For example, while chronicling the impact of the American Civil War and Reconstruction on the drive for Canadian Confederation, the role of the transcontinental railroads in bringing White settlers to the Prairies, and the shifting relationships locally, between Canada and the United States, and globally, within the British Empire, Robert Bothwell found only one occasion to mention African Canadians in *The Penguin History of Canada* between his recounting of the Underground Railroad in the 1850s and the reform of immigration laws in the 1960s. Alongside discussion of anti-Asian discrimination and violence in the first decade of the twentieth century, he noted only that "Blacks from the United States were also discouraged. Canada was, obviously but unofficially, to be white."[11]

A focus on demography, however, misses the lived experience of the African Canadians in this generation – and it elides the racist sensibilities that shaped both Canadian and US civil society at that time, which actively minimized and obscured the accomplishments of African Canadians from the historical record. A half-century ago, Robin Winks argued that retelling tales of the Underground Railroad combined with the height of White supremacist pseudoscience to keep African Canadians "virtually forgotten" in the decades after the American Civil War.[12] After the Civil War, abolitionists took a victory lap, regaling the public with stories of the Underground Railroad – and crowding out the realities of African Canadian life with stories of past escape that could only now be revealed.[13] Romantic tales of the Old South proliferated and minstrel shows continued apace in both the United States and Canada, tingeing even stories of fugitive resistance and survival with patronizing racism.[14]

"Canada was susceptible to the same pseudo-anthropology and pseudo-science that grew in western Europe, Britain, and the United States between 1870 and 1930," Winks wrote in 1971, noting (in dated language) how "the Negro in Canada found himself sliding down an inclined plane from mere neglect to active dislike." Winks cited how both professional and amateur Canadian historians "expressed their surprise at discovering, over and over again, that slavery had existed within Canadian territory." Though in the late nineteenth century Toronto attorney J. Cleland Hamilton "wrote and rewrote his articles on 'The African in Canada,'" Winks found that the research was utilized to claim "that the Negro had no place in Canadian society."[15]

Fred Landon and William Renwick Riddell became the first true scholars of the Black Canadian past, beginning their research just after World War I. Publishing in newspapers as well as the nascent *Journal of Negro History*, Landon and Riddell spent decades writing groundbreaking studies of the fugitive era and the enslaved people of eighteenth-century British North America and New France.[16] In Landon's accounts of Buxton and Amherstburg, published in 1918 and 1925, respectively, he noted how "today, more than half a century after emancipation, it [Buxton] is still a prosperous and distinctly Negro settlement" and that "even today, there are many coloured families resident in Amherstburg, descendants of those who came in the days before the Civil War and who did not leave their adopted home when the abolition of slavery and the downfall of the Confederacy made it possible."[17] However, Landon's only article solely regarding the post–Civil War years described the trials of a White Confederate fugitive living in Canada, Dr. Rufus Bratton.[18] We can only note ruefully that Landon documented the fugitive generation with expert detail and yet said so little about the post–Civil War generations of African Canadians he identified as still living in these communities. In 1941, Landon concluded an essay for the *Negro History Bulletin* with the following (unfounded) claims:

> But since 1865 the story of the Negro in Canada lacks those elements that stir the imagination. The reason is that he is simply a fellow-Canadian to

those about him and his life differs in no respect from that of hundreds of thousands about him. He is a citizen of Canada and as such he is entitled to all the privileges of citizenship. These cannot be denied him. He votes freely wherever and whenever he is qualified to do so; he suffers no discriminations in the franchise. His children attend the public schools of the province in which he resides and may go on to the collegiate institutes and high schools. Occasionally a Negro student enters a university; others attend normal schools and become teachers.

Few Negroes in Canada have gained wealth, but the great majority have comfort and all have the same security as their white neighbors. Comparatively few have entered the professions; most have found their life in humble occupations.[19]

Landon's erroneously rosy picture of African Canadian life after the American Civil War could be read as a blueprint of the very areas of ongoing struggle that the next wave of scholarship engaged.

In the late 1940s, an Amherstburg carpenter and community leader named Alvin McCurdy began collecting archival sources on African Canadian history, creating the pre-eminent collection of the Black experience in Ontario over the centuries.[20] In the 1970s and 1980s, Robin Winks, Daniel Hill, and James W. St. G. Walker published books that transformed our understanding of African Canadian history.[21] McCurdy's archive and these works – which drew on his collections as well as other sources, gathering and citing documentation with a newfound degree of precision – demonstrated an ongoing focus on the eras of slavery in Canada, the Loyalist influxes in the Age of Revolutions, the fugitive slave era, and then (in the cases of Winks and Walker) the civil rights struggles and Caribbean migrants of the twentieth century. These are all admirable and important subjects, many of which have an immediate appeal in the construction of a "usable" Canadian identity – as a refuge, on the one hand, or as just another European settler colony built on forced labour and racist ideals, on the other. But as attention is focused on these eras, the decades after the Civil War again go unremarked.

For his part, Winks sought to frame these decades after the American Civil War as a "nadir," when African Canadians retreated into Black churches, schools, voluntary associations, and a segregated press as institutions that would preserve their community until better times.[22] Yet such historical framing too easily adopts a Jim Crow–inflected, US-based framework for Black Canadian history that obscures more than it reveals. Winks ultimately agreed with Walker's critique that *The Blacks in Canada* was too often "a 'history of the Black man as an issue in white Canadian life,'" rather than the story of African Canadians.[23] The African Canadian poet and critic George Elliott Clarke has gone further, claiming that Winks "exhibits, purely, a small-l liberal, American bias. I would need an entire book to amend – one by one – his false precepts ... African-Canadian 'progress' must be read against Canadian cultural norms, not American ones."[24]

In Walker's most chronologically comprehensive work on African Canadian history, *A History of Blacks in Canada: A Study Guide for Teachers and Students* (1980), he discussed the Confederation generation on only three-and-a-half of the book's 181 pages.[25] Nevertheless, Walker noted the importance of US emancipation as a dividing line in Canadian history. He argued that "until 1865 black immigration into Canada was specifically caused by reason of colour." Further, he contended that "since the American Civil War, however, black immigrants have been motivated only coincidentally by their colour," pointing to "opportunities for self-fulfillment, or for the advancement of their children" as causes that then linked "black" and "gold, tan, or white" immigrants – while still noting their "highly visible characteristic" in the Great White North.[26] Walker eloquently described the logic of emigration in these years, noting the irony of how

> in the "segregated" United States there was a full black society from top to bottom, with black universities, black newspapers, black hospitals, black lawyers and doctors and tradesmen, as well as waiters, labourers and smaller farmers. But in "non-segregated" Canada blacks tended all to fit into one level of society, for the higher institutions and higher professions were tacitly reserved for whites. A black youth seeking a career in law or medicine had a greater chance of acceptance into a black American college than into a white Canadian one, and upon graduation he was more certain of a successful practice in the American black community than in Canadian society.[27]

Only with "New-Black Canadians," as Walker labelled them, after 1917 do the questions that link and divide later Canadian immigrants of African descent from the earliest Black Canadians accentuate the gaps in the narrative during the years between the Civil War and World War I.[28]

The existence of detailed bibliographies of African Canadian history allows us to quantify the size of the gap in the history of the Confederation generation. Even within a generally neglected field of Black Canadian history, the history of the Confederation generation is particularly limited. By analysing the entries in five of those bibliographies – by George H. Junne, Karolyn Smardz Frost, Hilary Bates Neary, Hillary Russell, and David C. Este, with each entry coded for the period that the history covered – I found that an average of 3.7 per cent of the entries consider the African Canadian experience between 1865 and 1914. In contrast, the fugitive slave era, which is discussed in somewhere between 13 and 85 per cent of the entries, clearly commands more than half of all scholarship on African Canadians.[29] (See table.)

The numeric disadvantage is compounded by the brevity and noticeable lack of detail in so many treatments of the African Canadian experience in the Confederation generation. In a rather representative, brief, and unsourced statement, a 1967 centennial history of African Canadians in Windsor noted only that "by the late eighteen hundreds, ... [African Canadians] were still proportionally small in number, but it is during this time that evidence of their business acumen begins to appear," and that "villagers of this race were also leading busy productive lives," before moving on to individual biographies and a list of "firsts."[30] Even a book-length biography of William Peyton Hubbard (1842–1935), the first Black alderman in Toronto, merely described the politics of the period from 1865 to 1914 as "a fiery swirl of opinion and controversy" that Hubbard avoided, as he focused on "hard work and dedication" alone.[31] In Gary French's *Men of Colour: An Historical Account of the Black Settlement on Wilberforce Street and in Oro Township, Simcoe County, Ontario, 1819–1949* (1978), the narrative concluded when the formal settlement sponsorship stopped in 1832; the author argued that "it was inevitable that the result would be a gradual elimination of Black settlers from the area."[32] But on the very next page, French noted that the local African Canadian population numbers were stable at least through 1871, the last year he addressed, and that "there are still one or two families of descendants of the Negro settlers in the area." The book title's dates derived from the fact that James Dizon Thompson (1877–1949) was the last African Canadian to live in the township proper, but the disconnect – between the continuation of African Canadian life in the region and French's declarations that "the settlement had, in effect, disappeared by 1900" – is jarring.[33]

In the 1990s, the sense that African Canadians were recent arrivals remained far too common. As the contributors to *"We're Rooted Here and They Can't Pull Us Up": Essays in African Canadian Women's History* wrote, "Black children entering the schools have no sense of Blacks being here for generations, and, hence, that there is a 400-year presence and contribution of African Canadians in this country. These children naturally feel invisible and marginalized."[34] The patterns also repeat in textbooks and curricula; even in *Towards Freedom: The African-Canadian Experience* (1996), the chapters that discuss the period after the American Civil War and before World War I included long sections on the experience

Table 4.1. Works on Black Canadian history by era

Bibliographer	Date of bibliography	Total number of entries	Pre-1763	1763–81	1781–1838	Era of US fugitive slaves, 1838–65	Confederation generation, 1865–1914	1914–45	1945–80	1980–publication	Works that discuss all periods	Total entries used for percentages	Percentage of entries on Confederation generation	Percentage of entries on era of US fugitive slaves
Bates Neary	1969	153	3	1	5	130	3	9	0	0	2	153	1.96	84.97
Russell	1990	348	26	5	46	173	11	24	7	1	55	348	3.16	49.71
Junne	2003	3244	n/a	n/a	120	443	31	28	17	5	n/a	644	4.81	68.79
Este	2008	31	5	1	1	4	1	3	0	2	14	31	3.23	12.90
Smardz Frost	2009	124	5	1	7	83	7	5	0	1	15	124	5.65	66.94
												AVERAGE	3.76	56.66

n/a: not available

Note on methodology: For all bibliographies except for Junne, every publication listed was categorized. Periodization was borrowed from traditional divides in the Canadian history survey. For Junne, which is not limited to histories but draws primarily from periodical articles, the counts were based on index and keyword searches, and both counts and the total include duplicated entries. The categorization was conservative; if the all-periods sources were included and subcategorized by content, the percentage of coverage of the era of US fugitive slaves would be even higher. While Neary's bibliography was completed in 2009, it catalogued only works by Landon, the last of which was published in 1969.

of African Americans in the US Colored Troops, US Reconstruction schools and politics, and Black homesteaders such as the "exodusters."[35] In contrast, the comments about African Canadian life in these years remain brief and vague: "The post–Civil War push and pull factors [listed elsewhere in the chapter as Civil War fighting, Reconstruction opportunities, and then the lack of in-migration and increasingly racist immigration regulations] had reduced Canada's black population to an insignificant phantom, a distant memory," the textbook claims, overstating the reality.[36] Claudine Bonner has noted how such attention to US events in these years leave out vital African Canadian stories. "The influx of American blacks to Canada, the way it changed many communities, and the low profile all of this has in our textbooks is definitely a Canadian tale," she wrote. "The gathering of the histories and stories of the communities which make up the nation is vital to an individual's self-understanding and identity, and should not be left to an annual celebration of black heritage, but rather be part of an inclusive curriculum that values all aspects of the history of the nation."[37]

Natasha Henry, Adrienne Shadd, Karolyn Smardz Frost, and Rosemary Sadlier are among the many scholars and activists who have been working to change how schoolchildren learn about African Canadian history, offering curricular supplements, primary source documents, and teacher training to build a more inclusive Canadian history.[38] According to Boulou Ebanda de B'béri, one of the lead researchers of the SSHRC-funded Promised Land Project, the initiative sought to move Canadian Black history beyond "a mythical version of the Underground Railroad."[39] The final publication of the project, *The Promised Land: History and Historiography of the Black Experience in Chatham-Kent's Settlements and Beyond*, and especially Afua Cooper's epilogue, grappled with the difficulty in telling new stories of African Canadian history within local, national, and global frameworks, even while the public wishes to rehear the stories of the Underground Railroad, half-listening, in order to celebrate heritage stories they assume they already know.[40] And yet the supposed disappearance of African Canadians in the Confederation generation is a persistent myth. In the 2010 edition of the generally strong multidisciplinary introduction to Black Canadians and the prejudices they face, *Black Canadians: History, Experience, Social Conditions*, Joseph Mensah emphasized how terrible it is for current Canadians to keep forgetting the country's slave past but then states that "by the end of the [American Civil] war, most Blacks had returned to the United States," saying nothing further about Black Canadian life in the Confederation generation.[41]

Though not the majority, and not comprehensive, there are some histories that have documented African Canadians in the Confederation generation and that point the way forward for new research. To begin again in British Columbia, Crawford Kilian's *Go Do Some Great Thing: The Black Pioneers of British Columbia* was first published in 1978, after Kilian – a White, American-born novelist – "learned only by chance that black people had been living in the province since the gold rush of 1858."[42] Beginning his in-depth research in the 1970s, Kilian wrote,

> I wondered why scarcely anyone seemed interested in their [Black British Columbians'] experience.
>
> ... In regional histories of such places as Saltspring Island, Kamloops, and the Peace River country, mention was made in passing of black pioneers such as the Starks, John Freemont Smith, and Daniel Williams. With few exceptions, these accounts treated such individuals as curiosities, mere anecdotes in the province's "real" history. When not romanticizing or patronizing the blacks, such accounts often betrayed outright racism. Even historians sometimes took as fact the bigoted opinions of the blacks' white contemporaries.
>
> In effect, the black pioneers of British Columbia had become what Orwell called "unpersons." They had played a key role in the early years of the colonies that became British Columbia, and yet the province had forgotten them.[43]

Kilian dedicated himself to doing better: gathering the incidents and anecdotes, researching their context, reaching the point where "the quarrels and annoyances that beset Victoria's blacks in the early 1860s seem comfortingly trivial" despite having been "played for laughs by the newspapers of the time." Looking beyond such sensationalism, Kilian described how "in the gold fields of the Cariboo and on Saltspring Island, blacks and whites lived and worked together with relatively little friction," despite the "subtle ways racism touched them all."[44] Work in mining was volatile and unpredictable no matter one's skin colour. Combined with the post–Civil War return of some Black Victorians to the United States, those who remained were a "shrinking minority," Kilian surmised; "black people by the turn of the century were so thinly scattered across the province that they rarely came to public notice."[45] Oral histories of White residents recalled that Black families "always kept at a respectful distance." As Kilian notes, this "indicates that the blacks had – after almost a half a century's contribution to the colony and the province – gained little more than tolerance."[46]

Now, more than forty years after Kilian's book was first published, Sherry Edmunds-Flett's decades of research documenting the lives of first generation African Canadian women in British Columbia will explain how African Canadians, especially in Vancouver's so-called vice districts, were targeted for prosecution.[47] Such work will help us understand how sexism and racism interacted in the Confederation era to prevent African Canadians from enjoying equal rights and opportunities.

A similar recovery came from the work of two African Canadian women in Ontario who compiled new comprehensive histories for their home communities. Arlie C. Robbins wrote *Legacy to Buxton* (1983) as a chronological narrative; in *Seek the Truth: A Story of Chatham's Black Community* (1989), Gwendolyn Robinson (assisted by her husband, John) followed the stories of individuals and institutions.[48] These books, written by lifelong members of these communities, had far more to say about the Confederation generation, as well as more assertions about the economic and social trends that shaped these years. In three chapters on these decades, Robbins described how "a generation of young free Blacks, many of whom had never known slavery and most of whom had received an excellent education in [founder of the Elgin Settlement, Reverend William] King's schools, had grown to adulthood." Some went to the United States as teachers during Reconstruction, some had joined "the Buxton migration to the American West," and some had moved elsewhere in Ontario or Michigan and sought their livelihoods.[49] At the height of the community's professional accomplishments, "councillors, trustees of the various school sections, path masters ... and Justices of the Peace were distributed among both races," Robbins noted. But "competing for jobs with their white counterparts" in rural southwestern Ontario, she surmised, led to "the recurrence of hostilities between the two races." White Canadians continued to expect African Canadians to go south, but "by the 1890s, it had become obvious that despite the suggestions ... the remaining black residents of North Buxton and Raleigh had no intention of going 'home.'"[50]

Enlistment for the Boer War and then World War I saw open discrimination against potential Black recruits in Canada; the Ku Klux Klan became active in the country, and the educational, social, and employment worlds for White and Black Canadians became ever more separate. Eloquently, Robbins concluded that, in these years, "once again we donned the mask," as Paul Laurence Dunbar's 1896 poem suggested, but "not nearly as gracefully as our parents had done, for we were educated, we were free and we were proud – ill-equipped to accept without question the racial slurs or the 'no coloured allowed' signs that now blossomed into prominence in a once friendly land." And, crucially for a history of this generation, Robbins found that community leaders "retreated behind an unbreachable wall of silence." In line with the other imbalances this chapter has noted, Robbins concluded that "many of us were told about our grandparents who had been slaves and maybe a few of us had heard about the Elgin Settlement but a far greater number of us were told little or nothing about our early home" in the difficult years between the Civil War and World War I.[51]

In Gwendolyn Robinson's account of Chatham, the larger community and county seat just north of Buxton, about a quarter of the biographies she included discuss residents during the Confederation generation and their successes in law, business, medicine, and the arts.[52] Robinson found economic competition to be the key barometer of African Canadian success in Chatham. When the Black community was small, it was "no longer perceived as a threat to the white community," she wrote, but when economic opportunities flowered, "black businesses and professionals began to be squeezed out," in a pattern that repeated in the 1860s, around 1900, and after World War I. Describing why so many moved away from the town that had once been celebrated as the "Black Mecca," Robinson concluded that "many decided that they had waited too long for a favorable change."[53]

Where Robbins and Robinson relied at times on anecdote and personal stories that burnish their authority as community insiders, demographic studies by Jonathan Walton, Colin McFarquhar, and Tracey Adams tracked trends in Black employment and other markers of community health through newspapers, city directories, and government records.[54] Walton and McFarquhar found that "considerable continuity" shaped African Canadian life in Ontario in the years 1870 to 1919, as "Ontario's white majority never truly understood the concerns of its black minority." In McFarquhar's words, "Little changed over this fifty year period because the underlying attitudes did not change."[55] McFarquhar noted that those African Canadians who were most successful – lawyers, doctors, city officials – were regarded as sui generis: "Whites could justify their presence by downplaying the significance of their race, or ignoring it altogether."[56]

For the most part, however, African Canadians were stuck in the same occupational categories, and they repeatedly made similar demands for greater respect and equal rights without much progress. In a detailed study of recorded occupations for African Canadian workers in London, Ontario, in the years 1861 to 1901, Adams found that, decade after decade, the vast majority of African Canadian men were listed as labourers, barbers, teamsters, plasterers, and farmers, while African Canadian women were servants, laundresses, and occasionally seamstresses.[57] She added,

> In this era of industrialization, professionalization, and the gradual expansion of the services sector, it is important to note what work African-origin men and women were *not* doing. They were not employed as store or office clerks, or as professionals, and they were not employed to any great extent in factories. While African Canadian men continued to work as teamsters and dray men, they were not employed as drivers of more modern vehicles (trolleys, automobiles). By 1901, then, African Canadian men and women remained concentrated in jobs that had been around for decades – low-skill, blue-collar, and service work – that were not attractive jobs for others. They were largely excluded from expanding fields and new industries.[58]

Interestingly, Adams found that African Canadians with more prestigious jobs tended to leave the province, or to die and not be replaced – the same men and women held the same jobs decade after decade, many without finding either an upwardly or downwardly mobile career path.[59] As she noted, "even the well-educated and trained were channeled into dead-end service jobs in the late 19th and early 20th centuries. In such an environment, it is not surprising that outmigration continued, and the size of the African Canadian population declined."[60]

But continuity and survival can be its own form of success, based in community organizing and hard-won relationships. Such history has to be studied community by community, through the hard work of recovering stories that were quietly celebrated in a time when White supremacy in Canada prevented anything from being commemorated more prominently. Sociologist Claudine Bonner's doctoral thesis uses oral histories to recover the experience of North Buxton during the Confederation generation. Following a research question of "What contributed to the evolution of North Buxton from 1873 to 1914 to make it a successful community?" Bonner specifically chose 1873 as a starting time for her study since it "[gave] those fugitives from American slavery wishing to return to America ample time to do so, and [allowed] those who would choose Buxton as their home time to decide they would remain there."[61]

While Sharon Roger Hepburn provided a professional historian's take on the early history of Buxton, Bonner noted that "the end of her [Hepburn's] study leaves the unanswered question, since many Buxtonites chose not to leave the community, what was life like for those living in the resulting community during these years? If life was so difficult and there were few opportunities, why did they choose to stay there?"[62] Bonner was able to provide the subtle details that hint at why the community survived: its isolated location strengthening community ties; the arrival of the railroad providing some jobs; educational, religious, and fraternal ties maintaining strong connections with those who moved away; and tax receipts demonstrating local success at farming that kept the community viable.[63]

Adrienne Shadd, who is both a scholar and a descendant of pre–Civil War African North Americans, similarly highlighted the incremental changes made through organizing and advances in education. In her book *The Journey from Tollgate to Parkway: African Canadians in Hamilton*, Shadd recounted how in 1885 Charles A. Johnson, a leader of the Black Hamiltonian community, offered two hundred Black volunteers to fight against Louis Riel; he was ignored.[64] In an 1889 letter to the editor published in the *Hamilton Herald*, another community leader, George Morton Jr., argued that while he and his fellow African Canadians merely sought equal opportunities, "the Caucasian draws the color line ... He draws it when he practically says we are good enough to vote, but not to hold office. The color line is drawn in public, in private, in pleasure, in business, in life, in death, in the busy marts of trade, and at the sacred altar."[65] Shadd related that Morton became a letter carrier in 1891, and fellow African Canadian Julia Berry held a modest job on Hamilton Mountain as a tollgate collector, but that African Canadians could still generally count more protests than successes.[66]

Blacks and Whites alike noted the advantage of a Canadian education for African North Americans, and it mattered, as Shadd noted, whether they sought employment as waiters or as doctors.[67] In Hamilton, Toronto, and London, public schools had allowed African Canadian children to attend since before the Civil War, but the segregation fights in the western Ontario communities, as well as in St. Catharines, continued into the twentieth century. Shadd has also chronicled the successful legal effort of the Kent County Civil Rights League to desegregate Chatham schools in 1893.[68] The larger percentage of skilled workers and independent entrepreneurs in the Black community of Hamilton in the late nineteenth century, in comparison with the opportunities in Chatham, gives testimony to the differences those gains in education could create – and to the historically uneven experience of African Canadians, including those of the Confederation generation.[69]

Individual biographies add even more testimony to these differences. Shadd highlighted the biography of Charles Roman, born in Williamsport, Pennsylvania, in 1864. After his family moved to Dundas, Ontario, Roman began working in the cotton mill at the age of eight. He was the first non-White student at Hamilton Collegiate Institute; he then worked as a schoolteacher and became an evening student at Meharry Medical College in Nashville, Tennessee. He eventually became president of the National Medical Association – the premier medical association of African Americans in those segregated years – and served as the first editor of its journal.[70] All of it was possible, Roman's biographer noted, because "even such preparation as he had had ... during his first twenty-one years in the North and in Canada ... gave him an advantage over most of his associates."[71] Similarly, genealogist and historian Hilary Dawson, in her account of Alfred Lafferty, an honours graduate of the University of Toronto and Chatham's first Black lawyer, described how "Lafferty rose, with the support of his family, his talents and hard work, from the slums of Toronto to the Chatham establishment," chronicling his social connections and his success in owning and maintaining an eleven-room brick house for decades.[72]

Colin McFarquhar has surmised that we might even be missing the story of some of the most influential African Canadians because the records go silent on race for the prosperous and successful – while always noting the race of a non-White Canadian under arrest.[73] The racial consciousness of the legal system has been a productive area of research for Barrington Walker, who has found case after case from the late nineteenth century where African Canadians were charged and tried. "Cases of property crime give us a window on the harsh realities of Black life in the nineteenth century," Walker wrote. "The death-penalty cases involving Black defendants ... were the result of the interplay of legal factors and social attitudes, the tension between the veneer of the rule of law and biologically and culturally rooted ideas about race in Canada." Walker urged more scholars to look into these legal records, as "the law, from the days of slavery to the difficult days of freedom, has profoundly shaped the Black experience in Canada," and hence "there is much more Black Canadian history in the legal archives" to be explored.[74] Legal archives – in their granular, case-by-case nature – can provide the shadow of the histories of community organizing, demonstrating how individuals suffered or struggled against a legal system built by and for White Canadians.

The complications of community-by-community history are multiplied by the changing geography of Black Canada in the late nineteenth century. While early Black Canadian history is best centred in the conquest of New France, the arrival of Black Loyalists and Jamaican Maroons, and the colonization of some Black British North Americans to Sierra Leone, in the Confederation generation Ontario came to dominate the history of the Dominion, overshadowing the Maritime provinces, Quebec, and the far different stories in the Canadian West. As George Elliott Clarke has written of Halifax, even in the twenty-first century, "from the standpoint of Toronto, my little community that numbers 30,000 people, which counts for about 10% of the Black Canadian total population, has little to contribute to the history and discussion of an African-Canadian presence. We literally do not count."[75]

While Black life in the colonial era was centred in the Maritimes and Quebec, these areas are even harder to document than Ontario in the era of Confederation, as Harvey Amani Whitfield noted in a recent essay on the history and historiography of the African diaspora in Atlantic Canada.[76] In two articles from 2012, Jennifer Harris has done the painstaking work of recovering the late nineteenth-century history of an African Canadian community in Westmorland County, New Brunswick.[77] Noting the merely passing references to Black New Brunswick after the Civil War in William Spray's *The Blacks in New Brunswick* (1972) and Greg Marquis's *In Armageddon's Shadow: The Civil War and Canada's Maritime Provinces* (1998), Harris delves far deeper, finding that while "the problems and challenges faced by Black Westmorlanders more generally were compounded by additional obstacles in education, housing, and the acquisition of property, ... it is not so much that Sackville's nineteenth-century Black community dissolved as it is that it relocated, reconfiguring itself in another space, bolstered by additional communal and structural supports, as well as by educational and financial opportunities."[78]

Harris is most successful at demonstrating these ties in the life story of Lalia Halfkenny (1870–97), the first Black woman to graduate from a seminary in Maritime Canada. Halfkenny obtained a teaching post at Hartshorn Memorial College in Richmond, Virginia, but Harris notes the "fundamental irony" in that Halfkenny, "like most other black Maritime graduates of the era," could succeed only "in isolation from the world where she had been raised, received her own education, and where her family still resided."[79] In Nova Scotia, Halfkenny's great-uncle could only be a janitor at Acadia University, but this meagre patronage allowed others in the community to attend and graduate from university. Harris does a marvellous job of recovering how the janitor position was passed down among members of the Black Nova Scotian community, creating a narrow avenue for success in the midst of a segregated and unwelcoming community.[80]

Even more path-breaking in geography, chronology, and scope is Sarah-Jane Mathieu's *North of the Color Line*, a history of Canada's railroad porters that suggests a radically different reading of African Canadian history in this period. When Canada called for homesteaders at the turn of the twentieth century, Mathieu documented that African Americans were eager to be those settlers – a possibility that Canadian officials tried to foreclose.[81] While some African Americans made it through the gauntlet of restrictions to settle in the West, most notably in Alberta's Amber Valley in 1911, Mathieu found that far more came as porters, as the Canadian Pacific Railway "clandestinely shuttled their own black immigrant workforce into Canada."[82] Documenting these new African Canadian communities, especially near railroad transfer stations in the cities of the Prairies, Mathieu counted 5,000 Black immigrants among the 1.8 million new arrivals in Canada between 1870 and 1914, leading to her argument that "in actuality, African Americans and West Indians migrated to Canada at consistent rates throughout this period, despite various measures to keep them out."[83] The porters were able to use their mobility to form transnational social and political alliances, despite both national and corporate efforts to make them an invisible servant class.[84] As Mathieu's history suggests, some porters experienced economic and social success – accomplishments just as hidden as the struggles in the Confederation generation.

Mathieu also argues that White Canadians in this period wished to see race as a question of unwelcome immigrants rather than to engage with established non-White Canadian communities.[85] In another irony that silenced the African Canadian populations, White Canadians stoked a nativist racial paranoia, even though, as Mathieu notes, "most white Canadians outside Toronto, Montreal, and Halifax would rarely have seen a black person before the Great Depression."[86] Once again, it was organizing within this labour community that allowed for gains in civil and political rights. Mathieu documented how the porters successfully challenged the de facto ban on Black servicemen in World War I, applying political pressure that led to the creation of the No. 2 Construction Battalion. Mathieu argued that this led to ever more successful labour organizing during the interwar years, civil rights victories, and a transnational human rights alliance through the labour movement in the decades that followed.[87]

African Canadian migration into the United States helped to shape the contours of the Confederation generation as families maintained economic, religious, and fraternal ties that stretched across the US-Canada border. In my larger project, I am reconstructing the personal stories of border crossers, adding their motivations and fears to what we know of African Canadian, African American, and a joint African North American history in these years.[88] Though my work is in its infancy, I can see how many social visits were reported in the *Chicago Defender* and other Black newspapers, charting lives that crossed from Michigan, Illinois, or Ohio across to Ontario, Nova Scotia, or elsewhere in Canada.[89] In their recent works on African Canadian soldiers in the Union army during the Civil War, both Richard Reid and Bryan Prince conclude with glimpses into the pension files that revealed family stories that included crossing back and forth over the US-Canada border in the decades following the war – work that my project will continue to explore. Pension files from Black Canadian veterans of the US Civil War also offer a significant amount of detail about African Canadian community life.[90]

Even a temporary sojourn in the United States came to shape the lives of some African Canadian veterans, and none more than Anderson Abbott. Abbott, who had been a contract surgeon to the US Army, returned to his family's real estate holdings in Toronto but remained an active observer of American life and a fervent devotee of his fellow veterans in the local Grand Army of the Republic post.[91] He also drew on his experience in both countries to make pronouncements on how best to achieve equality. At the turn of the twentieth century Abbott wrote, "Our youth evince a strong disposition to cross the borderline as soon as they acquire sufficient knowledge and experience to make a living ... By the process of absorption and expatriation the color line will eventually fade out in Canada."[92] By "absorption," Abbott meant advocacy for the full cultural and physical assimilation of African Canadians through "amalgamation" in mixed-race marriages.[93] Abbott himself, over the course of his life, married three White women. In some branches of his family, it worked: Abbott's descendant Catherine Slaney wrote a memoir about being surprised to learn of her African Canadian ancestry. Over the course of her research into Abbott, and then her interviews of and reunions with both "White" and "Black" Abbott descendants, Slaney eloquently examined why and how certain members of the family began to pass as White. Slaney argued that Abbott, despite his personal pride as a Black Canadian, never made room in his vision of Canadian identity for any path forward other than being completely swallowed up through assimilation into a "melting pot" Canadian identity.[94]

The history of African Canadians in the Confederation generation may never garner the attention given to the stories of the Underground Railroad, the twentieth-century civil rights struggles, and the earliest days of slavery in New France. Even oral histories today can fall victim to this focus. At the Buxton Homecoming reunion in 2015, I experienced this telescoping of historical priorities when I asked Fred Johnson, a ninety-year-old resident of southwestern Ontario and third-generation African Canadian, about his family's experiences between 1865 and 1930, stretching into his own childhood; he demurred, wanting to instead tell me about his ancestor's arrival as a fugitive fleeing the United States.[95] As Nina Reid-Maroney has noted, "The field of nineteenth-century African-Canadian history is just beginning to move beyond the constraints of a narrative so defined by the Underground Railroad that it has left little room for asking questions about what happened next."[96]

The first step in filling a gap in African Canadian history is acknowledging the existence of such a hole. For a whole host of reasons, we may never have a satisfactorily complete history of African Canadians in the Confederation generation. But an examination of the reasons these African Canadians have been forgotten, or ignored, or erased, can place us on the road to recovering them. Silences have plagued the study of African Canadians in the Confederation generation, but – as many of the best studies mentioned above have demonstrated – we can get beyond generalizations and guesses by re-examining the archival records, paying attention to local details, and listening closely to oral histories and the traces left by artefacts. In Black community archives, in data aggregation from church and government records and other demographic sources, from genealogies and memories and long-forgotten newspaper columns, more of the history of African Canadians in the years between the American Civil War and World War I is out there, waiting to be told. As this chapter has suggested, recovering African Canadian stories from the era of Confederation will fill this gap through painstaking but revelatory work.

NOTES

1 "British Columbia." *Daily Evening Bulletin* (San Francisco), September 25, 1877.
2 "Funeral of Sir James Douglas," *New York Times*, August 8, 1877, 2.
3 See, for example, "British Columbia," *Daily Evening Bulletin*; and *Daily Colonist* (Victoria, BC), January 3, 1866, 2, http://www.britishcolonist.ca/.
4 Crawford Kilian, *Go Do Some Great Thing: The Black Pioneers of British Columbia*, rev. 2nd ed. (Burnaby, BC: Commodore, 2008), 27, 111, 146. See also Adele Perry, *Colonial Relations: The Douglas-Connolly Family and the Nineteenth-Century Imperial World* (Cambridge: Cambridge University Press, 2015); Robin W. Winks, *The Blacks in Canada: A History*, 2nd ed. (Montreal and Kingston: McGill-Queen's University Press, 1997), 275.
5 Dred Scott, Plaintiff in Error, v. John F.A. Sandford, 60 US (19 How.) 393 (1857), majority opinion delivered by Justice Roger B. Taney, https://www.law.cornell.edu/supremecourt/text/60/393.
6 I use the term "African North Americans" to emphasize how these people of African descent crossed borders and did not identify themselves with only one English-speaking nation-state; for earlier use of the term, see Adam Arenson, "Experience Rather Than Imagination: Researching the

Return Migration of African North Americans during the American Civil War and Reconstruction." *Journal of American Ethnic History* 32, no. 2 (2013): 73–7; and Ikuko Asaka, *Tropical Freedom: Climate, Settler Colonialism, and Black Exclusion in the Age of Emancipation* (Durham: Duke University Press, 2017), 14. This chapter does not consider the experience of people of African descent crossing between the United States and Mexico, though that border also has a history of fugitive escapes, forced crossings by enslaved people, and use in crafting a new identity; see, for example, Sean Kelley, "'Mexico in His Head': Slavery and the Texas-Mexico Border, 1810–1860," *Journal of Social History* 37, no. 3 (2004): 709–23; and Alice Baumgartner, *South to Freedom: Runaway Slaves to Mexico and the Road to the Civil War* (New York: Basic Books, 2020).

7 See discussion in Kilian, *Go Do Some Great Thing*, 62–4, 111–13; see also Winks, *Blacks in Canada*, 279–80.

8 On White Canadian migration in this generation, see Bruno Ramirez, "Through the Northern Borderlands: Canada-U.S. Migrations in the Nineteenth and Twentieth Centuries," and Nora Faires, "Population Movements and the Making of Canada-U.S. Not-So-Foreign Relations," both in *Migrants and Migration in Modern North America: Cross-border Lives, Labor Markets, and Politics*, ed. Dirk Hoerder and Nora Faires (Durham: Duke University Press, 2011), 76–98, 129–49; and Faires, "Leaving the 'Land of the Second Chance': Migration from Ontario to the Upper Midwest in the Nineteenth and Early Twentieth Centuries," in *Permeable Border: The Great Lakes Basin as Transnational Region, 1650–1990*, by John J. Bukowczyk, Nora Faires, David R. Smith, and Randy William Widdis (Pittsburgh: University of Pittsburgh Press, 2005), 78–119. See also Philip J. Deloria, *Indians in Unexpected Places* (Lawrence: University Press of Kansas, 2004).

9 Winks, *Blacks in Canada*, 484–96; Michael Wayne, "The Black Population of Canada West on the Eve of the American Civil War: A Reassessment Based on the Manuscript Census of 1861," *Social History* 28, no. 56 (1995): 465–86. For Ontario, see "Census of 1861," Library and Archives Canada, last modified September 9, 2020, http://www.bac-lac.gc.ca/eng/census/1861/Pages/about-census.aspx.

10 Winks, *Blacks in Canada*, 486; K.G. Basavarajappa and Bali Ram, "Section A: Population and Migration," Statistics Canada, n.d., archived content, accessed July 5, 2021, https://www150.statcan.gc.ca/n1/en/pub/11-516-x/pdf/5500092-eng.pdf.

11 Robert Bothwell, *The Penguin History of Canada* (New York: Penguin, 2008), 251.

12 Winks, *Blacks in Canada*, 288.

13 Winks, 289, 234–41. On an abolitionist victory lap, see Scott Gac, *Singing for Freedom: The Hutchinson Family Singers and the Nineteenth-Century Culture of Reform* (New Haven: Yale University Press, 2007), chap. 1.

14 Cheryl Thompson, *Uncle: Race, Nostalgia, and the Cultural Politics of Loyalty* (Toronto: Coach House Books, 2021). Se also Winks, *Blacks in Canada*, 290–1; and K. Stephen Prince, *Stories of the South: Race and the Reconstruction of Southern Identity, 1865–1915* (Chapel Hill: University of North Carolina Press, 2014).
15 Winks, *Blacks in Canada*, 292, 297, 298.
16 Karolyn Smardz Frost, "Introduction," in *Ontario's African-Canadian Heritage: Collected Writings by Fred Landon, 1918–1967*, ed. Karolyn Smardz Frost, Bryan Walls, Hilary Bates Neary, and Frederick H. Armstrong (Toronto: Natural Heritage Books, 2009), 20–1.
17 Fred Landon, "The Buxton Settlement in Canada" (1918) and "Amherstburg, Terminus of the Underground Railroad" (1925), in Smardz Frost et al., *Ontario's African-Canadian Heritage*, 99, 66.
18 Fred Landon, "The Kidnapping of Dr. Rufus Bratton," *Journal of Negro History* 10, no. 3 (1925): 330–3.
19 Fred Landon, "The Negro in Canada," *Negro History Bulletin* 4, no. 7 (1941): 160.
20 These are now available as Alvin D. McCurdy fonds (1808–1986), Archives of Ontario, Toronto.
21 Winks, *Blacks in Canada*; Daniel G. Hill, *The Freedom-Seekers: Blacks in Early Canada* (Agincourt, ON: Book Society of Canada, 1981); James W. St. G. Walker, *A History of Blacks in Canada: A Study Guide for Teachers and Students* (Ottawa: Minister of State Multiculturalism, 1980). For earlier historiographic work placing Winks, Hill, and Walker as foundational texts, at times alongside others, see Karolyn Smardz Frost, "Ontario's African-Canadian Heritage: Sources and Resources," in Smardz Frost et al., *Ontario's African-Canadian Heritage*, 315–27; and David C. Este, "Black Canadian Historical Writing 1970–2006: An Assessment," *Journal of Black Studies* 38, no. 3 (2008): 388–406.
22 Winks, *Blacks in Canada*, chaps. 10–13, esp. 336–7.
23 James Walker, review of *The Blacks in Canada: A History*, by Robin Winks, *Dalhousie Review* 50 (Summer 1971): 285, quoted in Winks, xvii.
24 George Elliott Clarke, *Odysseys Home: Mapping African-Canadian Literature* (Toronto: University of Toronto Press, 2002), 63–4n9, as quoted in Daniel McNeil, "Afro(Americo)centricity in Black (American) Nova Scotia," *Canadian Review of American Studies* 35, no. 1 (2005): 57. For an additional detailed critique of Winks's work, see Harvey Amani Whitfield, "The African Diaspora in Atlantic Canada: History, Historians, and Historiography," *Acadiensis* 46, no. 1 (2017): 220–2.
25 Walker, *History of Blacks in Canada*, 66–9.
26 Walker, 66.
27 Walker, 67.

28 Walker, 67.
29 George H. Junne, *The History of Blacks in Canada: A Selectively Annotated Bibliography* (Westport, CT: Greenwood, 2003); Smardz Frost, "Sources and Resources"; Hilary Bates Neary, "A Bibliography of Fred Landon's Writings on Black History," in Smardz Frost et al., *Ontario's African-Canadian Heritage*, 295–314; Hilary Russell, *A Bibliography Relating to African Canadian History* (Ottawa: Historical Research Branch, National Historic Sites Directorate, Parks Canada, 1990); Este, "Black Canadian Historical Writing."
30 Charlotte B. Perry, *The Long Road: The History of the Coloured Canadian in Windsor, Ont., 1867–1967* (Windsor: Sumner, 1969), 19. A far more comprehensive history of Black communities in Windsor is Irene Moore Davis, *Our Own Two Hands: A History of Black Lives in Windsor from the 1700s Forward* (Windsor, ON: Biblioasis, forthcoming).
31 Stephen L. Hubbard, *Against All Odds: The Story of William Peyton Hubbard: Black Leader and Municipal Reformer* (Toronto: Dundurn, 1987), 20, 128.
32 Gary French, *Men of Colour: An Historical Account of the Black Settlement on Wilberforce Street and in Oro Township, Simcoe County, Ontario, 1819–1949* (Stroud, ON: Kaste Books, 1978), 45.
33 French, 46.
34 Peggy Bristow, Dionne Brand, Linda Carty, Afua Cooper, Sylvia Hamilton, and Adrienne Shadd, introduction to *"We're Rooted Here and They Can't Pull Us Up": Essays in African Canadian Women's History* (Toronto: University of Toronto Press, 1994), 3.
35 Ken Alexander and Avis Glaze, *Towards Freedom: The African-Canadian Experience* (Toronto: Umbrella, 1996), chaps. 4 and 5.
36 Alexander and Glaze, 93.
37 Claudine Y. Bonner, "This Tract of Land: North Buxton, Ontario, 1873–1914" (PhD diss., University of Western Ontario, 2010), 3–4.
38 See, for example, Natasha Henry's site, "Teaching African Canadian History," http://teachingafricancanadianhistory.weebly.com/; and Rosemary Sadlier, *The Kids Book of Canadian Black History* (Toronto: Kids Can Press, 2003).
39 Boulou Ebanda de B'béri, quoted in "Beyond the Underground Railroad: The *Promised Land Project* Reveals Forgotten Black History," Social Sciences and Humanities Research Council, February 28, 2013, https://www.sshrc-crsh.gc.ca/society-societe/stories-histoires/story-histoire-eng.aspx?story_id=163.
40 Boulou Ebanda de B'béri, Nina Reid-Maroney, and Handel Kashope Wright, eds., *The Promised Land: History and Historiography of the Black Experience in Chatham-Kent's Settlements and Beyond* (Toronto: University of Toronto Press, 2014), esp. Afua Cooper, "Reflections: The Challenges and

Accomplishments of the Promised Land," 193–210. On the interplay of history, heritage, and history education, see John Mack Faragher, "And the Lonely Voice of Youth Cries 'What Is Truth?': Western History and the National Narrative," *Western Historical Quarterly* 48, no. 1 (2017): 1–21.

41 Joseph Mensah, *Black Canadians: History, Experience, Social Conditions* (Halifax: Fernwood, 2010), 53.
42 "Crof," Crawford Kilian profile, accessed April 2, 2021, http://profile.typepad.com/crawford; and Kilian, *Go Do Some Great Thing*, 9.
43 Kilian, 9.
44 Kilian, 69. Comma between "ways" and "racism" silently removed.
45 Kilian, 115, 137.
46 Nan E. Tremayne, quoted in Kilian, 137, and Kilian's comments.
47 Sherry Edmunds-Flett, "The First Generation of Black Women in British Columbia," PhD diss., Simon Fraser University, expected 2022.
48 Arlie C. Robbins, *Legacy to Buxton* (North Buxton, ON: A.C. Robbins, 1983); Gwendolyn Robinson and John W. Robinson, *Seek the Truth: A Story of Chatham's Black Community* (self-pub., 1989).
49 Robbins, *Legacy to Buxton*, 89, 99, 127–8. Hepburn's concluding chapter draws on this account; see Sharon A. Roger Hepburn, *Crossing the Border: A Free Black Community in Canada* (Urbana: University of Illinois Press, 2007), 190, 196–8.
50 Robbins, 113, 106.
51 Robbins, 107, 110.
52 Robinson, 49–67.
53 Robinson, 3–5.
54 Jonathan William Walton, "Blacks in Buxton and Chatham, Ontario, 1830–1890: Did the 49th Parallel Make a Difference?" (PhD diss., Princeton University, 1979); Colin Stephan McFarquhar, "A Difference of Perspective: The Black Minority, White Majority, and Life in Ontario, 1870–1919" (PhD diss., University of Waterloo, 1998); Tracey Adams, "Making a Living: African Canadian Workers in London, Ontario, 1861–1901," *Labour/Le Travail* 67 (Spring 2001): 9–44.
55 Walton, "Blacks in Buxton and Chatham"; McFarquhar, "Difference of Perspective," iv, 311.
56 McFarquhar, "Difference of Perspective," 315.
57 Adams, "Making a Living," 41.
58 Adams, 41.
59 Adams, 35–7.
60 Adams, 42.
61 Bonner, "Tract of Land," 6, 8.
62 Bonner, 18.

63 Bonner, chaps. 4 and 5; see also 287–8.
64 Adrienne Shadd, *The Journey from Tollgate to Parkway: African Canadians in Hamilton* (Toronto: Dundurn, 2010), 183.
65 George Morton, "Justice Is Not Blind: The Color Line Drawn Even at the Sacred Altar," *Hamilton Herald*, December 27, 1889, 1, as quoted in Shadd, *Journey from Tollgate to Parkway*, 176.
66 Shadd, 149, 202.
67 Shadd, 201–2.
68 Shadd, 172, 170–1, based on Adrienne Shadd, "No 'Back Alley Clique': The Campaign to Desegregate Chatham's Public Schools, 1891–1893," *Ontario History* 99, no. 1 (2007): 77–95.
69 Shadd, *Journey from Tollgate to Parkway*, 168–9, 202.
70 Shadd, 197, 199.
71 William Montague Cobb, "Medical History," *Journal of the National Medical Association* 45 (1953): 301.
72 Hilary J. Dawson, "From Immigrant to Establishment: A Black Family's Journey," *Ontario History* 99, no. 1 (2007): 43.
73 McFarquhar, "Difference of Perspective," 316.
74 Barrington Walker, *Race on Trial: Black Defendants in Ontario's Criminal Courts, 1858–1958* (Toronto: University of Toronto Press, 2010), 183–4, 185.
75 Clarke as quoted in McNeil, "Afro(Americo)centricity," 72n2.
76 Whitfield, "African Diaspora in Atlantic Canada," esp. 216–18.
77 Jennifer Harris, "Black Life in a Nineteenth-Century New Brunswick Town," *Journal of Canadian Studies* 46, no. 1 (2012): 138–68; Harris, "'Ushered into the Kitchen': Lalia Halfkenny, Instructor of English and Elocution at a 19th-Century African American Women's College," *Acadiensis* 41, no. 2 (2012): 45–65.
78 Harris, "Black Life," 156.
79 Harris, "'Ushered into the Kitchen,'" 66.
80 Harris, 54–6.
81 Sarah-Jane Mathieu, *North of the Color Line: Migration and Black Resistance in Canada, 1870–1955* (Chapel Hill: University of North Carolina Press, 2010), chap. 1.
82 Mathieu, 14. See also R. Bruce Shepard, *Deemed Unsuitable: Blacks from Oklahoma Move to the Canadian Prairies in Search of Equality in the Early 20th Century, Only to Find Racism in Their New Home* (Toronto: Umbrella, 1997); Selwyn J. Jacob, dir., *We Remember Amber Valley* (Kelowna, BC: Filmwest, 1984), video recording, 24 min.; Deanna Bowen, *sum of the parts: what can be named* (2010), video of performed oral history, 18 min., http://www.deannabowen.ca/sum-of-the-parts-what-can-be-named; Colin A. Thomson, *Blacks in Deep Snow: Black Pioneers in Canada* (Don Mills, ON: J.M. Dent, 1979); and Jimmy Robert Melton (who is a descendant), "Amber

Valley: A Black Enclave in Northern Alberta, Canada" (MA thesis, California State University, San Bernardino, 1994). The railways also employed African Canadians, especially from the Maritime provinces; see Mathieu, *North of the Color Line*, 72–4.
83 Mathieu, *North of the Color Line*, 12, 395.
84 Mathieu, 5.
85 Mathieu, 11, 15–16.
86 Mathieu, 14.
87 Mathieu, esp. chaps. 3, 4, and 5.
88 For a précis, see Arenson, "Experience Rather Than Imagination."
89 For an example, see "Personals," *Chicago Defender*, Big Weekend Ed., May 21, 1910, 2.
90 For example, on veterans of the US Civil War who returned to live in Canada and filed for a pension from there, see Richard M. Reid, *African Canadians in Union Blue: Volunteering for the Cause in the Civil War* (Vancouver: UBC Press, 2014); and Bryan Prince, *My Brother's Keeper: African Canadians and the American Civil War* (Toronto: Dundurn, 2015). See also Karolyn Smardz Frost and Veta Smith Tucker, eds., *A Fluid Frontier: Slavery, Resistance, and the Underground Railroad in the Detroit River Borderland* (Detroit: Wayne State University, 2016); Smardz Frost, *Steal Away Home: One Woman's Epic Flight to Freedom – and Her Long Road Back to the South* (Toronto: HarperCollins Canada, 2017); and Arenson, "Experience Rather Than Imagination."
91 Reid, *African Canadians in Union Blue*, esp. conclusion.
92 Anderson Abbott, "Prejudice in Canada," Abbott Collection, Toronto Reference Library, quoted in Catherine Slaney, *Family Secrets: Crossing the Colour Line* (Toronto: Dundurn, 2008), 131, 130.
93 Slaney, 131.
94 Slaney, 131–3.
95 Fred Johnson, conversation with the author, Buxton Homecoming, 2015; biographical details confirmed by Shannon Prince, personal correspondence, July 2017. For another profile of Johnson, see "Photo Exhibit Examines Canadian Descendants of Slaves," CBC News, September 23, 2016, http://www.cbc.ca/news/canada/windsor/slave-descendants-photo-exhibit-1.3775232.
96 Richard Reid, review of *African Canadians in Union Blue: Volunteering for the Cause in the Civil War*, by Nina Reid-Maroney, *Canadian Historical Review* 96, no. 3 (2015): 440.

5
Petitioning Power: Canadian Racial Consciousness Meets Alabama Injustice, 1958

WENDELL NII LARYEA ADJETEY

> Negroes, of whom we have too many in Upper Canada ... are very prone to felonious assaults on white women; if the sentence and imprisonment were not very severe, there would be the great dread of people taking the law into their own hand.
>
> John A. Macdonald, 1868

On an August morning in 1958, southwestern Ontarians gathered within earshot of radios and listened to news unfolding within Canada and around the world. What captivated Canadian hearts and minds most on that fateful morning had nothing to do with the ongoing Arab-Israeli conflict in the Middle East or decolonization in sub-Saharan Africa or even a Cold War showdown between the superpowers. The place and the actors that captured the Canadian imagination on 28 August seemed less distant and more familiar than other drama unfolding around the globe.

The news that Jimmy Wilson, an African American man in Alabama, had been sentenced to death by electrocution in less than eight days for petty larceny shocked the radio listeners' liberal ideas of democracy and the rule of law. Within five days of hearing this news, Canadian citizens – homemakers, children and students, business owners, trade unionists, newly arrived immigrants – submitted over three thousand letters of petition to Alabama governor James Folsom that played a pivotal role in the campaign to stop Wilson's execution.

The petitions are replete with examples of Canadians denouncing the evils of US white supremacy. For example, Ken Young, a sixteen-year-old in Waterloo, Ontario, added his voice to the chorus of concerned Canadians discussing the unfolding civil rights legal crisis in Alabama. Despite his youth and lack of first-hand experience with southern racism, Young concluded that the egregious punishment of death for paltry theft in a country like the United States stemmed from racism and a blatant disregard for democratic values and the rule of law.[1] In his typewritten letter (an indication of his class privilege), he declared, "Although I am only 16 years old I know that the jury for Wilson should not have been all white. I don't suppose that if a white person did something wrong they would have an all Coloured jury." Young uncovered the root of southern racism and prejudice. "The Civil War," he concluded, "is over long ago and it's time the lazy old south woke up to that fact."[2] In subjecting African Americans to racial caste in the post-bellum era, the South violated their Thirteenth, Fourteenth, and Fifteenth Constitutional Amendment rights. To a Canadian observer, failure to overcome a past pockmarked with intolerance and racial violence seemed to be a uniquely US problem.

Less than 150 kilometres away in Oshawa, Ontario, self-identified Mrs. Freilleux heard the same alarming news and felt shock that the State of Alabama would execute a man for petty theft. She, like the thousands of white Canadian women who submitted letters of petition demanding clemency for Wilson, justified her outrage through words that are part and parcel of the Canadian imagination of the United States. "I am a Canadian and a proud one," she wrote, "and I know and am proud to say this action will never happen in Canada. And I know if I were living where this Negro man lives the same State and I being a white woman I would be ashamed." For this self-proclaimed proud Canadian, the chasm in racial tolerance between Canada and the United States had never been wider and more apparent. Her indictment of US racism included a critique of white womanhood in the South as lacking the empathy and respect for the rule of law that the petitioner believed white women should possess. "When I heard the story over my Radio," she added, "I just couldn't believe it was true. I feel sorry for this man and his people[;] maybe I should feel sorry for the white people who are wishing him to receive the death sentence." The petitioner considered her gender and brand of Canadian whiteness as one inclined toward liberalism and acceptance of racial minorities – a stark contrast to US racial politics.

That racial constructs of Blackness provided Canadians a language with which to engage their neighbours to the south matters to historians who conceptualize transnational forms of racism and resistance in twentieth-century North America. Resisting racism allowed white people and African North Americans to participate in a cross-border discourse that fundamentally shaped civil and human rights activism in Canada and the United States. These social processes underscore the value of integrating Canadian and US histories. This methodological approach is what scholars call "interactional history."[3]

Many Canadians who heard of Jimmy Wilson's impending execution jumped at the opportunity to voice their sententious critiques of the US racial order and showcase Canadian liberalism. Canadians also yearned to expose the divide in the United States between the rhetoric of republican ideals, on the one hand, and blatant racial injustice, on the other. This civil rights case serves as a window into post–World War II Canadian society, one that helps crystallize the ways that white Canadians conceptualized race and racial injustice. Moreover, the swiftness with which white Canadian petitioners repudiated the State of Alabama and the United States suggests, by default, that some believed Canada treated Black people better. In other words, a strong rebuke of US racism arguably absolved white Canadians of guilt regarding the second-class status of African Canadians.

This strategy reinforced the petitioners' individual and collective attempt to highlight Canada as a leader of liberal internationalism. As globally minded citizens, Canadians repeatedly framed their racial activism in a Cold War, geopolitical discourse that challenged Washington's legitimacy to lead the free world, considering that many of its constituent parts practised archaic laws that rivalled those of any communist country. Some petitioners hoped, too, that their embrace of liberal internationalism would give their country special status in a fraying British Commonwealth.

In illuminating the role that Canadians played in this sparsely documented event, it is helpful to revisit several factors. First, there was the nature of the alleged robbery and assault of which Wilson stood accused, and how the news made headlines and appeared on Canadians' social radar. Second, it is useful to examine Canadians' perception of Estelle Barker, the alleged victim, as an incredible witness. Third, Canadian moralism, the legacy of British abolitionism, underscored the enduring threat of US racism and Canadians' misgivings over US democracy and its rule of law. Finally, the public outcry in Wilson's favour offers lessons to historians about Canadian participation in and contribution to the Black freedom struggle in North America.

Making Headlines in the Canadian Press

The events that led to the planned execution of Jimmy Wilson and the media coverage that outraged Canadians began on a warm, unremarkable evening in the sleepy town of Marion, Alabama, on 27 July 1957. Wilson, a fifty-four-year-old African American handyman and occasional transient, worked odd jobs in sparsely populated Marion. The unequal distribution of economic opportunities, even after Emancipation, yoked poorly educated and semi-skilled Black people to their white counterparts in exploitative and dependent relationships.[4] In fact, it had become common, before the approbation of the Civil Rights Act of 1964 and Voting Rights Act of 1965, for African American men and women to contract out their labour to white employers in the Jim Crow South. Estelle Barker, an elderly white widow, sought cheap labour from African Americans like Wilson. In the months leading up to the alleged robbery and assault, the eighty-two-year-old Barker had occasionally hired Wilson to perform odd jobs around her house and yard. On the Saturday evening of 27 July, Wilson, according to trial transcripts of Barker's testimony, showed up unannounced at her home "and said he had come to do some work." Barker, in turn, responded "that it was too late."[5]

In the Jim Crow South, any unregulated interaction between a Black man and a white woman at a private dwelling, especially at night, constituted a dangerous flirtation with the colour line. Rather than removing himself from this peculiar situation, the handyman remained on the property, Barker claimed. The octogenarian testified that Wilson lingered about asking for a drink of water, so she directed him to the backyard where he normally quenched his thirst when he worked on her property. Wilson, according to trial transcripts, wanted more than to satiate his thirst for water that evening. After walking to the backyard, he entered the house through the rear door uninvited, alleged Barker. Referring to the case, legal historian Mary Dudziak writes, "She asked him what he wanted and he said he wanted her money." When Barker denied having any money, Wilson allegedly said, "Yes, you have too [sic]." After this exchange, Barker complied; she went to her bedroom closet and retrieved her purse. Wilson, according to Barker, then commanded her to "pour it out on the bed."[6] Barker emptied the contents of her purse as instructed, which amounted to less than four dollars.

It is what happened next that led to Wilson's condemnation in the court of Jim Crow public opinion. According to Barker, Wilson became physically and sexually suggestive in his threats and demands: "He threw me on the bed, pulled off my stepins, and attempted to rape me, that is what he did." Barker's testimony included stereotypical images of the lascivious and violent Black male who prowls in search of white women to devour.[7] The spurious threat of Black men raping white women has long occupied a significant place in the southern imagination. Metastasizing during US Reconstruction, white supremacists doubled down on their unfounded fear of Black male sexuality as the reason to topple, in violent coup d'états, the interracial southern governments of Black and white legislators.[8]

In punctuating her statement with "that is what he did," the elderly widow provided a small but significant window into her motivations. Barker's desire for credibility at a time and place – the Jim Crow South – when misguided ideas alone convicted Black men of rape is telling. She also stated that Wilson would have raped her had a neighbour not come to her aid. As Dudziak writes, "a light flashed outside … He jumped up and told her he would kill her if she opened her mouth and then ran out the door."[9] An all-white jury, after hearing Barker's testimony, handed Wilson a swift death sentence not for assault but for robbery.

This classic case involving an alleged African American robber and would-be rapist became known as "Death for a Dollar Ninety-Five." It captured worldwide attention and fuelled a critique of US race relations.[10] From London to Montevideo, from Copenhagen to Switzerland, and from Ghana to Jamaica, Europeans and racialized peoples peppered US consulates with petitions and published editorials in newspapers deriding the self-appointed leader of the free world for its shameful treatment of African Americans.[11] Not only did the Wilson case stoke the flames of the freedom struggle against colonialism and white supremacy in the Global South, but it also forced many white people in the West to scrutinize US credibility on the rule of law in a bipolar world undergoing rapid Soviet expansion. To borrow the words of Dudziak, the case, "feeding a global debate about the nature of American democracy" as it did, placed US domestic and foreign policy under the discerning eye of the international community.[12]

While Dudziak has explored the significance of the Dollar Ninety-Five case in a global, Cold War context, little analysis has been done regarding what it meant in terms of building a particular national identity that simultaneously challenged US preponderance. In Canada, the case helped to define the Anglo-Canadian identity as one that embraced racial equality with African descendants. It portrayed racial inequity in Canada as a non-issue, thus reinforcing a romantic image of the North Star – the celestial light that guided the disinherited and enslaved to a "free" Upper Canada.

The *Toronto Daily Star* broke the news in the Canadian print media one week before Ontario radio station CKEY declared to the masses that the State of Alabama would execute Jimmy Wilson for robbing an elderly white woman. On 20 August 1958, Martin "Marty" Goodman – an affable, up-and-coming twenty-three-year-old Jewish Canadian reporter – published an exclusive interview with Wilson while he waited on death row at a state penitentiary. On the front page of that Wednesday edition of the *Star* appeared several shocking headlines concerning violence that had occurred in southwestern Ontario the night before, including "Car

Bomb Kills Man Call It 'Vendetta'" and "The Little Witness," an article about a six-year-old who witnessed a robber shoot and kill a grocer. The newspaper also ran the headline "'Near Riot' as Trucks Enter Stelco Plant," on a story about dejected steelworkers whose shop-floor politics had evolved into violence outside a picket line.[13] The violent overtone of these headlines belied Canada's image as a harmonious place filled with mild-mannered people. Yet all the headlines paled in comparison to Goodman's sobering headline about Jimmy Wilson and the fate that awaited him inside an Alabama prison: "Star Meets Negro, to Die for $1.95 Robbery." Underneath, the subtitle read "Robs White Widow[;] Can't Read, Write[;] Aware He'll Die."[14]

To understand the nature of discrimination in Canadian society in the interwar and early postwar years is to appreciate the interracial alliance between Canadian Jews and African Canadians.[15] When fourteen-year-old Alan Kruger heeded the CKEY radio announcer's call to action on 28 August, his identity as a Jewish Canadian influenced his activism. In his west Toronto home, Kruger drafted a letter that demonstrated an acute awareness of racial injustice. "We all hear great propaganda about the free U.S.A. where everyone has an equal chance," he wrote. "Isn't this fact a little over emphasized[?]" Kruger continued, "I have read a lot about the situation in the South and I recall in my mind about a young Negro youth named Till who was attacked and killed by some white men for whistling at a white woman. They were all acquitted. A similar incident took place recently. That was in the U.S.A. where everyone has an equal chance." The Emmett Till reference might not be entirely coincidental: the date on which station CKEY announced Wilson's death sentence also marked the third anniversary of the lynching of Till by white supremacists in Money, Mississippi.[16]

Kruger's sober assessment of US racial injustice had much to do with his family's experience as racial minorities in postwar Toronto.[17] Kruger had grown "up in a house where everybody felt an obligation to equal rights." He explained that "there was a lot of prejudice in Toronto in the fifties. My father was very aware of it. There were a lot of exclusions. When you went to the beach there were signs that said no 'Dogs or Jews.'" As a boy, Kruger had accompanied his family to civil rights marches on the University of Toronto campus to show solidarity with African Americans in their struggle.[18]

Kruger's personal and familial experiences mirror those of *Star* reporter Marty Goodman. Goodman's family had fled to Montreal from western Canada in his childhood in response to the intolerable level of anti-Semitism there. These experiences in his formative years shaped his perception of racism. Investigating and chronicling racial injustice, therefore, was more than an occupation to Goodman. It was his life's calling. A childhood friend described him as "a principled man; a man who stood up for justice."[19] The stories of both Kruger and Goodman counter the benign narrative of Canadian racial tolerance, a trope that some white Canadians used as a rallying cry of sorts to distinguish Canada from the United States. Yet, Canadian society had to address its own problems in order to burnish its image as an alternative to US society during the Cold War. "Canadians hold themselves as superior to the Americans," Kruger pointed out, "but there was just as much discrimination here as in the United States."[20]

When the *Star* sent Goodman, a young correspondent, to cover the Wilson case in Alabama, his editors reasoned that his background had prepared him for this challenging assignment. As a Canadian whose family had experienced racial discrimination, Goodman was better positioned to convey the deeper human elements of racism than his colleagues who had never experienced such injustice. Shortly after arriving in Alabama, Goodman secured an exclusive interview with the condemned fifty-five-year-old Wilson. In doing so, he played a major role in circulating news to Canadians and around the world about Wilson's plight. "It wasn't considered major news," he wrote, "until The Star, a Chicago magazine and the Associated Press inquired into it."[21] Covering a story about racial injustice involving an African American accused of robbery and attempted rape in the volatile Deep South, a place unwelcoming to Black folks and Jews, underscores Goodman's conviction to fight racism.[22] For Goodman, discrimination against Jews and Black people symbolized a tyranny of sorts, and he might have seen similarities between anti-Semitism and anti-Black racism.

When Goodman travelled to Atmore State Penitentiary, roughly two hundred kilometres south of Montgomery, he sat with Wilson inside the warden's office and conducted the only interview with him while he waited in solitary confinement. Wilson had spent time in Atmore before: in 1954 he left the prison after serving a three-year sentence for larceny.[23] That a state prison, and not a lynch mob, planned Wilson's execution indicated a modicum of change to the South's archaic culture of vigilante justice, if for nothing else than symbolic reasons. So pervasive was the image of bloodthirsty white mobs in the southern consciousness that a local paper commented that the state institution in a distant town had deliberately imprisoned Wilson "for safekeeping."[24] Nonetheless, the façade of the legal proceedings, the all-white jury, and the presiding justice, all culminating in a guilty verdict and death sentence, symbolized more than a southern performance. It demonstrated that, although committed to the maintenance of a racial caste system, the architects of Jim Crow, too, understood the importance of appearing legitimate.[25]

For Goodman, the hour that he spent interviewing Wilson provided him with an intimate understanding of the plight of so many African Americans in the South. Wilson's current and past conflicts with the law, as the Canadian reporter discovered in his interview, resulted from a racist penal system and Wilson's illiteracy, the corollary of a racial order that kept African Americans in their "place." Goodman asked Wilson if he had ever heard of Toronto or, better yet, if he could locate it on a map. Wilson identified Toronto's location as "somewhere in Northern Alabama."[26] As an illiterate person, Wilson could not have grasped the impact that his case had on the United States and around the world, considering that many individuals expressed their outrage in writing. That a white reporter from a distant place like Toronto had travelled to Alabama simply to ask him scores of questions might have also confounded him.

Moreover, the fact that the overwhelming majority of letter writers protested with pens or typewriters signals their relative privilege to access information and concern themselves with international affairs. This explanation could help clarify why the voices of so many white Canadians, particularly women, are represented in the petitions. One Toronto petitioner, for instance, described herself as "just a housewife." Most working-class families could not afford to subsist on a single breadwinner's income; thus, it was likely that most of the women who wrote letters belonged to middle-class or upper-middle-class families. The petitioners represented not a cross-section of Canadians but those who could exercise agency and civic duty at a moment's notice. Some, who had experienced discrimination, like Goodman, had a vested interest at stake. Others, although well intentioned, saw Wilson as another recipient of Canadian benevolence and racial progressivism. Many reflected on their growing consciousness of global human rights, pointing out that the US racial order was anathema to a post-Holocaust world undergoing rapid decolonization.

Jimmy Wilson was a simple man. As an impoverished wanderer, life on the road had taken a toll on his fragile frame. Goodman, discerning the gravity of the situation in Wilson's countenance, painted a bleak image of him. It is perhaps one of the only descriptive accounts available: "His cheeks sunken, his eyes haggard, he perspired during our hour-long interview, though the warden's office was air-conditioned." As the *Star* correspondent probed into the alleged robbery and rape, he noticed Wilson's mannerisms: "He crossed and uncrossed his arms, patted his shoulders and scratched his short, gray fuzzy hair while puzzling two syllable words."[27] Wilson's anxiety was perhaps indicative of his lack of interaction with and/or suspicion of white professionals and definitely reflected his dread of execution.

As Goodman probed further, Wilson broke his silence, stringing together more than a two-syllable response, one that cast doubt on his conviction. "They never asked me anything," Wilson said repeatedly. "The policeman that arrested me ... he didn't ask. He say 'that's how it happened, wasn't it?' I say 'no.' He cuffed me until I say 'yeah ... that's how.'" The fact that Wilson had been alone with a white woman in and of itself made him a suspect. A diminutive man, he stood five feet seven inches tall and weighed 135 pounds. The image that Goodman painted of Wilson is not one of a threatening foe whose sheer stature alone would suggest potential harm, even in the rigid caste system of Jim Crow Alabama. If anything, the image in Goodman's account is one of the harmless Negro, a "Tommish" figure whose fear of white supremacy rendered him incapable of harming white people or mounting any direct opposition to the social structures that subjugated him.[28] As Goodman assessed Wilson's demeanour and stature, seeds of doubt sprouted in his mind about the alleged charge of robbery and the implication of sexual assault.

Wilson told Goodman that the sequence of events that unfolded on 27 July 1957 had begun the preceding Friday evening when Wilson and an acquaintance decided to celebrate after picking and then selling a day's worth of cotton. Wilson and the other man drank in celebration of their earnings and the upcoming weekend: "That was bad ... an old man like me ... but it was only drinking. All of a sudden I didn't have any more money." Having spent his earnings, Wilson realized he needed a few dollars to get through the weekend. On the following day, a Saturday, Wilson devised a plan that had succeeded in the past. "I had worked once for Mrs. Barker and she loaned me some money against my wages," he recalled. "So I went back. She refused. I thought about it all day and went back again. She must have been scared because she gave me some – about $1.50." This sum is nearly half the amount that the county solicitor alleged Wilson had robbed from Barker. Wilson ultimately spent this money on his return cab fare from Barker's house. Wilson said that when he returned to Barker's home for the second time on that Saturday, she "was sitting into a rocker ... *She told me to come in* [emphasis added]. I ain't lyin ... before God I ain't."

The account that Wilson gave Goodman in the warden's office contradicted Barker's court testimony. Wilson countered that he entered the widow's home only after he had received her verbal consent. He insisted that he did not go to Barker's home to commit robbery or rape. He was seeking a loan against his wages, because Barker had granted him one in the past. Wilson and Barker exchanged some words before she agreed to give him some money. "She reached inside her purse," Wilson recounted, "and threw the change on the bed. I asked for more but she said she didn't have no more." In desperation, he insisted, "I never touched her. I never broke in. I know I shouldn't have been drinking ... but I didn't do anything wrong. I know there isn't much good to me ... but I'm telling the truth. I don't want to die." Wilson ultimately perceived Goodman as a potential ally, an interlocutor who could convey his innocence to the public and potentially deliver him from impending capital punishment.

Unlike the witnesses who testified at the hour-long trial – including Barker, the two taxi drivers, and a state investigator – the court did not invite Wilson to testify, a true indication of his subordinate citizenship. In fact, Wilson's state-appointed counsel met with him just once prior to trial and did not interview him before or during trial, nor did he cross-examine the state witnesses. The shoddy judicial proceedings therefore resulted in the insinuation of the attempted rape of an elderly white woman without any pushback from Wilson's defence attorney. "Wilson was actually being tried for touching a white woman, not for robbery," averred a University of Alabama, Tuscaloosa law professor. "His lawyer could have attempted a defence. It doesn't sound as if he did anything but appear in court."[29] Considering that a Toronto reporter gave Wilson his only in-depth interview – indeed, his only opportunity to vindicate himself to the people of Alabama, the country, and the world – Wilson "steadfastly denied having made any attempt to assault the woman and added that the police had beaten him to confess that he had."[30]

Determining Culpability

Racial injustice in Alabama, as in all the former Confederate States of America, permeated every aspect of civil society, specifically law enforcement, the judiciary, and the political establishment. Goodman's depiction of it created such a firestorm in southwestern Ontario that it called into question not only the South's racial politics but also its gender politics. When station CKEY solicited letters to petition Governor Folsom, Barker's credibility emerged as one of the three prominent concerns that Canadians questioned. Goodman expressed a similar concern, too. In a single day of making private inquiries in Marion County, the journalist spoke with four witnesses who went on the record and provided character profiles of both Barker and Wilson.

As an outsider, Goodman understood that the surest method by which he could substantiate Wilson's claims, as well as Barker's trial testimony, was to become, in a sense, a private investigator who could extract insight from townsfolk. The witnesses with whom he spoke included "two persons who gave creditable character accounts of Wilson and two persons who know Barker and said her faculties may be impaired by age." A Birmingham resident, for instance, said she and other friends in her neighbourhood had hired Wilson to complete odd jobs in the past and that they considered him "the best worker [they] ever saw." She stated, "We had given him a radio and a little place to stay. He was proud of it and so neat. Then all of a sudden he disappeared."[31] In addition to affirming a positive image of Wilson, this account is indicative of the paternalism of southern society, the gross imbalance in power relations, and the common practice of compensating Black wage labour not with commensurate wages but with material goods.

Some of Barker's friends doubted her claims of robbery and sexual assault. One friend said Barker "sometimes takes strange fancies." The friend did not elaborate on what these "fancies" entailed, but given the context of the allegations and the pervasive fear of licentious Black men preying on unsuspecting white women, the elderly widow might have turned a pervasive southern fear into a well-scripted encounter that threatened to breach the colour line. The same friend stated that Barker "gets set on a thing and that's it. You know she's getting on."[32]

Canadian petitioners scrutinized the veracity of Barker's testimony in light of her age and, more important, the pervasive racial construct of the Black rapist. Together, the irrational fears of Black male sexuality and Barker's history of fabrication made her testimony sound fantastical. When Torontonian L. Horwood first read Goodman's exposé in the *Star*, "shock" overcame her. Horwood considered her petition an opportunity to exercise her independence of thought and womanhood. As she drafted her letter to Governor Folsom in her upper-middle-class Toronto neighbourhood, her class, gender, and racial privilege neither obfuscated her reasoning nor masked her objectivity. Like a few of her compatriots who followed the Wilson case with a sharp eye to detail, Horwood's response is nuanced and her critique urbane. "It soon became apparent to me," she wrote, "that this man was being executed not for robbery, but for the 'alleged,' mind you, just 'ALLEGED,' assault of a white woman."

Some Canadians found the news of an alleged Black rapist provocative and scandalous. One petitioner questioned the plausibility of a Black man sexually assaulting an elderly woman. In the words of one white Canadian woman, "And why? Should a man try to rape a [82] year old women [*sic*], who is she trying to kid?" The petitioner, a Toronto resident, further stated, "Why by the looks of things down there it seems to be a crime to walk down the street, talk to a white girl or go to a white school ... I'm glad I'm Canadian & not American." Most Canadians disavowed the notion that racism and the strict policing and surveillance of Black people existed in Canadian society. They considered discrimination a US phenomenon. C. King, another white Canadian woman and a resident of Tottenham, Ontario – a small, rural town northwest of Toronto – averred, "If he was going to rape anyone it would have been someone younger. I guess she [Barker] is mad because he didn't go all the way."

On the one hand, King's premise is troubling because it not only accepts the plausibility of the Black rapist but also suggests that Barker, not Wilson, acted sexually aggressively, a charge that would never hold up in a US courtroom. On the other hand, King's inference that Barker's unfulfilled sexual desires were the reason she accused Wilson of rape is reminiscent of a controversial claim that the eminent African American sociologist E. Franklin Frazier espoused. Arguing that race prejudice was a form of mental illness among southerners, Frazier asserted that fabrications among white women "often represent unacceptable sexual desires which are projected when they can no longer be repressed."[33]

Nevertheless, the judicious and at times sententious tone in which some white Canadians expressed outrage over foreign incidents of racial discrimination points to a society undergoing a shift in racial attitudes and one blinded to its own brand of racism. Ms. Cumming of Gilford, Ontario, about an hour's drive north of Toronto, noted, "As we do not know all the details we feel a suitable jail sentence would be recommendable." Another petitioner wrote, "I can understand the death sentence for murder, but not for robbery and unproven assault." A Toronto couple, Mr. and Mrs. Ardis, said that "it would be a crime to the human race to execute a man on such flimsy grounds, as prejudice is very obvious ... The people in the U.S.A. are terrible narrow-minded about the negros."[34] In a similar vein, three married couples in east Toronto pointed out in a single petition that "the alleged rape of a senile old woman who could possibly have manufactured her accusation due to a deep-rooted hatred of the colored race is a gross miscarriage of justice and contrary to the basic principles of our Christian beliefs." The perception of Barker as a "senile old woman" who harboured prejudice against African Americans was not a uniquely Canadian perspective but one that Barker's neighbours also expressed to Goodman.

These white Canadian couples believed unequivocally that an elderly white woman could fabricate a tale of robbery and assault to seize upon the prevailing fears of Black male sexuality. However, the sensibility and empathy that these petitioners displayed begs a fundamental question: Would they have acted differently if an African Canadian man stood accused of robbery and sexual assault within their own tightly knit, all-white communities? After all, the majority of petitioners, who resided in small towns in Ontario, might not have had any prior contact with Canadians of African descent. Because of the Underground Railroad, African descendants lived mainly in southwestern Ontario cities, such as Chatham, Dresden, Hamilton, Toronto, and Windsor. In the 1950s Ontario had five million residents, five to ten thousand of whom might have been of African descent.[35] African Canadians constituted the "other," hidden from non-city dwellers.

Canadian Moralism Meets US Democracy and the Rule of Law

It might have surprised most of the Canadian petitioners who questioned the plausibility of a Black man posing a sexual threat to an elderly white woman to learn that the fear of the Black male rapist also existed north of the forty-ninth parallel. In fact, nineteenth- and early twentieth-century Canadian constructs of Black masculinity reflected the southern image of libertine predators whose movements the state had to regulate with a watchful eye.[36] This perception had long loomed in the white Canadian imagination. So entrenched remained this fear that after Britain dropped the death penalty for punishments involving rape, the Canadian Dominion government refused to follow the metropole's lead, fearing that it would relinquish a deterrence against Black male sexuality.[37] The inaugural prime minister, John A. Macdonald, referred to the matter in 1868, as quoted at the start of this chapter. If Canada failed to protect the virtues of white womanhood, Macdonald reasoned, law-abiding citizens might feel compelled to check Black sexuality with mob violence, drawing comparisons to the American South.[38]

As historian Barrington Walker shows in his analysis of African Canadians in Ontario's criminal courts from the 1850s to the 1950s, law enforcement and the judicial apparatus feared Black male sexuality, even as elites within these establishments evoked the language of British "fair play" and strongly admonished lynch law.[39] Canadian notions of liberalism and justice supposedly inherited from British abolitionism did not prevent the courts from meting out the harshest forms of punishment to Black defendants accused of sexually assaulting white women. These defendants might have escaped lynch law, but at the same time, the state held a monopoly to execute those in cases it deemed justifiable and it exercised this prerogative throughout much of Canada's short history.[40]

Capital punishment for rape in Canada remained legal until 1954 in part, Walker argues, because of unfounded societal fears of Black men.[41] One of the petitioners of the Wilson case wrote, "I am glad we do not have a law like that [the death sentence for robbery] in Canada"; however, Canadian criminal law routinely dehumanized Black life. Nevertheless, the Wilson case compelled some Canadians to question, at least in the US context, the egregious construct of the Black male rapist. In so doing, some deployed the rhetoric of fairness. Mr. and Mrs. Hand of north Toronto noted that "it is inhuman to take a man's life, on the evidence of an old woman who had no bodily harm. We are white people and they (negros) [sic] have just as much right as anybody to fair justice."

Identifying wrongdoing and demanding fairness came easily to Canadians who scrutinized US race relations. When Toronto couple Mr. and Mrs. Mowbray petitioned the Alabama governor, they framed their remarks within notions of fairness: "We are white people and think it is terrible an old woman's word can have so much power[;] if the man had of [sic] been white the case would never of [sic] been heard of." Critical distance from the incident coupled with Canadians' perception that the American South remained an unredeemable place that treated Black men brutally helps explain why some Canadians viewed Wilson with such empathy.

The notion of British "fair justice" that pervaded twentieth-century Canadian society is a corollary of eighteenth- and nineteenth-century British legislation and military strategy that ostensibly favoured enslaved Africans and ultimately ended the institution of slavery. Chief Justice Mansfield's decision in the 1772 Somerset Case denied the moral and legal basis of chattel slavery in the metropole. The granting of safe passage to "Black Loyalists" in 1783, the nominal abolition of slavery in Upper Canada in 1793, the abolition of the transatlantic slave trade in 1807, the granting of safe passage again to Black Refugees from the War of 1812, abolition of slavery throughout the empire in 1833, and the emergence of Canada as a safe haven for fugitives in the 1840s and 1850s created a lore about Canada's inheritance of a British brand of racial progressivism.[42] For Canadians, the enduring legacies of these watershed events permeated notions of race, justice, and freedom. As such, some white Canadians in the twentieth century used race relations in the United States not only as a litmus test of sorts to disavow claims of racism in Canadian society but also as the standard by which critiques of subtle yet insidious forms of Canadian racism were delegitimized.

This romanticized national narrative helped shape the zeitgeist of Canadian society when a fifteen-year-old Canadian girl who lived near Niagara Falls, Ontario, drafted a petition on Wilson's behalf. As a teenager, she had received a patriotic education that extolled the virtues of Canadian justice and tolerance as unique qualities that differentiated Canada from the United States while glossing over the fact that slavery had once existed in her region of Upper Canada. It is also probable that the few African Canadians who lived in and around her hometown descended from fugitives and free persons. This fact would have served as a powerful testament to the myth of Canadian (or British) justice and freedom. Therefore, denouncing white supremacy in the United States without applying the same self-examination to her own community and country absolved her Canadian conscience. In other words, Anglo-Canadian exceptionalism – that is, the ability to see racism as a phenomenon in foreign countries – is a corollary of romantic tales of enslaved and persecuted Black folk finding refuge in British North America.

The fifteen-year-old petitioner wrote, "Your country is said to [be] free, a democracy and yet a coloured man because of stupid prejudice was sentenced to death where a white man would have been given a month in the county jail. Did you ever stop to think," she asked the governor, "that God made every living being on this earth from the same model, put the same blood into everyone's veins whether they be Negro, Chinese, Indian, Japanese or White[?]" She stated, "*We* the white race are no better or no worse than any other race in the world ... Life is a sacred thing[;] don't take it away without thinking of the consequent [*sic*]." In a final appeal to the governor, the teenage petitioner, perhaps out of naïveté that all adults are well intentioned, wrote, "Please you must be a good man or you wouldn't have the important job you have. Think about it a man is going to die for stealing $1.9[5]. We aren't living in Russia where ... a man is killed by [an executioner]." With the Cold War as a backdrop, this racial cosmopolitanism breathed life and sincerity into Anglo-Canadian exceptionalism.

The Wilson case even allowed naturalized Canadians to join the debate on racial injustice in the southern United States and around the world. At a time when colonized subjects in the Global South fought tirelessly to remove the yoke of colonialism, it became more challenging for Westerners to ignore the clear links between imperialism and white supremacy. When Englishman D.F. Sanderson immigrated in 1955 to Port Credit, Ontario, just a few miles west of Toronto, he acknowledged the racial tensions that were a hallmark of the postwar period. "I have strong, very strong views regarding the increasing problem of racial discrimination," he admitted. "Even in London, England, it is becoming increasingly evident that this modern world in which we live no longer has any connection with democracy." As a British subject and new Canadian, Sanderson's perspective, although critical of the metropole, did not scrutinize Canadian society in the same manner. For Sanderson, Canada, a former British colony with a dominant anglophone population, represented a *new* England free from racial tension. Canada's white supremacist immigration policies made racial conflict in Canadian society appear non-existent or better managed.[43]

Sanderson reserved his sharpest judgment for the United States – for its inability to break away from a racial caste system and the inequities that this perpetuated. "Who do these radical segregationists think they are? Who are they to say that a white man is better than a 'Coloured'?" He observed, "When a 'darkie' proves himself with some outstanding feat in sports or athletics or even in the entertainment field these same radical 'Little Fa[u]bus's' wildly acclaim them as Americans but just when it suits them the Coloured man becomes an outlaw." The reference to Arkansas governor Orval Faubus, who opposed nominal integration of the Little Rock School District, shows the extent to which notions of US white supremacy permeated the Canadian consciousness. Many front pages of Canadian newspapers carried weekly images and articles of the education crisis in Arkansas and other civil rights conflicts, exemplifying the type of foreign exposure given the Canadian public on race.[44]

Sanderson also critiqued the conditions that would, allegedly, compel Jimmy Wilson to commit robbery and sexual assault in the first place. "Why was the robbery committed? Was the offender unemployed or without funds at the time? If he was unemployed – why? The answer to these questions," Sanderson suggested, "would prove beyond doubt to any clear thinking court that the white man generally is guilty all the way. [As a white man] I feel very little pride in being any color at all." In a clear break from the overwhelming majority of petitioners, Sanderson prescribed a remedy that would help address the crucible of racism. "The solution to the entire affair," he argued, "is surely education [of those who hold prejudiced views]; education by some authority similar to the U.N. Council, after all, the problem is an International one." As a new and proud Canadian, Sanderson believed that the United Nations was best positioned to curtail racism, a view that aligned with postwar Canadian national and foreign policy that placed enormous import on multilateralism and liberal internationalist institutions. That a naturalized Anglo-Canadian man in the early postwar years critiqued US racism while also recommending that an international institution dominated by imperial nations be enlisted to stem the tide of racism is contradictory. Sanderson, in his position as an immigrant from England, Canada's most preferred country from which to recruit the ideal nation builder, found US racial oppression and injustice so egregious without for a moment questioning the structures of white supremacy that facilitated his immigration to Canada. Barriers to entry – such as climate suitability, arbitrary health examinations, and demands that prospective

Black immigrants, a majority of whom belonged to the British Commonwealth, demonstrate "exceptional merit" – frustrated prospective Black immigrants in the early postwar years.[45]

It is hard to deny that some of the petitioners, like Sanderson, felt sincerely about the evils of US racism. However, it is plausible that Sanderson and his new compatriots might not have critiqued American racism to the extent that they did had they been competing with African Canadians for scarce economic resources and residential space on the same scale as white people in some parts of the United States. The relative invisibility of African Canadians a corollary of unwelcoming attitudes and racist immigration policies, created a racial climate in which many white Canadians could express sympathy for and empathy with African Americans while disavowing the daily injustices and racial inequities that faced African Canadians and other racialized peoples in Canadian society.

In contrast to Sanderson's letter, that of E. Beck of Toronto offers insight into how a white, non-British immigrant woman embraced constructs of Anglo-Canadian exceptionalism in her critique of the Alabama governor. "I am a new-canadian [sic]," Beck wrote, "so please do excuse my spelling." She addressed her questions to the radio station staff, not Governor Folsom or his aides. "Please ask this ruler, what would happen, in his so beloved state, if he would put a white man, for the crime of taking $1.[95] into the electric chair?" To show empathy and worldly experience, she pointed out, "This administrator of government acts like a regime I very well remember and he is the one committing crime every hour of the day, one of those days justice will be than [sic] to him, I hope." Although Beck does not specify from which "regime" she fled, it is plausible – based on her surname, her description of government as a regime, and her recent immigration to Canada – that she had fled from Hungary or East Germany. Nonetheless, a reflection on the legacy of colonialism and ethno-racial discrimination in Canadian society is absent from Beck's letter. On balance, as an immigrant from a society where African descendants were an afterthought, it is understandable that Beck lacked a nuanced understanding of Canada's racial state.

Ignoring Canada's discriminatory immigration policies, many of the letters are replete with tacit notions of Canadian racial equality, an exceptionalism of sorts that Canadians desired to showcase to their US neighbours.[46] White Canadian petitioners seemed oblivious to the true racial climate in their country, on the one hand, and to the Canadian government's ongoing erasure from the national consciousness of the African Canadian or Indigenous experience, on the other. One Torontonian petitioner, who signed their name "A White Canadian, who speaks for *Justice for all*," wrote that "white Southerners practice a cowardly *racial discrimination and visciousness* [*sic*] much worse than any *Communist* could do, and which is far from civilized." Signing their petition "Disgusted," sisters Shirley and Lillian Jenssen of Toronto stated that it is "disgraceful and outrageous for the United States and the State of Alabama to pass such a sentence on Jimmy Wilson. The whole of Toronto and a good many others feel the same way."

Agnes Donaldson summed up the petitioners' deep-seated beliefs: "We in Canada are very different from the United States over the cases of the Coloured people." This belief of amicable race relations in Canadian society might have been linked to Canada's strict admittance of a nominal quota of Black women domestic workers after 1955. It is plausible, considering the likelihood that some of the petitioners belonged to the upper-middle-class families who hired Black women to perform housework, that the relatively calm space of domestic work and its imbalanced power dynamics that favoured employers led some petitioners to an inaccurate assessment of the racial climate in Canadian society.[47]

Some Canadians threatened an economic boycott of the South. According to a Mr. and Mrs. Smith, "We have made it a practice to spend our winters in the south for the last 5 years but if they execute a *coloured* man for stealing $1.95 we will find somewhere else to spend our holidays." The Smiths' class privilege as "snowbirds" (Canadians with the economic resources to migrate south for winter) calls into question the extent to which they had voluntarily exposed themselves to the South's rigid colour line. Why would one take an immediate and definitive stance against southern racism after ignoring five years of lynchings and other forms of racialized oppression? It is plausible that the Smiths' threat had more to do with a desire to invoke judgmental language to show their purported progressive racial attitude as Canadians than with boycotting the South; otherwise, it might have taken fewer than five winters in the sunny South for the Jim Crow racial order to offend their humanitarianism.

For some Canadians, Cold War politics meant attacking US democracy and its violation of the rule of law. Edward Matthews of Newmarket, Ontario, a suburb just north of Toronto, voiced such a concern. "This is a poor example to the world of American democracy," he wrote. "It is little wonder that American prestige has sunk into the gutter in the past few years ... Does not the law say that a man on trial shall be tried by an unbiased jury[?]" To underscore his assertion that Washington's moral authority was in decline, Matthews claimed that Canadians were "slowly losing their respect for Americans." Yet, some in Matthews's nearly all white Newmarket community had threatened to banish an interracial Black-white family in 1955. In addition, one teacher in the community used the epithet "nigger" when speaking to schoolchildren.[48]

Nonetheless, during the 1950s, Canadians overlooked local and national race relations, critiquing the hypocrisy in US domestic and foreign policy. When Mrs. Howard, a resident of a small town about thirty kilometres north of Toronto, appealed for Wilson's clemency she invoked language and sentiment on two topics that, when deployed together, proved most problematic to the US government during the Cold War: racial oppression and the spread of communism.[49] "The United States of America by this so called 'trial' has made a mockery of its constitution & destroyed the faith of peoples who looked upon their country as a living example of freedom & justice," Mrs. Howard asserted. "In a true democracy," she explained, "there cannot be laws that apply differently for white than for Colored people. In sentencing this man to death on the flimsy evidence presented at the so called 'trial,' the U.S.A has placed itself on the same level as Communist Russia who has shown in *its* 'trials' that it doesn't matter if the man sentenced is really guilty, just so long as his death serves as an example to anyone contemplating a similar act." Mrs. Howard had also managed to convince seven of her friends and neighbours to sign her petition. One Toronto woman summed up this sentiment: "They are being worse than the Communists if they call this justice."

Many letters reflected that Canadians no longer believed the US Cold War rhetoric of exceptionalism, being leader of the free world, liberal democracy, and anti-communism. Some openly challenged the foundation of US Cold War propaganda. This perceived lack of credibility fuelled a Canadian hubris that the United States should adopt Canada's system of justice and attitudes on race. F. Turner echoed this sentiment: "Here is one of the keys to why America is slowly hated by every country in the world including we neighbours in Canada. This attitude that you are displaying openly for all the world to see and all people to question is just the fuel for communist propaganda that they [communists] try to create." To many Canadians, the treatment of African Americans provided fodder to those who sought to undermine Anglo-Western hegemony. Speaking out against racial injustice in the United States allowed some Canadians to rebuff perceptions of Western hypocrisy during the Cold War.

Lessons from the Past

When radio station CKEY mailed the petitions to Governor Folsom's office in Montgomery, Alabama, few Canadians anticipated the immediate impact that their political activism would have on Jimmy Wilson's life. Mounting pressure on US diplomats around the world forced Alabama to pay closer attention to the currents of international affairs. Although the Alabama Supreme Court denied Wilson's appeal following a routine motion in August, the state had delayed his execution date to 24 October 1958. But by 13 September Governor Folsom had received over three thousand letters from CKEY and quipped that "he was snowed under with mail from Toronto demanding clemency." Folsom admitted that in his two terms as governor he had "never seen anything like it."[50] On 30 September, Governor Folsom granted Jimmy Wilson clemency.

In denouncing southern racism forcefully and openly, Canadians believed that they had demonstrated, yet again, their unwavering commitment to justice, freedom, and equality before the law, traits that distinguished them from their US neighbours. As one Toronto couple proclaimed, "We vote *life* not *death* for a Negro, who no doubt suffers only from his environment under a questionable democracy." The egregiousness and audacity of Wilson's intended punishment, coupled with Marty Goodman's impeccable investigative reporting and CKEY's call to action, compelled Canadians to live up to the moral rhetoric of British justice and fair play, which, in both theory and praxis, urged white Canadians to showcase their social primacy vis-à-vis their US counterparts. Canadians seldom showed their humanitarian impulse without acknowledging their superiority. As a result, postwar racial injustice piqued their interests. In this script, Canadians could freely tout their progressive attitudes and overlook the structures of white supremacy that undergirded their society and confined African descendants to subordinate citizenship.

Another, less conspicuous truth is that critiquing racial injustice elsewhere, but especially in the United States, gave African Canadians a false sense of security. When some Canadians denounced the most abject forms of racial oppression in the United States, they did it for themselves, for it absolved their own racist attitudes. As a result, Wilson and the tens of thousands of US enslaved fugitives and free persons who absconded to Upper Canada in the nineteenth century could be incorporated into a benign history that celebrates Canadian benevolence. This national narrative, where white people are the saviours of Black people, gave an embryonic Canada moral credibility, enabling it to adopt a stance of liberal internationalism during the Cold War. In the absence of lynch law, and when many viewed the United States as a failed model of race relations, Canada appeared utopic.

Furthermore, when properly historicized, the Wilson case illuminates the Canadian human rights climate that allowed ordinary citizens to exercise agency on his behalf. As a Jewish Canadian, whose family had experienced racial discrimination in Canada, Goodman's interest in Wilson was characteristic of the interracial coalition that Jews and African

Canadians forged with each other in the interwar and postwar years. In this vein, one could conclude that Goodman, and other Canadians of minority backgrounds, saw Alabama as a mirror of dominant white Canadian society, where the federal government forged citizenship rights and access to resources along racial and ethnic lines.

By holding up the mirror of racial inequity to the United States, Canadians would ultimately see themselves, even if they did not want to look, because Canada's racial minorities also agitated against discrimination and for fair play. Perhaps Canada appeared not as a country of amicable race relations but rather as a place where racial politics could undergo transformations. One Torontonian presciently echoed this sentiment: "Jimmy Wilson in reality is a symbol of our future. Our future can't be unstable and still proceed. Feelings of patriotism and loyalty will gradually be smothered, just because the scales don't balance." Perhaps US racial injustice taught some Canadians a lesson about the cost of condoning and ignoring racism, at least publicly. For Canadians, balancing their inherited scales of British justice would require deep national introspection on the question of racial minorities.

NOTES

1 On the Odell Waller case, an iconic case of southern violence and a miscarriage of justice, see Glenda Gilmore, *Defying Dixie: The Radical Roots of Civil Rights, 1919–1950* (New York: W.W. Norton, 2008), 329–36, 331–44. See also Jack Greenberg, *Race Relations and American Law* (New York: Columbia University Press, 1959), 313–42; Mark Tushnet, *Making Civil Rights Law: Thurgood Marshall and the Supreme Court, 1936–1961* (New York: Oxford University Press, 1994), 50–1; C. Vann Woodward, *The Strange Career of Jim Crow* (New York: Oxford University Press, 1957); and Stuart Banner, *The Death Penalty: An American History* (Cambridge, MA: Harvard University Press, 2002).

2 All of the letters quoted in this chapter were written in late August or early September 1958 and can be found in folders 1 and 2, container SG 13823, 1955–1959, Correspondence Re: Jimmy Wilson, 1958 – Letters to Canada's Station CKEY, J. Folsom Governor of Alabama, Alabama Department of Archives, Montgomery.

3 See Peter van der Veer, *Imperial Encounters: Religion and Modernity in India and Britain* (Princeton: Princeton University Press, 2001), 8; and Nico Slate, *Colored Cosmopolitanism: The Shared Struggle for Freedom in the United States and India* (Cambridge, MA: Harvard University Press, 2012), 3.

4 See Douglas Blackmon, *Slavery by Another Name: The Re-enslavement of Black Americans from the Civil War to World War II* (London: Icon, 2012); Jacqueline

Jones, *Labor of Love, Labor of Sorrow: Black Women, Work and the Family, from Slavery to the Present* (New York: Basic Books, 2010); Tera Hunter, *To 'Joy My Freedom: Southern Black Women's Lives and Labors after the Civil War* (Cambridge, MA: Harvard University Press, 1998); Gerald Jaynes, *Branches without Roots: Genesis of the Black Working Class in the American South, 1862–1882* (New York: Oxford University Press, 1986); Lorenzo J. Greene and Carter G. Woodson, *The Negro Wage Earner* (Washington, DC: Association for the Study of Negro Life and History, 1930); and Abram L. Harris and Sterling D. Spero, *The Black Worker: The Negro and the Labor Movement* (New York: Columbia University Press, 1931).
5 Mary L. Dudziak, "The Case of 'Death for a Dollar Ninety-Five': Miscarriages of Justices and Constructions of American Identity," in *When Law Fails: Making Sense of Miscarriages of Justice*, ed. Charles J. Ogletree Jr. and Austin Sarat (New York: New York University Press, 2009), 28.
6 Dudziak, 28.
7 On southern constructs of gender, see Crystal Feimster, *Southern Horrors: Women and the Politics of Rape and Lynching* (Cambridge, MA: Harvard University Press, 2009); and Glenda Gilmore, *Gender and Jim Crow: Women and Politics of White Supremacy in North Carolina, 1896–1920* (Chapel Hill: University of North Carolina Press, 1996). See also Stewart Tolnay and E.M. Beck, *A Festival of Violence: An Analysis of Southern Lynchings, 1882–1930* (Champaign: University of Illinois Press, 1995).
8 For a detailed analysis of how southern white supremacists disenfranchised African Americans after Reconstruction, see Gilmore, *Gender and Jim Crow*.
9 Dudziak, "Death for a Dollar Ninety-Five," 28.
10 Dudziak, 28.
11 Mary L. Dudziak, *Cold War Civil Rights: Race and the Image of American Democracy* (Princeton: Princeton University Press, 2000), 3–46.
12 Dudziak, "Death for a Dollar Ninety-Five," 26.
13 *Toronto Daily Star*, August 20, 1958.
14 Martin Goodman, "Robs White Widow Can't Read, Write[;] Aware He'll Die," *Toronto Daily Star*, August 20, 1958, 1.
15 On cooperation between Canadians of African descent and Jews, see Daniel Braithwaite, interview by Arleigh M. Holder, August 17, 1978, BLA-7181-BRA, Ontario Multicultural History Society (OMHS); Harry Gairey, interview by Kenneth Amoroso, July 9, 1977, BLA-1446-GAI, OMHS; Gwendolyn Johnston, interview by Ruth Lewis, February 22, 1979, BLAH-6901-JOH, OMHS; Stanley Grizzle, *My Name Is Not George: Personal Reminiscences of Stanley G. Grizzle* (Toronto: Umbrella, 1998), 32; and Donald Moore, *Don Moore: An Autobiography* (Toronto: Williams-Wallace, 1985), 32. For a critical analysis of Black-Jewish relations, see Jack Salzman and Cornel West, eds., *Struggles in the Promised Land: Towards a History of*

Black-Jewish Relations in the United States (New York: Oxford University Press, 1997).

16 See Timothy Tyson, *The Blood of Emmett Till* (New York: Simon & Schuster, 2017).

17 For additional reading on anti-Semitism in Canadian society, see Irving Abella and Harold Troper, *None Is Too Many: Canada and the Jews of Europe, 1933–1948* (Toronto: Lester & Orpen Dennys, 1982).

18 Alan Kruger, telephone interview by the author, April 10, 2013.

19 Marvin Goldsmith, telephone interview by the author, April 4, 2013.

20 Kruger interview.

21 Goodman, "Robs White Widow."

22 Considering the potential threats against African Americans and Jews in the Deep South, especially civil rights workers and reporters who investigated lynchings and other crimes, Goodman could have objected to this assignment based on fear for his safety, but he did not. On Jewish contributions to human rights in postwar Canada, see Ross Lambertson, "'The Dresden Story': Racism, Human Rights, and the Jewish Labour Committee of Canada," *Labour* 47 (2001): 43–82; and James W. St. G. Walker, "The 'Jewish Phase' in the Movement for Racial Equality in Canada," *Canadian Ethnic Studies* 34, no. 1 (2002): 1–29. See also Cheryl Greenberg, "The Southern Jewish Community and the Struggle for Civil Rights," in *African Americans and Jews in the Twentieth Century*, ed. V.P. Franklin, Nancy L. Grant, Harold M. Kletnick, and Genna Rae McNeil (Columbia: University of Missouri Press, 1998), 123–64; and Maurianne Adams and John Bracey eds., *Strangers and Neighbors: Relations between Blacks and Jews in the United States* (Amherst: University of Massachusetts Press, 1999).

23 Goodman, "Robs White Widow." The Jim Crow South used various dubious measures such as vagrancy laws to imprison African Americans unjustly. See Blackmon, *Slavery by Another Name*.

24 Dudziak, "Death for a Dollar Ninety-Five," 29.

25 See Jason Ward, *Defending White Democracy: The Making of a Segregationist Movement and the Remaking of a Racial Politics, 1936–1965* (Chapel Hill: University of North Carolina Press, 2011); and Michael Klarman, *From Jim Crow to Civil Rights: The Supreme Court and the Struggle for Racial Equality* (New York: Oxford University Press, 2004).

26 Martin Goodman, "'Liberal' Governor Seen as Negro's Only Hope to Escape '$1.95' Chair," *Toronto Daily Star*, August 21, 1958, 3.

27 Goodman, "Robs White Widow." All remaining quotations in this section are from Goodman's article.

28 A "Tom" or "Uncle Tom" is a derogatory noun that refers to African descendants who behave obsequiously. For a famous portrayal of this

archetype, see Harriet Beecher Stowe, *Uncle Tom's Cabin; or, Life among the Lowly* (Boston: John P. Jewett, 1852). Goodman's portrayal of Wilson as a helpless person likely influenced some Canadians to support his case.
29 Quoted in Goodman, "Robs White Widow."
30 Ibid.
31 Ibid.
32 Ibid.
33 E. Franklin Frazier, "The Pathology of Race Prejudice," *Forum* 70 (June 1927): 861.
34 Frazier, 861.
35 Canadian Census data historically underestimated African descendants in Canada. For figures on African Canadians, see Keith Henry, *Black Politics in Toronto since World War I* (Toronto: Multicultural History Society of Ontario, 1981), 13.
36 See Barrington Walker, *Race on Trial: Black Defendants in Ontario's Criminal Courts, 1858–1958* (Toronto: University of Toronto Press, 2010), 116–82; and Sarah-Jane Mathieu, *North of the Color Line: Migration and Black Resistance in Canada, 1870–1955* (Chapel Hill: University of North Carolina Press, 2010), 15, 25, 52–4.
37 Walker, *Race on Trial*, 116.
38 Macdonald cited in Constance Backhouse, *Petticoats and Prejudice: Women and Law in Nineteenth-Century Canada* (Toronto: Osgoode Society for Canadian Legal History and Women's Press 1991), 98; John A. Macdonald to William Johnston Ritchie, Nova Scotia Chief Justice, June 8, 1868, no. 854, MG 26A, Letterbook 11, Macdonald Papers, NAC (LAC), Ottawa.
39 Walker, *Race on Trial*, 24–88.
40 Walker.
41 Walker, 116, 141–82.
42 Britain promised liberty to enslaved Africans who defected from their US masters to aid His Majesty's forces during the US Revolutionary War and the War of 1812. See John Fabian Witt, *Lincoln's Code: The Laws of War in American History* (New York: Free Press, 2012); Gerald Horne, *Negro Comrades of the Crown: African Americans and the British Empire Fight the U.S. before Emancipation* (New York: New York University Press, 2012); and Simon Schama, *Rough Crossings: Britain, the Slaves, and the American Revolution* (London: BBC Books, 2005). See also Lawrence Hill, *The Book of Negroes* (Toronto: HarperCollins, 2007); Christopher Leslie Brown, *Moral Capital: Foundations of British Abolitionism* (Chapel Hill: University of North Carolina Press, 2006), 105–54, 209–58, 451–62; and James Walker, *The Black Loyalists: The Search for a Promised Land in Nova Scotia and Sierra Leone, 1783–1870* (Toronto: University of Toronto Press, 1992), 1–17, 271–330. The resettlement of "Black Loyalists" in Upper Canada and the Maritimes

after the Revolutionary War, on the one hand, and the enslaved Africans who accompanied their Loyalist masters from the Thirteen Colonies, on the other, exposed the limits of British benevolence. Whether nominally free or enslaved, racial caste denied African descendants their humanity in British North America. See Barry Cahill, "The Black Loyalist Myth in Atlantic Canada," *Acadiensis* 29, no. 1 (1999): 76–87; Harvey Amani Whitfield, *North to Bondage: Loyalist Slavery in the Maritimes* (Vancouver: UBC Press, 2016; Whitfield, *Blacks on the Border: The Black Refugees in British North America, 1815–1860* (Burlington: University of Vermont Press, 2006); Walker, *Black Loyalists*; Wallace Brown, "Negroes and the American Revolution," *History Today* 14, no. 8 (1964): 556–63; Barry Cahill, "Slavery and the Judges of Loyalist Nova Scotia," *University of New Brunswick Law Journal* 43 (1994): 73–125; and D.G. Bell, J. Barry Cahill, and Harvey Amani Whitfield, "Slavery and Slave Law in the Maritimes," in *The African Canadian Legal Odyssey: Historical Essays*, ed. Barrington Walker (Toronto: University of Toronto Press, 2012), 363–420. On the 1772 landmark Somerset case that refuted the legality of chattel slavery in the metropole and inspired African descendants in the Atlantic world, see Steven M. Wise, *Though the Heavens May Fall: The Landmark Trial that Led to the End of Human Slavery* (Cambridge, MA: Da Capo, 2005); and Vincent Carretta, *Equiano, the African: Biography of a Self-Made Man* (Athens: University of Georgia Press, 2005), 208–12. Abolitionist David Walker's description of the British is arguably the most nuanced statement that an African descendant made concerning the paradox of British oppression and benevolence. Walker wrote that the British are "the best friends the coloured people have upon earth. Though they have oppressed us a little and have colonies now in the West Indies which oppress us *sorely* – Yet notwithstanding they have done one hundred times more for the melioration of our condition, than all the other nations of the earth put together." See David Walker, "One Continual Cry," in *David Walker's Appeal to the Colored Citizens of the World, 1829–1830*, ed. Herbert Aptheker (New York: published by the author, 1965), 105–6.

43 See Agnes Calliste, "Race, Gender and Canadian Immigration Policy: Blacks from the Caribbean, 1900–1932," *Journal of Canadian Studies* 28, no. 4 (1993): 131–48; Vic Satzewich, "Racism and Canadian Immigration Policy: The Government's View of Caribbean Migration, 1962–1966," *Canadian Ethnic Studies* 21, no. 1 (1989): 77–97; and Harold Troper, *Only Farmers Need Apply: Official Canadian Government Encouragement of Immigration from the United States, 1896–1911* (Toronto: Griffin House, 1972).

44 For an analysis of postwar US media consumption in Canada, see Adam J. Green, "Images of Americans: The United States in Canadian Newspapers during the 1960s" (PhD diss., University of Ottawa, 2006).

45 See Agnes Calliste, "Canada's Immigration Policy and Domestics from the Caribbean: The Second Domestic Scheme," *Socialist Studies* 5 (1989): 133–65; and Satzewich, "Racism and Canadian Immigration Policy."
46 In a similar vein, northerners considered themselves superior to southerners. In fact, the way Canadians viewed US race relations is very similar to how the North viewed the South.
47 See Calliste, "Canada's Immigration Policy."
48 See Dan Hill, *I Am My Father's Son: A Memoir of Love and Forgiveness* (Toronto: HarperCollins, 2009), 49–55.
49 Thomas Borstelman, *The Cold War and the Color Line: American Relations in the Global Arena* (Cambridge, MA: Harvard University Press, 2001).
50 Dudziak, "Death for a Dollar Ninety-Five," 36.

SECTION THREE

Building Black Communities and Shaping Black Resilience

6

The Shiloh Baptist Church: The Pillar of Strength in Edmonton's African American Community

DAVID ESTE AND JENNA BAILEY

Introduction

In January 2017, Alberta's provincial government officially recognized Black History Month. David Shepherd, the only Black member of the Legislative Assembly, remarked, "Men and women of African descent have been part of Alberta's history for over 100 years. They homesteaded alongside settlers from around the world, helping to found our cattle industry and fighting through harsh winters and racial prejudice to build thriving communities."[1] In honour of the occasion, Black history events were organized in several locales throughout the province.

However, most Canadians are not aware of the long-standing existence of people of African descent in Alberta. The best known is John Ware, who was born as a slave in South Carolina. After the Civil War, he gained his freedom and made his way to Canada on a cattle drive in 1882. He remained in the province until his death in 1905.[2] It is important to note that in addition to Ware, a small number of people of African descent resided in the region prior to the twentieth century.[3]

According to the 2016 census, 129,390 Alberta residents identified as being Black, with the highest concentrations in Edmonton (57,815) and Calgary (54,190).[4] The community is extremely diverse, composed of members from an array of African and Caribbean countries, African Americans, and the descendants of the "Black Pioneers" who arrived in the 1900s.[5] Immigration has since contributed to the growth of the African Canadian community in the province.

Given the lack of attention to the African Canadian experience in Alberta, there are demands by members of the African Canadian community, especially in Edmonton, that their historical and contemporary experiences be incorporated into the educational curriculum as well as shared with the general public. For example, Bashir Mohamed, who is part of the Black Lives Matter movement in Edmonton, stated in an interview, "I wonder why it [Alberta's Black history] was overlooked ... I feel like this is a huge part of our identity that I guess has been almost forgotten and I wonder if there's a reason for that."[6] Similar views were echoed in a proposal submitted in 2016 by the Shiloh Centre for Multicultural Roots (SCMR), a group that represents descendants of Black settlers who migrated to Alberta in the early twentieth century, to the Alberta Human Rights Commission: "Our community has been and continue[s] to be treated as if we do not exist. There are policies and practices that ignore our historical preserve in Alberta and the contributions we have made to our country and province are marginalized. The first Blacks who migrated to Alberta have not been recognized."[7] Cheryl Foggo, a noted author, historian, and playwright, in commenting about the lack of knowledge about the African Canadian community in the province, voiced the following questions: "Why are those communities secret? Why don't we all know about them? Why aren't they a part of our knowledge of our history and heritage because if they were, I think we would stop repeating the cycles of ignorance that just seem to carry on and on."[8]

Not surprisingly, most writing on African Canadian history has focused on the experiences of people of African descent who have resided in Ontario, Nova Scotia, and Quebec. Settlement patterns and population size are two major factors contributing to this development. As several scholars have noted, including Joseph Mensah, Anne Milan and Kelly Tran, and Marcel Trudel, slavery began in Canada in the seventeenth century in New France. By the end of the century, Blacks were sold and bought at markets in Montreal and Quebec City.[9] Prior to the American War of Independence, at least one hundred slaves of African descent resided in Nova Scotia.[10] With the defeat of the British in 1783, enslaved Blacks were brought to the Maritimes with White Loyalists who settled in the region. The first major influx of African Americans to Canada occurred that year, when the British sent approximately 3,500 Black Loyalists to Nova Scotia after the War of Independence. This was followed by the arrival of Maroons from Jamaica in 1796.[11]

In Upper Canada, now Ontario, there was movement during the early 1790s to abolish slavery. In 1793, Lieutenant Governor John Graves Simcoe introduced legislation designed to ban the importation of enslaved people of African descent to the region. However, the bill was subjected to revisions including the agreement that once the children of slaves reached the age of twenty they were granted freedom. Slavery was eventually abolished in Canada in 1833.[12]

African Americans continued to migrate to Canada. After the War of 1812, those African Americans who had fought for the British (known as the Black Refugees) were given the opportunity to settle in Nova Scotia, where they faced varying forms of racism and discrimination. Some African American slaves escaped to Ontario through the organized Underground Railway network, while others made it on their own volition. They settled in different locations, including Toronto, Chatham, and Amherstburg.[13]

In the middle of the nineteenth century, approximately eight hundred African Americans left California and moved to Victoria, British Columbia. These African Americans felt that as free citizens in the United States their rights were threatened, and hence the migration to Canada.[14] The next influx of African Americans to Canada occurred in the 1880s. By this time, Montreal had emerged as the railway capital of Canada. Following the practice of American railroad companies such as Pullman, both the Canadian National and Canadian Pacific Railways expressed the desire to have men of African descent serve as porters on their trains. The two companies sent recruiting teams to major US cities such as New York and Philadelphia as well as the southern states to hire African American men. By 1900, Montreal's Black community had started to develop as a number of African American porters decided to make this city their permanent home.[15]

In Alberta, scholars such as Cheryl Foggo, Howard Palmer and Tamara Palmer, Bruce Shepard, Jennifer Kelly and Dan Cui, and Karina Vernon are bringing to light the history of African Canadians in the province through their respective works.[16] Further, Velma Carter, Wanda Leffler Akili, and Gwen Hooks, descendants of the original settlers, have published important works that record much of the local and family history.[17] Finally, the Black Settlers of Alberta and Saskatchewan Historical Society conducted a series of recorded interviews with relatives of Black Pioneers who settled in the two provinces, making an important contribution to the documentation of the experiences of people of African descent.[18] While important work has been and is being done to record and share the history of people of African descent in Alberta, one aspect of this history that could be explored further is the role of the Shiloh Baptist Church in Edmonton, which was founded by African Americans in Edmonton who ventured to Alberta between 1908 and 1912. This chapter therefore examines the role the church played for this community after it was established.

The chapter is organized in the following manner: The first part discusses the roles that Black churches played in early African Canadian communities. We then provide readers with a description of our research methodology. In the next part of the chapter, we establish the context for the discussion of the Shiloh Baptist Church by providing commentary on

(1) the African American presence in Oklahoma from 1840 to 1907 and (2) the migration and settlement of African Americans to the Canadian prairies. The remainder of the chapter focuses on the founding of the Shiloh Baptist Church in Edmonton and the various roles the church served for both the African Americans who settled in rural communities near Edmonton and those families who resided in the city.

Black Churches in Early African Canadian Communities

There appears to be a strong agreement within African Canadian historical literature that the Black Church emerged as one of the key institutions in the initial Black communities that developed in Canada. James Walker contends that "for the black pioneers and for generations of their descendants, the core of the community was the church. Church membership defined community, provided opportunities to participate in community affairs, and created networks for cooperative endeavour." Walker also stresses that Black preachers provided positive leadership and were instrumental in maintaining cohesive communities where community members faced racism on a daily basis.[19] In *The Freedom-Seekers: Blacks in Early Canada*, Daniel Hill emphasizes the pivotal role that Black churches played in the development of early Black communities in Ontario. He remarks, "Blacks began to come to Canada, first in small numbers, later on thousands. Their churches, which had been an important part of their life before they fled from the USA were quickly transplanted to Canadian soil and carried on their ministry. Their earliest and most important institutions in all Black Upper Canadian communities were the churches."[20]

Carol Duncan voices similar sentiments as she notes that "the Black church emerged as a central institution in the development of Black cultural life in North America both in Canada and the United States."[21] Rosemary Sadlier and Fiona Clarke, in their book entitled *The Black Church in Canada*, reinforce the message imparted by Hill, Walker, and Denise Gillard, which emphasizes how Black churches served as platforms to resist the secondary status that White society conferred on Black communities.[22] Philip Daniels, who produced a documentary called *Seeking Salvation* about the role of churches in African Canadian communities, remarks, "I believe that the impact of the institution of the church within black communities across our country [Canada] is probably deeper and its impact is probably a lot wider. Not only in a spiritual sense or in a religious sense ... It traditionally has been involved in education and literary efforts and it has been an organizing point for women in the community."[23]

Previously, David Este has argued that the early Black churches were fundamental.[24] As part of African Canadian communities these churches fostered social life through activities like the development of debate clubs, as well as events such as dances and picnics for community members. Furthermore, opportunities for leadership development occurred through the church, particularly for women. For example, the constitution of Union Church, which was founded in 1907 in Montreal, provided clear guidelines for the creation of an administrative system that encouraged this development: "the officers shall be a Pastor, not more than five deacons, seven deaconesses, a clerk, a treasurer, a superintendent of Sunday School, and auditor."[25] From a gendered perspective, the positions set aside for women reflected their importance in the affairs of the church and the community. Because the majority of men were employed by the railroad companies, the deaconesses provided services that ensured the ongoing operation of the church.[26]

Another key activity that the Black churches became engaged in was fighting anti-Black racism.[27] Este asserts that a major act of resistance against the anti-Black racism that Black Canadians experienced was the formation of churches in their communities.[28] In virtually every site where African Americans settled in Canada in the eighteenth and nineteenth centuries, some tried to attend White churches and were refused, while others did attend these churches but did not have any involvement in the daily operations of these institutions and had to sit in segregated pews. As a result, they established their own churches, and the ministers of these Black churches served as advocates on behalf of African Canadians in addressing the injustices that community members experienced on a daily basis. They stressed the importance of having employment and educational opportunities for African Canadians as well as access to public places – such as restaurants and, in the early twentieth century, theatres – as anti-Black racism was present in virtually every sector of Canadian society.[29]

Methodology

This chapter draws its findings from a larger study.[30] In the fall of 2016, the Shiloh Centre for Multicultural Roots received a grant from the Alberta Human Rights Commission to carry out a project entitled "Stories of Pioneer African American Canadians as a Catalyst for Reconciliation."[31] This project was conceptualized by Deborah Dobbins, who is the current president of SCMR and board member of the Shiloh Baptist Church. Dobbins is a third-generation African Canadian; her grandparents were part of the group that migrated to Canada from Oklahoma. Throughout the study, Dobbins served as the project coordinator. She was instrumental in promoting the project within the community and served as the primary recruiter, given her strong ties to the community. The primary purpose of the project was to document and reclaim the stories of the African Americans who migrated from Oklahoma, Texas, Missouri, Illinois, and other states to the Prairie provinces, particularly those who settled in Alberta and Saskatchewan during the 1905–12 migration wave. A second goal of the project was to explore the experiences of Black settlers and their descendants who faced racist and discriminatory behaviour and how they dealt with these forms of oppression while residing in the Prairie provinces. A final expectation of the project was to increase awareness of the presence and experiences of the African Americans who settled in the Prairie provinces between 1905 and 1912. As stated in the SCMR proposal, "our community has been and continues to be treated as though we do not exist."[32] Through this project, the SCMR intended to address the lack of knowledge about the Black settlers in Alberta.

From a methodological perspective, we engaged in oral history. Basically, oral history is the systematic collection of living people's testimony about their own experience. This type of history depends upon human memory and the spoken word. In describing the value of oral history, Graham Smith maintains that this approach "provides an opportunity to gain a greater appreciation of the multiple, often sharply contested historical perspectives that exist in memory."[33] According to the Oral History Association, "Oral history refers both to a method of recording and preserving oral testimony and to the product of that process ... Oral history interviews seek an in-depth account of personal experience and reflections, with sufficient time allowed for the narrators to give their story the fullness they desire."[34] A strength of oral history is the ability to understand how people make sense of their own lives and the ways in which they perceive events and experiences.[35] Finally, oral history can provide a platform to individuals and groups who are marginalized in conventional histories – the working class, women, and ethnic minorities.[36] Two of the limitations associated with oral history are the accuracy of the data collected and an individual's ability to recall experiences or events.[37] As a methodological balance to oral history, we used an array of books, book chapters, and peer-reviewed journal articles that focus on the settlement by and subsequent experiences of the African Americans who migrated to different sites in Alberta and Saskatchewan.[38]

In the effort to recruit participants for the study, the project coordinator made several announcements at a number of services and events at the Shiloh Church. This helped to inform the community – Black

Albertans in the Edmonton area – about the initiative. This publicity as well as the project coordinator's individual connections and relationships with fellow community members resulted in nineteen individuals who agreed to participate in the initiative.

The primary data collection method was semi-structured interviews, conducted by the two authors, with the descendants of those individuals and families who ventured to Alberta and Saskatchewan between 1905 and 1912. In describing this type of interview, Lioness Ayres notes that "it is a qualitative data collection strategy in which the researcher asks informants a series of predetermined open-ended questions."[39] Within the literature, there is strong consensus that the semi-structured interview format provides the interviewer with flexibility to gain an enhanced understanding of the experiences of the individuals who are being interviewed.[40] As was outlined in the consent forms, the interviews were videotaped for the purposes of creating a documentary. Therefore, the participants are not anonymous and provided informed consent to be filmed and/or quoted.

An initial interview guide was developed by the research team based on the objectives outlined in the project's proposal and in consultation with the project coordinator, who was quite knowledgeable about the migration of African Americans to Alberta from 1905 to 1912.[41] The guide was also reviewed by the project's advisory committee. As the interviews progressed, changes were made to the guide based on the initial analysis of the data. The interview guide questions focused on both the migration and settlement processes of the Black Pioneers. Examples of questions include the following: What prompted your family to leave the United States (Oklahoma) and venture to Alberta? What attracted your family to move to Alberta? What were the major challenges your family encountered as they attempted to adjust to living in a new country? What helped your family settle in the province?

A second set of questions explored the interviewees' experiences with racism and discrimination in various settings such as the school system, places of employment, and public spaces. Closely related were queries that centred on the impact of the racism that was manifested against study participants. The final question asked participants to suggest strategies or actions designed to deal with the racism that Black people living in Alberta experience on a daily basis.

An inductive approach was used for the analysis of the data.[42] As described by David Thomas, "inductive analysis refers to approaches that use detailed readings of raw data to derive concepts, themes, or a model through interpretations made from the raw data," with the constraints imposed by structured methodologies.[43] He maintains that this approach provides a convenient way of analysing qualitative data for many research purposes.

Once all the interviews were transcribed verbatim, we proceeded to read the transcripts several times to get a sense of what each individual interview contained that related to the primary goals of the project. We then engaged in a thematic analysis of the data; Victoria Clarke and Virginia Braun describe this type of analysis as "a method for identifying, analysing, and interpreting patterns of meaning ('themes') within qualitative data."[44] Our thematic analysis resulted in the development of an initial coding framework that served as the foundation for the in-depth analysis of the transcripts, which subsequently resulted in a more robust coding system. To create this coding system, the researchers first developed a set of codes or themes using the interview protocol as a guide when they first analysed the transcripts. As the researchers conducted further analysis of the transcripts, they refined, expanded on, and created new themes and subthemes from the initial codes.

A limitation of this study is that it focuses solely on the experiences of nineteen participants who were descendants of African American migrants who had settled in different locations in Alberta and Saskatchewan shortly after these provinces had become part of Canada, on 1 July 1905. Because of the sample size, the findings are certainly not generalized to the entire population of the descendants of the African Americans who ventured to the two provinces. A second limitation of this study is that the information about the Black Pioneers is drawn from second- and third-hand accounts by participants. The researchers attempted to mitigate this limitation through their access to historical documents of the families of those they interviewed that supported the commentary provided by the participants. These limitations exist, yet the importance of capturing these stories remains, as they contribute to our knowledge about this particular group of African American settlers who made their way to and settled in Canada.

Demographic Profile

Nineteen individuals with family members who had migrated from Oklahoma, Mississippi, Iowa, Tennessee, Kentucky, Missouri, and Texas to Alberta participated in the study as interview respondents. Of the nineteen participants, eight were men and eleven were women. Fourteen interviewees were second generation and five of the participants were third generation. The original pioneers settled in five rural locations – Wildwood (previously known as Junkins); Breton (previously known as

Keystone); Campsie, near Barrhead; Amber Valley (previously known as Pine Creek); and the Eldon District near Maidstone, Saskatchewan – as well as Edmonton and Calgary. We attempted to include participants from each of the rural communities and managed to attract individuals from four of the areas (Eldon District, Wildwood, Campsie, and Amber Valley). At the time of the interview, virtually all participants resided in the city of Edmonton or surrounding area. At least sixteen of the participants had some type of involvement or connection with the Shiloh Baptist Church.

During the series of interviews conducted by the research team, one of the consistent themes that emerged was the importance of the Shiloh Baptist Church – founded in 1910 in Edmonton – in the lives of the African Americans who settled in the city and neighbouring communities. Hence, the interviews became an important source of information about the church. This served as a major factor for pursuing additional research on Shiloh, which resulted in this chapter. In conducting further research on Shiloh Baptist Church, we had access to some of the original church documents, such as minutes of meetings and advertisements of the different events that were organized and held at the church, as well as newspaper clippings that focused on the importance of Shiloh to the "Black community" in Edmonton.

African Americans in Oklahoma

While individuals migrated to the prairies from several states, the vast majority of the families who settled in Alberta came from communities in Oklahoma, making it important to focus on what led these individuals to leave that particular state. African Americans have resided in the territory known as Oklahoma since the 1830s. In 1830, the federal government in Washington passed the Indian Removal Act, which annexed the land of several Native American communities in the southern state.[45] A collectivity of five of these groups – Cherokee, Chichasaw, Choctan, Creek, and Seminole – became known as the Five Civilized Tribes as a result of the Act. Members of these groups ventured to Indian Territory in Oklahoma and were accompanied by their African American slaves. It is estimated that between 4,500 and 5,000 Blacks were enslaved by the Five Tribes.[46] In describing how the slaves, many of whom were mixed-race, were used, Michael Doran states that "the slaves of this class of tribal citizens were quickly put to work upon their arrival, cutting timber, readying fields for cropping and raising buildings."[47] At the end of the American Civil War, the slaves with the Five Tribes were freed. Harold Troper describes the experiences of the slaves in the Creek Nation who resided in the eastern part of Oklahoma, noting that "the Negro was generally accepted and legally incorporated into the tribe, with blacks receiving a share in the redistributed Indian land holdings."[48]

According to scholars such as Paul Frymer, Sarah-Jane Mathieu, and Rachel Wolters, beginning in the 1890s Oklahoma as a territory became a popular destination for African Americans, especially those in the South.[49] As Mathieu writes, "With the spread of Jim Crow in the South and de facto exercise of segregation in most northern and western states, many African Americans increasingly sought asylum from white supremacist demagogues."[50] They were also attracted by land opportunities. In describing the situation, Frymer notes, "African American leaders such as E.P. McCabe encouraged the settlement of black communities, envisioning the movements of tens of thousands of people with the eventual possibility of even establishing an all-black state as refuge against southern oppression."[51]

Although African Americans who ventured to the territory were allowed to vote, they encountered some challenges. According to Frymer, "Black settlers struggled for opportunities to gain good lands and faced many of the same bureaucratic problems they faced decades earlier in attempting to claim public lands in the South – lacking money and finding their claims repeatedly rejected by local land commissioners."[52] Another barrier African Americans faced was the resistance that Native Americans put forth in response to the land claims made by members of the African American community. As a result, Oklahoma became the place where Blacks, Whites, and Native Americans competed for land. Yet, "Blacks were able to prosper in the region and even some integration occurred," Wolters notes, and "African Americans created as many as thirty-two towns." She adds, "Blacks in those towns operated their own businesses, provided markets for local farmers [and] created educational and religious institutions that provided opportunities for advancement."[53] However, in 1907 Oklahoma became a state, and with the influx of White southerners, Jim Crow legislation was passed that resulted in severe restrictions for members of the African American community. In 1910 African Americans lost the right to vote, which contributed to their increased marginalization in the state. As segregation became more entrenched, violence against African Americans increased. According to Wolters, between 1907 and 1915 fifteen Blacks were lynched in the state.[54]

Migration and Settlement of African Americans

Given the changing environment in Oklahoma, some African Americans began to consider the options that were available to them. Members of the community became aware of the possibility of migrating to western Canada, and that destination became more attractive as conditions for African Americans in the new state got progressively worse. Research respondents cited several reasons for the migration of their families to western Canada. One of the primary motivations was the increasing hostility African Americans faced in Oklahoma. One male participant explained, "There was a lot of white people that came into Oklahoma and they brought their customs with them, you know, of treating black people very bad and they introduced Jim Crow laws which took away the dignity of the black person because they could not vote after that ... They had separate schools, separate washrooms, separate drinking fountains, separate restaurants."[55] One female participant maintained that in the United States, "Blacks weren't really treated that well."[56] Another female participant noted that the African Americans from Oklahoma "had come from an environment where there was this expectation that you just did what you were told. You had no rights. You were just for a lot of them [White people] just chattel."[57] One female participant, whose grandfather had resided in a southern state and owned a hotel, commented on what forced her grandfather to migrate: "They were threatened. They had a lot of problems ... There was a hotel in the town where the white people were, and they were taking a lot of business away from him [the White hotelier] ... a neighbour told my grandfather that a group of white men were coming to get them [the family]. My grandfather had just had enough and he just left. They left the house. They left their business. Just packed wagons and left."[58] According to this research participant, her family would have been in danger if they had not departed.

Finally, in explaining several reasons for the migration, another male participant stated, "There was an advertisement in the newspaper down there [Oklahoma] about land being sold up in Canada for a filing fee of $10 and that seemed like a great thing when you are suffering second-class citizenship on a daily basis ... so there was a lot of black people especially in Oklahoma, that decided enough was enough. It is time to move North regardless of the cold weather, cold winters."[59] During the early 1900s in an attempt to populate western Canada after having forcibly removed the Indigenous populations from their traditional territories, the federal government advertised the availability of land for individuals who were interested in migrating, placing these ads in American newspapers including Black newspapers in Oklahoma.[60] One male interviewee stated, "My grandfather read in the local paper in Oklahoma that if you came to Canada, you would be given so much land ... I think the biggest attraction was the land which was not available to him in Oklahoma or

Tennessee."[61] Another male participant told of a similar scenario: "There was an ad run in the paper in Oklahoma and different parts of the states saying there was land – free land – well, it was not free. You had to pay $10 or $15 or something like that for a quarter of land, but you had to break so much of it ... the ad was run back in 1905 to 1910."[62] A female participant also supported these sentiments, explaining, "So they [Canadian government] sent out announcements to come to Alberta. You would get a piece of land for $10 for 60 acres and homestead here in Alberta."[63]

In commenting on the impact of the advertisements that were circulated in Oklahoma, Wolters states that "Black Oklahoma read with keen interest the promises of a good life in Western Canada."[64] However, scholars including Troper, Palmer and Palmer, and Walker argue that Canadian officials were surprised by the response by African Americans to the call for settlement of western Canada, as the federal government had hoped to attract White American farmers or ranchers.[65] However, the African American community in the new state viewed Canada as a place where they could flee from the discrimination and increasing violence that White Americans perpetuated against members of the community.

Similarly, the quest for freedom was an important motivator for the migration to Alberta. One female respondent remarked, "Most people came to Alberta by railway to experience freedom, to be able to contribute to a country in a free and safe way."[66] Another female participant noted, "My parents heard that Canada was a good safe place."[67] A male community member interviewed expressed similar sentiments: "They [my grandfather and great-uncle] decided, well, we are going to Canada because things look pretty bright up in Canada for a new future."[68] Hence, a variety of reasons precipitated the exodus out of Oklahoma and settlement in Alberta, which represented the first major migration of people of African descent to the province.

One way to travel from Oklahoma to Alberta was by first taking the train to the Canadian border. A female participant, in recalling what was relayed to her by a family member who was part of the migration process, remarked, "They were met with a lot of trouble at the border. When they came, Canadian officials did not realize that Black people were coming. They did not want Blacks in Alberta. They had the skills, they had everything that was on their [officials'] checklist so they had to let them in."[69] As Canadian immigration officials realized that African Americans were migrating to the Prairie provinces, they began to look for reasons to deny Blacks the opportunity to enter Canada.[70] One female respondent whose family resided in the most famous Black settlement, Amber Valley, stated that "the border officials were instructed to look for any slight medical imperfection that could be used to refuse their entry."[71] Indeed, the following excerpt from a Shiloh Baptist Church newsletter illustrates this treatment of African Americans at the border: "For example, medical examiners stationed at border crossings were instructed to scrutinize African American immigrants for any medical condition that would justify their exclusion, quietly offering a financial bonus to doctors for each African American immigrant rejected at the border."[72] Once they got to the border, some continued via train to larger cities from which they travelled to their final destination in each province by horse and buggy. A male interviewee, recalling the story of the migration that one of his aunts had shared with him, remarked, "So they [my relatives] came back to Edmonton in late fall. They came by train and when they got off the train, apparently they were almost waist-deep in snow."[73]

The African Americans who ventured to Alberta mainly settled in Edmonton, Calgary, or rural regions near Edmonton. In 1908, the first Oklahoma settlers arrived in Wildwood, which would eventually become the second-largest Black settlement in Alberta. In 1909, the Black settlement at Breton was founded by Bill Allen and Charlie King Sr.; by 1910, Campsie was settled by ten families; and finally Amber Valley, the largest Black settlement, was settled by African Americans brought that same year by Henry Sneed, who worked as a farmer and minister while residing in Oklahoma.[74] A female participant who was a long-time resident of Wildwood provided the following description of the village: "It was a small community and there were quite a few coloured people as we were called then ... It was an ordinary country life. Grandfather Smith, he has 325 acres of land."[75] In describing life in Amber Valley, one male participant commented that "life was sometimes very hard. We did not always have a lot of food." However, he also spoke about the social activities that brought community members together: "We played baseball. We had school and community dances. Picnics were held at least once during the summer."[76]

Walker provides a potential explanation for the pattern of settlement: "the pioneers appear to have selected their remote locations in order to avoid the racial hysteria which their arrival had evoked from the White majority."[77] The majority of study participants maintained that their parents or grandparents had positive relations with their White neighbours who were also farmers. One participant stated, "My parents really loved [living in Wildwood] because the neighbours were good ... white people help[ed] us with our farming needs."[78] Other study participants also stressed that while their families resided in the smaller communities such as Wildwood, Breton, Campsie, and Amber Valley, they did not frequently encounter acts of racism and discrimination. One male respondent recalled that when his father went into the town situated close to

Wildwood he would be addressed as "Hey big Nigger."[79] A female interviewee stated that she "only experienced racism when I came to [Edmonton]."[80] Similarly, in response to the question about experiences with racism, a second male stated, "I do not ever remember nothing being really prejudice ... And I do not recall being treated bad by the whites or anything like that."[81]

One of the reasons for the limited racism and discrimination encountered by the African American settlers in the rural communities was likely the fact that, as part of the farming community, they relied on their neighbourhood to assist them, especially when it came to harvesting the crops. A male participant stated, "We had good neighbours, friendly neighbours. We did everything to accommodate one another. My dad had purchased a steam threshing outfit and after we got our crops done, we did it for anybody else."[82] One female participant maintained that the African Americans who settled in the small communities fared better than their peers who resided in Edmonton, as the "people in the rural areas were able to have a few chickens, their pigs and gardens, so they were at least able to provide food for themselves, and they did not have to worry about having food for their families."[83]

Living in Edmonton

For those African Americans who travelled to Edmonton, their arrival resulted in severe backlash by the White community, which was supported and reinforced in newspapers. A clear sign that African Americans were not welcome in Edmonton was the circulation of a petition by the Edmonton Board of Trade that stressed that settlers from the United States were not suited to the Canadian weather, that they would have difficulty living in Canada, and that their presence would lead to "revolting lawlessness."[84] The petition was well supported by residents of the city and resulted in the Board of Trade passing a resolution demanding that the government of Canada prohibit any further Black migration.[85] In a letter to Prime Minister Wilfrid Laurier and Immigration Minister Frank Oliver, anti-Black sentiment was clearly expressed: "We, the undersigned residents of the City of Edmonton, respectfully urge upon your attention and upon that of the government of which you are the head, the serious menace to the future welfare of a large portion of Western Canada, by reason of the alarming influx of negro settlers."[86] Another section of the letter clearly asked the federal government to stop the migration: "We therefore, respectfully urge that such steps immediately be taken by the Government of Canada as will prevent any further immigration of negroes into Western Canada."[87] In response to the fears associated with the Black migration to the Prairies, the Liberal federal government approved Order-in-Council PC 1324 on 12 August 1911. The clear purpose of the order was to ban Black persons from entering Canada for a period of one year. The reason for this action was stated in the order, which targeted "any immigrants belonging to the Negro race" – specifically, that this "race is deemed unsuitable to the climate and requirements of Canada."[88] Hence, it became quite evident that Black immigrants were not welcome in Canada. However, the order was never implemented as the Canadian government did not want to damage relations with the United States. A second reason was political in nature; Laurier's government did not want to alienate African Canadians in an election year given the sizable Black communities in southern Ontario and Nova Scotia.[89]

Perhaps the strongest concerns among Alberta's White settlers in regard to the African American migration centred on fears of Black male sexuality, which in turn raised concerns about the safety of White women. Stereotypical beliefs and images that Black males "lusted" for White women contributed to this fear. As noted by Mathieu, "the arrival of black men in particular sparked groundless white paranoia especially among some white women's groups."[90] As a result of this negative reaction to the arrival of African Americans in western Canada, by 1912 the migration had come to an end.

Shiloh Baptist Church

Virtually every research participant whose family resided in the small rural communities close to Edmonton or who lived in the city with their families spoke about the Shiloh Baptist Church. Hence, this section of the chapter highlights the role of this church in the lives of the African American migrants.

As with their peers who settled in Quebec, Ontario, and Nova Scotia, the church was an important institution among the African Americans who migrated to Alberta, whether they settled in the small communities near Edmonton or made the city their home, as it had been in Oklahoma initially. The early group of Black Pioneers established small churches outside of Maidstone and in Wildwood, Amber Valley, and Breton. Those African Americans who resided in Edmonton were not welcomed at the White churches in the city. In commenting about the formation of the Shiloh Baptist Church in Edmonton, one female interviewee explained, "Now in 1909, there were other churches in existence in Edmonton. When our people went to attend those churches, they were not welcomed. And because God is, was such an important part of people's lives, they started to meet in the homes. In July 1910, the Shiloh Baptist Church was formally formed."[91] This account was supported by the words of a male participant who remarked, "It was a Black church. The folks from the United States wanted some place where they would worship by themselves."[92] Shiloh Baptist Church was formed out of the need for persons of colour to have a welcoming place to gather and worship.[93] Similarly, the Emmanuel African Methodist Episcopal (EAME) Church was also established by Black settlers in 1921.[94]

The existence of the church provided opportunities for community members to contribute. One male participant provided the following commentary about his mother: "Well, with mother she was a pretty strong individual for Shiloh. Very important, her faith was pretty big. She was the superintendent for Sunday school. She worked very hard for the church." This participant further remarked, "My mother would have never been given the role of superintendent if she was allowed to attend the white churches in the city."[95] Being superintendent for the Sunday school provided the opportunity for the participant's mother to develop and display her leadership abilities. Given the racism that the African Americans experienced in Edmonton, especially in the area of employment, one female participant revealed that "the church also provided members of the congregation the opportunity to meet and discuss their rights and how they were treated in Canadian society."[96] Similar sentiments were expressed by another female participant, who commented that "people would get together and talk about how things were unfair."[97]

As the church developed, the religious education of the community's youth became paramount and, as a result, Sunday school became a major priority. A consistent notation in the church minutes concerning activities that were held on Sundays was the acknowledgment that "Sunday School was called to order."[98] Sunday school also provided an opportunity for the younger members of the congregation to play together, thus assisting in the development of friendships and strengthening community relationships.

Women were actively involved in activities encouraged by the church. Some of the female participants mentioned the women's ministry, for example. One individual stated, "The women's ministry is where all the women in the church come together and they had their bible studies; they had different kinds of teaching that were related to women that helped them to grow and become strong in who they are."[99] Not surprisingly, music emerged as a major activity for members of Shiloh's congregation. One female participant noted that "Shiloh had the first gospel choir. Whenever anything black oriented came to Edmonton, and they needed to find someone to represent the blacks, they would come to

Shiloh. And the choirs sang at many places."[100] The Troubadours, the first black male gospel group in Alberta, also emerged from the church. Community members were provided the opportunity to sharpen their musical skills, and music lessons were provided to the youth associated with Shiloh.[101]

In 1938, members of the congregation formed the Colored Canadian Industrial Association (CCIA), whose membership included African Canadian men and women residing in Alberta. According to the association's constitution, the primary purposes of the group included the following: (1) to meet together regularly to study and discuss matters pertaining to the general welfare of our people, as a whole especially in Alberta; (2) to decide upon definite, concrete and legitimate methods of placing our united case before governing authorities; (3) to carry on a literary and debating club for the discussion of topics of general interest and to encourage the practices of public speaking; and (4) to procure the delivery of lectures on social, educational, political, economic and other subjects and to give and arrange musical and dramatic entertainments.[102] Entities such as the CCIA were important for community members as they realized their secondary status within the province. As well, the array of activities organized by the CCIA provided opportunities to socialize.

One of the contributing factors in the formation of the CCIA constitution was the strong presence of the Ku Klux Klan (KKK) in Edmonton during the 1930s. Under the leadership of John James Maloney, the KKK began to flourish in the city. Maloney began to canvass the countryside to establish new chapters and collect membership fees. The KKK was hostile toward a number of groups including immigrants, people of colour, and Catholics.[103] Another reason for the emergence of the CCIA was the need to advocate for better job opportunities. Basically, African Canadian men in Edmonton were limited to employment with the railway companies, working as porters where they were expected to be subservient to the White customers.[104] The majority of Black women were limited to working as domestics engaged in "days" work – cleaning the homes of members of the dominant group.[105]

Members of the association recognized the need to address the inequities that people of African descent experienced not only in Edmonton but in Alberta. They viewed the CCIA as a vehicle to advocate on behalf of the African Canadian community and confront the existence of racism and discrimination. Kelly and Cui have written about similar advocacy work that emerged out of the EAME church in Edmonton during the 1920s.[106] It is apparent that people of African descent residing in the province were keenly aware of their status and recognized the need for community advocacy to deal with racism and discrimination, especially in the urban centres. Secondly, through the organizing of literary and debating clubs, along with the provision of lectures, the CCIA appeared to foster both knowledge enhancement and educational skills for community members. These activities also contributed to a greater sense of community for the African American settlers and their descendants.

Conclusion

The African Americans who migrated to Alberta primarily from Oklahoma in the early 1900s were motivated to leave for three primary reasons. The first was to escape the increasing oppression that the African American community experienced once Oklahoma transitioned from a territory to a state. This resulted in losses for African Americans – loss of freedom and of their right to vote – and the imposition of Jim Crow laws formalized the segregation between the dominant White community and African Americans. Increasingly, African Americans became targets of such violent acts as lynching and destruction of personal property. In the eyes of the African Americans, then, Canada was perceived to be a country apparently void of the racial hatred that was becoming commonplace in Oklahoma. Finally, as farmers, having access to land to claim for themselves proved to be another attractor for the African American settlers.

As the majority of study participants noted, spirituality was an important aspect in the lives of those African Americans who settled in Alberta. Like their peers who migrated to provinces such as Nova Scotia, Ontario and Quebec, that desire to have their own place of worship became stronger as a result of the exclusionary practices they encountered when they attended White churches in Edmonton. The African American settlers turned inward and decided to form their own church in Edmonton, which was named the Shiloh Baptist Church. In a short period of time the church became the focal point not only for Blacks residing in Edmonton but also for members living in the small Black communities in the surrounding area.

Epilogue

In 2010, Shiloh's existence as the oldest Black church in Edmonton received attention from different types of media as the congregation celebrated one hundred years of existence. For example, some members of the church were interviewed as part of a video project documenting the history of Shiloh; the brief video can be seen on YouTube.[107] As well, the *Edmonton Journal*, one of the city's major newspapers, published several stories featuring the church.[108] The study conducted by the authors led to the development of two documentaries. The first is entitled *We Are the Roots: Black Settlers and Their Experiences of Discrimination on the Canadian Prairies*. The second, sponsored by the Aspen Foundation for Labour Education, is *Black Lives in Alberta: Over a Century of Racial Injustice Continues*; it focuses on the stories of four young Black adults who have lived in Alberta for their entire lives.

Shiloh Baptist Church continues to be a site where people of African descent, and especially the descendants of the "Black Pioneers," meet not only to share in worship but also to participate in an array of activities, such as musical and educational events. It is still considered to be a "Black church" despite the fact that its congregation is multiracial.

NOTES

1 Michele Jarvie, "Black History Month Marked in Alberta," *Calgary Herald*, January 27, 2017, http://calgaryherald.com/news/local-news/black-history-month-marked-in-alberta.
2 Robin W. Winks, *The Blacks in Canada: A History* (Montreal and Kingston: McGill-Queen's University Press, 1997), 70.
3 R. Bruce Shepard, "Diplomatic Racism: Canadian Government and Black Migration from Oklahoma, 1905–1912," *Great Plains Quarterly* 3, no. 1 (Winter 1983): 5–16; Shepard, *Deemed Unsuitable: Blacks from Oklahoma Move to the Canadian Prairies in Search of Equality in the Early 20th Century Only to Find Racism in Their New Home* (Toronto: Umbrella, 1997).
4 Statistics Canada, "Immigration and Ethnocultural Diversity: Key Results from the 2016 Census," *The Daily*, October 25, 2017.
5 Shepard, *Deemed Unsuitable*; Harold Martin Troper, "The Creek Negroes of Oklahoma and Canadian Immigration," *Canadian Historical Review* 53, no. 3 (1972): 272–88; Winks, *Blacks in Canada*, 305–6; David Este and Wek Kuol, "African Canadians in Alberta Connecting the Past with the Present," in *Multiple Lenses: Voices from the Diaspora Located in Canada*, ed. David Divine (Newcastle, UK: Cambridge Scholars, 2007), 29–45.
6 Kyle Muzyka, "Forgotten Identity: Alberta Black History Not Taught in Schools," CBC News Edmonton, February 1, 2017, http://www.cbc.ca/news/canada/edmonton/alberta-black-history-bashir-mohamed-1.3957084.
7 Shiloh Centre for Multicultural Roots (SCMR), "Stories of Pioneer African Canadians as a Catalyst for Reconciliation" (unpublished proposal, SCMR, Edmonton, 2016), 1.
8 David Bell, "Hidden History Explored in New Doc as Alberta Celebrates Black History Month," CBC News Calgary, February 1, 2017, http://www.cbc.ca/news/canada/calgary/black-history-month-alberta-1.3962796.

9 Joseph Mensah, *Black Canadians: History, Experience, Social Conditions*, 2nd ed. (Halifax: Fernwood, 2010), 45–58; Anne Milan and Kelly Tran, "Blacks in Canada: A Long History," *Canadian Social Trends*, no. 72 (Spring 2004): 2–7; Marcel Trudel, *Canada's Forgotten Slaves: Two Hundred Years of Bondage*, trans. George Tombs (Montreal: Véhicule, 2013).

10 Bidglal Pachai, *Blacks: Peoples of the Maritimes* (Halifax: Nimbus, 1997, 3).

11 Bridglal Pachai and Henry Bishop, *Historic Black Nova Scotia* (Halifax: Nimbus, 2006), 10–15.

12 Daniel Hill, *The Freedom-Seekers: Blacks in Early Canada* (Agincourt, ON: Book Society of Canada, 1981); Carl James, David Este, Wanda Thomas Bernard, Akua Benjamin, Bethan Lloyd, and Tana Turner, *Race and Well-Being: The Lives, Hopes and Activism of African Canadians* (Halifax: Fernwood, 2010); Gregory Wigmore, "Before the Railroad: From Slavery to Freedom in the Canadian-American Borderland," *Journal of American History* 98, no. 2 (2011): 437–54.

13 Hill, *Freedom-Seekers*; James et al., *Race and Well-Being*.

14 Crawford Kilian, *Go Do Some Great Thing: The Black Pioneers of British Columbia* (Madeira Park, BC: Douglas & McIntyre, 1978).

15 Dorothy Williams, *The Road to Now: A History of Blacks in Montreal* (Montreal: Véhicule, 1997).

16 Cheryl Foggo, *Pourin' Down Rain* (Calgary: Brush Education, 1990); Howard Palmer and Tamara Palmer, eds., *Peoples of Alberta: Portraits of Cultural Diversity* (Saskatoon: Western Producer Prairie Books, 1985); Shepard, "Diplomatic Racism"; Shepard, *Deemed Unsuitable*; Jennifer Kelly and Dan Cui, "Racialization and Work," in *Working People in Alberta: A History*, ed. Alvin Finkel (Edmonton: Athabasca University Press, 2012), 267–86; Karina Vernon, ed., *The Black Prairie Archives: An Anthology* (Wilfrid Laurier University Press, 2020).

17 Velma Carter and Wanda Leffler Akili, *The Window of Our Memories* (St. Albert: Black Cultural Research Society of Alberta, 1981); Velma Carter and Leah Suzanne Carter, *The Window of Our Memories*, vol. 2, *The New Generation* (St. Albert: Black Cultural Research Society of Alberta, 1990); Gwen Hooks, *The Keystone Legacy: Recollections of a Black Settler* (Edmonton, Bright Pebble, 1997).

18 The Black Settlers of Alberta and Saskatchewan Historical Society (BSAS) was founded in 2005 by four women who were all descendants of Black slavers and early Canadian pioneers. BSAS has researched, compiled, coordinated, and centralized the history of Black settlers in Alberta and Saskatchewan over the last century. Additionally, BSAS will archive and document material to educate, promote, and officially recognize the historic role Black settlers played in pioneering the lands that would become Alberta and Saskatchewan.

19 James W. St. G. Walker, "African Canadians," in *Encyclopedia of Canada's People*, ed. Paul Robert Magocsi (Toronto: University of Toronto Press, 1995), 153.
20 Hill, *Freedom-Seekers*, 130.
21 Carol B. Duncan, "Historical and Contemporary Perspectives on Multiculturalism and Black Christianities in Canada," in *Churches, Blackness and Contested Multiculturalism*, ed. R. Drew Smith, William Ackah, and Anthony G. Reddie (New York: Palgrave Macmillan, 2014), 240.
22 Rosemary Sadlier and Fiona Clarke, *The Black Church in Canada* (Toronto: Ontario Black History Society, 2015); Denise Gillard, "The Black Church in Canada," *McMaster Journal of Theology and Ministry* 1 (1998), http://www.mcmaster.ca/mjtm/1-5.htm.
23 Phillip Daniels, dir., *Seeking Salvation* (Toronto: Fandor Films, 2004).
24 David Este, "Early Black Churches in Canada: Sites of Activism and Resistance" (lecture, African Faith-Based Activisms in Canada and the Western World: Law, Politics and Socio-Economics, Osgoode Law School, York University, Toronto, 2016).
25 "Constitution and By-Laws," Union Congregational Church, 1907, Montreal.
26 David Este, "The Black Church as a Social Welfare Institution: Union United Church and the Development of Montreal's Black Community, 1907–1940," *Journal of Black Studies* 35, no. 1 (2004): 3–22.
27 Martha Kuwee Kumsa, Magnus Mfoafo-M'Carthy, Funke Oba, and Sadia Gaasim, "The Contours of Anti-Black Racism: Engaging Anti-Oppression from Embodied Spaces," *CAOS: The Journal of Critical Anti-Oppressive Social Inquiry* 1, no. 1 (2014): 21–38. According to Kumsa et al., anti-Black racism is racism directed specifically against Black people.
28 Este, "Early Black Churches in Canada"; David Este, Christa Sato, and Darcy McKenna, "The Coloured Women's Club of Montreal, 1902–1940: African-Canadian Women Confronting Anti-Black Racism," *Canadian Social Work Review* 34, no. 1 (2017): 81–99.
29 Este, "Black Church."
30 Author David Este possesses a long-standing interest in Black Canadian history, having completed a master's degree in the subject area. Since 2004, he has published a number of articles and book chapters exploring African Canadian contributions to Canadian social welfare history. He was a member of the research team that completed the "Racism, Violence, and Health" study conducted in Halifax, Toronto, and Calgary, which explored the impact of racism on African Canadian men, on their families, and at the community level at each site. See Este, "Black Church"; and Este, Sato, and McKenna, "Coloured Women's Club."
31 The Shiloh Baptist Church was the first "coloured" church and community centre in Alberta. It was founded on 7 July 1910, as a result of existing racial

discrimination practices during the early 1900s in Alberta. The Shiloh Centre for Multicultural Roots is an organization consisting of a distinct group of the descendants of Black pioneer settlers who were part of the roots of Alberta when it was declared a province in 1905. The SCMR was established in 2010 to commemorate the hundredth anniversary of the founding of Shiloh Baptist Church. Its mandate is to blend genres of the arts and other key talents to honour the roots and diverse heritage of Black pioneers and their descendants as well as to educate their youth to empower them for the future.

32 SCMR, "Stories of Pioneer African Canadians," 1.
33 Graham Smith, *Oral History* (Warwick, UK: Institute of Historical Research, Higher Education Academy, 2010), 4.
34 "Principles and Best Practices for Oral History," Oral History Association, adopted October 2009, accessed March 5, 2018, http://www.oralhistory.org/about/principles-and-practices/.
35 Alessandro Portelli, *The Death of Luigi Trastulli and Other Stories: Form and Meaning in Oral History* (Albany: State University of New York Press, 1991).
36 Elaine Batty, "Reflections on the Use of Oral History Techniques in Social Research," *People, Place and Policy* 3, no. 2 (2009): 109–21; Barbara W. Sommer and Mary Kay Quinlan, *The Oral History Manual* (Lanham, MD: AltaMira, 2002).
37 Batty, "Reflections on the Use."
38 Examples of the secondary material include Troper, "Creek Negroes of Oklahoma"; Palmer and Palmer, *Peoples of Alberta*; and Carter and Akili, *Window of Our Memories*.
39 Lioness Ayres, "Semi-Structured Interview," in *The SAGE Encyclopedia of Qualitative Research Methods*, ed. Lisa M. Given (Thousand Oaks, CA: SAGE, 2008), 811.
40 Catherine Marshall and Gretchen B. Rossman, *Designing Qualitative Research* (Thousand Oaks, CA: SAGE, 2016); Michael Patton, *Qualitative Research and Evaluation Methods* (Thousand Oaks, CA: SAGE, 2002).
41 An ethics application form was submitted to the Office of Research Ethics at the University of Lethbridge. The Human Subject Research Committee reviewed the submission and the project was approved on 15 November 2016.
42 Yvonna S. Lincoln and Egon G. Guba, *Naturalistic Inquiry* (Thousand Oaks, CA: SAGE, 1985).
43 David R Thomas, "A General Inductive Approach for Analyzing Qualitative Evaluation Data," *American Journal of Evaluation* 27, no. 2 (2006): 238.
44 Virginia Braun and Victoria Clarke, "Using Thematic Analysis in Psychology," *Qualitative Research in Psychology* 3, no. 2 (2006): 77–101; Clarke and Braun, "Thematic Analysis," *Journal of Positive Psychology* 12, no. 3 (2017): 297–8.

45 Michael F. Doran, "Negro Slaves of the Five Civilized Tribes," *Annals of the Association of American Geographers* 68, no. 3 (1978): 335–50.
46 Doran, "Negro Slaves."
47 Doran, 340.
48 Troper, "Creek Negroes of Oklahoma," 275.
49 Paul Frymer, *Building an American Empire: The Era of Territorial and Political Expansion* (Princeton, NJ: Princeton University Press, 2017); Sarah-Jane Mathieu, *North of the Color Line: Migration and Black Resistance in Canada, 1820–1955* (Chapel Hill: University of North Carolina Press, 2010); Rachel Wolters, "As Migrants and as Immigrants: African American Search for Land and Liberty in the Great Plains, 1890–1912," *Great Plains Quarterly* 34, no. 4 (2015): 335–55.
50 Mathieu, *North of the Color Line*, 23.
51 Frymer, *Building an American Empire*, 170; E.P. McCabe was a former politician from the state of Kansas who promoted migration to Oklahoma. He ventured to the territory in 1890. McCabe became actively involved in the political arena in Oklahoma. His primary goal was to create a "Black" state.
52 Frymer, 170.
53 Wolters, "As Migrants and as Immigrants," 337.
54 Wolters, 337.
55 Lawrence Mays, interview by the authors, Shiloh Baptist Church, Edmonton, February 27, 2017, 7–8. In all references to interviews, page numbers refer to the interview transcript.
56 Doris Mayes, interview by the authors, Shiloh Baptist Church, Edmonton, December 3, 2016, 4.
57 Trudy Taylor, interview by the authors, Shiloh Baptist Church, Edmonton, December 4, 2016, 33–4.
58 Marlene Ruth Jones, interview by the authors, Shiloh Baptist Church, Edmonton, February 27, 2017, 3.
59 Mays interview, 8.
60 Mathieu, *North of the Color Line*.
61 Ralph Taylor, interview by the authors, Shiloh Baptist Church, Edmonton, December 4, 2016, 3–4.
62 Neil Brown, interview by the authors, Shiloh Baptist Church, Edmonton, February 27, 2017, 2.
63 Debbie Leffler, interview by the authors, Shiloh Baptist Church, Edmonton, December 3, 2016, 2.
64 Mathieu, *North of the Color Line*, 335.
65 Troper, "Creek Negroes of Oklahoma," 272–88; Palmer and Palmer, *Peoples of Alberta*; Walker, "African Canadians."
66 Debbie Leffler interview, 2.

67 Jones interview, 4.
68 Daniel Anthony Payne, interview by the authors, Shiloh Baptist Church, Edmonton, February 26, 2017, 3.
69 Debbie Leffler interview, 3.
70 Wolters, "As Migrants and as Immigrants."
71 Debbie Leffler interview, 5.
72 Shiloh Baptist Church, "Celebrate Black History Month," *Special Issue* 1, no. 1 (2018): 6.
73 Payne interview, 4.
74 Palmer and Palmer, "The Black Experience in Alberta," in Palmer and Palmer, *Peoples of Alberta*, 374, 337; Shepard, *Deemed Unsuitable*.
75 Gladys Leffler, interview by the authors, Shiloh Baptist Church, Edmonton, December 3, 2016, 14.
76 Elmer Edwards, interview by the authors, Shiloh Baptist Church, Edmonton, February 26, 2017, 4, 5.
77 Walker, "African Canadians," 147.
78 Ralph Taylor interview, 14–15.
79 Ralph Taylor interview, 11.
80 Jones interview, 7.
81 Neil Brown interview, 5–6.
82 Ralph Taylor interview, 13.
83 Debrah Beaver, interview by the authors, Shiloh Baptist Church, Edmonton, February 26, 2017, 10
84 Letter to the Right Honorable Sir Wilfrid Laurier, April 18, 1911, para. 2, MS209, file 153, City of Edmonton Archives.
85 Mensah, *Black Canadians*, 54.
86 Letter to Laurier, para. 2.
87 Letter to Laurier, para. 3.
88 Eli Yarhi, "Order-in-Council P.C. 1911–1324 – The Proposed Ban on Black Immigration to Canada," *Canadian Encyclopedia*, last modified February 26, 2020, http://www.thecanadianencyclopedia.ca/en/article/order-in-council-pc-1911-1324-the-proposed-ban-on-black-immigration-to-canada/.
89 Yarhi, "Order-in-Council."
90 Mathieu, *North of the Color Line*, 24.
91 Debbie Leffler interview, 26.
92 Ralph Taylor interview, 17.
93 "Shiloh's History," Shiloh Baptist Church, accessed June 16, 2021, https://www.eshilohbc.com/history.
94 Dan Cui and Jennifer Kelly, "'Our Negro Citizens': An Example of Everyday Practices," in *The West and Beyond: New Perspectives on an Imagined Region*, ed. Alvin Finkel, Sarah Carter, and Peter Fortna (Edmonton: Athabasca University Press, 2010), 253–77.

95 Ray Lewis, interview by the authors, Shiloh Baptist Church, Edmonton, February 27, 2017, 27–9.
96 Trudy Taylor interview, 32.
97 Debbie Leffler interview, 29.
98 Shiloh Baptist Church Minutes, August 21, 1921 and October 6, 1935, Shiloh Baptist Church.
99 Marlene Brown, interview by the authors, Shiloh Baptist Church, Edmonton, February 27, 2017, 34.
100 Debbie Leffler interview, 28–9.
101 Debbie Leffler interview, 28.
102 "Constitution," Colored Canadian Industrial Association (CCIA), Edmonton, 1938, in the possession of Deborah Dobbins.
103 Allan Bartley, *The Ku Klux Klan in Canada: A Century of Promoting Racism and Hate in the Peaceful Kingdom* (Halifax: Formac, 2020).
104 Walker, "African Canadians," 147.
105 Geoff McMaster, "Descendant of Alberta's Black Settlers Documents Rich Heritage," *Folio*, February 3, 2017, https://www.ualberta.ca/folio/2017/02/descendant-of-albertas-black-settlers-documents-rich-heritage.html.
106 Cui and Kelly, "'Our Negro Citizens.'"
107 Edmonton Journal, "Western Canada's Oldest Black Baptist Church Turns 100," June 26, 2010, YouTube video, 4:18, https://www.youtube.com/watch?v=c21MYUnZbwc.
108 Jennifer Fong, "Shiloh Celebrates First Century," *Edmonton Journal*, June 26, 2010; Edmonton Journal, "Western Canada's Oldest."

7
Establishing Communities

AMOABA GOODEN

Introduction

"Establishing communities" uncovers, explores, and centres the Black experience in Canada while simultaneously contesting the oft-portrayed myth of Canada as innocent in acts of atrocities against First Nations, African-descended people, and other people(s) of colour. The presence of African-descended people in Canada is long and persistent, beginning as early as the seventeenth century; the first recorded evidence can be traced to Matthieu da Costa, a free person of African descent who served as a French interpreter in the early 1600s.[1] Black Canadian communities are also linked to various other Black populations including but not limited to free and enslaved Blacks in the Maritimes, Jamaican Maroons who arrived in 1796, African Americans who arrived in Nova Scotia after the War of 1812, and Caribbean migrants in the early and late twentieth century. In addition to the above, the presence of African-descended people in Canada is also linked to the institution of slavery, which, although often denied by the Canadian nation, existed for well over two centuries as a labour system. While slavery did not develop on a large scale as it did in the southern United States, it was institutionalized in Canada and shaped conceptions of class and race in the nation; its by-products – anti-Blackness, white privilege, and white power – framed Canada's "deep-rooted delusions of fascist superiority."[2]

As Robin Maynard establishes in her seminal text, *Policing Black Lives: State Violence in Canada from Slavery to the Present*, historical and contemporary racial violence experienced by Black Canadians challenges us to move beyond a rhetoric of a benevolent Canada so that we can unearth a distinct kind of deep-seated Canadian anti-Blackness, born not out of American influences but out of a racialized global colonial architecture.[3] This anti-Blackness forced a particular kind of Black Canadian resistance and resilience, which has been documented by scholars such as Daniel Hill, Bridglal Pachai, John Grant, Joseph Mensah, Amoaba Gooden, Karen Flynn, Charmaine Crawford, and Donald Clairmont. These scholars have traced African-descended communities' historical accounts of settlement, enslavement, betrayals, discrimination, vulnerability, and nascent nation-building.[4] Manifesting in a wide range of racialized phenomena, slavery's afterlife, which impacted the conditions under which Blacks were living, pushed Black Canadians to organize and create institutional and social spaces, some free from the white Canadian gaze, to address issues around freedom, identity, and oppression.

If we are to make meaning of the organizing efforts of Black Canadians we must "dig deep" into their organized social movements and political and social institutions, as well as their daily lives and communities. Yet, if we are going to understand Black Canadian communities in all their complexities, what questions do we ask? Do African-descended people in Canada make up a unified community? And if so, on what basis? What about context? Whose history do we draw on to map the action, strife, perspicacity, and worldliness of these communities? How do collective action and organizing factor into geographical and social spaces? And how do we "step into" and hold Black communities as multifaceted, diverse, and complicated so that we can understand the complexities of their lived experiences and resist romanticizing organizing and collective action? This chapter does not "disregard the diversity and conflict within groups," nor does it assume that the only meaningful struggle occurs within organizations.[5] It does, however, foreground agency, culture, gender, and race as central components in understanding how African-descended people established communities while also recognizing that interlocking systems of imperialism, capitalism, and racialized patriarchy have created unique realities for people of African descent. These conditions make it possible for Black Canadians to converge around a common struggle, primarily against anti-Black racism, through the process of "transversal politics."[6]

There are numerous examples of early institutions that demonstrate that Black Canadians, through individual and collective action, have, from the very beginning, participated as active citizens in the social fabric of Canada by converging or by advocating for social change. Organizations such as the Negro Citizenship Association (NCA) lobbied the Canadian government to change racialized immigration practices, thus fostering a stronger sense of community for Black Canadians and for the country in general as they pushed Canada toward a vision of fairness and equality. With a specific emphasis on Ontario, this chapter explores the organizing efforts of early and contemporary African Canadians. However, while Ontario is highlighted, by no means is this discussion meant to be exhaustive. One of the limitations of much of the available scholarship on Black Canada(s) is its focus on Ontario while downplaying or ignoring Black settlements in geographic locations such as Nova Scotia, Alberta, Saskatchewan, and Quebec. Recognizing the above geographic spaces, but viewing Ontario as an example for understanding diverse Black experiences across Canada, this chapter is sensitive to Rinaldo Walcott's appreciation of organizing by Blacks as a "refiguring of and elaboration" of the Canadian landscape and thus Black Canadianness. In essence, I suggest that it is from a presence of simultaneously belonging and unbelonging that Blacks expounded upon and ultimately transformed notions of Canadianness by organizing and building community.

Anti-Black Sentiments and Black Canada's Early Resistance

In the early 1800s, the majority of African Canadians were concentrated primarily in the Atlantic provinces, particularly Nova Scotia. Ontario's Black population remained relatively small until the early 1800s, when Ontario became a primary destination for American fugitive slaves, influenced in large part by legislated gradual abolition of slavery (in Upper Canada/Ontario) starting in 1793, the ending of slavery in the British Empire in 1833, and the 1793 and 1850 Fugitive Slave Acts in the United States.[7] As a result, Ontario increasingly became a last stop on the Underground Railroad. According to Hill, almost all of the southern states were represented in Ontario by the mid-1800s.[8] Those arriving in Ontario between 1817 and 1822 settled in smaller groups along farmland on the US-Canada border, present-day Windsor and Sandwich Township. Settlement tended to be where other African-descended people had established communities: Colchester, Elgin, Dresden, Dawn, Queen's Bush, Wilberforce, Hamilton, St. Catharines, Chatham, Riley, London, Malden, Amherstburg, Buxton, and Toronto.[9] Chatham and Dresden, in particular, became well known as terminals of the Underground Railroad. By 1860, estimates of Blacks in Ontario ranged from 15,000 to 60,000 and the larger national Black population was estimated to be approximately 110,000.[10]

Immediately upon entering Canada, Black migrants made building institutions a top priority. Some of the Black settlements mentioned above were supported with the help of philanthropy but failed or fell short of expected goals when they were unable to purchase land or assist in meeting even the subsistence needs of the settlers. The failure of these settlements pushed many Black women and men toward urban centres in hopes of securing employment; thus, Black urban communities were found in the cities of Windsor, London, Hamilton, and Toronto. Like Blacks in other parts of the country, Black Ontarians living in rural areas hired themselves out as axemen, servants, washerwomen, and farmhands. In urban areas, Blacks found themselves in menial low-paying jobs – servants, bellboys, porters, shoeshine boys, and general labourers, for example – and in trade skills building on knowledge learned on Southern plantations. These included such skills as barbering, carpentry, and blacksmithing, while a few became shopkeepers and clerks.[11]

As the Black population increased in various parts of the country, so too did the "Negrophobia" on the part of white Canadians, and as a result, systemic discrimination governed the socioeconomic and political lives of most Blacks.[12] Although some Canadians voiced sentiments of equality and justice, these same Canadians demonstrated Canada's pervasive, paternalistic, and racist response to African-descended peoples. For example, the Mission to the Free Colored Population claimed that they saw Blacks as equals yet also maligned Blacks with statements like "the real work of the Mission ... [was] to elevate and instruct" Blacks, who were full of "heathen ignorance."[13] The racism demonstrated by organizations such as the Mission reflected Canada's racist disposition. A hotel clerk in southwestern Ontario argued that "Niggers are a damned nuisance. They keep men of means away from the place. This town has got the name of 'Nigger town' and men of wealth won't come here. I never knew one of them that would not steal, though they never steal anything of the great amount ... [T]hey have been trained to steal in slavery."[14] Certainly, within Black Canadian communities there were differences, tensions, and conflicts, some largely influenced by ideologies of religion, gender, colourism, and class. These tensions notwithstanding, for the most part, it was the racially oppressive climate to which early Black Canadians were responding when they established organizations and institutions.

Pushing to build institutions and organizations in order to create a sense of community, Black Canadians established businesses along with churches, schools, and benevolent and fraternal organizations. The African Baptist Church, founded in Nova Scotia in 1832 by Reverend Richard Preston, served as both a church and a school for people of African descent. In British Columbia, when approximately four hundred Black families migrated from California in 1858, they established restaurants and various other businesses and became landowners.[15] African American immigrant women in Montreal, influenced by the Black women's club movement in the United States, founded the Coloured Women's Club of Montreal (CWCM) in 1902. The club operated as a social service club providing housing, food, and other support to the Black community. The CWCM particularly assisted members of the St. Antoine district (Little Burgundy) community and was also instrumental in forming Montreal's oldest Black church in 1907, the Union Congregational Church (the church later changed it name to Union United Church).[16] And by 1919, Black community members across the nation had established the Universal Negro Improvement Association (UNIA) in cities including Montreal and Toronto. Formed largely by African Caribbean people, the UNIA addressed both local and global issues facing Blacks, including a focus on racial pride, education, and social service needs such as housing, employment, and food, as well as a larger goal of reparations.[17]

In Ontario, the first Black institution on record was the First Baptist Church, founded in Toronto in 1826; in the 1830s, Black residents in Hamilton established St. Paul's African Methodist Episcopal Church. Both were fundamental to the survival of Blacks as they provided a place of respite and solace in times of spiritual and social need.[18] To resist anti-Blackness, other organizations were formed. The True Band Society, a self-help organization with fourteen chapters in Ontario, was founded in 1854 by Amherstburg's Black community. Natasha Henry points out that the organization supported the Black community by encouraging self-help and community building; it assisted with economic development and education and provided financial support for African American refugees from slavery.[19] In addition to the above, Ontario saw the establishment of the Kent County Civil Rights League in 1891, which was formed by Blacks in Chatham; the Canadian League for the Advancement of Coloured People (CLACP), started in 1924; the Coloured Literary Association of Toronto (1920s); the West Indian Progressive Association (1920s); the Toronto United Negro Association (TUNA) (date unknown); the National Unity Association (1948); the Negro Citizenship Association (1951); and the Canadian Negro Women's Association (1951).[20]

TUNA established a financial institution, the Toronto United Negro Association Credit Union, as well as the West Indian Federation (WIF), which served as both a social organization and the first recorded Black restaurant in Toronto. The WIF provided "shelter to the poor West Indian immigrant girls who didn't have anyone or know anyone ... they were school teachers, secretaries, some nurses, and they had ... come in as domestics, to get into Canada."[21] Institutions such as these allowed Blacks to participate in knowledge sharing and provided opportunities to collaborate within translocal and transnational spaces, thus fashioning avenues for democratic participation. For new arrivals, information about where to live, where to find employment, and how to survive in

Canada cultivated a Canadian variation of diasporic and transnational sensibility enhanced by the common ideology around freedom and equality. This knowledge sharing, which was an intentional community-building strategy and practice, allowed Blacks to circumnavigate the socioeconomic and cultural structure of the Canadian nation.

Also a strategy of intentional citizenship, community building was integral to the success of major Black Canadian leaders such as Fleurette Osborne, Donald Moore, and Rosemary Brown, who were leaders in the National Congress of Black Women (NCBW), the NCA, and the British Columbia Association for the Advancement of Coloured People (BCAACP), respectively.[22] The practice of intentional citizenship was also influential in establishing the Home Service Association (HSA), the Black Action Defence Committee (BADC), and, most recently, contemporary organizations like Black Lives Matter-Toronto (BLM-TO). In establishing these institutional/social spaces, African-descended people ultimately strengthened Canadian social structures by creating spaces where Black Canadians came together for leisure, cared for one another, fought for social, civil, and political rights, and carved out spaces away from the white gaze.[23]

Establishing Community Organizations in Ontario

In Ontario at the turn of the twentieth century, the Black population numbered about 8,935. This number remained relatively static until around 1911, when it dropped to about 6,747. Comprised of four distinct Black cultures – central Canadians, Maritimers, African Americans, and Caribbeans – the majority lived in large urban centres such as Windsor and Toronto, although they made up only a small fraction of each city's population.[24] Each group was integral to the community in cities in Ontario, creating institutions that reflected their social and historical realities. This section briefly looks at the characteristics of the different populations that formed a distinct Canadian Blackness that impacted organizing and community building.

The first group of African-descended people in Ontario, the Black central Canadians, traced their heritage back several generations. This population included "Old Torontonians" – families such as the Hubbards, the Abbotts, and others who had migrated from the United States and lived in Toronto and other parts of southwestern Ontario.[25] They represented a mixed socioeconomic class; a small portion of this group had attained some degree of economic success while others were unemployed or working class (working either on the railway or in service positions). They worked inside and outside of their own communities as barbers, tailors, seamstresses, saloon and shopkeepers, shoeshine boys, and maids.[26] The socioeconomic success of some Black Canadians was indicative of the economy's differential impact on Black people depending on their respective class positions, which, in turn, influenced how communities were established. Nevertheless, race and class were mirror images of each other. Many Blacks were denied employment in major companies. Harry Gairey, the Jamaican-born community activist who migrated from Cuba and whose organizing efforts led to Toronto's first anti-discrimination ordinance, recalls that in early Toronto many Blacks, regardless of their place of birth, "couldn't go to Eaton's and ask for a job, or to the Bell Telephone ... it was unheard of to go to a restaurant or a public dance ... you knew you weren't welcome. That's a known fact."[27]

While white supremacy restricted economic opportunities for Blacks in Ontario, these same limitations encouraged some Black men and women to establish businesses to serve the Black community. That is, because Blacks were barred from service in white businesses, they created their own, including barbershops and dry cleaners.[28] In addition to Black-owned businesses, the middle- and upper-class members of this group created social clubs and self-help organizations that set the initial tone for Black life in Ontario. Examples included a Black Masonry fraternity that dates back to 1914 and the Eureka Friendly Club, a benevolent organization that middle-class Black women established prior to World War I to help with the poor and the sick, and the Eureka Lodge #20.[29] Of greater importance, though, was the Home Service Club, which later changed its name to the Home Service Association. Created by the middle and upper echelon of the Black community in Toronto, the HSA was established to service the needs of Black soldiers during World War I and advanced a distinct Black Canadian social movement philosophy based on temperate action and social change.[30]

The second group of African-descended people in Ontario, Black Maritimers were a relatively mobile population as a result of economic hardship. Arriving in Ontario primarily after World War I, they made up a small core of the Black community in Toronto and its surrounding area. Nova Scotian migration to southwestern Ontario was particularly connected to Reverend Cecil Stewart, the Jamaican migrant who organized community members in southwestern Ontario. After visiting Nova Scotia and seeing the disparity and poverty in which Blacks were living, Stewart encouraged Black Nova Scotians to migrate to Toronto, where he felt there were better socioeconomic opportunities, either in the wartime industry or in service positions.[31] Violet Blackman recalls that "Reverend Stewart heard about the conditions of the sick people down in Nova Scotia and made the trip down there ... and he came back, he took up a collection, and he send down to help ... he had as many ladies as he could get a hold of to send down and bring out girls to work in the homes, and while they were here, they sent back and helped their family to come out."[32] It appears that Reverend Stewart established a church in which he temporarily housed migrants from Nova Scotia and ran a soup kitchen for poor Blacks. According to Bromley Armstrong, in 1930 Stewart formally organized the Afro Community Church, which later united with the Black Methodist Episcopal under the British Methodist Episcopal banner. The church acted as a community agency for the poor, providing food and supplies during the Depression era. Apparently quite tenacious, Stewart fought for and was successful in getting his community church to be accepted as a member in the Red Feather Agency. The agency was the precursor to the United Way of Canada, now one of Canada's largest contemporary social service organizations.[33]

The third group of Blacks in Ontario, African Americans, migrated into the province from the early 1900s to the mid-1950s to work in the wartime and postwar industries as cheap labourers, or to work on the railway. By 1924, this group had established the Canadian League for the Advancement of Colored People in numerous Ontario cities. Modelled after the US-based NAACP, its branches were located in Toronto, London, Niagara Falls, and Dresden. National in focus, the league's mandate was to fight Canadian anti-Black sentiments and unify institutions that supported Blacks.[34] The establishment of this organization reflected the ways in which the fight against anti-Blackness in Canada was connected, to some degree, by US and, later on, Caribbean and African formations against oppression.

The final group that made up the African-descended population in Ontario was African Caribbeans, whose presence was noticeable by the early 1900s. Although the Canadian government opposed Black immigration prior to the late 1960s, Blacks were allowed into Canada as domestics and reserve labour during the wars. For example, during both world wars, men from the British colonies of Barbados, Jamaica, Bahamas, British Guiana, Bermuda, Trinidad, and St. Vincent were recruited as soldiers, to work for the railway, or to work in the Maritimes either in the Dominion Steel mill or in the Cape Breton coal mines.[35] When returning white war veterans reclaimed their jobs, many Caribbean people moved to Toronto and Montreal from the Maritime provinces in search of employment. In southwestern Ontario many African Caribbeans entered service positions alongside Blacks from other parts of Canada, including the Maritimes and the United States, serving as bellhops, janitors, barbers, waiters, entertainers, railway porters, maids, and unskilled and semi-skilled labourers.[36]

Caribbean women were also among these early migrants to Canada. Although African Caribbean women began migrating later than men, the overwhelming majority of immigrants coming directly from the Caribbean were women.[37] After they settled, these early Caribbean migrants were joined by others including family members. It should be pointed out that African Caribbean women did not come as dependents of male migrants as is normally assumed in most migration literature on women. For instance, between 1916 and 1928, 238 Caribbean men came directly into Canada from the West Indies; of the 411 women who came into the country during the same period, 329 came to work as domestics and appeared to have settled initially in Montreal before some moved on to Toronto.[38] This differential migration pattern occurred primarily because Canada's gendered and racist labour recruitment programs directed demographic growth to meet the economic needs of the labour market. We can see this clearly by looking at the pattern of immigration history in Canada, which welcomed individual white men and women and families as settlers and limited Black migration to temporary labour needs. There was encouragement of northern and eastern Europeans to populate and open up western Canada from the late 1800s until the early 1960s, while African American, Caribbean, and Canadian-born Black men were recruited by the railway to serve merely as porters, often with restricted immigration status (families were initially denied entrance to Canada). There was also encouragement of British and other white men to fill the professional areas of the labour market while African Caribbean men and women and other people of colour were recruited to serve as temporary domestics or farm labourers, starting as early as 1911 with the domestic workers program. The Farm Workers Program, which began in the late 1960s, targeted Black men and other men of colour, who were brought in as farm labourers on temporary work visas. Jamaican farm workers were recruited by the federal government and started arriving in Ontario in 1966. They were the precursors of a migrant worker program that would eventually include nationals from Barbados and Trinidad and Tobago.[39]

This African Caribbean population, with women outnumbering men, would continue to grow slowly until the late 1960s, when changes in Canadian immigration policy increased migration from the Caribbean dramatically. This population would influence the creation and shaping of Black queer organizations like Blockorama/Blackness Yes! (formed in 1999); community health centres such as Women's Health in Women's Hands (1987) that are geared toward treating and supporting women of colour; and the development of the National Congress of Black Women (1973), a Black feminist association that brought together

African-descended women from across Canada to address common concerns including sexism, racism, underemployment, and a multitude of other issues that Black communities faced. This new Caribbean population would play an influential role in Black political mobilization with a working-class focus by pushing community organizing to consider issues of youth and gender, and by helping to shape a Black Canadian sensibility that would look to the Caribbean, Africa, and the United States to piece together the struggle against racial and class domination. As the discussion below on the UNIA and the HSA will demonstrate, Black Canadians were not a monolithic group. Yet, despite intraracial tensions, they pushed to create spaces, often unsuccessfully, that tried to hold the tension of difference associated with the diversity among Black Canadian voices and within organizations in hopes that they would advance ideals about community establishment, social spaces, and institutions.

Dreaming out of the Dark: UNIA, HSA, and Community Building in Toronto

Shaped by the above migratory groupings, particularly central Canadian and Caribbean-born Black populations, community building in the early to mid-1900s reflected the historical realities and particularities of each group. As mentioned earlier, two organizing projects – the HSA and the UNIA – and their complex interplay demonstrate the multiple ways Black Canadian organizations played a role in shaping social action and community building. Both the HSA and the UNIA, fashioned from the radical imaginations of Black Canadians, illustrate that organizing, as a specific political action, is non-monolithic and has at its core an unwavering awareness of the plight faced by African Canadians. Whether or not these organizations chose to address anti-Black racism and other oppressive restrictions facing the Black community reflected the specific contextual and sociopolitical negotiations around how they desired to contest the Canadian nation.

The Home Service Association (HSA)

The oldest Black social service organization on record in Ontario, the HSA was initially established to meet the needs of Blacks in the Canadian Armed Forces during World War I. Founded in 1913 by African Canadians who were small in number and living in a nation divided along linguistic lines, the HSA closed its doors in 1981.[40] The founding members were older, more financially established, and more conservative than the growing and younger African Caribbean population who were coming from nations where Blacks were the majority.[41] At its outset, the HSA was a cultural and recreational organization of considerable importance among Toronto's Black elite and non-Caribbean community. Membership consisted of African Canadian families such as the Hubbards, the Lightfoots, the Simpsons, and the Thompsons, who represented the Black elite of the day. It appears that in its early years, the HSA was similar to elite social clubs in the United States such as the Bon Ton Society of Washington, DC, and the Blue Vein Society of Nashville.[42] Stanley Grizzle recalls that it was "light-skinned" Black Canadians who controlled the HSA, and in confirming the alienation that dark-skinned Blacks felt from the organization, Gairey states that "at the time the Home Service Association was based on colour. The fairer you are, the more acceptable you become."[43]

Cognizant of its reputation among African Canadians migrants, many of whom were members of the UNIA, and recognizing that its reputation, as described above, hindered its ability to reach an increasingly diverse Black Canadian population, particularly the poor, youth, and the newly arrived African Caribbean migrant, the HSA aggressively worked to change its image. In 1936, it created an outreach program and began to advertise with flyers and posters. Hoping that it could "build a strong body of members who will be vitally interested in helping to bring about better conditions for their people," the association attempted to secure more representation across class and place of birth on its board.[44] In 1942, with the support of the Black community, the HSA raised enough funds to purchase its own building. As a result, Canada's first Black social service agency, focusing on war veterans and providing counselling and recreational activities, was opened. According to an HSA annual report, "All [were] welcome to this Community House."[45] Ownership of a physical space was an important step for community cohesion and organizing. Norman Grizzle recalls that Sunday nights in particular became significant for youth as the site served as a social space, bringing Blacks together from across the city, free from the white gaze. Events were free and included "entertainment, speakers," and food. This, according to Grizzle, lessened "division[s] brought on by cultural differences and place of birth" and ultimately helped to shape a Black Canadian sensibility.[46]

The Universal Negro Improvement Association (UNIA)

Caribbean organizations appeared in Toronto as early as 1919 with the creation of the Coloured Literary Association of Toronto (CLAT) and the West Indian Trading Company. While CLAT concerned itself with settlement and acculturation, the West Indian Trading Company, formed sometime between 1917 and 1920, was an investment company that imported Caribbean produce.[47] However, it was the establishment of the UNIA by young, working-class African Caribbean men and women in Toronto that symbolized how African Caribbean Canadians and first-generation African Caribbean people conceptualized and organized themselves both culturally and politically. Henry suggests that the large number of Black Caribbean people who formed the UNIA in Toronto and Montreal had re-migrated from Nova Scotia, where they had experienced a wide-ranging and disparaging form of anti-Black discrimination that had radicalized their approach to fighting racism.[48]

The UNIA was one of the first organized movements to challenge both the church and its pastoral leadership in the Canadian Black community and the conservative political beliefs of some Black Canadians. Later, organizations such as the Canadian League for the Advancement of Coloured People (1924) and Reverend Stewart's Afro Community Church (1936–7) would also challenge established Black conservative political positions. As an international organization, the UNIA used its transnational and Pan-African social and political philosophy to articulate the boundlessness of the African diaspora. Gender inclusive, the UNIA gave people of African descent "incentive[s] and taught [them to] love [their] Black skin."[49] In Dionne Brand's *No Burden to Carry: Narratives of Black Women in Ontario*, Violet Blackman and Gwen Johnston, both working-class African Canadian women, recall that the UNIA was "sort of a second home for us." Blackman, an officer of the UNIA, noted that "I was in everything in the UNIA ... I was the chairlady, anything I did had to go to the heads ... I was responsible for the things that goes on and for the money that [was] being made."[50]

Scholars such as Daniel Hill report that members of the UNIA thought Marcus Garvey brought a new "aggressiveness to the British Negro. He represented the first real leadership the Negro had seen, and he gave Negroes a social and economic consciousness they had never known ... Garvey showed ... that all Negroes should unite to fight [oppression]."[51] Utilizing Garvey's pan-African framework, the UNIA organized, advocated, and fundraised in order to secure enough capital to purchase a building under the UNIA banner as early as 1927, twenty years before the Home Service Association acquired its own building.

From its onset, the UNIA served as a diasporic secular space. Armstrong also recalls that "the UNIA was not just a place for its members to hold their meetings, it was a community center where Black adults and children went to socialize, attend debates, danced, and played music. In its edifice, leaders and members representing many different organizations gathered to plan the future direction of their community. When new arrivals and visitors to the city needed a place to go, they were referred to the UNIA ... All roads in the community led to ... the UNIA."[52] Thursday nights in particular were exceptional because the community came together to release the cares of the week; "there'd be a dance [because] that was the night the domestics got off ... you never cared about Friday morning. It was such a good time; it was dancing and meeting friends, and romance bloomed from there." Johnston notes that even though it was relatively popular "a lot of the church people didn't follow the UNIA," confirming the tension between some church and UNIA members.[53]

While the HSA and the UNIA were perhaps the most established organizations of the time, as discussed above, many other organizations were created prior to 1950. However, none of them, including the UNIA and HSA, functioned as lobbying agencies/organizations – that is, none operated as a grievance agency, a place where African-descended people could get legal support against the daily racism they were facing; in addition, none provided any educational or legislative support for Blacks. Yet, both the HSA and the UNIA were radical organizations for their time. They strategized and established concrete institutionalized structures from which people of African descent could carve out space in a hostile environment. Located in geographical areas where the majority of Blacks lived, the organizations were generally accessible and appeared to be supported by members of the Black community. And although initially exclusive, the HSA, through its own reflexive praxis, became more open and welcoming. However, it did remain a more conservative space than the UNIA, often remaining silent on issues of racism. For example, the HSA refused to join the NCA when it lobbied for changes to Canada's racialized immigration policy. And in 1955, when Daniel Braithwaite led the fight to ban the children's book *Little Black Sambo* from being used by the Toronto District School Board, the HSA refused to participate.[54] Still, both organizations were sites of resistance and community; they provided space for members of the Black community to celebrate, relax, and learn free from the white gaze.

The Winds of Change

In the decade preceding World War II, there was a small but significant settlement of Blacks in parts of southwestern Ontario. While there were no legal delimitations in terms of Black districts or any formal segregation of Blacks in residential areas, de facto segregation existed although some of this can be attributed to racial and cultural affinity. These areas attracted new Black immigrants as well as other immigrants because housing was relatively inexpensive. In Toronto, the majority of Blacks lived in the poorest areas: in particular, the west central district, bounded by Sherbourne and Bloor Streets, Lansdowne Avenue, and the waterfront (what is downtown Toronto today). Specific areas included (1) Cabbage Town, (2) along Queen and Adelaide Streets, and (3) on University Avenue, as well as on Sullivan, Lippincott, Augusta, Leonard, and Wales Streets.[55] Moreover, Blacks continued to be denied accommodation at certain hotels, and refusal of service was common at restaurants, theatres, recreational facilities, and other public places. Blacks remained restricted to low-wage positions as porters or in domestic service with little or no job security and very few opportunities for advancement.

It was not until about five years after World War II, when the Canadian economy needed migrant labour, that there was a significant increase in Ontario's Black population, the majority coming from the Caribbean.[56] This increase transformed southwestern Ontario racially and culturally and changed race relations in the province forever. In addition, this population would increase the capacity building of Black institutions, including the HSA and the UNIA, and shape the nature and function of these Black organizations. By the early 1950s, as Henry reports, there were approximately thirty-five Black organizations on record with the majority functioning primarily as social clubs and self-help organizations.[57]

Diasporic Sensibilities and Ambiguities

The increase in Ontario's Black population introduced new political and cultural temporalities that pried open notions of Blackness, forcing community organizing to focus, to varying degrees, on gender, class, and sexual politics. For example, the Canadian Negro Women's Association (CANEWA) – which was similar to, yet different from, the US-based National Association of Colored Women (NACW) – emerged around 1951 in Toronto from a pre-existing group called the Dilettantes, a social club made up primarily of Black, middle-class, Canadian-born (largely first-generation African Caribbean and long-established African Canadian) women. The CANEWA articulated a robust African Canadian diasporic sensibility that shaped later generations and various organizations, particularly as the number of Black citizens increased. Concerned with racial uplift and the anti-Black racism that African Canadian women, men, and children were experiencing, the CANEWA wanted "to become aware of, appreciate, and further the merits of the Canadian Negro."[58] As such, it established scholarships and bursaries for needy students and organized the first Canadian Negro History Week in 1967.

In addition, the CANEWA worked to establish an inclusive organization to alleviate the tensions around class, religion, and place of birth that persisted between Caribbean-born and Canadian-born Blacks. Working under the premise of diasporic sensibility, the CANEWA organized a Calypso Carnival in 1952 to bring various African Caribbean and African Canadian groups together to recognize and celebrate Africa and the Caribbean. There had been limited contact between long-established African Canadians and (recent) African Caribbean migrants, especially women, since the latter worked mainly as domestics or in other service positions and had little time to join social clubs or self-help organizations frequented by the middle class. The Calypso Carnival, which ran until 1964, offered Black Canadians the opportunity to celebrate and honour their cultural differences and similarities. The diasporic Calypso Carnival was the forerunner of the now world-famous Caribana and serves as an example of the ways in which the frameworks of Blackness in the Canadian context were expanding.[59] In resisting fixed notions of Canadian identity, the CANEWA was in actuality opening up possibilities of cultural hybridity in Black community building; that is, it saw community as inclusive and transnational.

This diasporic sensibility, which shaped the outlook, action, and vision of community, was also held by Black students, many of whom started arriving in Canada from the Caribbean on temporary visas during the 1920s. Their numbers increased dramatically after World War II.[60] According to Althea Prince, African Caribbean students in particular brought "a new sense of urgency to the work to be done at the level of community" as they realized that the "work to be done was building and maintaining community." She recalls that these students, including her, "met at house parties, in Caribbean nightclubs which sprang up around the city, and at community events. We formed bonds of friendship which helped somewhat to heal the wounds of racism."[61] This level of consciousness and action ushered in unprecedented social action and development in the Black community during the late 1960s and '70s.

In Toronto, Black students, regardless of place of birth, at York University, the University of Toronto (U of T), and Ryerson Polytechnic Institution were instrumental in community-building activities that took place during this time.[62] Horace Campbell, an African Caribbean graduate student at U of T, is credited for much of the initial work among the student population in the late 1960s and early '70s.[63] He was instrumental in the creation of the U of T Black Students' Union and, when an undergraduate at York University, the Black People's Movement at that institution. Both organizations were politically, socially, and culturally active in the wider Black community. The students marched and demonstrated against the "atrocities perpetrated against African peoples" in Canada, feeling charged with a "political mission and responsibility for community."⁶⁴

Such was the case in Montreal with the 1969 student uprising at Sir George Williams University (now Concordia University) as students reacted to the anti-Black racism that some students, particularly those from the Caribbean, were facing. A white faculty member, Perry Anderson, had failed the majority of African Caribbean students in his class the previous year. Between 29 January and 12 February 1969, approximately two hundred students (African Caribbean, African Canadian, and white allies) occupied the computer centre, inconveniencing businesses in downtown Montreal in hopes that the university would be pressured to respond; instead the police were called in to remove the students. A riot squad with tear gas, clubs, and shields entered the centre and forced the students out. Over $2 million worth of damages to buildings and equipment resulted. Ninety-six students (forty-five of whom were Black) were arrested, charged, and jailed. One of the students arrested was Anne Cools, who would later become the first Black senator in Canada. Black students were singled out as leaders and expelled from the university. Three African Caribbean students were deported after serving time in prison.⁶⁵

In the wake of increased student activism across Canada, but particularly the 1969 student uprising in Montreal, the National Black Coalition of Canada (NBCC) was established not only to reconcile what many saw as a lack of Black leadership in Canada, but also to address the schisms between Caribbean-born Blacks and African Canadians, and the inability of Black people to mobilize and shape the welfare of Blacks throughout the nation.⁶⁶ While Black institution building was well underway in Canada, as demonstrated by the number of organizations noted above, there were no groups that organized around race and addressed anti-Black racism at the national level. The NBCC was born to address this dearth. According to Jean Augustine, the vision of the NBCC "was to ... advocate on behalf of the concerns of Black people right across Canada ... We face racism, we have difficulties in empowerment, we have difficulties with our young people; we have challenges. Whether you're in Halifax ... Calgary ... Vancouver or Toronto; we found that our situations were the same and we felt that a national organization will give us an opportunity to bring our voices together."⁶⁷ Focusing on four major areas – human and civil rights, legal aid and defence, education, and immigration – the NBCC's three major aims and objectives were to create an environment in which Black Canadians could achieve their fullest potential, to ensure Black people were able to participate fully in shaping their society socially, politically, and economically, and to eradicate all forms of racism and discrimination.[68] The number of organizations that joined immediately – twenty-seven from across Canada, including the Jamaican Canadian Association in Toronto – suggests that significant institution building was well underway in 1969. However, it also suggests a recognition that place of birth and social service work could not be the main underpinnings of community building. An organization such as the NBCC, structured around race and all of its vestiges, was desired. By the early 1970s, over eighty organizations across the nation were members, with the largest numbers coming from Ontario.[69]

However, from its inauguration, members raised concerns over a lack of resources and tensions around the NBCC's sustainability and viability. In 1969 *Contrast*, the principal community-based Black newspaper at that time, reported, "While the manner of its inception leaves much to be desired in the minds of thinking people it is still a beginning. The possibilities of its usefulness and fidelity to our interests cannot be discredited ... there has been enough of suspicion and warring among ourselves as to each other's motives ... let us support each other's effort."[70] The NBCC ultimately failed not only for the reasons noted above, but also because it was an organization run primarily by middle-aged men and failed to articulate an African Canadian diasporic position on classism, anti-Black racism, and sexism. This fundamental failure, in addition to internal tension, conflict, and its reliance on government grants – it received over $173,000 from the federal government between 1978 and 1982 – fuelled its collapse in the mid-1980s.[71]

Building Alliances

Fighting the male leadership of the NBCC and embodying the diasporic sensibility that was held by students and that produced the Calypso Carnival, the CANEWA organized Canada's first national Black women's conference in 1973; the outcome of the conference was the National Congress of Black Women of Canada (NCBW).[72] Passing resolutions that highlighted female immigration, education, and issues facing single parents and seniors, the organization positioned itself to be a lobby group. For example, its resolution on immigration pushed for a reformation of immigration policies. In addition, the congress advocated for anti-racism training for teachers.[73] By 1980, NCBW had become a coalition of twenty-three chapters across Canada and consisted of members from both the working and middle classes. Diasporic and pan-African in nature, the NCBW was strongly committed to transformation of the ways in which the Black community organized unity, evident in its 1990 assertion that Black collective action must include concerns of Black lesbians.⁷⁴

The NCBW was dreaming of and organizing for new political and social relationships and new attitudes toward community. Today, community activists such as Angela Robertson and Debbie Douglas share the same dream as they organize and assist men and women in pooling resources (emotional and social capital) to build alliances and meet personal, family, social, political, and economic challenges. They interface with the social structure of Canada and try to buffer the social trauma that Black Canadians face. They fight for systemic change by addressing matters of immigration, gender, sexuality, health, childcare, violence against women, education, employment, and citizenship rights. Robertson, for example, is one of the co-founders of Blockorama/Blackness Yes!, a celebration of Black Pride for the queer community, while Douglas, the executive director of the Ontario Council of Agencies Serving Immigrants, lobbies the Canadian government on behalf of racialized individuals from all over the world.⁷⁵

Movements like Black Lives Matter–Toronto also exhibit the diasporic sensibility of Douglas and Robertson and are continuities of community-building and organizing efforts of Black Canadians that, in turn, are part of larger global national-liberation movements. The killing of Michael Brown in Ferguson, Missouri, was the catalyst for the BLM movement in the United States. The Black women who started the movement and created the hashtag #BlackLivesMatter – Patrisse Cullors, Opal Tometi, and Alicia Garza – articulate that an understanding of state-sanctioned violence was central to the movement.⁷⁶ Young Black Canadians connected the killing of Brown to racially motivated murders of Black Canadians like Jermaine Carby and many other Blacks and persons of colour. The connection that African Canadians have with one another and with Blacks in other places speaks to the complexity of Black lives. The slogan of BLM-TO in the fall of 2014 – From Toronto to Ferguson: Black Lives Matter – was fuelled by an African diasporic understanding of global violence and by deep historical grievances. Black Canadians are assaulted by anti-Black racism and state-sanctioned violence in a never-ending cycle of stop and frisk, arrests, harassments, and death.⁷⁷ BLM-TO organizes advocacy and support for the Black and Brown victims of carding and state-sanctioned violence, for Black trans bodies, and for all those who have lost their lives to white supremacy. As indicated earlier, it is from this presence (of simultaneously belonging and unbelonging) that Blacks have acted to transform notions of Blackness and Canadianness. As demonstrated by their demands, BLM-TO is able to express multiple intersecting identities (gay, straight, African Canadian), stand with Indigenous people and people of colour, and articulate a broader critique that places state violence within the interlocking systems of imperialism, capitalism, and patriarchy.[78]

With clear African diasporic strategies, BLM-TO draws strength from a cross-border connection with Ferguson, Baltimore, New York, and other places across the globe. The organization stood with Indigenous populations to protest the Dakota Pipeline at Standing Rock in the United States; halted the 2016 Toronto Pride parade until Pride Toronto agreed to multiple demands, including the removal of the Toronto Police from future parades; and continues to participate in numerous campaigns aimed at ending anti-Black oppression globally.[79] Most recently, Blacks in the United States have utilized BLM-TO's strategy and have asked their local Pride parade organizers to discontinue police booths/floats and to have more Black queer and trans participation.[80] Members of the BLM group in New York have indicated that "we stand in full solidarity with our siblings of the Toronto Chapter of #BlackLivesMatter. We have been inspired by the strategic moves made by the TO team, including the chapter's decision not to attend PRIDE this year in order to spotlight the reality of anti-Blackness in all areas of society."[81]

The social force that emerges out of BLM-TO's reconnection with Blacks in other places is a reminder that Black communities and identities are negotiated and conceptualized within local and transnational spaces.[82] Perhaps their actions can serve as a catalyst for thinking of the ways in which Black Canadianness is and has always been a part of the larger African diaspora.

Conclusion

At the end of slavery in the British Empire (1833), the Black Canadian community was firmly entrenched, yet continued to live, in a state of paradox.[83] Anti-Blackness was so deeply embedded in the social and economic bedrock of the Canadian nation that, while legally free, Blacks experienced "racial discrimination ... in virtually every aspect of their social and economic lives."[84] In their struggle against continued oppression, and born out of their racialized circumstances, African Canadians held on to dreams of freedom and full citizenship. These dreams were formed by and intersected with ideals of social justice, freedom, resistance, and inequality and set the parameters by which Blacks organized communities and created institutions. Within Black Canadian organizing, there were differences, tensions, and conflicts, some largely influenced by ideologies of religion, gender, and class. As such, the organizations were not monolithic – rather, they were full of contradictions that emerged as Black Canadians attempted to address specificities and commonalities in the Black struggle for social change. Yet these tensions were essential in helping some organizations identify, articulate, and act on the structural basis of oppression. These frictions facilitated new ways of thinking and organizing, and, ultimately, they either ended or moved organizations forward.

Current movements such as BLM-TO are patterns of continuities between the past and the present; such movements are the result of the afterlife of slavery and a simultaneous recognition that the legacy of colonialism impacts Black lives in vicious ways. Black Canadians use organizing, in and of itself, and the building of organizations as a social force in their demand for socioeconomic and political rights and in their articulation of ways that the Canadian nation can move forward and transform. Some organizations, such as the HSA and the UNIA, provided African Canadians with a sense of trust, solidarity, and sometimes nostalgia that helped solidify collective effort, while history, racial solidarity, and place of birth were factors that enabled these organizations to thrive. Yet other groups, such as the CANEWA, university students like Horace Campbell, the Congress of Black Women, and BLM-TO, expanded on and introduced other ways of organizing and building community. While Black Canadian organizing was not always seamless and coherent, African Canadians have transposed and utilized global political strategies, melding them into an organic whole, despite contradictions and tensions. They have negotiated, discarded, and combined strategies and approaches so that their communities remain works in progress. In doing so, they have emphasized that creating home is as much about fracture as it is about consistency and collective negotiation.[85] In the process, they reconfigure the possibility of the Canadian nation for Black people.

NOTES

1 Robin W. Winks, *The Blacks in Canada: A History*, 2nd ed. (Montreal and Kingston: McGill-Queen's University Press, 1997), 1; Daniel Hill, *The Freedom-Seekers: Blacks in Early Canada* (Agincourt, ON: Book Society of Canada, 1981), 3; Ken Alexander and Avis Glaze, *Towards Freedom: The African Canadian Experience* (Toronto: Umbrella, 1996), 38. Various scholars have noted that when da Costa arrived with the French traders in Nova Scotia, he was fluent in French, Spanish, and Mi'kmaq. The brief history of Matthieu da Costa is often quoted in numerous texts, articles, papers, and so forth on Black history in Canada but with no primary source referenced. Robin Winks points researchers to the *Dictionary of Canadian Biography*

(Toronto, 1966), 452, and other sources in turn point to Winks or use no reference at all. "Mathieu de Coste" is used, as is "Mattieu da Costa." Most suggest that da Costa was not a "permanent resident."

2 Stanley B. Ryerson, *The Founding of Canada: Beginnings to 1815* (Toronto: Progress Books, 1963), 238.

3 See Robin Maynard, *Policing Black Lives: State Violence in Canada from Slavery to the Present* (Halifax: Fernwood, 2017), chap. 1.

4 See, for example, Daniel Hill, "Negroes in Toronto – A Sociological Study of a Minority Group" (PhD diss., University of Toronto, 1960); Bridglal Pachai, *Beneath the Clouds of the Promised Land: The Survival of Nova Scotia's Blacks* (Halifax: Black Educators Association of Nova Scotia, 1990), 30; John Grant. *The Immigration and Settlement of the Black Refugees of the War of 1812 in Nova Scotia and New Brunswick* (Dartmouth, NS: Black Cultural Center, 1990), 96; Joseph Mensah, *Black Canadians: History, Experiences, Social Conditions* (Halifax: Fernwood, 2002), chap. 1; Amoaba Gooden, "'Betta Must Come': African Caribbean Migrants in Canada: Migration, Community Building and Cultural Legacies" (PhD diss., Temple University, 2005); and Charmaine Crawford, Karen Flynn, and Amoaba Gooden, "Constructing Black Canada," *Southern Journal of Canadian Studies* 5, no. 1 (2012): 8.

5 Robin Kelly, *Race Rebels: Culture, Politics, and the Black Working Class* (New York: Free Press, 1994), 4.

6 According to Patricia Hill Collins, within the assumptions of transversalism, participants bring with them a "rooting" in their own particular group histories but at the same time realize that in order to engage in dialogue across multiple markers of difference, they must "shift" from their own centres. See Hill Collins, *Black Feminist Thought: Knowledge Consciousness, and the Politics of Empowerment*, 2nd ed. (New York: Routledge, 2000), PDF, 245, https://uniteyouthdublin.files.wordpress.com/2015/01/black-feminist-though-by-patricia-hill-collins.pdf.

7 The 1793 antislavery bill created the idea of an ideological split between a free Canada and a slave-oppressive United States. It was enacted after an enslaved young African woman by the name of Chloe Cooley from Queenstown was bound and sold across the Niagara River to the United States. Outraged, the abolitionist community petitioned the government of Upper Canada. A compromise was established, entitled *An Act to Prevent the Further Introduction of Slaves and to Limit the Term of Enforced Servitude within this Province* (Ontario). Contrary to popular belief, this act did not ban slavery; in fact, it left the slave-owning legislators unaffected. The act freed the children of enslaved Africans only after they reached the age of twenty-five. This set the course for the coming of thousands of African Americans escaping slavery in the American South. See Alexander and Glaze, *Towards*

Freedom, 52; and Daniel Hill, "Black History in Early Toronto," *Polyphony* 6 no. 1 (1984): 28–30.

8 Hill reports that many of the families who settled in early Toronto brought with them money to purchase homes. They were from Virginia, where they had been working primarily in service positions as waiters, barbers, cooks, or servants. Hill acquired this information from the family records of W.R. Abbot. See Hill, "Negroes in Toronto," 76.

9 Charles L. Blockson, *The Underground Railroad* (New York: Prentice Hall, 1987), 289.

10 Samuel Gridley Howe, *The Refugees from Slavery in Canada West. Report to the Freedmen's Inquiry Commission, by SG Howe* (Boston: Wright & Potter, 1864), 17; see also Ida Cecil Greaves, *The Negro in Canada* (Montreal: Packet-Times Press for the Department of Economics and Political Science, McGill University, 1930), 44; Jason H. Silverman, *Unwelcome Guests: Canada West's Response to American Fugitives Slaves, 1800–1865* (Millwood, NY: Associated Faculty Press, 1985), 1; and Hill, "Negroes in Toronto," 36. Although early historians generally argued that the majority of enslaved African Americans who escaped were men, the first Upper Canada census (1851) counted 2,502 Black males and 2,167 Black females, a relatively small gender difference.

11 Wilbur Henry Siebert, *The Underground Railroad from Slavery to Freedom* (New York: Macmillan, 1968), 36.

12 "Negrophobia" was first used by Jason Silverman to imply the irrational fear of Black people by whites. Jason H. Silverman, *Unwelcome Guest: Canada West's Response to Black Fugitive Slaves, 1800–1865* (New York: Associated Faculty Press, 1985), 1.

13 M.M. Dillion, "Report of Rev. M.M. Dillon, Superintendent of the Mission," in *Mission to the Free Colored Population in Canada*, Occasional Paper No. 4, West London Branch of the Colonial Church and School Society, October 1855, 4, https://www.canadiana.ca/view/oocihm.55469/1?r=0&s=1; see also Colonial and Continental Church Society, "The Report of the Mission to the Coloured Population in Canada," Fugitive Slave Mission, Colonial and Continental Church Society, 1860, 5.

14 Peter C. Ripley, *Black Abolitionist Papers*, vol. 2, *Canada, 1830–1865* (Chapel Hill: University of North Carolina Press, 1987), 119.

15 "The Decommissioning of 823 Jackson Avenue, Once the African Methodist Episcopal Fountain Chapel," *Hogan's Alley Memorial Project* (blog), November 1, 2008, http://hogansalleyproject.blogspot.com/2008/11/on-26-october-2008-basel-hakka-lutheran.html.

16 "The Coloured Women's Club," Coloured Women's Club, last updated March 15, 2005, https://colouredwomensclub.tripod.com; see also David Austin, "All Roads Led to Montreal: Black Power, the Caribbean, and the

Black Radical Tradition in Canada," *Journal of African American History* 92, no. 4 (2007): 516–39.
17 Carla Marano, "'Rising Strongly and Rapidly': The Universal Negro Improvement Association in Canada, 1919–1940," *Canadian Historical Review* 91, no. 2 (2010): 233–59; Keith S. Henry, *Black Politics in Toronto since World War I* (Toronto: Multicultural History Society of Ontario, 1981), 18–19.
18 Hill, "Negroes in Toronto," 77–8.
19 Natasha L. Henry, *Emancipation Day: Celebrating Freedom in Canada* (Toronto: Dundurn, 2010), Kindle, 678–83.
20 A lack of historical records prevents an accurate accounting of dates for some of these organizations. For the only limited documentary evidence on the Toronto United Negro Association (TUNA), see Bromley L. Armstrong with Sheldon Taylor, *Bromley, Tireless Champion of Just Causes: Memoirs of Bromley L. Armstrong* (Pickering, ON: Vitabu, 2000), 38. TUNA endeavoured toward a broader membership base by attempting to incorporate Caribbean and Canadian members in its organization. Armstrong joined the organization in 1948 and recalls that it was established and headed primarily by middle-class African Caribbean people, although membership was inclusive of the general Black Toronto community. He reports that many of the members had migrated to Toronto in the prewar years and "through organizational development and a spirit of voluntarism, they had taken proactive roles in the helping to build their community." The organization created a Credit Union in the 1940s, and although Armstrong did not join the organization until after inception, by 1955, he was elected president.
21 Harry Gairey, *A Black Man's Toronto, 1914–1980: Reminiscences of Harry Gairey*, ed. Donna Hill (Toronto: Multicultural History Society of Ontario, 1981), 38–9.
22 Fleurette Osborn was the first president of the National Congress of Black Women and advocated on the behalf of women nationally and internationally. She migrated to Montreal from Barbados in 1960, and as a student at Sir George Williams University, she became an activist and worked with domestic Caribbean workers. For more on Osborn, see Adrienne Shadd, *The Journey from Tollgate to Parkway: African Canadians in Hamilton* (Toronto: Dundurn, 2010), 279–81; and Marcia Wharton-Zaretsky, "Black Woman Activists in Toronto from 1950 to 1990" (PhD diss., Ontario Institute for Studies in Education, University of Toronto, 1999), chap. 4. Donald Moore, also an immigrant from Barbados, was chair of the NCA. Moore migrated to Montreal and then Toronto via New York in the early 1900s. Over a three-year period, Moore, the NCA, and various other community activists organized and lobbied the local, provincial, and federal governments for changes to the Immigration Act. A thirty-five-member

delegation, including members of the Brotherhood of Sleeping Car Porters, travelled to Ottawa in 1954 to press for changes to the racist immigration policy. They urged immigration officials to use the NCA as an intermediary between persons held for deportation and immigration, and they advocated on behalf of individuals who faced difficulty or who were held awaiting deportation. In addition, the NCA recognized the vulnerable position Black women were placed in and lobbied for female guards. In response to the Canadian labour shortage of nurses, the organization acted as an advocate, securing jobs prior to the nurses' arrival, obtaining job letters for immigration officials, and even transporting Caribbean nurses to areas outside of Toronto once they arrived in the city. For more on Moore, see Donald Moore and Samuel Selvon, *Don Moore: An Autobiography* (Toronto: Williams-Wallace, 1985). Rosemary Brown was a feminist British Columbian activist who arrived via Montreal. Born in Jamaica, she was the first Black woman in Canada to be elected to a provincial legislature. She was also the first Black woman to run for leadership of a Canadian federal political party. She held the Order of Canada and the Order of British Columbia. Brown established the Vancouver Status of Women in 1972 and was an active member of the British Columbia Association for the Advancement of Coloured People.

23 For more information on the above organizations, see Gooden, "Betta Must Come," chap. 4; Amoaba Gooden, "African Canadian Leadership: Pan-Africanism, Transnationality, and Community Organizing," in *African Canadian Leadership: Continuity, Transition, and Transformation*, ed. Tamari Kitossa, Erica S. Lawson, and Philip S.S. Howard (Toronto: University of Toronto Press, 2019), 111–46.

24 See Keith Henry's discussion in *Black Politics in Toronto*. Greaves's study in 1930 also mapped the entire Black Canadian population; she classified Blacks in Canada in three categories (US, Canadian, and West Indians). She did not differentiate among Canadian Blacks (Maritimers vs. Blacks from Ontario or Quebec). See Greaves, *The Negro in Canada*, 46. Traditionally, Blacks from the Maritimes lived in the rural parts of the province and Blacks in Ontario/Quebec lived in the urban areas of the province. The terms "Caribbean" and "West Indian" are used here interchangeably to refer to people of African descent from the Caribbean. While the term "Caribbean" is preferred by the author, the term "West Indian" is used here in its historical context and to recognize the time period.

25 For more about "Old Torontonians," see Henry, *Black Politics in Toronto*, 6–9; see also Daniel Hill, "Black History in Early Toronto," 28–30; and Hill, "Negroes in Toronto, 1793–1865," Ontario Historical Society, 1963, 73–91.

26 Henry suggests that Black Toronto in the early 1900s was "marked by a solid institutional life and a degree of economic comfort and civic integration."

Many of the individuals who settled in Toronto brought money with them when they migrated to Canada. They were able to purchase real estate and set up various businesses in addition to social institutions and organizations. Henry, *Black Politics in Toronto*, 3. See also Hill, "Black History in Early Toronto," 28–30; "Negroes in Toronto, 1793–1865"; and Agnes Calliste, "Sleeping Car Porters in Canada: An Ethnically Submerged Split Labour Market," *Canadian Ethnic Studies/Etudes Ethniques au Canada* 19, no. 1 (1987): 2–3. For a history of the railway porters' union in Canada, see Stanley G. Grizzle, *My Name's Not George: Story of the Brotherhood of Sleeping Car Porters: Personal Reminiscences of Stanley G. Grizzle* (Toronto: Umbrella, 1998); and Ray Lewis, as told to John Cooper, *Shadow Running: Canadian Railway Porter and Olympic Athlete* (Toronto: Umbrella, 1998). See also Selwyn Jacob, dir., *The Road Taken* (National Film Board of Canada, 1996), https://www.nfb.ca/film/road_taken/; and Greaves, *The Negro in Canada*.

27 Harry Gairey, *A Black Man's Toronto, 1914–1980: Reminiscences of Harry Gairey*, ed. Donna Hill (Toronto: Multicultural History Society of Ontario, 1981), 9.

28 The Black churches at the time included the British Methodist Episcopal, the African Methodist, and the First Baptist Church.

29 Armstrong and Taylor, *Bromley*, 39.

30 See Edythe McGruder, *History of Home Service Association*, University of Toronto, Faculty of Social Work, Toronto, 1939; see also Gairey, *A Black Man's Toronto*.

31 Henry, *Black Politics in Toronto*, 5. Reverend Stewart appears frequently in memories and narratives of the Black experience in Toronto.

32 See Violet Blackman's interview in Dionne Brand, *No Burden to Carry: Narratives of Black Working Women in Ontario, 1920s to 1950s* (Toronto: Women's Press, 1991), 43–4.

33 Gairey (*A Black Man's Toronto*, 11) also mentions Stewart's brother who went to Hamilton, Ontario, where a church was named after him, the Stewart Memorial Church. We also find mention of Stewart's brother in Lewis, *Shadow Running*, 17. Lewis reports that the "Stewart Memorial church was one of the vital cornerstones of our family life."

34 Agnes Calliste, "The Influence of the Civil Rights and Black Power Movement in Canada," *Race, Gender & Class* 2, no. 3 (1995): 123.

35 Dwaine Plaza, "Migration and Adjustment to Canada: Pursuing the Mobility Dream, 1900–1998," *Society of Caribbean Studies Annual Conference Papers*, ed. Sandra Courtman, vol. 3 (2002): 4–6. The Caribbean migrants arriving on the Canadian east coast were primarily from Barbados; see also Grizzle, *My Name's Not George*, 29.

36 James W. St. G. Walker, *The West Indians in Canada* (Ottawa: Canadian Historical Association, 1984), 11.

37 The term "direct" is used particularly in this early period because many West Indian men went to work in England, the United States, or the Maritimes prior to their arrival in Ontario. This could have been because educated Black men from the Caribbean who wanted to come to Toronto and work at their vocation rather than on the rails had a difficult time being accepted directly from the West Indies. Many, like Gairey, travelled to the United States first. Gairey, *A Black Man's Toronto*, 5.
38 Greaves, *The Negro in Canada*, 56.
39 Indira Ganaselall, "Technology Transfer among Caribbean Seasonal Farm Workers from Ontario Farms into the Caribbean" (MA thesis, University of Guelph, 1992), 19; see also Robert Gerald Cecil and G. Edward Ebanks, "The Caribbean Migrant Farm Worker Programme in Ontario: Seasonal Expansion of West Indian Economic Spaces," *International Migration* 30, no. 1 (1992): 19.
40 McGruder, *History of Home Service Association*, 2; see also William Manning, *My Name Is Eva: A Biography of Eva Smith* (Toronto: Natural Heritage, 1996), 104.
41 Gairey, *A Black Man's Toronto*, 14; see also Leonard Johnston, interviewed by Huguette A. Casimir, Ontario, 1978, Multicultural Society of Ontario.
42 Kathy Russell, Midge Wilson, and Ronald Hall, *The Colour Complex: The Politics of Colour among African Americans* (New York: Anchor, 1992), 24–5.
43 Gairey, *A Black Man's Toronto*, 14.
44 McGruder, *History of Home Service Association*, 10.
45 Winks, *Blacks in Canada*, 422; See also Home Service Association annual reports, 1943, Toronto Public Library.
46 Norman Grizzle, interview by Donna Bailey, September 1, 1982, BLA-8797-GRI, African-Canadian collection, Oral History Collection, Multicultural Historical Society of Ontario.
47 Henry, *Black Politics in Toronto*, 2; Gairey, *A Black Man's Toronto*, 10.
48 Henry, *Black Politics in Toronto*, 3.
49 Gairey, *A Black Man's Toronto*, 12.
50 Brand, *No Burden to Carry*, 170, 40–1.
51 Hill, *Negros in Toronto*, 347.
52 Armstrong and Taylor, *Bromley*, 41.
53 Brand, *No Burden to Carry*, 170–1, 170.
54 Kevin Plummer, "Historicist: Banning *Little Black Sambo*," Torontoist, January 25, 2014, https://torontoist.com/2014/01/historicist-banning-little-black-sambo/.
55 Hill, *Negros in Toronto*, 344; Gairey, *A Black Man's Toronto*, 8. See also the narrative of Bertha Mcleer in Brand, *No Burden to Carry*, 82.
56 See Walker, *West Indians in Canada*, 8–9.
57 Henry, *Black Politics in Toronto*, 13.

58 Canadian Negro Women's Association, 1951, Papers of the Ontario Black History Society.
59 Hill, *Women of Vision*, 57.
60 Walker, *West Indians in Canada*, 11.
61 Althea Prince, *Being Black* (Toronto: Insomnia, 2001), 34, 55, 32.
62 Research on student involvement in building community in the 1960s and '70s is limited. Most of the writing about their efforts comes in the form of personal essays in books, such as *Being Black* by Althea Prince, or paragraphs in memoirs, autobiographies, and biographies. With regard to the lack of written texts, Prince suggests that "we were young and naïve enough not to think that our lives would be interesting to anyone: not even to ourselves. We were also suspicious of the media. So we did what was to be done, simply because it was there to be done." Prince, *Being Black*, 60.
63 Dr. Horace Campbell is now a professor of African American Studies and Political Science at Syracuse University. See Keren Brathwaite, "The Lessons the TYP Teaches US" (address on the twentieth anniversary of the Transitional Year Programme [TYP], University of Toronto, March 15, 1991); and Prince, *Being Black*.
64 Prince, *Being Black*, 59, 58.
65 See "Sir George Explodes," *Contrast*, February 1969, 1, and March 1969, 1. See also Dennis Forysthe, ed., *Let the Niggers Burn! The Sir George Williams University Affair and Its Caribbean Aftermath* (Montreal: Black Rose Books/ Our Generation Press, 1971).
66 Barrington Walker, "The National Black Coalition of Canada, 'Race,' and Social Equality in the Age of Multiculturalism," *CLR James Journal* 40, no. 1–2 (2014): 159–77. See also "Sir George Explodes"; Austin, "All Roads Led to Montreal"; and Forysthe, *Let the Niggers Burn!*
67 Jean Augustine, transcript from video, "National Black Coalition of Canada," Pushing Buttons, Pushing Stories, n.d., http://archives.library .yorku.ca/exhibits/show/pushingbuttons/black–caribbean-community /national-black-coalition-of-ca.
68 Paula Denise McClain, *Alienation and Resistance: The Political Behavior of Afro-Canadians* (Palo Alto, CA: R & E Research Associates, 1979), 55.
69 "Support for a Common Cause," editorial, *Contrast*, October 1969, 2.
70 "Support for a Common Cause," 2.
71 Walker, "National Black Coalition."
72 Report of First National Congress of Black Women, Papers of the Ontario Black History Society, April 6–8, 1973; see also Hill, *Women of Vision*, 62.
73 Report of First National Congress of Black Women.
74 Ron Fanfair, "Unity Urged," *Share*, March 16, 1995, 4.
75 Debbie Douglas, statement on Bill C-24 to Citizenship and Immigration Committee, 41st Parl., 2nd Sess., April 30, 2014, https://openparliament

.ca/committees/immigration/41-2/23/debbie-douglas-1/only/; Beverly Bain, "Right to Party: 20 Years of Black Queer Love and Resilience," *The Conversation*, June 29, 2017, http://theconversation.com/right-to-party-20-years-of-black-queer-love-and-resilience-80040.

76 On the early phase of the movement, see Keeanga-Yamahtta Taylor, *From #BlackLivesMatter to Black Liberation* (Chicago: Haymarket Books, 2016).

77 For a complex look at Canada's state-sanctioned violence, see Robin Maynard, *Policing Black Lives: State Violence in Canada from Slavery to the Present* (Halifax: Fernwood, 2017); and Wendell Adjetey, "Policing Race: Rethinking the Myth of National Exceptionalism in a Canadian Context," Humanity in Action, February 2015, https://www.humanityinaction.org/knowledge_detail/policing-race-rethinking-the-myth-of-national-exceptionalism-in-a-canadian-context/. For more about BLM-TO, see the Facebook page of Black Lives Matter – Toronto.

78 Julia Craven, "Black Lives Matter Toronto Stand by Pride Parade Shutdown," *Huffington Post*, July 6, 2016, https://www.huffingtonpost.com/entry/black-lives-matter-toronto-pride_us_577c15aee4b0a629c1ab0ab4.

79 Craven, "Black Lives Matter Toronto"; Katrina Onstad, "Rebel Rebel," *Toronto Life*, February 27, 2017, https://torontolife.com/city/rebel-rebel/; Black Lives Matter – Toronto, "These lists of demands have been developed ...," accessed June 26, 2021, https://blacklivesmattertoronto.ca/demands/.

80 Shanifa Nasser, "Black Lives Matter NYC 'Inspired' by Toronto Chapter's Call for Removal of Uniformed Police," CBC News, June 25, 2017, http://www.cbc.ca/news/canada/toronto/Black-lives-matter-toronto-pride-2017-1.4177554.

81 BlackLivesMatter NYC, "Not like This – #NoPrideHere," *Medium*, June 25, 2017, https://medium.com/@blmnyc/not-like-this-notopride-8b3f414a3d5a.

82 Solimar Otero, "Rethinking the Diaspora: African, Brazilian, and Cuban Communities in Africa and the Americas," *Black Scholar* 30, no. 3–4 (2010): 54–5.

83 Barrington Walker, *Race on Trial: Black Defendants in Ontario's Criminal Courts, 1858–1958* (Toronto: University of Toronto Press, 2010).

84 Clayton James Mosher, *Discrimination and Denial: Systemic Racism in Ontario's Legal and Criminal Justice Systems, 1892–1961* (Toronto: University of Toronto Press, 1998), 82.

85 Otero, "Rethinking the Diaspora."

8
Montreal's Black Renaissance

SEAN MILLS

"Black Power" had been inspiring dissidents in Montreal since the mid-1960s, but in the fall and winter of 1968–9, in the movement's cafés and avant-garde papers, in the teach-ins and cramped apartments, a new topic began creeping into conversations. Those who had considered themselves the Left, and who had compared their plight to that of American Blacks, were surprised by the sudden explosion of Black activism in the city. In the years leading up to the 1960s, discrimination ensured that Black Montrealers remained segregated in substandard living conditions and concentrated in unskilled and low-paying jobs. Montreal's Black population – with its history stretching back to the seventeenth century – had always found ways to resist racism, but now something new was taking place. From the perspective of Montreal's Black population, the 1960s – with political organizations continually being formed, public protests abounding, and a whole series of international conferences taking place – was a watershed in political organizing.[1]

In the second half of the 1960s, Black activists transformed Montreal into a major centre of Black thought, where many of the world's leading Black intellectuals converged with local activists to discuss the global context of race and imperialism. When an occupation of the computer centre at Sir George Williams University in February 1969 ended badly, with blows by riot police, the destruction of $2 million worth of property, and scores of arrests and criminal charges, a new era of Black activism began. The event reflected the heated atmosphere of the late 1960s, and in response to the open hostility that Blacks faced after the event, many members of the community began meeting regularly to discuss the need for autonomous institutions, sparking a political renaissance in the community.

The powerful surge of Black activism in Montreal cannot be understood outside of the larger international context of Black militancy in the late 1960s. Many activists were, after all, recent immigrants from the Caribbean who had come to Montreal to study, and all were profoundly influenced by the movement taking place in the United States. Although they framed their struggle in global terms, they also operated in a politically charged milieu. So even if they had wanted to, it would not have been possible for Montreal's Black activists to remain indifferent to the Quebec liberation movement unfolding all around them. The emergence of Black activism, I will therefore argue, operated simultaneously on many levels, generated many diverse meanings, and constituted a movement that was not only international in scope but also deeply embedded in the lived realities of Montreal.

Black Montreal and the 1960s

While the Sir George Williams Affair of 1969 acted as the immediate spark that set off a Black renaissance in the city, Black opposition to racism had originated deep in the city's past. From the everyday forms of resistance employed by those enslaved in New France, to the organization in 1919 of a division of the Universal Negro Improvement Association, to the unionization of the largely Montreal-based sleeping car porters of the Canadian Pacific Railway during World War II and the efforts of the Coloured Women's Club of Montreal, Montreal's Black residents had never accepted the racism and segregation they faced on a daily basis.[2] Yet racism persisted, limiting their employment prospects and the areas of the city in which they could live and ensuring their psychological and cultural segregation from mainstream society. Walking into downtown restaurants and cafés would often be a humiliating experience for Blacks, as they were met with cold looks and sometimes refused service altogether.[3] White passengers on public transit would refuse to sit beside Black people, bars and clubs sometimes turned them away, and they were almost always forced to work in jobs far below their skill level.[4]

Throughout the 1950s and early 1960s Montrealers were increasingly fascinated by the growing civil rights movement in the United States. Montreal's main civil rights organization, the Negro Citizenship Association (NCA), began denouncing continued discrimination and, in the mid-1960s, founded the journal *Expression*.[5] From its beginning in 1965, the journal opposed racism and advocated a lobbying campaign to the provincial and federal governments that aimed at both more comprehensive anti-discrimination legislation and a stronger enforcement of the laws already in place. While the NCA worked for civil rights, a new energy began to sweep into the city, capturing the imaginations of many young Blacks and especially students of Caribbean origin who had recently arrived in the city. Montreal's Black population had always included people of different origins, so it would be wrong to draw too clear a division between the community's various components.[6] But in the 1960s, it was Caribbean students – often intent on returning home to pursue political activity after their studies – who introduced anticolonial ideas into Black Montreal, at first upsetting many established members of the community but ultimately deeply affecting the way in which the community conceived of itself and understood its relation to the rest of Quebec society and the world at large.[7]

Increased immigration from the Caribbean began in the mid-1950s with the West Indian Domestic Scheme that allowed single women to immigrate to Canada if they agreed to act as domestic servants for about a year. And, while Britain began restricting non-White immigrants in the early 1960s, Canada began to undo some of the more overtly discriminatory aspects of its own policy, a process that would lead to its 1967 point-based selection criteria. As a result of the changes, the makeup of immigrants to Canada began to change. From 1966 to 1972, the proportion of immigrants from Latin America, the Caribbean, Africa, and the Middle East rose to 23 per cent (it had been 4.5 per cent from 1940 to 1950). Immigration from the English-speaking Caribbean rose from representing 1 per cent of Canada's immigration in 1960 to 10 per cent in 1971.[8] Often, in historian Dorothy Williams's words, the new immigrants brought "different values which did not quite mesh with Montreal's old stock black community," but eventually "these newcomers used their energies to refashion old community associations and create new ones."[9]

In the mid-1960s a group calling itself the Caribbean Conference Committee on West Indian Affairs formed the basis of a new Black intelligentsia in the city. It worked to develop new analyses of colonialism and neocolonialism in the Caribbean, laying much of the groundwork for Black politics in Montreal in the late 1960s and early 1970s.[10] As recent immigrants to Canada, group members felt alienated from the larger society. While their focus remained the future of the Caribbean, the committee also strove to oppose the daily realities of discrimination in Montreal, fully aware, as one member put it, that they were continuing in a tradition of what others in the city "had done before."[11] Troubled by the continued subjugation of their countries of origin by dominant Western powers, even after formal political independence had been achieved, the group set out to organize a series of international conferences to analyse both the history and the present-day realities of the Caribbean. Robert Hill, one of the group's most important members, recalls that the Conference Committee was formed at a time when recuperating Black history was seen as a revolutionary gesture. For its very first conference in 1965, the committee hoped to bring Martinican poet and political figure Aimé Césaire to Montreal but, when Césaire could not attend, Barbadian novelist and poet George Lamming took his place.[12] Lamming's speech revealed his profound belief in the possibilities opened up by the process of decolonization. He congratulated the young activists, assuring them that the effects of their work were being felt around the world.[13] In the exciting aftermath of this first conference, Trinidadian activist and intellectual C.L.R. James was invited to Montreal for another conference the following year. He would not only come to the 1966 conference but also become deeply involved with the committee, staying in Montreal for prolonged periods throughout the winter of 1966–7 and greatly influencing their intellectual work.[14]

Although Black nationalism – as opposed to the more theoretical work of the Conference Committee – would come to play an increasingly important role in Montreal, the effects of the group's activities continued to be felt. Perhaps even more important than its intellectual achievements was the change that the Conference Committee represented. By bringing together individuals who were both theoretically informed and highly committed to social justice and democracy, the committee began an ongoing discussion about the structural roots of racism and economic exploitation. Although the committee itself disbanded before the emergence of Black Power in Montreal at the end of the decade, the ideas it had developed in preceding years laid much of the groundwork for the movement.[15]

The end of the 1960s was a turbulent time for Blacks in North America. Because of the persistence of racism despite the legal victory of the American Civil Rights Bill, many young African Americans – like Martin Luther King himself – began rethinking the analyses and strategies of the civil rights movement.[16] In popular representations of the period, the civil rights and Black Power movements are often portrayed as being mutually exclusive, the former advocating racial integration and an end to legal segregation, the latter advocating racial pride and separation. What this perspective ignores are the ways in which the two movements emerged in response to similar problems, reflected the same pursuit of freedom, and perhaps most importantly, changed as the 1960s progressed.[17] Popularized by Stokely Carmichael in 1966, the term "Black Power" generally refers to attempts to overcome the psychological and material consequences of being Black in a society marked by institutionalized racism. Rather than appealing to the moral conscience of White America, the Black Power movement "affirmed black people, their history, their beauty, and set them at the center of their own worldview."[18] In response to racism, the argument went, Black people needed to organize independently and affirm their own priorities and needs. The earlier hope of integration into White society gave way to the idea of Black community building, one that meant moving beyond the narrow individualism that characterized mainstream society. It also meant transforming Blackness from a source of shame into a source of pride.[19]

The movement in the United States had a profound effect on politics in Montreal. No one single event, of course, marked the end of the civil rights era. But in the minds of many, the assassination of Martin Luther King on 4 April 1968 put an end to hopes of peaceful racial integration. King's assassination sparked a wave of violence that swept across most major urban centres in the United States. Many took to the streets in anger, and in the days of rioting that ensued, the National Guard was mobilized, curfews were established, forty African Americans were killed, and another twenty thousand were arrested.[20] In Montreal, while the actions were less dramatic, the anger was just as intense. Citizens organized a street protest to denounce the racism of both the United States and Canada. A crowd of six hundred gathered at the Hall Building of Sir George Williams University, and as the march proceeded to Dominion Square it swelled to over two thousand protesters. Many sang the civil rights anthem "We Shall Overcome," and a large picture of Malcolm X was carried at the front of the march. Protesters carried signs reading "Shake off your chains" and "Vive le pouvoir noir." One speaker spoke with approval of Carmichael, the figure most closely associated with Black Power, and another yelled out, "For 400 years, we've been exploited. We've been beaten. We've been shot." This exploitation did not only occur in "Raceland, U.S.A.," he argued. Blacks had also been discriminated against and exploited in Canada. Now, he continued, "is the time to put an end to the discrimination, the exploitation, the degradation."[21]

The pages of the NCA's *Expression* also revealed a more pronounced mood of anger. An editorial published right after King's assassination argued that if Montreal continued along its present road, it was "almost inevitable" that the city would witness fierce rioting in the years to come. If nothing was done, the journal warned, "Our ghettos will grow; we will fester under your noses; and, the dirty dunghills that you have created will, one day, explode with the thunder of many suns into your clean, unconcerned, lily-white faces." The editors warned that they were "tired of writing useless letters" to government officials and, presaging the uncompromising attitude to come, thundered that Blacks "are no longer duped" by "clever lies." "Behind the false facade of pleasantness, we can glimpse the murderous teeth of discrimination, we can spy the diseased head of prejudice, we can smell the putrid odour of their rotting and bankrupt souls."[22] This rage would soon be expressed by the city's Congress of Black Writers.

The Congress of Black Writers

By 1968, Black Montrealers were searching for new ways to overcome racism. Two conferences took place in the fall, both indirect successors to the conferences on Caribbean affairs. The first, held from 4 to 6 October 1968, dealt specifically with local problems. Held at Sir George Williams University, the conference featured speakers who discussed everyday problems of discrimination in housing and employment, the paucity of opportunities for marginalized people, and the social and cultural alienation of Blacks in Canada.[23] Many of the speakers reflected the prevailing mood in the city. John Shingler, a professor of political science at McGill University, argued that merely integrating into the larger capitalist system is to "entirely to miss the point of human liberation."[24] And in his keynote address Howard McCurdy spoke of the necessity for self-respect, arguing that it was necessary to get to "the roots of our blackness." Black Power, he maintained, meant "black solidarity" in Canada and throughout the world.[25]

The Congress of Black Writers, held at McGill from 11 to 14 October, was considerably more controversial. Dedicated to the memory of Malcolm X and Martin Luther King, and organized by a younger crowd of mostly students, the congress had the goal of fostering a "second liberation" for Blacks.[26] In the week leading up to the event, *Le Quartier latin*, the student newspaper of the Université de Montréal, wrote that it formed a logical continuity with the Congrès des écrivains et artistes noirs held in Paris in 1956, in Rome in 1959, and in Dakar in 1966; the *McGill Daily* called the event the "largest Black Power conference ever held outside the United States."[27] Co-chairing the congress were Elder Thébaud, a Haitian postgraduate student at McGill, and Rosie Douglas, a McGill graduate student from Dominica who had previously been involved in the Caribbean Conference Committee and who acted as a link between the two different cohorts of Black activists in the city.[28] They explained the goals of the event:

> In the face of this total colonial stranglehold, it is clear that the task of self-liberation involves much more than freedom from economic and social oppression. Genuine freedom can only come from the total liberation of the minds and spirits of our people from the false and distorted image of themselves which centuries of cultural enslavement by the white man have

imposed upon us all. The struggle for liberation of black people is accordingly not only an economic or political question, but also a cultural rallying cry, a call to re-examine the foundations of the white man's one-sided vision of the world, and to restore to ourselves an image of the achievements of our people, hitherto suppressed and abandoned among the rubble of history's abuses.

It is in this context that this Congress of Black Writers hopes to make its contribution. Here, for the first time in Canada, an attempt will be made to recall, in a series of popular lectures by black scholars, artists and politicians, a history which we have been taught to forget: the history of the black man's own response (in thought and in action) to the conditions of his existence in the New World; in short, the history of the black liberation struggle, from its origins in slavery to the present day. For the sake of tomorrow's victories, it is imperative that we take another look at the events of yesterday, in the Congress, black people will begin to rediscover themselves as the active creators, rather than the passive sufferers, of history's events; the subjects, rather than the objects, of history. It is only when we have rediscovered this lost perspective on ourselves that we can truly begin to speak of emancipation; it is only when we have returned to our authentic past that we can truly begin to dream about the future.[29]

The congress brought many of the world's most important Black intellectuals to Montreal, including Michael X, leader of the Black Muslims in England; Walter Rodney, prominent Guyanese intellectual; and American activist and intellectual James Forman. The congress also featured both C.L.R. James and Halifax-based activist Rocky Jones.[30] Jones, the only African Canadian to speak, endorsed an alliance between Blacks in Canada and other marginalized people in the country, including Indigenous peoples and francophone Quebeckers.[31] Eldridge Cleaver, the Black Panther Information Minister and author of *Soul on Ice*, had hoped to attend but was stopped because of his troubles with Californian law.[32]

While the conference caused much excitement, it was, as David Austin points out, "a product of its time, full of machismo and male bravado." "Tellingly," he argues, "women activists and writers were conspicuously absent from the roster of speakers, despite the fact that, behind the scenes, women played a crucial role in organizing the congress."[33] While some recognized the problematic gender politics of the conference, others denounced the continual reference to violence as a legitimate political weapon. One prominent Caribbean intellectual, Lloyd Best, felt that the conference was pitched at an "absolutely scandalous" intellectual level, dividing the world simplistically into "cowboys and Indians."[34]

Other members of the Black community felt ambivalent, recognizing the importance of the event while remaining uncomfortable with its tone and approach.[35]

The conference's various speakers lectured on African history and African civilization and on the necessity of fostering a pride in the beauty of Blackness. Forman, drawing on Fanon, denounced African bourgeois leaders as opportunists who had only their own interests in sight.[36] The biggest event of the conference was undoubtedly the appearance of Stokely Carmichael, the Trinidadian-born, American-raised civil rights and Black Power activist. After waiting anxiously in the Union Ballroom at McGill University, the overflow audience of two thousand – mostly made up of White students – stood in disbelief as Carmichael stepped onto the stage. He began by outlining the colonization of Black people throughout the world and vividly described its devastating effects.[37] He insisted on the need to globalize Black struggle, calling on people the world over to "create their own legitimations."[38] The electrified crowd repeatedly interrupted Carmichael, who spoke for over an hour, with cheers and applause.[39] The power of his speech brought seasoned activists "close to tears" and had a profound effect on C.L.R. James.[40]

Carmichael's speech was powerful, but it was also controversial. He made no secret of the way he felt that power needed to be achieved: "I don't think that white Canadians would say that they stole Canada from the Indians (laughter). They said they took it – and they did (applause and laughter). Well then, it's clear that we can't work for these lands, we can't beg for'em, so we must take them. Then it's clear that we must take them through revolutionary violence."[41] Carmichael's uncompromising militancy embodied the spirit of the conference: a new climate of anger that would lead, at least in part, to the Sir George Williams Affair.

Although Montreal's English-language newspapers denounced the gathering at McGill, many White activists attending the conference were fascinated by this local manifestation of Black Power. Among these were Stanley Gray, a lecturer involved with student politics at McGill and Gérald Godin, the radical poet and director of the Parti Pris publishing house.[42] Godin had long drawn on racial metaphors to describe the oppression of French Canadians and had even argued just two years earlier that francophone Quebeckers were "the Blacks of Canada."[43] But now, in the margins of his souvenir program, Godin began to make connections between the oppression and alienation of French Canadians and that of Blacks *in Canada*. When listening to Rocky Jones plead for Canadian Blacks to join forces with francophone Quebeckers and Indigenous peoples, Godin wrote "that's the way I feel," transcribing Jones's attempt to convey the psychological impact of racial oppression.

He went on to draw similarities between Blacks and francophone Quebeckers, adding a message of his own: "that's the way French Canadians feel."[44] Godin was so moved that he started planning to make a movie about Canadian Blacks.[45]

The congress undoubtedly had its greatest impact on a new generation of Black Montrealers. According to Barbara Jones, for them it was an "edifying experience," and they came to realize that their only hope lay "in a new era of black militancy and a new humanism."[46] Dennis Forsythe has recorded that many people claimed the conference was the biggest event of their lives and that it demonstrated "the emotional intensity of Blacks crying out in the wilderness." He observes, "The overall effect on the Black psyche was to inculcate a feeling of exhilaration and uplift; we had been christened in the holy cause. We now saw ourselves as makers rather than takers of our history. We saw ourselves as part of a great struggle, a historic struggle, from which we derived a peculiar feeling of exhilaration, uplift and pride, and a sense of power. We were sanctified as the makers of our own destiny."[47]

At the congress, according to Forsythe, as Blackness became "a symbol of rightness," then "the Whites present had to be, by definition, symbols of evil." Much controversy broke out at the conference when some wanted to exclude White people from sessions, while others wanted to ensure that White people did not wear Malcolm X buttons. Many speakers shocked the largely White audience by referring to Whites as "pigs" and "oppressors."[48] For the first time, many Whites felt "distrusted, excluded, [and] ignored."[49] Conference co-organizer Rosie Douglas noted that because there were Whites in the audience, "the speakers found themselves having to justify the need for liberation." He argued that it was therefore necessary to make a compromise: Whites were allowed in, but after every session there was an exclusively Black caucus.[50] In the months to come, the pent-up frustrations of Montreal's Black population would head toward a dramatic collision with one of the city's most important institutions.

The Sir George Williams Affair

The influx of Black Power ideas into Montreal had a great impact on the political dynamic of the city, but it was not until January and February of 1969 that this new militancy would be translated into action at Sir George Williams University.[51] The origins of the conflict dated back to the end of the 1967–8 school year, when a group of Caribbean students accused biology professor Perry Anderson of racial discrimination in grading and academic incompetence. On 29 January 1969, after months of heated controversy, the students felt that their charges were not being adequately addressed. Roughly two hundred protesters overtook a hearing into the matter and then proceeded to the ninth floor of the Hall Building to occupy the university's computer centre.[52] Tensions grew to a climax on the fourteenth day of the occupation when, feeling betrayed by the administration and cornered by the police, the students barricaded themselves in the computer centre. Realizing that the riot squad had been called in, the students threw paper and computer punch cards out of the ninth-floor window. Riot police broke down the doors and, in the confusion that ensued, a fire broke out and computers were destroyed.

In the end, ninety-seven protesters were arrested, criminal charges were laid, and the damage totalled over $2 million. Rosie Douglas and Anne Cools were seen as the ringleaders, and they each served significant jail time for their actions.[53] The media broadcast news of the event around the world, and protests against symbols of Canadian power erupted throughout the Caribbean. Students at the Cave Hill campus of the University of the West Indies in Barbados mounted a "symbolic burial of Anderson and the racist institution of Sir George Williams University."[54] The visit of Canadian governor general Daniel Roland Michener to the Caribbean on a "goodwill tour" set off a series of protests – he was even blocked by students from entering the University of the West Indies' St. Augustine campus – contributing to a period of political unrest in Trinidad.[55]

The Sir George Williams Affair has generally been left out of narratives chronicling political developments in Montreal during the 1960s. It has been seen as either an aberration or, at best, a matter of secondary importance to the struggle between two linguistic groups. When it is remembered, it is generally portrayed as an event having relevance only to Black Canadians and as a conflict that had little impact outside of the circles of Black Montreal. Such representations distort both the impact of this event on other sectors of society and the ways in which the protest formed part of a larger atmosphere of revolt that prevailed in the city. In addition, this interpretation overlooks the fact that the occupation had the support of many White students at the university, who actually formed the majority of those present.[56]

Black students, most of whom had come to Canada from the Caribbean to study, were keenly aware of both the international context and the local environment in which they lived.[57] Alfie Roberts, a member of the Caribbean Conference Committee and a participant in the Sir George Williams Affair, was aware of being part of a larger movement that affected nearly all aspects of life in Quebec. In 1962, the same year that he immigrated to Montreal from his native St. Vincent and the Grenadines, Roberts read Marcel Chaput's *Pourquoi je suis séparatiste* and realized that many people in Quebec were making claims to independence similar to those being championed by the nations of the Third World. Roberts described the meshing of international and local developments when he arrived in Montreal:

> So all of this was happening and there was a certain conjuncture of events. We are talking about the agitation, the effervescence, the emerging to the fore of the problems that Black people were having and were publicly agitating to have redressed in the United States; we are talking especially about the Cuban Revolution in 1959 with its bearded, olive green-clad combatants filling the newspaper pages and the works of guerrilla warfare by Che Guevara making the rounds; we're going back to Nkrumah in 1957 – the independence of Ghana; we're talking about Guinea in 1959; the works of Fanon. All of this had a tremendous impact on what was happening here in Quebec and I walked into all of it.[58]

Roberts argued that the many Black conferences of the 1960s could be considered as "a Black complement to the ongoing Québécois Quiet Revolution." When the Sir George Williams Affair erupted in February of 1969, he continued, it "announced loud and clear that Black people were here, and not only below the tracks, but inside the whole society." The event, Roberts explained, must be understood as coinciding with the "tremendous worker unrest" that prevailed in the province of Quebec at the time.[59] True, Roberts was something of an exception among those involved in the Sir George Williams Affair; he had arrived in Canada relatively early and was not a student at the time of the event. But the young students who were radicalized by the affair also came to recognize the importance of the local situation. The Sir George Williams Affair – with crowds of White people yelling "Let the niggers burn!" during the fire, and with the Black students being locked up separately from the White students once they had been arrested – provided many with a dramatic example of the discrimination that they faced more subtly on a daily basis.[60]

As Paul Gilroy has argued, racism needs to be understood not as a static essence that exists unchanged through history but rather as a process, as something that gains new characteristics and dimensions at different moments. Understanding racism depends on our "capacity to comprehend political, ideological and economic change."[61] Racism, to put it another way, does not "move tidily and unchanged through time and history. It assumes new forms and articulates new antagonisms in different situations."[62] The events of February 1969 grew out of tensions caused by racial injustice in Montreal and throughout the world. Local events acquired their meaning when read through larger narratives of anti-colonialism and anti-imperialism, as well as the civil rights and Black Power movements. And the Sir George Affair itself played an important role in causing many Montrealers to embrace Black Power as an intellectual framework.

The confrontation at Sir George Williams also changed the ways in which some francophone intellectuals thought about race. Gestures of support came from many in Quebec nationalist circles. During the occupation, a scheduled "Quebec Week," which was to feature many prominent nationalist figures, was cancelled in support of the occupation.[63] Student groups across the country came out in support of the occupation and against institutionalized racism. After the forced expulsion from the computer room and the vast property damage that ensued, however, many supporters disappeared. The students' society at Sir George Williams University attempted to distance itself from the events of 11 February, even firing the editor of *The Georgian*, the university's main student newspaper, and there was a backlash against those involved in the demonstration among the student body, including some Black students.[64] Nearly all of the main anglophone student organizations abandoned the protesters, and many faculty members did so as well (although some Black faculty members supported the students).[65] Nonetheless, there was some support from francophone circles. The Montreal Central Council of the Confédération des syndicats nationaux (CSN) called for the release of those being held in prison, declaring that the mainstream media "tends to forget that the material mess caused by the occupation of SGWU is nothing in comparison with the problem of racism."[66]

In the university newspapers, individual students wrote angrily about the events at Sir George. Speaking on behalf of students at the Université de Montréal, Romeo Bouchard wrote that, as both francophone Quebeckers and students, they were "brothers twice over" of the Black students at Sir George.[67] One author in *Le Quartier latin* wondered whether, by "blaming the ferocity of a cornered animal, we come to forget the ferocity of the animal that corners" and went on to question the operating priorities of the modern capitalist system: "These charred IBM computers acted as the very symbol of a consumer society that turns its universities into depersonalizing factories, manipulating and shaping humanity to its own needs." Those "who idolize the dollar as the Supreme Dispenser of peace and happiness are enraged to see $2 million go up in flames," yet these same people do not shed a tear when "the human spirit is suffocated in the cold bowels of the machine."[68] Jacques Maassen articulated the same sentiment in the pages of the *McGill Daily*, arguing that the very fact that such "havoc" was caused over "the destruction of a few computers" demonstrated "the corrupt sense of values infused into us by our 'great society.'" The destruction of a computer, he argued, was a symbolic act against "the image of the progression and evolution of this society."[69]

In the hall outside of the large courtroom where the arrested students were to appear, among the bright and colourful dashikis, many people wore "McGill français" buttons. A petition was passed around stating that "black students and French students are more or less fighting for the same things."[70] And a reverend who had travelled all the way up from Harlem for the trial distributed leaflets that had been given to him outside. The leaflet read:

> WE THE SUPPORTERS FOR ALL PEOPLES DEMAND THAT THE STUDENTS WHO ARE BEING ILLEGALLY HELD WITHOUT BAIL BE RELEASED IMMEDIATELY.
>
> THE ALLEGED DAMAGE DONE TO THE COMPUTERS READ TO THE AMOUNT OF TWO MILLION DOLLARS WHEREAS THE AMOUNT OF DAMAGE MANIFESTED BY INSTITUTIONALIZED RACISM IS INCALCULABLE.
>
> NOT EVEN IN RACELAND, U.S.A. WOULD THIS GRAVE INJUSTICE BE COMMITTED.
>
> WE WANT JUSTICE.

And, on the reverse side of many of the leaflets:

NOUS LES NÈGRES BLANCS D'AMÉRIQUE SOUTENONS NOS FRÈRES.[71]

Montreal's Black Renaissance

By bringing questions of racism and immigration to the forefront of public discussion, the Sir George Williams Affair challenged many of the established truths of the Montreal Left, but its most important and lasting impact was on Black Montreal. When Black activists and their supporters decided to take over the computer centre, they did so with the belief that the computer symbolized not only capitalist modernity but also the ravages that Western imperialism had wrought on the poor nations of the world. Through the control of technology, capitalism was transforming the world's population into consumers, and they conceived of their efforts as an attempt to bring democracy to the community, the country, and the world.[72] After the destruction of the computers and the riot squad's forceful removal of the students, various segments of Montreal's Black population came together as a community.[73] According to Forsythe, the affair was "a major event in the metamorphosis of Black people."[74] In the pages of *Expression*, an editorial argued that the events "had a profound influence on that institution and the entire Montreal community." It had become clear that Canada, "riddled with paradoxes and contradictions," was a country that championed "equality for all races" yet "condone[d] in silence the unequal treatment of its non-white peoples: the Indians, the Eskimos, the Japanese, the blacks." In the context of the heated aftermath of the Sir George Williams Affair, the battle for equality "can be considered nothing less than a revolutionary struggle to reformulate the basic and fundamental concepts, value judgments, and ways in which each racial group perceives the existence of all others."[75]

Black activists decided that they needed to move out of the university milieu and begin organizing the community in its entirety, especially those, like domestic servants, who were the most vulnerable. Alfie Roberts started the Caribbean International Service Bureau, which organized a conference, started a day care, and published a special issue of the *McGill Free Press* entitled "The Black Spark."[76] According to Leroy Butcher, Black activists and intellectuals were teaching people that they had the right to do things for themselves, and that they needed to believe in themselves and be proud of their history.[77] Members of the Black community began meeting on a weekly basis at what became known as the "Thursday Night Rally." The rallies started after the Sir George Williams Affair, when semi-weekly gatherings were held to relay information about the arrested students. As the meetings evolved, they became a forum for broad community discussions about race and racism. Before long, guest speakers were being invited regularly and a crowd of up to 175 people would commonly turn out for the event. Historian Roy States gave lectures on international Black history and on the history of Blacks in Canada. Films featuring the Black struggle were screened, speakers lectured on Africa and South America, and discussions about books like *Malcolm X Speaks* and *Soul on Ice* took place among young people struggling to find their place in the world.[78]

If uncompromising militancy and a belief in violence as an appropriate means of social change led in part to the destruction of the computer centre, the racist backlash after the event instigated the creation of a range of new organizations and institutions. The creation of communications media such as Black Is Television and, slightly later, *The Black Voice* were matched by new community organizations including the Côte des Neiges Black Community Association, the Lasalle Black Community

Association, the Black Coalition of Quebec, the Notre-Dame-de-Grâce Black Community Association, the Quebec Black Board of Educators, and others.[79] Other activities emerged, such as the Congress of Black Women, as well as Cultural Youth Workshops and Black Youth TV, and a group of university students formed the Black Action Party and set out to provide Afrocentric education for Black youth. Initiatives of grassroots organizing and alternative media proliferated, becoming a crucial element of Montreal life in throughout the 1970s.[80]

One of the most important legacies of the Sir George Williams Affair was *UHURU* (Swahili for "freedom"), a newspaper that became the dominant voice articulating Black activism in the city.[81] The paper began as a bulletin of the 11 Feb. Defence Committee, and through its very existence was seen as a concrete demonstration of Black Power ideals.[82] It provided a medium free from White control through which Black intellectuals were able to challenge the assumptions of Western society and develop their own understanding of themselves and of their community.

The paper, while always controversial, was an immediate success. Its circulation of roughly three thousand nearly matched that of *Parti Pris* of the mid-1960s, and the editors felt that the "demand is even more pressing."[83] *UHURU* even received a letter of congratulations from Stokely and Miriam Carmichael, thanking the paper for the service that it was rendering "to the Black world."[84] On 30 November 1969, over three hundred of its supporters celebrated the opening of its new office at 2554 Saint-Antoine. On the ground floor of an apartment building in the city's traditional Black neighbourhood, the office was identified by a big sign that hung in its window. The interior of the building matched its austere exterior. The walls, plastered with posters, were adorned with a painting, a map of Africa, and a donated electric clock; a picture of Eldridge Cleaver hung on the door to the toilet. In the combined workroom and library, the journal's writers sought to develop their own understandings of the origins of, and alternatives to, the injustice that surrounded them.[85]

Although those who wrote for *UHURU* articulated a variety of ideological positions, they agreed on a few central points. They had, for example, the conviction that to be Black was to be colonized and therefore to be on the side of those who were involved in the worldwide struggle against empire. And Montreal's radical Black writers – building on the work and insights of the Caribbean Conference Committee – were at the forefront of developing analyses of Canada's imperialist role in the Caribbean.[86] While many in the wider circles of the Left saw Montreal as a colonized city, Black writers began considering its role as an imperial metropole that undoubtedly formed part of the West and that therefore held its share of responsibility for the misery inflicted upon the poor nations of the world.[87]

Black writers in Montreal would continue seeing their condition through an anti-imperialist lens, analysing universities like Sir George Williams as institutions that fulfilled a "colonial role of conditioning young people (Bible in hand) under the guise of progress, civilization, democracy and christianity."[88] Viewed from this angle, the Sir George Williams Affair was an "unavoidable confrontation between colonizer and colonized."[89] Because capitalism had historically required slave labour, it was argued, racism and capitalism were connected. However, it was not capitalism per se but colonization – theorized explicitly as the experience and legacy of African slavery – that gave the Black liberation struggle "an autonomous vitality of its own."[90] Frantz Fanon's *Black Skin, White Masks* acted as a key work for Montrealers who sought to understand the meaning of racial oppression. Fanon had outlined ways in which notions of Black inferiority and White superiority had infused and shaped cultural systems and individual perceptions. For Fanon, "White" had come to represent morality, beauty, intelligence, rationality, and respect; "Black," on the other hand, symbolized "the lower emotions, the baser inclinations, the dark side of the soul."[91] Fanon helped to elucidate the "black sickness of mind," the "acquired belief" in "inferiority based on the enforced values of a white society" that so many Blacks had experienced.[92]

Maurice Tremblay, for example, wrote movingly in *UHURU* about how he devalued himself as a Black person growing up in Montreal and about the psychological trauma of constantly living under the gaze of White society. For Tremblay, the Sir George Williams Affair was a turning point. When the administration remained deaf to the students' concerns, and when the crowd yelled "Let the niggers burn" and other racist chants as the fire broke out in the computer centre, he began to understand that the task at hand was *not* to emulate White society but to celebrate and "rejoice in Black Identity."[93] Like many other writers featured in *UHURU*, Tremblay had become convinced that Blacks in Montreal could no longer allow their self-perceptions to be forged by others. Contributors to *UHURU* varied in the meaning they assigned to being Black. Some defended an essentialist position, arguing that Blacks formed a proud race that had been destroyed;[94] others gave a political and ethical definition to the word. But uniting the various attempts was the belief that Blacks *themselves* needed to do the defining, needed to come together and establish their own terms of reference.

Compared with those of many American cities, Montreal's Black community was extremely small, numbering no more than about fifteen thousand at the end of the 1960s.[95] And they were deeply aware that there was little hope of advocating complete separation from larger society.[96] Perhaps for this reason, pan-Africanism took on a heightened importance for Black activists in Montreal. Douglas explained the appeal of Carmichael's vision in this regard: Carmichael saw pan-Africanism as the "highest political expression" of Black Power and believed that "African people on the continent or scattered all over the world must define their working political framework in a manner which will enable us in our day to day struggle to relate our common heritage to the racist oppression which we all face irrespective of our socio-economic status."[97] As more and more Blacks in Montreal began to see the world this way, there was a great surge of interest in all things African. Groups began organizing cultural events like the "Journey back to Africa" and articles featured "authentic" African fashion. News of the "first real Afro-American wedding in Canada" even adorned the front page of the paper.[98]

Black Intellectuals and Montreal

UHURU may have framed its struggle as one between Black and White, but such a clear dichotomy ultimately could not hold given the complexities of empire in Canada. From its very beginning, *UHURU* acknowledged a tension between the conflation of the "colonized" with "Black" and the recognition that not all of those who were colonized were of African origin. In an issue arguing that the dominant legacy of the 1960s was the challenge to White supremacy, Asian and Latin American anti-imperial resistance was cited alongside struggles in Africa, the Caribbean, and Black North America.[99] And, perhaps not surprisingly, Black Power advocates in Montreal reached out to Indigenous Canadians in their first attempt to build solidarities across different movements.

The first non-Black person who lectured at a rally of the Black community at the UNIA Hall was Henry Jacks, an Indigenous man from Vancouver. In *UHURU*, Edmund Michael compared the plight of Indigenous peoples to that of Blacks. Jacks, Michael wrote, "has had to endure very much the same type of humiliations and dehumanization that the black man has had to endure in this country." He continued, "We as black people here in Canada must therefore turn a sympathetic eye to the plight of the red man and vice versa for, just as he is kept in place on his controlled reservations and in the ghetto and are always regarded as 'those damned Indians,' so too are we regarded as 'those damned niggers,' by whites." It was necessary for Black activists to make contact with Indigenous groups, for "after all it is they who were the original owners of N. America and we as black people were forced to work and build it all for the white people, who are our oppressors." He called on his readers "to develop the consciousness of our fellow blacks, while the reds strive to re-educate their people, and in this way, we can co-operate with each other in areas which can rebound to the mutual benefit of both peoples who constitute the 'wretched of the earth.'"[100] Another article mocked Cardinal Léger's plea for Catholics to conduct missionary work in Africa and argued that, in "view of the treatment meted out not only to Blacks in Canada but also to the indigenous Indians, one wonders whether Cardinal Leger and the Church should not transfer their missionary activities to the Canadian scene."[101] Following and extending the logic of Black Power, *UHURU* advocated Indigenous control over Indigenous communities. *UHURU* also covered the rising tide of militant Indigenous activism in the United States and clearly saw Red Power as a natural ally of Black Power.[102]

But Montreal also differed from other North American cities in that radicals of the *majority* population claimed to be colonized by a foreign power. Montreal's Black activists therefore faced a situation in which many in the White population surrounding them had drawn on the very same literature of Third World liberation and Black Power as they did to theorize themselves as being culturally, economically, and psychologically dominated by an imperial system of power. This basic fact of Montreal life in the 1960s could be neither ignored nor dismissed; at press conferences and in interviews, Black activists were repeatedly asked about their position on the "Quebec situation."[103] Still, as late as 1968 many Black leaders refused to acknowledge the legitimacy of the national liberation movement in Quebec. When three organizers of the Congress of Black Writers, Douglas, Thébaud, and Keith Byrne, were interviewed by the *McGill Daily* just before the opening of the congress, Douglas stated that one of the important landmarks of the event was that it brought both French- and English-speaking Blacks together in the same forum.[104] But when the interviewer of the *Daily* pushed further, asking about the "significance" of the bilingual nature of the conference – clearly implying that it was related to its location in Montreal – Thébaud merely reiterated that it was significant in that French- and English-speaking Blacks were getting together. That Quebec itself was bilingual, Thébaud stated, was of little importance. The interviewer kept pushing: "Some Québécois draw an analogy between the situation of the Blacks in the world and that of French-speaking Québécois. Do you [think that] the analogy is valid, and if so, do you see the possibility of co-operation between Québécois and blacks?" Thébaud remained intransigent: "Quebeckers like to call themselves the *nègres* of Canada, but we would like to highlight the fact that of all races, the black race has been the most humiliated. We therefore need first to organize among Blacks who have been divided by the colonizer. Collaboration between Blacks and oppressed Whites is desirable, but this is not the task of the moment." Thébaud and Douglas were adamant that it mattered little that the congress was being held in Montreal. When asked if it was important for people in Canada and Quebec to hear speakers on the subject of racial discrimination, Thébaud responded again: "No," it was important for "people generally." It was "incidental" that the congress was being held in Montreal, and it "could have been held anywhere."[105] Rosie Douglas quickly added that the congress could have been held "on Mars" for all that it mattered.[106]

It is not difficult to understand why Black activists would have been hesitant to recognize the political claims of French-speaking Quebeckers. Black people had been enslaved by French colonists from the earliest days of settlement, and they had been marginalized and debased ever since. They had been subject to the discrimination and racism of French- and English-speaking Montrealers alike, and it is easy to see how the struggle for Quebec liberation, which up until the late 1960s had been predicated on the language of francophone victimization, could be seen to be of little concern for them. What's more, with the rarest of exceptions, francophone intellectuals largely ignored the presence of Montreal's Black population.

The first opening toward mutual recognition came in the aftermath of the computer centre incident and amid the vicious language debates that were tearing the city apart. As mentioned earlier, the Montreal Central Council of the CSN publicly declared its support for the students and denounced the attitude of the courts in which they were being prosecuted.[107] And in the years following the Sir George Affair, Black intellectuals arrived at a deeper understanding of the complex power relations of Montreal society. In 1970, those responsible for the Thursday night rallies decided to set up a political committee to develop an analysis "of the political situation in Quebec."[108] They also recognized their ambiguous position in the language wars and the danger that they might be unwittingly drawn into the debate as tacit supporters of "English rights." When an English-language school attempted to use Black children to bolster their arguments for English-language education, *UHURU* reacted angrily. If "the white English at the Royal Arthur School want to fight the white French," the paper asked, "why use blacks to fight their war?" In educational debates, as in all other aspects of life, Black people needed to "act on decisions made by themselves and by their own initiation."[109] Racism, another article argued, existed in both francophone and anglophone communities, and it was necessary that Blacks abstain from the language wars; the article demanded that "both English and French be taught to our children."[110]

While *UHURU* always maintained that Blacks were the object "of discrimination from both English and French," the paper did recognize that Blacks and francophones were oppressed by the same forces in the province. In English-controlled companies, an editorial argued, "racist hiring policies ... have existed for years," and "French speaking Quebecois find it very difficult to make any headway in the economics of their country." It was therefore "difficult if not impossible to understand how blacks (the object of discrimination from both English and French) can find themselves doing any better than the French if at all as well."[111]

The 1970 provincial election campaign was the first in which the Parti Québécois (PQ), the new provincial sovereigntist party that had been founded in 1968, fielded candidates. The PQ's social democratic platform captured the hopes of a wide variety of activists, including labour unionists and members of neighbourhood citizens' committees. Opinion in the Black community was divided over both the election and the significance of the PQ. In an official editorial, *UHURU* noted that during the election, which ended up bringing the Quebec Liberal Party to power, "the white anglo-saxon (English speaking) voters panicked at the thought of independence in Quebec, not understanding what it is all about, fearing reprisals, loss of influence, and against the French majority assuming their rightful positions of responsibility (economic and otherwise) in their own province." When it came to the PQ, the editorial explained that the party's "platform is clear cut and should be viewed without fear since it simply calls for [francophone] Quebecers [to take] control of Quebec, which is the ambition and right of all nations and peoples." It even suggested that "Blacks must if they intend to stay in Quebec make up their minds to adopt at least a working knowledge of French."[112]

When Dennis Forsythe published *Let the Niggers Burn!* in 1971 about the Sir George Williams Affair and its aftermath, the very first sentence of the book – "Something happened here in Montréal on February 11th, 1969, which for different reasons neither Blacks nor Whites will ever forget" – reveals a change in the dialogue between Black and francophone activists. Unlike most anglophones, in this opening line Forsythe used the French spelling of "Montréal," thereby recognizing the primacy of the French language in the city.[113] For Forsythe, it was crucially important to understand that "Quebec is a tension-ridden environment, and that this state of affairs has increased over the last few years. Quebec, and Montreal specifically, is like a machine creaking at its seams, as witnessed by the increasing frustrations and resentment expressed by almost all segments of the society. In the last three years policemen, teachers, taxi-drivers, post-men, anti-poverty groups, students and women have all entered the 'long march' here in Quebec."[114]

According to Forsythe, one had to realize that, as "conservatism, capitalism and imperialism, to an even greater extent, do not respect national borders; so neither can radicalism respect frontiers." But although an incident such as the Sir George Williams Affair "could have occurred in many other places; that it erupted in Montreal, and at Sir George Williams University, is due to specific situational factors that emerged in Montreal."[115] While struggling with key questions of empire, imperialism, and colonization, many other Black Montrealers came to understand the cultural and material oppression of French-speaking Quebeckers. Some, like the writers of the Caribbean International Service Bureau, even began seeing the French-Canadian working class, who they hoped would intervene "on the side of black and oppressed people in their struggle for a new society," as potential allies in the political struggles in the years to come.[116]

Black writers introduced new analyses of race, community development, and democracy into the public sphere, adding and contributing to the complex and hybrid mixture of ideas and movements. In ways that were at times complex and at times contradictory, a new generation of Black intellectuals challenged dominant understandings of colonization and worked to reclaim the meaning of Blackness through a process of psychological, economic, and political decolonization. Yet Black Power in Montreal, like the larger world of Montreal radicalism of which it formed a part, rarely even recognized one of its most central contradictions. While advocating liberation for all human beings, Black Power was theorized as a "struggle for manhood," both explicitly and implicitly excluding women from any active role.[117] Winston Franco argued that "there are some black people who cannot see the institutionalized racism of our society." This was not such "a strange phenomenon," he continued, "since people who lose their balls in their infancy find it impossible to remember what it felt like to have had them."[118] Omowale wrote that "the dignity and manhood of black students at Sir George Williams University, was belittled in every way possible."[119] During one of the demonstrations of the occupation, Rocky Jones challenged the masculinity of White men, calling them "pansies, because they won't even fight for white folks."[120] And in the surge of Black Power activism after the event, one author wrote in *UHURU* that the "Black Man is the personification of strength, power, peace and love; the 'Father of Civilization,'" and even the very "essence of Manhood."[121]

But while Black men were called forth to reclaim their virility, Black women were expected to assume a passive role. True, women had been involved in Black politics from the start. The 1967-8 *Caribbean Conference Bulletin* highlighted the work of Anne Cools, Bridget Joseph, Gloria Simmons, and Jean Depradine as "the living indication that the Caribbean woman will be in the forefront of the movement for a new Caribbean."[122] More often than not, however, women were valued only as the reproductive force of the nation, a position sometimes advocated by women themselves.[123]

This was typical of left-wing politics in the 1960s. While theorizing national liberation, male activists were blind to the oppression many women experienced in their traditional roles. But at the end of the 1960s Black women began speaking out against the sexism of a movement that was ostensibly going to bring about "liberation," mostly through letters to the editor and to the advice column of *UHURU* and surely in many heated arguments in meeting places and private homes. Letter after letter complained that Black men continued to believe in the myth of White beauty. In addition, the men thought that being seen with a White woman was a symbol of success. Black women felt that they were perceived as slowing the progress of their husbands. Black men's search for White women, their "reaching out after whiteness," often affected Black women "to the point of trauma."[124] Many were left "sad and confused" with the hypocrisies of the movement.[125]

Black women argued that racism, with all of its devastating implications, did not operate in isolation. For one woman it was clear that "our so-called black brothers" did not seem to be practising what they preached. "These brothers," she argued, "have no morals, no manners, no etiquette, they treat the sisters like dirt." She had even come to believe "that all this black power bit is a farce."[126] Black women, another author wrote, experienced the same devaluation by Black men as Black men did from White society. "So that what he [the Black man] termed as 'violence' on the part of the white man," she argued, "he viciously practices in turn on the Black woman."[127] Anne Cools, who was both a member of the Caribbean Conference Committee and a participant in the Sir George Williams Affair, was one of the loudest voices to speak out. Through her work, she helped to build a new militancy among women, a militancy that was capturing the imaginations of women across North America.[128] In Montreal, as across the continent, individuals began recognizing the need to extend organizing and cultural self-affirmation to women. When they did so, Montreal politics would never be the same again.

NOTES

This chapter is a revised version of chapter 4 in *The Empire Within: Postcolonial Thought and Political Activism in Sixties Montreal* (Montreal and Kingston: McGill-Queen's University Press, 2010).

1 By far the most important accounts of Black political organizing in Montreal are those of David Austin, "All Roads Led to Montreal: Black Power, the Caribbean, and the Black Radical Tradition in Canada," *Journal of African American History* 92, no. 4 (2007): 516–39; and Dorothy W. Williams, *The Road to Now: A History of Blacks in Montreal* (Montreal: Véhicule, 1997), chap. 7, in which she discusses the "black cultural renaissance of the period" (130). For a look at the reactions of the French- and English-language media to Black activism, see Marcel Martel, "'S'ils veulent faire la révolution, qu'ils aillent la faire chez eux à leurs risques et périls. Nos anarchistes maisons sont suffisants': occupation et répression à Sir George-Williams," *Bulletin d'histoire politique* 15, no. 1 (2006): 163–78. Since the original publication of this chapter in 2010, a number of new works have dealt with the events discussed. See, in particular, David Austin, *Fear of a Black Nation: Race, Sex, and Security in Sixties Montreal* (Toronto: Between the Lines, 2013); Austin, ed., *Moving against the System: The 1968 Congress of Black Writers and the Making of Global Consciousness* (Toronto: Between the Lines, 2018); and Ronald Cummings and Nalini Mohabir, eds., *Fire That Time: Transnational Black Radicalism and the Sir George Williams Occupation* (Montreal: Black Rose, forthcoming).

2 On the topic of slavery in New France, see Marcel Trudel with Micheline D'Allaire, *Deux siècles d'esclavage au Québec* (Montreal: Hurtubise, 2004). Also see Daniel Gay, *Les Noirs du Québec, 1629–1900* (Sillery: Septentrion, 2004); and Sarah-Jane (Saje) Mathieu, "North of the Colour Line: Sleeping Car Porters and the Battle against Jim Crow on Canadian Rails, 1880–1920," *Labour/Le Travail* 47 (Spring 2001): 9–41. On the political organizations of Black women, see Shirley Small and Esmeralda M.A. Thornhill, "HARAMBEC! Quebec Black Women Pulling Together," *Journal of Black Studies* 38, no. 3 (2008): 427–42.

3 Williams, *Road to Now*, 39. Also see James W. St. G. Walker, *Racial Discrimination in Canada: The Black Experience* (Ottawa: Canadian Historical Association, 1985). On systemic racism in Canada's past, see Walker, *"Race," Rights and the Law in the Supreme Court of Canada: Historical Case Studies* (Waterloo, ON: Osgoode Society for Canadian Legal History and Wilfrid Laurier University Press, 1997).

4 David Austin, "Contemporary Montréal and the 1968 Congress of Black Writers," *Lost Histories* 24, no. 1 (1998): 59.

5 For an outline of the history and outlook of the NCA, see Richard E. Leslie, "Editorial," *Expression* 1, no. 1 (1965): 5.
6 While divisions existed within the larger community, all groups shared common experiences of racism in Canadian society. According to James Walker, "When white Canadians express discriminatory tendencies they do so on the basis of colour, making colour a unifying characteristic for West Indians of African descent and giving them a community of experience with other black Canadians. Even the Haitians, who are distinguishable by language, report strikingly similar experiences to those of their anglophone counterparts." James W. St. G. Walker, *The West Indians in Canada* (Ottawa: Canadian Historical Association, 1984), 20.
7 Williams, *Road to Now*, 111, chap. 7.
8 Micheline Labelle, Serge Larose, and Victor Piché, "Politique d'immigration et immigration en provenance de la Caraïbe anglophone au Canada et au Québec, 1900–1979," *Canadian Ethnic Studies/Études ethniques au Canada* 15, no. 2 (1983): 8–11.
9 Williams, *Road to Now*, 100.
10 According to David Austin, in "the 1960s and 1970s, the Roberts' apartment on Bedford Street in the Côte-des-Neiges district of Montreal was a political stomping ground where books could be borrowed by friends, Caribbean students, political activists, and aspiring politicians. It was a place where dusk till dawn discussions were held on a wide array of subjects, and where political strategies were mapped out. Alfie and his wife Patricia hosted many sessions in their Montreal home, earning it the name 'The University of Bedford,' and many people, including several future Caribbean prime ministers, came of age politically in their living room." Austin, "Introduction," in *A View for Freedom: Alfie Roberts Speaks on the Caribbean, Cricket, Montreal, and C.L.R. James*, by Alfie Roberts (Montreal: Alfie Roberts Institute, 2005), 20.
11 Roberts, *View for Freedom*, 77.
12 Robert Hill, "The Caribbean Island of Montreal: The Caribbean Conference Committee and the Black Radical Tradition" (lecture, Rebellion, Protest, and Change: Reflections on the 1960s and the Development of Montreal's Black Community, UNIA Hall, Montreal, 18 February 2006), video recording (available through the Alfie Roberts Institute, Montreal).
13 George Lamming, address at the 1965 Conference on West Indian Affairs, Université de Montréal, audio recording. My thanks to Anne Cools for providing me with this recording.
14 For a vivid description of the conference committee, and a discussion of the political atmosphere in Black Montreal during the 1960s, see Roberts, *View for Freedom*, 65–73. According to Austin, "It was as a result of the CCWIA

activities in Montreal that James was eventually permitted to re-enter the United States for the first time since his expulsion in 1953. James returned to Montreal for the Congress of Black Writers in October 1968 and on several other occasions between 1968 and the early seventies" (p. 72, editorial note).

15 For further discussion on these points, see Austin, "All Roads Led to Montreal."

16 Jeffrey O.G. Ogbar, *Black Power: Radical Politics and African American Identity* (Baltimore: Johns Hopkins University Press, 2004), 197. This new outlook is articulated in King's speech against the Vietnam War, "Beyond Vietnam: A Time to Break Silence," delivered at the Riverside Church in New York City on 4 April 1967. Also, in "Black Power Defined," appearing in the *New York Times Magazine*, King argued that "We must frankly acknowledge that in past years our creativity and imagination were not employed in learning how to develop power." And, he went on, it was now necessary to "take the next major step of examining the levers of power which Negroes must grasp to influence the course of events." Both of these texts are reproduced in Martin Luther King, *I Have a Dream: Writing and Speeches That Changed the World*, ed. James M. Washington (San Francisco: HarperSanFrancisco, 1992).

17 For just one example of an author who argues for a re-examination of the divisions between the civil rights and Black Power movements, see Timothy B. Tyson, *Radio Free Dixie: Robert F. Williams and the Roots of Black Power* (Chapel Hill: University of North Carolina Press, 1999).

18 Ogbar, *Black Power*, 156.

19 For a moving account of one person's journey through the civil rights movement and its aftermath, see the epilogue to John Howard Griffin, *Black Like Me* (New York: Signet, 1976). For some of the main arguments of the emerging Black Power movement, see Stokely Carmichael and Charles V. Hamilton, *Black Power: The Politics of Liberation in America* (New York: Vintage, 1967).

20 Clayborne Carson, *In Struggle: SNCC and the Black Awakening of the 1960s* (Cambridge, MA: Harvard University Press, 1981), 288.

21 Quoted in Bill Bantey, "Montreal Mourned and Cried with Black and White Together," *Montreal Gazette*, 8 April 1968, 13.

22 "Editorial," *Expression* 3, no. 1 (1968): 3–5.

23 "Sir George Hosts Black Conference," *The Georgian*, 1 October 1968, 3. Dennis Forsythe, "The Black Writers Conference: Days to Remember," in *Let the Niggers Burn! The Sir George Williams University Affair and Its Caribbean Aftermath*, ed. Dennis Forsythe (Montreal: Black Rose Books/Our Generation Press, 1971), 58–9; Williams, *Road to Now*, 118–19.

24 John Shingler, "Panel Discussion," *Expression* 3, no. 3 (1969): 21.

25 McCurdy also spoke of the necessity of forming an alliance with "the Indians," their natural allies. Howard McCurdy, "Problems of Involvement in the Canadian Society with Reference to Black People," *Expression* 3, no. 3 (1969): 13–14; Daniel Hill, "Panel Discussion," *Expression* 3, no. 3 (1969): 18. McCurdy was not alone in his defence of Indigenous Canadians. Montreal economist Barry Mayers spoke of the necessity of confronting discrimination on all fronts, for "if we can justify discrimination, either by silence or otherwise, of the Indians, of the Eskimos, of the French Canadians, of the English Canadians, then there is no reason why the society can't justify discrimination against Negroes." The problem was largely one of poverty, and the Canadian population "will never get any kind of meaningful involvement unless we change the whole social structure of the Canadian Society and so make it possible to remove from isolation not only the Negro but the Indian, the Eskimo and, in a general sense, the entire population." Myers, "Panel Discussion," *Expression* 3, no. 3 (1969): 25–6.
26 Forsythe, "Black Writers Conference," 60.
27 Stanley Aleong, "'Dynamique de la libération noire': Congrès des écrivains noirs – McGill, 11–14 octobre," *Le Quartier latin*, 8 Octobre 1968, 12; "Black Power Is Coming," *McGill Daily*, 27 September 1968, 1. The McGill West Indian Society was not pleased, however, by the fact that the *Daily* described the conference as a "Black Power conference" and demanded a retraction, to which the *Daily* consented. "Letter to the Editor," *McGill Daily*, 9 October 1968.
28 Leroy Butcher, "The Sir George Williams Affair and Its Aftermath" (Rebellion, Protest, and Change: Reflections on the 1960s and the Development of Montreal's Black Community, UNIA Hall, Montreal, 18 February 2006), video recording.
29 Elder Thébaud and Rosie Douglas, "Editorial," Souvenir Program of Congress of Black Writers, McGill University, 11–14 October 1968, Gérald Godin fonds, 81p–660:02a/16, Université du Québec à Montréal (hereafter, Godin fonds).
30 Souvenir Program of Conference on Black Writers, McGill University, 11–14 October 1968, Godin fonds.
31 Austin, "Contemporary Montréal," 58.
32 Forsythe, "Black Writers Conference," 63.
33 Austin, "All Roads Led to Montreal," 523.
34 Cited in Austin, 523.
35 Letter signed by the Negro Community Centre Inc., Negro Theatre Arts Club, Montreal Negro Alumni Group, The Jamaica Association of Montreal, Canadian Conference Committee (Black Organisations), and the Trinidad and Tobago Association (Montreal), Godin fonds.

36 An edited version of Forman's speech can be found in James Forman, "Black Writers Hail Frantz Fanon," *Guardian*, 23 November 1968, 20–1.
37 Mike Boone, "Stokely Preaches Violent Revolution," *McGill Daily*, 15 October 1968, 2.
38 Forsythe, "Black Writers Conference," 62.
39 Boone, "Stokely Preaches," 1.
40 See the account of Ekwueme Michael Thelwell in *Ready for Revolution: The Life and Struggles of Stokely Carmichael (Kwame Ture)* (New York: Scribner, 2003), 544.
41 Quoted in Austin, "All Roads Led to Montreal," 525.
42 Stanley Gray, interview by the author, Hamilton, 10 June 2005.
43 Gérald Godin, "La folie bilinguale," *Parti Pris* 3, no. 10 (1966): 56.
44 Annotations on Souvenir Program of Conference on Black Writers, Godin fonds.
45 Gérald Godin, untitled document, 16 October 1968, Godin fonds.
46 Barbara Jones, "A Black Woman Speaks Out," *McGill Reporter*, 4 November 1968.
47 Forsythe, "Black Writers Conference," 62–6.
48 Forsythe, 64.
49 Editors, "Black Militants and Red Guards," *McGill Reporter*, 4 November 1968, 1.
50 Rosie Douglas, Rita Sherman, and Robert Chodos, "No Time for Coalitions," *McGill Daily*, 21 October 1968, 5.
51 The Congress of Black Writers also had important international ramifications. The international nature of the struggle was made clear when Walter Rodney, lecturer at the University of the West Indies in Jamaica, was banned from returning to Jamaica after his appearance at the conference in Montreal. News of the ban quickly spread to Jamaica, where angry crowds took to the streets. Police unleashed clouds of tear gas and made generous use of guns and clubs. The riots left downtown Kingston in shambles; fifty buses were burned, and three people were killed in the confrontations. At a mass rally held at Sir George Williams University in support of Rodney, Rodney himself took to the podium. He insisted that the violence was not a mere student uprising but a "revolutionary manifestation of social malaise" on the part of the entire population of Kingston. The audience listened intently as Rodney spoke of his dedication to working with lower-class Blacks. These people, he stated, humbled him with their knowledge about heritage and culture and about the beauty of Black people. The audience, clearly moved, repeatedly broke into enthusiastic applause, and when Rodney concluded his speech by saying that they will "celebrate victory with black drums," the crowd burst into a standing ovation. Robert Wallace, "Local Rally Supports Jamaican Students," *McGill Daily*, 21 October 1968, 1. It should be noted as well that after the Congress of Black Writers, Bobby Seale of the Black Panthers came to the city for the Hemispheric

Conference to End the War in Vietnam at the end of November 1968. "Bobby Seale Makes It ...," *McGill Daily*, 2 December 1968, 3.
52 "SGWU Hearing Folds: 200 Students Occupy Computing Center," *McGill Daily*, 30 January 1969, 1.
53 Rosie Douglas received an eighteen-month sentence, and Anne Cools a four-month sentence. Austin, "All Roads Led to Montreal," 531–2.
54 Carl Lumumba, "The West Indies and the Sir George Williams Affair: An Assessment," in Forsythe, *Let the Niggers Burn!*, 179.
55 See Lumumba, 181; and Austin, "Introduction," n12.
56 According to the editors of *UHURU*, "most" of the students arrested were Black, but in fact only forty-two of the ninety-seven people arrested were Black. See "Editorial: Deep Ramifications," *UHURU*, 16 February 1970, 2. The event has received virtually no attention in works dealing with the Quiet Revolution.
57 The Sir George Williams Affair had ramifications that spread far beyond the Canadian border, initiating a series of political revolts throughout the Caribbean. See Forsythe, *Let the Niggers Burn!*
58 Roberts, *View for Freedom*, 57–8.
59 Roberts, 73, 81–2.
60 Austin, "Contemporary Montréal," 59. In both the short-term and medium-term aftermath to the incidents of 11 February, many different groups began speaking up against the racist backlash that was occurring. The West Indian Students Association, for example, wrote, "We cannot accept the hysterical cries of 'hoodlums,' 'rioters,' 'dangerous agitators,' 'foreigners,' 'Red Chinese agents,' and 'let the niggers burn.' We reject the overt racism and anti-student sentiment comparable in many ways to the witch-hunt atmosphere of McCarthyism in the early 1950's." West Indian Students Association memo, n.d., Anderson Affair fonds, William Ready Division of Archives and Research Collections, McMaster University.
61 Paul Gilroy, "*There Ain't No Black in the Union Jack*": *The Cultural Politics of Race and Nation* (Chicago: University of Chicago Press, 1991), 27.
62 Gilroy, 11.
63 See *The Georgian*, 4 February 1969.
64 For examples of this backlash, see the many articles in the 19 February 1969 edition of *The Georgian*. For an example of a West Indian student speaking about how many West Indian students were opposed to the occupation, see A.R. Ali, "The Price of Courage to Disagree," *The Georgian*, 19 February 1969, 8.
65 "SGWU Pulls Out of UGEQ," *McGill Daily*, 17 February 1969, 1. See also "Fired Georgian Editor to Receive Cup Verdict," *McGill Daily*, 26 February 1969, 3. For the letter from the "radical faculty," see "An Open Letter to Leftwing Faculty and Students at Sir George Williams University from

a Group of Radical Professors," 1969, Statements, Dr. Marsden Papers, Concordia University Archives. See also Eugene Genovese, *In Red and Black; Marxian Explorations in Southern Afro-American History* (New York: Pantheon Books, 1971), v–vi.

66 "Sir George Williams et le cas de Charles Gagnon: les Deux Masques de la Répression," press release, 21 February 1969, publications, Conseil central des syndicats nationaux de Montréal (CCSNM) fonds, Archives, Confédération des syndicats nationaux (ACSN). On the occasion of a conference held on the twentieth anniversary of the Sir George Affair, on 11 February 1989, Michel Chartrand gave a paper entitled "The Affair and Quebec's National Question." See "The Computer Centre Incident 20 Years Later: Feb. 11, 1969–Feb. 11, 1989," Alfie Roberts Institute, Montreal.

67 Roméo Bouchard, "Vous êtes des nègres," *Le Quartier latin*, 11 February 1969, 2.

68 Kenneth-Charles De Puis, Jacques Michon, and Pierre Larivière, "On soutient toujours son frère et sa sœur," *Le Quartier latin*, 25 February 1969, 12.

69 Jacques Maassen, "Values and the Computer," *McGill Daily*, 14 February 1969, 4.

70 Dorothy Eber, *The Computer Centre Party: Canada Meets Black Power* (Montreal: Tundra Books, 1969), 271, 220.

71 Eber, 152, 157.

72 Butcher, "Sir George Williams Affair."

73 Williams, *Road to Now*, 121.

74 Dennis Forsythe, "By Way of Introduction: 'The Sir George Williams Affair,'" in Forsythe, *Let the Niggers Burn!*, 8.

75 "Canadian Liberalism: Fact or Fiction," editorial, *Expression* 3, no. 3 (1969): 3–6.

76 See Caribbean International Service Bureau (CISB), "Black Spark Edition," *McGill Free Press: Black Spark Edition* (1971): 1.

77 Butcher, "Sir George Williams Affair."

78 Brenda Dash, "Thursday Night Rally Re-Opens," *UHURU*, 12 January 1970, 7.

79 See Austin, "All Roads Led to Montreal," 535.

80 For an overview of many of these developments, see Williams, *Road to Now*, chap. 7.

81 Because of its radical tone, *UHURU* did not, of course, speak for all of Montreal's Black community. At the first national meeting of the Canadian Conference Committee in Toronto, in October 1969, a major confrontation erupted between Montreal radicals – who demanded that the fallout of the Sir George Williams Affair be discussed as a priority – and other Black organizations. Through the pages of the new publication *Umoja*, a frustration with those involved in the Sir George Williams Affair is palpable.

According to Clarence S. Bayne, "a black community cannot be built on the basis of people who are continually living in a state of returning to the West Indies, who are not committed to making this country theirs." "Editorial Note: Black Unity," *Umoja* 1, no. 1 (1969): 1; "A Programme of Action for the National Black Coalition," *Umoja* 1, no. 2 (1969): 1, 4; C.S. Bayne, "A Report on the Canadian Conference Committee," *Umoja* 1, no. 1 (1969): 3.

82 "Focus on UHURU," *UHURU*, 8 December 1969, 4; Omowale, "The Brother on the Corner," *UHURU*, 31 July 1969, 5.

83 "Focus on UHURU," 4. The print run of *Parti Pris* in the mid-1960s stood at roughly four thousand. "Lettre au lecteur," *Parti Pris* 2, no. 1 (1964): 18.

84 Stokely Carmichael and Miriam Carmichael, "Letter to the Editor," *UHURU*, 2 February 1970, 2.

85 "Focus on UHURU," 4–5.

86 In an October 1968 publication by members of the Conference Committee meant to coincide with the Congress of Black Writers, several authors spoke of the neocolonial role that Canadian capital and Canadian companies played in the Caribbean. See, for example, A. Eustace, "On the Economism of the 'Movement ... As the West Indian Society for the Study of Social Issues,'" *Caribbean International Opinion: Dynamics of Liberation* 1, no. 1 (1968): 26–31; and Feleon, "On Haiti," *Caribbean International Opinion: Dynamics of Liberation* 1, no. 1 (1968): 61–4.

87 Powerful analyses of race and of the connections between Canada and the Caribbean sometimes even made their way into other leftist writing. "SGWU Blacks Get a Taste of Just Society," *Last Post* 1, no. 3 (1970): 5–7.

88 "Sir George and O'Brien," *UHURU*, 18 August 1969, 1.

89 LeRoi [Leroy] Butcher, "The Anderson Affair," in Forsythe, *Let the Niggers Burn!*, 106.

90 Rosie Douglas, "Solidarity Day against Canadian Racism and Beyond," *UHURU*, 23 March 1970, 4.

91 Frantz Fanon, *Black Skin, White Masks*, trans. Charles Lam Markmann (1952; New York: Grove Press, 1967), 190.

92 "The Sixties: Revolution or Evolution?," *UHURU*, 12 January 1970, 4.

93 His title drew explicitly on a chapter from *Black Skin, White Masks*. Maurice Tremblay, "The Facts of Blackness," *UHURU*, 1 June 1970, 6–8.

94 See, for example, Omowale, "The Need for a Black United Front in Montreal," *UHURU*, 18 July 1969, 4.

95 Williams, *Road to Now*, 109.

96 For Howard McCurdy, "we cannot look at black power as based on numbers in this country." McCurdy, "Problems of Involvement," 14.

97 Rosie Douglas, "Stokely Carmichael Returns to U.S.," *UHURU*, 13 April 1970, 1.

98 See *UHURU*, 31 July 1969, 5, and 2 September 1969.

99 See *UHURU*, 12 January 1970.
100 Edmund Michael, "'Red Power in Canada,'" *UHURU*, 29 September 1969, 3.
101 "Check Point: Montreal," *UHURU*, 12 January 1970, 6.
102 Asher, "Red Nationalism on the Rise," *UHURU*, 2 March 1970. The 12 January 1970 edition of the paper also noted the occupation of Alcatraz Island in San Francisco Bay.
103 At a meeting held at Sir George Williams University in November 1968, for example, American civil rights activist Floyd McKissick and history professor Arvarh Strickland spoke to a crowd of two hundred students and were immediately asked whether the plight of Blacks could be related to the struggles of francophone Quebeckers in Canada. McKissick, clearly caught off guard, could only muster a confused reply. According to *The Georgian*, "Mr. McKissick replied that his concern was with the immediate, local racial problems and that he considered racism to differ from region to region, not necessarily along Marxist class lines." "'White Racist System Ain't Healthy for Whites or Blacks'– McKissick," *The Georgian*, 26 November 1968, 6.
104 Rosie Douglas, in "Black Writers Congress: The Organizers Talk ...," *The Review* (*McGill Daily* supplement), 11 October 1968, 2.
105 Elder Thébaud, in "Organizers Talk," 4–5.
106 Douglas, in "Organizers Talk," 5.
107 Fernand Foisy, "Rapport du sécrétaire – décisions du comité exécutif," 19, Congrès 1969, CCSNM fonds, ASCN.
108 Sister Obiageli, "Thursday Night Rally Revival!," *UHURU*, 2 March 1970, 6.
109 "C.B.C. Use Innocent Black Children," *UHURU*, 27 April 1970, 1, 8.
110 Charles, "Black Children and Bilingualism," *UHURU*, 13 April 1970, 7.
111 "Editorial," *UHURU*, 27 April 1970, 2.
112 "Editorial," *UHURU*, 11 May 1970, 2. For a more radical position that rejects the PQ, advocating instead the ideas of Quebec decolonization associated with Charles Gagnon and Pierre Vallières, see Rosie Douglas, "The Irrelevance of the Quebec Elections," *UHURU*, 27 April 1970, 6.
113 Dennis Forsythe, preface to *Let the Niggers Burn!*, 3.
114 Forsythe, "By Way of Introduction," 10.
115 Forsythe, 14, 12.
116 CISB, "Black Spark Edition," 1.
117 Butcher, "Anderson Affair," 77.
118 Winston Franco, "Two Views of the Conference of Black Writers – II," *Expression* 3, no. 3 (1969): 43–4.
119 Omowale, "Respectable Faces Students Twelve Charges," *UHURU*, 18 August 1969, 7.
120 Cited in Eber, *Computer Centre Party*, 126.
121 "Dear Brother Black," *UHURU*, 14 October 1969, 6.

122 Quoted in Austin, "Introduction," 21, editorial note.
123 "Dear Brother," *UHURU*, 22 December 1969, 6.
124 "Letter to the Editor," *UHURU*, 8 December 1969, 2.
125 "Letter to the Editor," *UHURU*, 24 November 1969, 2.
126 A Black Sister, "Dear Sister," *UHURU*, 15 September 1969, 6.
127 "Letter to the Editor," *UHURU*, 8 December 1969, 2.
128 According to Akua Benjamin, who arrived in Toronto from Trinidad in the middle of Toronto's radical upsurge, "Anne Cools came to one of these meetings, and she blasted the men. She challenged us women in the room as to why we were not talking. In those days, I just sat quietly in the back of the room. I would sit there and sweat. I was afraid to speak, afraid that I would get shut down. Anne cursed the men out, saying, 'fucking' this and 'fucking' that. We had never heard a woman talk like that. She really empowered me. After that I thought, 'I'm going to raise my voice.'" Quoted in Judy Rebick, *Ten Thousand Roses: The Making of a Feminist Revolution* (Toronto: Penguin, 2005), 9–10.

SECTION FOUR

Controlling Black (Working) Bodies

9
"Likely to become a public charge": Examining Black Migration to Eastern Canada, 1900–1930

CLAUDINE BONNER

> Vessels from [the] West Indies are carrying Negroes landing them at different ports of Nova Scotia with little or no means and without inspection. Customs officers should be immediately instructed as to their duties as these West Indians are daily becoming a charge province.
>
> W.F. Annand, June 1909

Upon receipt of this telegram from W.F. Annand in June 1909, Immigration Branch Superintendent W.D. Scott responded by sending J.B. Williams, the department's "travelling border inspector," to investigate the matter of West Indian illegal immigrants entering Nova Scotia.[1] Williams visited Port Hawkesbury, Point Tupper, Sydney, and North Sydney before sending a detailed report back to Ottawa. In this report, Williams outlined the fact that between 1 April and 8 June 1909 fifty-one West Indians had passed through Port Hawkesbury, all bound for Sydney.[2] The discovery of this practice led to an odyssey beginning in 1909 and continuing well into the 1920s, reflecting the ways in which the Canadian state struggled with and questioned notions of race, identity, and, on the basis of these, access.

Today Canada is a geographically large immigrant-receiving society with over 37 million residents settled mainly across the southern edge of the nation. The Indigenous population comprises less than 5 per cent of the nation's inhabitants, meaning that most Canadians are descendants of immigrants (or are themselves immigrants). As a result, it should not be surprising that writing about immigration has long been an aspect of Canadian historical scholarship, mapping the various waves of migration into the contemporary period. Recent historical writing has evidenced acknowledgement of Canada as a nation of immigrants as Canadian historians have grappled with interpreting how each new wave of immigrants has been received and treated on Canada's shores.[3] The last two decades have seen a growing body of literature and renewed interest in the histories of race and immigration.[4] There also appears to be a better understanding of the role that White settler society played in subjugating the Indigenous peoples, as well as the ways in which race, class, and gender have worked to shape our history. In her look at ethnic immigration historiography up to the late 1990s, Franca Iacovetta calls for a more integrative approach to the study of immigrants and minorities and of race and ethnicity in Canadian history. While much remains to be done, with these developments being evident perhaps we are seeing a change in the ways we conceptualize and write about history in Canada.[5]

As a result of changes in the scholarship about race and immigration in Canada, one of the things we have seen is the production of historical writing that recognizes the arbitrary creation and maintenance of a racist hierarchy.[6] This hierarchy was initially based on biological notions of innate differences between peoples, arising in the European Enlightenment and premised on a process of ordering and placing humans using physiological and mental criteria. These notions allowed natural historians to include humans in the process of classification of the natural world, turning perceived physical differences into justifications for relations of domination. As Europeans extended their presence globally, they used these understandings of personhood and place to justify their treatment of the racial "Other." Their original understanding of "race" as biologically determined evolved through its use as a sociopolitical construct to maintain this hierarchy – one that placed Whites at the top as full citizens and non-Whites in subordinate positions.[7] This ordering can be seen in terms of the access given to the immigrant worker. British and American Whites and western Europeans were readily admitted and sought-after immigrants. Eastern and southern Europeans, while still decidedly "foreign" and less welcome because of their strange languages and customs, were still more readily accepted than Blacks and Asians. Canadian industry used Black and Asian migrants as a source of cheap, dispensable labour that could be tapped into during times of worker shortage.[8] Prevailing notions of the unassimilability of these groups, the belief in their biological and moral inferiority (and lack of character), fuelled the creation and maintenance of a systemically racist nation. Evidence can be found in the immigration and judicial records of the period, records that have become a source of understanding more about our nation through the application of micro-analyses centring race.

This chapter examines the ways in which the province of Nova Scotia dealt with attempts at entry into Canada by people of African descent in the early decades of the twentieth century and, in so doing, adds to a growing body of immigration literature. It explores the ways in which the

Canadian state's relationship to this migration required the deployment of an extensive cohort of customs and other officers and years of work on the part of the Immigration Branch in its role of determining admissibility.[9] During the period under investigation, Nova Scotia worked to promote the exclusion of additional Black migrants by the application of stringent policing. The existing extensive collection of letters and other documents from the Immigration Branch makes Nova Scotia a good case for examination, as the collection includes several cases specific to that province and provides insight into the processes and rationale of the branch and its staff during this period.

The chapter begins with a review of some of the ways labour migration became embedded in the fabric of Caribbean life. This will demonstrate to the reader how Canada, as a site of both arrival and departure, connects to the history of the broader African diaspora and, hence, why there was a movement of African-descended people into Canada in the period under examination. To come to a better understanding of the ways that Nova Scotian ports were implicated in the process of gatekeeping, the chapter then outlines the ways Black migrants (and, for much of the time under examination, particularly Black migrants from the Caribbean) were systematically surveilled and restricted by immigration authorities during their migration. The chapter ends with a look at the creation of a new Black community in Sydney that emerged despite the policies and behaviours of exclusion, in an area known as Whitney Pier.

Early Twentieth-Century Black Migration in the Americas

Between 1900 and 1930, people of African descent, originating in the British West Indies and the United States, made their way to different parts of Canada, including the remote location of Sydney, Nova Scotia. The majority were part of a transnational industrial workforce that moved throughout the Americas in response to opportunity. This group was affected by many of the same global pushes and pulls that had brought Italians, Ukrainians, Poles, and other Europeans across the continent and into Canada.[10] The African Americans were part of what would become known as the Great Black Migration, as waves of southern African Americans made their way to the urban North and Far West in the early years of the twentieth century, forever changing much of American life.[11] Those coming from the Caribbean and Latin America were part of a wave of migration that had begun with the legal end of slavery in the region. Regions of the British West Indies experienced a catastrophic decline in their sugar industry in the decades after emancipation as they were unable to compete with what was being produced in Cuba and Brazil by slave labour (as well as the production of beet sugar in Europe itself). The price of sugar from the Caribbean dropped significantly in the late 1800s when it ceased being the main source of sugar on the market.[12] As a result, workers on British Caribbean islands were laid off and forced to seek employment in other places that could use their skills in sugar production. In the case of Barbados, overpopulation and unemployment led the government to help people to emigrate after having initially tried to keep people on the island as cheap sources of labour. Beginning in the 1860s, the Barbadian government began sponsoring emigration from the island.[13] Workers left their homes and ventured to places where they endured the hardships of Jim Crow policies, disease, high death rates, discrimination, and ill treatment, for a chance at economic and social stability.[14] By leaving, they could send remittances home to their families, build homes on their native islands for their later return, and thus create lives they would not have otherwise had.

While a need for better economic circumstances pushed migrants out of their home countries, the availability of jobs and opportunities determined where they went. Initially moving to other Caribbean islands and countries in South and Central America whose plantation economies were perhaps better able to sustain them, migrants travelled to places such as Cuba, the Dominican Republic, Guatemala, Venezuela, and Costa Rica. Major construction projects also shaped the movement of people throughout the Caribbean. In 1850, the building of the railway in Panama led to a mass migration of Jamaican workers to that country. Thirty years later, men and women from all over the Americas flocked to Panama again, this time for the building of the Panama Canal. The final years of the 1800s and the first decades of the twentieth century were marked by the constant movement of bodies within this region, as migrants flocked to new locales.[15] Ports throughout the Americas were kept busy with this labour migration; according to historian Lara Putnam, cities like Kingston, Jamaica, saw so much activity that by 1908 several steamship lines were traversing the region, bringing skilled and other labourers and others seeking adventure from that port to a number of ports in South, Central, and North America.[16] People learned of new, lucrative places to find work from sailors passing through towns or returnees sporting new clothing and shoes – or by listening to the songs of the day, the lyrics of which spoke of these places, travel, the jobs, and potential earnings.[17]

Included in the myriad of places to consider for employment possibilities was Sydney. Late nineteenth-century steelmaking and coal transportation had transformed Sydney into a nationally important industrial city, incorporated in 1904. Because of the new burgeoning industry, Sydney offered vital opportunities to labourers the world over, creating a new set of labour migration possibilities for people of African descent in the Americas.

Among these possibilities was work in the new steel industry. Henry Melville Whitney, a Boston capitalist, had consolidated the ownership of several Nova Scotia coalfields in 1893. This provided him with the opportunity to enter the business of steelmaking in an enterprise that allowed use both of coal from his mines to fuel the furnaces and of ore from his Wabana mines on Bell Island, in Newfoundland, as raw materials.[18] In 1901, Whitney opened Dominion Iron and Steel Company (DISCO) in Sydney and the company would employ hundreds of local and immigrant workers for decades. With the birth of this new industry, thousands flocked into the new city, spawning new services and other supporting enterprises.

Among its early employees, DISCO hired African American steelworkers who had extensive experience in the industry and were considered skilled workers as a result of their experience working in the American steel belt.[19] With American management and state-of-the-art American technology at DISCO, the most sensible hiring practice was to seek out men who had worked in the industry, and even men who had already worked with these managers. John H. Means, Superintendent of Furnaces at DISCO starting in 1901, recruited his workers from the network he had developed in Alabama, Buffalo, Tonawanda, Maryland, and Pittsburgh.[20] With the opening of DISCO there appears to have been no problems in the process of recruiting or hiring African Americans at this time. As Donald Avery has noted, Canadian immigration policy at times reflected the needs of industry more so than the nation's prevailing politics on racial exclusion. Thus, when the Canadian government – as well as agricultural, railroad, mining, and other industries – needed cheap labour, the state responded to these needs despite nativist ideas surrounding who was not to be let into the country.[21] However, many of the workers Means hired did not stay for very long in the Sydney community; this was something he had somewhat expected, as he noted in a letter in 1901 in reference to African American workers: "I fear the men will be unable to stand this climate."[22] With their departure, the company sought to replace them and other American labourers with ethnic Europeans and Caribbean workers.

Canada seemed an ideal place to settle since, starting in 1896, the federal Department of the Interior sought out new immigrants to homestead on the Canadian prairies. The department mounted extensive advertising programs across Europe and the United States, bringing in over a million new immigrants between 1896 and 1914.²³ Among them, Americans with money to invest and skills to impart were the most sought after – that is, *White* Americans with money and skills. The political climate clearly favoured converting Canada into a truly "White" country (although the presence of its Indigenous population meant that Canada was never exclusively White), and the state worked to keep non-Whites out. The Great Black Migration coincided with this period of recruitment of immigrants from the United States into Canada. Black Oklahomans were among those seeking to settle in the Canadian Prairie provinces, disillusioned by their failed attempts at settlement in their new American state, which had instituted its own Jim Crow policies. This arrival of African Americans at the borders of western provinces in the early 1900s created distress and confusion. Both within the civil service and among the public, fears of an influx of Black migrants from the United States abounded in the early years of the twentieth century. Canadian immigration officials worked to place whatever obstacles they could in the way of African Americans to discourage and prevent them from entering the country, and it was made clear that "the fertile lands of the West will be left to be cultivated by the white race only."²⁴ For African Americans, the obstacles were minor in comparison with the racial terror they sought to escape, as Jim Crow practices spread throughout the South, state laws became more rigid in the North, and the practice of segregation became normalized throughout the country.²⁵

Black Immigration in Eastern Canada

The new threat of Black immigration from the Caribbean through the Atlantic gates simply added to the fears planted by the threat of Black migration coming from the American South.²⁶ Customs officers began relying on the 1906 amendments to the Immigration Act and called upon immigration officers to use their discretion in recognizing that Black migrants were likely to become public charges (noted as "l.p.c." on their immigration documents) and hence burdens on the state. This revised Immigration Act worked to impose more stringent regulations and included an expanded list of prohibited immigrants, including those with physical and mental impairments, as well as the destitute, the impoverished, and anyone else likely to become a public charge. The act allowed for anyone included in the prohibited classes to be deported within two years of arrival in Canada. On the basis of this list, Caribbean migrants were denied entry into the country. They were also labelled as being morally and physically unfit and there was evidence to suggest that in a climate where Canada sought to welcome agriculturalists, these Black

Caribbean migrants had not shown themselves to be capable farmers.[27] When faced with Caribbean women attempting to enter the country, an argument Immigration Superintendent W.D. Scott made against their entry was that "nearly all West Indian girls suffered from some combination of tuberculosis, immorality and insanity."[28] This perspective arose out of the existing stereotypes and understandings of Black bodies as hypersexual and diseased. By virtue of their race as well as their gender, these women were seen and understood as flawed and hence inadmissible.[29] As Jared Toney notes, these scientific "truths" about Blackness were being used to "maintain the racial integrity of the nation."[30]

While these beliefs about Blackness abounded, Black people continued to be brought into the country for work. For example, as White Canadian women were leaving domestic service for jobs in the new manufacturing and service sectors, a demand arose for cheap domestic labour in Quebec, the Maritimes, and Ontario. As a result, in 1910, Canada instituted its first domestic scheme, bringing in one hundred young women from Guadeloupe. Compared with other domestics at that time in Canada, who were paid twelve to fifteen dollars for the same work, these young women were paid a monthly wage of five dollars. In addition to this clear discrimination in wages, according to Agnes Calliste, this immigration scheme was laced with paternalism and ethnocentrism, and the women experienced a "fourfold form of oppression" in terms of how their immigration status interacted with their race, class, and gender.[31]

The women in the domestic scheme were among few people of colour who were sought out or allowed to enter the country during this period. Most Black persons attempting to enter Canada through maritime ports were turned away. Calling on dozens of civil servants in small port locations across Nova Scotia, the Immigration Branch worked to marshal the power of the state against what was being labelled as an assault on the nation by people who were seen as, and understood to be, unassimilable. A review of incidents and documents related to race and immigration reveals the extent to which government officials sought to limit Black migration into Canada in the years between 1909 and 1925.

The report from Williams to Superintendent Scott in 1909 that opened this chapter appears to have been innocuous, but it ended on an ominous note that provides insight into the ways Black migrants attempting to enter Canada would experience immigration in this region for the next decade. Williams reported that Port Hawkesbury seemed to be the main port other than Halifax at which West Indian passengers disembarked after travelling to Nova Scotia aboard schooners from Barbados at a cost of twenty dollars per head, an amount with which their government appeared to assist them. The tone of the report was positive. Williams reported that John Hennessy, Collector of Customs at Port Hawkesbury, thought those passing through the town were of a "better class" and "well dressed." The fact that the West Indians appeared to be employed, or going to seek employment, in Sydney should have provided reassurance that none of them would become a public charge, the prospect that seemed to have initially driven the investigation. Yet, Williams told Scott that "the chief port where these negroes have been landing will be watched."[32] This marks the beginning of a period of surveillance and assessment of Black immigrants in the Nova Scotian ports to determine their admissibility. A look at the roster of customs officers at ports of entry and preventive stations across Nova Scotia during this period provides insight into how much was invested in this process of policing the border. In this period there were close to two hundred collectors, sub-collectors, preventive officers, and other staff at work in the province. Almost every port, large or small, had a customs office.

Over the next few years, many of these civil servants within the Immigration Branch, both in the small port offices and in the central Immigration Office in Ottawa, worked to track down and confirm rumoured landings of illegal Black migrants across the province. Even with the vast network of officers at their disposal (or perhaps because of it), it could take days or weeks for letters or telegrams to be received, or answered, so confusion and misinformation were abundant. A good example of this concerned the ship the *Marion* in Port Hawkesbury. Upon its arrival at Port Hawkesbury in May 1910, W.L. Barnstead wrote a letter to the Immigration Office: "I learn on good authority ... that the Sch. Marion from Barbados landed at Port Hawkesbury twenty-five Negros, for points in Cape Breton. Of course these may have been properly examined by an officer, but as this is the time of year that quite a number of them come in schooners I thought it well to advise you."[33]

In response, L.M. Fortier, for the Department of Immigration, sent a letter to J.J. Williams, immigration inspector in Port Hawkesbury, on 31 May asking the following questions: "Will you please advise me immediately whether this is so, and if so, whether the negroes were admitted by you after inspection, as required by the Immigration Act. If they were you should send me a copy of the ship's manifest with all the particulars we require noted thereon. In any event I would like to hear from you in this matter without delay. Who are the owners of the Marion, and where is she now?"[34] When Williams replied a few weeks later, he claimed the report of the ship's landing was false: "No such vessel as the Marion has been reported, or has landed, negroes here, this season. All negroes landed here have been reported in my regular monthly statements. Any information you may have received to the contrary is false."[35]

This exchange of letters, as well as the number of individuals involved, highlighted the anxiety created at the possibility of twenty-five Blacks having landed illegally in the region, as well as the ways in which the Immigration Office responded to such a possibility. However, while the story of the landing of the *Marion* had been disproven, several other ships were determined to have bypassed the 1910 Immigration Act, which further encouraged the use of the discretionary powers of government to regulate the flow of immigrants into Canada, reinforcing and expanding the exclusionary provisions outlined in the *Immigration Act* of 1906.[36]

In some cases, the names of the arriving West Indian passengers were known, while in others, the ship records only depicted numbers. For example, documents pertaining to the *Yolando*, or *Yalondo*, which arrived at Saint John, New Brunswick, on two occasions in 1912, reveal only numerical data for the human cargo from Barbados: thirty-eight passengers on 7 May and twenty-five passengers on 25 July.[37] The ship had no living accommodations aside from those for the master and crew, which meant the owner had violated the 1910 Immigration Act's requirement to provide this accommodation. In this instance, the *Yolando* was charged one hundred dollars for the infraction.[38] Throughout this period the staff of the Immigration Branch was working to keep up with what appears to have been a steady, lucrative process of clandestine immigration of Blacks, made necessary by the refusal of the state to see Blacks as admissible to the nation. Nothing in the documents from this period suggests a focus on Caribbean or other migrants who were not Black; instead, there occurred a constant scrutiny of seemingly Black Caribbean migrants to ascertain whether or not they should be classified as such.

On 23 May 1914 a letter was received by W.D. Scott again regarding ship captains illegally bringing passengers from Barbados and other places. The letter was sent by James C. Lantz, mate of the *H.R. Silver* and resident of Mahone Bay, Nova Scotia. In his letter, Lantz stated that his captain was bringing far more than the allowed four passengers on the *Silver* on his return from Barbados (he was alleging there had been twenty-one on the boat's most recent trip).[39] Further, Lantz wrote that the passengers were coming in unsafe, crowded conditions, fraudulently signed on as ship's crew in the Caribbean, and secreted off the boat at small ports in Nova Scotia, usually under cover of night. According to the Immigration Act, passengers were not to leave a vessel before permission had been granted by an immigration agent, and there was also a penalty if vessels carried passengers who were not officially entered on the list of passengers. Lantz provided the Immigration Branch with the names of the real crew, as well as a list of the eleven passengers and how much each had paid for his passage.[40] Lantz's letter ignited another major investigation within the branch, led by Inspector of Agencies L.M. Fortier, who was left with the realization that this was not a singular incident but in fact a common practice. The owners of the *H.R. Silver* were fined seven thousand dollars for the fourteen Barbadians whom Captain Gerhardt admitted to having smuggled into the country.[41]

During this same period, Fortier, in another letter, warned Scott about "the state of the labour market in the Sydneys." Since unemployment is already high, he suggested, "the Department should maintain an unyielding attitude in the matter of the West India Negroes."[42] Inspector Fortier appeared to have become obsessed with closing any loopholes that were allowing Caribbean Blacks into Nova Scotia (perhaps increasingly so after his investigation into the case of the *H.R. Silver*). According to historian John Schultz, for Fortier the goal was to ensure that roadblocks were placed in the way of West Indians to prevent them from landing in the Maritimes. The department, with him as its agent, saw no benefit to these people entering the country.[43]

One thing that becomes abundantly clear upon a close reading of the immigration files is that even though the main rationale put forward in the years between 1900 and 1930 relates to the Immigration Branch's fear of Black migrants becoming public charges, this was simply an excuse, since even those with jobs or who met the requirements in other ways were provided with obstacles to entry. Even if one had the means of support, this did not mean one would be admitted. For example, at the end of July 1914, Fortier noted in a letter to Scott that his instructions to customs officers had changed from allowing Caribbean migrants into the country if they passed the required medical examination, had twenty-five dollars, and had a ticket to their destination in Canada. He believed this to be insufficient toward proving that they would not become public charges. He believed there were too many of them already in the province, acknowledged several hundred were working in the Dominion Iron and Steel Company, and noted a plan to ascertain how every single DISCO worker from the Caribbean had made his/her way into the country, to ensure none had found a loophole: "I am procuring a detailed statement from both the Dominion Iron & Steel Co. and the Dominion Coal Co., of all West Indian Negroes taken into their employ since the first of January, 1914. There will be something over two hundred names in these lists, but Mr. Young will examine them all, for a purpose of discovering how and under what circumstances they got into Canada with a view to finding out and stopping up loopholes."[44]

These companies employed hundreds of other ethnic and foreign workers during the period, but the branch's investigation would be directed solely at Caribbean men who, as employees of DISCO, were clearly earning money and able to support themselves. It is reasonable to argue that this was not about a likelihood of the men becoming public charges; it was about Blackness. As had others within the branch, Fortier had clearly appointed himself a guardian of Canada's racial purity.[45]

Industry did not always agree with the perspective of the Immigration Branch, and there were several times in this period where the needs of industry were believed to outweigh the needs for a "White" nation and, at times, superseded immigration policy. During those periods, regardless of the prevailing discourses, companies sought out the bodies they needed to complete the work.[46] In Sydney at the turn of the century, with the opening of DISCO and the need for a viable workforce, the company sought permission to bring in foreign workers on multiple occasions.[47] While not always successful, as they were thwarted by the leadership in the Immigration Branch, these occasions provide examples of how industry sought out cheap labour, regardless of race. In the years before World War I, DISCO sent Barbadian men to Barbados as recruiting agents; this had become part of company practice – sending ethnic workers back home to recruit on the company's behalf.[48] With the difficulties in procuring employees during the war years, in 1916 DISCO requested and was given permission to import one thousand Caribbean workers. Scott justified this concession in an internal letter to Fortier of the Immigration Branch as being for the greater good of the nation: "The production of steel and coal must go on even at some expenses to the country, and the concession is made on the principle of being the lesser evil. You can readily understand how unwilling we would be here to make the concession under any but the strongest reasons."[49]

It was clearly understood within the branch that Canada would only entertain bringing in Black workers under the most desperate of conditions. According to Calliste, it appears that these 1,000 workers were never recruited from the Caribbean, as DISCO may have filled its quota from 1,300 Austrians who had been released from internment camps in Quebec and Ontario.[50] Whether through official or unofficial means, however, DISCO continued to provide employment to workers from the Caribbean.

Those from the Caribbean who were already resident in Canada were limited by the demands of the Immigration Branch if they tried to leave the country on vacation or for any other reasons. Several wrote letters to clarify their situation if they returned to the Caribbean, since they were uncertain as to their admissibility upon their return because the limitations on access kept changing. Immigration Superintendent Scott clarified their position, indicating that they "would be entitled to land in Canada as a matter of right, provided they had acquired and had not lost Canadian domicile."[51] This highlighted the fact that the new requirements of admissibility (maintaining Canadian domicile) could now prevent Caribbean workers from being eligible to re-enter the country, and thus they could find themselves listed as "l.p.c." upon their return, despite having homes and jobs in Canada. Since the branch was well aware that there was an illegal practice of entering the country, this was another way of seeking to remove those who had bypassed the system into Canada. Unless there was an amnesty for illegal immigrants, they could not risk leaving the country. For those who had been admitted into the country legally, they would have to meet new requirements that they might not have had to meet on their original arrival.

Even men who had been working at DISCO and who went home when there was a slowdown in work availability would not be guaranteed access if they tried to return to Canada. According to Scott, they would have to provide sufficient proof from the steel plant that they would have permanent employment upon their return, but he noted that "the above immigrants will be rejected if such action can properly be taken under the provisions of the Immigration Act."[52] So once again, providing proof that they would indeed not be "likely to become public charges" was insufficient. Whatever provision the Immigration Branch could find under the act would be used to reject them. In part, since these were mostly male labourers, one might wonder if these refusals were also gendered and simply aimed at keeping mainly Black men out of Canada. This is a distinct possibility when one considers that in May 1915 Scott indicated that "domestic servants, however, from the British West Indies, who can pass the medical inspection and have sufficient money to qualify, may be admitted, provided ample evidence is submitted that they are going to assured employment and are not persons who are likely to become a public charge."[53]

This provision suggests that women meeting these requirements might be admissible. But just over a month later, Scott seemed less permissive of admitting West Indian domestics. In response to a letter, he noted that "the government does not encourage coloured immigration of any sort, and I think Mr. Sutton should be advised to secure white help if possible, as such help is likely to be a permanent asset to the country, whereas coloured immigration constitutes a problem for all time to come."[54] Thus, Caribbean immigration, regardless of gender, was being limited. Over the next few years the correspondence remained much the same, with Scott and his staff maintaining their understanding of who had rights of access to the nation.

In 1917 the Canadian trade commissioner in Barbados contacted Mr. O'Hara, Deputy Minister of Immigration, to express concerns that "illegal discrimination was being practiced by the Canadian Authorities against coloured passengers from the West Indies to Canada." He noted that even White persons suspected of having "a taint of colour" were being challenged. O'Hara contacted the Immigration Branch in an attempt to ensure that persons coming to Canada received their documents from the steamship company at the place of embarkation and did not arrive in Canada only to have to be returned home. In response Scott took a different tone from before and noted, "Persons of the African race are not suited for the climate of this country ... There is no regulation discriminating against colored immigrants any more than whites."[55] The bar had shifted, and despite there having been a Black presence in Canada since the 1600s, Scott was drawing on the rules under the new Immigration Act amendment of 1910, which served to both expand and reinforce the exclusionary provisions outlined in the Immigration Act of 1906. This new amendment increased the list of prohibited immigrants and also gave the Governor-in-Council more leeway in determining who was admissible to Canada. Among the new categories allowing for the arbitrary denial of access was the determination of one's unsuitability "to the climates or requirements of Canada," a rule that seems to have been interpreted as being directed to all Blacks wishing to enter the country.[56]

In 1918 concerns were noted by then governor of Newfoundland Sir Charles Alexander Harris in a letter to Canada's governor general, the Duke of Devonshire, about coloured Barbadians not being given access to Canada. According to Harris's letter, a Black Barbadian by the name of Fitzgerald Nightingale had arrived in Newfoundland on a sailing vessel and his attempt to enter Canada had been denied. Harris sought to determine whether there were exclusions in Canadian immigration legislation for people from that country. He also noted the duty performed at the front during the Great War by many West Indians, in the West Indian Regiment and the West Indian Transportation Corps, and wondered if perhaps they should be given access to the nation, having clearly proven themselves as British subjects.[57] As in the incident with the *Marion*, receipt of this letter led to a flurry of investigation to determine exactly what had happened and to ensure it was understood that the provisions of the Immigration Act were applicable to all citizens of all countries, including British subjects from Great Britain, and that no special regulation excluded immigrants from Barbados. Several letters were sent to customs offices following up on this incident, and while the individual who denied Nightingale access does not appear to have been found, the various customs offices all pointed to the "new" Order-in-Council that would have prevented immigration for anyone not coming to Canada directly from their homeland. By this they were referring to an amendment made to the Immigration Act in 1908, termed the Act of Direct Passage, or the continuous journey regulation.[58] Thought to have been instituted to limit immigrants from India and Japan and other "Asiatics," since their countries did not offer direct passage to Canada, the act prohibited the landing of any immigrant not coming to Canada by continuous journey from the country to which they were native. If they had not purchased a single ticket from that country to Canada, they were to be denied entry. The act had been challenged several times in Canada, most famously in 1914 when the *Komagata Maru* was refused landing in Vancouver.[59] Customs officers' suggestions that they could have used this act to deny Nightingale access to Canada had they encountered him in 1918 highlights the ways in which officials continued to place obstacles in the path of racialized persons including Caribbean immigrants, the vast majority of whom were of African descent.

In the years after World War I, the economic turmoil being experienced in Canada and its effect on the labour market were the explanations Scott and his staff used most in response to inquiries regarding West Indian access to Canada. While noting that Canada was still not encouraging West Indian immigration, Scott was clear that the country was accepting few from any country. For example, in 1916 in response to rumours, the Passenger Traffic Manager of the steamship service of the United Fruit Company sent a letter to the Department of Immigration inquiring as to whether it was true that Canada had "recently passed a law prohibiting the immigration of coloured people from Jamaica, B.W.I. into Canada."[60] Scott responded that there was no such legislation but that the country "does not encourage coloured immigrants to come to Canada."[61]

This was not the final such letter that Scott's office received over the next decade, and the responses remained consistent in terms of the provisions of the Immigration Act. What appeared to change, depending on the audience, were the additional explanations as to why West Indians, and in particular, West Indian Blacks, were not to be admitted to Canada. For example, in 1919 a Jamaican agent wrote to the Minister of Agriculture because he had heard there was a need for agriculturalists in Canada, and he sought to serve as an agent in this regard in Jamaica.[62] Scott wrote back with what appeared to be the latest set of reasons for deterring West Indians, telling the gentleman that the "cessation of hostilities" had greatly changed the labour conditions in Canada, and therefore Canada was "not encouraging the immigration of any class of workers from the West Indies, and very few from any country."[63] Not long after this exchange, there was a letter from the Charge d'Affaires in Santo Domingo asking if he should issue passports to "coloured British labourers who desire to go to Canada in search of employment."[64] Scott's response was somewhat different here than his last, in that he noted that Canada was not accepting immigrants "*except* agriculturalists and domestics *of European origin and of allied and friendly nationalities* [my emphases]."[65] In 1922, this position changed slightly as the job clause became the means of admission for agricultural and servant classes – but only those from the British Isles, Newfoundland, and self-governing dominions, as well as wives and minor children of Canadian residents.[66] The contradictions in the process of decision-making were clear; for example, in addition to the previously mentioned idea that West Indians had not proven themselves to be agriculturalists, Scott noted that Canada was only accepting agriculturalists and domestics of European origin and of allied and friendly nationalities. The role of West Indians as British subjects in the war, and the fact that the British West Indies and Canada were both parts of the British Empire, appear forgotten or ignored – and what constituted allied and friendly nationalities remains unknown.

These arbitrary methods of discrimination were acknowledged and challenged in different quarters. Companies like DISCO that relied on cheap West Indian labour were not the only ones to push back against the discriminatory practices of the Immigration Branch; there was also pushback from Canadians with business interests in the Caribbean, and from the islands themselves, where local media challenged the Canadian government on the discriminatory practices of immigration officials. For example, the Canada-West Indian League, a lobby group based in Montreal that was highly critical of Scott, wrote to him to ascertain the rationale behind the increasingly stringent policies related to Blacks from the West Indies. The league noted that people in the West Indies were becoming aware that Canada did not want "coloured immigrants" and that this could have "very harmful effects on Canadian trade."[67] As noted in the correspondence above, shipping companies also challenged what they had come to recognize as a system stacked against the West Indian migrant and, hence, working to reduce their customer base and affect their bottom lines. In another letter, from the Royal Mail Steam Packet Company in 1923, an official noted that in the immigration regulations, "no provision is made for the entry of the coloured West Indian in any capacity whatsoever."[68] The lobbying groups and those pushing back against the practices of the Immigration Branch caused the branch to become somewhat more discrete in its practices, but those measures did not cease.

Creation of a Community

Despite the extremes to which the Immigration Branch went to keep them out of the country, West Indians and African Americans continued to make their way into Nova Scotia. They entered a nation that was struggling to deal with the changes that came with modernity and where they would be relegated to a second-class status. They were coming into a context where they would be the racial or ethnic "other," but it was a place filled with opportunity. Most newcomers to Sydney were attracted by the possibility of high wages and better living conditions.[69]

The first set of Black skilled workers to migrate to Sydney, the African Americans mentioned earlier in this chapter, arrived in 1901 to work at DISCO. They had been promised good, decent accommodations and the opportunity to bring wives, cooks, or washerwomen with them on their arrival. Instead, once there, they were placed in company shacks and other types of rooming houses. These shacks were in a section of Sydney known as Whitney Pier, named for DISCO's founder, Henry Melville Whitney, and were situated close to the operations. The steel company provided these shacks for the foreign unskilled workers to live in at different parts of the grounds. Evidence suggests that the shacks were poorly kept. The area where the African Americans settled came to be known as "Cokeville" or "Cokovia" because of its proximity to the coke ovens and, while convenient to the employers for housing men who worked in this area of the plant, this was the least desirable part of Whitney Pier for people to live in.[70] According to historian Kristoffer Archibald, its undesirability included the heavy smoke from the steel mills and blasting furnaces, as well as the fact that the area around the coke ovens was extremely polluted as a result of the coke processing. The results of exposure would become evident decades later, with residents developing cancers and other illnesses.[71]

Upon arrival in the community, most immigrant workers, legal and illegal, settled into poorly insulated, substandard spaces oftentimes not fit for habitation. Craig Heron suggests that the Newfoundlanders came to be termed "shackers" because of the lifestyle they had adopted, living in temporary shacks on the edge of town. My exploration has shown that this designation applied not just to Newfoundlanders but to anyone living in this kind of accommodation, as numerous men from Barbados are also listed as "shackers" in the 1911 census; it shows six large households with Caribbean men listed as shackers and seven households with three or more Caribbean "lodgers."[72] In his discussion of men living in similar situations in the Sault in Ontario, Heron suggests that the men chose to live in these settings out of frugality in a context with little choice – living this way would limit expenses, allowing for greater savings or remittances to be sent home. The frugality would pay off not only for the worker but for the company, as it need only pay these transient workers a small stipend.[73]

Life in this quarter quickly evolved to resemble a community, and by the time the groups of Caribbean immigrants started arriving en masse around 1909, a vibrant, colourful community had begun to be established. Starting with the African Americans and the few local African Canadians working in the steel industry, and with the introduction of Caribbean workers, the new Black quarter created its own microcosm of the social world, its members quickly organizing or joining churches, creating lodges and mutual aid societies, forming sporting leagues and teams, and developing a rich musical life.

Conclusion

From 1900 to 1930, people of African descent in the Caribbean left their home countries for a multitude of reasons, chief among them the realities of high unemployment and extreme poverty in their homelands. Many travelled as part of a transnational industrial workforce to places in the Spanish Caribbean and throughout the Americas to find employment – including to work on large construction projects brought about by a new and burgeoning transportation industry. Among the ports to which they sought entry were those of the Canadian Maritimes. The records providing a window into their movement suggest that Canada, as prospective host country and, for some, their new home, was not readily accessible and, at least initially, not accepting. The state – through the work of an army of bureaucrats, and in many instances in response to nativist fears being voiced by alarmed Canadians – set out to limit access to Caribbean migrants, most of whom were of African descent. On the surface, it appeared that men like Fortier, Williams, and, in particular, Scott appeared to have personal vendettas when it came to their relationship to and treatment of potential Caribbean immigrants. Their attitudes, however, reflected the general mindset and belief systems of both the time and the department in which they were employed. They toed the line between bigotry and liberal sentiment, always keeping (or attempting to keep) within the dictates of immigration policy.

Even after Scott's retirement and subsequent replacement by F.C. Blair, the entrenched beliefs that particular groups were undesirable remained and could be seen in continued arbitrary denials of access, based on the presumed needs of the nation. It is in this that we are reminded that immigration policy is the means by which national gatekeepers dictate who else may be allowed in and, by those rules, the kinds of people who are not considered to be part of the nation-building process. As James Walker points out, "immigrants provide the raw material for the national identity."[74] Therefore, if decades were invested in keeping people of

African descent outside of what was to be used to define our national identity, what does it mean for these same people inside Canada today? How does Black presence disrupt this taken-for-granted national identity, and what meaning does the ambivalence with which the presence of people of African descent has been greeted, historically, hold in terms of this identity? After all, throughout its history, and as has been highlighted throughout this chapter, Canada has maintained an uneasy relationship structured on the need to embrace Black residents as cheap, unskilled labour, while not wanting to include them as permanent fixtures within the Canadian populace.

NOTES

1 W.F. Annand to W.D. Scott, 12 June 1909, Immigration Branch Records, RG 76, vol. 566, file 810666, pt. 1, Library and Archives Canada (hereafter, LAC). Throughout this chapter, the terms "West Indian," "Caribbean," "Negro," and "Black" are used interchangeably to refer to people of African descent from British colonies of the Caribbean. I am not suggesting that all people from the Caribbean are Black or of African descent, nor am I assuming that all of those who migrated to Canada from the Caribbean would have necessarily identified, or been identified, as such. However, I do this with the recognition that most individuals under discussion here were of African descent and that an understanding of the social construction of race holds that some, regardless of personal identification, during the period under investigation, were read or understood as "Black" or "African" simply by being from this region. I recognize that within this collective label there are a myriad of experiences and that its use can be seen as problematic in many ways; based on shade or level of perceived Whiteness, for instance, one's historic position in the social hierarchy differed. The ways in which colourism shaped Caribbean migration during the period is something that warrants further investigation.
2 J.B. Williams to W.D. Scott, 29 June 1909, Immigration Branch Records, RG 76, vol. 566, file 810666, pt. 1, LAC.
3 See, for example, Ninette Kelley and Michael Tebilcock, *The Making of the Mosaic: A History of Canadian Immigration Policy*, 2nd ed. (Toronto: University of Toronto Press, 2000); and Franca Iacovetta with Paula Draper and Robert Ventresca, *A Nation of Immigrants: Women, Workers, and Communities in Canadian History, 1840s–1960s* (Toronto: University of Toronto Press, 2000).
4 See, for example, Barrington Walker, *The History of Immigration and Racism in Canada: Essential Readings* (Toronto: Canadian Scholars, 2008); and Karen Flynn, *Moving beyond Borders: A History of Black Canadian and Caribbean Women in the Diaspora* (Toronto: University of Toronto Press, 2011).

5 Franca Iacovetta, *The Writing of English Canadian Immigrant History*, Canada's Ethnic Group Series, Booklet No. 22 (Ottawa, 1997), 21.
6 Donald H. Avery, *Reluctant Host: Canada's Response to Immigrant Workers* (Toronto: McClelland & Stewart, 1995), 7–9; Sarah-Jane Mathieu, *North of the Color Line: Migration and Black Resistance in Canada, 1870–1955* (Chapel Hill: University of North Carolina Press, 2010), 6–7.
7 Michael Omi and Howard Winant, *Racial Formation in the United States*, 3rd ed. (New York: Routledge, 2015)
8 Craig Heron, *Working in Steel: The Early Years in Canada, 1883–1935* (Toronto: University of Toronto Press, 1988), 73–111; Mathieu, *North of the Color Line*, 62.
9 The Immigration Branch oversaw immigration and settlement issues within the federal Department of the Interior from 1892 to 1917. From 1917 to 1936, a separate Department of Immigration and Colonization was created to take over the work of the Immigration Branch. For more on the governance of immigration in Canada, see Kelley and Trebilcock, *Making of the Mosaic*.
10 See, for example, John E. Zucchi, "The Italian Immigrant Presence in Canada, 1840–1990," in "The Columbus People: Perspectives in Italian Immigration to the Americas and Australia," special issue, *Centre for Migration Studies Special Issues* 11, no. 3 (May 1994): 368–80; Walker, *History of Immigration;* and Iacovetta, *Nation of Immigrants*.
11 On the Great Black Migration, see James M. Gregory, *The Southern Diaspora: How the Great Migration of Black and White Southerners Transformed America* (Chapel Hill: University of North Carolina Press, 2005); and Steven A. Reich, *The Great Black Migration: A Historical Encyclopedia of the American Mosaic* (Santa Barbara, CA: Greenwood, 2014).
12 Peter D. Fraser, "Nineteenth-Century West Indian Migration to Britain," in *In Search of a Better Life: Perspectives on Migration from the Caribbean*, ed. Ransford W. Palmer (New York: Praeger, 1990), 19–38.
13 Christopher Stuart Taylor, *Flying Fish in the Great White North: The Autonomous Migration of Black Barbadians* (Halifax: Fernwood, 2016), 56–68.
14 This reference to Jim Crow is not just to the United States, as, according to Barrington Walker, "Canada also had its own version of Jim Crow ... pervasive beliefs about the biologically rooted and intractable nature of Black racial inferiority within the context of a liberal order which was based on ideas of formal legal equality and a belief that the lower races could be advanced under the right conditions of tutelage." Walker, *Race on Trial: Black Defendants in Ontario's Criminal Courts, 1858–1958* (Toronto: University of Toronto Press, 2010), 4n4.
15 Violet Mary-Ann Johnson, "*The Migration Experience: Social and Economic Adjustment of British West Indian Immigrants in Boston, 1915–1950*"

(PhD diss., Boston College, 1993); Barry B. Levine, ed., *The Caribbean Exodus* (Westport CT: Praeger, 1987); Lara Putnam, *Radical Moves: Caribbean Migrants and the Politics of the Jazz Age* (Chapel Hill: University of North Carolina Press, 2013); Olive Senior, *Dying to Better Themselves: West Indians and the Building of the Panama Canal* (Kingston, Jamaica: University of the West Indies Press, 2014).

16 Putnam, *Radical Moves*, 26.
17 Bonham C. Richardson, *Panama Money in Barbados* (Knoxville: University of Tennessee Press, 1985), 155. People in the Caribbean coined the term "Panama money" to refer to lucrative opportunities abroad and not only in Panama. Being able to leave home to earn one's Panama money was a common goal in this period.
18 David Frank, "The Cape Breton Coal Industry and the Rise and Fall of the British Empire Steel Corporation," *Acadiensis* 7, no. 1 (1977): 10; Don MacGillivray, "Henry Melville Whitney Comes to Cape Breton: The Saga of a Gilded Age Entrepreneur," *Acadiensis* 9, no. 1 (1979): 44–70; Mary Elizabeth Keating and Elizabeth Beaton, *From the Pier, Dear! Images of a Multicultural Community* (Sydney, NS: Whitney Pier Historical Society, 1993).
19 Heron, *Working in Steel*, 50–72. The discussion of technology and skill is beyond the scope of this project. However, Heron provides more insight into the ways in which technology factored into understandings of the skill involved in steelmaking.
20 Elizabeth Beaton, "An African-American Community in Cape Breton, 1901–1904," *Acadiensis* 24, no. 2 (1995): 72–4.
21 Avery, *Reluctant Host*, 82–107.
22 Means to Turner (General Passenger Agent, Baltimore), 23 August 1901, DISCO Letterbooks, Beaton Institute.
23 Avery, *Reluctant Host*, 24.
24 Mathieu, *North of the Color Line*, 29.
25 Mathieu, 23.
26 Mathieu, 26.
27 F.C. Blair to Royal Mail Company, 20 September 1922, Immigration Branch Records, RG 76, vol. 566, file 810666, pt. 2, LAC. This idea that migrants from the Caribbean were not agriculturalists is never challenged, despite the reality of most of the Caribbean population having spent over four hundred years working the land in the building of empire.
28 John Schultz, "White Man's Country: Canada and the West Indian Immigrant, 1900–1965," *American Review of Canadian Studies* 12, no. 1 (1982): 58.
29 For further discussion of the representations of Black womanhood, see Evelyn Brooks Higginbotham, "African-American Women's History and the Metalanguage of Race," *Journal of Women in Culture and Society* 17, no. 2 (1992): 251–74.

30 Jared G. Toney, "Locating Diaspora: Afro-Caribbean Narratives of Migration and Settlement in Toronto, 1914–1929," *Urban History Review* 38, no. 2 (2010): 75–88.
31 Agnes Calliste, "Canada's Immigration Policy and Domestics from the Caribbean: The Second Domestic Scheme," in *Race, Class, Gender: Bonds and Barriers*, ed. Jessie Vorst et al. (Toronto: Between the Lines, 1989), 136–68.
32 Williams to Scott, 29 June 1909.
33 W. Barnstead to W.D. Scott, 26 May 1910, Immigration Branch Records, RG 76, vol. 566, file 810666, pt. 1, LAC.
34 L.M. Fortier to J.J. Williams, 31 May 1910, Immigration Branch Records, RG 76, vol. 566, file 810666, pt. 1, LAC.
35 J.J. Williams to L.M. Fortier, 15 June 1910, Immigration Branch Records, RG 76, vol. 566, file 810666, pt. 1, LAC.
36 Valerie Knowles, *Strangers at Our Gates: Canadian Immigration and Immigration Policy, 1540–1997* (Toronto: Dundurn, 1997), 85. The *Immigration Act* of 1910 further enhanced the discretionary powers of government to regulate the flow of immigrants into Canada, reinforcing and expanding the exclusionary provisions outlined in the *Immigration Act* of 1906.
37 W.D. Scott to Dr. Ellis and Mr. Lantalum, 23 May 1912, and Mr. Lantalum to W.D. Scott, 25 July 1912, both in Immigration Branch Records, Immigration Branch Records, RG 76, vol. 566, file 810666, pt. 1, LAC.
38 J. Millar-Smith to W.D. Scott, 9 August 1912, Immigration Branch Records, RG 76, vol. 566, file 810666, pt. 1, LAC.
39 An Act Respecting Immigration and Immigrants, 1906, *Statutes of Canada*, 6 Edward VII, c. 19. This act outlines the permissible number of passengers relative to the size of any vessel entering Canadian ports.
40 J. Lantz to Department of Marine and Fisheries, 12 May 1914, Immigration Branch Records, RG 76, vol. 566, file 810666, pt. 1, LAC.
41 W.D. Scott to V.C. Smith and Co., 27 July 1914, Immigration Branch Records, RG 76, vol. 566, file 810666, pt. 1, LAC.
42 L.M. Fortier to W.D. Scott, 12 August 1914, Immigration Branch Records, RG 76, vol. 566, file 810666, pt. 1, LAC.
43 Schultz, "White Man's Country," 56.
44 L.M. Fortier to W.D. Scott, 27 July 1914, Immigration Branch Records, RG 76, vol. 566, file 810666, pt. 1, LAC.
45 Shultz, "White Man's Country," 53.
46 Avery, *Reluctant Host*, 74, 29–36.
47 Agnes Calliste, "Race, Gender and Canadian Immigration Policy," *Journal of Canadian Studies* 28, no. 4 (1993–4): 134, 135. In 1916 there was a request to bring 150 workers from the Caribbean to work in the mines in Springhill and Sydney. In 1920–1, DISCO recruited 61 labourers to work in the mines.
48 Calliste, "Race, Gender," 135.

49 W.D. Scott to L.M. Fortier, 10 August 1916, Immigration Branch Records, RG 76, vol. 566, file 810666, pt. 1, LAC.
50 Calliste, "Race, Gender," 134.
51 W.D. Scott to Pickford & Black Ltd., 11 February 1915, Immigration Branch Records, RG 76, vol. 566, file 810666, pt. 2, LAC.
52 W.D. Scott to Pickford & Black Ltd., 17 March 1915, Immigration Branch Records, RG 76, vol. 566, file 810666, pt. 2, LAC.
53 W.D. Scott to J.J. Williams, 15 May 1915, Immigration Branch Records, RG 76, vol. 566, file 810666, pt. 2, LAC.
54 W.D Scott to Pickford & Black Ltd., 17 June 1915, Immigration Branch Records, RG 76, vol. 566, file 810666, pt. 2, LAC.
55 W.D. Scott to Deputy Minister O'Hara, 30 July 1917, Immigration Branch Records, RG 76, vol. 566, file 810666, pt. 2, LAC.
56 Knowles, *Strangers at Our Gates*, 85.
57 Sir Charles Alexander Harris to the Duke of Devonshire, 23 December 1918, Immigration Branch Records, RG 76, vol. 566, file 810666, pt. 2, LAC.
58 An Act to Amend the Immigration Act, 1908, *Statutes of Canada*, 7–8 Edward VII, c. 33.
59 Hugh J.M. Johnston, *The Voyage of the Komagata Maru: The Sikh Challenge to Canada's Colour Bar* (Delhi: Oxford University Press. 1979). On May 23, 1914, a crowded ship from Hong Kong carrying 376 passengers – most being immigrants from Punjab, British India – arrived in Vancouver's Burrard Inlet, on the west coast of the Dominion of Canada. The passengers, all British subjects, were challenging the "continuous passage" regulation, which stated that immigrants must "come from the country of their birth, or citizenship, by a continuous journey and on through tickets purchased before leaving the country of their birth, or citizenship." Their bid was unsuccessful, and only 24 were allowed to remain in Canada. The ship and the remaining 352 passengers departed Vancouver in July 1914.
60 M. Lowrey to Department of Immigration, 23 October 1916, Immigration Branch Records, RG 76, vol. 566, file 810666, pt. 1, LAC. Here, "B.W.I." refers to British West Indies.
61 W.D. Scott to M. Lowrey, 27 October 1916, Immigration Branch Records, RG 76, vol. 566, file 810666, pt. 1, LAC.
62 M.H. Edwards to Minister of Agriculture, Canada, 3 March 1919, Immigration Branch Records, RG 76, vol. 566, file 810666, pt. 2, LAC.
63 W.D. Scott to M.H. Edwards, 15 March 1919, Immigration Branch Records, RG 76, vol. 566, file 810666, pt. 2, LAC.
64 Mr. Fisher, Charge d'Affaires, to Minister of Immigration and Colonization, 12 May 1919, Immigration Branch Records, RG 76, vol. 566, file 810666, pt. 2, LAC.

65 W.D. Scott to Mr. Fisher, 7 June 1919, Immigration Branch Records, RG 76, vol. 566, file 810666, pt. 2, LAC.
66 F.C. Blair to Royal Mail Steam Packet Company, 9 September 1922, Immigration Branch Records, RG 76, vol. 566, file 810666, pt. 2, LAC.
67 Secretary, Canada-West Indian League, to Commissioner of Immigration, 29 August 1914, Immigration Branch Records, RG 76, vol. 566, file 810666, pt. 1, LAC.
68 Royal Mail Steam Packet Company to F.C. Blair, 5 February 1923, Immigration Branch Records, RG 76, vol. 566, file 810666, pt. 2, LAC.
69 Beaton, "African-American Community," 73.
70 Beaton, 81–2.
71 Kristoffer Archibald, "Bodily Health, Contaminants, and the Environment: Recognizing the Impacts of Industrial Pollution in Deindustrializing Sydney, Nova Scotia" (PhD diss., Concordia University, 2016), 17–21.
72 For the 1911 census, the applicable Sydney (Cape Breton South) subdistrict is 18, and most of the entries indicating "shackers" begin on page 22. https://www.bac-lac.gc.ca/eng/census/1911/Pages/about-census.aspx.
73 Heron, *Working in Steel*, 81.
74 James Walker, *"Race," Rights and the Law in the Supreme Court of Canada: Historical Case Studies* (Waterloo, ON: Osgoode Society for Canadian Legal History and Wilfrid Laurier University Press, 1997), 248.

10

"... not likely to do well or to be an asset to this country": Canadian Restrictions of Black Caribbean Female Domestic Workers, 1910–1955

MICHELE A. JOHNSON

Non-familial workers, including persons of African descent, enslaved and free, were tasked with domestic labour beginning with the establishment of the settler communities/colonies in the places that would coalesce into the Canadian nation-state.[1] Whether in New France, Nova Scotia, or Upper Canada (Ontario), Black workers toiled in the households of their enslavers and employers, replicating an association across the Americas among Black bodies, labour, and servitude that would become fixed in the Canadian imaginary by the twentieth century.[2] That Black women, in particular, would become materially and discursively tied to the physical and emotional labour of domestic service constituted their lived realities whether they were among the established communities across the country or were migrants who tended to be based in the country's large urban centres. Building on the seminal research of scholars such as Frances Henry, Agnes Calliste, Abigail Bakan, Daiva Stasiulis, Tanya Schecter, and Makeda Silvera who examine the intersections between Black womanhood and domestic service in Canada, this chapter focuses on the recruitment of women from the Caribbean – most of whom were Black – to perform domestic work in Canada during the first half of twentieth century.[3]

The chapter begins with a brief assessment of the first domestic labour scheme, which recruited women from Guadeloupe (1910–11) and which has been examined by some scholars;[4] it ends just before the launch of the second scheme (1955–67), which recruited women from the (British) "West Indies" and British Guiana and which has received significantly more attention.[5] While the two labour schemes have rightly attracted scholarly attention, this chapter focuses on the period between the schemes – which were themselves severely limited, highly regulated, and closely surveilled – and argues that despite the demand by some Canadian employers for "coloured girls" from the Caribbean to perform domestic service, Canadian officials used a variety of means to restrict the movement of Black female bodies into what was imagined as "White" Canadian spaces. Through a close analysis of legislation, Orders-in-Council, and written and applied immigration policies, as well as official correspondence among and between Canadian and Caribbean officials, the chapter demonstrates that Canadian immigration and other authorities sustained a deliberate and racist rejection of Black female immigration into the Dominion. As they acted on gender-based anxieties about the "problems" that Black female bodies presented – with their potential to reproduce and extend Blackness into "White" Canada – Canadian officials also reinforced ideas that these women (and the families they would produce) "were not likely to do well or to be an asset to [the] country."[6] Perceived as intrinsic liabilities who were unassimilable, when Black Caribbean women sought to enter Canada in order to fill domestic service positions, Canadian authorities spent considerable energy to erect barriers to their arrival. Government officials, and the (White) population on whose behalf they acted, believed that the women added to the spectre of an enlarged and augmented Black Canada with the potential of exposing and disrupting the much-vaunted myth of the liberal and progressive, the politically and racially tolerant Great White North.[7]

Although the European settler population and their political and administrative representatives were determined to imagine the Canadian nation-state as "White" despite the presence of communities of Indigenous and other racialized peoples, the periodic need to recruit labour from non-White sources sometimes temporarily disrupted the narrative of Whiteness. As a result, in the early twentieth century, in addition to male workers from the Caribbean who, according to Calliste, were recruited to work in "the hottest, most physically demanding, and lowest paid jobs" in the steel mills in Nova Scotia, "by 1909 there were several Caribbean women working as domestics" in that province. While (White) Canadians left domestic service as soon as they were able because of what Calliste describes as "deplorable working conditions – low pay, long hours, hard labour, low status, isolation, and lack of independence and respect ... most Caribbean women remained in domestic service since other areas of employment were closed to them."[8]

This is not to suggest that the immigration into Canada of Black Caribbean women who were willing to perform domestic service early in the twentieth century occurred without significant hurdles. Indeed, the Immigration Act of 1910, which outlined nine "prohibited classes" of persons who were barred from the country, also stated that the Governor-in-Council (the federal cabinet) could issue conditions for landing "that immigrants and tourists shall possess in their own right money to a prescribed minimum amount, which amount may vary according to the race, occupation or destination of such immigrant or tourist."[9] The Governor-in-Council could also, by proclamation, whenever it was believed to be "necessary or expedient," prohibit the landing of "immigrants belonging to any race deemed unsuited to the climate or requirements of Canada, or of immigrants of any specified class, occupation or character."[10] Along with the "prescribed" monetary requirements that could be determined by a migrant's "race" (and which seemed to operate without clear guidelines or limitations), the tropes of climatic unsuitability – despite long-existent and contributing communities of African descent in Canada – as well as an alleged inability to fulfil (undefined) Canadian requirements were used as effective barriers to prevent the movement of Black bodies into "White" Canadian spaces.

It was into this context that, according to Calliste, "J.M. Authier, a former American consul in Guadeloupe," recruited one hundred women to work as domestic workers in the households of "Quebec's middle class." Between September 1910 and April 1911, the women arrived from the Caribbean and – after careful examinations by immigration officials regarding "their desirability as immigrants and their likelihood of success as domestics" resulting in reports that they were "'a good class' of immigrants who were likely to succeed" – were placed "to work in Trois-Rivières, Montreal, and Quebec City."[11] When ninety-six employers were surveyed about the domestic workers in their employ, most of the fifty-five who responded "expressed satisfaction with their employees," because in addition to being "devout Catholics" who spoke French, "they were cheap, intelligent, industrious, devoted, fond of children, docile, polite, submissive, and, unlike some white domestics, 'they knew their place.'"[12] But not everyone was pleased. According to Calliste, one employer did not believe that "these girls will ever be capable of rendering any good service to our Canadian families ... they do not wish to submit, have not a good will and are very exacting," while another complained of "the fact that [the employee's] climatic indolence was backed by a strong dose of bad will which rendered her quite unsuitable."[13]

It is not clear what impact these negative assessments may have had on W.D. Scott, Superintendent of Immigration in Ottawa, who recommended the suspension of that Caribbean Domestic Scheme, supposedly because "the women were 'not all of good moral character.'"[14] He may also have been influenced by false reports like that in *Collier's Magazine* that the Guadeloupean women had been "met at the Windsor Station by redlight district women who spirited them away to serve as prostitutes" and by public sentiments such as those captured in a letter to C.A. Magrath, MP, that raised concerns about these "negro women" who would "certainly be mothers some day."¹⁵ While the former falsehood pointed to prevalent discourses about and expectations of Black women's inherently illicit sexuality, the latter reference to their potential roles as mothers – who would expand and extend Blackness in/to "White" Canada – unveiled what Dana Whitney Sherwood and Boulou Ebanda de B'béri refer to as Canada's fear of "the reproductive and community-building capacities of the black female."¹⁶ Both concerns centred the bodies of Black women as subjects upon whom restrictions ought to be placed.

In addition to these specific fears of Black womanhood, it is important to note that the Guadeloupean women employed in the first scheme to recruit Caribbean women for domestic service were also caught up in a larger, virulent tide of anti-Black racism in the early twentieth century that was symbolized by the passage of an Order-in-Council (PC 1324) on 12 August 1911. Over the signature of Prime Minister Wilfrid Laurier, the order stated that for one year after that date "the landing in Canada shall be and the same is prohibited of any immigrants belonging to the Negro race, which race is deemed unsuitable to the climate and requirements of Canada."¹⁷ The Order-in-Council, an echo of the 1910 Immigration Act but applicable specifically and exclusively to "the Negro race," was rescinded in October 1911 for what Calliste describes as "political reasons." These included "undesirable diplomatic problems with the Caribbean and American governments," the antagonism of Black voters in Ontario and Nova Scotia, and the effectiveness of informal restrictions to exclude Black individuals and communities.¹⁸ There is little doubt that the perceptions and ideologies that had resulted in the passage of the Order did not decline, dissipate, or disappear; this was borne out by the suspension of the first scheme and the deportation of some of the remaining Guadeloupean workers.¹⁹

Although the first recruitment scheme for women from the Caribbean to perform domestic service in Canadian households was abruptly terminated, some Canadian employers continued to look to the region for potential household workers. They were convinced of the unavailability of (White) Canadian women to perform paid domestic labour. This was heightened during World War I when some Canadian women were able to find employment in the war industries vacated by men who had joined the armed forces and when European women experienced difficulties in emigrating to Canada to work as domestic servants. Perhaps, then, some coloured/Black women – who would also fulfil the North American stereotype of Black bodies in service to White households – would be ideal to fill those gaps.

In April 1915, James Gilchrist, Superintendent of Immigration in the Department of Agriculture in Saint John, New Brunswick, contacted

W.D. Scott to thank him for "giving permission for Mr. W.H. Lance to bring a colored girl from the West Indies for domestic service." Referring to previous correspondence in which Scott had asked about Lance "getting help locally," Gilchrist responded,

> This is out of the question, for our rural districts are simply starved for the want of domestic help. While there is a fair supply in our cities and towns, it is impossible to get a girl to work in a farm house, no matter what the conditions or pay, as they are determined to stay in the towns, and I am positive that if we had one hundred of these colored girls in the country districts, they would not displace any of our own help, but would be a great blessing to our women in general.[20]

While many of the "colored" women from the Caribbean were recruited for work in urban contexts, Gilchrist's letter on Lance's behalf reminds us that this was not always the case. One can imagine that "work in a farm house" would involve isolation and hard labour as well as a blurred line between house and farm work. Gilchrist's belief that one hundred of "these colored girls" would be welcomed into the rural areas of New Brunswick spoke to the desire for assistance felt among rural (White) Canadian women who, in keeping with prevailing gender ideologies and expectations, were responsible for the care (physical, social, emotional, and otherwise) of their households and families; the unwillingness of White Canadian women to perform the hard, tedious, and poorly paid labour of domestic service; and the belief that the "colored" girls would be able to fulfil those requirements. It also indicated the gendered, racialized, and infantilized nature of the proposed recruitment by Lance and others; after all, it was "colored *girls*" who would work for "our *women.*" But Gilchrist did not stop there.

Although Scott had previously given his permission for Lance to recruit "this girl," the process had not flowed smoothly. Gilchrist reported that Mr. J.V. Lantalum, who worked in the immigration office, said he required "instructions direct[ly] from [Scott] before he would permit one to land." Gilchrist asked Scott to "kindly issue these instructions, for which I will be extremely grateful."[21] Later that month, Scott replied to Gilchrist "respecting the proposed immigration of a coloured girl from the West Indies for domestic service in the home of Mr. W.H. Lance," where his instructions to Mr. Lantalum were included.[22] While we can presume that in this instance Scott's direct instructions resulted in the admission of the "coloured girl," his stated preference for "getting help locally" remained unshaken. And, lest anyone doubt exactly what that meant, in short order he would state his position clearly.

In June 1915, Pickford & Black Ltd., a shipping company in Halifax, Nova Scotia, contacted Scott on behalf of David Sutton of Cornwallis about "the admission of a coloured maid from Barbados."[23] Scott's response was unambiguous:

> As you are aware, the Government does not encourage coloured immigration of any sort, and I think Mr. Sutton should be advised to secure white help if possible, as such help is likely to be a permanent asset to the country, whereas coloured immigration constitutes a problem for all time to come. If a coloured servant arrives in good health and [is] able to qualify financially and otherwise with the immigration regulation and is going to definite employment, she will be permitted to enter, but not otherwise; in other words, if the regulations will debar any person of that sort then these will be applied under the policy of preventing the immigration of any class not likely to do well or to be an asset to this country.[24]

Since Sutton was, in fact, providing "definite employment," the bases on which the "coloured maid from Barbados" could be excluded included financial requirements and qualifications "otherwise with the immigration regulation" – a phrase vague enough to give enormous power to Canadian officials to reject prospective Black immigrants without publicly invoking "race." Scott and those who determined the policies and procedures of immigration assumed that this "coloured" woman was "not likely to do well or be an asset" to Canada. Since he offered no reasons besides a difference in colour (race) for the "permanent asset" that "white help" would represent but that "coloured" help would not, it is reasonable to conclude that Scott viewed Black women as inherently problematic "for all time to come."

In order to ensure that the possible immigration of Black women – deemed *not* to be assets to the nation – was tightly controlled, Scott ensured that his office oversaw those applications. In September 1915, Scott was contacted again by Pickford & Black, this time regarding "the admission to Canada of one Flora Reece," who was supposed to be "going to Mrs. Learmont at Trure" in Nova Scotia. The application had been given tacit permission by Mr. F.W. Hetherington, Assistant Dominion Immigration Agent at Halifax, in a letter to Pickford & Black that stated that "Mrs. A.H. Learmont of Trure, N.S., has engaged a coloured girl named Flora Reece of Georgetown, Demerara. She will be admitted upon passing the usual medical examination and having twenty five dollars in her possession."[25] Scott's annoyance with this conditional permission – which would have fallen in line with contemporary immigration requirements but would have allowed the immigration of "a coloured girl" – was clear. In a message to W.L. Barnstead, Dominion Immigration Agent in Halifax, he wrote, "I wish you would say to Mr. Hetherington that under no consideration is he to write such a letter, in fact, any letter guaranteeing or promising the admission of any person to Canada. There is a great danger in the issuance of these letters and the Department has already had trouble over such letters being issued. If any of the steamship companies or steamship agents apply for a special concession or a letter of any kind, they should be referred here."[26] While Scott did not state that his objection to Hetherington's letter was because the potential immigrant was a Black woman, given his letter to Pickford & Black only three months prior it might be argued that the race-based ideas that framed his earlier statement regarding a policy of exclusion continued to be at least a factor.

This seemed to be confirmed when Scott was contacted by a steamship and touring company about attempts by Mrs. Henderson, a Canadian employer, to transport a domestic worker from the Caribbean. Scott's response was sharp:

> It would be well to advise Mrs. Henderson that the Government does not look with favour upon the immigration of coloured people and no encouragement is offered. I understand that there are a great many domestics in Canada who find it rather difficult to secure positions especially in some of the cities ... If we have not enough European domestics in Canada it will not be difficult to get more in view of conditions on the other side [in Europe]. It is somewhat difficult just at the present moment to procure sailings but as soon as conditions clear up we will be able to get a number of a class of domestics who would be a permanent asset in this country instead of bringing in coloured women who create a problem rather than become an asset.[27]

While it is doubtful, Scott's reference to "a great many domestics in Canada" in urban areas who were having difficulty finding placements – and who presumably should have been among the potential workers sought by employers like Henderson – may well have included African Canadian women, the majority of whom spent their working lives in domestic service.[28] However, his statement that, in spite of the challenges to migration resulting from the ongoing international war, the recruitment of European domestic workers who would be "a permanent asset" was preferable to "coloured women" who were believed to be intrinsically problematic was telling. There is little doubt that the Superintendent of Immigration was acting on the government's (unpublicized) policy to restrict or prevent Black immigration, and the government was, in turn, taking its cue from a more general public sentiment.

While Scott seemed able to offer his frank position to the principals in companies like Pickford & Black, where the general public was concerned he was much more careful and circumspect. In April 1916, after inquiries by Geo. Howland Esq. of Toronto about "the admission to Canada of female coloured labour from Jamaica," Scott replied,

> I beg to state there are no special regulations prohibiting the entry of immigrants from Jamaica, but as a large number of immigrants of this class have become public charges in Canada and consequently have had to be deported at considerable expense to the Department, the regulations are strictly enforced in the matter of all such applications. In addition to the monetary requirements and medical examinations, all coloured immigrants must furnish absolute evidence to the effect that they are coming to assured permanent employment in Canada, otherwise they will be rejected.[29]

Walking that fine line between denying that "special regulations" had been passed or applied in the cases of potential Black Jamaican female workers and insisting that whatever regulations *were* in place would be strictly upheld for "this class," Scott presented a face of reasonable bureaucracy. Claims that the women could (and, given the alleged history of "immigrants of this class," likely *would*) become "public charges" were, as Claudine Bonner argues in this volume (chapter 9), part of a larger discourse pointing to the burden that Blackness threatened to impose on hardworking (White) Canadian communities. However, even when no such threat existed or was greatly mitigated because the women fulfilled all the requirements and were offered positions in domestic service, the Canadian authorities still discouraged Black women's immigration since they were allegedly destined to become problems to the nation. Scott and his ilk wielded an enormous amount of power in being able to interpret and implement policies on behalf of the government and people of Canada. As such, they operated as sociocultural and racial gatekeepers of how Canadian identity was to be defined and structured (as White) as well as the filters through which the purported problems of Blackness – including intrinsic inferiority, uncivility, liability, and an inability to assimilate – would not be allowed to pass easily.

Despite the deep reservations indicated by Scott, the desire among some Canadian employers to recruit Black Caribbean women for domestic service remained. In April 1916, a bureaucrat in the Immigration Branch of the Department of the Interior reported, "On several occasions I have been approached by citizens of Brockville [Ontario] who wish to bring coloured girls, as domestics, from St. Kitts in the British West Indies, explaining to me that they are required to make applications to bring them in, and to send passage money etc. before the steamship companies will accept them as passengers for Canada, and have inquired for forms used for that purpose." Since the writer was "not familiar ... with cases of this kind," he sought some direction from Scott.[30] Although Scott's reply is not (yet) available, we can assume that it followed along the lines of his forthright discouragement of immigration into Canada for Black women.[31]

Although it is unclear why the citizens of Brockville seemed to be partial to Kittitian women working in their homes, their "wish" for "coloured girls" to perform domestic service was in keeping with a larger association in Western societies among Black womanhood, personal/domestic service, and expectations of servility.[32] This is especially the case in societies in the Americas, all of which exploited the labour of enslaved women of African descent; and Canada was no exception.[33] Despite its history as a society that utilized the labour of enslaved Black women who worked as domestic servants, and despite the fact that Black women in Canada were almost always restricted to domestic service, Scott wanted nothing to do with an expansion of the pool of Black women who might perform as paid domestic workers. Although some Canadian employers may have wished to recruit a cheap, racialized workforce whose exclusive relegation to domestic service served and confirmed prevailing ideas about "Black servitude," Scott and the immigration department were obligated to a more pressing concern: to exclude Black (female) bodies, and all their potential "problems," from "White" Canadian spaces.

That was certainly apparent in October 1916, when Scott responded to an inquiry by Sir Herbert Ames, MP, "suggesting the advisability of the admission of Maude Lee, a coloured girl, to work for D.L. Campbell, Financial Manager of Messrs. Farquhar, Robertson, Limited, of Montreal." Scott informed Ames that Campbell had previously written to him directly and that he had informed Campbell that "we were not seeking the immigration of coloured people and that the only way Maude Lee might be permitted to enter would be if she complied in every particular with the provisions of the Immigration Act."[34] Further, said Scott,

> If the Department offered the slightest encouragement to the entry of coloured women, I am of the opinion, judging by the number of letters that come to me enquiring about coloured domestics, that we would soon have a coloured girl in about every other home where servants were employed. I am quite aware that the demand for servants is very great and that wages are increasing, but this is inevitable under present abnormal conditions when women workers are in demand in almost every possible occupation. As soon as the War ceases, I conclude that it will be possible to get with

little or no effort all the desirable women workers that Canada can absorb. The preponderance of women over men in European countries will be marked – as indeed it must be already – and I think it better that people in Canada suffer some little inconveniences now than agree to the admission of a class of help which cannot be regarded as any permanent asset to the Country.[35]

It is not clear where Maude Lee was based, or if her potential employer – who lived in Montreal – required a French-speaking worker. What *was* clear was that Scott's negative response to the possible immigration of "coloured people" seemed even sharper when the prospective immigrants were Black women. He confirmed that "several" inquiries had been made about the possibility of gaining access to the labour of "coloured domestics" and that the servant-employing classes would recruit large numbers Black women as servants if they were available. Scott pointed to the extraordinary context of the war, which had absorbed (White) female workers who would otherwise have been available for domestic service, and promised that when the war ended, the Canadian authorities would be able to recruit "all the desirable women workers that Canada can absorb." He urged Ames (and Campbell) to "suffer" the inconvenience of waiting for acceptable White women as domestic workers rather than to support the immigration of "a class of help which cannot be regarded as any permanent asset" to Canada. It was not, then, that Canada had no ability to absorb Black female domestic workers, or that Canadian employers did not want to employ them – quite the contrary. Rather, in Scott's (and the government's) view, Black women simply did not have anything positive to offer the country. Further, if they were admitted at the rates at which employers wanted to recruit them, it was likely that the face of (White) Canada would be irrevocably changed. And still further, if the anxieties about their Black *womanhood* (and likely fertility) that lurked behind declarations about immigration policies were realized, they and their families would expand Blackness in Canada in ways that were not to be countenanced.

The Montreal-based Jules Howe Travel Agencies contacted Scott regarding a newspaper article that pointed to the prohibition of immigration of Black women from the Caribbean to perform domestic service, and Scott replied in October 1916:

I beg to state that there is no clause in the Immigration Act prohibiting the immigration to Canada of coloured people from Jamaica. The newspaper article to which you refer evidently originated from the fact that this Department does not encourage the immigration of coloured persons, and

> we have repeatedly advised enquirers to that effect. The Department is very often asked for permits in [sic] behalf of coloured domestics from the West Indies, Jamaica and the Barbadoes [sic], and our reply in all such cases is to the effect that no such permit can be given, and that the domestics in question must comply fully with the Immigration Regulations.[36]

Speaking for the immigration department, Scott confirmed that the government's position was deliberately ambiguous: there was no legal barrier to Black immigration, but it was not encouraged. Thus, Canadian immigration laws managed to appear fair, transparent, and even-handed and, simultaneously, to imagine and portray Canada as the Great *White* North where Blackness was discouraged by entrenched – and yet largely hidden – policies and the anti-Black attitudes that informed them. The correspondence also confirmed there were several Canadian employers who wanted to recruit "coloured domestics" from the Caribbean; facing the lack of encouragement (about which Scott was clear), these employers sought "permits" to ease the process of immigration. However, as Scott indicated, these permits were not a part of the regular immigration process, with which the prospective immigrants had to "comply fully." And given the department's stated lack of encouragement and the superintendent's negative stance, the women's ability to reach full compliance would not be assisted by the Canadian authorities.

In the wake of World War I, the resulting upheaval, fear of communism, and suspicion led the government of Canada to pass *An Act to Amend the Immigration Act,* 1919, which sought to control movement into the country even more tightly. In addition to barring a range of groups from entry, the legislation included the prohibition of

> immigrants belonging to any nationality or race or of immigrants of any specified class or occupation, by reason of any economic, industrial or other condition temporarily existing in Canada or because such immigrants are deemed unsuitable having regard to the climatic, industrial, social, educational, labour or other conditions or requirements of Canada or because such immigrants are deemed undesirable owing to their peculiar customs, habits, modes of life and methods of holding property, and because of their probable inability to become readily assimilated or to assume the duties and responsibilities of Canadian citizenship within a reasonable time after their entry.[37]

The legislation prevented the immigration of a number and range of groups and provided additional policies and guidelines by which prospective immigrants of African descent could be, and often were, excluded.

In addition to the increasingly restrictive legislation, the Canadian government passed Orders-in-Council that gave the authorities the power to act whenever it was believed to be necessary. One Order-in-Council passed in 1923 pointed to the "unemployment conditions ... existing in Canada" and prohibited the landing of "all classes and occupations," except for persons in six groups. These included agriculturalists with the means to begin farming, farm labourers and domestic servants with "reasonable assurance of employment," wives and minor dependents of legal immigrants, and US citizens provided their labour or service was required, as well as "any British subject entering Canada directly or indirectly from Great Britain or Ireland, Newfoundland, the United States of America, New Zealand, Australia or the Union of South Africa" who satisfied an immigration officer that "he ha[d] sufficient means to maintain himself until employment [was] secured."[38] The British subjects who would be admitted were assumed to be male and to be limited to those from "White" British colonies and the United States; however, since domestic servants were among the groups exempted from prohibition and since Canada seemed ready to welcome migrants, some Caribbean workers – being British citizens – assumed that they could enter the Great White North once they fulfilled the requirements of immigration. But this was not the case.

In April 1925, James Comack, the Canadian Trade Commissioner based in Jamaica, wrote to W.J. Egan, Deputy Minister of Immigration and Colonisation, to address "a peculiar situation" that had cropped up in the island "from time to time."[39] To illustrate, Comack said he had been approached by the secretary of the Jamaican Young Women's Christian Association (YWCA), who had brought in "a young Jamaican lady aged about 22, well dressed and to all appearances white," who, "finding little chance of advancement" in Jamaica, "desire[d] to emigrate to Canada to undertake domestic service if needs be, but hope[d] ultimately to get a position as a nursery governess, for which she [was] eminently fitted." According to Comack, this woman had "apparently enough money to buy her ticket and satisfy all the requirements as to landing money, and to spare." However, "the local agents of the Canadian Government Merchant Marine – the only direct passenger service from here to Canada – [had] take[n] up the attitude that they w[ould] not sell her a ticket to Canada unless she produce[d] a 'permit' from the Canadian Government." So, Comack asked the following questions:

(a) Are the shipping agents right in refusing to a British subject with the requisite qualifications of education, money, health and education [*sic*], a ticket to Canada without this "permit," when Canada is advertising for immigrants of the class in question, and when, so far as I can see, every immigration regulation is complied with?

(b) Just what are your requirements in regard to immigrants from Jamaica to Canada?

Comack continued,

> It would appear to me that the position taken up is ... about as "clear as mud." It is doubtless very convenient to place the responsibility on the intending immigrant, but it puts me in a very awkward position here when they come and complain. All the time the people are reading that Canada wants desirable immigrants, and a closer rappoachment [sic] between Canada and the British West Indies is loudly advocated. Can I tell Jamaicans that they are not wanted in Canada? The situation is doubtless difficult, but I should be very glad to know fully what is the Canadian Government's position. What I want is something cut and dried, so that I do not have to continue hedging. If the Department do [sic] not want Jamaicans to settle in Canada under any circumstances, I think this should be definitely stated – or else clearly refuted. If there are any exemptions, I should be much obliged if you would let me have them in detail.[40]

The questions raised by Comack on behalf of this Jamaican woman – who was likely to have been read by the Canadian authorities as Black although she was "to all appearances white" – and her advocate from the YWCA indicated that she was unable to satisfy the requirements of Canadian immigration, even though, according to Comack, "every immigration regulation [had been] complied with." She was educated, healthy, in possession of more than the required funds, and willing to work as a domestic servant – yet, she was barred from emigrating to Canada unless she had a "permit." This fictive permit (to which so many persons referred) seemed to be another means by which women who originated from "Black" spaces such as the Caribbean were prohibited from entering Canada, since shipping agents informed prospective employers and domestic workers that these permits were needed, but the immigration department said this was not the case. Further, if Comack seemed confused by the prohibition of migration by a British subject from one British colony (Jamaica) into another (Canada), the Canadian officials who oversaw the country's immigration policy could point to both the 1919 amendment to the Immigration Act, which referenced race, climate, and assimilability, and the 1923 Order-in-Council that limited acceptable sources of Britishness to make their case for the woman's exclusion.

Nor was 1923 the last time that Orders-in-Council would be used to limit the possibilities of Black immigration. An order passed in August 1930 and another in March 1931 over the signature of Prime Minister R.B. Bennett confirmed the expanded prohibition of "all classes and occupations," as well as the limited definition of British subjects who were allowed to immigrate.[41] Importantly, the 1931 Order-in-Council removed farm labourers, domestic workers, and close relatives of Canadian residents from the list of those exempted from exclusion.[42] As a result, British subjects who were not from White settler colonies were effectively barred from Canada. And while it would be interesting to know if persons of colour originating from those so-called White colonies were among those admitted, what is clear is that for the residents of the British colonies in the Caribbean, their British-ness and sisterhood with Canada within the imperial realm meant little or nothing as their immigration was largely prohibited.

During the second half of the 1930s, as the Caribbean remained mired in deep structural inequities that resulted in extremely poor socioeconomic conditions in a context of limited political representation for the vast majority of citizens, the British colonies in the region witnessed a series of confrontations between the working classes and the colonial authorities.[43] The West India Royal Commission, which was struck "to investigate social and economic conditions" in the region and "to make recommendations," advocated remedies that were supposed to be delivered through the Colonial Development and Welfare Organisation, established in 1940.[44] However, the upheaval of World War II only served to exacerbate the problems of underdevelopment and, in particular, chronic unemployment across the Caribbean region in the period.[45] As they had in the second half of the nineteenth century and the early twentieth century, Caribbean governments and peoples looked to migration as an answer to the enduring problems of poverty and inequality.[46] And since a second domestic labour scheme was believed to present a (partial) solution, Caribbean governments attempted to persuade the Canadian authorities to relax their barriers to Black immigration.

According to G.H. Scott, in 1946 the Executive Council of the Jamaican government inquired, by way of the High Commissioner for the United Kingdom in Canada, about sending a delegation to the Dominion "to explore the possibilities of recruiting Jamaicans for agricultural and domestic work in Canada."[47] In March 1947, J.J.S. Garner, Deputy High Commissioner for the United Kingdom, who was stationed in Ottawa, wrote to the Canadian government on behalf of the Jamaican government to ask whether "opportunities may arise for the employment of Jamaican labour in Canada." Referring to the successful experiment in which "many thousand West Indian labourers" were recruited to work in the United States during World War II, Garner explained that the Jamaican government wondered "whether a similar scheme could be under contract in industry and agriculture, and whether opportunities may also exist for the employment of Jamaicans in domestic service here," and whether the Canadians would entertain a Jamaican government delegation to discuss the possibility.[48] In response, the Undersecretary of State for External Affairs said the Director of Immigration, Department of Mines and Resources, and the Department of Labour had discussed the matter, and "the conclusion reached was that there will be no need to draw on this source of labour." Further, the undersecretary wrote, "There are other factors in this matter which would make it inadvisable to admit Jamaican labourers. These people are not assimilable and the climatic conditions of this country, generally speaking, are not favourable for them." As a result, there was "no advantage in a Jamaican delegation proceeding to Canada to discuss the proposal in question."[49] As had been the case when individual Canadian employers, prospective domestic workers, or shipping agents contacted the Canadian authorities regarding the possibilities of Black immigration, the response was negative. That Caribbean people (read as Black) were unassimilable and unable to cope with the harsh climate of the Great White North would remain among the tropes of exclusion.

Although they had been rebuffed in 1946, in 1954 the Jamaican government once again approached the Canadian authorities about the possibilities of launching labour schemes for agricultural and domestic workers. Pointing to the "applications from prospective employers of Jamaican domestic workers in Canada" that the Jamaican Labour Department and Minister of Labour had received, G.H. Scott expressed confidence that given an opportunity, such workers would prove satisfactory but stated that "due to immigration restrictions ... it is not possible to take advantage of these offers."[50] Lauding the "creditable record of Jamaicans in the USA both as agricultural and domestic workers, as a consequences of which there is an increasing demand for them," Scott argued that "the time may be opportune to approach the Canadian authorities again to enquire whether they would now be prepared to consider a scheme for the migration of selected Jamaicans for employment in the Dominion."[51] However, as they had done in 1946, the Canadians – through the office of the British West Indies (BWI) Trade Commissioner in Canada – rejected the Jamaican government's proposal, arguing that "the entry of labour on a temporary basis into Canada interferes with the standing regulations governing the entry of labour on a permanent basis and is a question which in all probability would be resisted in official quarters." With that response, J.A. McPherson, Jamaican Minister for Labour, "suggested that no further action be taken in the matter for the time being."[52]

The Jamaican government was not the only colonial administration in the Caribbean that believed a formal immigration agreement with Canada – in particular, one promoting labour schemes – could help to curb the chronic unemployment and underdevelopment that characterised much of the region. In 1954, the Barbadian government also made a request for a domestic labour scheme to Canada. According to C.E.S. Smith, the director of the Department of Citizenship and Immigration (Immigration Branch), in a meeting with the Barbadian Deputy Minister of Labour (Mr. A.H. Brown), the Minister of Trade and Labour (Mr. Mapp), and the Commissioner of Labour (Mr. Arthur Pickwood), Mapp reportedly "outlined the problems in ... Barbados wherein he stated there was a surplus population and a serious unemployment situation." Smith reported that "these gentlemen ... requested information as to whether there was a shortage in Canada of domestic help" and were told that "it was not nearly as acute as it had been in the past few years but that there was still a steady demand for qualified domestics." As they had done in the case of the Jamaican request, Canadian officials informed the Barbadian government officials that Canada's immigration regulations did "not permit persons coming here under temporary status to accept employment unless by permit," whereupon the Barbadians stated that they wanted to investigate migration "to relieve situations in the various occupations and that it was really their intention to have these people migrate on a permanent basis." Focused on their desire to promote labour emigration, Mapp and Brown hypothesized about a case of a Canadian tourist in Barbados who "obtained the services of a domestic" and asked whether the worker would be allowed to return to Canada with the family. They were informed that "under the present regulations only close relatives and meritorious cases were being dealt with" and that such requests "would have to receive the consideration of [the Immigration] Minister in relation to the migration of persons from the West Indies as a whole rather than from only one Island." Although Mapp and Brown also made inquiries about the admission of student nurses and coopers, given the focus of the discussions, Smith concluded, "No doubt we can expect to hear from these gentlemen in the form of a letter to our Minister regarding the granting of admission to domestics."[53] Smith did not have long to wait.

A few months later, in November 1954, the governor of Barbados, Sir Robert Duncan Harris Arundel, appealed to the Canadian Minister of Citizenship and Immigration regarding the "many thousands of unemployed and under-employed" in the island. Acknowledging that "the vast majority of the inhabitants are racially negroid and British by tradition and culture," Arundel made the case for labour schemes to Canada: "The need for outlets, permanent or temporary, is extremely acute, and the Island can produce a force of a thousand or more domestic servants, or of semi-skilled or unskilled workers, as well as a smaller number of other workers with a secondary education."[54] Anticipating the usual excuse of the climate as a deterrent for immigration from the island, Arundel argued that "past experience has shown that although the Island is in the Tropics its people who have migrated to temperate climates have not been adversely affected by the change." The governor pressed further:

> It is understood that Canada is presently in need of immigrants. The loyalty of Barbadians to the British Crown is a historical fact and it is felt that Barbadians could settle as workers, either permanently or temporarily, in Canada, a fellow member of the British Commonwealth of Nations, with profit to Canada and credit to themselves. Indeed, several Barbadians served with the Canadian forces during the last World War with credit, and many of these have elected to remain in Canada.
>
> It is further understood that at present immigrants are admitted from Barbados on a temporary basis, when employed as domestic servants by Canadians returning from a visit to the Island. As it appears that vacancies exist in Canada for domestic servants, it is possible that an organised scheme could be evolved whereunder suitable selected immigrants could be sent to Canada on a temporary basis to fill known vacancies.[55]

The Canadian response was, once again, negative. Explaining that there was "no longer a demand for seasonal farm workers from outside Canada," Minister J.W. Pickersgill stated, "As for the temporary admission to this country of domestics, our regulations do not permit persons to come here with temporary status to accept employment unless by special permission which is given only in exceptional circumstances." And, to ensure that any perceived loopholes were closed, Pickersgill was clear: "At the present time, our immigration policy provides only for the admission from Barbados of close relatives of legal residents of Canada and persons whose circumstances have exception merit. I fear it would not be realistic for me to hold out much hope of any fundamental change in the present policy in the near future."[56] Although he had invoked the British citizenship, culture, loyalty, employability, and service to the empire of Barbadians, as well as challenged the usual barrier of "climate," perhaps none of Arundel's arguments could counteract his statement that the island's population was "racially negroid," which from the Canadian perspective made them neither truly British (given Canada's narrow list of properly British places of origin) nor able to *become* Canadian.

While the Caribbean political leadership would have been disappointed by the responses to their initial attempts to initiate labour schemes, they were not dissuaded. In February 1955, Barbadian officials Mapp and Pickwood contacted Canadian officials at Canada House, in London, where, along with "Mr. Anderson, a representative of the British Colonial Office," they once again presented their case for a labour emigration scheme from Barbados to Canada. The Acting Director of Canadian Immigration subsequently reported that he and Mr. Hudd, the Official Secretary to the Canadian High Commissioner, "listened sympathetically to the Barbados representatives but made no commitments whatever, and advised that we would inform our respective departments concerning the matter."[57]

No doubt, the stalling mechanism was expected to precede the usual rejection of the proposed labour scheme. However, having been accompanied to the meeting at Canada House by a representative of the British Colonial Office, the Barbadians seemed to have leveraged their status as a (loyal) British colony in need of support, to have convinced that office of the merit of their campaign, and, perhaps, to have offered to Britain a (partial) solution to their own growing problem of an influx of Caribbean immigrants.[58] Quickly following up on the meeting between Mapp and Pickwood and the Canadian officials at Canada House, Assistant Secretary in the British Colonial Office W.I.J. Wallace also contacted the Canadian authorities and thanked them for "giving such sympathetic consideration" to the "problems and suggestions" the Barbadians had outlined during the meeting. Wallace took the opportunity "to emphasise that the Barbados Government fully realize that other people also have their employment problems and do not wish to suggest anything in the way of a mass migration, or indeed anything that would cause difficulties in Canada. However, they would welcome anything in the way of a controlled scheme, either for domestic workers or for any other category of emigrant and, naturally, we in the Colonial Office would be happy to see any such scheme inaugurated."[59]

In the accompanying "Proposal for controlled emigration from Barbados of specified types of Worker," Wallace made the case for labour immigration schemes from the island to Canada. Echoing Governor Arundel's earlier message to the Canadian Minister of Citizenship and

Immigration, the proposal offered information about Barbados's population, the "vast majority" of whom were described as "racially negroid but British by three centuries of tradition and culture" and loyal to the British Crown.[60] According to the proposal, "the need for outlets for emigration from Barbados [was] acute and the Island [could] produce a force of many hundreds of domestic servants, and a large number of semi-skilled or unskilled workers, as well as a smaller number of other workers with a secondary education." Pointing out that earlier in the twentieth century Barbadian workers had emigrated for work on the Panama Canal and in the United States, but that these "traditional outlets [were] now closed" and thus the government was "seeking alternatives," the proposal anticipated one popular Canadian argument and observed (in parentheses) that "although Barbados is in the Tropics, its people have shown themselves to be well able to withstand cold climates."[61] Again anticipating the objection of the Canadian authorities, the proposal argued,

> It is recognised that there is a danger that girls once admitted might leave domestic employment and seek higher wages in industry. This danger is always present in schemes of controlled emigration of this kind, and no doubt a small percentage of girls would leave domestic employment in this manner. It is suggested, however, that the Canadian Government would possess a very potent sanction to prevent abuse of the scheme, since if the rate of wastage became too high they could declare the scheme to be a failure and notify their decision not to admit any more domestics. This would provide a very real incentive to the Barbadians to stick to the terms of their employment.

Finally, a closing request was made that "the Canadian Government should give sympathetic consideration" to the proposal.[62]

Although the Jamaican and Barbadian governments had made a series of appeals for a labour scheme to allow for the emigration of women from the islands to perform domestic service in Canada, they met with consistent resistance from the Canadian authorities. However, only a few months after the refusals of the Jamaican and Barbadian requests, the unproductive meetings between the Barbadians and Canadians in Ottawa and London, and the intervention of the Colonial Office, there was a reversal in the Canadian position. Perhaps the intervention of the British Colonial Office, which sought "controlled emigration" of Barbadians to Canada that "naturally ... the Colonial Office would be happy to see ... inaugurated," had sharpened the focus of the Canadian authorities. Perhaps Canada's participation in World War II – a war that had demonstrated the horrors of strident race-based ideologies – had made the country more reticent about publicly championing racist immigration policies. And perhaps Canada was involved in a re-evaluation of the country's national interests. A *controlled* labour scheme that recruited women from the Caribbean to perform domestic service in (White) Canadian households seemed to answer a range of concerns.

After decades of resistance to the idea of a second domestic scheme, in May 1955 government bureaucrat W.W. Dawson declared that the proposed scheme was "workable ... provided that there is proper care in selection and that domestic activities be made compulsory for the full period of residence in Canada." Arguing for the scheme, which he suggested should begin with "a trial group of 100 girls," Dawson outlined five "factors favourable of a plan of this kind":

(1) The supply of domestics from European sources is diminishing and is inadequate to meet the demand in Canada.

(2) There would be greater continuity of employment in a movement of this kind than is possible under ordinary immigration plans. This would be particularly true if the agreement relating to acceptance of a girl clearly indicated that failure to remain in domestic employment would mean immediate return to point of origin.

(3) We have adequate facilities at St. Paul l'Ermite for reception and distribution, and through the N.E.S. [National Employment Service] have placement facilities, and girls brought forward under this programme could be handled with very little additional cost.

(4) On several occasions over the years, Canadians who have resided in the West Indies have reported their desire to bring girls from there for domestic employment.

(5) Some improvement in relationship with the West Indies would probably result, and this might in turn over the long haul improve trade between these countries and Canada.[63]

Although the Jamaican and Barbadian officials had previously offered some of these same points, which had been rejected, perhaps it was the fifth – improved relationships and trade – that was pivotal. Perhaps it was only coincidental that the Canadian Alcan Bauxite Mining Company had built the first alumina processing plant in Jamaica at Kirkvine in Manchester and had begun shipping the ore in 1952, joining the Bank of Nova Scotia (established in Jamaica in 1889), among other Canadian commercial concerns.[64] After years of rejecting the very notion of a domestic scheme, in June 1955 the government of Canada agreed to the "admission of coloured domestics" from the Caribbean – "75 from Jamaica and 25 from Barbados, on an experimental basis."[65] The second West Indies Domestic Scheme (1955–67) would introduce a new phase of *limited* and *controlled* immigration of Black women, who would, despite the attempts to regulate their movement, employment, and lives, help to change the face of (parts of) Canada.

For the first half of the twentieth century, Canadian officials utilized a variety of means to restrict the immigration of Black Caribbean women who sought positions as domestic workers in Canadian households. As Calliste argues, the immigration policies that Canada's government passed and implemented were "structured by a dialectic of economic, political, and ideological relations: the demand of employers for cheap labour and the state's desire to exclude blacks as permanent settlers." This was, says Calliste, because "the immigration branch perceived black people as likely to cause difficult economic and race-relations problems in the country."[66] Where Black women from the Caribbean who were willing to work as domestic workers were concerned, the reasons for excluding or restricting their access to Canada were linked, as Sherwood and de B'béri argue, to "the fear of black family and community and the accompanying fear of black women as the centre of both."[67] For many Canadians, whose own fears galvanized their officials, Black womanhood introduced the spectre of the literal and discursive reproduction and expansion of Blackness in Canada; to borrow from David Austin, it was this "fear of a black nation" that inspired Canadian immigration and other officials to construct, reinforce, and maintain barriers to Black immigration and the possibilities of residence and citizenship.[68]

After a reassessment of its national interests in 1955, Canada decided to launch a second West Indies Domestic Scheme, which would grant to thousands of Canadians the ability to hire Black women from the Caribbean to perform domestic service and thereby confirm the prevailing expectation that Black women in the Dominion were almost always domestic workers.[69] As I have argued elsewhere, the second scheme as it was constructed and maintained allowed both the Caribbean governments (which were anxious for its success, both to relieve unemployment and for the possibilities of remittances and later family emigrations) and the Canadian government (which was determined the control the "type" of women entering the country) to screen the applicants closely and to scrutinize and manage their (working and personal) lives.[70] By implementing strict quotas for the emigration of domestic workers, the second scheme limited and controlled the movement of Black women, and even though the annual recruitment did not exceed 280 women (250 from the British colonies in the Caribbean and

30 from British Guiana), the Canadian authorities could simultaneously answer critics who (correctly) pointed to discrimination in the country's immigration policies. In addition, the second scheme allowed the Canadian authorities to cultivate goodwill among members of the public in the Caribbean – including those competing for the coveted spots – and within regional governments that got political mileage from the widely publicized annual competition, as well as with members of the Black communities in Canada, many of whom were voters. Despite these tight controls and barriers, however, as well as deeply entrenched and systemic anti-Black racism, significant numbers of these Black women and their families would force an interrogation and re-evaluation of Scott's prediction about their inability to do well or become assets to the country. As they and their compatriots from Africa and its far-flung diasporas expanded and extended Blackness in/to Canada, they would become part of a movement whose (unintended) consequences included unsettling the Great White North.

NOTES

1 According to Marcel Trudel, the local records indicate that there were about 3,604 enslaved persons in New France in 1759; the majority were Indigenous and 1,132 were "Negroes." Trudel, *L'esclavage au Canada français: Historie et conditions de l'esclavage* (Quebec: Les Presses Universitaires Laval, 1960); Robin W. Winks, *The Blacks in Canada: A History*, 2nd ed. (Montreal and Kingston: McGill-Queen's University Press, 2000), 1–23. See also Kenneth Donovan, "Slaves and Their Owners in Ile Royale, 1713–1760," *Acadiensis* 25, no. 1 (1995): 3–32; William Riddell, "The Slave in Canada: Before the Conquest," *Journal of Negro History* 5, no. 3 (1920): 263–72; and Riddell, "Notes on the Slave in Nouvelle-France," *Journal of Negro History* 8, no. 3 (1923): 316–30.

2 Historians estimate that by 1776 there were about two thousand enslaved persons of African descent in Nova Scotia alone. Enslaved Africans were also to be found in Cape Breton, Prince Edward Island, Newfoundland (where they were used in the fisheries), Lower Canada (Quebec), and Upper Canada (Ontario). See Winks, *Blacks in Canada*, 24–60; Roy F. Fleming, "Negro Slaves with the United Empire Loyalists in Upper Canada," *Ontario History* 45, no. 1 (1953): 27–30; Frank Mackey, *Black Then: Blacks and Montreal 1780s–1880s* (Montreal and Kingston: McGill-Queen's University Press, 2004); William Riddell, "The Slave in Upper Canada," *Journal of Negro History* 4, no. 4 (1919): 372–95; Riddell, "Slavery in the Maritime Provinces," *Journal of Negro History* 5, no. 3 (1920): 359–75; and Riddell, "The Early British Period," *Journal of Negro History* 5, no. 3 (1920): 273–92.

3 Frances Henry, "The West Indian Domestic Scheme in Canada," *Social and Economic Studies* 17, no. 1 (1968): 83–91; Agnes Calliste, "Race, Gender and Canadian Immigration Policy: Blacks from the Caribbean, 1900–1932," *Journal of Canadian Studies* 28, no. 4 (1993–4): 131–48; Calliste, "Canada's Immigration Policy and Domestics from the Caribbean: The Second Domestic Scheme," in *Race, Class and Gender: Bonds and Barriers*, ed. Jesse Vorste (Toronto: Garamond, 1991), 136–69; Abigail B. Bakan and Daiva Stasiulis, eds., *Not One of the Family: Foreign Domestic Workers in Canada* (Toronto: University of Toronto Press, 1997); Tanya Schecter, *Race, Class, Women and the State: The Case of Domestic Labour in Canada* (Montreal: Black Rose Books, 1998); Makeda Silvera, *Silenced: Talks with Working Class Caribbean Women about Their Lives and Struggles as Domestic Workers in Canada* (Toronto: Sister Vision, 1989).

4 In particular, please see Calliste, "Race, Gender." See also Dana Whitney Sherwood and Boulou Ebanda de B'béri, "Unsuitable to Become Canadian: Change and Continuity in Racial Discourse in Canadian Political Consciousness, *A Mari Usque Ad Mare*, 1850–1965," in *Women in the "Promised Land": Essays in African Canadian History*, ed. Nina Reid-Maroney, Boulou Ebanda de B'béri, and Wanda Thomas Bernard (Toronto: Women's Press, 2018), 181–210.

5 For some of the scholarship that refers to or focuses on the second scheme to recruit women from the Caribbean to perform domestic service, see Abigail B. Bakan and Daiva K. Stasiulis, "Foreign Domestic Worker Policy in Canada and the Social Boundaries of Modern Citizenship," *Science and Society* 58, no. 1 (1994): 7–33; Bakan and Stasiulis, "Making the Match: Domestic Placement Agencies and the Racialization of Women's Household Work," *Signs: Journal of Women in Culture and Society* 20, no. 2 (1995): 303–35; Bakan and Stasiulis, eds., *Not One of the Family: Foreign Domestic Workers in Canada* (Toronto: University of Toronto Press, 1997); Calliste, "Canada's Immigration Policy"; Rina Cohen, "A Brief History of Racism in Immigration Policies for Recruiting Domestics," *Canadian Woman Studies* 14, no. 2 (1994): 83–6; Patricia Daenzer, *Regulating Class Privilege: Immigrant Servants in Canada, 1940s–1990s* (Toronto: Canadian Scholars, 1993); E.M.K. Douglas, "West Indians in Canada: The Household Help Scheme: A Comment," *Social and Economic Studies* 17, no. 2 (1968): 215–17; Wenona Giles and Sedef Arat-Koç, eds., *Maid in the Market: Women's Paid Domestic Labour* (Halifax: Fernwood, 1994); Ruth Lynette Harris, "The Transformation of Canadian Policies and Programs to Recruit Foreign Labor: The Case of Caribbean Female Domestic Workers, 1950's–1980's" (PhD diss., Michigan State University, 1988); Henry, "West Indian Domestic Scheme"; Michele A. Johnson, "'… to ensure that only suitable persons are sent': Screening Jamaican Women for the West Indian Domestic Scheme in

Canada," in *Jamaicans in the Canadian Experience: A Multiculturalizing Presence*, ed. Carl E. James and Andrea Davis (Halifax: Fernwood, 2012), 36–53; Audrey Macklin, "On the Inside Looking In: Foreign Domestic Workers in Canada," in Giles and Arat-Koç, *Maid in the Market*, 13–39; Schecter, *Race, Class, Women*.

6 W.D. Scott (Superintendent of Immigration, Ottawa) to Messrs. Pickford & Black Ltd., Halifax, 17 June 1915, RG 76, vol. 566, file 810666, pt. 2, microfilm C-10646, "Immigration from the British West Indies, 1909–1949" (hereafter, IBWI, 1909–49), Library and Archives Canada, Ottawa (hereafter, LAC).

7 As James Walker argues, where persons of African descent are concerned, a great deal of this myth of tolerance is tied to Canada's participation in the Underground Railroad: "that the North Star led not just out of slavery, but into freedom, equality, and full participation in Canadian life, that the Promised Land was fulfilled in Canada ... The North Star myth was, however, a liability for Canada, for it prevented any sincere examination of the situation faced by blacks ... It allowed most Canadians to believe that Canada had no 'race problem,' that Canadian blacks were satisfied with conditions here, that there was no cause for concern or for corrective action." James W. St. G. Walker, *Racial Discrimination in Canada: The Black Experience*, Historical Booklet No. 41 (Ottawa: Canadian Historical Association, 1985), 6. While the North Star myth became solidified and reupholstered as the trope of the Great White North (constructed as geographically and racially White and pure), some scholars have started to challenge the Great White North discourse. See Andrew Baldwin, Laura Cameron, and Audrey Kobayashi, eds., *Rethinking the Great White North: Race, Nature, and the Historical Geographies of Whiteness in Canada* (Vancouver: UBC Press, 2011).

8 Calliste, "Race, Gender," 140.

9 "Regulations as to Monetary and Other Requirements from Specified Classes of Immigrants," An Act Respecting Immigration, 1910, *Statutes of Canada*, 9–10 Edward VII, c. 27, s. 37. The nine "prohibited classes" (s. 3) included persons who were "mentally defective," "diseased," "physically defective," "criminals," "prostitutes and pimps"; persons who sought to procure prostitutes, women, or girls "for the purpose of prostitution or other immoral purpose"; professional "beggars or vagrants, or persons likely to become a public charge"; persons sponsored by charitable organizations; and persons not complying with regulations.

10 *An Act Respecting Immigration, 1910*, c. 27, s. 38(c).

11 Calliste, "Race, Gender," 140.

12 Calliste, "Race, Gender," 141. Calliste quotes Scott to F. Oliver, 2 June 1911; G. Boudrias to Scott, 23 May 1911; G. Marsolais to Scott, 20 May 1911; E. Dufresne to Scott, 20 May 1911; C. Laurendeau to Scott, 23 May 1911; and

R. Morin to Scott, 29 May 1911, all in RG 76, file 731832, Public Archives of Canada (PAC) [now LAC].

13 Calliste, "Race, Gender," 142. Calliste quotes W. Tremlay to Fortier, 29 May 1911; and P. Couture to Scott, 17 June 1911, both in RG 76, file 731832, PAC.

14 Calliste, "Race, Gender," 142. Calliste quotes Scott to Oliver, 17 June 1911, RG 76, file 731832, PAC. W.D. Scott was also quite active in the attempts to exclude African Americans from migrating to the Prairie provinces in the same period. See R. Bruce Shepard, "Plain Racism: The Reaction against Oklahoma Black Immigration to the Canadian Plains," in *Racism in Canada*, ed. Ormond McKague (Saskatoon: Fifth House, 1991), 15–31; Shepard, *Deemed Unsuitable: Blacks from Oklahoma Move to the Canadian Prairies in Search of Equality in the Early 20th Century Only to Find Racism in Their New Home* (Toronto: Umbrella, 1997); and Karina Vernon, "Black Civility: Black Grammars of Protest on the Canadian Prairies, 1905–1950," *CLR James Journal* 20, no. 1–2 (2014): 83–96.

15 See Calliste, "Race, Gender," 140.

16 Sherwood and de B'béri, "Unsuitable to Become Canadian," 184.

17 *Orders in Council – Décrets-du-Conseil*, PC 1911-1324, 12 August 1911, RG2-A-1-a, vol. 1021, LAC.

18 Calliste, "Race, Gender," 142–3.

19 According to Calliste, some of the remaining domestic workers from Guadeloupe were deported (they were labelled as "likely to become public charges" or had "illegitimate" children while in Canada). They and other Caribbean Blacks were deported at such a rate by the Canadian authorities that, as Calliste argues, between 1913 and 1915 they experienced "the highest deportation rate in Canada." Calliste, "Race, Gender," 143.

20 James Gilchrist (Superintendent of Immigration, Department of Agriculture, Saint John, NB) to W.D. Scott, Esq. (Superintendent of Immigration, Ottawa), 16 April 1915, RG 76, vol. 566, file 810666, pt. 2, microfilm C-10646, LAC.

21 Gilchrist to Scott, 16 April 1915.

22 W.D. Scott to James Gilchrist, Esq., 26 April 1915, RG 76, vol. 566, file 810666, pt. 2, microfilm C-10646, LAC.

23 Scott to Pickford & Black, 17 June 1915. According to the Nova Scotia Archives (NSA), "The firm of Pickford & Black was established by Robert Pickford and William Anderson Black in 1876 … At the time of its inception, Pickford & Black was a ship chandlery and hardware firm outfitting fishing and other vessels." In time, the firm purchased a wharf, and by 1887 the firm was involved with the steamship business and with shipping and trading services between Halifax and Cuba, Bermuda, Turks Island, and Jamaica. The firm also acted as agents for "several leading marine insurance underwriters including Lloyd's of London, and were

agents for numerous European steamship lines." Archival description, Pickford & Black Ltd. fonds, NSA, accessed 4 June 2021, https://memoryns.ca/pickford-black-ltd-fonds. See Pickford & Black Ltd. fonds, MG 3, vols. 1561–718, and MG 7, vols. 43–55, NSA.
24 Scott to Pickford & Black, 17 June 1915.
25 W.D. Scott to W.L. Barnstead, Esq. (Dominion Immigration Agent, Halifax), 21 September 1915, IBWI, 1909–49, LAC.
26 Scott to Barnstead, 21 September 1915.
27 W.D. Scott to [illegible], Davis Steamship and Touring Company, [date illegible], IBWI, 1909–49, LAC.
28 See Suzanne Morton, "Separate Sphere in a Separate World: African-Nova Scotian Women in Late 19th Century Halifax County," *Acadiensis* 22, no. 2 (1993): 61–83; Dionne Brand, "A Working Paper on Black Women in Toronto: Gender, Race, and Class," in *Returning the Gaze: Essays on Racism, Feminism and Politics*, ed. Himani Bannerji (Toronto: Sister Vision, 1993), 220–42; Bakan and Stasiulis, *Not One of the Family*; Giles and Arat-Koç, *Maid in the Market*; Silvera, *Silenced*; Linda Carty, "African Canadian Women and the State: 'Labour Only, Please,'" in *"We're Rooted Here and They Can't Pull Us Up": Essays in African Canadian Women's History*, coord. Peggy Bristow (Toronto: University of Toronto Press, 1994), 218–19.
29 W.D. Scott to Geo. Howland, 7 April 1916, RG 76, vol. 566, file 810666, pt. 2, microfilm C-10646, Immigration Branch, LAC.
30 [Name illegible] (Brockville) to W.D. Scott, 11 April 1916, IBWI, 1909–49, LAC.
31 Scott's reply was not available in the files consulted at Library and Archives; however, it may yet be located.
32 See Victoria K. Haskins and Claire Lowrie, eds., *Colonization and Domestic Service: Historical and Contemporary Perspectives* (New York: Routledge, 2015); Rebecca Sharpless, *Cooking in Other Women's Kitchens: Domestic Workers in the South, 1865–1960* (Chapel Hill: University of North Carolina Press, 2010); Kimberly Wallace-Sanders, *Mammy: A Century of Race, Gender, and Southern Memory* (Ann Arbor: University of Michigan Press, 2008); Micki McElya, *Clinging to Mammy: The Faithful Slave in Twentieth-Century America* (Cambridge, MA: Harvard University Press, 2007); Elizabeth Clark-Lewis, *Living In, Living Out: African American Domestics in Washington, D.C., 1910–1940* (Washington, DC: Smithsonian Institution Press, 1994); Susan Tucker, *Telling Memories among Southern Women: Domestic Workers and Their Employers in the Segregated South* (Baton Rouge: Louisiana State University Press, 1988); Elizabeth Fox-Genovese, *Within the Plantation Household: Black and White Women of the Old South* (Chapel Hill: University of North Caroline Press, 1988); Daniel E. Sutherland, *Americans and Their Servants: Domestic Service in the United States from 1800 to 1920* (Baton Rouge: Louisiana State

University Press, 1981); and David M. Katzman, *Seven Days a Week: Women and Domestic Service in Industrializing America* (New York: Oxford University Press, 1978).

33 See Reid-Maroney, de B'béri, and Thomas Bernard, *Women in the "Promised Land"*; Afua Cooper, *The Hanging of Angélique: The Untold Story of Canadian Slavery and the Burning of Old Montréal* (Toronto: HarperCollins, 2006); Maureen Elgersman, *Unyielding Spirits: Black Women in Slavery in Early Canada and Jamaica* (New York: Garland, 1999); and Bristow, *"We're Rooted Here."*

34 W.D. Scott to Sir Herbert Ames, MP, 11 October 1916 (file 909404 Imm.), IBWI, 1909–49, LAC.

35 Scott to Ames, 11 October 1916.

36 W.D. Scott to Messrs. The Jules Howe Travel Agencies, Montreal, 21 October 1916 (file 884741), IBWI, 1909–49, LAC.

37 An Act to Amend the Immigration Act, 1919, *Statutes of Canada*, 9–10 George V, c. 25, s. 13. Among the amendments in the new legislation, "mentally defective" persons who were so labelled "at any time previously" (s. 3(2)) were prohibited, as were persons convicted of or admitting to "any crime involving moral turpitude" (s. 3(4)); persons judged as "likely to become a public charge" (s. 3(6)); those with "chronic alcoholism" or "constitutional psychopathic inferiority"; persons who believed in or advocated the overthrow of the government, the assassination of public officials, or the unlawful destruction of property; persons guilty of treason; and persons who had committed any offence "in connection with the war against any of the allies of His Majesty" (s. 3(6)).

38 *Orders in Council – Décrets-du-Conseil, PC 1923-183, 31 January 1923, RG 2-A-1-a, vol. 1322, LAC. This Order-in-Council rescinded the Order-in-Council of 9 May 1922 (PC 717).*

39 James Comack (Canadian Trade Commissioner, Commercial Intelligence Service, Department of Trade and Commerce, Kingston) to W.J. Egan, Esq. (Deputy Minister of Immigration and Colonisation), 9 April 1925 (file D-5), IBWI, 1909–49, LAC.

40 Comack to Egan, 9 April 1925.

41 According to PC 1957 of 14 August 1930, "paragraphs 2, 3, 7 and 8 of the Regulations made by Order in Council P.C. 183 of the 31st January, 1923, as amended by P.C. 642 of the 11th April, 1923, and P.C. 534 of the 8th April, 1926, are hereby rescinded." *Orders in Council – Décrets-du-Conseil, PC 1930-1957, 14 August 1930, RG 2-A-1-a, vol. 1465, LAC.*

42 *Orders in Council – Décrets-du-Conseil*, PC 1931-695, 21 March 1931, RG 2-A-1-a, vol. 1479, LAC.

43 See Gordon K. Lewis, *The Growth of the Modern West Indies* (Kingston, Jamaica: Ian Randle, 2004); Colin A. Palmer, *Freedom's Children: The 1938 Labor Rebellion and the Birth of Modern Jamaica* (Chapel Hill: University of

North Carolina Press, 2014); O. Nigel Bolland, *The Politics of Labour in the British Caribbean: The Social Origins of Authoritarianism and Democracy in the Labour Movement* (Kingston, Jamaica: Ian Randle, 2001); and Ken Post, *Arise Ye Starvelings: The Jamaican Labour Rebellion of 1938 and Its Aftermath* (The Hague: Nijhoff, 1978).

44 Walter Edward, Baron Moyne, et al., *West India Royal Commission Report*, Presented by the Secretary of State for the Colonies to Parliament by Command of His Majesty, July 1945 (London: His Majesty's Stationery Office, 1945; Kingston: Ian Randle, 2011), xi.

45 For example, see C.J. Burgess, "A Review of Economic Conditions in Jamaica, 1939–1948," Jamaica Bureau of Statistics, 31 March 1949; and Owen Jefferson, *The Post-War Economic Development of Jamaica* (Mona, Jamaica: Institute of Social and Economic Research, University of the West Indies, 1972).

46 See Velma Newton, *The Silver Men: West Indian Labour Migration to Panama, 1850–1914* (Mona, Jamaica: Institute of Social and Economic Research, University of the West Indies, 1984); and Annette Insanally, Mark Clifford, and Sean Sheriff, eds., *Regional Footprints: The Travels and Travails of Early Caribbean Migrants* (Mona, Jamaica: Latin American-Caribbean Centre and Sir Arthur Lewis Institute of Social and Economic Studies, University of the West Indies, 2006).

47 G.H. Scott, for Minister for Labour, "Executive Council Submission: Recruitment of Jamaicans for Agricultural and Domestic Work in Canada," Ministry of Labour, Government of Jamaica, copy 3203, 20 January 1954, 1B/31/14, Jamaica Archives.

48 J.J.S. Garner (Deputy High Commissioner for the United Kingdom, Ottawa) to Mr. Pearson, 14 March 1947 (file 942/25), IBWI, 1909–49, LAC.

49 CPH (Undersecretary of State for External Affairs) to J.J.S. Garner Esq. (Deputy High Commissioner for the United Kingdom, Ottawa), 15 April 1947, IBWI, 1909–49, LAC.

50 Scott, "Recruitment of Jamaicans."

51 Scott, "Recruitment of Jamaicans."

52 J.A. McPherson, Minister for Labour, "Executive Council Submission: Recruitment of Jamaicans for Agricultural and Domestic Work in Canada," Ministry of Labour, Government of Jamaica, copy 3203, quoting BWI Trade Commissioner in Canada, 21 April 1954, 1B/31/342, Jamaica Archives.

53 C.E.S. Smith, Director, Department of Citizenship and Immigration (Immigration Branch), Memorandum, "Meeting with Deputy Minister of Labour and Minister of Trade and Labour and Commissioner of Labour, Barbados" (file 810666), 9 August 1954, 1–2, RG 76-1-B, vol. 830, file 552-1-644 – Coloured Immigration: Policy and Instructions, pt. 2: 1953–8 (hereafter CIPI, pt 2: 1953–8), LAC. According to Smith, the Barbadian

contingent inquired as to whether the student nurses, once trained, would be "permitted to remain permanently in Canada." They were informed that an arrangement for their acceptance into hospitals "was made privately" and that where remaining in the country was concerned, each case would be determined "on its individual merits." Regarding the case of coopers, the Canadian officials pointed out that "the use of barrels for the handling of certain produce was diminishing" (p. 3).

54 Governor Robert Duncan Harris Arundel, "Letter to the Minister of Citizenship and Immigration, Ottawa," Government House, Barbados, 17 November 1954, CIPI, pt 2: 1953–8, LAC.
55 Arundel, "Letter to the Minister of Citizenship and Immigration, Ottawa."
56 J.W. Pickersgill, Canadian Minister of Citizenship and Immigration, "Letter to His Excellency Brigadier Sir Robert Duncan Harris Arundel, N.C.M.G., O.B.S., Governor of the Windward Islands," 16 December 1954, CIPI, pt 2: 1953–8, LAC.
57 A/Director, United Kingdom, to Chief, Operations Division, Ottawa, Department of Citizenship and Immigration, Immigration Branch, "Emigration from Barbados, B.W.I.," file 23-353 Ch. 1 or 810666, 28 February 1955, CIPI, pt 2: 1953–8, LAC.
58 See Ransford W. Palmer, ed., *In Search of a Better Life: Perspectives on Migration from the Caribbean* (New York: Praeger, 1990); and Barry B. Levine, ed., *The Caribbean Exodus* (Westport, CT: Praeger, 1987).
59 W.I.J. Wallace, Assistant Secretary, British Colonial Office, "Letter to Frederic[k] Hudd, Esq., C.B.E.," 24 February 1955, WIS 552/2/01, CIPI, pt 2: 1953–8, LAC.
60 According to the Barbadians, "the latest manifestation" of their loyalty to the British Crown was "the great welcome given to H.R.H. the Princess Margaret." Wallace to Hudd, 24 February 1955, attachment: "Proposal for controlled emigration from Barbados of specified types of Worker," 1.
61 Wallace to Hudd, 24 February 1955, "Proposal," 1.
62 Wallace to Hudd, 24 February 1955, "Proposal," 2.
63 W.W. Dawson to Mr. A.H. Brown, memorandum, "Jamaican Domestics," 10 May 1955, 1, 2 (Original No. 553-36–644), CIPI, pt 2: 1953–8, LAC. St. Paul l'Ermite refers to the facilities in Quebec in which the recruited women could be given temporary accommodation until they were placed with their employers.
64 "Development of the Bauxite/Alumina Sector," Jamaica Bauxite Institute, accessed 1 February 2019, http://www.jbi.org.jm/pages/industry; Carlton E. Davis, "60 Years of Bauxite Mining in Jamaica, Part 1," *Gleaner*, 5 June 2012; "The Story behind Scotiabank Jamaica," Scotiabank, accessed 1 February 2019, https://jm.scotiabank.com/about-scotiabank/inside-scotiabank/the-story-behind-scotiabank-jamaica.html.

65 J.W. Pickersgill, Minister of Citizenship and Immigration, and M.F. Gregg, Minister of Labour, confidential memorandum to Cabinet, "Admission of Coloured Domestics," 23 March 1956, Movement of domestics (coloured) from British Guiana, 1956–1966, Canada Immigration Division/Division de L'Immigration du Canada, RG 76, vol. 838, file 553-36-556, LAC.
66 Calliste, "Race, Gender," 145.
67 Sherwood and de B'béri, "Unsuitable to Become Canadian," 186.
68 David Austin, *Fear of a Black Nation: Race, Sex, and Security in Sixties Montreal* (Toronto: Between the Lines, 2013).
69 Agnes Calliste, "Canadian Immigration Policy and Domestics from the Caribbean: The Second Domestic Scheme," in *Canadian Women: A Reader*, ed. Wendy Mitchinson, Paula Bourne, Alison Prentice, Gail Cuthbert Brandt, Beth Light, and Naomi Black (Toronto: Harcourt Brace Canada, 1996), 136–68.
70 Johnson, "'... to ensure,'" 36–53.

SECTION FIVE

"Schooling" Black Canadians

11

Stories from *The Little Black School House*

SYLVIA D. HAMILTON

This chapter explores the history and memory of Canada's all-Black segregated schools and the attendant struggle of African Canadians to ensure that their children had access to the full educational opportunities promised by Canadian society. Through advocacy and a legacy of resistance, and by dint of committed work, teachers, community leaders, and parents fought for many generations to turn the "promise" of freedom into reality.

Canadians can no longer engage in the dance of denial about the misery caused by the forced evacuation of Indigenous children when they were ripped from their families only to be placed in separate, segregated residential facilities that, while called "schools," bore little resemblance to the caring, nurturing educational environment this word evokes. Rather, they were locations, *sites of memory*, where abuse and racism reigned. Why did this happen? In a word, race – the socially constructed, not biological, category that has stratified and negatively affected humans for generations and that theorist W.E.B. Du Bois spoke of when he said "the problem of the Twentieth Century is the problem of the color line."[1] What is not widely known or remembered is that in two Canadian provinces a large number of African Canadian children, because of their race, were also required by law to attend separate, segregated schools.

Legal scholar Constance Backhouse explains that from the middle of the nineteenth century, Black and white students could be separated by law. Legislation in both Nova Scotia and Ontario allowed this division.[2] Historian James W. St. G. Walker further points out that "by circumstance and public attitude, a colour line was drawn in Canada which affected the economic and social life of the blacks. The various attempts to give legal sanction to the line failed universally except in one important area: blacks were denied equal use of public schools in Nova Scotia and

Ontario, and this division was recognized by the law. The most important manifestation of colour prejudice in Canadian history is in education."[3] These all-Black schools were set up in rural areas of Nova Scotia and southern Ontario and, although not by law, there were a limited number of Black schools in New Brunswick, Alberta, and Saskatchewan, where smaller populations of African-descended people lived.[4]

"Colour prejudice" directed against people of Asian and African descent was codified in government documents and by various actions taken to discourage their entry into Canada. The prevailing racial attitudes in the early part of the century were exemplified by Prime Minister Mackenzie King's declaration in 1908 that Canada was a "white man's country."[5]

By 1849 Ontario had changed its School Act, which regulated all public schools, to permit separate schools to be set up for Black children. In Nova Scotia, legislation to allow officials to create separate schools was on the books by 1865.[6] In spite of evidence – experiential and documented – to the contrary, we still face a prevailing assumption that in Canada, unlike the United States where race is a defining characteristic of American society, race plays a lesser role. If we in any measure accept this analysis, it becomes easier to be shocked and surprised when racial conflicts or racist events, such as a white teacher in *blackface* in a video, a cross burning, or people donning KKK outfits, make the national news. They are characterized as "isolated incidents" or intended as a joke.[7]

The logic works if we convince, or have convinced, ourselves that race is an insignificant indicator and that it has played a limited negative role in the Canadian nation. We can condemn such events without an understanding of the historical roots of racism.[8] Racial segregation in education is deeply mired in concepts of white supremacy. The behaviours and actions that arose from these beliefs lead to the dehumanization of Indigenous peoples, the segregation of African and Asian Canadians, and the immoral treatment of the most vulnerable members of any society: children.

While the way in which children of colour were treated cannot be collapsed or directly compared with the horrific experiences of Indigenous children, the core racist beliefs that yielded separation by race were the same, and this did not abate even after the adoption and proclamation of the Universal Declaration of Human Rights (UDHR) on 10 December 1948, of which Article 26 reads:

> Everyone has the right to education. Education shall be free, at least in the elementary and fundamental stages ... It shall promote understanding, tolerance and friendship among all nations, racial or religious groups, and

shall further the activities of the United Nations for the maintenance of peace ... Parents have a prior right to choose the kind of education that shall be given to their children.⁹

For many Canadian students this right was denied solely because of their race. Racial prejudice, coupled with severe economic circumstances, meant that many Black people growing up in the first half of the twentieth century ended their formal schooling before finishing Grade 9; some left before reaching Grades 5 or 6. For these students, aspirations to higher learning and to various professions were quashed because the doors were usually closed. Educator and African Baptist minister Dr. W.P. Oliver in 1949 put it bluntly when he said, "Segregated schools are a barrier to good inter-group relations. They are a visible symbol of separation, and a denial of the right 'to belong.' Such schools became the stamp of approval of the mental apartheid that exists in many white minds."¹⁰

Within Black communities throughout Canada, education has always been constructed as society's passport to a better life, and children viewed as our most precious resource, the jewels in our crowns. Education has been and continues to be held up as a fundamental right, as articulated in Article 26 of the UDHR. How then does one explain why some children would have been allowed a level of resources that others were denied? Why was it deemed to be in the "best interest" of Black children and white children that they be separated by race?

The desire for education on the part of African Canadians across decades was matched by the equal desire of some Canadians to keep the races apart. For example, in 1843, even though Black parents in Hamilton, Ontario, had paid taxes, they were barred from sending their children to public schools. They petitioned Governor General Lord Elgin after receiving little help from the local officials and eventually won their rights. Yet, in the same region, Amherstburg parents were less successful. Hostility was so strong that local white school trustees threatened drastic action should Black students attend the school. They were quoted as saying that rather than send their own children "to School with niggers they will cut their children's heads off and throw them into the road side ditch." Although African Canadian parents could hold no hope of consistent application of laws that would uphold their rights, they nonetheless continued over time to do all that they could to press government officials to do so.¹¹

During the research and subsequent production of my documentary film *The Little Black School House*, the links between segregation in education and the contours of segregation within the rest of society were starkly underlined. The historic practice of segregating groups of African Canadian students within the educational system reflected the broader segregation extant in Canadian society. In short, setting students apart in separate schools was no different from the denial of other public services.

Retired University of Windsor professor and former Member of Parliament Dr. Howard McCurdy states that during his childhood years, his family confronted direct racism in Amherstburg, Ontario. He lived in two towns in the same province, yet his experiences had a marked difference: "In London at St. George's school that I attended, my sister and I were the only Black students there. Where, I wasn't conscious of race in London, when I moved to Amherstburg, I became immediately conscious of it. Employment discrimination in Windsor and Amherstburg was widespread. In Amherstburg, Black people did not work in the town."[12]

Former museum curator Elise Harding-Davis's parents faced similar unsettling experiences. They were not permitted to buy a house in Windsor, Ontario, because of the restrictive covenants that prevented Black people and Jews from buying property. She explains that following World War II, Black soldiers in uniform who had just returned from fighting for democracy abroad were denied entry into some establishments in their hometown of Windsor.[13]

Overt and covert segregation in Canada continued into the 1960s. Research documents the persistence of negative racial attitudes over time and across generations. Parents and educators continually express concerns about high dropout rates and the streaming of students into special programs.[14] At the same time as students were being segregated, general curriculum material either ignored African-descended people or presented them in a stereotypical fashion. The segregated system fostered such attitudes within the broader community. Advocates within African Canadian communities were concerned not only with the quality of education offered their students but also with the representations of Black people in school texts that were available to all students in the public educational system.[15] Generations of African people fought against racist content in the school curriculum and the invisibility of African people in discussions about Canadian nation-building.

Historical Background: Go Back and Fetch What You Forgot

In this ahistorical, highly disposable age, it is fundamental that we maintain our efforts to underline the importance of history and its relevance to our lives today; we need to stop, reflect, and reconsider who we are and how we arrived at this place at this time. The Akan people of West Africa articulate a concept called Sankofa: *Se wo were fin a wo Sankofa a yenkyi*, which means, "It is not a taboo to return and fetch it when you forget."[16]

I am interested in two questions: first, what memories have we failed to represent, and second, what memories do we not want to represent and why? The enslavement of African-descended people in Canada sits at the cusp of these troubling questions.

In a text titled *History and Memory in African-American Culture*, editors Geneviève Fabre and Robert O'Meally use French historian Pierre Nora's *lieux de mèmoire*, or *sites of memory*, as the theoretical framework for an examination of the simultaneous themes of history and memory. For them this idea pointed to a new set of potential historical sources – such as paintings, buildings, dances, journals, novels, poems, orality – which, taken together, linked individual memories to create collective, communal memories of African American culture and life. This concept brings together the private, through oral storytelling and family histories, and the public, as found in archival documents.[17] This reading gave me a wider lens for viewing and understanding these elements within an African Canadian context.

Whether we wish to remember or not, the educational segregation of children of African descent in Canada and elsewhere is a direct by-product of the colonial system of chattel slavery, an institution whose goal was to strip African people of their dignity and humanity in order to use them as vehicles of cheap labour for a profit-making system. In several of my film projects I have referenced slavery and, in post-screening discussions with predominantly white audiences, have been questioned about it. In many cases people are just astounded – how come they did not know this? I face silence when I explain that ministers, church leaders, and key political figures owned slaves and that there are wills on record bequeathing women, children, and men as part of household property to heirs and successors for ever and ever and ever; that the women and girls were looked upon for their capability to breed more property, as it were. The first enslaved people in what we now know as Canada were people of the First Nations who were enslaved by French colonists, who later replaced them with African people.

When I walk along the Halifax waterfront I think of the young children who were bought and sold there – of a young African girl child sold along with hogsheads (barrels) of rum. When I stand beside Halifax's St. Paul's Church, I think of the enslaved Africans who were baptized to "save their souls" but whose Black bodies were not their own. Their voices silenced, their memories haunt me still. African people in early

Canada acted on their thirst for education, in spite of the predominant societal attitude summed up by the common saying that if you educated a "slave" you made him unfit for service.[18] In my high school during the 1960s there were so-called *slave auctions*, where students could be bought for a few days, or a week, to be the slave for another student. The *slave* would carry the *owner's* books and do whatever was requested. Whether they were held as fundraising events or part of winter carnival activities, I can't remember, or rather, my memory refuses to. As one of a handful of Black students in the high school, I kept my distance, as did they.

Talking about slavery in Canada is taboo. The generalized narrative asserts that African-descended people arrived in Canada via the Underground Railroad. The *runaway slaves* followed the North Star to freedom with Harriet Tubman's words, "Live Free or Die," ringing in their ears. A Heritage Minute tells the Underground Railroad story that is indeed true.[19] Tens of thousands of African-descended people arrived in Upper Canada from the United States, especially after the passage of the *Fugitive Slave Act* of 1850. However, the promotion of the Underground Railroad story as *the* narrative explaining how Black people came to Canada obscures vital parallel narratives: those that speak about the enslaved African people in the provinces now known as Nova Scotia and Quebec and, at the same time, those of the so-called *runaways*, people whom I call the *freedom runners* entering Canada. These were bold people who took their lives into their own hands, who reclaimed ownership of their bodies. Historian Afua Cooper's *The Hanging of Angélique*, the story of the enslaved African woman Marie-Joseph Angélique and the Montreal fire she was accused of starting, has cracked open a discussion of slavery in Canada. It includes an examination of the burial grounds of enslaved people in Nova Scotia, Ontario, and Quebec.[20]

These *lieux de memoire* or *sites of memory*, by their very existence, challenge the dominant narrative and the resultant image that Canadians hold of themselves, especially in comparison with their neighbours in the United States. Slavery in Canada, when acknowledged, is argued away on the basis of a comparison and on the question of numbers. Smaller numbers were supposed to have made the practice more palatable, less harsh. We are supposed to learn all that is important and significant as bodies of knowledge in our educational systems from the primary to postsecondary levels. Yet, only in recent years have we seen glimmers of information about African peoples in Canada showing up in public schools – all too often relegated to events during February, Black History Month. Significantly, for many generations we have learned nothing of Canada's history of all-Black schools, segregated by law and geography, in Ontario and Nova Scotia, two provinces with long-standing, historic populations of African-descended people. I consider the locations and the extant former schoolhouses as sites of memory; generations of invisible stories are embedded in these geographic sites and in the memories of the students, teachers, parents, and trustees who were the schools' communities.

The segregated schools were a direct legacy of the enslavement of Black peoples and the conscious and unconscious racist societal attitudes that are intertwined with that heinous system. Traces linger in our language: *slave driver*, *working like a slave*, and *whip into shape* are common phrases uttered without much thought to their origins or how they might sound to a listener who is of African descent.

The geography of Black settlements in Canada, and most particularly in Ontario and Nova Scotia, can be traced to the residual political and racial attitudes toward African people that began during slavery and colonization. Considered second- or lower-class citizens (the term *citizen* is used advisedly here as rarely were they accorded the benefits and rights assumed by other Canadians), they were allotted land accordingly. Nonetheless, from the earliest periods of settlement, African people created their own institutions, two primary ones being churches and schools. Denied access to common or public schools, they created their own at the same time as they fought for the right to send their children to public schools. Elise Harding-Davis can trace seven generations of her family history to 1798 when her ancestors crossed the Detroit River to Canada to start new lives.

She explains that they came with nothing, "And so we often first built a church building. And we would use that as a school, a social center. Education was the most important facet of Black life."[21] Nova Scotia judge Corrine Sparks, who attended a segregated school, points to the same primary connection for early Black settlers in Nova Scotia: "Education and religion in an African Nova Scotian context are intricately related. Family life revolved around the church. Generally speaking, the more educated people in the community would be the deacons and of course you'd have a minister who was really the leader of the community. So a lot of the educational grounding came from the organizational framework of the Black church."[22]

The link between church and school was not only philosophical, it was geographical; the schools shared the same land and were constructed beside the churches. In my home community of Beechville, located near Halifax, our two-room school was constructed on nearby property allocated by elders of the African Baptist Church. The desire of Black parents to educate their children was palpable, as evidenced by the countless petitions they filed with governments to have their children attend common schools and, when denied access, for funds to build their own schools. For example, in 1820, parents in the Black Refugee community of Preston, Nova Scotia, petitioned the authorities for financial help to pay for a teacher. Twenty-five years later, in 1845, eighteen families in Windsor, Nova Scotia, urged provincial authorities to assist them in establishing a school for their children.[23]

Site of Memory: *The Little Black School House*

When racial flare-ups at Nova Scotian schools topped the national news in the late 1980s, few watching were aware of the story's deeper background. Among members of the media reporting the incidents, and even among the teaching and administrative staff of the schools involved, few knew the history and experience of some of the parents and grandparents of the Black students involved in the turmoil.

Few knew of the long-standing struggle against racist practices in the educational system, nor of their origins. In September 1990, a group of retired teachers who had taught in Nova Scotia's segregated schools organized a weekend reunion during which they participated in a variety of activities, including a bus tour to the sites of several former schools in Halifax County. The footage I filmed during this memorable event was lost in a massive fire in 1991 at the National Film Board in Halifax. The stories recalled, the places visited, and the commitment to not forget this history stayed with me.

After the fire I completed a short film titled *Speak It! From the Heart of Black Nova Scotia*, about Black youth, race, identity, and empowerment.[24] However, its important backstory – one inspired by the reunion – still had to be told. *The Little Black School House* is a one-hour documentary film that tells the story of segregated schools in Canada, the teachers who taught there, and the students they taught.[25] It is also the story of the struggle of African Canadians to achieve dignity and equality through the pursuit of education. Segregation in education is always associated with the United States or South Africa. In 1954, while the US Supreme Court was moving to prohibit racial segregation in schools by its landmark ruling in the *Brown v. Board of Education of Topeka* case, schools segregated by race were in full operation in communities in Nova Scotia and Ontario.[26]

Structurally, the film is a multivoiced narrative. Two categories of people appear: individuals who taught in or were students at or whose children attended segregated schools, and knowledgeable historians and educators who situate these schools within the broader sociopolitical context. They engaged in this public act of remembering, one where the individual stories taken together shape a collective memory.

This memory holds a complicated truth about segregation and what that meant: forced exclusion on the basis of race, lack of basic physical and educational resources, and limitations on access to further education. However, at the same time, for the most part, Black teachers who were fiercely devoted taught the students well, held them to the highest standards, inculcated a strong work ethic, and did all that they could to equip them to live in a society that might reject them because of their race. They displayed creativity, innovation, and resilience. Many of the teachers, after having attended teachers' college, were limited in the teaching options open to them. Rarely would they be hired in schools other than those that were segregated. The oral testimonies of the film participants consistently maintain an emphasis on education, a legacy passed down from generation to generation, as demonstrated by the focus on education within the African United Baptist Association (AUBA) of Nova Scotia. Its education committee gave annual reports at association meetings, such as one held in 1948 when Chair Rev. A.F. Skinner stated, "All Negro schools are staffed by Negro teachers almost all of whom have had special training for the work. They come to know intimately the needs of their pupils, and take pride in endeavoring them."[27]

The documentary was filmed in several locations in Nova Scotia and Ontario in the fall of 2006 and was first screened in September 2007.[28] Within the film, there are intergenerational scenes involving high school students in conversation with community Elders. In one, a surprised student listens intently as an Elder speaks about her early school days: "From grade one to grade five. That's as high as the grades went. We just had the two teachers ... Just one classroom. There's lots of times we didn't get to school on account of the snow storms or somebody would drive us with the horse and sled or something like that. No school buses. On foot."[29] They were so engaged with each other, as they sat on a school bus touring sites of former schools in Guysborough County, Nova Scotia, that they seemed unaware that this rare and fleeting moment, where memory was passed on, was being captured on film. The weekend we filmed in this district, members of the Tracadie United Baptist Church welcomed me and my crew to their 184th anniversary, a milestone of survival and history that we recorded for the film.

Legislation, cited earlier, that enabled segregated schools was routinely applied in areas with what were deemed significant Black populations. Thus, rural areas in Ontario and Nova Scotia where there was de facto segregation were confirmed in their long-standing practices by law. In towns and cities where the Black population might be more numerous in particular areas, children would attend the nearest school, often located in a less affluent section of the city or town. There they faced streaming, isolation, and, in the case of the Willow Street school in Truro, Nova Scotia, separate bathrooms.

Mercer Street School in Windsor, Ontario, attended by former teacher Lois Larkin when she was young, was a case in point. Remembering her experience when interviewed, she explained that she had one teacher at this inner-city school who was supportive but, for the most part, children of colour were not encouraged. Subsequently, "many of our children were streamed into what was called the opportunity class and these children carried those labels and sadly as a result many of them did not go on to secondary school."[30] James Haines remembers his troubling experience at the Gagetown public school in New Brunswick: "Gagetown school was terrible. The teacher was very prejudiced. She punished us by putting soap in our mouth, strapping us. I do not want to remember those years and those things. I do not have good memories about those years. For example when Mrs. Alexander from the school board came to school she always said, 'How are my little darky children.' Even Santa Claus used the same word, 'darkies.'"[31]

During my research and production process I was reminded of the compelling stories told in Isabelle Knockwood's *Out of the Depths: The Experiences of Mi'kmaw Children at the Indian Residential School at Shubenacadie, Nova Scotia*. She recounts the harrowing experiences of the children who were forced to eat spoiled potatoes and meat from tin plates while priests were served the best food. At five she was taken to the school along with her sisters where they were issued uniforms with numbers. She could only look forward to the weekly visit from her parents, who walked five miles from the reserve each Sunday to see them. Knockwood's interviews showed that it was the children who did not have regular visits from parents who suffered the most abuse:

> Nearly always, when I taped interviews with former students, they would begin to cry as they recalled their experiences at the school. One man showed me physical scars that he still bore. I began to feel that I was carrying their pain, as well as my own, around with me ... For me too the ruined school began to take on its own individual personality. Even in its derelict state it seemed menacing. I spent a lot of time up on the hill, walking around the school grounds, looking at the decayed building. It was if I wanted it to talk to me.[32]

We learn about the intense amount of physical labour required of students in direct contrast to the minimal amount of academic work offered. There was little preparation for careers or work beyond the school. Knockwood, like other girls who reached Grade 5, regardless of age, was required to work in the school's kitchen. Some worked for a month; others remained there permanently.

Out of the Depths combines Knockwood's personal story with that of other survivors of the school; by incorporating them into her memoir, she offers a collective history, much as I was attempting in constructing *The Little Black School House*. The prickly challenge of *The Little Black School House* is in its counter-memory – it presents historical events, experiences, contained in the individual and collective memory of African Canadians that run counter to the stories in the popular imagination about Canada and its system of education and about segregated schools. "Canada" and "segregated schools" are words that rarely appear in the same sentence; many assume they never existed in our country. Consider the power of the photographic images of Black children, stalked by angry white parents and surrounded by members of the US National Guard, as they are taken to school. These images, along with those from the white supremacist apartheid regime in South Africa, defined our Canadian understanding of segregation in education. The United States, being our closest neighbour geographically and, to some extent, culturally, represented our yardstick – indeed, our definition of segregated schools.

I chose not to use any archival footage from the United States or South Africa in this film to ensure that the story would be clearly seen and defined as a *Canadian story*, a made-in-Canada experience, one hardly admitted and never before told on film. The sense of place, the geography, is of the utmost importance in *The Little Black School House* precisely because it is a Canadian story and must be understood as such. The question then is this: How can a memory be vivid, emotional, almost palpable, as if of yesterday, among one sector of Canadian society and yet not even apparent to another? I say *apparent* since it is hard to understand such absences in the memory of those who – given their proximity, geography, and time period – should have known.

This story has not been told in the foundational texts where such knowledge is codified and therefore "known" and taught. Throughout the various film production stages, from research to launch, people who were not of African descent asked how it was that they did not know this story and its many dimensions: a parallel (unequal) system of public education and the multigenerational resistance and struggle of parents and community leaders against segregation and exclusion. African Canadians simply said, "Finally this story will be told."

The Little Black School House was released during the period when the Toronto District School Board was considering a proposal from Black parents to create a Black-focused school as one effort to halt their children's high dropout rate and disengagement from the city's public schools. While a discussion of this proposal and its aftermath is beyond the scope of this chapter, it bears mentioning that many who were opposed to the school cited segregation and "turning the clock back" as reasons for opposing it.

The proposal called for a curriculum that focused on the history and contributions of people of African descent and for teachers who understood and were knowledgeable of this ethic/approach; the school would be open to students of African descent and to students from any background who wished to attend, a fact lost during the raging public debate. Few seemed to know the actual history of legalized segregation and, therefore, were not able to make a distinction in what the parents were advocating nor able to draw the obvious connection to the long-standing existence of publicly funded Catholic or alternative schools in Toronto. While references to "race" were removed from the Ontario education legislation, religion was not. In Nova Scotia, the late Wade Smith, then a school vice-principal and an engaged, thoughtful Black educator, while commenting on the high dropout rate of Black students in Halifax schools, was taken to task by media commentators and educational officials for suggesting that an alternative school rooted in a Black cultural experience might help to stem this tide. In both cases, Toronto and Halifax, the strongest voices decrying the suggestion of Black-focused schools offered few alternatives, nor did they display any understanding or knowledge of the historical, tenacious roots of racism within the educational system, as exemplified by forced, legal segregation, exclusion, and lack of parental choice.[33]

A Legacy of Resistance

The educational experiences of several racialized groups in the early years of the twentieth century – for example, Chinese, Japanese, and African Canadians – were marked by racial isolation and exclusion. These communities shared the negative categorization of *the other*, equated with inferiority. This racism, which also led to Indigenous children being placed in residential schools, was grounded in beliefs, conscious or not, of white superiority. Why else would these children be set apart?

Significantly, active resistance to racism and exclusion was common throughout these communities over several generations. Ontario writer Adrienne Shadd's research uncovered the case of parents in Chatham, Ontario, who in 1891 took direct action against their local school board's rule that required all Black children to attend one school in Chatham, no matter where they lived in the city. After filing a petition in an organized action, parents proceeded to take their children to the school of their choice; the result was the desegregation of Chatham's schools.

In 1921, the Chinese community in Victoria, British Columbia, resisted efforts by the city's school board to segregate them into specific schools. Parents organized a student strike to force officials to allow their children to attend schools where they were registered. They kept their students out of school the entire year and set up their own school in defiance in order to maintain the strike and to provide an education for their children.[34] Parents in Three Mile Plains, Nova Scotia, pulled their students from school in 1926 in protest over the poor conditions and thereby closed the school. Their move forced the government and the local gypsum company, a main employer in the district, to produce funds to pay for repairs.[35] As late as 1964, parents and community leaders in South Essex County, Ontario, petitioned the local school board to allow their children to attend a new school that was under construction in the town of Harrow. Their school, SS #11 Colchester South, was in extremely poor condition and was the last segregated school in Ontario. The petitioners wrote, "On behalf of parents and ratepayers, the residents have been patient for more than three decades. The fear and silence identified with the past has been supplanted with courage and determination to make certain that their children are going to receive the best possible education on an integrated basis equal to the standards established for other children."[36]

These remembered and uncovered acts of resistance stand as sites of memory, the documentary evidence of the ongoing struggle against racism and for human dignity. Historical context was the canvas for this story, but contemporary witnesses – the teachers, the students, the community leaders – gave it life, dimension, and meaning based on their lived experiences. Their faces, their bodies, and their memories became the landscape of *The Little Black School House*. What the people who appeared in this film – or who were involved in the decades-long fight for justice for former residents of the Black community of Africville, a village destroyed in the 1960s by the city of Halifax in the name of urban renewal and for which the city has now formally apologized – remember, they remember for all Canadians.[37]

In Nova Scotia, the multigenerational advocacy around educational concerns led to successful, historic changes within the educational system and governmental agencies: designated seats for African Nova Scotians on every school board; a provincial advisory council to the Minister of Education; the African Canadian Services Division in the Nova Scotia Department of Education; a government minister responsible for African Nova Scotian Affairs with a fully staffed office; and credit courses in

African Canadian Studies, Grade 11, and English 12: African Heritage are open to all Nova Scotian students at the high school level. Yet parents and educators, while applauding these valuable, long overdue institutional developments, caution that *we are not there yet*. Much remains to be done to ensure that, as Dalhousie Law School professor Michelle Williams says, "whatever they [children] can dream they can do."[38]

NOTES

This article first appeared in *Cultivating Canada: Reconciliation through the Lens of Cultural Diversity*, edited by Jonathan Dewar, Mike DeGagné, and Ashok Mathur, in the Aboriginal Healing Foundation's Research Series published in 2011. In 2018, Nova Scotia eliminated all elected school boards in the province, consequently the designated seats for African Nova Scotians were dissolved.

1 W.E.B. Du Bois, *The Souls of Black Folk* (Chicago: A.C. McClurg, 1903; Project Guterberg, 1996), 11, https://www.gutenberg.org/files/408/408-h/408-h.htm.
2 Constance Backhouse, *Colour-Coded: A Legal History of Racism in Canada, 1900–1950* (Toronto: University of Toronto Press, 1999), 250–2.
3 J.W. St. G. Walker, *A History of Blacks in Canada: A Study Guide for Teachers and Students* (Ottawa: Minister of Supply and Services Canada, 1980), 107. For a comprehensive discussion of the history of African Canadians see Walker, "African Canadians," in *Encyclopedia of Canada's Peoples*, ed. Paul Magocsi (Toronto: University of Toronto Press, 1999), 139–76.
4 Lenetta Tyler taught for a term at Fredericton's Elm Street School in 1929. The school had no bathroom and the children had to collect wood for the stove. The school covered Grades 1 to 5. Tyler, research interview by the author, Development Report for *The Little Black School House*, 2003. In Saskatchewan and Alberta, where the migration of African people from Oklahoma took place at the turn of the century, the new settlers set up their own schools. A small community developed north of Maidstone in the Eldon district of Saskatchewan around 1908. Although there were enough families for a school, local authorities were reluctant because it would mean that Black and white children would be housed together. Eventually a school was set up in 1915 but the boundaries were such that white children were excluded. After the outmigration of the Black settlers in the 1920s, the school ceased to be segregated. In Alberta, Black families settled near Athabasca, in the Amber Valley area, where by 1913 they had built their own school, which continued into the 1950s. In her memoir, Calgary writer Cheryl Foggo chronicles what it was like growing up Black in western Canada, where her family has lived for four generations. Foggo, *Pourin Down' Rain* (Calgary: Detselig, 1990). For further information on the

settlement of Oklahoma Blacks in western Canada, see Alberta's Black Pioneer Heritage, accessed 16 June 2021, http://wayback.archive-it.org/2217/20101208160316/http://www.albertasource.ca/blackpioneers/.

5 "That Canada should desire to restrict immigration from the Orient is regarded as natural, that Canada should remain a white man's country is believed to be not only desirable for economic and social reasons, but highly necessary on political and national grounds." W.L. Mackenzie King, *Report by W.L. Mackenzie King, C.M.G., Deputy Minister of Labour, on Mission to England to Confer with the British Authorities on the Subject of Immigration to Canada from the Orient, and Immigration from India in Particular*, Sessional Papers No. 36a (Ottawa: S.E. Dawson, 1908). For details on the 1911 Order-in-Council prohibiting "Negroes" from entering Canada, and on the impact of the 1910 immigration act on Black immigration to Canada, see Walker, "African Canadians," 114.

6 Robin W. Winks, "Negro School Segregation in Ontario and Nova Scotia," *Canadian Historical Review* 50, no. 2 (1969): 164–91. See also Backhouse, *Colour-Coded*, 250–2.

7 In March 2007 a white teacher in a school in Charlottetown, Prince Edward Island, appeared in blackface in a video, made by three teachers and shown at a staff meeting, that mocked a member of the staff who was of African descent. The CBC quoted the school's principal as saying, "It's a minor incident gone awry." "Black-Face Video Offends School Teacher," CBC News, 9 March 2007, https://www.cbc.ca/news/canada/prince-edward-island/black-face-video-offends-school-teacher-1.654422. Two incidents of people wearing KKK outfits made national news, in 2007 and 2010. First, for Halloween in October 2007, three students came to Cornwall Collegiate Vocational School wearing KKK garb and at least one carried a noose. "Ku Klux Klan Costume Shocks Schoolmate," CBC News, 1 November 2007, https://www.cbc.ca/news/canada/ottawa/ku-klux-klan-costume-shocks-schoolmate-1.641895; second, the first-prize winner in the Campbellford, Ontario, Legion October 2010 Halloween costume party was dressed as a Klansman, carrying a Confederate flag and rope with a noose, at the end of which was a man in blackface. "KKK Costume at Legion Halloween Party Disgusts Many in Ontario Town," *Globe and Mail*, 2 November 2010, https://www.theglobeandmail.com/news/national/kkk-costume-at-legion-halloween-party-disgusts-many-in-ontario-town/article569545/. Furthermore, a cross burning on the lawn of an interracial couple in Hants County, Nova Scotia, in February 2010 generated much national attention and outrage. It is imperative to state that these last two events caused much public outcry and disgust and, in Nova Scotia, a major public rally in support of the couple. Along with the widespread outrage that surrounded the suspension of an Ontario minor hockey coach for taking a stand against racial taunts directed at one of his players, these public responses may be

significant indicators that some attitudes are shifting. "N.S. Couple Shaken by Cross Burning," CBC News, 22 February 2010, https://www.cbc.ca/news/canada/nova-scotia/n-s-couple-shaken-by-cross-burning-1.880988. For evidence of shifting attitudes, see Kate Allen, "After Suspension, Coach Returns to Ice a Little Wiser," *Toronto Star*, 6 January 2011, https://www.thestar.com/news/gta/2011/01/06/after_suspension_coach_returns_to_ice_a_little_wiser.html.

8 See Backhouse, *Colour-Coded*, 15. Backhouse argues that Canadians maintain a sense of "racelessness" that is in direct contrast to the historical record. Her exhaustive examination of "hundreds of statutes and thousands of judicial decisions that use racial constructs as a pivotal point of reference" lead her to conclude that, "Collectively, these legal documents illustrate that the legal system has been profoundly implicated in Canada's racist history. Legislative and judicial sources provide substantial evidence to document the central role of the Canadian legal system in the establishment and enforcement of racial inequality." Historian James W. St. G. Walker also addresses this subject, in *"Race," Rights and the Law in the Supreme Court of Canada: Historical Case Studies* (Waterloo, ON: The Osgoode Society for Canadian Legal History and Wilfrid Laurier University Press, 1997).

9 United Nations, General Assembly, *Universal Declaration of Human Rights*, UN Doc A/810 at 71 (10 December 1948), https://www.un.org/en/about-us/universal-declaration-of-human-rights.

10 Cited in Colin A. Thomson, *Born with A Call: A Biography of Dr. William Pearly Oliver, C.M.* (Dartmouth, NS: Black Cultural Centre for Nova Scotia, 1986), 102. A paper written by Dr. William P. Oliver in 1949 and presented at a meeting of the Canadian Humanities Council in Halifax offers a compelling snapshot of the status of Black people in Nova Scotia at the time. The paper is both direct and candid. Oliver lists the number of people in various jobs and discusses the poor educational opportunities arising from the segregated school, such that, at the time of writing, he stated, "During the 135 years of their settlement here, there is a record of only nine negro university graduates, and of these nine only three can really be called direct descendants of the early settlers." W.P. Oliver, "Cultural Progress of the Negro in Nova Scotia," *Dalhousie Review* 29, no. 3 (1949): 296. Interviewed in *The Little Black School House*, nurse and business owner Geraldine Browning, who grew up in East Preston, Nova Scotia, states that after Grade 8 it was the end of the road in the segregated school; students had to travel far from their communities to enter Grade 9.

11 See Winks, "Negro School Segregation," 172. Backhouse cites a number of historical legal cases in Ontario where officials used different tactics to prevent Black children from attending the common schools. See, especially, Backhouse, *Colour-Coded*, 414.

12 Howard McCurdy, MD, interview, *The Little Black School House*, 2007.
13 Elise Harding-Davis, interview, *The Little Black School House*, 2007.
14 Annette Henry, "Missing: Black Self-Representations in Canadian Educational Research," *Canadian Journal of Education/Revue canadienne de l'education* 18, no. 3 (1993): 206–22; see also her detailed reference list, which includes Keren Braithwaite, "The Black Student and the School: A Canadian Dilemma," in *African Continuities/L'heritage African*, ed. S.W. Chilungu and S. Niang (Toronto: Terebi, 1989), 195–216; and Stephen Lewis, *Consultative Report on Race Relations* (Toronto: Ministry of Citizenship, June 1992). On Nova Scotia, see Black Learners Advisory Committee (BLAC), *BLAC Report on Education: Changing Inequality in Education* (Halifax: Black Learners Advisory Committee, 1994).
15 In Nova Scotia, individuals such as Delmore "Buddy" Daye, Pearleen and William Oliver, and Carrie Best were challenging formal and informal exclusion of Black people from educational opportunities, employment, housing, and public services. From challenging a barbershop's refusal to cut a young boy's hair to protesting racist material in the school curriculum, these leaders were forthright and outspoken. Pearleen Oliver launched two challenges: one against the colour bar that prevented Black women from entering nursing, the other for the removal of the text *Little Black Sambo* from the province's schools. She was successful in both actions. In 1944 she worked with community leader Mr. B.A. Husbands, who on behalf of the Coloured Citizens' Improvement League wrote to then premier A.S. MacMillan objecting to use of the book *Little Black Sambo* in Nova Scotia's schools: "Whereas the little children of our public schools get their introduction to the colored race as far as public education is concerned, at an impressionable age, in the grade 2A, reader; And whereas the references in the story of 'Black Sambo' appearing where it does, holds the colored race up to ridicule, causing deep pain among our children, and presenting our race in such a manner as to destroy respect: Therefore be it resolved that the Provincial Department of Education be asked to eliminate this objectionable material from the text book. And be it further resolved that the story be substituted by the authentic history of the colored people and stories of their great men and their contributions to Canadian Culture." Colored Citizen's Improvement League to A.S. MacMillan, 1944, Nova Scotia Archives and Records Management, Halifax (hereafter, NSARM).
16 Christel N. Temple discusses the Sankofa concept in "The Emergence of Sankofa Practice in the United States: A Modern History," *Journal of Black Studies* 41, no. 1 (2010): 127.
17 G. Fabre and R. O'Meally, introduction to *History and Memory in African-American Culture*, ed. G. Fabre and R. O'Meally (New York: Oxford University Press, 1994), 8, 15.

18 See Walker, "African Canadians," esp. sections on migration and on arrival and settlement. For a detailed examination of slavery in Canada, see T. Watson Smith, "The Slave in Canada" (Halifax: Nova Scotia Printing Company, 1899), https://archives.gnb.ca/exhibits/forthavoc/html/Slave-in-Canada.aspx?culture=en-CA. On slavery in French Canada, see Marcel Trudel with Micheline D'Allaire, *Deux siècle d'esclavage au Québec* (Montreal: Hurtubise, 2004).
19 "Heritage Minutes: Underground Railroad," Historica Canada, accessed 16 June 2021, https://www.historicacanada.ca/content/heritage-minutes/underground-railroad.
20 Afua Cooper, *The Hanging of Angélique: The Untold Story of Canadian Slavery and the Burning of Old Montréal* (Toronto: Harper Perennial, 2006). Burial sites include the Redhead Cemetery in Guysborough County, Nova Scotia; Priceville in Grey County, Ontario; and a place marked by a large stone, called "Nigger Rock," in St-Armand, Quebec. On the Priceville site in particular, see Jennifer Holness and David Sutherland, dirs., *Speakers for the Dead* (National Film Board of Canada, 2000), https://www.nfb.ca/film/speakers-for-the-dead/.
21 Harding-Davis interview, *Little Black School House*.
22 Judge Corrine Sparks, interview, *The Little Black School House*, 2007.
23 Preston Petition, 11 November 1820, RG 1, vol. 422, doc. 22, NSARM; Windsor Petition, 13 February 1845, RG 5, series P, vol. 74, no. 51, NSARM.
24 After the reunion my late mother, Dr. Marie Nita Waldron Hamilton, who was president of the group, steered a project to compile short biographies of the various teachers; her colleagues published it after her death. See Doris Evans and Gertrude Tynes, *Telling the Truth: Reflections: Segregated Schools in Nova Scotia* (Hantsport, NS: Lancelot, 1995); Sylvia D. Hamilton, dir. and writer, *Speak It! From the Heart of Black Nova Scotia* (National Film Board of Canada, 1992), https://www.nfb.ca/film/speak_it_from_heart_of_black_nova_scotia/.
25 Sylvia D. Hamilton, dir. and prod., *The Little Black School House* (Grand Pre, NS: Maroon Films, 2007).
26 See Brown v. Board of Education of Topeka, 347 U.S. 483 (1954).
27 African United Baptist Association (AUBA), Minutes of the AUBA (1948), 18, in author's personal files. The Acadia University Archives, in Wolfville, Nova Scotia, has a collection of AUBA minutes dating from 1854 when the organization was founded. Nova Scotia Archives and Records Management also holds some original copies of minutes from AUBA meetings.
28 The documentary was filmed in the following locations: Halifax, Dartmouth, Cherrybrook, Five Mile Plains, Inglewood, Guysborough, and Antigonish Counties, Nova Scotia; and Toronto, Windsor, and Amherstburg, Ontario.

29 Guysborough Elder, interview, *The Little Black School House*, 2007.
30 Lois Larkin, interview, *The Little Black School House*, 2007.
31 James Haines, research interview by the author, Development Report for *The Little Black School House*, 2003, 19.
32 Isabelle Knockwood with Gillian Thomas, *Out of the Depths: The Experiences of Mi'kmaw Children at the Indian Residential School at Shubenacadie, Nova Scotia* (Lockport, NS: Roseway, 1992), 27, 56. For an examination of the impact of European colonization on the Mi'kmaq, see Elder Dr. Daniel N. Paul, *We Were Not the Savages: Collision between European and Native American Civilizations*, 3rd ed. (Halifax: Fernwood, 2006).
33 Regarding Toronto's Africentric school, see "Africentric Alternative School," Toronto District School Board, accessed 16 June 2021, https://schoolweb.tdsb.on.ca/africentricschool. On Black student achievement in Toronto, see Robert S. Brown and Erhan Sinay, *2006 Student Census: Linking Demographic Data with Student Achievement – Executive Summary* (Toronto: Toronto District School Board, April 2008), https://www.tdsb.on.ca/Portals/research/docs/reports/2006StudentCensusLinkingAchievementDemoFinal-Email.pdf. On Nova Scotia, see BLAC, *BLAC Report on Education*. The BLAC site contains the original report and a review and status update. On Wade Smith, see Carsten Knox, "A Matter of Principle," *The Coast*, 7 June 2007, http://www.thecoast.ca/halifax/a-matter-of-principle/Content?oid=960870.
34 See J. Timothy Stanley, "White Supremacy, Chinese Schooling, and School Segregation in Victoria: The Case of the Chinese Students' Strike, 1922–1923," *Historical Studies in Education/Revue d'histoire de l'education* 2, no. 2 (1990): 287–305.
35 For a discussion of the Chatham case, see Adrienne Shadd, (2007). Interview, *The Little Black School House*. See also Shadd, "'No Back Alley Clique': The Campaign to Desegregate Chatham's Public Schools, 1891–1893," *Ontario History* 99, no. 1 (2007): 77–95. Finally, see David States, research interview by the author, Development Report for *The Little Black School House*, 2003.
36 Elise Harding-Davis, Dr. Howard McCurdy, and former student Elrita Mulder discuss the successful campaign to close SS #11 in *The Little Black School House*. The school was closed and students went to the new school in 1965, the next academic year. In 1964, references to race were removed from the Ontario provincial legislation through an amendment introduced by Leonard Braithwaite, an African Canadian member of the Ontario legislature. Nova Scotia changed its legislation in 1954 to remove references to race; however, the segregated schools did not all close at that time since individual school districts were in charge of school consolidation. The last segregated school to close was in 1983 in Guysborough County, one of the locations featured in *The Little Black School House*.

37 Within the span of three months in 2010, Canadians witnessed two public apologies made in Nova Scotia. On 24 February 2010 the city of Halifax apologized for the destruction of the community of Africville. (The apology, the terms of the agreement reached with the Africville Genealogy Society, and a backgrounder may be found at Halifax, "Apology," accessed 16 June 2021, https://www.halifax.ca/about-halifax/diversity-inclusion/african-nova-scotian-affairs/africville/apology.) Also in 2010, the Province of Nova Scotia announced an official apology and a free pardon to the late Viola Desmond for her wrongful imprisonment. Ms. Desmond had been thrown in jail in 1946 for sitting in the white section of a New Glasgow movie theatre. A free pardon, rarely used, is granted on the advice of the lieutenant governor and is given in the case of wrongful convictions. See Nova Scotia, Premier's Office, "New Glasgow Presented with Free Pardon, Record of Conviction," press release, 16 August 2010, https://novascotia.ca/news/release/?id=20100816003. Desmond had unknowingly taken a seat in the white section; it was happenstance. However, what is less widely known is that New Glasgow's Carrie M. Best, who would later found her own newspaper and host radio programs, launched a deliberate challenge to segregated seating at the very same Roseland Theatre on 29 December 1941. She took her young son Calbert with her and sat in the white-only section. She refused to leave and was arrested. For a full account of her challenge and her court case against the Roseland, see Constance Backhouse, "'I Was Unable to Identify with Topsy': Carrie M. Best's Struggle against Racial Segregation in Nova Scotia, 1942," *Atlantis* 22, no. 2 (1998): 16–26.

38 Michelle Williams, interview, *The Little Black School House*, 2007. See the websites of the Nova Scotia Department of Education, African Services Division (ACSD) (http://acs.ednet.ns.ca); African Nova Scotian Affairs (ANSA) (https://ansa.novascotia.ca); and the Council on African Canadian Education (CACE) (http://www.cace.ns.ca).

12
Black Education: The Complexity of Segregation in Kent County's Nineteenth-Century Schools

DEIRDRE McCORKINDALE

The topic of racial segregation in the nineteenth and twentieth centuries is often limited to the post-emancipation American South or the apartheid policies of South Africa. These two examples are the standard by which racist policies are measured and are often treated as unique examples of racial oppression reflective of the respective racist cultures, founded on White supremacy, that exist in these particular geographical areas. Despite the emphasis on these two regions, Canadian racial segregation predates both American Jim Crow and South African apartheid policies.[1] In fact, nineteenth-century schools in Canada West were subject to a unique form of legal segregation. It is usually addressed negatively in this context, yet segregation also contributed to the peculiar phenomenon of improved education for some Black students but substandard education for others living in the same areas.[2] The Common Schools Act of 1850 contained the conditions for the legal establishment of separate public schools in Canada West.[3] However, even prior to the act's passage, Canada West had already engaged in de facto racial school segregation.[4] In particular, this practice was especially prevalent in Kent County's communities because of its large Black population. This new governmental legislation entrenched ongoing practices of racial separation, which were rooted in anti-Black racism, and as a consequence made any attempts at racial integration of schools in the county even more difficult. However, the activism of the Black communities that existed in nineteenth-century Kent County paved the way for Black innovation and advancement in education in the region. Segregated Black schools in nineteenth-century Kent County represented – and were a consequence of – both White supremacy and paternalism, but these schools were also a result of Black resistance to these same racist ideologies.

Located in modern-day southwestern Ontario, Kent County was well known as a terminal on the Underground Railroad and as an area of settlement for free people of colour.[5] It was the site of two major planned fugitive slave settlements: Dawn, located in present-day Dresden, and the Elgin Settlement, located in present-day North Buxton. Moreover, while it was not a planned settlement, the city of Chatham also developed a significant Black community by the nineteenth century; by 1850 roughly one-third of the population of Chatham was Black and resided predominantly in the city's east end. Regrettably, owing to the region's association with the Underground Railroad, there existed – and still exists – a mythology that centres on these communities. The stories about these communities are often concerned only with the journeys of fugitive slaves to freedom and have promoted what some scholars, including James Walker, refer to as the "North Star Myth," which perpetuates the idea that once enslaved African Americans entered Canada in the nineteenth century they were free from the prejudices that had existed in the United States.[6] George Elliott Clarke suggests that generally an avoidance of acknowledging racial tension in Canada is unsurprisingly natural, in that Canadians prefer to see themselves as morally superior to residents of the United States "with their messy history of slavery, civil war, segregation, assassinations, lynching, riots, and constant social turmoil."[7] The lack of attention to the realities of race in Canada contributes to the North Star Myth. Walker has also argued that a focus on the North Star Myth has prevented a "sincere examination of the situation faced by Blacks and other visible minorities" throughout Canadian history.[8] Thus, not only is the North Star Myth inaccurate, but it has also contributed to a lack of historical scholarship on Canadian anti-Black racism. This is especially true in Ontario, the focus of this chapter. The North Star Myth has been applied to other Black populations in Canada; however, the Black communities that existed in nineteenth-century Canada West are particularly notable because of their relationship to the Underground Railroad.

Anti-Black Racism in Canada West

It is important in this analysis to examine racial attitudes toward people of African descent in nineteenth-century Canada West in order to fully comprehend the problems and policies that would arise over issues of education. In this discussion, an analysis of the institution of slavery is critical to understanding some of the racial prejudices in Canada that would later manifest in Ontario's educational institutions. Prior to the nineteenth century, only a few Canadians would have had some limited contact with Blacks, and those who did, for the most part, may have associated them with enslaved persons. Britain abolished slavery in the empire in 1833, and in the 1850s the Black population in Kent County increased, primarily as a result of movement along the Underground Railroad. This influx of new Black residents to Kent County who were fleeing American slavery in turn reaffirmed the pre-existing connection between Blackness and slavery in the region, which resulted from the practice of slavery in Canada West. The slavery that existed in Canada West prior to abolition has often been characterized as more benign or less harsh than in other places in the Atlantic World, as the numbers of enslaved people in Canada West were comparatively smaller than in more plantation-heavy areas of the Atlantic World, where slaves and slave labour were often the economic backbone of the economy.[9] However, while these enslaved people existed outside of plantation slave societies, the same racial hierarchies that existed in those systems were in place in Canada West; there was an entrenched belief in the inherent inferiority of Black people and a sense that this inferiority is what justified their enslavement, regardless of the type of labour in which they were engaged.

Given the conceptions of race that surrounded and accompanied Black slavery, it is unlikely that between 1833 and the arrival of larger numbers of Blacks in the 1850s the residents of Canada West would cast off their beliefs about race in which Blacks were designated as inherently inferior. This belief in Black inferiority, rooted in slavery and its legacies, would be one of the key reasons driving White opposition to integration in Canadian society. Furthermore, scholars such as Robin Winks have noted that a lack of slavery or even an aversion to the institution was not an indication of attitudes supporting racial equality. For example, many of Kent County's White residents were active in colonization efforts in West Africa, which was a practice often criticized for its racist tendencies.[10] In addition, objections to Black settlement and integration were often followed by the assertion that while the area's White inhabitants may have objected to integration, they were, of course, staunchly anti-slavery. For example, when the Elgin Settlement in Kent County was proposed, a meeting held in 1849 at the Royal Exchange Hotel in Chatham was largely made up of people who opposed the settlement but who also resolved that they "abhor[red] slavery and [were] ready and willing to assist in its abolition by every possible means in their power."[11] However, allowing Black settlements in their own regions was apparently excluded from the White citizens' consideration of "every possible means" of assistance. Therefore, the presence of abolitionist sentiment in places like Kent County did not translate into a welcoming and integrated environment for free Blacks and former enslaved persons making their homes in Canada West.

By the mid-nineteenth century the Black population had increased to the point where Whites feared competition over jobs and land as well as the consequences of Black demands for social equality. As one contemporary observer noted, Blacks in Canada "cease[d] to be interesting Negroes and bec[a]me Niggers."[12] Dawn, which was home to one of the larger Black populations in nineteenth-century Kent County, was consistently referred to as a "Nigger hole" by White commentators outside of the settlement.[13] The increased population caused Whites to become more critical of the Black settlements, often attributing any failure to some innate deficiency of the Black race.[14] Benjamin Drew, in his 1856 collection of former slave narratives, refers to a former slave who noted that he was under a great deal of pressure from Canada West's White population, feeling that any action taken by individual Blacks in Canada West was projected onto the entire Black community. He claimed that "if a coloured man does anything out of the way, his fault is tacked to the whole of us."[15] Such a generalized, monolithic attributing of qualities from the singular to the whole exemplifies the perpetual difficulties experienced by the Black communities in Kent County.

The acceptance by both local communities and government authorities of fugitive slaves into Canada West appears to have had little to do with any tacit or explicit suggestion of full equality. Winks has suggested, rather, that the acceptance of fugitive slaves into Canada had much more to do "with an ambivalent anti-Americanism." Canada West's toleration of the fugitive slave was utilized as a means "to demonstrate the superiority of British liberties and to strike at the republic economically as well as morally."[16] This supposed moral superiority of the British identity was also reinforced by the belief that the racism that Blacks in Canada West experienced, in all its myriad forms, was a result not of any British or Canadian prejudices but rather of American influence and immigrants. Reverend Proudfoot of London, Ontario, for example, noted that "the prejudice against coloured people is growing here, but it is not a British feeling; it does not spring from our people, but from [Americans] coming over here."[17] This attribution of anti-Black racism in Canada to Americans was also suggested by Henry Ford Douglass, who commented in the *Provincial Freeman* in 1857 that "separate schools and churches are nuisances that should be abated as soon as possible" and that "they are dark hateful relics of Yankee Negrophobias."[18] The use of the term "Yankee" here suggests Douglass felt that school segregation was indeed a product of American racism rather than something organic to Canada West. Egerton Ryerson, the Superintendent of Public Instruction, referred to the racism in Canada West as "the American Feeling that still exists in this country."[19] Moreover, such an admission of racism in Canada West was often followed by the theory of American influence. Making a specific point on this Canadian tendency, Samuel Gridley Howe's *Report to the Freedmen's Inquiry Commission* refers to this kind of justification as the "theory of 'contagion' from Americans."[20] The fact that Howe had a term for this phenomenon suggests that at least in the communities he visited, such as London, Windsor, and Kent County, the deflection of anti-Black racism onto an American presence was relatively common.

However, this sentiment was dismissed by Black abolitionist Samuel Ringgold Ward, who argued that Canadian racism was in fact not simply a product of American immigrants. Rather, he stated, Canadian prejudice was something native-born and unique to the country. In his 1855 autobiography, Ward contended that there was a difference in what he called "Negro Hate" between the United States and Canada: specifically, American prejudice "is sanctioned by the laws and the courts, the latter is *not*."[21] Ward suggested that the major difference between the two countries was that there were laws and courts in Canada that could protect Black citizens, but the laws were simply not practised or often enforced. Ward also stated that pro-slavery influences existed within Canada, apparently originating from both American immigrants and former slave owners from the West Indies – a statement that not only lends itself to the idea of American contagion but reiterates that this sentiment was not Canadian in origin. However, Ward's autobiography suggests that much of the prejudice he saw and experienced actually came from native-born Canadians. For example, he recalled a Black couple travelling in Canada West during 1851 and 1852 who were "denied admittance at some dozen public taverns" on the basis of their skin colour. When writing about these taverns, Ward stated that Canadians were "apeing the bad character of their Yankee neighbours"; this again lends itself to the theory of American contagion. However, he also states that Canadians had not been as influenced by anti-slavery efforts as Americans, leading to a more initially hostile racial climate. Ward stated that the "Canadian is beneath and behind the Yankee feeling," arguing that American ideology may have influenced Canadian racism but was not the sole cause of it.[22]

Many of the White citizens of Canada West tried to stop Blacks from entering the province. Residents of Chatham and the surrounding area suggested that a special tax, called the "provincial tax poll," be applied exclusively to Blacks who wanted to live in the area. Various members of the communities surrounding the county's fugitive slave settlements would repeatedly suggest the implementation of this tax.[23] When the Elgin Settlement was being proposed, White inhabitants of the area sent a petition to the legislative community detailing their fear that a Black settlement would limit the area's prosperity and lead to the deterioration of the morality of the people living there. In addition, Edwin Larwill, a town councillor and school board member, offered a host of reasons – some legal, some economic – why the Elgin Settlement should be stopped, and he even went so far as to say that the climate would be unfavourable to any Black settlers. Many in Kent County seemed to agree with Larwill and made claims to lawmakers and immigration officers that Blacks should not be allowed into Canada West because the region was too cold.[24] Climate was a common argument levied by White Canadians (and many northern American states as well) to prevent Black entry; the argument claimed that Blacks were not suited to cold weather and as such should be settled in hotter climates such as Jamaica or Liberia.[25]

The Canadian arguments against Black settlement are telling, providing a small picture of the racial climate that awaited fugitive slaves and free people of colour in nineteenth-century Canada West, a place with some legal protections for Black residents but not full equality. As the numbers of Black immigrants increased, the areas with the densest Black populations became even more hostile toward Black settlement in what had previously been predominantly White living spaces. However, these efforts to keep Blacks out did not stop Black settlement, the outcome being both formal and informal racial segregation in Kent County.

Racial segregation appeared in many forms in Canada West. Some forms were legally sanctioned, such as in education, while others were practices of social convention. Often Blacks and Whites went to separate churches, partly owing to residential segregation in cities, but also because of discrimination against Blacks by White churches.[26] Kent County was no exception to this kind of segregation. Some communities, including the Elgin Settlement, were segregated by virtue of having been established for the assistance of fugitive slaves, but within other cities, like Chatham, the Black population often had little choice but to congregate because of financial constraints or because Black individuals were not allowed to live outside of the Black communities. Ward criticized Blacks throughout Canada West for settling in segregated communities, as he felt that the way to equality was through White exposure to examples of "enlightened progressive coloured people."[27] Unfortunately, Ward seemingly failed to realize that the segregation he witnessed in Chatham and other cities in Canada West was not necessarily voluntary.

Ward was not the only person to observe the racial climate. Mrs. Isaac Riley, a fugitive slave who settled in Buxton, recalled that when she arrived in Canada she noticed the cold indifference of White people toward the Black community, stating that "it seemed as if the white people did not want to speak to us."[28] Thomas Cross of Chatham noted that because of the prejudice in town, Chatham's Black residents were "generally speaking confined to a particular locality of town." One resident of Chatham, Mr. Sinclair, stated that in Orford Township, Kent County, Blacks were not allowed to settle; he recalled an incident where a Black man tried to build a home but "as fast as he built it in the day time, the White people would pull it down at night."²⁹

Early in Kent County's history, Black residential integration was actively opposed. In 1835 the Crown granted William Harvey, a Black man, land on Chatham's King Street North, which did not have any Black residents, and Harvey proceeded to build the first frame house in the town. However, Harvey was required to submit a petition to the city council stating that "the townspeople had no objection to a black man building his home" in the specified area, because the result would be residential integration. However, when he presented the petition, along with the first instalment of the land purchase, only one magistrate would give his signature; the petition was refused and Harvey was forced to sell the land instead of settle on it.³⁰ An examination of the obstacles placed before Black settlers indicates why so many benevolent mission societies were established in Canada West, particularly in Kent County, which was often the most limited in terms of settlement opportunities for Blacks. These mission societies helped to establish Black settlement in areas where Blacks were not fully welcomed. While this aided Black communities in responding to pre-existing racial segregation, it also led to increased segregation, because the result was that many Blacks could *only* settle within these Black communities.

Black Education in Canada West

The field of education offers a very unique view of Canada West's racism and segregation because, unlike the other forms of segregation discussed earlier, such as housing, the segregation of schools came to be a legal part of Canada West's education policy. There is a common misconception that legal school segregation of Blacks in North America had its roots in the southern United States; however, according to Charles L. Glenn, "racial segregation of schools is an invention of the North [northern United States] and Canada."³¹ In 1850, the province enacted the Common Schools Act in Canada West. This new legislation contained the conditions for the legal establishment of separate public schools. This was originally designed for Catholics and Protestants so that they could establish separate schools for each denomination. However, the law was quickly adapted to deny Blacks an education in White schools. Clause XIX of the Common Schools Act allowed for the establishment of separate schools not only for Roman Catholic and Protestant denominations "but also of coloured people."³² This act stated that any group of twelve Black families could petition for a separate Black school.

The legislation was lauded for protecting the rights of Black children by allowing Black communities the option of having their own schools if they wished. However, the 1850 act was less than liberating for Canada West's Black population. It also meant that board trustees could establish separate schools *against* the wishes of Black residents and could legally require Black children to attend them instead of an available White school. Under this act, segregation became a legally sanctioned practice in Canada West's schools.

White residents gave many reasons for establishing separate Black schools. In a report in 1862 of the subcommittee to the school trustees in the city of London, it was argued that "the negro differs ... essentially from the Caucasian race in organic structure."[33] The report went on to argue that Black and White children should not be housed in the same schools because the learning environment would be much too hostile. The report stated that the White children expressed a "dislike to being seated with their coloured classmates; and sometimes this feeling of repugnance is so strongly shown as to require the intervention of the teacher's authority to suppress it." It also argued that the teachers (assumed to be White) would not feel a natural connection with the Black students and therefore "the little coloured child feels ... disappointment mingled with grief"; further, said the report, though the Black children were young, "they [were] not placed on the same footing as others."[34] The headmaster of a London high school asserted that "the White children refuse to play with them in the playground."[35] Thus, the experience of Black marginalization in integrated schools in London was used to argue for school segregation. In an unusually open and explicit statement of Canadian anti-Black sentiment, White parents in Amherstburg promised to "cut their children's heads off and throw them into the roadside ditch if they were forced to attend school with niggers."[36]

The abhorrence of integration, even if hyperbolic, indicated a significant contingent of White residents who strongly and vocally opposed Black integration. One integrated school in Chatham that started with fifty students was left with nine after White parents withdrew their children in 1860.[37] After a fire burned down their school in 1888, members of the Black community in Dresden asked the city if their children would be allowed to attend the White common school until theirs was rebuilt.[38] They were denied entry, and those hoping to send Dresden's Black children to White schools "were threatened with being mobbed if they attempted it."[39] Eventually, a school for Black children was set up in the town hall, but the conditions were substandard.

Rather than being identified as a consequence of prejudice, the segregation of Black students was treated as a choice made by Black citizens.

Indeed, some prominent Black leaders, such as Mary Ann Shadd, denounced the practice while seemingly overlooking the fact that, for many Black residents, educational segregation was not a choice willingly made but rather a necessity if their children were to attain any formal education at all. Nevertheless, Shadd maintained that integration was necessary for equality and that the segregated schools were stunting any progress toward that goal.[40] This was because the continuation of segregated schools set Black children apart from Whites at a young age and fostered further segregation into adulthood. Formerly enslaved African American William Henry Bradley was upset by the establishment of segregated schools and noted that while some of the Black residents of Dresden had asked for them, "many coloured people have prayed against them as an infringement of their rights."[41] However, while integration was a goal that many Black residents yearned for, the resulting segregated schools that some members of the Black community had requested – as well as those that had been imposed upon them – were crucial to educating Black youth, and often their only option.

Egerton Ryerson, the Superintendent of Public Instruction from 1844 to 1876, was responsible for establishing separate Black schools largely as a result of petitions from Black residents from Hamilton, the Wilberforce settlement north of London, and St. Catharines, although these were not the only areas with segregated schools. These petitions were sent to Ryerson because Black parents felt that their children were being denied their educational rights as citizens. The shared complaint of these petitions was that Black children had not been allowed to attend the common schools that were available, "with the result that these children were receiving no formal education."[42] In the 1861 case of *Simmons v. Chatham*, a court confirmed the total exclusion of Black pupils from the town's schools.[43] In fact, in many areas of Canada West school taxes were refunded to Black taxpayers, as their children were not allowed to attend the schools.[44]

Samuel Gridley Howe noted, with respect to public schools, that many Blacks regretted their pleas for Black schools, because once they had been established, Whites would not allow the Black residents to give them up.[45] This was the case in Malden Township, where a Black school was acquired for the Black population, but after three months of operation Blacks in Malden requested admittance to the common school because of the poor conditions of the Black school. Whites in the area blamed the school's poor conditions on Black negligence and reaffirmed their commitment to keep the schools in Malden segregated.[46] In addition to those who petitioned for separate schools, Blacks who did not support segregated schooling and those who lived closer to a common school were often forced to attend Black schools. Dennis Hill, a resident of Kent County, legally challenged segregation in the 1850s by requesting that his son be allowed to attend the nearby White common school rather than have to travel four miles to the Black school. In a letter to Ryerson in November of 1852, Hill noted that he owned three hundred acres of land and was one of the largest taxpayers in the school section, but his son was denied his "rights of school privilege for no other crime then [*sic*] that my skin is a few shades darker than some of my neighbours."[47] Hill eventually lost his case when Chief Justice John Beverly Johnson ruled that because separate Black schools existed, Blacks must attend them.[48]

With respect to segregation Black Canadians were placed in difficult situation; both before and after the creation of the 1850 Common Schools Act, Whites in Canada West would not allow Black children in their institutions, forcing Black parents to request their own schools or to rely on private schooling offered by the few (often expensive) schools established by mission societies. However, according to Clause XIX of the Common Schools Act and subsequent court rulings, once a separate Black school was established, Black children were often forced to attend the school. As a result, Blacks were placed in the circumstance of relying solely on segregated schooling or receiving no schooling at all. Segregated schooling offered a great deal of promise for Blacks if they were funded by private mission societies that prioritized education and would allow poorer Blacks to attend. Often, segregated Black schools provided with public funds reflected the very prejudice that created them in the first place. Since Whites viewed Black Canadians as a threat, accordingly, the schools that Blacks were provided with were largely inferior.

Kent County's Black Communities and Abolitionist-Funded Schools

Of the privately funded abolitionist schools in Canada West, three of the most highly regarded were located in Kent County: the British American Institute (BAI) in Dresden, the Wilberforce Institute of Chatham, and the Buxton Mission School in North Buxton. These schools were often upheld by contemporaries as examples of segregated education provided to Black students that were equal to, or even surpassed, White institutions. These were schools built with the needs of fugitive slaves in mind and funded by religious abolitionist societies in Britain and the United States. Because so many fugitive slaves came into Canada with very little in terms of education or skilled trades, many of the founders of these institutions believed that, in addition to education, fugitive slaves needed assistance in the form of land and shelter upon entering

Canada. As the discussion above makes clear, these institutions were deemed especially necessary in the face of the hostility of Canada West's White residents.

Despite the educational opportunities that it offered, the Dawn Settlement has often been portrayed as a failure because of the controversy surrounding the closure of the British American Institute in 1868 due to funding issues. Marie Carter points out that what is problematic about past scholarship on Dresden as a whole is that historians have tended to begin and end their scholarship about Blacks in the area with Josiah Henson and the BAI.[49] Carter argues that because the story of Henson as a former enslaved person (and alleged inspiration for the character of Uncle Tom in Harriet Beecher Stowe's *Uncle Tom's Cabin*) overshadows Black settlement in the area, other aspects of Black settlement in Dresden have been largely overlooked. One of the most important factors overlooked here is that a Black community existed in what is now Dresden prior to the purchase of land by Henson and his associates, as fugitive slaves are said to have settled along the south bank of the Sydenham River prior to 1830. Carter also argues that the Dawn Settlement and the BAI tend to be used by historians and contemporaries as interchangeable terms for Black settlement in the Dresden area.[50] This is problematic because it can at times be difficult to discern whether sources are speaking about the planned settlement of the BAI or Black settlement in the Dresden area in general.

The British American Institute refers both to the lands and the school established by Hiram Wilson, Josiah Henson, and James Canning Fuller out of a concern for the illiteracy of the fugitive slaves coming into Canada.[51] Blacks did not settle solely on the three hundred acres of the BAI; there were farmers and labourers who made their living outside of the institute. For example, Carter notes that Weldon Harris, a Black man who lived next to the institute, did not identify himself as a Dawn resident.[52] Many members of the area's Black community were previously free men and women, some of whom had attained some measure of wealth and social status.[53] The connections and skills that the free people possessed, such as professional services, businesses, and financial support, were important to establishing a well-rounded community consisting of both former slaves and free people that existed outside of the BAI. Therefore, it is important to note that while the BAI contributed to both the settlement and education of Blacks in the area, it was not the only settlement.

The BAI was established along the Sydenham River in Dresden in 1842 with twelve students in attendance. The school was a one-and-a-half-storey log building with an upstairs living area for students. In addition, apart from resident students, students over fifteen years old were able to enter the school free of cost. Blacks were also able to buy land around the area of the school. Within the first ten years of its establishment, there was a blacksmith shop, a sawmill, a grist mill, and a shoemaking shop. These shops were established in order to teach formerly enslaved refugees trades to further promote Black self-reliance. However, due to a lack of funding and allegations of fraud, the school eventually fell into disarray. Although many historians, such as Robin Winks and Jacqueline Tobin, have debated the reasons for the decline of the school, the general opinion appears to point to mismanagement and debt.[54] Henson was often away, touring to promote business for the institute and using his fame from his association with Stowe's novel to raise funds; in 1857 John Scoble, a White British-born abolitionist who helped to form the British and Foreign Anti-Slavery Society, which aimed to abolish slavery throughout the West, was sent from England to manage the institute. Despite his efforts, Scoble was not able to save the institute or the settlement. Daniel Hill has argued that once Scoble arrived at the BAI he began to take over all of the deeds of the institute. Hill also claims that Scoble used the institute for his own benefit, shipping the settlement's wood to Detroit and claiming the best house in the settlement and livestock on the land. It should be noted that Scoble was also accused of racism by Kent County residents, which added to the controversy around the settlement.[55]

The BAI was an example of segregated schooling being used for positive means through the teaching of skilled trades and basic literacy skills to both children and adults. However, not all members of the Kent County Black population saw the institute as something positive; Black activists opposed the BAI, criticizing it for being racially segregated as well as for its constant solicitation of funds.[56] The school was established prior to the Common Schools Act of 1850, but even after would have been a welcome addition since there were few common schools that would accept Black children in Kent County. The BAI offered an alternative to no education for formerly enslaved people and their children, with a chance for local Blacks to learn a trade, but it also provided Black residents with an opportunity to purchase land on the institute grounds and gain some measure of independence. In addition, it should be noted that the BAI offered an education to former adult slaves who would have been denied access to common schools based on age as well as colour. Owing to its location and the ambitions of the BAI to teach basic literacy and trades, the institute brought many needed advancements to the emerging community of Dresden. For example, the establishment of the grist mill at the BAI was important because prior to the 1830s, residents of the Black community would have had to travel for miles for access to mills.[57] Thus, the BAI provided mills, workshops, and a manual labour school to a developing area.

The closing of the institute did not mean the failure of the community itself, however. Dresden maintained a considerable Black community after the BAI's lands were sold. In his 1861 report entitled "The Colored People of Canada," William Wells Brown, when discussing the Black community in Dresden, observed that there were at least five hundred Black residents in the area but that none had anything to do with the institute. This is important to note because the failure of one Black educational institute was perceived as a failure to educate the Black community as a whole. Brown also argued that many of the Black residents in the region "have farms that would do honor to any race."[58] After its closure, the remaining lands of the BAI were sold for forty thousand dollars and the money was used to establish Chatham's Wilberforce Educational Institute in 1871.[59] This meant that even though the BAI did not fulfil its purpose in the Dresden area, when it was sold the resulting funds were still used to foster Black education in Kent County. This suggests that despite the controversies associated with the BAI, there nevertheless remained a commitment to the importance of Black education.

Buxton, or the Elgin Settlement for Black Refugees, founded in 1849 near Chatham by the Irish-born Reverend William King, was in the nineteenth century regarded by some Blacks, such as Samuel Ringgold Ward, to be the model settlement of Blacks in the Kent County area.[60] This was largely because of its longevity and the success of its school. Arlie Robbins argues that it was because Buxton was the last of the major Black settlements that was attempted in Canada, and so it benefited from the lessons learned from past mistakes. Robbins also argues that King was a proven leader through his work with Edinburgh youths and plantation owners and made good use of his skills in establishing the Elgin Settlement.[61] In addition, it should be noted that King was also very selective about which Blacks were allowed to settle in the area: potential Black residents were asked to provide character references and it has therefore been suggested by some historians, including Headley Tulloch, that "most of the families accepted could have done well anywhere."[62]

The Buxton Mission School opened in 1850 and, much to the surprise of the Black settlers, two White children who lived in the area were soon enrolled there. This was unusual considering the overwhelming White support for segregated schooling. However, given the school's reputation as an academic institution, the enrolment of White students at the Buxton Mission School may have been explained by the proximity of the school and the advantages that it offered. The students at the settlement were guided toward secondary education and "those who showed ability were sent to college."[63] Unlike the more practical, skills-based education at the BAI, education at Buxton Mission School was meant to be academic to push the Black settlers into college levels of education. Buxton resident Henry Johnson noted that he had left the United States to benefit from Canada's citizenship rights but he chose to settle in Buxton specifically "to educate my child."[64] Many children were sent from as far away as the southern United States because of the education they could receive at the Buxton Mission School. Buxton was at one point so popular that a local White common school was forced to close because so many of the White students were sent to the mission school.[65] Buxton therefore found itself in a unique educational situation: the school had been established for Black settlement at Buxton, but it came to be attended by students of other races and ethnicities and from other localities. While this seems like a harmonious example of early integration, the White students who attended the Buxton School were sent by their parents individually and there is no indication of a larger trend toward integration. Instead, Buxton was an example of integration established through superior education, not legislation or Canadian benevolence. Furthermore, Buxton served as a successful example of integration that resulted from Blacks opening their own institution, rather than from common schools opening their facilities to Black children. In other words, the success of this school as an educational facility resulted in White children integrating with Black children into a Black school, rather than the reverse.

The school boasted some early academic success stories as well. By 1856, several of its graduates were ready for college. Alfred Lafferty went on to graduate with one of the highest standards at Trinity College. Jerome Riley also graduated with honours and helped establish the Freedmen's Hospital of Washington, DC. After graduation Riley returned to Florence, Alabama, as "one of the few educated Blacks in Alabama, [where] he became a member of the State Legislature, taking an active part in the Constitutional Convention of 1867."[66] It should also be noted that Reverend King joined with Mayor Thomas Cross of Chatham to establish a high school in Chatham. With the number of students coming to the mission school it became important that students would have higher educational opportunities once they graduated. Robbins states that the "needs of the Buxton children combined with the needs of the Chatham children were responsible for the first high school in Kent County."[67] Therefore, the advances of Black education through the Buxton Mission School, a private institution, were able to advance Black education in the larger Black community and in the even larger Chatham community. Much as with the BAI, educational successes in Buxton's Black community extended opportunities for education in surrounding areas.

The City of Chatham and Education

Despite an overwhelming historiographic focus on the Underground Railroad, Chatham's Black community was made up of more than fugitive slaves. Between 1855 and 1865, Chatham had several practising Black doctors, including Martin Delany, Anderson Abbott, Thomas Joiner White, Amos Aray, and Samuel C. Watson. The city was also home to several Black businesses, which were located on blocks that were named for or by noteworthy Black residents, such as Old Jacobs Pork Row, Hunton Block, Charity Block, Boyd Block, and Murray Block.[68] Old Jacobs Pork Row was a series of small, one-storey businesses attached together. Hunton Block was built by Stanton Hunton, a carpenter, and held several businesses, including the practice of Dr. Abbott. Charity Block was owned by James Charity, a shoe store owner, and housed the Black newspaper, *Provincial Freeman*.[69] Boyd Block was named after Grandison Boyd, a Black resident who owned and operated a mill and warehouse that was one of the major milling businesses in Chatham. Murray Block was named for Nathanial Murray, who owned a shoe store as well as a crockery and a furniture store. Adding to the list of notable Chatham residents was James Monroe Jones, who was the son of a former slave and was a skilled gunsmith who moved to Canada West in 1849. For his craftsmanship Jones was awarded first prize for the best assortment of firearms at the Montreal Grand National Exhibition in 1860. Jones also became a magistrate in Chatham in 1874.[70] One of the more prominent illustrations of the vibrant Black population in Chatham is the publication of *Provincial Freeman* from 1855 to 1859. *Provincial Freeman* was a newspaper edited by Mary Ann Shadd, which was started in Windsor, then moved to Toronto, and eventually came to Chatham in 1855. Shadd's paper advocated self-reliance and Black immigration to Canada West and provided its readers with news of the achievements and setbacks of Blacks in both Canada and the United States.[71] These are only a few examples of Chatham's diverse and vibrant Black community, but they are a testament to the strength of that population. Rather than being a city peopled by a primarily refugee slave population, Chatham was a city made up of established Black professionals, fugitive slaves, and White citizens alike. This particular mixture of populations, both socially and residentially, is what made the issue of racially segregated schooling unique in the area. The Black community in Chatham was notably successful, yet despite these successes, educational opportunities in the city remained racially segregated.

The mixture of labourers and professionals within Chatham's Black population was also reflected in the schools established there. In the city of Chatham there were two notable schools that were in many ways opposites: the Princess Street School and the Wilberforce Institute. These schools were established decades apart but they were some of the only formal educational opportunities available in Chatham in the nineteenth century for people of African descent. They both also represented two different outcomes regarding segregated education. The Princess Street School, established in 1824, represented a separate but unequal school, granted by the city of Chatham, which constantly struggled for equality. The Wilberforce Institute, established in 1872, was a private school built by the Black community to provide higher-quality academic education to train Black professionals rather than to offer an industrial skills education.

As William Wells Brown pointed out in "The Colored People of Canada," Chatham was one of the first areas in Canada West "to exclude the children of colored parents from the common schools."[72] The Princess Street School was originally a log cabin built on one acre of land granted to the Board of Education by the Crown in 1824, significantly before the Common Schools Act. Princess Street was a common school that provided a basic education for the Black community rather than an academic and professional one like Wilberforce. Credit for the building of the school has been attributed to Israel Williams, who had escaped slavery in Virginia and settled in the Chatham area, where he established a farm and later a slaughterhouse, making him one of the city's earliest butchers. Williams wished for his six children to receive an education, but they were denied entry into one of Chatham's common schools. When he approached a teacher at the school to question this decision, he was informed that "she was afraid of displeasing her employer and exciting White parents if she allowed his children access to the classroom."[73] Upset with this explanation, Williams, along with other members of the community, agitated for their children's right to an education, ultimately resulting in the creation of the Princess Street School.[74] In Chatham, many members of the community understood the importance of education for their children, and when denied access to the common school they sought alternatives in pursuit of these goals.

This does not mean that Chatham residents and Black activists were content with a segregated institution; quite the opposite was true. Shadd argued that the Princess Street School should not even exist because Blacks and Whites should be attending school together.[75] The school was founded not as an outcome of Black self-segregation but out of necessity after all other efforts at integration – and its promise of access to education – were exhausted in the 1820s. However, its establishment did not mean the end of difficulties. Many of the Black citizens of Kent County complained about conditions at the school, such as overcrowding, poor instructors, and lack of plumbing and proper heating. The school built an addition, at a cost of $299, in an attempt to remedy overcrowding; however, this addition proved substandard, being only "a frame structure without any foundation or plumbing."[76] The Princess Street School was often in various states of disrepair and was not always given the best resources from the administration. In the late 1850s it obtained a new stove and new equipment, such as globes and maps, that did make conditions better, and by 1873 the log cabin had been completely replaced by a brick structure.[77] Despite its condition, by the 1850s the school had about eighty pupils enrolled with over fifty attending regularly. Throughout the years the community never stopped demanding equal education for their children, and they consistently advocated for better conditions in the schools their children were attending.

One of the most damning pieces of evidence against Chatham's Black schools is found in a letter on behalf of the Black citizens of Kent County to the Minister of Education in August of 1888. While the letter is not clear as to which Kent Black school was being discussed, judging from the description provided the Princess Street School was most likely the school the residents referred to as "ours." In this letter, the citizens argued that there were numerous problems with the school system. For example, because the children were segregated and the number of separate schools was small, some children had to travel upwards of two miles to attend school and on the way had to "pass by others to which they were denied admittance." The letter complained that despite the fact that the Black school in Chatham was certified by the board, it was not properly inspected. Community members argued that a number of staff members were posted at their school after having been deemed incompetent to teach in the White common schools. They pointed out that one principal, who had been dismissed from the all-White Central School for incompetence, was paid a salary of $750 "and yet it was well known to members of the board that he would from the feebleness of age, sit and sleep in his chair during school hours for half an hour at a time." They also noted that this principal's successor had been fired from his position in Dover Township and also from his minor position at Central School for incompetence and "then was thrust upon us."[78] It is therefore clear that the education of Black students in the city of Chatham was not a high priority for the school board, but it was for local Black residents.

The Princess Street School was arguably both an accomplishment for the Black community and also a hindrance. Anti-Black racism established the need for the institution, and the Black community's efforts built it to fill an educational void, and while it was a school that received heavy criticism, it also held an important place in the community. The school was one of the places where abolitionist John Brown held meetings when he visited Chatham in the 1850s before his assault on Harpers Ferry.[79] In addition, when the school was closed, it became the site of the Woodstock Industrial Institute in the early twentieth century, thus continuing to be used by the community as a meeting place and educational site. Woodstock was an industrial school established by the Black community that, like Wilberforce, was open to non-Black students. At Woodstock, students were taught skills such as painting, blacksmithing, nickel plating, dressmaking, sewing, music, and eventually wireless telegraphy for a time. The school remained open until 1927 when it became the J.G. Taylor Community Centre, named for one of the founders of the Woodstock Industrial Institute.[80] Therefore, while the Princess Street School began as a segregated institution and faced many challenges, it also served as an important part of Chatham's Black community, making the story of segregation in Chatham more complex than simply one of separation.

Princess Street was not the only option for Black students in the late nineteenth century, as the Wilberforce Institute was built in 1873. The Wilberforce Institute came together when the BAI merged with the Nazery Institute, a short-lived Black school established in 1869 in Kent County by Bishop William Nazery of the British Methodist Episcopal Church. In 1872, prior to the merger, the Nazery Institute had six teachers and sixty-eight students, which suggests that despite its short operational period, the community was nevertheless invested in its potential as an educational facility. The Wilberforce Institute, newly established from these two institutions, was situated on the corner of Princess Street and Wellington Street East in 1873, placing it within Chatham's Black community. In 1873 the institute had one hundred pupils, the capital of the institution was $36,000 in invested funds, and according to reports from local residents, this school was indeed better equipped than others in Chatham, Black or White.[81] The school was established to enable its students to enter higher education and advance to professional occupations such as doctors, lawyers, and teachers, a service that Blacks were not easily afforded in the nineteenth century. It should be noted that while the Wilberforce Institute was an institution started by and for the Black community, it accepted all students. Wilberforce demonstrates that Black educational institutions in Canada could be equal to their segregated White counterparts, but this often required the work of Black officials and a considerable amount of private funding. The city's White officials consistently proved themselves either unable or unwilling to work on behalf of the Black community to improve educational institutions and facilities for Black students, and so the burden of educational progress had to be carried by those invested in the success of the Black community.

Contemporary Black community members such as Shadd and Ward criticized the BAI, Wilberforce, and the Buxton Mission School for fostering a paternalistic environment for Blacks and placing them in yet another form of dependence on Whites – this time on abolitionists and ministers who established and sought funding for schools, rather than on slave masters. However, Blacks in Kent County during the nineteenth century were placed in a difficult position of having to choose between either no schooling or segregated schooling. Many Black schools in Canada West were inferior institutions that, according to Jason Silverman, often closed after a short period of time "for want of teachers and a means of supporting them."[82] While Kent County boasted some of the better educational opportunities for Blacks in the province, it too suffered from poor conditions and many of its schools had little to no abolitionist or private backing. This was especially evident in the case of the Princess Street School, which was well known for its "uncomfortable" and poor conditions.[83] Thus, in the case of Kent County, while allegations of paternalism for some of the private schools may have been accurate, the conditions of governmental schools, such as the Princess Street School, suggest that these White-funded Black private schools may have been preferred alternatives to public schooling in the face of a hostile and segregationist White community. Many of the schools in Kent County (private and public alike) were advocated for by the Black population at a time when they were denied access to integrated education. This suggests that education was very important to both fugitive slaves and the free Black populations that settled in Kent County. Through establishing the schools discussed, Blacks in Kent County were able to gain education and training that were often denied to their counterparts in the United States and other parts of Canada.

Conclusion

Many Black communities in Canada West adopted racially segregated education out of necessity, as White hostility over Black settlement in the region resulted in a lack of Black integration into educational institutions. Being denied a proper education in public schools caused Black communities in Kent County to establish their own educational institutions, with mixed results. In Kent County, racial segregation resulted in both excellent schools and subpar schools existing either side by side or in succession. While the spectre of segregation as a racist practice is an important point, it is also significant that many of Kent County's Black schools were established because of community involvement. They were, in many cases, the result of a combination of efforts by both Blacks and Whites inside the community (and from outside of the community) pooling resources in order to remedy the problems that school segregation had caused. While educational segregation in Kent County was a result of White officials, students, residents, and parents, and of racist attitudes applied toward educational policies, the successful educational responses to such segregation came about as a result of joint investment by the Black community and sympathetic Whites who were willing to fund or otherwise aid the Black community's pursuit of education. In the nineteenth century, many Black settlements and communities throughout Canada and the United States were fighting just to get one adequate school with one teacher to educate Black students. In the same period, Kent County had several Black schools with multiple teachers, and whenever one closed, the community came together to try to open a new school, or to cobble one together out of the former's ashes. Thus, while it is important to note the effects of White supremacy on Black people in Canada West, it is equally important to consider the ways in which Black communities – each with its own unique history – responded and resisted.

NOTES

1 Named for a minstrel character from the 1830s, "Jim Crow" refers to the state and local laws (written and unwritten, official and unofficial) that legislated segregation in the United States following emancipation in the nineteenth century. "Apartheid" refers to the system of institutional and social segregation that was established in South Africa in the late 1940s and developed fully into a system of racial separation in the twentieth century.
2 "Substandard" in this instance refers to conditions such as overcrowding, lack of resources, and unfit faculty.
3 Kristin McLaren, "'We Had No Desire to Be Set Apart': Forced Segregation of Black Students in Canada West and Myths of British Egalitarianism," in *The History of Immigration and Racism in Canada Essential Readings*, ed. Barrington Walker (Toronto: Canadian Scholars, 2008), 74.
4 As early as 1824 the city of Chatham had established the segregated Princess Street School for Black residents.

5 Kent County, now a historic county in Ontario, was amalgamated into the municipality of Chatham-Kent in 1998.
6 James W. St. G. Walker, *Racial Discrimination in Canada: The Black Experience* (Ottawa: Canadian Historical Association, 1985), 6.
7 George Elliott Clarke, foreword to *The Hanging of Angélique: The Untold Story of Canadian Slavery and the Burning of Old Montréal*, by Afua Cooper (Toronto: HarperCollins, 2006), xii.
8 Walker, *Racial Discrimination in Canada*, 6.
9 Robin W. Winks, *The Blacks in Canada: A History*, 2nd ed. (Montreal and Kingston: McGill-Queen's University Press, 2000), 50.
10 Efforts toward colonization by White abolitionists contributed to anti-Blackness in North America because repatriation to Africa was often viewed as a way of avoiding integration. This was problematic because many of the free and enslaved persons that abolitionists and other proponents of repatriation wanted to relocate to Africa had lived in North America over several generations, giving them little connection to West Africa. Thus, colonization was seen as a way of combating slavery while not having to integrate or interact with people of African descent. Jonathan William Walton, "Blacks in Buxton and Chatham, Ontario, 1850–1890: Did the 49th Parallel Make a Difference?" (PhD diss., Princeton University, 1979), 37, ProQuest.
11 "Elgin Association for the Improvement of the Colored Race," *Kent Advertiser*, August 23, 1849.
12 Samuel Gridley Howe, *The Report to the Freedmen's Inquiry Commission, 1864: The Refugees from Slavery in Canada West* (Boston: Wright and Potter, 1864), 40.
13 Victor Lauriston, *Romantic Kent: The Story of a County, 1626–1952* (Chatham: County of Kent, 1952), 383.
14 In the nineteenth century, conceptions of race became more streamlined, sometimes using science and history to argue for a lack of intelligence in people of African descent, claiming that people of African descent had no history and had made no significant contributions to the world, which in turn justified their lowered status in North American societies. Therefore, according to this line of reasoning, any failure within established Black communities – such as lack of funding, mismanagement, or even the failure of a business venture – was often attributed to Blackness rather than to other factors.
15 Benjamin Drew, *The Refugee: Or the Narratives of Fugitive Slaves in Canada* (1856; Toronto: Prospero, 2000), 235.
16 Winks, *Blacks in Canada*, 149.
17 Howe, *Report to the Freedmen's Inquiry*, 39.
18 Henry Ford Douglass, "The Duties of Colored Men in Canada," *Provincial Freeman*, March 28, 1857.

19 Howe, *Report to the Freedmen's Inquiry*, 40.
20 Howe, 49.
21 Samuel Ringgold Ward, *Autobiography of a Fugitive Negro: His Anti-Slavery Labours in the United States, Canada and England* (London: John Snow, 1855), 73.
22 Ward, 73.
23 Headley Tulloch, *Black Canadians: A Long Line of Fighters* (Toronto: NC Press, 1975), 116.
24 Jason H. Silverman, *Unwelcome Guests: Canada West's Response to American Fugitive Slaves, 1800–1865* (Millwood, NY: Associated Faculty Press, 1985), 64, 68.
25 James Oaks, *A History of American Slaveholders* (New York: Random House, 1982), 131.
26 Daniel Hill, *The Freedom-Seekers: Blacks in Early Canada* (Agincourt, ON: Book Society of Canada, 1981), 104.
27 Ward, *Autobiography of a Fugitive Negro*, 100.
28 Mrs. Isaac Riley narrative, in Drew, *The Refugee*, 299.
29 Howe, *Report to the Freedmen's Inquiry*, 44.
30 Gwendolyn Robinson, *Seek the Truth: A Story of Chatham's Black Community* (self-pub., 1989), 25.
31 Charles L. Glenn, *Afro American/Afro Canadian Schooling from the Colonial Past to the Present* (New York: Palgrave Macmillan, 2011), 109.
32 J. Donald Wilson, "The Ryerson Years in Canada West," in *Education in Canada: An Interpretation*, ed. E. Brian Titley and Peter J. Miller (Calgary: Detselig, 1982), 81.
33 "Extract from a Report of a Sub-Committee to the School Trustees," 1862, 191, Education File, Chatham Kent Black Historical Society.
34 "Extract from a Report," 192.
35 Howe, *Report to the Freedmen's Inquiry*, 48.
36 Paul Axelrod, *The Promise of Schooling: Education in Canada, 1800–1914* (Toronto: University of Toronto Press, 1997), 79.
37 Axelrod, 79.
38 A common school was a public school usually governed by locally elected school trustees.
39 Nathaniel Murray to the Minister of Education, 1888, RG 2-42, Department of Education select subject files, Archives of Ontario.
40 Jacqueline L. Tobin, *From Midnight to Dawn: The Last Tracks of the Underground Railroad* (Toronto: Doubleday, 2007), 68.
41 William Henry Bradley narrative, in Drew, *The Refugee*, 313.
42 Wilson, "Ryerson Years," 81.
43 Hill, *Freedom-Seekers*, 103.
44 Winks, *Blacks in Canada*, 371.

45 Howe, *Report to the Freedmen's Inquiry*, 50.
46 Hill, *Freedom-Seekers*, 102.
47 Dennis Hill to Egerton Ryerson, November 22, 1852, in *The Black Abolitionist Papers*, vol. 2, *Canada, 1830–1865*, ed. Peter C. Ripley (Chapel Hill: University of North Carolina Press, 1986), 243.
48 Peter C. Ripley, preface to Hill to Ryerson, in Ripley, *Black Abolitionist Papers*, 243.
49 Josiah Henson was an author, abolitionist, minister, and former enslaved African American from Maryland. He escaped slavery in 1830 with his family and settled in Canada West. It is claimed that his autobiography, *The Life of Josiah Henson, Formerly a Slave, Now an Inhabitant of Canada, as Narrated by Himself*, was the inspiration behind the character of Uncle Tom in Harriet Beecher Stowe's 1852 novel *Uncle Tom's Cabin*. There is some controversy as to whether this is true. Historian Robin Winks suggests that it is unlikely that Stowe ever met Henson and notes that she never fully declared him as the inspiration behind the character. Winks, *Blacks in Canada*, 181–95.
50 Marie Carter, "Reimagining the Dawn Settlement," in *The Promised Land: History and Historiography of the Black Experience in Chatham-Kent's Settlements and Beyond*, ed. Boulou Ebanda de B'béri, Nina Reid-Maroney, and Handel Kashope Wright (Toronto: Toronto University Press, 2014), 188, 179.
51 Hiram Wilson was an abolitionist from New Hampshire who worked to improve the lives of formerly enslaved people in Canada West. James Canning Fuller was a Quaker and Underground Railroad abolitionist.
52 Carter, "Reimagining the Dawn Settlement," 177.
53 Marie Carter and Jeffrey Carter, *Stepping Back in Time: Along the Trillium Trail in Dresden* (Chatham: Chamberlain Mercury, 2003), 38.
54 Winks, *Blacks in Canada*, 203.
55 Hill, *Freedom-Seekers*, 73.
56 Tobin, *From Midnight to Dawn*, 35.
57 Carter and Carter, *Stepping Back in Time*, 44.
58 William Wells Brown, "The Colored People of Canada," in Ripley, *Black Abolitionist Papers*, 477.
59 Winks, *Blacks in Canada*, 203.
60 Tobin, *From Midnight to Dawn*, 124.
61 Arlie C. Robbins, *Legacy to Buxton* (Chatham: Ideal, 1983), 55.
62 Tulloch, *Black Canadians*, 117.
63 Robbins, *Legacy to Buxton*, 62.
64 Henry Johnson narrative, in Drew, *The Refugee*, 307.
65 Roger E. Riendeau, *An Enduring Heritage: Black Contributions to Early Ontario* (Toronto: Dundurn, 1984), 19.
66 Robbins, *Legacy to Buxton*, 62.
67 Robbins, 64.

68 In this context a "block" refers to a large building that housed several businesses.
69 Robinson, *Seek the Truth*, 105
70 Robinson, 32.
71 Robinson, 105.
72 Brown, "Colored People of Canada," 470.
73 Robinson, *Seek the Truth*, 50.
74 Robinson, 88.
75 Robinson, 88.
76 Hill, *Freedom-Seekers*, 154.
77 Robinson, *Seek the Truth*, 88.
78 Murray to Minister of Education, 1888.
79 John Brown believed that armed insurrection was the only way to end slavery in the United States. In 1859 he led a raid on the federal arsenal in Harpers Ferry, Virginia, aiming to start a movement to liberate enslaved people. When planning this assault, Brown travelled to Chatham seeking supporters. This attack failed; Brown was tried for treason and hanged.
80 Robinson, *Seek the Truth*, 94.
81 Robinson, 91.
82 Silverman, *Unwelcome Guests*, 133.
83 Robinson, *Seek the Truth*, 88.

13
"We have to strive for the best": The High Aspirations of Black Caribbean Canadian Youth of the 1970s and 1980s

CARL E. JAMES

> They [Whites] give us so much pressure that you get nowhere. So, you have to just stay at the highest Black level that they allow us to have. We have to strive for the best.
>
> Kirk, age 19, 1985

Data reported by the Toronto District School Board (TDSB) in 2018 indicate that Black students were among the least likely to be enrolled in a Grade 9 Academic Program, to have graduated from high school after five years, and to have pursued postsecondary education.[1] While cumulatively 18 per cent of Black students had been suspended one or more times by the 2017–18 school year, only 7 per cent of their non-Black counterparts were.[2] Were things any different for Black youth of the 1970s and '80s, many of whom were among the group of first generation Canadians?[3] Did they face a social, educational, and occupational context that, as Kirk (quoted above) said, "got them nowhere"? Were they, as is the case now, a generation later, confronted with racism and discrimination that conspired to limit their opportunities, aspirations, and outcomes – keeping them at, as Kirk termed it, "the highest Black level" allowed, despite "striving for the best"?[4]

In this chapter, I reflect on the Canadian social and cultural context of the 1970s and '80s, noting the experiences, career plans, and ambitions of Black Canadian youth of Caribbean parents – particularly how they navigated the Toronto schooling system with aspirations of attaining an education that would get them "high-level" careers. This was a time when studies were reporting on the precarious job prospects for young Canadians. One study showed that well over one-half (60 per cent in Canada and 54 per cent in Ontario) of the "emerging generation" of Canadian youth viewed unemployment as their most serious social problem.⁵ Other researchers wrote that during that period of "economic decline when jobs are in short supply, youth especially teenagers are the most severely affected."⁶

Commenting on the fact that Black youth might be denied employment because of the colour of their skin or foreign accents – and without consideration of their actual abilities – Frances Henry and Effie Ginzberg proffered that they were likely to become alienated and frustrated. These scholars went on to say, "We know from experiences of other countries such as Great Britain, that such feelings can lead to social unrest and disorder which no society can justify or endure."⁷ Further, in an address to a conference on multiculturalism, then Ontario attorney-general Roy McMurtry observed that studies consistently demonstrated that "visible minority" youth faced "significantly higher levels of unemployment than the rest of the population." And he cautioned that "if thousands of racial minority individuals in this country are given reason to believe that they face perpetual, widespread unemployment and second-class status because of the colour of their skin, very serious social unrest could result."⁸

This discussion is predicated on the idea that the experiences, plans, aspirations, and achievements of individuals involve a complex series of interrelated processes. These include social identities (related to race, age, social class, and citizenship/immigrant status), individuals' sense of belonging (mediated by their interactions with majority/host members of the society), existing societal conditions (in terms of educational, social, and occupational opportunities), and individual, institutional, and societal obstacles and/or barriers (such as prevailing laws, policies, and rules that inform attitudes and practices). In what follows, I present a profile of Toronto's Black population of the 1970s and 1980s and go on to discuss the Canadian social context at that time with reference to the social, educational, and employment experiences, perceptions, and attainment of Black people generally, and the youth in particular. This will be followed by a discussion of Black youth's schooling experiences, their aspirations, and their achievements, noting the ways in which racism and discrimination affected them.

The Social Context of the 1970s and 1980s

According to Statistics Canada, in 1981 the Black population of Canada numbered about 249,850, of which 126,330 or 51 per cent lived in metropolitan Toronto; they constituted an estimated 4.2 per cent of the Toronto population.⁹ Despite limitations, the census data provide the best or at least fairly reasonable and comprehensive information on the Black

A Profile of the Black Population of Toronto

During the 1970s through to the 1980s, Toronto was home to the majority of Canada's Black population, with almost one-half of the population being under twenty-four years old. As table 13.1 shows, the male/female representation was almost even (51 per cent male and 49 per cent female), which was about the same as the general Toronto population. In comparison with other Torontonians, Black people were much more likely to be single (58 per cent of the Black population compared with 43 per cent of Torontonians) than married (36 per cent of the Black population 47 per cent of Torontonians); on average, the Black family was made up of about 3.9 persons, compared with 3.6 persons in a Toronto family. Also, 60 per cent of the city's Black population were Canadian citizens, but only 20 per cent of them were Canadian-born. A majority (68 per cent) of the population were immigrants from the Caribbean and South America

Table 13.1. 1981 characteristics of the Toronto Black population (percentage)

	Blacks (%)	Total Toronto (%)		Blacks (%)	Total Toronto (%)
Sex			**Marital Status**		
Male	51	49	Single	56	43
Female	49	51	Married	36	47
			Widowed	2	5
			Separated	4	2
			Divorced	2	2
Age			**Persons in Family**	3.9	3.6
0–9 years	18	13			
10–14 years	9	7	**Canadian-Born**	20	62
15–19 years	13	9			
20–4 years	9	9	**Citizenship**		
25–9 years	10	9	Canada	60	85
30–64 years	39	44	Country of birth	30	11
65+ years	2	9	Other	10	4

(*Continued*)

Table 13.1. Continued

	Blacks (%)	Total Toronto (%)		Blacks (%)	Total Toronto (%)
Foreign-Born Period of Immigration			**Birthplace**		
Before 1945	-	7	Canada	20	62
1945–54	1	17	US	1	1
1955–64	5	23	Europe	3	25
1965–9	28	18	Asia	1	6
1970–4	31	16	Africa	6	1
1975–7	21	11	Caribbean and S. America	69	5
1978–81* *first five months of 1981	14	8	Other	1	-
Education			**Occupation**		
Individuals 15+			**High White Collar**		
Less than Grade 9	11	16	Managerial, admin.	6	11
Grades 9–13	28	27	Natural science, engineering, math	3	4
No sec. cert.	13	13	Social science and related	1	2
Trades cert./dipl.	4	3	Teaching and related	1	4
Other Non-Univ.			Medicine and health	1	4
No cert./dipl.	8	6	Artistic, literary, rec.	1	2
Trades cert./dipl.	9	6	**Low White Collar**		
No univ./cert./dipl.	14	8	Clerical and related	27	25
University			Sales	5	9
No cert./dipl.	4	5	Service	14	11
Univ. or non-univ.	4	4	**Manual**		
BA or higher	5	12	Processing, machining, assembly, repair	21	11
			Construction	4	4
			Transportation	1	3
			Other	6	7
Labour-Force Activity			**Total Income***		
Participation % of 15+ years	75	71	Average ($)	9,287	12,410
Unemployed % of participant	5	4	Income from wages average ($)	10,782	13,614

* "Total income" includes all sources of income. The average is obtained by dividing the total income of all individuals fifteen years and older. "Income from wages" is gross wages before deductions. The average is obtained by dividing the total income by all individuals who are fifteen years and over and who are in the labour force (this excludes students, pensioners, etc.)
Source: Statistics Canada, 1981 Census of Canada, Public Use Sample tapes.

who had immigrated mostly between 1965 and 1977. Other areas from which Black people in Toronto had immigrated were Africa, Europe, and, in a very small proportion, the United States.

Table 13.1 also indicates that the high school and trade education of Black youth fifteen years of age and older tended to mirror that of the general Toronto population – except that Black youth were less likely to have a Grade 9 education (11 per cent of Black youth compared with 16 per cent of Toronto youth). And Black Torontonians were more likely than Torontonians in general to be engaged in non-university or trade education – resulting in more Black youth (14 per cent) than overall Toronto youth (8 per cent) obtaining trade and non-university certificates and diplomas. In fact, Black Torontonians over fifteen years old were half as likely as Torontonians in general to hold a bachelor's degree or higher. The low number of degree holders might be a reflection of the young age of the Black population (40 per cent were ten to nineteen years old, compared with 29 per cent of the Toronto population) and the recency of their settlement in the country, meaning that it was still early to quantify their participation in postsecondary education. It was also the case that Black adults (slightly more males than females) were twice as likely as non-Black Torontonians to participate in education on a part-time basis.

In terms of employment, Black people were just as likely as other Torontonians to be employed but were more likely to be found working in machining, assembly, repair, and service occupations; those in professional occupations were largely concentrated in the medical health area (table 13.1). Like the rest of the population, about one in four Black people was employed in clerical or clerical-related occupations, and more than one in ten (14 per cent) were in service occupations. Further, the 1981 census data indicates that the average total income of Black people from all sources was about $3,000 less than the average earned by Torontonians (table 13.1). While the average income of Torontonians in 1981 was between $12,410 and $13,614, for Black people the average income was between $9,287 and $10,872.

In terms of the population of Black Toronto youth, table 13.1 shows that in 1981, 22 per cent of them were between the ages of fifteen and twenty-four. Of this group, as shown in table 13.2, about 9 per cent were born in Ontario and about 2 per cent in Nova Scotia. Over 85 per cent of the youth were born outside of Canada: 75 per cent in the Caribbean and South America, and 5 per cent each in Africa and the United Kingdom. A large majority of the foreign-born Black youth had immigrated to Canada between 1966 and 1981, with 43 per cent having immigrated during the peak period of 1971 to 1975. Table 13.2 also shows that in 1981 almost half (47 per cent) of the Black youth population was attending

Table 13.2. 1981 census profile of Black youth (15–24) in Toronto

	Blacks (%)	Total Toronto (%)		Blacks (%)	Total Toronto (%)
Birthplace			**Immigration**		
Canada	11	76	Before 1960	–	5
Nova Scotia	(2)	(1)	1961–5	3	13
Ontario	(9)	(68)	1966–70	25	27
United States	1	2	1971–5	43	26
United Kingdom	4	4	1976–81	29	29
Africa	5	1			
Caribbean and South America	76	4			
Attending School			**Education**		
No	46	46	Less than Grade 9	3	4
Yes, full-time	47	47	**Grades 9–13**		
Yes, part-time	7	7	Secondary certificate	18	19
			No secondary cert.	49	43
			Trade cert./dipl.	2	1
			Other Non-Univ.		
			No cert./dipl.	9	8
			Trade cert./dipl.	3	2
			No univ./cert./dipl.	6	6
			University		
			No cert./dipl.	7	10
			Univ. or non-univ. cert./dipl.	1	2
			BA or higher	2	5

Source: Statistics Canada, 1981 Census of Canada, Public Use Sample tapes.

school full time, and fewer than one in ten was attending school part time. These figures are identical to the school attendance rate of the general Toronto population. Black youth were also similarly represented (6 per cent) at the postsecondary non-university level of education. Specifically, like other Toronto youth, the proportion of Black youth participating in and graduating with trade education was basically the same. However, compared with their Toronto cohorts, fewer Black youth (fifteen to twenty-four years old) received a university education, and they were half as likely as their peers to hold a bachelor's degree or higher. Further, in 1981 while the majority (59 per cent) of Black young people (under eighteen years old) were Canadian-born, they were mainly children of Caribbean immigrants to Canada (see table 13.3).

Table 13.3. Place of birth of the Black population in Toronto by age

Birthplace	Over 24 years (%)	15–24 (%)	Under 18 (%)
Nova Scotia	1	1	1
Quebec	1	1	1
Ontario	2	9	59
United States	1	1	2
Africa	6	5	3
Caribbean and S. America	84	75	31

Source: Statistics Canada, 1981 Census of Canada, Public Use Sample tapes.

The data on the Black population indicate that they were predominantly immigrants from the Caribbean largely working in low white-collar and service occupations. In fact, being one of the most recent immigrant groups in a society that historically has viewed Black people as "unassimilable," their "visibility" (or designation as a "visible minority") operated as a marker of their immigrant status.[11] John Porter points out that it is the perception of biological qualities upon which immigration has been historically based and, as such, has operated "in the building up of a class system and in the social process of assigning newcomers in the economic system."[12] However, in a survey, Black men mostly perceived their group to be hardworking and ambitious (see table 13.4) – qualities they identified as necessary for their success in their new society. Motivated by their "immigrant dream" and desires, Caribbean immigrants sought to access the opportunities necessary to realize those aspirations.[13] Writing of Caribbean immigrants in the United States, Janet Brice points out, "Even if they are not well educated, they come to hope, and sometimes expect, that their children and grandchildren will achieve more" than they do.[14]

The notion of hope ostensibly helped to structure how Black community members tended to perceive of their pathways toward the realization or fulfilment of their dreams. To this end, they banked on a positive sense of self (or self-concept), tolerant attitude, and high aspirations, not only as defences against the racism and discrimination they faced or expected to face but also as qualities that would help them secure the high educational and occupational/career achievements necessary for social mobility (or social and economic success) in the society.[15] The fact is, as numerous Toronto studies have demonstrated, the societal virus of racism against which Black people have had to inoculate themselves continuously accounted for their limited social and economic opportunities and, by extension, their achievements.[16]

Table 13.4. Male West Indians' view of themselves and their group

	1 (%)	2 (%)	3 (%)	4 (%)	5 (%)	
Respondents' View of Themselves						
Warm	57	27	13	2	1	Cold
Competitive	30	26	23	8	13	Non-competitive
Independent	57	23	16	3	1	Conforming
Ambitious	65	20	11	3	1	Not ambitious
Cautious	46	19	15	7	13	Adventurous
Hardworking	80	12	6	1	1	Lazy
Noisy	8	8	19	24	41	Quiet
Proud	24	12	26	7	7	Humble
Respondents' View of Their Group						
Warm	60	22	14	3	1	Cold
Competitive	23	33	36	4	4	Non-competitive
Independent	30	22	30	10	8	Conforming
Ambitious	43	28	22	4	3	Not ambitious
Cautious	19	19	35	15	12	Adventurous
Hardworking	43	29	24	3	1	Lazy
Noisy	31	23	36	5	5	Quiet
proud	30	18	34	6	12	Humble

Source: *Project: Ethnic Pluralism in an Urban Setting, 1978–1979*, Survey Research Centre, Institute for Social Research (ISR), York University, Downsview.

For instance, based on a sample of 617 White Torontonians, Frances Henry reported that from as early as the mid-1970s, 35 per cent thought that "there are too many Blacks in Toronto"; in addition, a "rather high proportion" (41 per cent) of the White respondents believed that "Blacks did not work as hard as White immigrants."[17] Black people were also stereotyped as poorer, more religious, more humorous, less ambitious, and better at sport than Whites.[18] As for the perceived class backgrounds of Black people, 75 per cent of Henry's White participants "thought that Black immigrants were working class and only 19 percent said they [Blacks] were middle class and above."[19] And the respondents Henry labelled as "racist" stereotyped Black people as "sloppy, slow moving and like to drive big cars."[20] Respondents indicated that Black people needed to be educated or retrained to better their situation.[21] It is understandable, then, that a study of "West Indians' view of themselves and their group" by York University's Survey Research Centre in 1979 would find that 40 per cent of the respondents had experienced discrimination (table 13.5) and a majority (75 per cent) had experienced "some

Table 13.5. Perceptions of prejudice and discrimination in Toronto

Ethnic Group (Male Side)	West Indian (%)	Chinese (%)	English (%)	German (%)	Irish (%)	Italian (%)	Jewish (%)	Portuguese (%)	Scottish (%)	Ukrainian (%)
SUBJECTIVE RESPONSES										
Discrimination against Your Group by Employers? % Some + a lot	75	57	9	19	3	33	43	36	4	27
Ever Faced Racial Discrimination? % Yes	40	31	16	26	8	26	45	10	8	25
OBJECTIVE RESPONSES										
Rate Social Standing of Group: % Excellent + Very Good	6	22	68	36	51	31	46	13	55	35

Source: *Project: Ethnic Pluralism in an Urban Setting, 1978–1979*, Survey Research Centre, ISR, York University, Downsview.

discrimination" or "a lot of discrimination" by employers. In what was considered an "objective evaluation" of the social standing or prestige of West Indians (read: Black people) in the society, most (non-West Indian) respondents agreed that West Indians did not have a good standing (table 13.5).

Many studies during this period investigated the employment activities and opportunities of Black people.[22] On this subject, researchers found that Black job applicants experienced a higher rate of rejection than Whites.[23] In their landmark study, Henry and Ginzberg revealed that even with the same credentials and employment background, a Black job applicant received one job offer to every three a White applicant received.[24] As well, Raymond Breton reported that a substantially higher proportion (28 per cent) of Black people than of any other ethnic group members (except Chinese, at 29 per cent) recounted having experienced discrimination when trying to get a job.[25] Similarly, in Wilson Head's 1975 study, a majority of Black respondents reported that they had been subjected to varying types of "unfair treatment" and "unfair restrictions" – including having more work demanded of them, being told that they had "little chance or no chance for promotion," not getting the sick leave and holidays they were due, and being subject to frequent layoffs. In addition, it was reported that more discrimination was experienced at the higher levels (e.g. supervisor) than at the lower levels of employment, and in higher status jobs, even when the qualifications of applicants were equal, discrimination was quite prevalent.[26]

In their study of the employment experiences of Black and other non-White MBA graduates, Elia Zureik and Robert Hiscott found that, compared with Whites and other non-White groups in the same period of employment (five to seven years), Black people earned less: an average of $25,660, while the salaries of other groups ranged from $32,000 to $39,000.[27] Of all the groups examined, a substantially higher proportion (20 per cent) of Black respondents reported that their rate of progress within their companies was "less rapid than expected." A significant 80 per cent of the Black respondents – more than any other ethnic or racial group – reported that they were considering leaving their jobs largely as a result of unhappiness because of discriminatory experiences such as not gaining job promotions. It is not surprising, then, that the Ontario Human Rights Commission's 1984–5 annual report would show that the commission received and settled more employment complaints from Black Canadians than from members of any other ethnic or racial group. Specifically, of 177 employment complaints (based on race) that were filed with the commission, 111 were filed by Black people; of the 104 cases settled, 63 were from Black complainants. Their complaints included problems in the areas of recruitment, hiring, terminations, and altercations during their employment – and understandably, employment termination was the problem about which Black people complained the most (58 per cent).[28]

Studies pertaining to the conditions of schooling and education for Black youth revealed that racial attitudes and discriminatory practices – evidenced in attitudes of teachers and peers toward Black students – affected not only their school participation, academic performance, and educational attainment but also to their emotional state and psychological well-being.[29] Some of Head's research participants perceived the school system to be "degrading and racist" in the ways it represented the historical presence and cultural contributions of Black people to Canadian society, thereby making it difficult for Black students to cultivate self-respect and positive racial identity – a situation that caused them to feel alienated from their schooling process. It was found that teachers' stereotyping of Black students as intellectually inferior and as slow learners led to many of them being placed into non-academic programs and some of them encouraged to concentrate on sports rather than academic work. For instance, it was reported that one male student, having expressed to his teacher his desire to become an engineer, was told, "You are a good basketball player and the school needs basketball players. Why don't you become a professional and forget about the engineering?"[30]

Basically, Head's research findings indicate that the majority of adults and young people alike claimed that many teachers discouraged Black students from entering high-level educational programs while directing them into technical, vocational, or commercial programs.[31] This is because, as one adult respondent put it, "Teachers see blacks as working with their hands rather than with their heads. Sometimes their accent causes a barrier, and the kids themselves take advantage of this, and do not apply themselves." Other research respondents observed that "black students must work harder and write better essays than white students in order to get decent grades."[32] Essentially, discrimination operated as a paradox, in that it caused some Black students to excel academically because of their determination to "work harder," and others, in resisting their school's deficit notion of their learning abilities, to calculate that it was not worth the incredible effort they put into their work for relatively little reward. Therefore, for these students, racism and discrimination operated to stifle their initiative and ambitions.[33]

In writing of the consequences of racism on Black Canadians in the early 1970s, Jules Oliver reasoned that

> the type of oppression that the Black race has gone through, and in many, many, ways still experience, is a form of mental genocide. It destroys the very fabric of human dignity and motivation. It has had a devastating impact upon our personality and our very sense of being. When studying our history it can be easily seen that from slavery to a system of discrimination, segregation, and slum communities, the Black man [sic] in Canada is left with a status not much better than that of a slave even in contemporary society. The position of second class citizen is the ideal state that the White society desires us to remain in. We are no threat to their vested interest, and of course, do not jeopardize the myth of White supremacy.[34]

Oliver further argues that it is difficult for Black Canadian youth to develop positive and strong self-concepts because being Black in a predominantly White society causes them to feel alienated and, as a consequence, like they are second-class citizens. Accordingly, the "psychological deprivation for the black child is not so much that he lives in an impoverished community, but rather, that he exists in an environment which perpetuates white values and white dominance." This alienation "perpetuated by the educational system" also results in "a condition of racial schizophrenia ... brought about by the mental genocide of racism which results in a black person never really accepting his racial origin completely."[35]

It is within this historical, political, social, and cultural context that Black youth of the 1970s and 1980s sought to establish and affirm their presence in Canada as they transitioned to adulthood. Significant to this process were the schooling and employment experiences, aspirations, and achievements of these youth of Caribbean descent. This is discussed in the following section.

Schooling and the Experiences, Aspirations, and Agency of Black Youth

The large influx of Black immigrant students into the school system in the early 1970s became a dilemma for many school authorities and educators who, for years, searched for ways to respond to the social and educational "problems," challenges, and needs of their new charges. To this end, studies were conducted by Toronto-area school boards, including, Toronto, York, and North York;[36] as well as independent researchers such as Subhas Ramcharan, W.W. Anderson and Rudolph S. Grant, and Christopher Beserve;[37] and social service agencies including the Children's Aid Society and Family Services Association.[38] A predominant assertion of these studies of the needs of Black "West Indian" youth was that their "problems," or the challenges they faced, resulted from them adjusting to a new society and concurrently to their parents – mostly mothers only – whom they had joined in Canada and barely knew (the parent had immigrated years earlier) and who resided in low-income reconstituted families (sometimes with siblings and step-parents). The data showed that less than half of these youth were living in homes where both parents were present (see table 13.1), and their experiences with discrimination were due to race, language, and cultural differences.[39] Anderson and Grant point out that language, accent, pronunciation, and intonation created communication problems for West Indian students, thus contributing to their learning difficulties.[40]

For a considerable number of years, from the late 1970s to the mid-1980s, these studies were the major sources of information about Black youth of Caribbean descent; as such, they fostered the notion that most of the experiences and problems of these youth had to do with their adjusting to and coping with family life in a new society and simultaneously with a school system that was unaware of and unresponsive to their needs and concerns.[41] But Toronto-area parents – witnessing that even into the 1980s their children were placed in general and vocational (or basic) level programs, consequently making them less likely to attend postsecondary institutions and more likely to be unemployed – organized (forming the Organization of Parents of Black Children, or

OPBC) and advocated that the school boards address the low rates of school participation, educational performance, and low achievement of their children.[42] In doing so, parents and community members sought to change the narrative of Black students as lacking interest in school, charging that it was instead the inequitable and alienating schooling system that was responsible for the situation these young Canadians were in.[43]

This move by parents reflected their strong belief – and that of their children – in education as the means by which they would be able to fully participate socially and economically in the society. Indeed, in their 1982 study of Grade 8 students in the Toronto Board of Education (TBE), Sylvia Larter and her colleagues found that Black students were the only group that rated education as "most important" to them. Yet, the two groups with the largest percentages in special education classes were Black (35 per cent) and "West Indian" (19 per cent) students. Nevertheless, these students still aspired – in some cases supported by their impoverished single parents – to obtain high levels of education because, for them, formal education was an opportunity and the only means to self-realization.[44] Further, despite the high value placed on education, research also showed that in 1983–4, of 460 Black Grade 9 students in the TBE, the majority, 53 per cent, were enrolled in basic-level (22 per cent) and general-level (31 per cent) programs, with just over one-third (36 per cent) in advanced programs. And Black students were second to Indigenous students in being most highly represented in basic-level programs.[45] This suggests that fewer than one-third (30 per cent) had the necessary requirements to pursue postsecondary studies, while the others would have had to do upgrading. These percentages help to explain why Black students were generally underrepresented at universities and, as table 13.4 indicates, why proportionately fewer Black folks (compared with other Torontonians) attained university degrees.[46]

In his 1975 study, Head found that a significant proportion of his Black adult respondents (36 per cent) perceived that a "great amount of discrimination" operated to prevent them from gaining employment.[47] Young people, by contrast, tended to be simultaneously more prudent and optimistic about the existence of discrimination and its effect on their opportunities. Actually, a large proportion of young respondents (45 per cent) felt that there was "some discrimination in job situations," and only 26 per cent felt that there was a "great amount." A further 26 per cent of the youth believed that there was "very little employment discrimination." And while Black respondents in general believed that with higher educational qualifications, they would more likely increase their chances of achieving their career goals, for youth the belief was that "with a university degree, options increase" and that there were "good" and even "very good" opportunities for employment. To this end, Head's young respondents suggested that "black students should prepare themselves for positions wherever they are available and without restrictions" – particularly in the areas of managerial and professional positions. Generally, the feeling was, "Aspire to the highest!" But there was a minority of young people who reckoned that, because of discrimination, "There's nothing to work for." They questioned, "Is the hassle worth it?"[48]

But then again, studies showed that, for some youth, careers in sport were seen as a viable alternative to careers requiring demanding academic preparation.[49] In fact, there was a tendency among working-class Black male youth in Toronto to have a keen interest in sport, and as such, some entertained the idea that they could eventually become professional basketball or football players.[50] Such aspirations, as has already been noted, were encouraged by teachers and school coaches, leading some youth to believe that their success in life was more likely to come through sport than through academic pursuits.[51] And as I argued then, "We cannot underestimate the powerful role of the media, especially television which beams sports programs into Canada showing the achievements and successes of Black American male athletes. It is possible, therefore, that lacking Black role models, and finding themselves in similar disadvantaged situations in Canada as in the United States, Black youth here are likely to idolize sports as well as Canadian and American athletes believing that they too can become successful through sports."[52]

Nevertheless, during the 1970s and 1980s, the predominant view of young people – if we go by Head's research participants – was one of optimism or hopefulness. Understandably, this characteristic of young people is in accordance with their need to believe that through their efforts and determination, they will be able to realize their aspirations.[53] Indeed, Head did find that the majority (two-thirds) of his respondents felt that their skin colour would not influence "the attainment of their personal goals." Essentially, most (80 per cent) of the youth believed that individual effort, qualifications, and ability were more important, and that it was up to them not to allow discrimination to stand in their way or make "colour" a barrier. According to one respondent, "It isn't colour which is important, nothing can stop you if you are willing to try."[54]

Ostensibly, filled with their Caribbean immigrant parents' motivation and optimism to make a success of their lives, the young people seemed to have calculated that the racism and discrimination they faced were primarily based on individual attitudes and not societal or institutional structures.[55] So, even during a period when racism-related incidents were evident, and when Torontonians (particularly White people) were coming to terms with the considerable numbers of racialized people settling in the city, most (60 per cent) of Head's young respondents still believed that discrimination would decrease in the future because, from their perspective, their non-Black peers were adopting more liberal and open-minded attitudes. In the words of one respondent, racism is "not worth bothering about. It will disappear in the future generation."[56]

In the study *Making It*, in which I examined the high aspirations and optimism of sixty Black Toronto youth (ages seventeen to twenty-two) in 1984 and 1985, I used their career aspirations as an indicator of their educational and social desires and goals. Findings showed that a large number of the youth reckoned that being Black meant they had to be conscious of their race since it influenced the circumstances and opportunities they experienced, and could expect to experience, in the society where, as one participant put it, "We're a visible minority." Another stated, "You'd be a fool to ignore that you're Black. A lot of people would be saying things to put you down and you wouldn't understand." Furthermore, when asked about the significance of race to him, another youth replied, "Not only is it significant; it's frightening."[57] The young people asserted that they were "labelled" as "less intelligent," "less ambitious," only having "interest in athletics," and being "from the islands," and as such, had to deal with the expectations associated with these stereotypes.[58] So, in cases where they were able to, as one young man proffered, "overcome the fact that I'm Black" – that is, do well educationally – White people would say to him, "Well, that must have been tough, how did you do it, kid?" In addition, a significant proportion of women identified that their gender and race made them "have two strikes against [them] ... that makes things challenging." The men concurred. In the words of one male respondent, "Blacks have to fight, and for a Black woman, it's even worse. She has both against her." Both the young women and men claimed that, based on their observations, Black women would experience more difficulties in achieving their ambitions, because gender and race are closely related, but sexism added to racism makes things "more deadly, challenging and difficult, and a double setback."[59]

The research participants noted that one of the most important ways they could cope with their situation was to "be realistic" and understand that the racism and discrimination they experienced was "just a part of life." As such, they felt that they needed to "always be on guard, be extra careful and extra polite" to White people.[60] Some respondents indicated that they tried "to ignore" the attitudes and behaviours toward them by seeing themselves as "a person first" in their attempt not to be solely defined by their Blackness.[61] In addition to using education as a means of realizing their ambitions, and to "prove to White people that we can do something," participants admitted to employing other strategies: "work twice as hard," "set a plan," and "be independent and strong-willed" – all of which, many of them admitted, took "self-confidence" (some of which came from participation in sports) as well as determination and strength.[62] Observing that Black people were sometimes used as "tokens," participants claimed they would exploit the practice of tokenism, especially when trying to gain employment.

Conclusion

With the significantly increased levels of migration of Caribbean people to Canada in the 1970s, the Black population in Toronto grew to about 4 per cent of the city's population. As relatively recent immigrants, the immigrant drive of Black youth combined with their hopes, aspirations, strong will, and determination (and those of their parents) served to inform and influence their educational, occupational, and social trajectory in the society.[63] Further, their small numbers notwithstanding, with their attitudes, agency, and activism they had relative impact on the social, educational, cultural, and political landscape of Canada, thereby setting the stage for many of the reforms we have seen in the educational, political, and social welfare systems of Toronto and Canada generally. Parents and community members generally could not have acted otherwise, particularly at a time when Black youth made up approximately one-quarter of the Black population.[64] Consequently, the young people could not have been ignored, for it is possible that their inability to meet the challenges that beset them would not have affected only them educationally, psychologically, and socially but also their community and, by extension, the society as a whole.

This chapter has shown that in the 1970s and 1980s, much as in the first two decades of the twenty-first century, Black youth experienced an inequitable education system sustained by racism and discrimination that was inherent in the Canadian sociopolitical structure. While such a context might have contributed to feelings of alienation and pessimism among the youth (and their parents), these feelings seem not to have been predominant. Instead, Black youth generally had high career aspirations, and they believed that the achievement of their goals involved adopting a set of strategies that would counteract the anti-Black racism they faced. The vast majority of youth, like their parents, viewed education as the most important resource and skill to have. But for some, athletics (in a few cases, in combination with education) was perceived as a viable alternative for achieving social success and social mobility. Generally, Black youth perceived self-confidence as an important attribute in their efforts to build and facilitate their high scholastic and athletic competences.

NOTES

1 As set out by the Ontario Ministry of Education, Advanced Program students took mainly academic subjects that gave them the broadest educational and occupational opportunities upon graduation; most went on to university and some to community college. General Program students were provided with a broad program of academic subjects that was expected to enable them access primarily to community colleges or, in some cases, to the Ontario College of Arts and Ryerson Polytechnical Institute. Basic Program students were given fundamental educational skills in preparation for work (Toronto Board of Education (TBE), *A Time to Choose*, [Toronto, 1984]). Other students who were more underrepresented in Academic Programs were Indigenous students, at 32 per cent compared with Black people at 54 per cent. Least likely to graduate after five years of high school were Indigenous students (45 per cent compared with 78 per cent for Black and Latin American students). And Black students (69 per cent) were among the three groups of students (Latin Americans at 64 per cent, Indigenous students at 32 per cent) who were least likely to apply to pursue postsecondary education after five years of high school (Robert S. Brown and G. Tam, "Grade 9 Cohort Graduation Rate 2011–2016," Fact Sheet 1, Toronto District School Board, November 2017). See also Carl E. James and Tana Turner, *Towards Race Equity in Education: The Schooling of Black Students in the Greater Toronto Area* (Toronto: Faculty of Education, York University, 2017).
2 C.E. James and Robert S. Brown, *The Detailed Black Subgroups of the Toronto District School Board (TDSB): A Ten-Year Comparison, 2006–07 and 2016–17* (TDSB and Jean Augustine Chair in Education, Community and Diaspora, York University, 2021).
3 "First generation" here refers to students who were born outside of Canada.
4 Carl E. James, *Making It: Black Youth, Racism and Career Aspiration in a Big City* (Oakville: Mosaic Press, 1990), 60.
5 Reginald W. Bibby and Donald C. Posterski, *The Emerging Generation: An Inside Look at Canada's Teenagers* (Toronto: Irwin, 1985).
6 Martha Friendly, Saul V. Levine, and Linda Hagarty, "Adolescents in the Urban Social Context," in *The Child in the City: Change and Challenges*, ed. W. Michelson, Saul V. Levine, and Ellen Michelson (Toronto: University of Toronto Press, 1979), 309.

7 Frances Henry and Effie Ginzberg, *Who Gets the Work: A Test of Racial Discrimination in Employment* (Toronto: Urban Alliance on Race Relations and the Social Planning Council of Metropolitan Toronto, 1985), 5.
8 Elaine Carey, "McMurtry Fears Jobless Race Violence," *Toronto Star*, November 11, 1984, A1.
9 At that time the census did not ask racial origin, but it did have a category for ethnic origin. The Public Use Sample Tapes identify Black people by origin in so far as respondents, whether as a single or multiple response, stated they are Canadian Black, Caribbean, Haitian, other Black (not elsewhere specified [n.e.s.]), other African (n.e.s.), or African Black. This population was reported to be 78,445. However, John Kralt further estimated that an additional 47,885 of the Toronto population was Black. This latter estimate included those people who were born in the Caribbean and Guyana and who reported "British" or "French only" as their ethnic origin and whose reported religion is not Hindu, Islam, or Sikh, (Linda L. Schachter, "Defining the Minority Population," *Currents: Reading in Race Relations* 2, no. 4 1984–5): 30–1.
10 Given the subjective reporting, and the fact that the census only asked persons to report their ethnic origin and not racial background, what we have is an estimate of the Black population. And insofar as Statistics Canada used birthplace – such as Africa and the Caribbean (West Indies), the main areas from which Black people immigrated – to assign people to the Black category, a number of Black people were likely to have been omitted from the sample. This categorizing is likely to have excluded those Black people who were born in Britain, the United States, South and Central America, and other places and who did not report themselves as Black. Thus, these citizens would have been grouped not as Black but as "British," "American," and so forth. On this point, Judge Rosalie Abella, in the Commission on Equity in Employment report, noted, "Black immigrants identified themselves as primarily from the Caribbean, including Guyana, and nearly all Caribbean immigrants reported only a single ethnicity. But almost as many Caribbean immigrants reported themselves as Black" (Canada, Royal Commission on Equity in Employment, *Equality in Employment: A Royal Commission Report* [Ottawa: Ministry of Supply and Services, 1984, 93]). It should be noted that the Guyana and Trinidad figures likely included a high proportion of Christian "East Indians" given their population in these countries. Also, while particular identity variables were used to ascertain Black from other Caribbean migrants such as white/European, Chinese, etc., it is possible that some did get counted as Black owing to regional origins. See also Linda Demers and John Kralt, *On the Comparability of the Census Mother Tongue Data, 1976–1981* (Ottawa: Statistics Canada, Housing, Family and Social Division, 1984).

11 Jean Burnet, "Myths and Multiculturalism," in *Multiculturalism in Canada: Social and Educational Perspectives*, ed. Ronald J. Samuda, John W. Berry, and Michel Laferrière (Boston: Allyn and Bacon, 1984). Writing during this period, Kubat and colleagues suggested that immigrants tended to be used as "scapegoats for the problems of urbanization and the concomitant ills of megalopolises" (Daniel Kubat, Ursula Merhländer, and Ernst Gehmacher, *The Politics of Migration Policies: The First World in the 1970s* [New York: Center for Migration Studies, 1979, 22]). See also Clifford J. Jansen, "Problems and Issues in Post–World War II Immigration and Its Effects on Origins and Characteristics of Immigrants," Paper presented at the annual meeting of the Canadian Population Society, Dalhousie University, Halifax, June 1981.
12 John Porter, *The Vertical Mosaic: An Analysis of Social Class and Power in Canada* (Toronto: University of Toronto Press, 1965), 66.
13 Carl E. James, *The Challenge of Making It: Youth's Aspirations and Perceptions of Their Chances to Succeed* (Ph.D. diss., York University, 1986).
14 Janet Brice, "West Indian Families," In *Ethnicity and Family Therapy*, ed. M. McGoldrich, Joe Giordano, and Nydia Garcia-Preto (New York: Guildford, 1982), 127.
15 Agnes Calliste, "Educational and Occupational Expectations of High School Students," *Multiculturalism* 5, no. 3 (1982): 14–19; Wilson Head, *The Black Presence in the Canadian Mosaic* (Toronto: Ontario Human Rights Commission, 1975); James, *Challenge of Making It*.
16 Wilson Head, "Historical, Social, and Cultural Factors in the Adaptation of Non-White Students in Toronto Schools," in Samuda, Berry, and Laferrière, *Multiculturalism in Canada*, 266–79; Head, *Black Presence*; Frances Henry, *The Dynamics of Racism in Toronto: Research Report* (Toronto: York University, 1978); Henry and Ginzberg, *Who Gets the Work*; Subhas Ramcharan, "Special Problems of Immigrant Children in the Toronto School System," in *Education of Immigrant Students: Issues and Answers*, ed. Aaron Wolfgang (Toronto: Ontario Institute for Studies in Education, 1975); Ramcharan, *Racism: Nonwhites in Canada* (Toronto: Butterworth, 1982); Elia Zureik and Robert Hiscott, *The Experience of Visible Minorities in the Work World: The Case of MBA Graduates* (Toronto: Ontario Human Rights Commission, 1983).
17 Henry, *Dynamics of Racism*, 38, 41.
18 Henry, 46–7.
19 Henry, 36.
20 Henry, 45.
21 Henry, 41.
22 Brenda Billingsley and Leon Muszynski, *No Discrimination Here? Toronto Employers and the Multi-Racial Workforce* (Toronto: Social Planning Council of Metropolitan Toronto, 1985); Raymond Breton, *The Ethnic Community*

as a Resource in Relation to Group Problems: Perceptions and Attitudes (Toronto: Centre for Urban and Community Studies, University of Toronto, 1981); Henry and Ginzberg, *Who Gets the Work*; Head, *Black Presence*; Ramcharan, *Racism*; Jeffrey G. Reitz, Liviana Calzavara, and Donna Dasko, *Ethnic Inequality and Segregation in Jobs* (Toronto: Centre for Urban and Community Studies, University of Toronto, 1981); Anton H. Turrittin, "Social Mobility in Canada: A Comparison of Three Provincial Studies," *Canadian Review of Sociology and Anthropology* 12 (1973): 163–86; Zureik and Hiscott, *Experience of Visible Minorities*.

23 Head, *Black Presence*; Henry and Ginzberg, *Who Gets the Work*; Zureik and Hiscott, *Experience of Visible Minorities*.

24 The researchers also noted that "for the first time in Canada, there is direct and concrete evidence of some of the ways in which non-whites are denied equal access to employment. The results of this study clearly indicate that there is very substantial discrimination affecting the ability of members of racial minority groups to find employment." Henry and Ginzberg, *Who Gets the Work*, 4.

25 Breton, *Ethnic Community*, 15.

26 Head, *Black Presence*, 166.

27 Zureik and Hiscott, *Experience of Visible Minorities*.

28 Ontario Human Rights Commission, *Annual Report, 1984–1985* (Toronto: Ministry of Labour, 1985), 71.

29 Head, *Black Presence*; Head, "Historical, Social, and Cultural Factors"; Ramcharan, "Special Problems."

30 Head, *Black Presence*, 89.

31 Head, 88–9.

32 Head, 169, 59–60.

33 James, *Challenge of Making It*.

34 Jules Oliver, "The Black Child and White Education," in *Must Schools Fail? The Growing Debate in Canadian Education*, ed. N. Bryne and Jack Quarter (Toronto: McClelland & Stewart, 1972), 218–19.

35 Oliver, 221. Racial schizophrenia, Oliver suggests, may be manifested in such behaviour "as passive acceptance of racial discrimination or fierce denial of its existence ... to the concept and philosophy of Blackness, groveling for White praise and accepting it without question; but also, a readiness to question and challenge the demands and arguments that Blacks put forward for the development of the Black race" (222).

36 Before amalgamation in 1998, Toronto was made up of six boroughs with their respective school boards. Studies conducted in Toronto include Jan Schreiber, *In the Course of Discovery: The West Indian Immigrants in Toronto Schools* (Toronto: Toronto Board of Education, 1970); and Ann-Marie Stewart, *See Me Yah: Working Papers on the Newly-Arrived West Indian Child in*

the Downtown School (Toronto: Toronto Board of Education, 1975); in York: John Roth, *West Indians in Toronto: The Student and the Schools* (Toronto: York Board of Education, 1973); and in North York: Isabel Fram, G. Broks, P. Crawford, J. Handscombe, and A.E. Virgin, *"I Don't Know Yet": West Indian Students in North York Schools: A Study of Adaptive Behaviours* (Toronto: North York Board of Education, 1977).

37 Ramcharan, "Special Problems"; W.W. Anderson and Rudolph W. Grant. *The New Newcomers: Problems of Adjustment in West Indian Immigrant Children in Metropolitan Toronto Schools* (North York: York University, 1975); Christopher Beserve, "Adjustment Problems of West Indian Children in Britain and Canada: A Perspective and Review of Some Findings," in "Black Students in Urban Canada," ed. Vincent D'Oyley and Harry Silverman, special issue, *T.E.S.L. Talk* 7, no. 1 (1976).

38 A task force established by the Children's Aid Society of Metropolitan Toronto examined the extent to which its services adequately catered to the youth in various ethnic groups in Toronto. It concluded that although ethnic groups – such as Chinese and other Asians, Greeks, Indo-Pakistanis, Indigenous people, and Black Caribbean people – altogether comprise about 19 per cent of the society's clients, there was a serious lack of information and resources about the youth that would allow staff to effectively assess and provide services for them. Particularly lacking was information on Caribbean youth, who made up 12.9 per cent of its client population – twice as many as the combined total of other groups. Task Force on Multicultural Programmes, *Final Report* (Toronto: Children's Aid Society of Metropolitan Toronto, 1982), 15. One of the few investigations into the social service needs of youth of Caribbean descent was conducted by social service practitioners Juliette Christensen, Anne Thornley-Brown, and Jean Robinson (1980), who were more concerned with the "cultural lack" of families and youth resulting from family reunification than the effects of racism. Christensen, Thornley-Brown, and Robinson, *West Indians in Toronto: Implications for Helping Professionals* (Toronto: Family Services Association, 1980).

39 Anderson and Grant, *New Newcomers*; Beserve, "Adjustment Problems"; Granville A. da Costa, "Counselling and the Black Child," in D'Oyley and Silverman, "Black Students"; Roth, *West Indians in Toronto*; Edgar Norman Wright and Gerry Kazuo Tsuji, *The Grade Nine Student Survey, Fall 1983* (Toronto: Board of Education for the City of Toronto, 1984).

40 Anderson and Grant, *New Newcomers*.

41 James, *Challenge of Making It*.

42 Carl E. James, *Colour Matters: The Experiences, Education, and Pursuits of Black Youth* (Toronto: University of Toronto Press, 2021). See also Post-Secondary Education Consultative Committee, *Post-Secondary: Opportunities for Students*

in Basic and General Level Programs – Discussion Paper (North York: North York Board of Education, 1983); and Wright and Tsuji, *Grade Nine Student Survey*.

43 In Head's study, respondents had expressed that a general perception of Black students was that they "are more socially than educationally oriented;" and that for them "It isn't 'hip' to care about school." Head, *Black Presence*, 92.

44 Sylvia Larter, Maisy Cheng, Sarah Capps, and Marianne Lee, *Post-Secondary Plans of Grade Eight Students and Related Variables*, No. 165 (Toronto: Board of Education for the City of Toronto, 1982), 53.

45 See note 1 for what the three programs provide students. See also Wright and Tsuji, *Grade Nine Student Survey*, 56.

46 Helen Hatton, *Employment, Funding and Accessibility Survey (1982)* (Hamilton, ON: McMaster Student Union, 1983). According to the Special Committee on Visible Minorities in Canadian Society, minority group members look to education as the means by which they can increase their participation in the society and thus ameliorate the problems of race relations. But access to postsecondary education for these group members was hindered by the fact that they were faced "with a number of obstacles to participation, low expectation by teachers and lack of respect for, and recognition of, the learners' past experience." Special Committee on Visible Minorities in Canadian Society, *Equality Now: Participation of Visible Minorities in Canadian Society* (Ottawa: Supply and Services, March 1984), 116, 133.

47 Forty per cent of the respondents said there was some discrimination, and 11 per cent reported "very little." Head, *Black Presence*, 153.

48 Head, 156–7, 97, 92.

49 Head; James, *Challenge of Making It*. Further, writing on the US context, Barry McPherson contended that "sports is salient for the Black, partly because of societal and subcultural expectations that he excel in and be interested in sports; partly because of early socializing experiences wherein he observes significant others enacting similar behaviour; and partly because of lack of opportunity to experience and internalize alternative activities." McPherson, "The Black Athlete: An Overview and Analysis," in *Social Problems in Athletics*, ed. D.M. Landers (Chicago: University of Illinois Press, 1976), 126.

50 Carl E. James, *Multicultural Programming for Youth: A Reference for Community Work* (unpublished manuscript, Secretary of State, 1982).

51 Head, *Black Presence*.

52 James, *Multicultural Programming*, 10.

53 James, *Making It*.

54 Head, *Black Presence*, 98.

55 Brice, "West Indian Families"; James, *Challenge of Making It*.

56 Head, *Black Presence*, 160.

57 James, *Making It*, 10, 41, 47.

58 Other stereotypes noted were being seen as "dancers" and "pimps."
59 James, *Making It*, 82, 21.
60 James, 32.
61 One female stated, "Obviously, I'm Black, but I don't make it an issue, I don't push it." James, 34.
62 Referencing a newspaper article, one participant commented, "Just a couple months ago, the *Toronto Star* ran an article on the number of Black Jamaicans students saying that they are not doing very well in the Canadian school system ... It makes me feel bad in a way, but it gives me the incentive to push on and to do better to surpass." See James, 36–7.
63 It should be noted that the presence of Black people in Canadian society dates back to 1628, but restrictive immigration policies prevented a large increase in their population until the late 1960s and early 1970s. However, over the years a number of Caribbean people had migrated to Canada – largely to Toronto to work as domestic servants, sleeping car porters, and service workers; see Cecil Foster, *They Call Me George: The Untold Story of Black Train Porters and the Birth of Modern Canada* (Windsor, ON: Biblioasis, 2019); Michele A. Johnson. "'... to ensure that only suitable persons are sent': Screening Jamaican Women for the West Indian Domestic Scheme," in *Jamaica in the Canadian Experience: A Multiculturalizing Presence*, ed. C.E. James and Andrea Davis (Halifax: Fernwood, 2012), 36–53; and Makeda Silvera, *Silenced: Talks with Working Class Caribbean Women about Their Lives and Struggles as Domestic Workers in Canada* (Toronto: Williams-Wallace, 1983).
64 Interestingly, the 2016 census indicates that 26.6 per cent of the Black population is aged fifteen years and younger, while for the Canadian population as a whole it is 16.9 per cent – indicating that, with about one-quarter of its population fifteen years and younger, the Black population is a young population. Deniz Do and Hélène Maheux, *Diversity of the Black Population in Canada: An Overview*, Statistics Canada, Catalogue no. 89-657-X2019002 (Ottawa: Minister of Industry, February 27, 2019), https://www.150.statcan.gc.ca/n1/en/catalogue/89-657-X2019002.

SECTION SIX

Creating New Diasporic Communities: Continental African Experiences

14
Creating Spaces of Belonging: Building a New African Community in Vancouver

GILLIAN CREESE

Introduction

This chapter examines the history and recent growth of an African community in metro Vancouver. The earliest settlers of African descent have been in the area for more than 150 years. The Black community has historically been very small, and its recent growth is largely due to immigration from countries in sub-Saharan Africa. The ethnic and national origins of African immigrants in metro Vancouver are diverse, but common experiences of marginalization, linked to processes of racialization, are creating pan-African identities and building community links that cross diverse African heritages.

The first Black community in what would become British Columbia emerged in the middle of the nineteenth century.[1] At the invitation of the governor of Vancouver Island, James Douglas, a man of mixed African and European descent, and with the desire to escape increasingly difficult conditions in California, six hundred members of the San Francisco Black community migrated to Vancouver Island in 1858. Some were drawn by the Fraser River gold rush, but others settled in Victoria and nearby Salt Spring Island, bought land, started businesses, and played a key role in civic life. They formed the first communities of African descent on the west coast of the colony, although many later returned to the United States after the Civil War ended with the legal abolition of slavery.[2] In 1881, the number of Black residents recorded in the census for British Columbia had declined to just under three hundred.[3]

By the turn of the twentieth century, Black families had begun to settle in the growing city of Vancouver. Most of the small Black population settled in the East Side neighbourhood of Strathcona, particularly in Hogan's Alley, which ran between Union and Prior Streets. Hogan's Alley was close to the railway, where many Black men worked as railway porters.[4] The community created businesses, established restaurants and music venues, founded the first Black church in the area in 1908, and created the Independent Coloured Political Association in 1914.[5] In the 1940s, the Black population of Strathcona was estimated at 800, mostly in and around Hogan's Alley.[6] In 1958, the BC Association for the Advancement of Coloured People was founded, compiling a "census" that listed 950 Black people living in British Columbia.[7]

The growth of the local African Canadian community in Vancouver was hampered by racist immigration policies intended to establish a White settler society on unceded Indigenous lands. White migrants were encouraged to come to Canada, especially those from Britain, northern Europe, and the United States. By the early twentieth century, "desirable" newcomers expanded to include people from southern and central Europe, while non-Europeans were excluded through various measures; during this time, legislation was passed to prevent further migration from India (1908), Japan (1908), and China (1923).[8] The Immigration Act of 1910 prohibited "immigrants belonging to any race deemed unsuited to the climate or requirements of Canada, or of immigrants of any specified class, occupation or character."[9] The rationale of being "unsuited to the climate" was used to exclude people of African descent from settling in Canada, although exceptions were sometimes made when workers from the Caribbean made convenient sources of much-needed labour, such as steelworkers in Nova Scotia and domestic workers in Ontario and Quebec.[10]

Without growth through immigration, Vancouver's historic Black community remained very small. In the 1960s, suburban redevelopment and plans for a highway through Strathcona to the downtown core promised to cut Strathcona in two and threatened to demolish Hogan's Alley, considered a slum area by local politicians. As Wayde Compton notes, the deterioration of Hogan's Alley was a direct result of the 1931 rezoning of the area as industrial rather than residential land, which then made it impossible to attain mortgages or loans for home improvement. As a result, the Black community began to move out of the area sometime in the late 1950s. Few Black families still resided there in 1971 when Hogan's Alley was finally destroyed during construction of the Georgia Viaduct, the first phase of a freeway that residents of Strathcona successfully mobilized to stop.[11] The destruction of Hogan's Alley marked the end of an identifiable Black community space in Vancouver, and the small population has remained dispersed throughout the region.

Canadian immigration policies changed in the mid-1960s, abandoning a focus on race and country of origin as the chief criteria for immigration and moving to a points system that emphasizes postsecondary educational credentials and occupational skills.[12] This change opened new possibilities of migration from countries in Africa, Asia, Latin America, and the Caribbean, which, over time, produced increasingly diverse urban centres across the country. Largely as a result of changes in immigration, the Black population in Canada grew from just over 32,000 in 1961, to almost one million in 2011, increasing from less than two-tenths of 1 per cent (0.17%) of the total Canadian population to almost 3 per cent (2.9%)[13] During this time period, the proportion of immigrants originating from countries in Africa slowly increased, from 1.9 per cent of all immigrants prior to 1971 to 7.3 per cent in the 1990s, 10.3 per cent from 2001 to 2006, and 12.5 per cent from 2006 to 2011.[14] Korba Puplampu and Wisdom Tettey argue that "neoracist" practices, such as the location and number of Canadian immigration offices, still shape migration patterns in ways that constrain immigration from sub-Saharan Africa.[15]

The growth in populations of African descent was and continues to be uneven across the country, producing much larger communities of African descent in Toronto and Montreal than in Vancouver. The vast majority of new Canadians from Africa settle in those cities, alongside large Black communities from the Caribbean as well as multigenerational African Canadians. Two-thirds of all Canadians who identify as Black live in Toronto (42 per cent) and Montreal (23 per cent); only 2.5 per cent of people who identify as Black live in Vancouver.[16]

According to the 2011 National Household Survey, there were 28,160 immigrants from Africa living in metro Vancouver, accounting for 1.2 per cent of the population.[17] The largest groups have migrated from South Africa (8,035), Kenya (3,905), and Ethiopia (1,440). A larger number of residents claim an African ethnic origin. In 2011, 32,475 people in metro Vancouver, or 1.4 per cent of the population, claimed an African ethnic origin.[18] The largest numbers identify origins in southern and east Africa (see table 14.1), including 6,000 people who identify their ethnicity as South African, constituting the single largest group citing an African ethnicity.

Not everyone who migrates from Africa or claims African ethnicity is racialized as Black. The number of Vancouverites who identified as Black in 2011 was considerably smaller; 23,545 people, or 1 per cent of the population, identified as Black. Of this number, 45 per cent were born in Canada and 55 per cent had an immigrant background.[19] Most Black immigrants in Vancouver have come from sub-Saharan Africa, though a smaller number of migrants are from the Caribbean, the United States, and other countries.[20] The Canadian-born population of African descent includes the second generation in the new African diaspora alongside others whose Canadian lineage may span several generations. Although

Table 14.1. African ethnic origins, Vancouver Census Metropolitan Area (CMA), 2011

African origins	Percentage of those who identify an African ethnic origin
Central & Western Africa	11
North Africa	16
Southern & East Africa	41
Other Africa	32
Total	100

Source: Statistics Canada, "2011 National Household Survey Profile, Vancouver CMA, Ethnic Origin."

numbers are relatively small, the growth in immigration from sub-Saharan Africa has fuelled the development of a self-identified African community in Vancouver. As Khalid Koser argues, the new African diaspora has a direct lineage to postcolonial countries in sub-Saharan Africa, making it distinct from people of African descent who do not have a recent connection with the African continent.[21]

By any measure, then, the new African diaspora in Vancouver is small but growing. No identifiable neighbourhoods or spaces are associated with this community; members are spread throughout the region and, like other immigrants, increasingly living in the suburbs where housing is more affordable. Although small in number, as individuals they are highly visible even amid the diversity of the city. Overall, 40 per cent of residents of metro Vancouver are immigrants, and 45 per cent identify as people of colour, but the vast majority of the latter have origins in Asia; the largest communities are Chinese, South Asian, and Filipino/a, which account for 75 per cent of all people of colour in Vancouver.[22] The development of a self-identified African community emerges in this context, where only 1 per cent of the population is racialized as Black and most are immigrants from sub-Saharan Africa and their Canadian-raised children.[23]

Negotiating Settlement, Creating Community

The mere presence of migrants from any particular ethnicity, nationality, or region does not automatically create a diasporic community. Diasporas form out of struggles to define themselves in relation to notions of homeland and current home and in the context of groups coexisting in the same space.[24] In some contexts, pan-African communities emerge across the diverse languages and ethnic and national backgrounds of migrants from different countries in Africa.[25] A pan-African community is emerging in Vancouver, bound together through small numbers from any specific ethnic or national origin, notions of Africa as a common continental homeland, shared experiences of racialization and marginalization in Canada, and diverse practices of solidarity and community building.[26] For the most part, there is little awareness of, and few links to, a historic Black community in Vancouver. Perhaps not surprisingly, the concerns of this new African community tend to focus on issues that affect the first generation of new migrants as they carve out spaces of belonging in an environment that is often unwelcoming.

Whether migration is a choice made by highly skilled and educated people entering under Canada's immigration points system or, for refugees, searching for asylum after fleeing violence and oppression in one's homeland, settling in another society is accompanied by loss and dislocation alongside new challenges and opportunities.[27] Settlement processes are gendered, affecting women and men in different ways, and challenging expectations around appropriate gender relations and parenting the next generation in Canada.[28] Settlement is also shaped by processes of racialization. The history of British and French colonialism, the subjugation of Indigenous peoples, and a century of immigration policies designed to recruit White settlers combine to affirm a White subject at the centre of the "imagined community" of Canada that contemporary discourses of multiculturalism have not dislodged.[29] This is the case for all migrants of colour, but in addition, those racialized as Black have to contend with discourses of Blackness refracted through the politics of race and the history of slavery in Canada and the United States.[30] As a result, scholars have pointed to ways in which migrants from Africa undergo a process of "becoming Black" in Canada, as new identities are produced in response to differential treatment bound up with histories of White privilege and anti-Black racism.[31]

The new African community in Vancouver is by no means defined solely by the hardships its members have encountered. The resilience of its members is evident in the diverse practices of community building that have emerged in the last two decades to address some of the challenges faced. Below, I outline some of the ways that immigrants from sub-Saharan Africa are marginalized in Vancouver, including their exclusion from the imagined community of Canadians and its impact on identities in the first and second generations. Next, I explore informal and formal practices that have created bonds, often across diverse African origins, that work to bring an African community into existence in Vancouver. This discussion draws on two qualitative research projects, one based on interviews with adult migrants from sub-Saharan Africa and a second project interviewing adult children of migrants from Africa who grew up in metro Vancouver, where they were usually one of the only Black and African children in their neighbourhoods and schools.[32]

Experiencing Marginalization

Members of the new African diaspora in Vancouver experience marginalization in a number of ways, and one of the most significant is in difficulty finding meaningful employment linked to education and training. Integration into the local labour market is central to broader processes of integration. More than a means to provide for one's family, though this is extremely important, employment is also a marker of productive citizenship, social status, and self-esteem. And yet routine employment practices privilege the local and penalize international attributes, resulting in the systemic marginalization of most recent immigrants in the Canadian labour market. Two such marginalizing practices are the requirement of Canadian educational qualifications and of Canadian work experience. Employers routinely privilege educational credentials attained in Canada, disadvantaging immigrants who received postsecondary education abroad (unless it was in the United States or the United Kingdom) even though these credentials are central to selection through the immigration points system.[33] Employers also privilege work experience in Canada and usually undervalue work experience abroad, though this prior work experience is rewarded in the points system.[34] Highly skilled jobs, such as professionals and managers recruited through immigration policies, are most affected by demands for Canadian credentials and work experience.

In my study published in 2011, titled *The New African Diaspora in Vancouver*, I found that three-quarters of the sixty-one people interviewed had experienced significant downward mobility although most were highly educated: 83 per cent of men and 74 per cent of women had postsecondary education. A majority of men (53 per cent), though fewer women (32 per cent), were in professional and managerial jobs prior to coming to Canada; only 10 per cent were similarly employed in Vancouver. Instead, a majority of men and women were employed in low-wage and often precarious employment, with men mostly in blue-collar manual labour and women more often in white-collar or semi-professional care jobs related to additional training in Canada (such as nurse aides).[35] This pattern of downward mobility among recent immigrants from Africa follows a long history of limited employment opportunities in Canada for peoples of African descent.[36]

Yalala's[37] experience is illustrative of the situation facing many in his community. A former CEO in Nigeria, with a degree in business administration, Yalala works "odd jobs" as a labourer. After seven years in Canada he concludes that, for African immigrants, "You don't get the job that requires your qualifications here, you just work to pay rent and to survive."[38] Similarly, Lwanzo was unemployed for most of the three years prior to our interview even though she had a local degree in environmental engineering, from the BC Institute of Technology, and prior postsecondary education and work experience in related fields in Zimbabwe. The devaluation of her prior credentials led Lwanzo to pursue another degree within Canada, but even her Canadian qualifications had not translated into good job opportunities. She critiques the immigration points system that accepts newcomers who are highly educated even though employers only offer positions that are low skilled: "They are accepting people who are educated, and when they come there, they treat them like uneducated people. What's the use? Why not take people who are not educated then, if what you want are janitors."[39]

In addition to employers' discounting international credentials and work experience, employment is also affected by discounting the competence of those who speak English with accents that are different from Canadian accents. As Pierre Bourdeau reminds us, linguistic capital is a form of embodied capital that is "[mis]recognized as legitimate competence."[40] Put simply, the power of speech is linked to the power (or lack of power) of the person speaking.[41] The legacies of colonialism in Canada result in privileging local English accents such that "foreign" accents that are not British imply lack of competence.[42] This has consequences in jobs that involve serving the public, including most traditional lower-skilled women's employment in service, retail, and clerical jobs, and so it particularly affects women in the African community.[43]

African immigrants in Vancouver experience the erasure of their English linguistic capital, which contributes to the difficulty in finding jobs commensurate with their qualifications, as well as frequent and demeaning encounters with strangers and acquaintances who challenge their grammar and pronunciation. As Ntombi explains so eloquently, "It's like the moment you start speaking the language, because the accent came out, you don't know anything."[44] Similarly, Bizima notes, "Since we can't talk like them, it's really hard to convince them that you can talk sense, when they find out what accent you have."[45] Discrimination against African English accents not only contributes to immigrants' marginalization in the labour market but also marks them as outsiders within civil society, as perpetual "foreigners" who are not perceived as Canadians.

Exclusion from the imagined community of Canadians is an important aspect of marginalization. Bodies are read for signs of recognition as belonging to this space or as being out of place, delineating insiders from outsiders in both material and psychic terms.[46] Frequent interrogation – specifically, "Where are you from?" – from strangers or acquaintances is widely interpreted in the African community as evidence that Black bodies are perceived to not belong in Canada no matter how long they have lived here. As Wetu observes, although in many respects he has come to think of himself as Canadian, other people make it clear to him that this cannot be so:

> Even though I change that [my identity], I will be Canadian, but somebody I pass, by my colour, he'll ask me, "Where are you from?" ... Because you can be a citizen here for many years, you have been here for twenty, thirty years. But you still feel that there are some areas which the colour is playing a part ... Just the colour is that we don't see you as a Canadian.[47]

Tungu explains that the persistence of such queries affects not only the first generation, for whom accents are a telltale sign that they originally lived somewhere else, but also their children. As a result, she believes that neither she nor her Canadian-born children are accepted as Canadians. Tungu explains,

> I cannot say I am Canadian when they don't support I am Canadian ... Here you are Black. If you are twenty [years here], you born here, nothing. They say, "Where are you from?" They will still ask you ... "I am Canadian." "No, where are you from? You born here?" "Yes." "Where are your parents from?"[48]

This view is borne out in research with second-generation African Canadians in Vancouver, where many participants frame their identities in relation to others' demands to know "where are you from."[49] These queries persist in spite of the second generation's embodiment of local accents and locally acquired cultural capital. For some in the second generation, this leads to a rejection of Canadian identity. For example, Shukre, who has been in Canada since she was an infant, identifies only as Somali because "as long as I keep getting asked where I'm from, I'm not from here, you know. As that question is *the first thing people ask me*, I'm not from here." Similarly, Maxwell identifies as African and as Ugandan but not as Canadian because "I've just come to the realization that this is not my country." Others among the second generation respond to these queries by acknowledging their African heritage and making simultaneous claims to their Canadianness, like Jessica ("Oh well, my parents are from Ghana") and Betty ("I'm from Ethiopia but I grew up here"). And some in the second generation try to disrupt the expected narrative by refusing to name anything other than a local origin, like Emily: "I tell them Vancouver ... and they'll say 'Oh, but like, where? Like where are your parents from?' And I'm like 'Does that matter?'"[50]

It is these types of shared experiences of marginalization – as Black and as migrants, or the children of migrants, from sub-Saharan Africa – that have fostered the development of support networks that build community within and across diverse African ethnic and national origins. As we will see below, diverse forms of community building have emerged over the past two decades that are all part of claiming spaces of belonging and that serve as a response to broader exclusionary practices within Canadian social spaces.

Building Community

The self-identification most common among members of the new African diaspora in metro Vancouver is that of seeing themselves as part of the "African community." This pan-African identity coexists with more specific national and ethnic identities and has particular salience in the local context. Developing a sense of pan-African identity is based on common experiences of marginalization in Canada and bonds that develop between migrants from diverse countries in sub-Saharan Africa. These bonds develop in the local context but extend to a belief in shared values that are perceived to permeate the African continent.[51] Fulani explains, "We are recognized as African community, so not Ugandan community necessarily. So I feel like I belong to the African community."[52] Similarly, Laziati identifies primarily as African and not as Swazi:

> It doesn't matter where you come from, you know, they just lump you in one thing. And, of course, I am not going about what people dictate to me. But for me, as an African, I have always felt more of a bond [with] other Africans, fellow Africans. So for me, I am an African first before my own country.[53]

As Laziati's comments suggest, a pan-African identity emerges out of commonalities shared, as well as how immigrants from Africa are treated in Vancouver, where "they just lump you in one thing." In an environment where daily interactions are overdetermined by processes of racialization, ethnic and national identities may become less central. As Kivete puts it, "The White man sees us as Africans. We are all the same, we are just Africans. You are a Black man, you are a Black man." Black bodies render ethnic and national heritage invisible. As Sangara observes, "You see an African lady, you don't see Nigerian. That's when you see me, you see an African."[54] In this context, the development of a pan-African identity is both a product of external homogenization and also an active process of building community solidarity.

Among the first generation, dis-identification with what they see as pejorative representations of African Americans leads to an emphasis on their Africanness and on dissimilarities from a larger Black community.[55] This is much less so among the second generation, who are immersed in North American popular culture from a young age. Teenage boys, in particular, often feel more affinity with a larger Black community and with African Americans, who dominate representations in popular culture, sharing the heightened surveillance in public spaces and in encounters with authorities. At the same time, as young adults, the second generation retains an awareness of their Africanness, often including identities that navigate both pan-African and national African heritages (as Ugandan, Somali, Ethiopian, etc.), and most also negotiate multiple or hybrid identities as Canadian.[56]

In the context of migration, building bonds of community among those from sub-Saharan Africa is embedded in orientations to both the "homeland" in Africa and "homemaking" in Canada. Avtar Brah describes the homeland as "a mythic place of desire in the diasporic imagination," in contrast to "the lived experience of the locality" in which day-to-day homemaking occurs.[57] Community activities associated with maintaining links to the homeland receive more public recognition and are more often undertaken by men.[58] Women predominate in homemaking activities in Canada, many of which are less visible aspects of community building.[59] Nevertheless, the African community in Vancouver is created through diverse practices oriented to diasporic homelands and homemaking in local spaces.

Some members of the African community are involved in creating formal organizations oriented toward their homelands, and these activities also help build community in the local context. There are several nationally focused organizations among the larger components of the African community, including organizations linked to Congo, Ethiopia, Ghana, Nigeria, South Africa, and Uganda.[60] These organizations are typically intended to maintain ties to the homeland and preserve cultural traditions in Canada. National organizations also hold periodic social functions and festivals that build community among co-nationals and the wider African diaspora in the local context.[61] In addition, several nonprofit organizations have emerged that focus on development in various parts of Africa, supporting projects such as building and running schools and medical clinics and providing safe drinking water in home villages. These development organizations are typically run by men connected to these villages and help them maintain their status as important members of those communities.[62]

Women are less likely to be centrally involved in organizations that focus on the homeland. Women are engaged in a broad range of informal networks to provide support to one another, including advice on parenting in Canada, how to navigate local schools, health care, and social services, providing gifts and food for new mothers, babysitting one another's children, offering support for bereaved families, and providing the emotional support found in commiseration with others facing similar challenges.[63] Although most have also developed friendships beyond the African community, often with women from other immigrant backgrounds, support among African women is central to developing bonds of community. As Bizima explained, she knows she can count on other African women when she needs help:

> The support is so much, you know. You find people phoning you, yeah. And if we need help, you know. We don't have money to babysit your kid; you just phone an African and she's going to help you with no charge at all ... Yeah, because we are really, you can really tell your problems to an African, and she is going to understand.[64]

Women have also organized more formal women's groups to meet a range of needs, including supporting AIDS orphans in Africa, forming lending circles to pool limited resources, organizing community meetings for problem solving, and providing information to new immigrants.[65] Some of these support networks are organized along national lines – for example, there are specific Nigerian, Congolese, and Sudanese women's groups in Vancouver – but most provide support to women who have diverse origins in Africa.[66]

With the vast majority of African immigrants in Vancouver identifying as Christian, churches are an important locus of African community development.[67] Many in the community attend multi-ethnic churches, but several African churches have also emerged. In 2010 we identified twelve separate churches that can be described as African churches, led by African pastors, with congregations in which African members predominate. No stand-alone African churches have emerged; each finds space to use in other churches or multi-purpose buildings. However, there has been some fundraising to build a church that various African denominations can use. African churches have also become an important source of support for new immigrants, providing information and referrals to settlement agencies, as well as a place to build critically important friendship networks.[68]

The African community plays an important role in providing settlement services for newer immigrants and refugees from Africa. In 2010, there were more than thirty African settlement workers, mostly women, working in a broad range of non-profit multicultural settlement organizations and schools in metro Vancouver. As Media commented, it was critical to have "some people from Africa representing us when you go and say an issue or a problem."[69] Two new settlement organizations were also created specifically to address the needs of this small but diverse group. The Centre of Integration for African Immigrants (CIAI) and Umoja Operation Compassion Society both emerged to provide targeted settlement services to immigrants and refugees from Africa, were founded and run by men in the community, and were largely staffed by members of the community as well.[70] Although CIAI no longer provides services, and Umoja now provides services to people from many parts of the world, these settlement agencies helped to raise the profile of the local African community in the wider society.[71]

Creating businesses that cater to the local community and/or profile African heritage is another facet of community development. Though no doubt an underestimation of entrepreneurialism in the community, in 2010 we identified eleven African restaurants, seven salons for hair and beauty products, and two specialty supermarkets, in addition to a handful of other home-based businesses.[72]

The African community has become more visible at the cultural level. African dance companies, theatre groups, and storytelling groups have been created in metro Vancouver, and a francophone African radio program was established. By the early twenty-first century, African-focused peace festivals, music festivals, film and arts festivals, and soccer tournaments were all part of the local cultural landscape.[73] Some of the latter spaces also foster links beyond the self-defined African community to connect with the larger Black diaspora in metro Vancouver.

Something that has not been accomplished yet, but has considerable community support, is the creation of an African cultural centre. As Omure notes, an African cultural centre would provide a stronger community presence in metro Vancouver: "A place we can say, 'This is African place. Oh, this is our cultural area.' We are going to be known in this place."[74] An African cultural centre is envisioned as a place to gather, connect, showcase African heritage, and pass on cultural values to the next generation. Men in the community complain about the lack of places for them to congregate, and they envision an African cultural centre filling this gap.[75] The small size of and limited financial resources within the African community make this goal more difficult to achieve than it was for much larger and more established communities that have built cultural centres in Vancouver.

Conclusion

The small Black community in Vancouver in the first half of the twentieth century was affected by discriminatory immigration policies that limited its growth and urban redevelopment that destroyed the only space once associated with the community. Today, the 1 per cent of metro Vancouver residents who identify as Black are scattered throughout the region. The majority are recent immigrants from sub-Saharan Africa and their children, with little awareness of, or links to, a historic Black community. This new African diaspora, with recent roots in diverse postcolonial African nations, experiences marginalization on many levels, including discrimination in the labour market, erasure of their English linguistic capital, and exclusion from the imagined community in which White bodies remain centred. In this context, a community of *Black African immigrants* is being forged as a self-defined "African community" in metro Vancouver.

The new African community is created through diverse practices, ranging from informal support to the development of formal organizations, with some oriented toward the diasporic homeland and many other activities concerned with homemaking in the local context. These diverse community-building activities, most of which cross national and ethnic lines, emerge as members navigate their new homes and come together to create new spaces of belonging. Coming together in these ways challenges everyday racism and marginalization, demonstrates the resilience, resourcefulness, and contributions of community members, and raises the African community's visibility in the wider society. Practices of building community are also central to claiming spaces of belonging, both physical sites and psychic spaces, in the quest to be recognized as full members of the larger imagined community and not perpetual strangers who should be grilled about "where are you from." Hence, belonging remains contested and will remain so until others recognize that members of the new African community are Canadians, actively engaged in homemaking in Vancouver, and not visiting from somewhere else.

NOTES

1 Crawford Kilian, *Go Do Some Great Thing: The Black Pioneers of British Columbia* (Burnaby: Commodore Books, 2008); Joseph Mensah, *Black Canadians: History, Experiences, Social Conditions* (Halifax: Fernwood, 2002).
2 Kilian, *Go Do Some Great Thing*, 11–27, 39.
3 Jean Barman, *The West beyond the West: A History of British Columbia* (Toronto: University of Toronto Press, 1991), 100.

4 Wayde Compton, *After Canaan: Essays on Race, Writing and Region* (Vancouver: Arsenal Pulp Press, 2010), 87–9.
5 Kilian, *Go Do Some Great Thing*, 139–40.
6 "About," Black Strathcona, accessed July 20, 2017, http://www.blackstrathcona.com/about/.
7 Kilian, *Go Do Some Great Thing*, 143.
8 Augie Fleras, *Immigration Canada: Evolving Realities and Emerging Challenges in a Postnational World* (Vancouver: UBC Press, 2015); Freda Hawkins, *Critical Years in Immigration: Canada and Australia Compared* (Montreal and Kingston: McGill-Queen's University Press, 1991); Peter Li, *Destination Canada: Immigration Debates and Issues* (Don Mills, ON: Oxford University Press, 2003); Alan Simmons, *Immigration and Canada: Global and Transnational Perspectives* (Toronto: Canadian Scholars, 2010).
9 Quoted in Hawkins, *Critical Years in Immigration*, 56.
10 Agnes Calliste, "Race, Gender and Canadian Immigration Policy: Blacks from the Caribbean, 1900–1932," *Journal of Canadian Studies* 28, no. 4 (1993–4): 131–48.
11 Compton, *After Canaan*, 90–8; *Black Strathcona*.
12 Fleras, *Immigration Canada*; Hawkins, *Critical Years in Immigration*; Li, *Destination Canada*; Simmons, *Immigration and Canada*.
13 In 1961 the Black population in Canada was 32,127. Mensah, *Black Canadians*, 53. In 2011 the Black population in Canada was 945,670. Statistics Canada, "2011 National Household Survey: Data Table, Visible Minority Population Canada," Statistics Canada Catalogue no. 99-010-X2011029.
14 Statistics Canada, *Immigration and Ethnocultural Diversity in Canada*, National Household Survey 2011, Statistics Canada Catalogue no. 99-010-X2011001 (Ottawa: Minister of Industry, 2013), 8.
15 Korba Puplampu and Wisdom Tettey, "Ethnicity and the Identity of African-Canadians: A Theoretical and Political Analysis," in *The African Diaspora in Canada: Negotiating Identity and Belonging*, ed. Wisdom Tettey and Korba Puplampu (Calgary: University of Calgary Press, 2005), 33–4.
16 Statistics Canada, *Immigration and Ethnocultural Diversity*, 16; Metro Vancouver, "Metro Vancouver Population by Visible Minority, 2011 NHS," accessed July 12, 2017, http://www.metrovancouver.org.
17 Statistics Canada, "2011 National Household Survey Profile, Vancouver CMA, Immigration and Citizenship."
18 Statistics Canada, "2011 National Household Survey Profile, Vancouver CMA, Ethnic Origin."
19 Statistics Canada, "2011 National Household Survey (NHS): Data Table, Vancouver CMA, Visible Minority, Immigrant Status and Period of Immigration."

20 For example, there were 1,980 immigrants from Jamaica, 2,045 from Trinidad and Tobago, 895 from Guyana, and 275 from Haiti in Vancouver in 2011, and there were also 26,240 immigrants from the United States in 2011. However, how many of these people identified as Black is unknown. Statistics Canada, "2011 National Household Survey Profile, Vancouver CMA, Immigration and Citizenship" and "2011 NHS: Data Table, Vancouver CMA, Visible Minority, Immigrant Status and Period of Immigration."

21 Khalid Koser, "New African Diasporas: An Introduction," in *New African Diasporas*, ed. Khalid Koser (London: Routledge, 2003).

22 Statistics Canada, "2011 NHS: Data Table, Vancouver CMA, Visible Minority, Immigrant Status and Period of Immigration."

23 The African community in Vancouver self-identifies as those who come directly from countries in Africa and are racialized as Black; specifying sub-Saharan Africa is often used to emphasize the importance of race. African migrants who are not racialized as Black in Canada, whether White or of Asian or Arabic heritage, are not usually considered to be part of this community. Gillian Creese, *The New African Diaspora in Vancouver: Migration, Exclusion, and Belonging* (Toronto: University of Toronto Press, 2011), 193.

24 Avtar Brah, *Cartographies of Diaspora: Contesting Identities* (London: Routledge, 1996); Rogers Brubaker, "The 'Diaspora' Diaspora," *Ethnic and Racial Studies* 28, no. 1 (1995): 1–19; James Clifford, "Diasporas," *Cultural Anthropology* 9, no. 3 (1994): 302–38.

25 Mattia Fumanti and Pnina Werbner, "The Moral Economy of the African Diaspora: Citizenship, Networking and Permeable Ethnicity," *African Diaspora* 3, no. 1 (2010): 3–12; Nicole Gregoire, "Identity Politics, Social Movement and the State: 'Pan-African' Associations and the Making of an 'African Community' in Belgium," *African Diaspora* 3, no. 1 (2010): 160–82; Pnina Werbner, "Many Gateways to the Gateway City: Elites, Class and Policy Networking in the London African Diaspora," *African Diaspora* 3, no. 1 (2010): 132–59.

26 Creese, *New African Diaspora*; Gillian Creese, "Gender, Generation and Identities in Vancouver's African Diaspora," *African Disapora* 6, no. 2 (2013): 155–78.

27 The term "African immigrant" is used here to refer to all newcomers from Africa who are racialized as Black regardless of whether they came through the immigration or refugee systems. Like skilled workers selected through the points system, government-assisted refugees selected abroad also tend to be highly educated and arrive with permanent resident status. In contrast, a smaller group of asylum seekers make refugee claims within Canada, often wait years to resolve their status, and receive little in the way of state support. With the exception of asylum claimants within Canada, research

suggests that in most respects the experiences of African immigrants and refugees in Vancouver are very similar. Creese, *New African Diaspora.*

28 Katherine Donato, Donna Gabaccia, Jennifer Holdaway, Martin Manalansan, and Patricia Pessar, "A Glass Half Full? Gender in Migration Studies," *International Migration Review* 40, no. 1 (2006): 3–26; Helma Lutz, "Gender in the Migratory Process," *Journal of Ethnic and Migration Studies* 36, no. 10 (2010): 1647–63; Patricia Pessar, "Engendering Migration Studies: The Case of New Immigrants in the United States," in *Gender and US Immigration: Contemporary Trends*, ed. Pierrette Hondagneu-Sotelo (Berkeley: University of California Press, 2003), 20–42.

29 Himani Bannerji, *The Dark Side of the Nation: Essays on Multiculturalism, Nationalism and Gender* (Toronto: Canadian Scholars, 2000); Harald Bauder, *Immigration Dialectic* (Toronto: University of Toronto Press, 2011); Eva Mackey, *The House of Difference: Cultural Politics and National Identity in Canada* (Toronto: University of Toronto Press, 2002). Benedict Anderson coined the term "imagined community" to refer to popular ideas about which people belong as members of a nation-state and which people are perceived as outsiders. Anderson, *Imagined Communities* (London: Verso, 1991).

30 David Este, "Black Canadian Historical Writing 1970–2006: An Assessment," *Journal of Black Studies* 38, no. 3 (2008): 388–406; Jennifer Kelly, *Under the Gaze: Learning to Be Black in White Society* (Halifax: Fernwood, 1998); Kelly, *Borrowed Identities* (New York: Peter Lang, 2004); Atsuko Matsuoka and John Sorenson, *Ghosts and Shadows: Construction of Identity and Community in an African Diaspora* (Toronto: University of Toronto Press, 2001).

31 Awad El Karim Ibrahim, "Becoming Black: Rap and Hip-Hop, Race, Gender, Identity, and the Politics of ESL Learning," *TESOL Quarterly* 33, no. 3 (1999): 349–69; Kelly, *Borrowed Identities*; Abdi Kusow, "Migration and Racial Formations among Somali Immigrants in North America," *Journal of Ethnic and Migration Studies* 32, no. 3 (2006): 533–51; Philomina Okeke-Ihejirika and Denise Spitzer, "In Search of Identity: Intergenerational Experiences of African Youth in a Canadian Context" in Tettey and Puplampu, *African Diaspora in Canada*, 205–24.

32 The first project is based on interviews conducted in 2004 with sixty-one women and men living in metro Vancouver who had migrated from twenty-one countries in sub-Saharan Africa; this research is reported in Creese, *New African Disapora.* The second project is based on interviews conducted in 2011 and 2012 with thirty-five men and women who went to high school in metro Vancouver and whose parents came from twelve countries in sub-Saharan Africa; this research is reported in Gillian Creese, *"Where Are You From?": Growing Up African-Canadian in Vancouver* (Toronto: University of Toronto Press, 2020). Funding for both projects was obtained from the Social Sciences and Humanities Research Council of Canada.

33 Marc Frenette and René Morissette, "Will They Ever Converge? Earnings of Immigrant and Canadian-Born Workers over the Last Two Decades," *International Migration Review* 39, no. 1 (2005): 228–58; Li, *Destination Canada*; Philip Oreopoulos, "Why Do Skilled Immigrants Struggle in the Labor Market? A Field Experiment with Thirteen Thousand Resumes," *American Economic Journal: Economic Policy* 3, no. 4 (2011): 148–71; Jeffrey Reitz, Josh Curtis, and Jennifer Elrick, "Immigrant Skill Utilization: Trends and Policy Issues," *Journal of International Migration and Integration* 15, no. 1 (2014): 1–26.

34 Abdurrahman Aydemir and Mikal Skuterud, "Explaining the Deteriorating Entry Earnings of Canada's Immigrant Cohorts: 1966–2000" (Statistics Canada Analytical Studies Branch Research Paper Series, No. 225, Catalogue no. 11F0019MIE, May 2004); Oreopoulos, "Why Do Skilled Immigrants Struggle"; Garnett Picot and Feng Hou, "The Rise of Low-Income Rates among Immigrants in Canada" (Statistics Canada Analytical Studies Branch Research Paper Series, No. 198, Catalogue no. 11F0019MIE, June 2003); Garnett Picot and Arthur Sweetman, "The Deteriorating Economic Welfare of Immigrants and Possible Causes: Update 2005" (Statistics Canada Analytical Studies Branch Research Paper Series, No. 262, Catalogue no. 11F0019MIE, June 2005).

35 Creese, *New African Diaspora*, 30–1; Gillian Creese and Brandy Wiebe, "'Survival Employment': Gender and Deskilling among African Immigrants in Canada," *International Migration* 50, no. 5 (2012): 56–76.

36 For historical examples, see Dionne Brand, *No Burden to Carry: Narratives of Black Working Women in Ontario, 1920s to 1950s* (Toronto: Women's Press, 1991); and Calliste, "Race, Gender." For slightly more recent examples, see Frances Henry, "Two Studies of Racial Discrimination in Employment," in *Social Inequality in Canada: Patterns, Problems, Policies*, 3rd ed., ed. James Curtis, Ed Grab, and Neil Guppy (Scarborough, ON: Prentice Hall, 1999): 226–35; and Mensah, *Black Canadians*, 140–73.

37 All respondents identified in this chapter are referred to by pseudonyms.

38 Creese and Wiebe, "Survival Employment," 10–11.

39 Creese and Wiebe, 12.

40 Pierre Bourdieu, "The Forms of Capital," in *Handbook of Theory and Research for the Sociology of Education*, ed. John Richardson (Westport, CT: Greenwood, 1986), 245.

41 Pierre Bourdieu, "The Economics of Linguistic Exchanges," *Social Science Information* 16, no. 6 (1977): 645–68.

42 Gillian Creese, "Erasing English Language Competency: African Migrants in Vancouver, Canada," *Journal of International Migration and Integration* 11, no. 3 (2010): 295–313; Creese, *New African Diaspora*, 33–60; Gillian Creese and Edith Ngene Kambere, "'What Colour Is Your English?,'" *Canadian*

Review of Sociology and Anthropology 40, no. 5 (2003): 565–73; Tracey Derwing, Marian Rossiter, and Murray Munro, "Teaching Native Speakers to Listen to Foreign-Accented Speech," *Journal of Multilingual and Multicultural Development* 23, no. 4 (2002): 245–59; Henry, "Two Studies"; Rosina Lippi-Green, *English with an Accent: Language, Ideology and Discrimination in the United States* (New York: Routledge, 1997); Murray Munro, "A Primer on Accent Discrimination in the Canadian Context," *TESL Canada Journal* 20, no. 2 (2003): 38–51; John Willinsky, *Learning to Divide the World: Education at Empire's End* (Minneapolis: University of Minnesota Press, 1998).
43 Creese, "Erasing English Language Competency"; Creese, *New African Diaspora*.
44 Creese, *New African Diaspora*, 33.
45 Creese, "Erasing English Language Competency," 303.
46 Sara Ahmed, *Strange Encounters: Embodied Others in Post-coloniality* (London: Routledge, 2000); Brah, *Cartographies of Diaspora*.
47 Creese, *New African Diaspora*, 200.
48 Creese, 199.
49 Gillian Creese, "'Where Are You From?' Racialization, Belonging and Identity among Second-Generation African-Canadians," *Ethnic and Racial Studies* 42, no. 9 (2019): 1476–94.
50 Creese, 1483–4, 1486, 1488, 1487.
51 Values that research participants defined as "African" include the importance of extended families and communal relationships, lifelong deference to elders, especially fathers, and hierarchical gender relations. Creese, "Gender, Generation and Identities."
52 Creese, *New African Diaspora*, 195.
53 Creese, 196.
54 Creese, 196, 194.
55 Creese, 192–209.
56 Gillian Creese, "Growing Up Where 'No One Looked like Me': Gender, Race, Hip Hop and Identity in Vancouver," *Gender Issues* 32, no. 3 (2015): 201–19; Creese, "'Where Are You From?'"
57 Brah, *Cartographies of Diaspora*, 192.
58 Luin Goldring, "The Gender and Geography of Citizenship in Mexico-U.S. Transnational Spaces," *Identities: Global Studies in Culture and Power* 7, no. 4 (2001): 501–37.
59 Creese, *New African Diaspora*; Creese, "Gender, Generation and Identities."
60 Creese, *New African Diaspora*, 217.
61 In 2009 the United African Communities of BC was formed to unite these diverse nationally focused organizations, though it soon folded for lack of resources. Creese, *New African Diaspora*, 224.
62 Creese, "Gender, Generation and Identities."

63 Creese, *New African Diaspora*, 210–14.
64 Creese, 211.
65 The group supporting African AIDS orphans was the only example we found of a women's network that focused on addressing issues in the homeland.
66 Creese, *New African Diaspora*, 211–12.
67 In 2010, we estimated that 90 per cent of African immigrants in Vancouver identified as Christian. At that time we were unable to identify any mosques with a significant population of sub-Saharan Africans. Creese, *New African Diaspora*, 214.
68 Creese, *New African Diaspora*, 214–17.
69 Creese, 227.
70 Creese, 227–8.
71 Changes in government funding, moving away from ethno-specific organizations and mandating new partnerships between settlement agencies, made some smaller operations financially unsustainable. CIAI closed its services in 2011. Umoja continues to provide settlement services but no longer with a focus only on those from sub-Saharan Africa. Umoja also has a second focus: development in the homeland that includes development work in Uganda and Tanzania.
72 Creese, *New African Diaspora*, 229.
73 Creese, 226.
74 Creese, 225.
75 It is striking that in the interviews most men raised the need for an African cultural centre as a priority, but no women mentioned it at all. It is unclear why this is so, but it may be that women had other priorities and/or may be less keen on providing men in the community with a place to congregate. Creese, 225–6.

15
"The part of you that's Rwanda": Creating a Rwandan Diaspora Community in the Greater Toronto Area in the Early Twenty-First Century

ANNA AINSWORTH

To be part of the Rwandan diaspora in the Greater Toronto Area (GTA) is to be engaged in ongoing processes of translation, re-imagination, and reconstruction of the category of "Rwandan." It is to be an inheritor of a national cosmology yet to be simultaneously rewriting this cosmology and altering its constitutive categories to fit new day-to-day experiences and multiple forms of individual identity. Those who belong to this group are subject to didactic messages from the Rwandan state that are potent in shaping who belongs and who does not and the terms of that belonging. The collective trauma of the 1994 genocide has generated an overdetermined national narrative, powerfully enforced by the Rwandan state. The Rwandan diaspora is especially exposed to the powerful homogenizing narrative because this shared trauma has generated a collective identity that imagines the diaspora as vulnerable; those who become leaders in the Rwandan GTA community thus perceive that they need the protection and favour of the home state, for fear that they could, once again, face genocide. Nonetheless, individual identities are never shaped from above alone; among this group, as among any other, individual members contest, challenge, and engage the narratives that they inherit and receive. Thus, the Rwandan diaspora in the GTA serves as a site of construction of the notion of "Rwandan." Yet, simultaneously, even as the idea of Rwandese identity is being constructed and contested, those who participate in this process are racialized as Black in the Canadian polity. In some ways, Rwandanness becomes the antidote to the obliterating and homogenizing gaze that racializes those who identify as Rwandan and as Black, in the context of Canadian multiculturalism.

As Rogers Brubaker argues, ethnicity, race, and nation are not groups or entities but "practical categories, situated actions, cultural idioms, cognitive schemas, discursive frames, organizational routines, institutional forms, political projects and contingent events."[1] In moments when Rwandans meet as Rwandans, all these interrelated categories, actions, frames, routines, projects, and events work to instantiate Rwandan ethnonationalism and generate the perception that it is a thing in the world. Yet, at the same time, as Brubaker proposes, this imagined reality is challenged by those who are thus classified. Consciously or otherwise, they offer understandings of themselves and the world that do not neatly fit the narratives of the nation. Among the Rwandan diaspora in the GTA this dialectical process was most evident during community events when those who identified as Rwandans met *as* Rwandans. In these moments, institutions, be they cultural or ethnic associations or the Rwandan state, imposed normative understandings of what constituted Rwandanness. The following chapter will lay out the history of Rwandan institutional organizing in the Greater Toronto Area, outline the moments of apparent unity and cohesiveness, and then examine the fractures, challenges, impositions – in short, the micropolitics of naming the Rwandan diaspora in the GTA.

The following discussion is based on primary, ethnographic research conducted between 2011 and 2015 among those who identified as part of the Rwandan diaspora in the Greater Toronto Area. I conducted thirty-one in-depth semi-structured interviews ranging from one and a half hours to six hours in length, as well as participant observation of community events and analysis of textual and visual sources. All names that appear are pseudonyms in order to protect the privacy of the participants. It is also worth noting that although I bear an Anglo name, I am also a migrant, from Poland. This shared commonality of migration, usually established early in the conversation when the participant would comment on my apparent "Canadianness," invited contrasts between the experiences of a white woman migrant and migrants who are racialized as Black, as will be discussed later.

History of Rwandan Diaspora Organizational Life in the GTA

Unfortunately, most documents relating to the early organizational life of the GTA Rwandan organizations were lost during leadership transitions. Thus, the following account relies primarily on oral testimony. The first Rwandan migrants to the GTA were young, well-educated men who had refugee status from the United Nations High Commissioner for Refugees (UNHCR) and were granted asylum in Canada in the mid- to late 1980s. They largely originated in the diasporic Rwandan communities in Uganda, Kenya, and Tanzania that were the product of successive violent expulsions from Rwanda of Tutsis by the Hutu majority dating from 1959. Yet, these men shared a sense of historical connection to the imagined homeland of Rwanda and most spoke Kinyarwanda.[2] These young men, initially about a dozen or so, also shared a family history of exile from Rwanda (most were born outside of Rwanda) and a lack of an alternate national identity as the African states that had received the refugees had refused to grant them citizenship and a new nationality.[3] They had found one another through personal contacts or, in at least one case, by hearing someone speak Kinyarwanda on a Toronto street, and they bonded over their isolation and visibility in a dominant white society that, though purportedly multicultural, positioned them as "other" and outside the realm of belonging, as will be discussed in the latter part of this chapter.

These young men's shared sense of isolation in the new homeland was paired with a sense of connection to their imagined homeland. In particular, those who had never lived in Rwanda expressed a "longing to go back."[4] Thus, when the Rwandan Patriotic Front (RPF)[5] formed in 1987 and began military incursions into Rwanda in 1990, these young men eagerly watched.[6] They wanted to help with what they called "the struggle" but understood that to declare themselves members of the RPF would open them up to legal scrutiny by the Canadian state, as the RPF was perceived as a terrorist organization at the time. Instead, they formed the Rwandese Canadian Culture Association (RCCA).

The RCCA was both a social club and an information-sharing space where the latest news from friends and family in the struggle was related. Those who participated in the early years of this organizing fondly recall the sense of closeness within the organization; "the community was small but very tight" and members of the group "really had a sense of community." Initially, without a designated space, the group met on the campus of York University, in empty classrooms or in the university's parkland. A few members of this group were attending the university and lived nearby, so "we took York like our own community" and used its semi-public space to socialize, play music, dance, and talk. As a group made up of young men, it was little different from any other single-gendered social group in that the members laughed, joked, and danced together but, in the midst of this social bonding, there were larger purposes at play as the politics of the RPF-instigated war further knitted the members together. News from siblings fighting "in the bush" was relayed, remittances were sent to support the struggle, and some members of the group even travelled to Uganda and joined the ranks of the RPF.[7] Thus, the young association was directly linked to the war and the members' sense of connection to one another and their burgeoning collective identity was tightened by their link to experiences of violence.

The RCCA also took on the role of a settlement agency for Rwandans who, beginning in the early 1990s, began arriving in increasing numbers. After the genocide, in late 1994, the tide of new Rwandan migrants rose. According to the 1996 census, there were 1,070 individuals in Canada who identified as Rwandan; by the 2006 census, that number had risen to 5,570.[8] It is worth noting that many chose not to identify as Rwandan upon arrival in Canada, so census numbers underestimate the population. In the mid-1990s, the RCCA took over the lease of a house near York University, which became known as Rwanda House, and this venue served as both a meeting place and a shelter for new migrants. Through telephone communication with family and friends in Africa, community members knew whenever a new migrant was arriving and would pick the migrant up from a shelter and offer him or her housing in Rwanda House. Thus, many new migrants who arrived in the GTA were automatically enfolded into what was becoming a significant community of those who identified as Rwandan.[9] The joint imperatives of supporting a nationalist struggle and of welcoming new migrants turned what had largely been a social club into a formal organization with political alliances and interests.

When the genocide ended and the RPF formed the transitional government in Rwanda in 1994, those who felt closely connected to the now-governing regime could join the RPF. A number did so, and a rift appeared in what had been presumed to be a shared identity. The RCCA had been made up of anyone who chose to be a member, because it was a "cultural group" and any Rwandan could join. However, to be a member of the RPF, one had to ask permission of the RPF leadership in Kigali, which suggested not only that those who desired membership wanted a closer affiliation with the regime but also that the regime was beginning to look for allies abroad. Beginning in 1995, those who were close to the new regime began returning to Rwanda.[10]

Concurrently, according to the participants, the Rwandan High Commission in Ottawa reached out to the organization and suggested that there was no need to have the RPF (represented by the High Commission) and RCCA as distinct entities. The leadership of both factions agreed and out of that emerged a new organization: the Rwandan Canadian Association (RCA) of Greater Toronto.[11] Because key members of the leadership of the now-defunct RCCA had left the country and returned to Rwanda without passing on the information about membership, bank accounts, and so forth, the new leadership of the RCA had trouble maintaining continuity. According to the participants, the financial records and membership rolls were lost.[12] Thus, the new RCA began its life with the assumption that every Rwandan was a member, but in fact few explicitly chose to become members. None of the participants of this study were able to explain why this was the case. So, during the latter 1990s the organization lost steam.

In the late 1990s and the early 2000s, even as the numbers of new Rwandese migrants grew, there was no clear sense of a shared identity as a unified community as a result of the various upheavals, foremost among them the genocide. Individuals and families were still connecting, but there was a lack of a unified, collective sense of an ethnonational community. During the early 1990s, said Mathieu, "we were very close," but by the end of the decade, "people were separated," largely owing to demographic diversity of the new migrants.[13] Some families intentionally chose to not associate with other Rwandans, fearing their own trauma.[14] Instead, people were connecting based on other loci of identification. Women created their own group, Umurage, which met in individual homes and served the particular needs of women primarily related to the domestic sphere, as well as their own conception of the community. While the RCA sought to generate a sense of shared identity through cultural activities, Umurage focused on specific needs, such as language instruction for children, social support for families struggling with the upheaval of migration, and the day-to-day struggles of racialized women in the Canadian state.[15] Other individuals who identified as Rwandans formed branches of opposition political parties, not aligned with the RCA and the regime in Rwanda, in support of what appeared to be democratization in Rwanda.[16] Yet others moved away from those who identified as Rwandan and created their own social worlds, unconnected to any sense of ethnonational affinity. Still others chose to return to Rwanda in hopes of starting over. During these years, Rwandanness, as a national/ethnic category, failed to crystallize in the GTA, despite the efforts of what Brubaker has called "ethnopolitical entrepreneurs" and resulting at least in part from the ongoing elite-level ethnopolitical conflict in the remembered homeland.[17]

Emergence of a "Diaspora"

In early 2007, the cabinet of Rwandan president Kagame declared that a Diaspora Office ought to be created to connect Rwandans in the "diaspora." This resulted in the creation of the Diaspora General Directorate in 2008 under the auspices of the Ministry of Foreign Affairs. The new directorate had a mandate to "mobilize Rwandan Diaspora for unity/cohesion among themselves targeted for the promotion of security and socio-economic development of their homeland."[18] The directorate established branches of a new umbrella organization called the Rwandan Diaspora Global Network in all the states where a significant number of those who identified as Rwandans resided. Under this 2008 initiative, branches were established in Senegal, Kenya, Burundi, Malawi, South Africa, Zambia, the United Kingdom, Germany, Switzerland, Denmark, Belgium, France, Poland, Austria, Luxembourg, the Netherlands, Canada, the United States, India, China, South Korea, and Australia.[19] The Rwandan High Commission to Canada launched the new organization in Canada with branches in all the urban centres where there existed a significant number of residents who identified as Rwandan. Thus, Rwandan Diaspora Global Network (RDGN) replaced the RCA and presented itself as the organizational body of Rwandans in Canada. It was the conduit for the Rwandan state, via its High Commission to Canada, to connect to individuals who identified as Rwandese and lived abroad.[20] Its primary function was to organize the annual genocide commemoration and other, less formalized community events, like summer retreats for youth.[21] These events were part of an active effort by institutions, the state among them, to call into being the "diaspora" as a community.

Aside from its formal capacity, the RDGN also offered settlement support to new migrants. This kind of service was assumed to be part of the normal functioning of the organization but not its primary mandate. Partly this was a consequence of the fact that by 2011 there were fewer newcomers from Rwanda than there had been in the previous two decades.[22] This was further compounded by the fact that the UNHCR revoked refugee status for refugees from Rwanda in June of 2013.[23] Thus, to migrate to Canada, Rwandans needed to apply under the categories of skilled workers, family sponsorship, business or student visas, or live-in caregivers.[24] According to informants, this policy change limited the numbers of Rwandese newcomers to Canada, though census figures to support this were not yet available.[25]

Performing Unity

At formally organized events hosted by the RDGN, there was usually an active narration of the nation, often closely linked to the Rwandan state's narratives of self.[26] The annual genocide commemoration served as the central rallying point for the community and as an active moment of nation-building as the genocide and the subsequent nation were narrated. These events were future focused, allowing for the memory of the dead but looking toward an imagined future. These were also performances of unity in a community that was internally divided by ethnicity, gender, and age. These were moments when markers of difference were sublimated and re-articulated as markers of shared values and shared ways of seeing.

No one who feels a connection to Rwanda either by birth or by ancestry is liable to forget the genocide. Especially survivors recall the genocide every year during the month of April, often despite themselves, as the physical and psychological symptoms of trauma invade and overturn their lives. As Grace recalled, "So, seriously I cannot forget that because it's 25th April that always, in my mind is a shock."[27] The genocide will not be forgotten by those who lived it, nor by their children, who live their lives under the shadow of the trauma, much like the children of Holocaust survivors lived with "the 'elephant in the room' – a subject barely spoken but nonetheless unavoidably present."[28] Before the inauguration of the RDGN in 2007, small groups organized their own ceremonies of remembrance. People met on the occasion of the anniversary and together remembered the events and those they had lost. Harnessing people's memories into a centralized performance of remembrance, as the RDGN has sought to do, was not about remembering, as that was already an active process. It was primarily an opportunity to create a sense of group cohesion and to generate ethnonational narratives. In this case, the Rwandan state, acting through the High Commission in Ottawa, actively worked to rewrite the history of the genocide in order to reinscribe a version that posited the RPF as the saviours of the nation and denied any of the atrocities committed by the RPF.[29] The formally ascribed motivation for the genocide commemoration is remembrance of genocide and resolution of trauma, yet neither appeared to be the outcome.

In Rwanda, commemorations are moments of nationalized mourning, which are designed to forge a "new, unified national identity around a single understanding of the genocide and a single version of Rwandan history."[30] Likewise, in the diaspora, the commemoration was a site of reinforcing the Rwandan mythico-history and the "correct" telling of the narrative of the genocide. Fidèle explained that the official commemoration was "a government thing, but it's not about to remember people. And even if you go there, there's a few survivors. You see people from Uganda, from here."[31] The point he was making was that those who were in Uganda or in Canada during the genocide were not survivors, yet they were the ones who attended the commemorations, possibly to claim a space of belonging in the new Rwanda. There was an understanding, at least among some, that the official commemorations were no longer about remembrance but about nation-building. This even extended to identifying those who were now deemed "genocide deniers," an increasingly long and problematic list including those who questioned that the genocide occurred, as well as jurists and academics who pointed to RPF atrocities, raised questions about the shooting down of the presidential plane, and otherwise disrupted the tidy narrative of the new state.[32] While there has been an active and violent campaign to deny the fact of the genocide, the Rwandan state has used a very broad definition of "denier" to include anyone who disrupts the official history.[33]

The 2013 commemoration, titled "Let's Commemorate the Genocide against the Tutsi as We Strive for Self-Reliance," explicitly excluded references to any deaths other than Tutsi deaths. Subsequent RDGN commemorations strongly reinforced the message that only Tutsis were victims. As one informant explained, "I've not been in three years, because for me, I don't see it as a commemoration anymore, it's a government show-up."[34] As the title of the event suggests, there is no room at this moment of myth-making for the remembrance of any dead except Tutsi, dead at the hands of the *génocidaires*. Thus, for those who carry the burden of remembering the Hutu or Tutsi dead at the hands of the RPF, this commemoration obliterated their memories. In this retelling of the genocide, the voices of those whose experiences did not fit the national narrative were silenced and their grief, terror, and loss negated, again. It also served the purpose of narrating a fictionalized unity of the community both to members of the community and to outsiders.

Internal Contestations

Even as individuals were actively performing unity, there were underlying contestations and challenges playing out about what it meant to be a Rwandan in the diaspora community of the GTA. The deeply riven divide between those who identified as Tutsi and those who identified as Hutu was one of the most potent and visible points of contestation among those who belonged to the community. The performances of nation at community events were always ostensibly ones of Rwandan nationalism, but the subtextual performance was of Tutsi identity writ large as Rwandan identity. Nearly all the community leaders, speakers at events, and event organizers were Tutsi (as I learned in interviews), though they rarely publicly identified themselves as such because they echoed the Rwandan state's narrative that "we are all Rwandan." Yet it seemed that there was a dearth of those who identified as Hutus at commemorations and other community events. When I broached this topic during interviews (with mostly Tutsis) I was told that Hutus were present, but no one could point any out to me. They always seemed to be just beyond my peripheral vision, and so I came to perceive them as peripheral in the community as well. This interpretation was reinforced by the few Hutus with whom I had the opportunity to meet and speak.

Community leaders commonly told me that although the ethnic identities of Hutu and Tutsi were relevant in the past, now "we are all Rwandese." One such community leader, Janvier, explained it thus:

> We are all Rwandese. We are Rwandese. And really, as a social scientist, you can hardly take the Hutu and Tutsi, if people speak the same language, inhabited the same geographical area, intermarry, and as a practice, how do you tell who is a Hutu and a Tutsi? Okay? In the past, the moment a Tutsi would be, if his cows would die, under a certain number he would become a Hutu. You see, when you move from one ... Yes, there were Tutsis, you can see them through physical structure, yes there are Hutu, but now, we would rather be Rwandese.[35]

Janvier was drawing from the state's script that frames the division between Hutus and Tutsis as a division of class recognized by ownership of a certain number of cows, whereby Tutsis owned more cattle. Yet, he also points out the ostensible physical features that mark the supposedly non-existent difference. This narrative closely echoed the framing of national reconciliation that the Rwandan state had been promoting since 2001. As a key tenet of its mandate to foster reconciliation, the Rwandan government officially erased ethnicity by declaring that "ethnic identity would no longer be an official factor in the bureaucratic life of citizens or the state."[36] In keeping with that position, on numerous occasions, President Kagame stated that there were no more ethnic identities in the new Rwanda. During an interview with Al-Jazeera's Rhiz Khan, Kagame explained as follows:

> When we banned the use of the identities that were used to divide the people of the country – erroneous though, because people think we have tribes, yet we don't have tribes. We simply have social classes made up of people who were farmers, those who used to keep cattle and those who were dealing in handicrafts. This is how the society is divided. But we said: "You can call yourself whatever you want to call yourself, but you cannot use it against somebody who is different from you. Above all, we are all Rwandans. You can say you are Hutu, Tutsi or Twa – but you cannot use it politically to the detriment of the other one who is different from you."[37]

The parallels between Kagame's oft-repeated formulation and the statement by a GTA community leader are striking. Both statements identify the distinction between Hutus and Tutsis as "social classes" and that these "classes" had been demolished in favour of a unified narrative of "we are all Rwandans." On the surface, these statements point to a surprisingly successful reconciliation program that appeared – in the space of merely twenty years since the genocide, when these identities were invoked as motivation – to have extinguished Hutu and Tutsi as ethnic identities and made them social classes. Thus, the idea of a uniform "Rwandese" ethnicity could be crystallized as older ethnic narratives were reformulated into other social categories, without challenging the hegemony of ethnicity. Rather than understanding ethnicity as a construct and thereby undermining the ideological basis of the state, this reframing allowed the state, as embodied in the figure of the president, to claim that those who had previously identified ethnically as Hutu and Tutsi were mistaken in their perception of their own identity. They were actually referring to class distinctions, and their ethnic identity was all along Rwandese. Despite the emotive appeal of this logic, in the Rwandese community in the GTA tensions around ethnic identity remained a significant source of conflict.

As one participant explained, many in the community disagreed with the official line that "we are all Rwandese" because it concealed the ethnicization of the new regime. Thus, as he argued, Tutsi make up 10 per cent of the overall population of Rwanda, yet "they work at 90 per cent [of government positions], so if you say there's no ethnic, and even if you see the whole government is Tutsi, you can't say the Tutsi have more power."[38] Those who pointed out this disparity did not do so out of a sense of altruism or even justice but because they genuinely feared that the post-genocide governing regime was recreating conditions for another genocide by marginalizing and excluding the majority Hutu. Yet, despite these simmering anxieties, ethnic affiliation had become a taboo subject.

There was a public consensus to avoid discussing ethnic identities and, conscious of the taboo, I did not pose any questions directly related to ethnicity; thus, many of the participants in my study did not identify their presumed ethnic background or discuss the presumed ethnicity of others. Based on this initial observation, it would appear that the ethnic categories of Hutu and Tutsi had indeed receded in importance in day-to-day life. Yet, despite the oft-repeated claim that "we are all Rwandans," as I gained trust within the community, a number of participants in the study directed our conversation toward inherited ideas about ethnicity. Many among the community in the GTA explained that because it was relatively small, everyone knew who was a Tutsi and who was a Hutu. Indeed, "here in Canada it's much easier to know who's a Hutu or Tutsi than in Rwanda. Because in Rwanda now, the government is trying to avoid it, it's not like they are so successful about it."[39]

Community members "know" through a complex set of cognitive associations that rely on the cosmology that they inherited from their immersion in Rwandese culture. Those who grew up in Rwanda before the genocide had an extensive social map of familial and community associations. So, for instance, Simon explained that he "knew" that a young woman was Hutu because he had known her uncle in Rwanda, where ethnic identity was determined and marked on identity cards under the previous regime, and thus knew the family's presumed ethnic identity – a continuation of the previous state's ethnocultural map. Based on this knowledge he extrapolated her identity and understood her to be Hutu. However, those who grew up outside of Rwanda would not have had access to this kind of lived memory since they did not have day-to-day experience in a neighbourhood of Hutus and Tutsis. So, how would they have learned, upon first sight, who was Hutu and who was Tutsi?

Natalia, a young woman who had grown up in Canada, offered insight into how this kind of classification can be learned and inherited despite not encountering individuals from the ostensibly other ethnic group.

NATALIA: I can tell who's Rwandan. We just have these traits that I can identify. The forehead, the eyes, you know, the long face, the skin, the legs. There's just so many things. So I can tell what someone is. Sometimes it's hard. You don't know. When you go to those events, there's some people you meet and you're like – "You're a Rwandan?"

INTERVIEWER: Does that challenge your presumption of what it means to be Rwandan?

NATALIA: It does and no, because at the end of day, it's like you went to Somalia, or Ethiopia, which are the countries known to have a specific type. There's a look. You can just tell. So, once we tell.

INTERVIEWER: Really you're talking about Tutsis?

NATALIA: I am, I am, I don't know … that's what pisses me off, because I can't differentiate it. Of course, Hutus, we were brought up to think they were the shorter, darker, scruffier, everything feature wise, they were more wide.

INTERVIEWER: So you were taught that too?

NATALIA: Well, no, I wasn't, I just read it from the research. My mom would not talk about – my mom would not describe it. But my mom would be like, she saw one, she'd be like – "he is Hutu."

INTERVIEWER: So you had a visual image of what that means.

NATALIA: Yeah, but most of the people that I see, I could just … it's weird, it's interesting that you say that, I could, I know the differentiation between and Tutsi and a Hutu, but when I see a Rwandan, I just say they're Rwandan. I don't think there's a Hutu or there's a Tutsi – I think "Oh, there's a Rwandan, and I speak English." At the end of the day, there is something different about both people because of that.

What is interesting about Natalia's account is the degree to which she had been trained to see a physiological type, yet when she met people who were identified as Hutu, she often found that they did not match these presumed physiological characteristics. However, rather than lead her to question the existence of the type, she was "pissed off" *because* she "can't differentiate." Yet, she was simultaneously echoing the narrative of "we are all Rwandans." This cognitive dissonance seemed to be easily glossed over. Even as migrants from Rwanda taught their children the new ethnonational identity, they continued to inscribe ethnic differences onto individuals.

These ostensible "ethnic" differences dictated silences at social and community gatherings. Jean-Paul, a young man who survived the genocide as a child and had since migrated to Canada on his own, explained that when he socialized with his Rwandan friends, a group of young men who, like him, had migrated relatively recently, they shared the "happy memories." They discussed childhood memories (though not genocide narratives – "childhood" here means their early youth, before 1994), but the moment "someone wants to mix that with some political situation, about how things are going now, then we stop." They would share "information about what happens, but not the analysis, the whole thing."[40] They avoided offering their individual understandings and opinions of current politics in Rwanda because the group was mixed; it was made up of Hutus and Tutsis and the understanding was that ethnic identity would lead to conflicting interpretations of events, so, to keep ties, they created spheres of silence. The interaction came with the cost of carefully choreographed silences and omissions, as those who identified as Tutsis were sometimes aware of the power of the genocide narrative and the subsequent framing of all Tutsis as victims and all Hutus as perpetrators.

As an example of this tendency, Christophe, as a Tutsi, would not discuss anything to do with the genocide – the single greatest marker of Rwandanness in the contemporary moment – with his Hutu friends. He explained that "no matter what, that kid is going to know his ethnic affiliation" and when the frame was that "Hutus killed Tutsis," that Hutu friend may say that "I was not even born, I don't even know about these things."[41] So, to avoid alienating his friends, Christophe chose to keep the silences. He avoided imposing his presumed monopoly over truth, stemming from his ethnic identification, onto his friends. Yet he used that same power to establish himself as an expert who spoke publicly in schools about the genocide and whose interpretation of the events was inherently legitimate because he was a Tutsi, even as he echoed the state's narrative of the genocide.

In the GTA community, Tutsis were the dominant group in terms of both numbers and relative social power. They were perceived by most external audiences as the only victims and survivors of the genocide, which granted them latitude and a significant measure of social authority in the community. They also tended to be associated with the current governing regime, thus granting them institutional support and legitimacy. According to the Rwandan state's narratives, Hutus were always read as guilty, as murderers by association, and Tutsis were always read as innocent, as victims by association.[42] A number of Hutus were also allied with the regime, but their affiliation depended upon their full acceptance of the state's mythico-history, as the expulsion and exile of many Hutu members of the early post-genocide parliament indicated.[43] Tutsis likewise were not permitted to dissent, but they did not face the same risks as Hutus. As Fidèle explained, "In my position, it's safe what I do because I am a Tutsi and I am a genocide survivor, so I can't be genocide denier, because I'm survivor ... A Hutu can't be in my position – they can say anything to him, but they can't say anything to me."[44]

Many of those who identified as Tutsi perceived it to be their duty to police the boundaries of ethnicity and, when they encountered a Hutu passing as something else, for instance, Congolese, to expose them. Olivia, as a Tutsi woman who often encountered Rwandan newcomers in her professional capacity, took it upon herself to expose what she perceived to be a lie. She explained that when she met migrants from the Great Lakes region in Africa who claimed to be Congolese, for example, but carried Rwandan names and spoke Kinyarwanda, she confronted them with what she understood to be their deception: that they were in fact Rwandan Hutus. She acknowledged that some may have been choosing not to identify as Rwandan because they did not wish to carry the stigma of others' crimes, but she still understood their deception to be evidence of their guilt, if only by association. Yet, in the same conversation, Olivia maintained that in the community the terms "Hutu" and "Tutsi" were no longer used, as all saw themselves as Rwandan.[45]

Angelina also recounted deep-rooted tensions that she had observed within the community. In the years after the genocide, the local, largely Tutsi community in the GTA feared holding social events, because "if we bring this social gathering, who knows, some Hutu might just come and say 'I'm going to put a bomb here and kill all these people.'" The generalized fear of the other was difficult to overcome, but, twenty-odd years since the violence, it had abated. Most cited the sense of day-to-day safety that they experienced in Canada, as well as the rule of law that served to deter acts of violence. Nonetheless, individual fears remained and, as Angelina expressed, there were very many Tutsis in the community who "can't stand being with a Hutu, because they're still resenting that, they can't let go," and Hutus who weren't "sure whether you're going to accept them either, or whether you associate with them, even if they have nothing to do with the killing that happened in that country ... so they withdraw ... and they form their own group."[46]

Those who identified as Hutus faced social policing of boundaries and surveillance if they chose to remain part of the community. As Angelina explained, many chose to separate themselves and form their own social circles and groups where they could feel more at ease. Yet many others sought out the larger community and wished to collectively identify as Rwandese. Georges, a Hutu man who was studying in Europe during the time of the genocide (and thus is exempt from accusations of being directly involved but who might still be presumed "guilty" by ethnic association) and who lost close family members at the hands of the RPF, was one of those who desired to remain in the larger Rwandan community. Yet he was very aware of the dangers that he faced. He knew many others who had chosen not to connect because "especially Hutus who took refuge in Congo and then came here, it would be difficult. I know there's some good innocent people, they are here, I meet them ... They keep a low profile."[47] He was referring to the anxiety of being accused of being a perpetrator in the genocide, which had the power to destroy one's life, both in the confrontation with the legal system and through the damage to community bonds.

Despite external performances of unity, the "inherited" and actively propagated division between those who identified as Tutsis and those who identified as Hutus remained a deep divide within the community. Very many in the community were actively trying to come to terms with this divide and wanted to share a sense of identity and peoplehood with those whom they perceived as the other. But this desire was very often paired with fear and anxiety that remained too difficult to overcome. Yet others, while extolling a unified national Rwandan identity, actively worked to demarcate those who were Tutsi, and thus understood to be innocent, and those who were Hutu, and thus understood to be at least suspect, if not guilty. The desire to generate a shared sense of identity based on Rwandanness was particularly potent in light of the racialization that all members of this group faced in their new homeland, Canada.

Confronting Racialized Multiculturalism

As the Rwandan community in the GTA struggled with imposed and constructed narratives of identity and history, individuals were also subjected to racialization in the new homeland, even as they wanted to believe in the promise of multiculturalism. Although, according to Peter Li, multiculturalism as a federal state policy "remains obscure and the program content of multiculturalism is periodically modified," it is perceived as appealing because it signifies a perception of tolerance. As an ideology, among Canadians there is general perception that "it is a desirable idea" but no clarity about what it refers to or how it is enacted.[48] This very ambiguity also leaves space for individual interpretation. In conducting this study, I heard the participants in the study express numerous interpretations of Canadian multiculturalism. Even as multiculturalism framed them as the eternal other, those who identified as Rwandan in the GTA filled it with their own hopes and expectations for belonging.

Those who identify as Rwandan in the GTA are inheritors of a larger history of Black peoples' migration to this part of North America, which dates back more than four hundred years. The legacy of the slave trade and the outright racist policies of the Canadian state against Black people form a long history of oppression, confronted by resistance and resilience of Black Canadians.[49] After the 1967 immigration reform, which shifted away from the overtly racist quota system of immigration to an ostensibly non-racist system based on points accrued for specific skills, continental Africans began to migrate to Canada in increasing numbers.[50] The Rwandan diaspora is one of the new communities that have emerged since then.

Many participants spoke warmly and often uncritically of Canadian multiculturalism. Patrice juxtaposed Canadian multiculturalism to Rwandan monoculturalism as he explained that in Toronto he met "white people, Arab people, you know from other countries from Africa, and that's something also about Toronto, there's a lot of variety of people that you can meet. I meet all type of people, all type of ages. It is good, because I'm thinking I like that, I like new people." Patrice framed Canadian multiculturalism explicitly as encompassing a greater plurality than just ethnic diversity when he identified "all type of people, all type of ages." In his understanding, it was this very plurality that enabled him to feel safe, as he perceived that in Canada "difference" was not dangerous the way it had been in Rwanda. Indeed, he explained that the degree of plurality was protective, unlike in Rwanda where difference was cast as either Hutu or Tutsi and only those two ethnic identities were perceived as significant. Yet, even as he appreciated plurality, Patrice was aware of the tensions between ostensibly different "cultural" groups: "I work with different type of people and when we go out, we cannot go together, because when we are together, some people feel so isolated, on the side, because they don't like the music I listen to, or, they have different background, different life. When you live with them more, you enjoy with them, whenever you go out of work and share a drink, it's a problem."[51] Interestingly, he did not perceive the tensions between people of different ethnic backgrounds in terms of a clash of cultures, but rather in more quotidian terms, as divergent musical preferences, for example. Yet these fractures were significant enough that they caused tension and "problems," preventing a deeper interpersonal engagement with co-workers outside of work.

Like Patrice, Seraphine also identified plurality as a prominent and progressive feature of life in the GTA. She also contrasted this plurality to a monocultural society, when she stated, "I love other, like diversity of people, I don't like to be in one, uhh, because I value other people, I value other nations and we have uhh [pause] one of the good things with Canada is that it has diversity of people, it's multicultural, you meet people from other nations, whether you don't know them, but you get a chance to connect with them, knowing you, 'cause I love to know about other cultures."[52] The implicit contrast, stated in "I don't like to be in one" ("one" referring to one culture/ethnicity), is to the remembered homeland, which for Patrice and Seraphine was traumatic as they were both survivors of the genocide. Thus, for both of them, the plurality that they encountered was reassuring and comforting. In both their accounts, there lay the assumption that as long as they were one of many who were different, they would not be targeted as the group that is too different to be tolerated and be re-subjected to genocidal violence. This assumption ignores the genocidal history against Canada's Indigenous populations, but it is a comforting notion to those who survived genocide elsewhere.

Christophe also lauded Canadian multiculturalism as he explained that in his workplace he encountered individuals from a variety of nationalities. Thus, "in my department I'm from Rwanda, I have another colleague from Eritrea, I have another colleague from Pakistan, another is from India, another one is from Jamaica, I have another one is from Filipino, so that kind of stuff. You know we enjoy it, we have the same kind of connection, we respect each other. Yeah we live it every day ... Yeah, yeah so that that tells you how diverse Toronto is."[53] The absence in this litany of "diversity" was most striking to me – he did not mention any people from Europe, and all the ethnonational groups that he identified are racialized minorities in Canada. In this account of "diversity," whiteness is the background and norm against which Christophe and his colleagues' racialized difference played out. They were rendered different by virtue of non-belonging to the white majority group. This is actually an account of the manner in which racialization marks men and women who are understood as non-white as the visible externalized face of multiculturalism. It is also important to note that the workplace in question was a call centre, which is generally a low-wage, low-skill workplace. Thus, Christophe's account also demonstrates the degree to which the low-wage, low-skill service-sector industry in the GTA is staffed by racialized people.

The inherent contradiction of multiculturalism as both including all manner of ethnic difference and only marking racialized peoples from the so-called Third World may be one of the push factors for individuals choosing to engage with others who identify as Rwandese, despite the potential for trauma and rejection. It may be that in the GTA, Rwandan identity can be liberating from the restrictions and pathologies of racialization. Theodore perceived this lack of "open-minded[ness]," but he also saw it as his responsibility to challenge these closed systems of thought. He explained,

> But you know there are some people they are not uhh, I cannot call open-minded, they don't understand that the country of Canada is big, that people from all over the place, so that's why I have to explain myself. But someone who knows that this country belongs to everybody, like you came from Poland, I came from Africa, someone from India, together we build this country, so it doesn't matter where we are from, or the, the colour of your skin, you know? We build this country together, so you have to explain to them and you have to understand them, that's reality that people are facing.[54]

Interestingly, Theodore perceived that it was up to him, and other migrants like myself, to explain Canadian multiculturalism to those who are not "open-minded." He did not see it as a completed project that granted space and belonging to all new migrants but as an ongoing process necessitating patience and understanding on the part of the migrant. Rather than perceiving multiculturalism as having created space and understanding for him and his family, he understood it as his responsibility to inform the insiders, or, in other words, the keepers of the nation. While many in the study expressed disappointment with the incomplete welcome extended to them, Theodore was unfazed by it and happily took up the challenge of building and explaining the nation. This perspective stood in sharp contrast to Olivia's account of migrants exhausting themselves trying to "to go to school, to do this, to go to work, to make money and to contribute to society, but then you meet all the systemic barriers in terms of not being able to go to school because you don't have your immigration papers yet, and not being able to hold a job in your career because your diploma or credentials are not accepted here" – all obstacles that will be addressed later in the chapter.[55]

Reminders of Non-belonging: "What's Your Background?"

One of the most common means by which those who are racialized are reminded of their place outside the nation is through the ubiquitous query "What's your background?" Many participants in this study explained, with grim humour, the perennial sprouting of that pseudo-polite question and its very clear, though implicit, meaning:

> THEODORE: It's not like you, because what are they going to ask you when they see your name, but for me, if they sees me, they says, "ah, you're a Canadian, where are you from, where's your background"?
> INTERVIEWER: What's the difference?
> THEODORE: The difference in term of colour, people think because you are white, to be Canadian is normal. You see that's reality where we are coming from.[56]

Theodore's matter-of-fact explanation of the meaning of this question echoed what many others also understood to be the underlying message: you do not belong here *because* you are Black and therefore cannot be part of the Canadian nation. Revocata, facing this question, explained that she was not ashamed to explain her Rwandan origin but understood that the question meant that "even though I call myself Canadian, I am not treated like a Canadian."[57] To be Black in the GTA is to be perpetually framed as external to the nation's imagination of self; it is to be the eternal other that those who belong can mark and remind of her non-belonging. Theodosia argued that "Canada has its good own things to offer. But still, in Canada we don't belong. We are still immigrants. We don't belong." After over fifteen years of living in the GTA, she stated that she and others like her – implicitly, those who are likewise racialized – "are still immigrants."[58] Many, if not most, had attained citizenship status (and proudly proclaimed it), yet they remained framed as perpetual immigrants, because of their Blackness. As Rinaldo Walcott puts it, "the impossibility of imagining blackness as Canadian is continually evident even as nation-state policies like multiculturalism seek to signal otherwise."[59]

Racialization in the Host/Homeland

The reminders of Blackness as outlined above serve as a form of othering and situate the parameters of difference for Rwandans in Canada. These day-to-day, subtle practices are part of a broader set of practices of classification and identification of who belongs and who does not in Canadian society. Those who identify as Rwandan in the GTA are racialized as Black in a dominant white society. "Racialization" refers "to the process, and the structures that accompany such a process, that produce and construct the meaning of race." It classifies and marginalizes individual people but also refers to "specific traits and attributes as, for example, accent, diet, name, beliefs and practices, and places of origin," which are interpreted as "abnormal and of less worth" than those of the dominant culture.[60] The other side of racism, often obscured, is the privilege that the dominant group exercises precisely because it is able to dominate other groups. Thus, in Canada, whiteness has been read as normative and those who are racialized as white are granted privilege.[61] In contrast, those who are racialized as other are subject to scrutiny, surveillance, overattention, avoidance, marginalization, and neglect.

Those who identify as Rwandan were racialized as Black, which in the GTA carried specific assumptions about criminality, immorality, vulgarity, loudness, and visibility.[62] They are also racialized as Black African, which was associated with primitivism, violence, tribalism, and a general backwardness.[63] These cognitive frames pre-dated the Rwandan community in the GTA, yet those who were part of this community found themselves read, measured, and, often, believed to be lacking, according to those stereotypes. Men, women, youth, and children, though subject to the same ideas about who they are based on how they look, experienced racialization in gendered and age-specific ways. Both young and older men were assumed to be criminals, but the manner in which this assumption played out differed. Older men spoke of being the subject of covert, nervous glances, white hands tightening on purses, security guards or police following them, unmerited police stops, and the day-to-day undermining of their authority in workplaces. Richard recalled vividly the experiences of "you walk in the elevator ... women – they shrink away from you and clutch their purse," people on the streetcar intentionally bumping into him and referring to him as "one of those," being detained at a shopping mall on accusations of theft, and many other day-to-day incidences of overt racism.[64] Young men discussed being perceived to be "Black youth" and thus subject to police surveillance, as well as to overt and coercive performances of dominance from figures of authority, like school principals. Mathieu recalled that during his adolescent years "I was really connected with fellow Black students. So I know, a lot of times, the way I would dress, the way I spoke, when we were together, we went around together, and a lot of times there was somewhat of a negative perception by authorities ... I remember getting questioned a few times by police, never for really doing anything."[65]

Compared with their male partners, brothers, and sons, women were less likely to be assumed to be criminal, but they faced sexualization, surveillance, oversight, and disregard. Women discussed being ignored in classrooms, being overlooked for placement or promotions in workplaces, and having their sexuality surveilled, commented upon, and judged. Marie faced the assumption that "you like to have children" – thinly veiled code implying that Black women are more likely to have multiple children with multiple partners.[66] Angelina was commonly asked by her employers, "How come you don't behave like a Jamaican?" and when she pressed and asked her boss why he had asked her this question, he replied that she had "a different demeanor." She understood this to mean not only that she did not fit narratives about "louder" and "vocally aggressive" Black women but that she was in a stable marriage.[67] Thus, in her workplace, rather than be judged on her merit as a worker, she was assessed for her conformity or nonconformity to racist scripts about behaviour and sexual patterns. She was then lauded and appreciated for *not* acting "Jamaican," which is a stand-in for "Black," suggesting the depth of racism in the workplace.

Parents often spoke of their fears and anxieties about their children's place in the new homeland based on the stories and experiences their children brought home. Olivia discussed her son's experience of racialization thus:

> I remember and experience where my son, my middle son, he was what, maybe 5, or 6? He went to school, in the class there was no other Black kids, and uh, the kids were never exposed they come from rural area of [city of residence], they, they were never exposed to colour and they would touch him thinking he's dirty. They would say "If you wash yourself really well, would the dark come off?" [chuckles, a bit bitterly] and he came home very, and he says "Mom, these kids are so ignorant." He was only 5 or 6. But he did not take it personally, he says "They touch my hair, they touch my skin, and they think I don't shower." And I says, "How did you react to that," and he says well, "They're just ignorant, they don't know." I said, "You can't blame them, they've never been exposed," so they, so they overcame.[68]

The children in the classroom, implicitly called parochial by Olivia, exhibited simultaneous desire and repulsion; they were drawn to her son, needed to touch him, yet presumed his colour to be dirt and imagined that if he bathed, he would look more like them. They were enacting, on the small stage of a kindergarten classroom, the drama of the colonizer and colonized, the drama of the Black body seen, perceived, known, and rejected through the eyes and touch of whiteness. Yet Olivia was insistent that neither she nor her son "blame" the children, as the children were merely "ignorant" rather than well versed in racial mythology that places Blackness hierarchically below whiteness.

Olivia's insistence is also interesting in light of the fact that while rural Ontario remains largely white, it is not a space without Blackness, in that media and popular culture inform these spaces with larger racist mythologies and narratives. Olivia's insistence on the need to educate and "expose" the kindergarten class to her son's difference must be read as her desire/need to not be read as a victim of racism. Though she was well aware of racism and had many other stories to tell, each narration emphasized that the source of these incidences was ignorance, not hate. Yet she was clearly harmed by the events and worried over her children's ability to cope and have full lives in a white-dominated society. As she explained, her other children had also faced racism in the classroom: one had been called the n-word after a lesson on the harm that the word carries, and her other child had faced daily belittlement of her surname. All three incidences were narrated as moments, as passing phases, rather than as evidence of pervasive racist mythology built upon the assumption of a white nation. Possibly, Olivia chose to interpret these as moments so as to be able to continue to function in her communities and retain her own sense of self-worth. This surveilling of her identity may also be one of the reasons that she polices the identity of those she perceives as hiding their Hutu past, as discussed earlier. Yet, the toll of confronting these mythologies was evident as Olivia recognized that "we always have to work harder, justify ourselves, confirm ourselves, try to just be accepted, because people judge you before they even see."[69]

Richard tried to protect his children by teaching them that "you should be proud of who you are – it will never change, it will never change you being a Canadian, however, you should be proud of your complexion, you should proud of your hair."[70] His attempt to broaden the narrative of who is "Canadian" to include his Black children is the only remedy he has available to shield them, yet it is an ineffectual rebuff when in nearly all other social interactions his children are reminded that they are different and that their difference, their Blackness, their "nappy" hair, are outside the nation's narration of self and they are framed as external to normalized whiteness. Perhaps the perpetual outsider status in the new homeland fuels the desire for a connection to Rwandanness as a protective space, insulating Richard and his family.

One participant joked that he preferred the racism of the 1980s and '90s because it was more explicit and he knew how to respond to it, while now he worries that his reading of a situation is subjective and someone else would not think he was being racialized.[71] This anxiety over the interpretation of an event was a common theme; a number of participants, when asked if they had experienced discrimination, hedged that they had, but could not directly explain how, and seemed to fear that I, as a white listener and therefore a beneficiary of white privilege, would not believe them because they could not point to a clear event or moment. Bernard explained that "it's not open. It's not direct because of laws, it's not like in other countries, but, people are not free of discrimination. You can see by, by action, you can see it, by the way they talk, or the action, but it's not open. Not like in other countries, like in Europe, here it's there, but ..."[72] The subtlety of racism has the secondary effect of making its victims feel that they are imagining the event and that they are exaggerating. Thus, not only are they harmed by the instance of racism, but they are also then doubly harmed by being led to question whether they imagined the event and thus unable to address it.

Accent Discrimination

One of the socially acceptable forms of pointing out someone's difference in the GTA is to comment on their non-regional accent. This too is a form of racialization as it serves to denote that that person with the purported accent does not belong and needs to be reminded of this. This admonition serves to remind not only of non-belonging but of the hierarchically lower position of the speaker. As Gillian Creese argues, persons with accents are "perceived to be less competent (or, indeed, incompetent) and have more difficulty being heard or having speech taken seriously." Similar to Creese's argument regarding the experiences of Africans in Vancouver, the ability to speak English in the GTA is a form of social capital and "Native speakers in predominantly White English-speaking nations remain its privileged purveyors" and possess the power to "define legitimate forms of knowledge or expression." This power is enacted in "practices of misrecognition, trivialization, and the 'refusal to hear' non-standard accents," which are "everyday forms of linguistic domination" and systematically deny the racialized minority upward mobility.[73]

Many in the study spoke fluent French if they had completed secondary school in pre-1994 Rwanda or had lived in the Democratic Republic of Congo or Burundi. Those who had lived in Kenya, Tanzania, or Uganda usually spoke English upon arrival. There were also some who lacked linguistic capital in either official language but possessed unrecognized linguistic skills, as many spoke at least two African languages, such as Swahili and, of course, Kinyarwanda. Given the time of migration of most in this study – the late 1980s or early 1990s – those who spoke

French often found work relatively quickly, predominantly in customer service. Yet, many others struggled to find employment as a result of accent discrimination, and even those who did find employment were disciplined for their accents, by, for instance, having customers demand to speak to "someone who speaks better English."[74] Among the participants in the study, it was predominantly women who spoke of being disciplined for having a non-standard accent. That few men mentioned this suggests that their greater social power relative to Rwandan women protected them somewhat from this form of othering. Seraphine recalled that "it was tough to get a job, very very tough. Like, you, the, the, minute you go for the interview, they hear the accent ... It was a big barrier. A big one. I think I lost like how many jobs ... and they are very polite, they tell you, 'oh thank you, we will call you if something comes up' and right then I knew there was no job for me."[75] This systematic denial of access to employment because of a non-Western accent contributes to the economic marginalization of new migrants.

Theodosia recalled that even though she found work in customer service and thus was able to contribute to her family's economic well-being, she still faced regular discrimination:

> I used to be [a] customer service agent on the phone. When I speak with the Canadian people, people who speak Canadian English, they would say, "Oh, you have an accent." I said, "Yeah, thank you, I know that, how can I help you?" You know? You move on, you know? And, sometimes when I speak to them, they say, "Oh, can I speak to someone who speaks better English." And then the question is – is it better English you are looking for, or you are looking for someone who can service your needs? Right? So there you get hassled. But hey, you get to live with it and you bypass it. I still do have an accent for sure, but I don't need to be told because I know.[76]

The perpetual reminder of Theodosia's accent was another racial code signifying, effectively, "Ohh, you're Black." It serves no other purpose than to signal to the speaker that the listener is aware of the speaker's presumed difference and presumed inferior status.

"Blacking Yourself"

An interesting reading of day-to-day racialization comes from Simon, who described working in a "completely white" town where "knowing that I was from Africa, it was like everyone wanted a small piece of me – to touch me, to talk to me."[77] In this experience, which he recalled fondly and shared with me in order to demonstrate that he had experienced moments where he was prized for his difference, Simon was *desirable* for his Blackness. He was valued not because he was competent at his job but *because he was a Black man* doing the job. While he recalled this warmly, it too was an example of racialization. And, though Simon did not perceive it as harmful, it still served to underscore his difference based only on his physical traits. In a way, he internalized this racialization, explaining that

> the discrimination might be there, but at the same time, the only way for me, the only way I see to be successful, is to avoid discriminating yourself. When you start seeing others as different, you behave in a way that you Black yourself and you don't reach out, you don't open yourself to others, and I can see, even within the community, there's people who have been here for so many years, but they're always by themselves.[78]

His reading of "Black[ing] yourself" puts the onus on the person who is being racialized to not only pretend not to see the racialization but also not be affected by it. Thus, Simon criticized those who "don't reach out," "don't open yourself to others," as, in effect, causing their own isolation and marginalization. This criticism, which I also heard from others, points to a troubling dynamic whereby community members buy into narratives about the decline of racism and racialization and then, if someone points it out its continuance, are presumed to be "Black[ing]" themselves. This idea of "Black[ing]" oneself is interesting as it suggests both the understanding that Blackness is constructed through day-to-day practices and the negative association with African Americans and others of African descent. This flip in agency is damaging as it proposes that those who are systematically denied access are themselves to blame for this denial. It also silences those who speak out against racialization, thus denying them the power to name their experience and offer a potent critique of Canadian society. Yet, given the traumatic history of politicized ethnicity contributing to genocide, it may not be surprising that Simon sought commonality and rejected the idea of difference. He knew intimately the cost of extrapolating and politicizing difference in ways that are not comprehensible to those of us who have not experienced genocide.

In each of the above illustrations of racialization, the individuals framed and proscribed by racist myths refused to comply and found sites of resistance. In doing so, they not only practised their agency but also produced counternarratives that worked to call into question the racist mythologies of the Canadian multicultural state. In their day-to-day interactions they sought to chip away at the edifice of difference and create new spaces where alternate visions of self and other could exist and where individuals and families could thrive.

To be part of the Rwandan diaspora in the GTA is to be subject to didactic and often oppressive narratives from the Rwandan state about who belongs and on what terms, even as one is haunted by genocide. It means navigating the politically and personally fraught terrain of ethnic affiliation even as the ethnic identities of Hutu and Tutsi are erased from public discourse. Yet it also means to confront racialization as Black, and therefore other, in the Canadian body politic. Nonetheless, many of those who seek belonging in the community of Rwandans in the GTA hold out hope for the healing of trauma and a community that includes all who identify as Rwandan, despite their personal and political history. They also hold out hope for a multiculturalism that is not premised upon white privilege but rooted in the idea of many cultures, together, shaping our communities.

NOTES

1 Rogers Brubaker, *Ethnicity without Groups* (Cambridge, MA: Harvard University Press, 2006), 11.
2 Gérard Prunier, *The Rwanda Crisis: History of a Genocide* (London: Hurst, 1995), 64–7.
3 Mahmood Mamdani, *When Victims Become Killers: Colonialism, Nativism, and the Genocide in Rwanda* (Princeton: Princeton University Press, 2001), 159–85.
4 Mathieu, interview by the author (transcript), 19 July 2013, coffee shop.
5 The Rwandan Patriotic Front was the Ugandan-based rebel militia that would invade Rwanda and eventually stop the genocide to then become the basis for the contemporary Rwandan state.
6 Prunier, *Rwanda Crisis*, 73–91; Simon (interview transcript), 31 July 2013, participant's home.
7 Simon, interview by the author (transcript), 31 July 2103, participant's home.
8 Statistics Canada, "Ethnic Origins, 2006 Counts, for Canada, Provinces and Territories – 20% sample data," accessed 21 January 2014; Statistics Canada, "Topic-Based Tabulation: Ethnic Origin (232), Sex (3) and Single and Multiple Responses (3) for Population, for Canada, Provinces, Territories, Census Metropolitan Areas and Census Agglomerations, 1996 Census – 20% Sample Data," accessed 21 January 2014.
9 Simon, interview transcript.
10 Janvier, interview by the author (transcript), 13 June 2012, mall cafeteria.
11 Simon, interview transcript.
12 Janvier, interview transcript; Simon, interview transcript.
13 Mathieu, interview transcript.

14 Natalia, interview by the author (transcript), 7 May 2013, coffee shop.
15 For a broader discussion of Rwandan women in the GTA diaspora, please see Ainsworth, "The Cracks and the Crevices: Rwandan Women in the Diaspora," in *Africa in the Age of Globalisation: Perceptions, Misperceptions and Realities*, ed. Edward Shizha and Lamine Diallo (London: Routledge, 2015), 171–84.
16 Fidele, interview by the author (transcript), 17 October 2013, restaurant.
17 Brubaker, *Ethnicity without Groups*, 12.
18 "Rwandan Diaspora Global Network," Republic of Rwanda, accessed 13 March 2014 (site discontinued).
19 "Rwandan Diaspora Global Network."
20 The participants in this study used "Rwandan" and "Rwandese" interchangeably.
21 Mathieu, interview transcript.
22 Statistics Canada, "Ethnic Origins, 2011 Counts, for Canada, Provinces and Territories – 20% sample data," accessed 21 January 2014.
23 "Returnees," UNHCR Rwanda, last modified 2018, http://www.unhcr.org/rw/returnees.
24 "Immigrate to Canada," Citizenship and Immigration Canada, accessed March 2014, http://www.cic.gc.ca/enGlIsH/immigrate/index.asp.
25 Jean-Paul, interview by the author (transcript), 23 May 2012, restaurant.
26 For an extended discussion of the new Rwandan state, see Mahmood Mamdani, *When Victims Become Killers: Colonialism, Nativism, and the Genocide in Rwanda* (Princeton: Princeton University Press, 2001); and Jennie E. Burnet, *Genocide Lives in Us: Women, Memory and Silence in Rwanda* (Madison: University of Wisconsin Press, 2012).
27 Grace, interview by the author (transcript), 25 August 2012, church.
28 Arlene Stein, "Trauma Stories, Identity Work, and the Politics of Recognition," in *Sociology Confronts the Holocaust: Memories and Identities in Jewish Diasporas*, ed. Judith M. Gerson and Diane L. Wolf (Durham: Duke University Press, 2007), 87.
29 Burnet, *Genocide Lives in Us*.
30 Burnet, 92.
31 Fidèle, interview transcript.
32 "Let's Commemorate the Genocide against the Tutsi as We Strive for Self-Reliance," pamphlet, 19th Genocide Commemoration, Ryerson University, Toronto, 2013.
33 Peter Erlinder, "'Genocide Denial' in Rwanda, Questioning the Official History" (unpublished paper, Centre for Research on Globalization, 2014).
34 Georges, interview by the author (transcript), November 7, 2013, coffee shop.
35 Janvier, interview transcript.
36 Burnet, *Genocide Lives in Us*, 155.

37 "Transcript of President Kagame's Interview with Al Jazeera's Riz Khan," 28 January 2011, Office of the President, accessed 29 June 2021, https://www.paulkagame.com/transcript-of-president-kagames-interview-with-aljazeeras-riz-khan-26812036/.
38 Fidèle, interview transcript.
39 Simon, interview transcript.
40 Jean-Paul, interview transcript.
41 Christophe, interview by the author (transcript), 30 June 2012, restaurant.
42 Mamdani, *When Victims Become Killers*; Burnet, *Genocide Lives in Us*; Danielle Beswick, "Managing Dissent in a Post-Genocide Environment: The Challenge of Political Space in Rwanda," *Development and Change* 41, no. 2 (2010): 225–51.
43 Filip Reyntjens, "Rwanda, Ten Years On: From Genocide to Dictatorship," *African Affairs* 103 (2004): 180–2.
44 Fidèle, interview transcript.
45 Olivia, interview by the author (transcript), 6 May 2013, her vehicle.
46 Angelina, interview by the author (transcript), 20 January 2013, coffee shop.
47 Georges, interview transcript.
48 Peter S. Li, "The Multiculturalism Debate." in *Race and Ethnic Relations in Canada*, ed. Peter S. Li (Don Mills, ON: Oxford University Press, 1999), 149, 164.
49 Puplampu and Tettey, "Ethnicity and the Identity of African-Canadians," 33–4.
50 Ali A. Abdi, "Reflections on the Long Struggle for Inclusion: The Experiences of People of African Origin," in Tettey and Puplampu, *African Diaspora in Canada*, 25–48.
51 Patrice, interview by the author (transcript), 23 March 2013, coffee shop.
52 Seraphine, interview by the author (transcript), 21 October 2012, church meeting room.
53 Christophe, interview transcript.
54 Theodore, interview by the author (transcript), 28 October 2012, church meeting room.
55 Theodore, interview transcript.
56 Theodore, interview transcript.
57 Revocata, interview by the author (transcript), 10 March 2012, by phone.
58 Revocata, interview transcript.
59 Rinaldo Walcott, *Black Like Who? Writing Black Canada* (Toronto: Insomniac, 2003), 48.
60 Vijay Agnew, "Introduction," in *Racialized Migrant Women in Canada: Essays on Health, Violence and Equity*, ed. Vijay Agnew (Toronto: University of Toronto Press, 2009), 8.
61 Camille A. Nelson and Charmaine A. Nelson, "Introduction," in *Racism, Eh? A Critical Inter-disciplinary Anthology of Race and Racism in Canada*, ed. Camille A. Nelson and Charmaine A. Nelson (Concord: Captus, 2004), 3.

62 Frances Henry, *The Caribbean Diaspora in Toronto: Learning to Live with Racism* (Toronto: University of Toronto Press, 1994).
63 V.Y. Mudimbe, *The Invention of Africa: Gnosis, Philosophy and the Order of Knowledge* (Bloomington: Indiana University Press, 1988).
64 Richard, interview by the author (transcript), 29 June 2013, participant's home.
65 Mathieu, interview transcript.
66 Marie, interview by the author (transcript), 13 August 2012, coffee shop.
67 Angelina, interview transcript.
68 Olivia, interview transcript.
69 Olivia, interview transcript.
70 Richard, interview transcript.
71 Richard, interview transcript.
72 Bernard, interview by the author (transcript), 3 September 2013, coffee shop.
73 Gillian Creese, *The New African Diaspora in Vancouver: Migration, Exclusion and Belonging* (Toronto: University of Toronto Press, 2011), 34, 35, 36.
74 Theodosia, interview by the author (transcript), 17 February 2013, church meeting room.
75 Seraphine, interview transcript.
76 Theodosia, interview transcript.
77 Simon, interview transcript.
78 Simon, interview transcript.

SECTION SEVEN

Locating Historical Black Presences in Cultural Artefacts

16
Race, Community, and the Picturing of Identities: Photography and the Black Subject in Ontario, 1860–1900

CHERYL THOMPSON AND JULIE CROOKS

In May 2017, I (Julie Crooks) curated a photographic exhibit at the Art Gallery of Ontario (AGO) called "*Free* Black North." The exhibit featured twenty-seven tintype photographic portraits of African Canadians – men, women, and children – who lived in southwestern Ontario (then called Canada West) in the mid-to-late nineteenth century. Many of the sitters were descendants of African Americans who, after fleeing the United States, established communities in Canada West. Although they had migrated to areas across the region, these newly arrived "freedom seekers" mostly settled in cities and towns near the Canada-US border such as Amherstburg, Windsor, St. Catharines, Chatham/Buxton, Toronto, and London.

The photographs in the AGO's exhibit spanned the 1860s through the 1890s, a period that is significant for several reasons. First, as Marcus Wood observes, because of the comparatively recent dates of slavery abolition in the United States (1865) and across the British colonies (1834), many photographs recording the process and experiences of emancipation – daguerreotypes, glass negatives, albumen prints, tintypes, and *cartes de visite* (all different types of photographic processes) – constituted "a wholly new and different emancipation archive from that which went before."[1] When we think of the visual culture of slavery, most people envision either the archetype of slaves working on cotton plantations in the American South or sugar plantations in the Caribbean or the fugitive slave following the "North Star" to Canada, an iconographic depiction of Black men and women post-1850. Second, there are very few visual representations of Black people in nineteenth-century Canada sitting for photographs in their "Sunday best." Photographic historian Deborah Willis once observed that between 1840 and 1900, African American photographers produced "idealized glimpses of family members set in romanticized or dramatic poses. Photographers sought to integrate elements of romanticism and classicism into their work, echoing the work of painters in the eighteenth century." Most of these early photographs, she writes further, were taken to commemorate a special occasion in the sitter's life, such as birth, confirmation, graduation, courtship, marriage, military service, anniversaries, death, or some social or political success.[2] Shawn Michelle Smith observes that "men, women, and children usually wore their best street garments for nineteenth-century photographic portraits, often including hats, coats, and shawls, as incongruous as such articles might seem within an interior parlor setting"; however, there are few such depictions of African Canadians.[3] Thus, nineteenth-century photographs of Black subjects require contemporary readers to understand not just the cultural import of their existence but also the sociocultural milieu in which they were created.

The period from the 1860s through the 1890s was marked by the widespread circulation of racial caricatures and debased images of Black women, men, and children not only in art but also in commodity advertising, scientific literature, and theatrical minstrel shows.[4] And in Canada West, in particular, while there is a mythology applied to the region that it accepted all its African American residents with open arms, and that it was the friendly terminus of the "Underground Railroad," there was deeply rooted anti-Black prejudice in communities along the Detroit and Niagara Rivers. Thus, the approximately thirty photographs in "*Free Black North*" were not just "glimpses" into the past; they were displays of resistance and illustrative of the power of images in reshaping one's sense of self amid a sociocultural milieu that was prohibitive to Black self-expression. As bell hooks observes, "In the world before racial integration, there was a constant struggle on the part of black folks to create a counter-hegemonic world of images that would stand as visual resistance, challenging racist images."[5] The question this chapter aims to explore, then, is this: What do nineteenth-century photographs of Black Ontarians, taken at professional studios, tell us about Black agency and resistance? By analysing these photographs, how might we begin to articulate the ways in which Black people saw themselves, how others might have seen them, and the dialectical relationship between viewer and subject in nineteenth-century photography?

In *The Cultural Work of Photography in Canada* (2011), a collection on photography in Canada, great emphasis is placed on photographs of immigrants from the early twentieth century, frontier photography, and Indigenous perspectives on photography, but little is said of African Canadians.[6] In "Imaged Communities: Putting Canadian Photographic History in its Place" (2015) – a sixty-page journal article co-written by six members of Canadian Photography History/Histoire de la photographie canadienne (CPH/HPC), a research team based at Concordia University in Montreal – there are no mentions of African Canadian photographers, sitters, or images. In the article's introduction, Martha Langford writes, "We seek to demonstrate that the writing of Canadian photography history is a matter of recognition, interpretation, and expansion on the great variety of documents that already exist, and we further affirm that each of these documents needs to be understood in relation to contemporaneous displays of photographic knowledge."[7] In this chapter, we similarly seek to demonstrate that Black subjects deserve recognition, interpretation, and expansion inasmuch as they have historically been ignored in the Canadian visual cultural record. By the vast number of photographic images culled from collections at Brock University and the Archives of Ontario for the "*Free* Black North" exhibit, we know that Black people had their photographs taken in Ontario, many during and after Confederation, and yet there is a consistent pattern of ignoring African Canadians, not only in visual culture histories but also in Canada's national history. Our analysis considers the ways in which Black women and men self-represented through photography – the way they dressed, wore their hair, and appeared "fashionable." We also interrogate the role of gender in representation. These images reveal plenty about both the sociocultural milieu of nineteenth-century Canada and the strategies that Black women subjects used to self-fashion and self-style through images.

European contact with Africans, and the subsequent conquest and control of the Black body through transatlantic slavery, irrevocably changed the course of modern history. In the context of the Atlantic World, racial distinctions based on supposed truths of colour and blood were made and confirmed in slavery; as a result, Blackness, as Nadine Ehlers asserts, "became synonymous with servitude and whiteness with freedom." Those who possessed the phenotypic markers of White skin, straight hair, an aquiline nose, and thin lips were typologized as "Caucasian" and in opposition to those possessing "black skin-pigment, 'woolly' hair ... [and] thick lips," who were identified as part of the "Negroid race."[8] The bodily distinctions in hair, skin colour, and phenotype between Black and White women gained intrinsic meaning in the institution of slavery, and in the post-slavery decades of the nineteenth-century photographic images became an outlet for Black people to construct a sense of self that contradicted the image of Blackness (i.e., that of slave) that circulated within the dominant Western visual culture. In the 1850s, for example, Dr. Robert W. Gibbes, a nationally recognized US palaeontologist, hired local daguerreotypist Joseph T. Zealy to make photographic records of first- and second-generation slaves on plantations near Columbia, South

Carolina, for Swiss-born Louis Agassiz, the natural scientist and zoologist from Harvard University. Using the frontal/profile combination that was first used in ethnographic photography, Zealy documented Black slave women and men in half- and full-length views stripped to the waist or, in the case of some of the men, totally naked. The result was a denial both of Black women's (and men's) humanity and of their control over the representation of their bodies, thereby removing all agency and power from their naked bodies.[9]

This chapter responds to these historical legacies and aims to bring the photographic images of African Canadians into plain sight; we aim to elucidate the counterhegemonic world of images created by Black women and men who lived across southwestern Ontario in the mid-to-late nineteenth century. In the first instance, we will engage with histories of the "Underground Railroad" and African Americans escaping enslavement in the United States to find their "freedom" in Canada. In the second instance, this chapter outlines the system of meaning in the visual repertoire of these "freedom seekers" as symbolized in their photographic images.

Photography allowed people of African descent to self-represent and to reimagine themselves in the absence of a visual culture that celebrated who they were, but these images also raise important questions about the breadth and parameters of freedom in the nineteenth century. To date, cultural historiographies of the African Canadian experience have scarcely explored the role of photography, not only in the emancipatory act of embodying freedom but also as a mirror onto which communities were reflected and formed and the African Canadian body was reimagined, reinscribed, and reinvented amid a sociocultural milieu where theories of scientific racism, commodity stereotypes, and blackface minstrel ephemera circulated widely. African American and Caribbean scholars of slavery, including Tina Campt, Sylvia Wynter, Hortense Spillers, and Saidiya Hartman, have argued that by re-inscribing the meaning of "Black" as *fugitive* and *captive* rather than as *slave* of the Americas, it allows for the ambiguities of the terms "captivity" and "fugitivity" to complicate our understanding of "freedom" and, in the case of this book, the "North," as a geographic space connotatively demarcated as morally superior to its geographic other, the "South." As Campt writes, "photography plays a critical role in articulating Black people's complex relationship to cultural identity and national belonging ... The photographic image has played a dual role in rendering the history of African diasporic communities, because of its ability to document and simultaneously pathologize the history, culture, and struggles of these communities."[10]

Slave Laws, Abolition, and African American Settlement in Canada West

In 1791, New France was renamed Lower Canada (Quebec), and Upper Canada (Ontario) was given its official name. A year before this division, the British Parliament passed a law allowing Loyalists and other potential Canadian residents to bring their slaves with them as long as they had the permission of the lieutenant governor.[11] The signing of the Treaty of Paris in 1763 introduced British laws and institutions in Lower Canada, and as the implementation of those laws and institutions spread into Upper Canada, there were multiple stages of its success. After Upper and Lower Canada were divided, and John Graves Simcoe was appointed the first lieutenant governor of Upper Canada, his first legislative piece of business was to move the capital of Upper Canada from Newark (Niagara-on-the-Lake) to York (Toronto) on the northern shore of Lake Ontario. It is interesting to note that one of the first "Lists of Inhabitants" of York, which included the townships of Scarborough and Etobicoke, provided a count of those who were Black but did not distinguish between slaves and free people.[12] When an enslaved Black woman named Chloe Cooley was observed being forced, bound and gagged, into a boat near Queenston, on the shores of Lake Erie, it was reported to Simcoe because of his known opposition to slavery. The incident is often thought to be the driving force behind Canada's first and only anti-slavery law.[13]

In 1793, Lord Graves passed *An Act to Prevent the Further Introduction of Slaves, and to Limit the Terms of Contracts for Servitude within This Province.* As a gradual abolition bill, the legislation did not end slavery outright; it maintained existing slaveholder property rights, while stipulating that the children of slaves would be considered free after the age of twenty-five, and their own children would be considered legally born free. Officially passed on 9 July 1793, the law made slaveholding unattractive because slave owners were wholly responsible, without much benefit to themselves, for the welfare and upkeep of two generations of slave offspring.[14] That same year, the United States passed its first Fugitive Slave Law, which tightened the parameters of slavery by stipulating that slave owners had a right to recover their slaves in any state, and that states had the right to apprehend fugitive slaves and return them to their owners. This law essentially made it a crime to assist a fugitive slave, and those who were caught doing so anywhere in the United States faced prosecution. After 1793, even free Blacks living in northern states, like New York, Pennsylvania, Illinois, Delaware, Ohio, and Michigan, could be captured and sold into slavery, even if they had been born free. As Sharon Hepburn explains, "one long-term result of these two historic laws of 1793 was that fugitive blacks, fearing recapture in the northern states, sought freedom in Canada."[15] The perception of Canada as a safe haven originated with these two opposing laws; at the same time, most historians ignore the draconian laws of the northern states that created push factors that forced many African Americans to head into Canada in the first place.

Using a variety of legal measures, states in the "Old Northwest" – particularly Ohio, Indiana, and Illinois – enacted "Black Codes" that deprived African American residents of their legal and civil rights, with the dual purpose of discouraging free and fugitive Blacks from the South from settling in their states and encouraging them to also leave. These "Black Codes" barred African Americans from gaining full citizenship rights with regard to immigration, residency, suffrage, militia service, education, jury duty, and testimony in court. As Hepburn explains further, "Such laws, designed to reserve those states for whites, compelled blacks seeking legal residence to meet onerous requirements ... Regardless of their enforcement, however, these laws remained on the books, representing a constant threat to the black population and a reminder of the dominance of white society."[16] Beyond that of Canada as a terminus on the "Underground Railroad," the other mythology around African Americans who fled north is that they were arriving from the Deep South, a region otherwise known as "Dixie," which included 11 Confederate States that had succeeded from the Union during the US Civil War: South Carolina, Mississippi, Florida, Alabama, Georgia, Louisiana, Texas, Virginia, Arkansas, North Carolina, and Tennessee. On the contrary, most fugitive slaves who entered Canada arrived from Michigan, Delaware, Maryland, Ohio, and Kentucky.[17] The North created an environment that became increasingly less inhabitable for African Americans through the first decades of the nineteenth century, which explains why "freedom seekers" comprised those who were "fugitive slaves" (having fled a plantation in the South), those who had become "free" (either by purchasing their freedom or through self-emancipation), and those who were "free-born" (had been born in the North and were never enslaved).

In 1850, the United States passed a second Fugitive Slave Law, designed to strengthen the earlier 1793 law. This new law vastly extended the powers of the US federal government by setting up machinery to assist in the return of fugitive slaves, regardless of the state laws. Before and after slavery was abolished throughout the British Empire in 1834, and with the passage of the 1850 Slave Law, thousands of fugitive slaves arrived in Canada, either alone or through the routes of the "Underground Railroad." As a result of this migration, Canada garnered its reputation as the "promised land." Some historians estimate that by 1860, one hundred thousand slaves had escaped to freedom in the North and about thirty thousand of those had found it in Canada.[18] The 1850 Fugitive Slave Law and the new generation of slave catchers it spawned sent a wave of fear through northern cities, where many African Americans had been living peaceful lives in their first or second generation of freedom. Almost all at once, the slow but steady migration across the Canadian border became a flood, and within weeks of the law's passage cities like Baltimore reported a problem in staffing hotels: all the Black waiters and porters had gone to Canada. Black churches in Buffalo and Rochester also complained that their congregations had nearly all fled.[19] Amid this sociocultural milieu, the cities and towns across Canada, the United States, and Britain became saturated with novels, theatrical performances, and scientific theories that all aimed to affirm the inferiority of Black people, even as some (like abolitionists, many of whom were Quakers and Methodists) abhorred the institution of slavery.

In the early nineteenth century, biological racialists, including phrenologists, craniologists, physiognomists, anthropometrists, ethnologists, polygenesists, and Egyptologists, worked to establish innate biological differences between Whites and Blacks. Contrary to the eighteenth-century race theorists who preceded them, and who had generally attributed racial distinctions to environmental conditions, this new breed of scientists were particularly eager not only to establish differences between the races but also to "prove" the moral and intellectual superiority of the Anglo-Saxon race.[20] Nineteenth-century scientists even went so far as to disseminate theories to prove that "the Negro's head was covered with wool rather than hair."[21] Significantly, British scientist Francis Galton, cousin of Charles Darwin, often proclaimed that Anglo-Saxons represented "a modern racial pinnacle to which those of African descent would never rise."[22] Nineteenth-century travellers and missionaries also viewed women's beauty as a function of race, "and because appearance and character were considered to be commensurate, the beauty of white skin expressed Anglo-Saxon virtue and civilization – and justified white supremacy in a period of American expansion."[23] Black women's bodies were thus positioned as non-virtuous and viewed through a prism of absence – of civility, beauty, and refinement.

Commodity racism, as Anne McClintock observes, "became distinct from scientific racism in its capacity to expand beyond the literate, propertied elite through the marketing of commodity spectacle." One of the consequences of centuries of colonial domination was that Whiteness functioned as both spectacle and desire in capitalist production. McClintock asserts that in the manufacture of soap, which had burgeoned into an imperial commerce at the beginning of the nineteenth century, "Victorian cleaning rituals were peddled globally as the God-given sign of Britain's evolutionary superiority, and soap was invested with magical, fetish powers." The cult of domesticity positioned White women's bodies within the domestic space, but the imperialist production of soap advertising equated monogamy ("clean" sex) with industrial capital ("clean" money), Christianity ("being washed clean"), and class control ("washing and clothing the savage").[24] Soap companies used caricatures of Black children to sell Whiteness as "clean" and conversely, Blackness as "degenerate."[25] In 1844, for instance, the N.K. Fairbanks Company introduced the cartoon images of two Black children, the Gold Dust Twins (Goldy and Dusty), to promote its brand of soap. In Canada, an advertising print produced by John Henry Walker (1831–99) depicts the stereotype of Sambo covered in buttermilk, a symbolic representation of a Black child subsumed in Whiteness.[26] As Thomas Hine aptly notes, "these racist images ... that reflected ethnic stereotypes, provided products with personalities that were apparently unthreatening. They were a kind of servant just about anyone could afford, with the frequent exception of people who belonged to the groups shown on the package."[27]

In addition to advertisements, literature also became part of the colonial enterprise connecting race, capitalism, and imperialism. Harriet Beecher Stowe's *Uncle Tom's Cabin* (1852) was the first mass-produced and widely distributed novel of the nineteenth century. It was first published in the *National Era* as a weekly serial between June 1851 and April 1852, and Stowe allegedly made up the story as she went along; most scholars agree that she likely borrowed in large part from the life of Josiah Henson, an escaped slave whose biography, *The Life of Josiah Henson, Formerly a Slave, Now an Inhabitant of Canada* (1849), overlapped with that of the character of "Uncle Tom" and who also corresponded with Stowe during the composition of *Uncle Tom's Cabin*.[28] As Wood observes, "[Henson] also featured in [Stowe's] *Key to Uncle Tom's Cabin*, a *post facto* attempt to provide a historical source for every character and event in the novel."[29] Using sentimental and romantic devices, Stowe galvanized the abolition cause by encouraging her White readers to identify with the characters in her book. Slaves were portrayed as "human beings" who suffered inhumane indignities and felt the same pain and anguish that Whites would have felt.[30] At the same time, however, novels like *Uncle Tom's Cabin* did not refute widely held beliefs about the supposed inferiority of Blacks; instead, these books, along with commodity and scientific racism, played a pivotal role in entrenching beliefs about racial difference.

Stephen Johnson explains that small-scale minstrel show productions of *Uncle Tom's Cabin*, which toured in New England and New York State, had come across the border into Canada West by the 1860s, and these so-called "Tom Shows," in general, "attracted a large segment of the population that otherwise would never expose themselves to the ... theatre."[31] Shortly after the serialized version first appeared in 1851 in the *National Era*, two panoramas of *Uncle Tom's Cabin* were presented at Toronto's St. Lawrence Hall; then, in May and June 1853, there were hundreds of performances in the city at the Toronto Lyceum.[32] The two plots – the romantic and the sentimental – played out through the juxtaposition of slave escape and martyrdom.[33] *Uncle Tom's Cabin*, appearing at the height of the Underground Railroad and shortly after passage of the 1850 Fugitive Slave Law, essentially transformed the "realism" of the runaway slave notice into a sentimental (fictional) narrative.

Race and Nineteenth-Century Photography

In order to grasp the sociocultural import of the photographic images discussed in this chapter, the aforementioned milieu is essential to the story. As previously noted, photography had, since its invention in 1839, served an imperialist role in documenting racial difference in the Americas. In her examination of how photography functioned as an important medium for the construction and communication of a modern Brazilian national identity related to empire, Margrit Prussat points out that many of the first photographers in Brazil were European or of European descent, and in their photographs of urban slavery, "people are represented mainly as street-vendors, household-slaves, or carriers – professions that were very common among the African population."[34] Circulating photographs served an imperialist function similar to that of novels and travel narratives because a daguerreotype was still a luxury item at midcentury, and given the plate size (one half of a full plate), it would have been quite expensive and was typically made for a wealthy client or the daguerreotypist himself.[35] Thus, the viewers of the vast majority of photographic images in the first decades of its invention were majority White, middle-to-upper class, and mobile.

The photographic portraits of African Canadians ultimately provide us with a visual sense of how enslaved and freed Black people represented themselves in the emergent medium. Unlike the portrait painter, who had to undergo extensive training in order to create a portrait in the likeness of a person, the photographer outfitted with a camera and a tripod only had to aim and shoot, producing an easily identifiable likeness.[36] Compared with portrait paintings, these photographs are a more historically accurate picture of what Black people in colonial Canada looked like, of how they wanted to appear and be *seen*. However, it is still important to recognize the performative nature of all photographic imagery. For example, in her reading of James Van Der Zee, the African American photographer who took hundreds of photographs of Black women and men in Harlem in the 1920s, Elizabeth Sheehan observes that "photographs dramatize this process of transforming specific subjects into 'types' through their composition, as [Van Der Zee's] studio space and props transform his sitters into the protagonists of recognizable bourgeois domestic scenes."[37] As Susan Sontag once observed, while the point of the standard portrait in the bourgeois household of the eighteenth and nineteenth centuries was to confirm an ideal of the sitter (proclaiming social standing, embellishing personal appearance), "the photograph-record confirms ... that the subject exists; therefore, one can never have too many."[38] Importantly, many photographers also produced idealized glimpses of family members set in romanticized or dramatic poses; thus, some photographers integrated elements of romanticism and classicism into their work, echoing the work of eighteenth-century painters.[39] While these photographs provide us with a "real" record of African Canadians, they should also be read as "idealized" representations that might not necessarily reflect the realities of everyday life for the sitters.

While our analysis of nineteenth-century photographs includes both Black men and Black women, it is important to understand how (and why) images of Black men and women differ. On the one hand, all images created by Black people should be "read" through a prism of agency and self-representation, even as some of the depictions may have been idealized or staged, but on the other hand, when images of Black men and Black women appeared in the popular culture, they carried different cultural import. Nineteenth-century visual representations of the enslaved Black male body, for example, frequently idealized the emancipation moment by exulting semi-nude male figures whereby Black men held up broken manacles and kneeled in gratitude to formally clad Whites.[40] Albert Boime states further that "images of emancipation, like rituals and ceremonies, were designed to emphasize the dependence of the emancipated slaves upon their benefactors as well as their ongoing need for the culture and the guidance of their liberators."[41]

The early nineteenth-century public exhibition of Saartjie Baartman, or Sarah Bartmann, Saat-Jee, or the "Hottentot Venus," played a pivotal role in the positioning of the Black female body as Other. Baartman became the most widely circulated visual depiction of Black womanhood, and as a result, Sander Gilman explains, "while many groups of African blacks were known to Europeans in the nineteenth century, the Hottentot remained representative of the essence of ... the black female."[42] Baartman, a South African Khoi or San woman of "mixed blood," was exhibited as a curiosity in Europe, first in London and then Paris, from 1810 to 1815. She became an emblem of European fascination with the body and sexuality of Black women.[43] Baartman occupies a special position in the nineteenth-century genealogy of a racialized and gendered visual culture, as an arbitrary starting point, which precedes photography because she was essentially the first Black woman to be documented through drawings, watercolours, writings, and the preservation of her private organs, all for the sake of promulgating the notion that there were innate differences between the races.[44] Since European concepts of feminine beauty were bound up with notions of purity, delicacy, modesty, and physical fragility, the Black woman was viewed as physically strong, exuding an "animal sensuality," which many scientists conceptualized as evidence of her inferiority.[45] The nineteenth century was ultimately a period filled with contradictions.

While the domestic sphere increasingly became a site of agency in terms of consumption, it simultaneously remained a site of patriarchal oppression.[46] Behind an image of White middle-class gentility, the domestic interior also masked slavery's exploitation of Black women (and men). With advancements in photography in the latter part of the century, Black people acquired the means to self-represent and an ability to create counter-images that challenged scientific racism, blackface minstrelsy, and the image of Blackness in the sentimental novel. Photographic portraits of Black subjects thus give us an ability to contend with Black subjectivity in and out of slavery and freedom and a sense for how sitters used their agency, however little they may have had, to express the human condition, in new and expanding ways. The photographs also provide a window into respectability politics in a Canadian milieu. In the United States, as Evelyn Brooks Higginbotham writes, "the politics of respectability emphasized reform of individual behavior and attitudes both as a goal in itself and as a strategy for reform of the entire structural system of American race relations." By claiming respectability through their manners and morals, Higginbotham asserts further, "poor black women boldly asserted the will and agency to define themselves outside the parameters of prevailing racist discourses."[47] What follows is one of the first attempts to contend with African Canadians' individual behaviour and attitudes in relation to a structural system of Canadian race relations.

Photographic Portraits of African Canadians in Nineteenth-Century Ontario

"*Free* Black North" ran from 29 April to 1 October 2017 at the AGO. The exhibition featured photographs of men, women, and children – descendants of former slaves with familial ties to Black settlements in St. Catharines and Amherstburg, Ontario – in the mid-to-late 1800s. Such ties can be traced to the collectors of the material, who were themselves descendants of African Americans who had escaped to the North. Their formidable archives are illustrative of Black visuality and transnationality across the Canada-US border. The show examined a historical moment in the development of Black photographic culture within the broader milieu of mid-to-late nineteenth-century southwestern Ontario. The featured photographs reflected the historical development of the medium and included rare tintypes, *cartes de visite*, and cabinet cards. The images represented in "*Free* Black North" were found objects located in the Alvin McCurdy fonds at the Archives of Ontario and the Rick Bell Collection located in the special collections at Brock University in St. Catharines. All constituted a form of vernacular photography. Vernacular photography, as curator Brian Wallis observes, is "banal photographs often recorded by the most ordinary photographers, small town studio operators, professional photographers on assignment." Wallis urges scholars of Black diasporic culture to view vernacular photography as a "politicized element of everyday life to help us understand its role in any individual's contested daily social, political and personal interactions."[48]

From the 1850s onward, itinerant photographers and those who owned local studios photographed countless Black subjects in southern Ontario. A range of local personalities and anonymous community members sat for portraits from which carefully cultivated and crafted images of respectability were produced. The images circulated as both private and public objects in the form of ambrotypes, cabinet cards, *cartes de visite*, and tintypes. The images are precious objects that offer a critical opportunity to consider how Black individuals used photography to assert their presence in small African Canadian communities in border towns such as Amherstburg and inland locales like Toronto. Asserting and self-fashioning a presence was imperative given the pervasive racialized environment of Upper Canada in the mid-nineteenth century. The photo-artefacts in "*Free* Black North" undermined such damaging representations by depicting the self-possession and agency of individuals, some of whom may have been only ten or fifteen years removed from enslavement.

One of the questions raised during the exhibition concerned the dearth of identifiable subjects. All of the photographs are portraits, indicating private and intimate commissions to be shared with friends and loved ones and not for public consumption. Thus, many of the photographs remain unlabelled and the sitters' names unknown. It was common for family members on both sides of the border to share photographs, in turn creating a widely circulating network of objects over 150 years. Harvey Young argues that the circulation of photographs such as these has "allowed the past to be assessed in the present and the present to be captured for the future."[49] bell hooks notes further that "for black folks, the camera provided a means to document a reality that could if necessary, be packed, stored, moved from place to place. It was documentation that could be shared, passed around. And, ultimately, these images, the worlds they recorded, could be hidden, to be discovered at another time."[50] So, while little is known about many of the subjects featured in the exhibition, their presence opens the possibilities for further research and future discoveries.[51] It also turns a spotlight on the lack of attention, prior to the opening of the exhibition, that was paid to Black lives in the Canadian visual historical record.

In 1849, just ten years following the invention of the daguerreotype, African American statesman and abolitionist Frederick Douglass expounded on the notion of the power of images (both negative and flattering) to shape perception. In his essay originally published in the *North Star*, Douglass asserted that "Negroes can never have impartial portraits, at the hands of white artists ... It seems impossible for white men to take likenesses of black men, without most grossly exaggerating their distinctive features ... [They] associate with the Negro face, high cheek bones, distended nostril ... thick lips, and retreating foreheads."[52] Douglass's prescient statement reveals the opportunity for Blacks to use photographic technology as a means of countering negative representations and to thereby shape their national identities as citizens. John Ernst poignantly observes that "historians have sought to delineate the various ways by which black Americans developed and performed a sense of community, through public observances and events, religious practices, publications, and their involvement in antislavery efforts and other social reform movements."[53]

We assert that photography similarly helped African Americans and African Canadians alike to cultivate a sense of community through images. Douglass's statements also point to the emancipatory possibilities of photographic portraiture, which allowed for potential Black sitters (as paying clients) to exert control over the process of the sitting and their likenesses. Of most import for Douglass was the use of photography as a tool in the representation of both free and self-emancipated Blacks as individual subjects unencumbered by the damaging visual economy of racist images. Thus, for Douglass, "The process by which man is able to posses[s] his own subjective nature outside of himself – giving it forms, color, space, and all the attributes of distinct personalities – so that it becomes the subject of distinct observation and contemplation is at bottom of all efforts, and the germinating principle of all reform and all progress."[54] His statements on the power of photography to resist not only one-dimensional characterizations of the enslaved but also the ability of the portrait to form a distinct (human) personality are profound. It is important to note that Douglass's ideas were formed at the height of the enactment of the 1850 Fugitive Slave Act when thousands of self-emancipated Blacks, seen as chattel in the southern United States, sought refuge in Canada West.

Douglass made use of the genre of the studio portrait to be photographed prolifically. In his 1861 speech "Pictures and Progress," in which he formulated a theory on photographic portraiture, he praised the democratization of photography and its availability to all people regardless of race and social stature.[55] Both Harriet Tubman and Sojourner Truth also used the medium as means of political engagement to foreground the abolitionist cause. Neither was as photographed as Douglass; however, according to Barbara Krauthamer and Deborah Willis, Truth was probably the first Black woman to wilfully distribute images of herself. Truth skilfully used her likeness in the form of *cartes de visite* to, as she noted, sell "the shadow to support the substance."[56] The same argument can be made of images of Mary Ann Shadd Cary (1823–1893), who was born into a free family in 1823 in Wilmington, Delaware, but had by 1851 established a home in Windsor, just across the river from Detroit. Alongside African American author and abolitionist Henry Bibb (1815–1854), Shadd Cary opened a school for fugitive slaves, which was run by Mary Bibb. She helped to established Canada's first Black newspaper, the *Voice of the Fugitive*, in 1851, a paper that circulated both in Canada and the United States. In 1853, Shadd Cary became the first woman to edit a newspaper in North America when her name was listed on the masthead of the *Provincial Freeman*, which she operated with Samuel Ringgold Ward (1817–1866), a Black abolitionist who also resided in Canada West.[57] In one of the only known images of Mary Ann Shadd Cary, found in the photographic archives of the Library of Canada and taken at some point in the late 1840s or early 1850s, the well-known abolitionist faces the viewer with a direct gaze wearing a buttoned-up dress. Her hair is parted down the middle. It is a living example of the kind of embodied emancipatory photography that African Americans living in Canada in the nineteenth century were able to achieve. Thus, the collections from which the work exhibited in "*Free* Black North" was pulled present the gendered nature of studio photography during the mid-to-late nineteenth century in southern Ontario, revealing the particularities, conditions, and contexts for self-fashioning by Black subjects – though our focus is primarily on Black women, who are too often nameless and/or unmarked in the historical record.

They were not public figures like Frederick Douglass or Sojourner Truth, but the women and girls featured in "*Free* Black North" in tintypes and cabinet cards were also acutely aware of the power of photography as a way to counter increasing racist sentiment. The exhibition design provoked discussions of selfhood, biography, and presence by situating the objects in small cases (as captured in the installation view of the exhibition). In the exhibition smaller cases were used to give the viewer a sense of the precious nature of these rarely seen photographs. Each portrait was given its own space in order to tell a specific and unique counternarrative to the prevailing stereotypical notions of peoples of African descent. The tintype process was itself unique, producing a positive image, one of a photograph on metal that could not be reproduced. The process lends itself to deeper reflections about its suitability as singular photo-object for a range of Black subjects. Each tintype features an individual and not a stereotypical representation. The range of individual subjects, especially Black female sitters, speaks to the heterogeneity of the communities in which they lived but also points to how important self-imaging had become to Black subjects by the late nineteenth century.

While many of these sitters were non-citizens, in terms of lacking full enfranchisement, landownership, and wealth, it was still important for them to capture their likeness in an image and to preserve that image generation after generation within their family record. As Smith points out, "the family photograph album offered individuals a colloquial space in which to display practices of national belonging. Through repeated codes of dress, props, and poses, amateur photographers ... could link themselves to others whom they would never meet through the increasingly standardized rituals of photographic self-representation." She writes further, "Using the same photographic technologies and tropes, individuals could mutually affirm their places in an imagined community rooted in discursive fantasies of national character."[58] Thus, photographs of African Canadians in the nineteenth century also point to the fantastical power of photography to allow for the possibility, however real or imagined, to link bodies to wider discussions around belonging – both to one's community and to the nation. "*Free* Black North" asked viewers to reflect on what the nineteenth-century studio photography experience might have been for these subjects, some of whom were descendants or perhaps former fugitive slaves themselves. How were they posed? What, if any, props were used? How did they comport themselves? In other words, how did these images become politicized objects that were instrumental in shaping everyday lived experiences in often hostile environments?

"*Free* Black North" adds to the discussion of the history of photography in Canada by using tintypes, a form popular between the 1860s and the turn of the century that was inexpensive and durable, making it available to many. Large numbers of extant tintypes can be found in collections both north and south of the border indicating that the process was extremely popular among people of African descent. Other names for the process are "ferrotype" (*ferro* meaning iron) and "melainotype" (*melaino* meaning dark or black). The special attributes of the tintype formed variant tones of dark purple, brown, and grey on the metal, which, when enhanced by the studio lighting, enriched the natural skin tones of the sitters. While some contemporary viewers of these tintypes become overly fascinated with the technology, it is important to remember that in the nineteenth century, photographic technologies were constantly changing and improving; to focus on the technology of the photography is to lose sight of the important fact that African Canadians were clearly attuned to their times, and also deeply embedded in the material culture of the period as Whites in Canada West would have been. The portable nature of the tintype and the ease of its circulation were central to their use as counternarratives to dominant ideologies and representations of Blackness. For the subjects featured in "*Free* Black North," photography and specifically the tintype was used as a weapon to control one's image and to proclaim "this is who I am."[59]

For both the free and the self-emancipated, portrait photographs became "fugitive images" that defied and transgressed archetypal representations of Black bodies. Steven Kasher writes that each tintype is an image created by its subject, a statement of, "this is how I choose to be seen."[60] Several images in the "*Free* Black North" exhibit speak to the power of photography not only as an emancipatory tool but also as a representational window into the black experience. The photograph of the "servant girl" featured in the exhibition, for instance, seems to confirm Douglass's claims about the democratization of photography. As he observed, "The servant girl can now see a likeness of herself, such as noble ladies could not purchase fifty years ago. But now ... such pictures are placed within easy reach of the humblest members of society."[61] We know precious little about the unidentified woman featured in a tintype from the Rick Bell Collection. She wears a distinctive white pinafore, which may designate her status as a domestic worker. Staring resolutely at the camera, her pose suggests complete ease with the photographic process that used the medium to shape the way she wished to be seen. As evidenced in this photograph, working-class Black women were interested in their appearance and in their ability to represent their status as "free" people and the accompanying exigencies in a White settler society.

For middle-class Black Canadian women such as Mary Branton-Tule, self-commissioned photography offered a means to commemorate personal achievements and define themselves within a wider world. Importantly, we use the term "middle-class" to denote not necessarily a socioeconomic status but more aptly a higher level of educational attainment and occupation than was available to African Canadians who worked as labourers, domestics, and/or servants. Branton-Tule was born in Chatham, Ontario, in 1860. She became an orphan as a teenager and went to live with family in Amherstburg, Ontario. Branton-Tule was educated in Atlanta at Spelman Seminary, a college founded for women preparing for missionary life. In the portrait of Branton-Tule by African Canadian photographer I.H. Lewis, taken in 1890 on the eve of her departure to South Africa to begin her work as a Baptist missionary, she wears an "Africa for Christ" banner across her chest, symbolizing her role in and commitment to the Christian missionary project.[62] Branton-Tule expresses herself as an independent and educated Black woman countering the stereotypical representations of Black women as only "domestic labourers and servants" in Canadian popular culture at the time.[63] The photograph also highlights the complicated engagement with Africa among many Black diasporic missionaries: they believed that Africans needed to be saved from European colonization, while also adhering to the Christian missionary ideology.[64] Lewis frames Branton-Tule as self-empowered and conscious of her upcoming journey as she directs her gaze to the future and her missionary objectives. She continued her missionary activity for several years in South Africa and then Liberia until her death in 1923.[65]

The struggle for self-representation also persisted among freed Black men living in border towns including Amherstburg and St. Catharines. Many held jobs such as pastors, labourers, and cooks, among other occupations, despite the forces of exclusion and racism that they continued to experience. For example, Reverend Horace Hawkins, who escaped from Kentucky, eventually resided in Amherstburg. Hawkins faced ongoing systemic racism and recalled such hostility: "A coloured man cannot get accommodated at any of hotels in Canada or on any line of the railroad ... I think the root of the prejudice is to be found in the fact that the coloured people came in here rapidly and the whites got the impression that the coloured people would become a majority in the Western county."[66] Hawkins's sentiment runs counter to the narrative of Canada as the benevolent place of refuge for escaping Blacks. Hawkins is also featured in the "*Free* Black North" exhibition, in a cabinet card taken between 1871 and 1880 at the Westlake Brothers studio in London, Ontario. The back of the card is inscribed as follows: *Reverend Horace Hawkins (also barber) born in Newport Kentucky in slavery escaped to Canada and lived in Amherstburg.*[67] The brevity of the inscription recounts Hawkins's life as once enslaved, a fugitive, and little else. However, Hawkins lived a fascinating life as a university-educated abolitionist and pastor who, eventually, bought his freedom from his former master in Kentucky. Hawkins had also acquired considerable wealth by the time of this photograph. Here, he is dressed in trim attire associated with his pastoral duties, with the collar a visible component of his ensemble, and his pose is commanding yet informal. Despite his experiences with racism, the three-dimensional space of Westlake studio situates Hawken's autonomy and sense of belonging in a specific Canadian local that belies the relentless inscription of his former fugitive status.

The portraits of Reverend Hawkins, Mary Branton-Tule, and the unknown "servant girl" displayed in "*Free* Black North" reflect kinship ties and transnational links, forming a range of tintypes, cabinet cards, and *cartes de visite* that present the complexities and ambiguities of transnational identities, of Black visuality. The photographs represent fragments that form a minute sampling of a larger archive of materials (over three thousand objects). The corpus of photographs presents moments of subjectivity and agency that are far removed from the myriad of visual media that typically depicted the violent outcomes of antebellum slavery on Black bodies. These images are generative of particular moments whereby the emergence of Black identity, "becoming" and "being," in a racialized Canadian landscape is realized. Stuart Hall's notion of identity formation as bound up in a process of becoming as well as being is useful for articulating the complex identities and subjectivities of self-emancipated Black Americans who escaped to Canada and adopted Canada as their new "home."[68]

Both the Alvin McCurdy and Rick Bell collections constitute fugitive archives built in wilful defiance of the threat of erasure. Art historian and queer activist David Deitcher considers defiance as a crucial component for any project of historical reclamation. He argues that "resistance compels the historian to unearth precious traces of the past. Through such acts of recuperation ... the historian helps to ensure the continued availability of that past as a source of validation." He notes that "a more measured defiance also informs the salvage of these photographs which the majority culture has found unworthy of preservation and study, consideration and care."[69] "*Free* Black North" assisted in recuperating "absent subjects," histories, and photographic objects on both sides of the border. While many of the images defy easy readings, they highlight how a visit to the photography studio played a critical role in asserting one's identity in nineteenth-century Black transnational communities. Collectively, they illuminate a tradition of early Black photography and how it contributes to broader narratives about the medium's history in Canada.

NOTES

1 Marcus Wood, "Marketing the Slave Trade: Slavery, Photography, and Emancipation: Time and Freedom in 'The Life of the Picture,'" in *A History of Visual Culture: Western Civilization from the 18th to the 21st Century*, ed. Jane Kromm and Susan Benforado Bakewell (New York: Berg, 2010), 255–66.
2 Deborah Willis, *Reflections in Black: A History of Black Photographers, 1840 to the Present* (New York: W.W. Norton, 2000), 3.
3 Shawn Michelle Smith, *Photography on the Color Line: W.E.B. Du Bois, Race, and Visual Culture* (Durham: Duke University Press, 2004), 66.
4 See Anne McClintock, "Soft-Soaping Empire: Commodity Racism and Imperial Advertising," in *Imperial Leather: Race, Gender and Sexuality in the Colonial Conquest* (New York: Routledge, 1995), 207–31; Arthur Riss, *Race, Slavery, and Liberalism in Nineteenth-Century American Literature* (New York: Cambridge University Press, 2006); and Eric Lott, *Love and Theft: Blackface Minstrelsy and the American Working Class* (New York: Oxford University Press, 1993).
5 bell hooks, "In Our Glory: Photography and Black Life," in *Picturing Us: African American Identity in Photography*, ed. Deborah Willis (New York: New Press, 1994), 46.
6 Carol Payne and Andrea Kunard, eds., *The Cultural Work of Photography in Canada* (Montreal and Kingston: McGill-Queen's University Press, 2011).
7 Martha Langford, Karla McManus, Elizabeth Anne Cavaliere, Aurèle Parisie, Sharon Murray, and Philippe Guillaume, "Imaged Communities: Putting Canadian Photographic History in Its Place," *Journal of Canadian Studies/Revue d'études canadiennes* 49, no. 2 (2015): 301.
8 Nadine Ehlers, *Racial Imperatives: Discipline, Performativity, and Struggles against Subjection* (Bloomington: Indiana University Press, 2012), 32, 25.
9 Deborah Willis and Carla Williams, *The Black Female Body: A Photographic History* (Philadelphia: Temple University Press, 2002), 23.
10 Tina Campt, *Image Matters: Archive, Photography, and the African Diaspora in Europe* (Durham: Duke University Press, 2012), 5.
11 Maureen G. Elgersman, *Unyielding Spirits: Black Women and Slavery in Early Canada and Jamaica* (New York: Garland, 1999), 25–6.
12 Adrienne Shadd, *The Journey from Tollgate to Parkway: African Canadians in Hamilton* (Toronto: Natural Heritage Books, 2010), 30.
13 Karolyn Smardz Frost, *I've Got a Home in Glory Land: A Lost Tale of the Underground Railroad* (New York: Farrar, Straus and Giroux, 2007), 195; Shadd, *Journey from Tollgate*, 29.
14 Smardz Frost, *I've Got a Home*, 196.
15 Hepburn, "Following the North Star," 95.
16 Hepburn, 97, 98.

17 See Boulou Ebanda de B'béri, Nina Reid-Maroney, and Handel Kashope Wright, eds., *The Promised Land: History and Historiography of the Black Experience in Chatham-Kent's Settlements and Beyond* (Toronto: University of Toronto Press, 2014).
18 John Boyko, *Blood and Daring: How Canada Fought the American Civil War and Forged a Nation* (Toronto: Alfred A. Knopf, 2013), 19.
19 Boyko, 25.
20 Shawn Michelle Smith, *American Archives: Gender, Race, and Class in Visual Culture* (Princeton: Princeton University Press, 1999), 30.
21 Riss, *Race, Slavery, and Liberalism*, 98.
22 Smith, *Photography on the Color Line*, 52. Darwin's *On the Origin of Species* (1859) and *The Descent of Man* (1871) had triggered a general interest in the documentation of the "other" in the scientific fields of anthropology, ethnography, and ethnology.
23 Kathy Peiss, *Hope in a Jar: The Making of America's Beauty Culture* (New York: Metropolitan Books, 1998), 31.
24 McClintock, "Soft-Soaping Empire," 209, 207, 208.
25 The juxtaposition between Whiteness as "clean" and Blackness as "unclean" continues in the present. In 2017, skin-care brands Dove and Nivea released advertising campaigns that echoed nineteenth-century soap advertisements.
26 See John Henry Walker, *Sambo and the Buttermilk*, c. 1850–85, wood engraving, ink on paper on supporting paper, 9.5 x 14.1 cm, Paintings, Prints and Drawings, McCord Museum of Canadian History, Montreal.
27 Thomas Hine, *The Total Package: The Evolution and Secret Meanings of Boxes, Bottles, Cans, and Tubes* (Boston: Little, Brown, 1995), 91–2.
28 See Boyko, *Blood and Daring*, 24. See also Moira Ferguson, "Mary Ann Shadd Cary (1823–1893)," in *Nine Black Women: An Anthology of Nineteenth-Century Writers from the United States, Canada, Bermuda, and the Caribbean*, ed. Moira Ferguson (New York: Routledge, 1998), 203.
29 Marcus Wood, *Blind Memory: Visual Representations of Slavery in England and America, 1780–1865* (Manchester: Manchester University Press, 2000), 195–6.
30 Robert C. Toll, *Blacking Up: The Minstrel Show in Nineteenth-Century America* (New York: Oxford University Press, 1974), 88–9.
31 Stephen Johnson, "Uncle Tom and the Minstrels: Seeing Black and White Stage in Canada West prior to the American Civil War," in *(Post)Colonial Stages: Critical and Creative Views on Drama, Theatre and Performance*, ed. Helen Gilbert (London: Villiers, 1999), 56–7.
32 Frost, *I've Got a Home*, 283.
33 Eliza Harris saves her son from slavery by crossing the icy waters of the Ohio River to join her fugitive husband, George, while Tom, a devout Christian, accepts his fate patiently until he's required to punish other slaves, whereupon he refuses and his owner beats him to death.

34 Margrit Prussat, "Icons of Slavery: Black Brazil in Nineteenth Century Photography and Image Art," in *Living History: Encountering the Memory of the Heirs of Slavery*, ed. Ana Lucia Araujo (Newcastle: Cambridge Scholars, 2009), 207.
35 Willis and Williams, *Black Female Body*, 51.
36 Smith, *American Archives*, 60.
37 Elizabeth M. Sheehan, "The Face of Fashion," in *Cultures of Femininity in Modern Fashion*, ed. Ilya Parkins and Elizabeth M. Sheehan (Hanover: University Press of New England, 2011), 182–3.
38 Susan Sontag, *On Photography* (New York: Picador, 1977), 165.
39 Willis, *Reflections in Black*, 3.
40 See Kirk Savage, *Standing Soldiers, Kneeling Slaves: Race, War, and Monument in Nineteenth-Century America* (Princeton: Princeton University Press, 1999), 65.
41 Albert Boime. *The Art of Exclusion: Representing Blacks in the Nineteenth Century* (Washington, DC: Smithsonian Institution Press, 1990), 171.
42 Sander L. Gilman, "Black Bodies, White Bodies: Toward an Iconography of Female Sexuality in Late Nineteenth-Century Art, Medicine, and Literature," *Critical Inquiry* 12, no. 1 (1985): 206.
43 Willis and Williams, *Black Female Body*, 59.
44 Michele Wallace, "The Imperial Gaze: Venus Hottentot, Human Display, and World's Fairs," in *Black Venus 2010: They Called Her "Hottentot,"* ed. Deborah Willis (Philadelphia: Temple University Press, 2010), 150.
45 Barbara Bush, *Slave Women in Caribbean Society, 1650–1838* (London: James Currey, 1990), 15.
46 Karen Sánchez-Eppler, *Touching Liberty: Abolition, Feminism, and the Politics of the Body* (Berkeley: University of California Press, 1993), 41.
47 Evelyn Brooks Higginbotham, *Righteous Discontent: The Women's Movement in the Black Baptist Church, 1880–1920* (Cambridge, MA: Harvard University Press, 1993), 187, 192.
48 Brian Wallis, *African American Vernacular Photography* (New York: ICP, 2006), 18.
49 Harvey Young, *Embodying Black Experience: Stillness, Critical Memory, and the Black Body* (Ann Arbor: University of Michigan Press, 2010).
50 bell hooks, *Art on My Mind: Visual Politics* (New York: New Press, 1981), 60.
51 During the run of the exhibition, an individual with roots in Windsor and Amhertsburg recognized a descendant whose photograph was part of the Alvin McCurdy collection.
52 Frederick Douglass, "A Tribute for the Negro," *North Star*, April 7, 1849, 2.
53 John Ernest, *A National within a Nation: Organizing African-American Communities before the Civil War* (Chicago: Ivan R. Dee, 2011), 14.
54 Frederick Douglass, "Pictures and Progress" (December 3, 1861), in *The Frederick Douglass Papers, Series One: Speeches, Debates, and Interviews*, vol. 3, ed. John W. Blassingame (New Haven: Yale University Press, 1979), 452–73.

55 Douglass, 452–3.
56 Barbara Krauthamer and Deborah Willis, *Envisioning Emancipation: Black Americans and the End of Slavery* (Philadelphia: Temple University Press, 2012), 39.
57 Ferguson, "Mary Ann Shadd Cary," 203.
58 Smith, *American Archives*, 6.
59 Steven Kasher, "Democratic Visages: The Tintype and America," in *America and the Tintype*, exhibition catalogue (New York: ICP, 2009), 50.
60 Kasher, 49.
61 Douglass, "Pictures and Progress," 379.
62 The important contribution by I.H. Lewis in the field of photography is the subject of ongoing research by Dr. Julie Crooks, one of the co-authors of this chapter.
63 Wendy J. Porter, "A Quartet and an Anonymous Choir: The Remarkable Lives and Ministries of Four Black Baptist Women in Late Nineteenth Century Ontario," in *Canadian Baptist Women*, ed. Sharon M. Bowler (Eugene, OR: Pickwick, 2016), 98.
64 Nina Reid Maroney, "African Canadian Women and New World Diaspora, c. 1865," Canadian Woman Studies 23, no. 2 (2004): 92–6.
65 Porter, "Quartet," 97.
66 Horace Hawkins, "American Freedmen's Inquiry Commission Interviews, 1863," in *Slave Testimony: Two Centuries of Letters, Speeches, Interviews, and Autobiographies*, ed. John W. Blassingame (Baton Rouge: Louisiana State University Press, 1977), 443.
67 Cabinet card of [Reverend?] Horace Hawkins, [c. 1890s], F 2076-16-3-4, Alvin D. McCurdy fonds, Archives of Ontario.
68 Stuart Hall, "Cultural Identity and Diaspora," in *Theorizing Diaspora: A Reader*, ed. Jana Evans Bradiel and Anita Mannur (Malden, MA: Blackwell, 2003), 225.
69 David Deitcher, "Looking at a Photograph, Looking for a History," in *The Passionate Camera: Photographs and Bodies of Desire*, ed. Deborah Bright (New York: Routledge, 1998), 31, 33.

17
Hogan's Alley Remixed: Wayde Compton's *Performance Bond* and the New Black Can(aan) Lit

PAUL WATKINS

The future is always here in the past
                              Amiri Baraka, "Jazzmen," 255

I. Canaan: False Freedom Land

I dreamed a dream ...
a fitful dream.
The life I lived so long ago,
in 'Canaan' land.
False 'Freedom' land –
strained welcome –
subtle hatred –
covert discrimination –
Slavery ... Canadian style.
           George A. Borden, "Fashions of Slavery," *Canaan Odyssey*, 7

Hogan's Alley was a neighbourhood in downtown Vancouver, British Columbia, and while it was home to many immigrant communities, this chapter focuses on the Black Canadian population that had established itself there by the early 1920s.[1] In 1967 the City of Vancouver began to level the western half of the neighbourhood to build a freeway, which displaced the communities living there. Combining spoken word, poetry, images, excerpts from oral histories, a playlet, an audio CD recording, and a newspaper clipping, Vancouver poet/writer/educator Wayde Compton's 2004 poetry book *Performance Bond* reanimates both the community and the destruction of Hogan's Alley. Compton's mash-up methodology brings Hogan's Alley back to life in literary form.² By engaging with Compton's historical resonances, mash-ups, and remixes of Hogan's Alley, we can recover Hogan's Alley as (*living*) metaphor and even – idealistically – imagine the kind of work we do in (historically based) scholarship as a kind of sampling and/or engaged poetics that helps facilitate more inclusive notions of citizenship, multiculturalism, and community. Moreover, given that Hogan's Alley is in the midst of a real memorialization (via the Northeast False Creek Plan), Compton's poetic and activist work – and our engagement with Vancouver's historical Black community – is essential to imagining and creating dynamic spaces that redress the past and reflect the current needs of Vancouver's Black population.³ Before delving into Compton's remix poetics and his creative engagement with Hogan's Alley, this chapter challenges early conceptions of Canada as a promised land (in reality, Canada is deeply rooted in the legacies of slavery and colonialism). In the final section I compare the erasure of historically Black communities to the elision of Black writers in Canadian literature (CanLit). Hogan's Alley and Black creative praxis offer portals for engaging with an analogue past in a digital present; collectively, we can work to actualize more expansive notions of Black Vancouver and Black cultural production in CanLit and, as scholars and activists, we must do so if we want to redress past wrongs and build a more equitable future.

There is a need, as George Elliott Clarke states in *Directions Home*, for literary scholars "to accept the historical (or 'indigenous') African-Canadian population and its cultural production as a constitutive element."⁴ A deeper understanding of Black cultural production in Canada needs to include historical figures (people like Mathieu da Costa, the first recorded free Black person in Canada, and Viola Desmond, who challenged racial segregation at a cinema in Nova Scotia in 1946) and Black communities put under erasure such as Africville and Hogan's Alley, as well as the nascent canon of Black Canadian writers dealing with contemporary experiences.⁵ Creating space for these histories are, as poet Dionne Brand attests, "redemptive and restorative; inasmuch as it binds us in a common pain it binds us in a common quest for a balm for that pain."⁶ As Cherokee writer Thomas King explains, "Most of us think that history is the past. It's not. It's the stories we tell about the past. That's all it is."⁷ Engaging with the stories that continue to ripple in the present involves an understanding of Canada's xenophobic, racist, and colonial past, including historical lacunae around slavery and the ongoing legacy of White supremacy.

Afua Cooper asserts that slavery is "Canada's best kept secret, locked within the National closet."⁸ Most Canadians, to borrow from Yvonne Brown, suffer from a "collective amnesia" and fail to take into account that the Middle Passage – the capture of Africans and the brutal crossing of the sea into the New World – was a holocaust that ruptured, damaged, or destroyed the lives of some twelve million African people. Brown describes the Middle Passage as a "collective amnesia" because "a history that involved those fourteen European nations could be omitted completely, an event that lasted 350 years – omitted completely."[9] In Canada, slavery was not officially denounced until 1793 and was not formally abolished until 1834. Across the border in America, at the Constitutional Convention in 1787, delegates decided that slavery should be allowed to continue on American soil, laying the foundation for the Fugitive Slave Acts of 1793 and 1850. The Underground Railroad, a surreptitious underground network of paths and safe houses that led to the slave-free northern states and Canada, was a result of these acts. According to a conservative estimate by historian Robin Winks, up to thirty thousand fugitive slaves (between 1830 and 1860) survived the journey from the United States to Canada – to Canaan land, that heaven coded in the African American spirituals.[10] For myriads of escaped slaves, Canada represented reprieve from a life of dehumanized imprisonment experienced on the brutal plantations, offering freedom from what abolitionist Frederick Douglass described as "the hell of slavery."[11]

And while Canada continued to congratulate itself on being different from the United States in providing a fugitive haven for slaves "under the lion's paw," the escaped slaves soon learned otherwise. They encountered very direct racism from "anti-slavery Negro hater[s]" (though it was often described as subtle), devastating poverty, segregation, and found the vestiges of a slavery system.[12] This is what Saidiya Hartman refers to as "the afterlife of slavery": "skewed life chances, limited access to health and education, premature death, incarceration, impoverishment."[13] "Negroes," Canadians presumed, were a monolith, comprising visitors, others, and not a people fit for integration into Canadian society.[14] Nevertheless, the escaped slaves founded their own Canaans (a moniker that underlines their identification with the biblical promised land) – Dawn, Wilberforce, the Refugee Home Society, and Elgin – and continued to plant their hopes and dreams into the soil of Canadian society. And so, while Canada was not the place that the astute Frederick Douglass had envisioned, where "the wild goose and the swan repaired at the end of winter" and not "the home of man," it was nonetheless, for many, a chance for a new beginning.[15] The survivors of the crossing not only survived in Canada, but many thrived, despite the hegemonic centre's historical imperative to erase Black communities and histories.

One of the earliest Black communities in Canada was Africville, located on the southern shore of the Bedford Basin, in Nova Scotia. Despite the promise of Africville as a safe haven – a Canaan – the Black settlers there were treated with persistent prejudice and were "assailed by bureaucrats and politicians desiring either to rid Halifax of a so-called 'segregated ghetto' or to hijack precious waterfront property for industrial use ... a village which was condemned, again and again, as a 'slum' before it was finally condemned to die."[16] In 1964, the land in Africville was expropriated for industrial use and within a period of five years its residents had been relocated and their homes demolished.

Ana Maria Fraile-Marcos writes that the treatment of Africville and its residents "underlines Canadian hypocrisy regarding the management of race and difference."[17] Thus, it is the work of scholars, poets, and activists to commemorate and reimagine these communities so that they may exist more fully in the present. The original site of Africville was declared a National Historic Site of Canada, and a replica of the Seaview Baptist Church (demolished in 1969) opened as a museum in 2011. While Black Loyalists and Refugees were given land in 1775 and 1812, they were not given any title/deed, which has only very recently been addressed – in 2017 – as the Nova Scotia government announced funding to help people from five historically Black communities to gain legal ownership of land that had been in their families for generations.[18] These acts of repatriation are important, as "commemorative events in relation to Halifax's Africville" have facilitated a "surge of interest in African Nova Scotian History" and an "outpouring of attention to New Brunswick's Black populations."[19]

The history of Hogan's Alley has many parallels with that of Africville, as we shall see later in this chapter: both were largely self-sustaining communities with their own schools, churches, a post office, music venues, and shops. Despite a great deal of cultural production in both neighbourhoods, both were seen, from the view of the White gatekeepers of their respective cities, as blighted communities in need of "urban renewal" (a term Compton discusses in relation to "negro removal"). Activism makes change possible, and poetry, at its best, allows us to imagine the shape of that change, as evidenced in Compton's remixing of Hogan's Alley: a remix that opens portals and spaces for cultural, political, and ethical dialogue, and even social change.

II. History as Remix: Compton's Schizophono Poetics

> We had to learn that the history is always there to be found/out-about, to learn, and to make.
> Clifton Joseph, "Recollections: A Seventees [sic] Black RAP," 20

In his poem "The Reinventing Wheel," Compton samples Ziggy Marley's words from "Tomorrow People," writing, "My family history is fractured, impure,/history imported with deft warp and weft./You don't know your past, you don't know your future./History imperative."[20] The alliterative "warp and weft" refers to weaving – the weft (yarn carried by the shuttle) is drawn through the warp (lengthwise yarn) – which is a perfect metaphor for how Compton spins and weaves histories together. Compton's interwoven approach to history lends an immediacy to the past that makes it active, as he acknowledges that history, especially Black Canadian history, is often "fractured." Black Canadian history as remembering – even if that history is fractured and then run through samplers and turntables – is a creative act that urgently seeks innovative ways to remember and remix the past in a way that occasions new forms of knowledge production in Canada.

Compton "perpetually beat juggl[es] history and ethnicity" to respond to "the brokenness [of] the tradition." History and tradition are imperative to Compton's DJ poetics because, for him, his postmodern panache is about the repetition of traditions that survive insurmountable odds that date back to the slave ships. Hence, Compton writes, "We have archived ourselves," as Black history becomes an act of echo/feedback/repetition that survives in the "intractable track/of the word." Compton hears sonic Black traditions from the ancients to Jimi Hendrix as he plugs himself into his mixer: "I/am plugged into my mixer, lashed, with wax/stopping my ears. Tracking/into Tradition … I am plugged into the tradition."[21] So, while conceptual poetry uses appropriation as a means to create a "new" work focused largely on the concept rather than the final product, Compton's appropriations (or, more accurately, samplings and traditional methods) are invested in the creation/memory of histories that mesh to recover the past.[22] For Compton, his liberation is largely directed toward the neglected and rooted/re-routed history of Black British Columbia.

In his work *Bluesprint: Black British Columbian Literature and Orature*, which was the first literary anthology of its kind to archive BC's Black communities, Compton describes how "black pioneers had come to Canada not only for economic relief, but to fulfill their dreams of full citizenship and equality under British law, which was – on paper, at least – non discriminatory." The stories in *Bluesprint* document that in British Columbia, Black people encountered segregation, racism, and political corruption "that accounted for such things as the spurious cancellation of black ballots in an election." As Compton describes, "B.C.'s black history has been one of continued exodus, immigration, settlement, exploration, miscegenation, communitarianism, integration, segregation, agitation, uprooting and re-rooting and re-routing."[23] Travel and exodus are essential parts of Canada's immigrant history, and we can think of Compton's scratching – his poetic dissonance and versifying – as lines of ruptured movement that inscribe over written histories that attempt to erase (white/out) Black histories.

"The history of BC is the history of whiteness," as Compton writes in the poem "Performance Bond."[24] The Blackness of the first governor of British Columbia, James Douglas, was the subject of rumour and speculation; historical records show that Governor Douglas was of mixed-race ancestry but passed as White his entire life.[25] Like the "scratched" microfiche that screams out BC's own mixed history, Compton's "JD" (about Douglas), which scratches over rumour with historical imperative and record (like a vinyl record), sounds a potent reminder that history itself (like JD's ancestry) is always mixed (between written and oral accounts and differing cultural perspectives). Although Indigenous people were in British Columbia tens of thousands of years before Europeans arrived, Indigenous history, like Black history in BC, has been reduced to footnotes by some White scholars. The issues of citizenship, settler and Indigenous relations, identity, White/Black/mixed-race, and Canadian and American borders are much more complex once you realize that BC is a site of diasporic and transnational identifications. As the monoliths and institutions of Vancouver's Black history are glossed over – or demolished, as in the case of Hogan's Alley – diasporic spaces become increasingly important representations, particularly in the mixed-race identities Compton circumspectly explores in the outer peripheries of cultural geography and group solidarity.

These expanding peripheries of cultural experience and group solidarity can be read through what Kamau Brathwaite terms "tidalectics," a theory counter to Hegel's dialectics, which provides an Africanist model for thinking about history. Discussing tidalectics in an interview with Nathaniel Mackey, Brathwaite describes how we can see history as cyclical: "In other words, instead of the notion of one-two-three Hegelian, I am now more interested in the movement of backwards and forwards as a kind of cyclic, I suppose, motion, rather than linear."[26] Compton's history ripples in time and his tidalectical approach is inspired by Brathwaite, who "liberates us from [the old dialectic, and] says, 'No, you're just part of the chain, your just part of this long chain of things. Even if you're innovating, you are still part of this long series of things.'"[27] While Compton's *Performance Bond* clearly concerns the history of British Columbia, it does so within the tidalectical nexus that considers and welcomes the larger diaspora and memories of geopolitical Black thinking across time and borders/continents. Compton shows how it is vital to remember the past in order to build the foundations for a more sustainable future.

Compton's Schizophonic Poetics

Various DJs, producers, and archivists use recorded material in inventive ways that show they are highly aware of the improvised nature of history and cultural practice. Sampling, like quotation, provides diacritical difference, *détournement*, carnival, wildstyle, and parade, and, as Paul D. Miller (DJ Spooky) suggests, it allows "people to replay their own memories of the sounds and situations of their lives ... sampling is dematerialized sculpture."[28] The rise of the DJ fits within the postmodern desire of contemporary masses to bring things closer. Technology changes culture. The invention of the Technics 1200 series of turntables, manufactured from October 1972 until 2010 (and then resumed in 2016) by Matsushita (and later known as Panasonic), made DJ culture largely possible in the first place, even though the Technics 1200 was never intended to be repurposed as a musical instrument. Then again, Adolphe Sax, who invented the saxophone in 1846, would probably never have imagined Charlie Parker playing "Koko" or Coltrane playing "Giant Steps" on his instrument. The Technics 1200s (in hip-hop they are often referred to as "Tec 12s," "Wheels of Steel," and the "Ones & Twos") with their direct-drive high-torque motor design initially made them suitable for cueing and starting tracks on the radio, although young DJs in New York would soon realize just how much they could do with a turntable and some records. As Compton writes in "The Reinventing Wheel," "the author was born in 1972" – a direct reference to the invention of the Technics 1200 turntable, the primary signifier of hip-hop and remix culture.[29]

Winfried Siemerling suggests hip-hop in Compton's work functions as a "literary structural metaphor and practiced improvisational form."[30] Through the improvisational and intertwined forms of hip-hop and remix, Compton creates a unique mix that plays with various traditions – oral and written, sonic and visual, African and European, Black and White, local and global, Canadian and American – in order to provide more nuanced critiques of power, identity, and history. By using various intertexts, like a vessel/DJ, Compton challenges existing discourses, introduces neglected histories (such as the Black community of Hogan's Alley), and connects these various voices together like the meta-turntable, which dually functions as a traditional and postmodern signifier. In an email conversation, Compton told me that he borrows "from the history of turntablism to create poetry in the way that early hip-hop deejays began to create music out of a medium that was not meant to create music, but rather to merely be a vessel for it."[31] As a vessel for the many voices, across the diaspora, that appear in *Performance Bond*, he confronts globalization and the commodification of Black culture.

However, Compton remains particularly skeptical about the emancipatory potential of hip-hop music, even as he applies hip-hop aesthetics to his writing, largely because he finds that the influence of hip-hop on small, culturally isolated communities, such as those in BC, is not only overly pervasive but might at times be a form of American imperialism. As he told Nigel Thomas, his poem "The Reinventing Wheel" (which he had not yet published at the time of the interview) is actually "anti-hip-hop in certain ways, and most of what has come out of it are my criticisms of hip-hop and of the passive reception of hip-hop in Canada. It has forced me to think more and more about American culture."[32] Compton particularly embraces many of the cultural aspects of hip-hop – notably, hip-hop turntablism as a possible metaphor "in and of itself, for a reflective *mise-en-abyme* of influences"[33] – but critiques the tone of much of hip-hop as emotionally limited, citing anger as the primary expression. Much of the hip-hop lingo in the poem both connects and intentionally falls a little flat when situated in the geographical and psychological experience of Vancouver: "Take us home. Keep it real. Word is bond." Compton performs with tidalectical reverence for the cyclical nature of influence: "The ancestors we have honoured/will be born as our descendants/to remember us."[34] Compton's strategy is hip-hop inspired, even as he acknowledges the limits of the form to speak to Black experience in British Columbia.

Like Brathwaite, Compton works to "find non-clichéd ways to describe what a lot of people call experimental, or avant-garde ... work that doesn't just happily receive and then carry on."[35] In his essay "Turntable Poetry, Mixed-Race, and Schizophonophilia," Compton defines "schizophonophilia" as the "love of audio interplay, the pleasure of critical disruptions to natural audition, the counter-hegemonic affirmation that can be achieved through acoustic intervention."[36] I particularly like the notion of acoustic intervention, of disrupting the pretense of naturalism, which for Compton is relevant in a context where race and mixed-race are being explicitly addressed. In 2010 in Vancouver I saw Compton cast his own poetry from *Performance Bond* in tidalectical relation to other works that deal with notions of hybridity, DJ culture, and Canadian citizenship, emulated via the music's own polyphonic and hybridized layering of sound and thematic. This performance involved a sampler and three turntables: the sampler played a vocal sample of Compton reading from his poem "The Reinventing Wheel," while the entire performance was cued to various electro and hip-hop beats with the aid of co-performer and turntablist Jason de Couto. The performance included an out-of-print vinyl of *Alex Haley Tells the Story of His Search for Roots* on one turntable, which was followed directly on another turntable by an excerpt from Margaret Atwood's *The Journals of Susanna Moodie*, read by actress Mia Anderson. The excerpt focused on a moment where "Atwood's Moodie re-perceives her whiteness." Here, as Compton suggests, "sampling provides the power of focus and re-contextualization" and reminds us that identity is a remix project.[37]

Envisioning rupture as a creative act, Compton employs postmodern remix culture as a democratic principle that polymetrically sounds citizenship. Compton's useful neologism, "schizophonophilia," appropriates and contests what Canadian acoustic ecologist and composer R. Murray Schafer terms "schizophonia." Schafer defines "schizophonia" as a "dislocation of the voice from the body through recording technologies, and electronic amplification."[38] Schafer views such technological manipulations as negative; Compton argues that Schafer believes schizophonia "disrupts the natural flow of life and breaks our connection to an ecologically contiguous world." However, through the unsettling nature of being mixed-race in North America, Compton embraces this rupture between the natural world and the decentralized body and author precisely "because it is unsettling." The phonograph/turntable is the perfect medium for this split/disembodied message of acoustic intervention, as Compton describes the phonograph as "a machine turned inside-out; a machine whose workings are always visible, whose interface is literally tangible, and whose production of sound is visceral. The body of the phonograph, like the body of a racialized object, can never close."[39] Through the medium of disembodied sound, mixed-race subjectivity is made sonically tangible by showing how race and identity formation never fully close.

Like a DJ sampling a record, Compton shows how a reference can be lifted to complicate our understanding of how we remember the past. Compton's poem "Performance Bond" opens with a reference to the song "As Time Goes By," made popular in the film *Casablanca*, by replacing the word "fundamental" with "multicultural": "The multicultural things apply/as time goes by."[40] This mis-duplication of the chorus of "As Times Goes By" further recalls the song's famous opening line, "You must remember this," which emphasizes that as time goes by, immigrant and migrant histories are often written over or forgotten. Compton reminds us that in British Columbia – and in Canada, with the exception of Indigenous people – "Everybody's a migrant. Every body gyrates/to the global bigbeat ... and multiculturalism can't arrive/by forgetting, but remembering ... because those who don't remember/repeat."[41]

Disturbing the punctum of official state history and state-sponsored multiculturalism, Compton connects the migrant and multicultural experience to the diasporic embodiment of the "global bigbeat." Using the cut-up method (although more Grandmaster Flash than Burroughs),[42] Compton emphasizes – through a synecdoche where "Everybody" embodies a physical "body" that gyrates, and even though Vancouver exists on the peripheries "of empire, and time has/gone by"[43] – that bodies and physical stories still inhabit the geography and are in need of recovery/sounding.

As Joanne Leow writes, in relation to "Performance Bond," "issues of geography are implied here, whether these are hectares taken from First Nations peoples or non-white communities in Vancouver who lost their neighbourhoods to urban redevelopment."[44] Remembering becomes a transnational act of recovery at the crossroads of erasure, and while Compton's poetics are cadenced with sonic repetitions, by contrast, forgetting signifies an illusory broadcasting of multiculturalism that dooms one to repeat the mistakes of the past. Compton backcues the historical record, spinning "the ready-made blues in the backwoods, backwards" to find a spiral "root through."[45] By entering into his schizophonic mix we can travel with him through the archives of Hogan's Alley and resound a vibrant community that was dealt a great injustice.

III. Rune: Hogan's Alley Remixed

> Those who cannot remember the past are condemned to repeat it.
> George Santayana quoted in Miller, *Rhythm Science*, 9

Hogan's Alley (see fig. 17.1) was the local, unofficial name for Park Lane, a T-shaped alley that ran through the southwestern corner of Strathcona in Vancouver during the first six decades of the twentieth century. It ran between Union and Prior Streets from approximately Main Street to Jackson Avenue. Hogan's Alley was not solely a Black neighbourhood; Italian immigrants also trace their history there, and it was right on the edge of Chinatown.[46] The history of Black immigrants arriving in British Columbia, mostly from California, dates back to 1858. Most of these Black settlers initially settled in Victoria and on Salt Spring Island, but eventually many moved to Vancouver as it gradually became the economic epicentre of British Columbia. In Vancouver, they made their homes on the East Side in the southern part of Strathcona, a working-class neighbourhood that would become known as Hogan's Alley.[47] By the 1920s the Black community had built an African Methodist Episcopal Church and

Figure 17.1. Hogan's Alley, 1958. City of Vancouver Archives, #Bu P508.53. Photo by A.L. Yates.

opened various businesses, and by 1940 the Black population may have reached some eight hundred people.[48]

The close-knit Black community of Hogan's Alley was largely a result of the community's proximity to the train stations, since sleeping car porters were predominantly Black men.[49] All the major vaudeville acts passed through Vancouver as circuits moved by train. Further, the musical scene in Hogan's Alley – which included many local acts, like the Crump Twins[50] – prefigured what we now refer to using the cliché "Hollywood North" and featured some of the biggest names in music, who would pass through to perform in the bars there, including Sammy Davis Jr., Ella Fitzgerald, Count Basie, Louis Armstrong, and Duke Ellington. For a period of time, a number of cross-cultural musical mavericks, such as Jelly Roll Morton and Jimi Hendrix, even made Vancouver's Downtown Eastside their home. At the Patricia Hotel, jazz legend Jelly Roll Morton joined the house band and played there between 1919 and 1921. Nora Hendrix, a former vaudeville dancer and the paternal grandmother of Jimi Hendrix, immigrated to Vancouver in 1911 and helped found the church in Hogan's Alley. Jimi Hendrix would often visit Vancouver and even lived there during the winter of 1962–3, practising and often playing in nightclubs.[51] Today, in Vancouver's Downtown Eastside there is a shrine dedicated to Jimi Hendrix. Despite their American origins, both Morton and Hendrix deserve honorary Canuck status; like British Columbia's own history of flux, both musicians represent music as a crossing of unbound possibility.

While Vancouver provided a more hospitable environment to Black people than the United States, Vancouver could be particularly hostile to racial others. In "Inlet Holler," from *Performance Bond*, Compton further implicates his own unease as a settler – his ancestors did not arrive as slaves – viewing the Vancouver inlet as "no more mine than yours," writing that like others he just happens to be here: "I am a settler/I am uneasy/there is nowhere to go."[52] Reflecting on the nature of belonging in Vancouver, Compton's poem "Illegalese: Floodgate Dub" engages with the media backlash against the Fujianese migrants who arrived in Canada by ship. In the summer of 1999, nearly six hundred Chinese migrants arrived on the BC coast in four dilapidated boats and one shipping container. The majority had paid at least $30,000 to smugglers for their passage, and many had not survived the trip. While every migrant was given due process (although certainly not fair process), 444 of the 577 refugee claims were rejected. Critic Larissa Lai addresses the crisis as one around legitimacy, particularly asking, Who has the right to say who comes and goes?[53] Compton remixes this incident, writing, "if you arrive in the belly of a rusting imagination, there are grounds to outlaw you." He points out the hypocrisy of a country like Canada that likes to remember itself as a haven for the runaway slave, but then asks, "why is it villifiable for Chinese migrants to hide in the belly of a dream/now?"[54] *Performance Bond* provides voice to those who are considered illegal and without citizenship status, interrogating Canada's history of exclusion, focalizing around the historical community of Hogan's Alley.[55]

Compton's inspirational home/community/hood of Hogan's Alley exists in the ghosting of history and the portals of retold stories: "It's a thin lane/between Hogan's Alley and self-hatred./My ghosthood, those old standards."[56] Compton's own disembodied voice – he often performs "The Reinventing Wheel" by manipulating a recording of himself reading sections of the poem – speaks to the loss of a community that was put under erasure; through a resampling/ghosting process, he demonstrates that community can never be erased. Compton's recovery of Hogan's Alley is an attempt to fortify the community and remember the past in the present moment. Compton's imaginative and schizophonophilic engagement with Vancouver's Black history (specifically in "Rune," the final section of *Performance Bond*), contests the historical and physical erasure of Hogan's Alley (an act of "Negro removal") by providing counternarratives that refortify that community.

Compton writes in his essay "Seven Routes to Hogan's Alley and Vancouver's Black Community" that "Vancouver's Black community suffered what their American cousins, punning on the term 'urban renewal,' called 'Negro removal' – the destruction of the politically weakest community of a city for large modernist planning schemes." Compton's renewal is the antithesis to the forced removal of Vancouver's historic Black community. Hogan's Alley was likely named after Richard Outcault's cartoon entitled *Hogan's Alley*, published between 1894 and 1896, which featured a fictional New York ghetto with crowded streets and urban squalor.[57] This depiction fits the public perception of Hogan's Alley, described by journalist Jack Stepler as standing for three things: "squalor, immorality and crime."[58] And while Hogan's Alley was hardly perfect – Compton reminds readers we must be careful not to romanticize it, having been told he was lucky to have not grown up there[59] – Hogan's Alley was brimming with honest labourers, Black businesses, a newspaper press, and a church. The removal of the community under the guise of an "urban renewal" project – specifically, the proposed building of an overpass – was, as Compton describes, "old-fashioned racism: freeways were invariably run through black neighbourhoods or Chinatowns, poor districts whose populations were least able to lobby civic governments."[60] Hence, citizenship afforded different rights to those living in the more prosperous (predominantly White) West End of downtown Vancouver than it did to those living in Vancouver's East Side.

In a 2013 interview with Compton, I probed him to think about the trajectory of his work around Hogan's Alley and Black BC history, particularly in relation to a larger national or transnational project. He told me that his initial need to work on the recovery of Black BC history came out of a raw necessity "to understand black history in the province, in Western Canada ... We were at first focused on a memorial, a public memorial, and then as we got rolling we quickly realized we didn't know much. So then it became more about information, consciousness raising, and information gathering."[61] Compton's performance of making Hogan's Alley come to life again is a historical imperative to present a fuller and more multicultural understanding of Vancouver than history books often depict.

Rune

"Rune," the title of the final section of *Performance Bond*, is a word with multiple meanings that appropriately animate Compton's magical, cryptic, and performative lament for Hogan's Alley: "onward movement"; any "of the letters or characters of the earliest Germanic alphabet"; "a similar character or mark believed to have mysterious or magical powers"; or, as a verb, "to compose or perform poetry or songs; to lament."[62] "Rune" also sounds apocalyptically close to *ruin*, recalling the ruins and visual remains of Hogan's Alley. "Rune," as Jonathan Dale Sherman contends in "The Hip-Hop Aesthetics and Visual Poetry of Wayde Compton's *Performance Bond*," "creates a union of hip-hop aesthetics and visual poetry to create a space for Vancouver's historical and present black community."[63] Essentially, Compton creates visual poetry by including graffiti signs, Vodou symbols, pictures, a simulated newspaper facsimile of a *Vancouver Daily Province* article, and various typographic characters that do not necessarily come from written words. In the book's acknowledgments, Compton writes that while much of "Rune" riffs on historical record, the section contains some "fictitious elements: a newspaper article, four landmarks, and two transcribed interviews."[64] He elaborates that "Rune" is "about the memory of Hogan's Alley, and specifically the problem of how to remember Hogan's Alley … The poem deals with the ambivalences of looking back, and the enduring curiosity of those times and conditions." He opts for an elliptical remembering ("semi-hoaxes" based on "actual corollary") rather than a realistic representation, since a realistic representation is itself a kind of imaginative impossibility.[65] By staging and mis-duplicating various historical works (articles, oral histories, and so on) concerning Hogan's Alley, Compton's "Rune" provides, as Leow suggests, "dense layers of historical, literary, and theoretical intertexts" that allow Compton "to have them interact and create new ways of understanding his contemporary contexts."[66] Hence, it makes sense that the first poem in "Rune" concerns the various historical and physical blank spaces of Hogan's Alley. Through creative interplay, Compton imaginatively fills those lacunae.

The poem "Blight" opens with an invitation to the reader to fill in the empty and abandoned spaces of the poem, much like the missing landmarks of Hogan's Alley: "When _____ take _____ pictures of _____, there are no people there; the decay will speak for itself."[67] Compton cleverly uses blank spaces – silence – to show how Hogan's Alley has been historically blighted. Blank spaces in the poem represent missing details, abandonment, and erasure, as well as a historical whitewashing as words in black ink have been replaced by white spaces that Compton then rebuilds into new structures and sites of performance: "There are whole languages built out of how _____ aren't./Absences chopped down, hewn into beams, and raised."[68] The blank spaces in the poem also function like a "cloze test," a psychological exercise "in which a person is required to supply words which have been deliberately omitted from a passage."[69] Given that cloze tests are often used in learning language and facts, Compton's poem suggests it is important to remember and recall the blighted history of Hogan's Alley. Building inspectors and the city described Hogan's Alley as a blighted neighbourhood that was essentially diseased and needed to be cut out from the city for fear the squalor would spread. Historians might deliberately omit important passages of a people's history, but those deliberate omissions can, at times, be creatively recovered, providing an opening or a closing: "instead of a shutter/it could have been an opener./A closer. A closure. A cloze test./A flutter." Compton's playful literary consonance, arriving at a cloze test that then erupts into a flutter – a taking off – recalls how easily portals, like a shutter (a screen, or a camera device allowing light to pass), are closed and opened. And while he sings an "occlusion blues," a closure in the vocal tract, "Blight" is ultimately about reinscription and remix "in/_____ ever-lovin way."[70] Like the DJ improvising a mix, inviting listeners to put their own interpretive mix together – each person will, after all, fill the blank spaces differently – Compton's recovery poetics, his audio-interplay, has more meaning when we participate in the imaginative performance of Hogan's Alley.

The same creative act of filling in blanks is displayed in Compton's visual poems/re-creations of "Lost-Found Landmarks of Black Vancouver." By including visual images within "Rune" – such as, in "Lost-Found Landmarks of Black Vancouver," the mirror images of "Forme and Chase," a photograph titled "Vividuct," and the graffiti tag of "Rev. Oz" taking up an entire white page in "Ghetto Fabulous Ozymandias" – and the various runes throughout *Performance Bond*, Compton creates a visual poetry that resists typical poetic inscription. Visual poetry, according to painter Lazlo Moholy-Nagy, seeks to "liberate literature from the disparateness of eye and ear, from the monotony connected with the dullness of regular typography."[71] Compton's photographic staging of Black Vancouver is not intended, as he explains, "to hoax readers, but rather to at once allegorize the ontological feelings emanating from the social and historical conditions ... and to experiment formally with cultural memorialization as a representational act." Understandably, he feels anxious creating manufactured images "of a community in the midst of a difficult 'real' memorialization," but the process, much like the "cloze test," is intended to engage readers in the process of fiction, which imitates history and a lack of action by official city councillors around what they have come to believe is an ambiguous Black populace.[72] Despite the apparent invisibility of the experience of Black people in Vancouver – past and present – photography represents one way to remember that actual people made Hogan's Alley home.

Figure 17.2. Georgia Viaduct construction on the old Hogan's Alley site, 1971. City of Vancouver Archives, CVA 447–374. Photo by Walter E. Frost.

The physical rupture and displacement of the inhabitants of Hogan's Alley for an overpass (the Georgia Viaduct) remains in the ruins of the failed "urban renewal"/ "negro removal" project. The construction of the Georgia Viaduct (figure 17.2) was part of the first phase of a planned interurban freeway that would run through Hogan's Alley and much of Chinatown and Gastown. The freeway was stopped by an alliance of Strathcona community activists and Chinatown businesspeople. While the construction of the freeway (which would have involved demolishing buildings throughout the Downtown Eastside and Chinatown) was blocked, the Georgia Viaduct overpass was ultimately completed, causing most of Hogan's Alley to be demolished and the most vulnerable people there to be displaced. While the work of activists should be rightly celebrated, the damage to Hogan's Alley was done and Vancouver would never again have such a concentrated Black community. Compton's concrete poem (informed by the form of concrete) "Forme and Chase" mirrors the image of two viaducts in a piece titled "Vividuct" on the page beside the poem and, like a viaduct, provides a crossing, a ghosting, between the past and present.[73] "Forme and Chase" mirrors the viaduct and uses a typewritten font to emphasize the loss of an entire analogue community, as if the history of Hogan's Alley was buried under the bridge.

Consisting of two stanzas that parallel two viaducts on the photo on the next page, Compton's poem depicts that while structures degenerate and cities change, memories and the histories of people continue to phantom the present, like the spectre haunting his font and dictation, much like "the ghosts in these Technics" embodying his turntable poetics.[74] Compton's choice to use the archaic spelling of form, "Forme," with the word "Chase," a printing term referring to the arrangement of text, emphasizes that while he is concerned with finding new ways to speak to the past, his "bastard grapholect" shows that written words are but a bridge, a portal, that often mimics what can be only partially recovered.[75] Then again, the image of the viaducts is itself a graphic representation of where a vibrant community once lived, whose imprints remain, like the graffiti on the viaducts: erased, and then rewritten, since Compton's neologistic spelling of viaduct as "Vividuct" comes from the Latin *vivi* – to live, to be alive, to survive.

Compton's tidalectical spinning of the past with the present is, as he describes in "The New Station," "alchemical work, spinning/meaning out of meandering ... I go over/the remains; I transform,/I translate." Compton's translation is very much an analogue one into a digital present; that is, he takes the absences of a faded past and transforms the remains/ruins/runes into a digital mix that speaks to the very mixedness of his own arrival. The poem "The New Station" is dedicated to *"Clarence Clemons, a black longshoreman beaten to death by Vancouver police in the alley behind New Station Café in 1952,"* *"Kary Taylor, a black dentist beaten by Burnaby RCMP in 1999,"* and *"my high school buddies ... who became Lower Mainland police officers, all of them Asian."* In the poem Compton takes us through various stations, describing a near collision in a car at age seventeen, recalling the experience "every time I cross this overpass. I'm keying/on my PC now towards this terminus ... between the old train station rising/at Terminal Ave. and the vanished/New Station Café."[76] Stations vanish and new ones crop up, recalling the passage of runaway slaves on the Underground Railroad toward their terminus in Canada. Time changes the stations, and given that Kary Taylor was beaten because the officer responsible (in his words) *"saw a black man in a nice car with an Oriental female, and, given the area, he wasn't sure if it was possibly a prostitute-pimp situation,"* it is one fitting justice that Compton's Asian Canadian friends are now police officers.[77] Racism in Vancouver still exists (and persists); Compton's "Illegalese: Floodgate Dub" and other poems announce this much, but we have also entered a multicultural era: many of the stations are liminal spaces between worlds, spaces of possibility, hope – digital spaces of remix.

"Ghetto Fabulous Ozymandias," the final poem in "Rune," riffs on Percy Shelley's sonnet "Ozymandias," even reading the poem within the poem. Shelley's poem contrasts the inevitable decline of leaders and empires with the lasting power of art and contains the often quoted lines engraved on the statue of Ozymandias: "My name is Ozymandias, King of Kings;/Look on my Works, ye Mighty, and despair!"[78] Around the colossal wreck of Ozymandias nothing remains, as the poem speaks to the arrogance of empire, except that the site of ruin for Compton is Hogan's Alley. In Compton's poem, the speaker, who is in dialogue with Rev. Oz, a homeless preacher, explains that "'Shelley's poem was about arrogance'" while "'this place – the community that was here – they were driven/out. Their neighbourhood was flattened by the City. There's nothing/left here because of an injustice. It doesn't make sense/to call the targets of this unfairness "arrogant."'" Rev. Oz replies, in one of the most telling moments in *Performance Bond*, that it does make sense, since "It is arrogant to disappear."[79] We can try to forget the past, but as Compton poignantly puts it, such a gesture would be an act of extreme arrogance.

Today Vancouver has over twenty thousand Black residents.[80] Compton points out that the "perceived absence of blacks in Vancouver is an optical illusion: black people today represent a higher percentage of the total population than they did fifty or a hundred years ago."[81] Yet, the majority of Vancouver's population understands very little of the history – or existence even – of Hogan's Alley. Compton, as "a person who has more white than black biological ancestry" and few direct familial ties to the area itself, has devoted so much time to the Hogan's Alley memorial project because he sees himself as "an afterimage of our history."[82] The work of Compton and others has not gone unnoticed: a plaque was put up in 2013 to commemorate the community, which Compton says "speaks loudly about a community that people too often seem surprised exists at all."[83] Canada Post, as part of Black History Month in 2014, commemorated Hogan's Alley on a stamp – featuring Fielding William Spotts Jr., the first Baptist in western Canada, and Nora Hendrix, grandmother to Jimi Hendrix and cook at Vie's Chicken and Steak House in Hogan's Alley – which Compton described as a substantial success: "knowing that generations that are coming up now are going to have this as part of the regular landscape is very satisfying."[84] In 2014, visual artist Stan Douglas created an app for iOS devices with which you can walk through Hogan's Alley circa 1948. In 2016, Telus released a short and highly informative documentary called *Secret Vancouver: Return to Hogan's Alley*. And, perhaps most fruitfully, depending on how the project plays out, are plans for an actual space that revives the community of Hogan's Alley. There are plans to remove the Georgia viaducts (although much is in flux; see note 3), and the city of Vancouver has hired American architect Zena Howard to help with the revitalization project.[85]

These efforts by activists and artists, and recent commitments by the city, gift future generations who will have these works, memorials, and possibly an actual area to gather and remember Hogan's Alley as part of their cultural landscape. The past matters because Compton, and all of us, remembers in the present tense. To think that a historically Black community in British Columbia (however small) that was forcibly removed doesn't matter to everyone is arrogant. We can only build a more multicultural future, a more nuanced remix, by first standing at the crossroads and understanding what has come to pass, but which is never fully past.

IV. From Analogue to Digital: Engaging with the New Black Can(aan) Lit

> The past is neither inert nor given. The stories we tell about what happened then, the correspondences we discern between today and times past, and the ethical and political stakes of these stories redound in the present. If slavery feels proximate rather than remote and freedom seems increasingly elusive, this has everything to do with our own dark times. If the ghost of slavery still haunts our present, it is because we are still looking for an exit from the prison.
> Saidiya Hartman, *Lose Your Mother: A Journey along the Atlantic Slave Route*, 133

As this epigraph suggests, the past is hardly static: the spectre of slavery still haunts the present. Therefore, the stories we tell are crucial to building a more ethical and equitable future for all citizens. Compton combines various historical, theoretical, and literary intertexts (from the Bible to Vodou) to sound a more inclusive version of Canadian citizenship that opens up space for those – like the historical Black community of Hogan's Alley – who have been pushed aside from official history. If the past is represented as "analogue" and the present as "digital," then we must consider both as part of the tidalectical process of creating the future, especially since, as Amiri Baraka puts it, "The future is always here in the past."[86] Moving between analogue and digital – in search of what C.L.R. James calls "new verse, new passwords"[87] – Compton's poem "Véve" features a dialogue (like a play script) between Analogue and Digital beside the Georgia Viaduct, at the former site of Hogan's Alley, and concerns the liminal space between worlds and technology, mixing the past and present together in tidalectical fashion to explore how boundaries limit fruitful dialogue. Véve is a Vodou religious symbol, and in the poem, using Digital's bag of trail mix, Analogue draws a version of

Legba's symbol on the sidewalk.[88] Within a few minutes, pigeons come by and eat the symbol, which causes Digital to inquire about more permanent types of writing, such as ink; they discuss Brathwaite's poem, also titled "Vévé," and the ritual power of writing and culture.

As Brathwaite writes in his poem, "So on this ground,/write:/within the sound/of this white limestone *vévé*, talk/of the empty roads, vessels of your head, claypots, shards, ruins."[89] For Brathwaite, whose poem invokes earthy and ephemeral images, Vévé becomes a poetic rite and figure of the act of writing. Digital states that the problem with that kind of writing is it "will eventually get mussed up," while Analogue contends that it's not quite writing but, more specifically, what "Brathwaite means is that it's the *beginning* of writing, or the urge to make a new kind of language to the New World." Compton's poem suggests that both analogue and digital offer creative potentials and that both are kinds of portals – that digital technology is, according to Analogue, "nothing new ... They just needed the tools to make you real."[90] Like a trickster, much like the coyote who is misrecognized as a dog by Digital and Analogue in the same poem, Compton's performance – his bonding of technologies – crafts new spaces and alternatives as means to think about the past and space and to envision how new and traditional methods are needed to create the future. To engage in the revolutionary potential of language, we need to find new ways to rework the past in the present moment.

Compton's use of multimodal and turntable poetics is a technique that allows him to explore the form's literary potential, and it provides a challenge to the very monocultural model (and garrison mentality) that has dominated CanLit for so long.[91] As Linda Hutcheon has said, "History leaves its mark on our literature, it always has."[92] But certain stories of history can be oppressive; hear Compton riffing on Countee Cullen: "What is Britannia to me?"[93] It is precisely this divergence between the inescapable mark of history coupled with the indifference toward a certain strand of enforced history that Compton disavows, and it is within (and between) these ruptures, fissures, and fragmentations that we as engaged scholars can create more nuanced sonic literary mixes. History is the border in the way a book contains story, and in scholarship it is where Black Canadian literature sits, a border of historical possibility that writers like Compton navigate. Historically, Black Canadians have struggled for equal citizenship and the right to control their cultural depictions; one need only look at French-Canadian artist François Malépart de Beaucourt's 1786 painting *Portrait of a Negro Slave or Negress*, now known as *Portrait of a Haitian Woman*, to see how Black people have historically had their representations depicted for them.[94] Thus, there is particular value to disturbing limited historical representations and creating representations that are more expansive and inclusive.

It is a kind of sanguine utopianism to assume that the old xenophobic myths of Canada as a White androcentric settler nation are gone from CanLit (David Gilmour and others of his ilk uphold such views).[95] If we look more closely, we see that being born in CanLit are multiple genuinely authored multicultural texts that interrogate Canada's past to dream of a more just society. Texts by Black Canadian authors like M. NourbeSe Philip, George Elliott Clarke, Lawrence Hill, André Alexis, Austin Clarke, Dionne Brand, d'bi.young.anitafrika, David Chariandy, Dany Laferrière, Suzette Mayr, Nalo Hopkinson, Chelene Knight, Afua Cooper, Claire Harris, K'naan, Wayde Compton, and countless others do not just teach us to be better listeners (citizens even) but make us more "Canadian" – that is, they take us more into Canada's margins to expand and challenge the notion of margins and where we historically place value.

We need to engage with what Smaro Kamboureli describes as a collaborative rethinking of "the disciplinary and institutional frameworks within which Canadian literature is produced, disseminated, studied, and taught."[96] It would be myopic to assume that White people do not have an advantage in society, and the same goes for White writers in CanLit. White privilege needs to be understood within settler colonialism: it is not some artefact of history but a process that continues to unfold in society. In "Institutionalized Racism and Canadian History," Adrienne Shadd reminds us that Black "descendants, particularly in the Maritimes, have been living in quasi-segregated communities for over 200 years."[97] A similar case could be made about Black writers being studied and taught in Canadian universities. The New Canadian Library, which compiles classic works of CanLit, contains but one work by a Black author: Austin Clarke's *Amongst Thistles and Thorns*.[98] Rinaldo Walcott has stated that he is quitting CanLit since it "fails to transform because it refuses to take seriously that Black literary expression and thus Black life is foundational to it. CanLit still appears surprised every single time by the appearance of Black literary expression and Black life."[99] As Darcy Ballantyne, Paul Barrett, Camille Isaacs, and Kris Singh write – reflecting on the fact that zero people showed up for their 2017 ACCUTE panel on Austin Clarke, ironically titled "Austin Clarke's Critical Neglect" – "CanLit is still very much an anti-black space."[100] And yet, how can you study and understand the shape of Canadian literature and history without engaging closely with the work of CanLit trailblazer Austin Clarke or with that of more contemporary writers like Wayde Compton?

People, like language, are heterogeneous, and citizenship in relation to a truly or genuinely multicultural country must reflect that, even if the wheel has to be reinvented in the process. Hogan's Alley was put directly under erasure, and the same thing has happened in mainstream CanLit with Black-authored texts. Much of the innovative, engaging, and brilliant writing in this country is happening in Black writing and in Indigenous writing: few texts are as layered and complex as Afrosporic Caribbean poet M. NourbeSe Philip's *Zong!* (2008) or Nisga'a poet Jordan Abel's *Injun* (2016). "Canada is," as Compton writes in "Illegalese: Floodgate Dub," "a remix B-side chorus in the globalization loop."[101] Compton's words depict the negative ethos of globalization, as well as the possibility for continued remix in the musical loop of a Canada that is always changing as new people and ideas enter into the mix. Compton remixes the past and combines various historical, theoretical, and literary samples to sound a more inclusive version of Canadian citizenship that opens up space for those – like the historical Black community of Hogan's Alley – whom official history have elided.

In his poem "Declaration of the Halfrican Nation," Compton asks, "is a black/rose natural? is it indigenous to this/coast?"[102] Compton's framing of a black rose as natural speaks to Black experiences in Canada as being as ontologically Canadian as anything else that is *inauthentically* authentic in Canada. Not necessarily in practice, but in theory (and idealistically, in legislation), Canada belongs equally to all of its citizens. Aside from Indigenous people, we are all uneasy settlers here. We have an opportunity to resist the politics of division and accept that our story is one of fragmentation but also one of multicultural possibility. I'm not sure how the "just" society might ultimately sound, but I do know that the history of Hogan's Alley, like other blighted histories, must be part of its conception. Like DJs attuned to the historical archive, we have a chance to engage and understand the past in order to build a more equitable future. For the future of Hogan's Alley that should include a real memorialization and public space that honours the past as a way forward. As engaged educators, students, and citizens we can see ourselves as consummate remixers entering into the larger Canadian sound mix. Collectively, when we work together to remember and reinvigorate the past – as Compton and others have done with communities like Hogan's Alley – we work against the politics of division and look for ways to heal the ruins of the past, ultimately providing avenues forward. Read, listen, and act: Hogan's Alley *lives*.

NOTES

1 This essay is built from a chapter of my doctoral dissertation, "Soundin' Canaan: Music, Resistance, and Citizenship in African Canadian Poetry"

(University of Guelph, 2015), as well as public talk on Compton's poetics and Hogan's Alley I gave at Vancouver Island University in 2016.

2 Mash-ups, as critic Lisa Coulthard outlines, "rub sources against each other, layering incongruous cultural products and reworking references through new combinations, associations and contexts." Coulthard, "Great Artists Steal," in *MashUp: The Birth of Modern Culture*, ed. Daina Augaitis, Bruce Grenville, and Stephen Rebick (Vancouver: Vancouver Art Gallery; London: Black Dog, 2016), 238.

3 The Northeast False Creek Plan (NEFC) "provides an opportunity to reconnect through reconciliation, replacing the Georgia and Dunsmuir viaducts with strong cultural, social and physical linkages." City of Vancouver, *Northeast False Creek Plan* (Vancouver, February 2018), 2, https://vancouver.ca/files/cov/northeast-false-creek-plan.pdf. The plan from the city includes a brief historical section on Hogan's Alley and Vancouver's Black community and, among other things, states the intention to "establish a Cultural Centre on the 898 Main Street block (Hogan's Alley block). The Cultural Centre will be a focal point for the Black Community, and will be welcoming and inclusive to all – a place 'from the community, for the community'" (p. 23). In a Facebook conversation I had with Wayde Compton (January 12, 2019), I was informed that "one political slate, Coalition Vancouver, was actually campaigning on killing the Northeast False Creek Plan." There continues to be a frustrating amount of ignorance in Vancouver about the historical Black community at the viaducts. As Compton went on to explain, "there was a lot of silence from the other parties, left and right, about the plan and the city's commitments in it to the Hogan's Alley Working Group [which included Anthonia Ogundele as a general city planning consultant and some thirty or so other people, including some former Hogan's Alley residents] and its successor, the Hogan's Alley Society. (The notable exceptions were Vision, whose plan it was to begin with, and One City, who explicitly supported Hogan's Alley restitution at the viaduct site.) We worked for two years in consultation with the City of Vancouver, but during the election, Vision Vancouver collapsed, and so it is not clear what the current council will do with the NEFC plan, or the Hogan's Alley portion of it." Compton then informed me that there is some promise, as one member of the Hogan's Alley Working Group is now on the council – Pete Fry, who is Trinidadian – and that there are a number of other important supporters, including Jean Swanson, a Vancouver city councillor and anti-poverty activist. More promising, as Compton pointed out, was that the Black community is now organized in a way it has not been since the 1990s and there is more understanding and support from the larger community for an official centre and a land trust. The Hogan's Alley Working Group, which has morphed into the Hogan's Alley Society,

continues to pressure the city to complete the promised plan. As Compton says, "The Hogan's Alley Society is functional and active and will be pushing for the completion of our part of the plan." The Society is being run by dedicated people like June Francis, Stephanie Alley, Adam Rudder, and Randy Clarke (a former resident of Hogan's Alley).
4 George Elliott Clarke, *Directions Home* (Toronto: University of Toronto Press, 2012), 4. To not look into the history and legacy (over 350 years) of African Canadian people – including the various social and cultural vicissitudes – is, in the words of George Elliott Clarke, to opt for a "veritable intellectual treason." Clarke, *Odysseys Home: Mapping African-Canadian Literature* (Toronto: University of Toronto Press, 2000), 198.
5 There were many other Black communities in Canada beyond Africville and Hogan's Alley; see Karina Vernon, ed., *The Black Prairie Archives: An Anthology* (Waterloo, ON: Wilfrid Laurier University Press, 2019).
6 Dionne Brand, *Bread out of Stone* (Toronto: Vintage, 1998), 37.
7 Thomas King, *The Inconvenient Indian* (Toronto: Anchor Canada, 2012), 2–3.
8 Afua Cooper, *The Hanging of Angélique: The Untold Story of Canadian Slavery and the Burning of Old Montréal* (Toronto: Harper Perennial, 2006), 68. Dionne Brand describes how in her own experience she was forced to read and learn about White writers in the academy and hardly at all about African American and Black Canadian writers. Brand, *No Burden to Carry: Narratives of Black Working Women in Ontario, 1920s to 1950s* (Toronto: Women's Press, 1991), 29. This sentiment is echoed by James W. St. G. Walker, who attests that "the student of Canadian history can go right through our school system, university courses, and even graduate school, without ever being exposed to the history of blacks in Canada." Walker, *A History of Blacks in Canada: A Study Guide for Teachers and Students* (Ottawa: Minister of State Multiculturalism, 1980), 3. See also Joseph Mensah, *Black Canadians: History, Experience, Social Conditions* (Halifax: Fernwood, 2002), 45.
9 Yvonne Brown, quoted in Wayde Compton, *Bluesprint: Black British Columbian Literature and Orature* (Vancouver: Arsenal Pulp Press, 2001), 155. Also, for a detailed account of how prevalent, rampant, manifest, and yet subversively subdued slavery was and is in early Canadian history, see the first two chapters of Robin Winks's seminal work *The Blacks in Canada: A History*, 2nd ed. (Montreal and Kingston: McGill-Queen's University Press, 2000). On the Middle Passage, see SlaveVoyages, "The Trans-Atlantic Slave Trade – Database," https://www.slavevoyages.org/voyage/database.
10 Winks, *Blacks in Canada*, 235. There is much to admire about Winks's text, yet as scholar David Austin describes, "Winks leaves little room for self-activity or self-organization of Blacks – that is, their own efforts to organize themselves in order to humanize their existence or confront Canadian racial oppression." Austin, *Fear of a Black Nation: Race, Sex, and Security in*

Sixties Montreal (Toronto: Between the Lines, 2013), 139. Winks makes the point that investigations of southern slave songs show that Canaan, the promised land, was equated most often with Africa and seldom with Canada (Winks, *Blacks in Canada*, 237). However, theologian and scholar James H. Cone argues that Canaan had multiple associations: "Heaven referred to Africa, Canada, and the northern United States." Cone, *The Spirituals and the Blues* (Maryknoll, NY: Orbis Books, 2009), 80. Whether or not the slave songs – the spirituals – were directly associated with Canada, the use of Canaan to refer to Canada as heaven continues to this day and carries important mythic value for Black Canadian writers.

11 Frederick Douglass, *Narrative of the Life of Frederick Douglass, an American Slave* (1845; New York: Penguin, 1986), 51.
12 Mary Ann Shadd Cary (1852), quoted in Jason H. Silverman, *Unwelcome Guests: Canada West's Response to American Fugitive Slaves, 1880–1865* (Millwood, NY: Associated Faculty Press, 1985), 158. Dorothy Nealy argues that "the racism in Canada is so subtle, and so elusive you can't really pin it down," a statement amplified by Dorothy Sylvia, who argues that "the Negro is better off in the much-maligned Southern United States than in Canada." Nealy quoted in Compton, *Bluesprint*, 119; Sylvia quoted in Sarah-Jane Mathieu, *North of the Color Line: Migration and Black Resistance in Canada, 1870–1955* (Durham: North Carolina University Press, 2010), 209. Racism in Canada is, as Cecil Foster describes, not as open as in the United States but certainly as pervasive; it is "racism with a smile on its face, as Canadian Blacks like to call the brand they live under. A racism that nonetheless still saps dreams and leads to despair about the future." Foster, *A Place Called Heaven: The Meaning of Being Black in Canada* (Toronto: HarperCollins, 1996), 320. In addition, see Mary Ann Shadd, *A Plea for Emigration, or, Notes of Canada West*, ed. Richard Almonte (Toronto: Mercury, 1998). While settler's guides like Susanna Moodie's *Roughing It in the Bush* (1852) have been studied as paradigmatically Canadian, Shadd's *Plea for Emigration* (1853), published at roughly the same time, sheds new light on lived African Canadian realities in the nineteenth century. Shadd often suggests, given the dangers of the Fugitive Slave Law, which made life dangerous for American Blacks, that Canada West is an ideal place to start a new life – a just society and a good place to earn a decent living: "If a coloured man understands his business, he receives the public patronage the same as a white man ... There is no degraded class to identify him with, therefore every man's work stands or falls according to merit, not as is his colour ... [Canada is] a country in which slavery is not tolerated, and prejudice of *colour* has no existence whatsoever" (pp. 59–60). Shadd's rhetoric is largely about the possibilities in Canada as antithetical to those of the United States, and often the realities of Canadian racism very clearly manifest in

her straightforward prose as she describes White residents moving away from Black residents as they formed the settlement of Elgin, about ten miles from Chatham, Ontario: "When purchase was made of these lands many white families were residents ... At first, a few sold out, fearing that such neighbours might not be agreeable" (p. 68). And so, White Canadian racism remains subtly – and yet very clearly – couched within Shadd's text.

13 Saidiya Hartman, *Lose Your Mother: A Journey along the Atlantic Slave Route* (New York: Farrar, Straus and Giroux, 2007), 6.
14 Winks, *Blacks in Canada*, 24.
15 Frederick Douglass, *The Life and Times of Frederick Douglass* (1881; New York: Dover, 2003), 110. This belief is echoed throughout much of Black Canadian and American literature, as Martin Luther King Jr. (in his Massey Lectures) praises Canada as more than a neighbor to the Negro: "So standing today in Canada I am linked with the history of my people and its unity with your past." King, *The Trumpet of Conscience* (Boston: Beacon, 2010), 3. However, for many of the escaped slaves, or for those who fought on the side of the Loyalists, it became apparent that Canada was something else, and not quite the heaven on earth many thought it to be. This disappointment is reflected in Austin Clarke's 1964 novel, *The Survivors of the Crossing*, which begins in the Caribbean with a letter from a friend describing "Canada [as] a real first-class place!" and later notes, "Life up here in Canada is the same thing as living in Goat-heaven and Kiddy-kingdom." Clarke, *The Survivors of the Crossing* (Toronto: McClelland & Stewart, 1964), 31, 57. The letter provides the Barbadian protagonist (Rufus) with the strength to stage a protest in the cane fields in Barbados, which ultimately fails because it is predicated on what Clarke sets up as a fictitious Canadian heaven. Towards the end of the novel the friend sends a more honest letter that describes the racism and unemployment the Black man faces in Canada, calling it the very same type of racism he had hoped to escape: "I sorry to paint a technicolour picture o' the place but, Jesus Christ, man! I couldn't let you know that here in this country is the same slavery as what I run from back in the island" (p. 104). This is also apparent in Benjamin Drew's interviews of formerly enslaved African Americans in the 1850s: *A North-Side View of Slavery: The Refugee: Or, The Narratives of Fugitive Slaves in Canada. Related by Themselves, with an Account of the History and Condition of the Colored Population of Upper Canada* (Boston: John P. Jewett, 1856; University of North Carolina at Chapel Hill, 2000), http://docsouth.unc.edu/neh/drew/drew.html.
16 Clarke, *Odysseys Home*, 288.
17 Ana Maria Fraile-Marcos, "The Transcultural Intertextuality of George Elliott Clarke's African Canadianité: American Models Shaping George & Rue," *African American Review* 47, no. 1 (2014): 115.

18 Sherri Borden Colley, "After 200 Years without Land Title, Nova Scotia Black Communities Offered Hope," CBC News, September 28, 2017, https://www.cbc.ca/news/canada/nova-scotia/legal-title-black-loyalists-north-preston-1.4309505.
19 Jennifer Harris, "Black Life in a Nineteenth-Century New Brunswick Town," *Journal of Canadian Studies/Revue d'études Canadiennes* 46, no. 1 (2012): 141.
20 Or, perhaps he samples Public Enemy, since a vocal clip in the opening of *Fear of a Black Planet* (1990) contains the same phrase. Wayde Compton, *Performance Bond* (Vancouver: Arsenal Pulp Press, 2004), 106–7. This is echoed by poet Marlene NourbeSe Philip, who writes, "Without memory can there be history?" Philip, *She Tries Her Tongue, Her Silence Softly Breaks* (Charlottetown: Ragweed, 1989), 97.
21 Compton, "The Reinventing Wheel," in *Performance Bond*, 102, 103, 104, 105, 104, 105.
22 For example, see the controversial Kenneth Goldsmith reading titled "The Body of Michael Brown" that used Brown's autopsy report as poetry. Goldsmith's performance lacked self-reflexivity, ultimately re-dissecting Brown's body under the guise of conceptualism.
23 Compton, *Bluesprint*, 18, 20
24 Compton, *Performance Bond*, 20.
25 Compton's poem "JD" looks at James Douglas as mixed-race ("father Scottish, mother from British Guyana") and passing as White. Compton asks, "O James Douglas, / did you ever see yourself / in us? / did you ever stop / in your war versus the wilderness / and think / we?" The poem mixes Black and White identifications as the crossfader blends "shuffling passports," a balancing act too much for nineteenth-century Douglas, who encouraged Blacks to come to British Columbia from California but then withdrew his support when they arrived. A few poems later, Compton inverts the title "JD" as "DJ," inviting the reader into the mix as a co-performer of the poem. Compton, *49th Parallel Psalm* (Vancouver: Arsenal Pulp Press, 1999), 18–19.
26 Nathaniel Mackey, "An Interview with Kamau Brathwaite," *Hambone* 9 (1991): 44. This motion of crashing tides moves from the Barbadian beaches (on one side in the Caribbean Sea and the other on the Atlantic Ocean) and in time becomes the waters of the BC shoreline. This mixing also speaks to a cyclical understanding of time. As Christian Habekost argues in *Verbal Riddim*, "the black tradition emphasizes [time] as crucial means of distinct improvisation and extemporization ... circulation and cyclical development, as opposed to the European principle of progression." Habekost, *Verbal Riddim: The Politics and Aesthetics of African-Caribbean Dub Poetry* (Amsterdam: Rodopi, 1993), 94.
27 Wayde Compton, interview by Paul Watkins, "'Schizophonophilia': An Audio-Interplay between Wayde Compton and Paul Watkins," *Improvisation*,

Community, and Social Practice, August 2013, 4, http://www.improvcommunity.ca/sites/improvcommunity.ca/files/research_collection/1049/Wayde_Compton_transcription.pdf.
28 Paul D. Miller, *Rhythm Science* (New York: MIT Press, 2004), 28–9.
29 Compton, *Performance Bond*, 106.
30 Winfried Siemerling, "Transcultural Improvisation, Transnational Time, and Diasporic Chance in Wayde Compton's Textual Performance," *West Coast Line* 63 (March 2010): 32.
31 Wayde Compton, personal communication, October 2009.
32 Nigel H. Thomas, *Why We Write: Conversations with African Canadian Poets and Novelists* (Toronto: TSAR, 2006), 71. Further, in an email conversation I asked Compton about his use of hip-hop as a medium, and he responded by saying, "I can say that I place my audio art within the long tradition of black diasporic orality more so than the more limited and recent innovation of hip hop. *Performance Bond* is largely about the anxiety of the globalization of hip hop. Is it a form of American sub-imperialism? Or does the diaspora cut across borders in a way that makes hip hop identification political resistance?" Compton, personal communication, October 2009. However, given that hip-hop has more than fifty years of history, and shows no signs of slowing down, I would have to say that the larger cultural practice of hip-hop is not limited in its approach as a diasporic orality.
33 Wayde Compton, "The Reinventing Wheel: On Blending the Poetry of Cultures through Hip Hop Turntablism," *Horizon Zero* 8 (June 2003) (site discontinued). *Mise-en-abyme* (from French, meaning essentially "to put in the abyss") is a technique in which a work references, or mirrors, itself in some way, such as an image containing a smaller version of that same image within itself, or a story containing elements of a similar story within that story.
34 Compton, *Performance Bond*, 102, 104.
35 Compton, interview by Watkins, "'Schizophonophilia,'" 3.
36 Wayde Compton, "Turntable Poetry, Mixed-Race, and Schizophonophilia," in *After Canaan: Essays on Race, Writing, and Region* (Vancouver: Arsenal Pulp Press, 2010), 199.
37 Compton, 197.
38 In Compton, 194.
39 Compton, 195, 199.
40 Compton, *Performance Bond*, 42.
41 Compton, 42.
42 Beat generation writer William S. Burroughs used a cut-up technique to cut up and rearrange texts in innovative ways that challenge institutional discourse. Grandmaster Flash is one of the early innovators of DJing, hip-hop, and scratch. His breakthrough, "The Adventures of Grandmaster Flash

on the Wheels of Steel" (Sugar Hill Records, 1981), displays Flash's virtuosic turntable skills over the course of seven minutes.

43 Compton, *Performance Bond*, 42.
44 Leow, "Mis-mappings," n.p.
45 Compton, *Performance Bond*, 110.
46 Compton paraphrased in *Secret Vancouver: A Return to Hogan's Alley*, a short documentary film produced by Melinda Friedman (Calgary: Spotlight Productions, 2016), https://www.youtube.com/watch?v=B-8lgpvj0Hg.
47 See the interactive website Black Strathcona (http://blackstrathcona.com/) for pictures, a chronology, video links, and a detailed history of Vancouver's Black community.
48 Numbers taken from the "About" section of the Black Strathcona website (http://blackstrathcona.com/about).
49 "Chronology" section of the Black Strathcona website (http://blackstrathcona.com/chronology); see also Mathieu, *North of the Color Line*.
50 See the insightful documentary *Secret Vancouver: Return to Hogan's Alley*, which includes an interview with the Vancouver entertainers the Crump Twins and background regarding their musical importance.
51 See Taraneh Jerven, "Vancouver's Legendary Jimi Hendrix Shrine Now Open for Summer," *Inside Vancouver*, June 11, 2013, http://www.inside vancouver.ca/2013/06/11/legendary-vancouver-jimi-hendrix-shrine-now-open-for-summer.
52 Compton, *Performance Bond*, 21.
53 Larissa Lai outlines the grassroots efforts in Vancouver to contest the media backlash against the Fujianese migrants who arrived in Canada by ship in 1999. Lai, "Asian Invasion vs. the Pristine Nation: Migrants Entering the Canadian Imaginary," *Fuse* 23, no. 2 (2000): 30–40.
54 Compton, *Performance Bond*, 31.
55 Compton's *Performance Bond* riffs on the word "bond," from an "appearance bond" (to appear in court) to the various performative acts that bond us together, often across geographical and imaginative spaces. The collection opens with an excerpt on detention from the Enforcement on Detention from Citizenship and Immigration Canada, referencing the "performance bond form," required when a guarantor is necessary to ensure compliance. The excerpt puts emphasis on establishing a detainee's identity, providing steps for how to do so, particularly for a foreign national. By opening a highly performative text with a document that suggests how citizenship is both performed and surveilled in Canada, Compton establishes that citizenship is something that is conferred by official law, and then undermines the law and state by complicating what exactly comprises a citizen, especially for those whose citizenship status is historically in flux. For those in the process of immigrating to Canada it remains a mystery

for them whether or not they will be granted entry and passage to become a citizen, or will have their status deemed as "illegal," or as a deportable person.
56 Compton, *Performance Bond*, 108.
57 Wayde Compton, "Seven Routes to Hogan's Alley and Vancouver's Black Community," in *After Canaan*, 84, 92.
58 Quoted in Compton, "Seven Routes," 91.
59 Compton, 109.
60 Compton, 93.
61 Compton, interview by Watkins, "Schizophonophilia," 4.
62 *Oxford English Dictionary Online*, s.v. "rune," accessed May 28, 2021, https://www.oed.com.
63 Jonathan Dale Sherman, "The Hip-Hop Aesthetics and Visual Poetry of Wayde Compton's *Performance Bond*: Claiming Black Space in Contemporary Canada" (MA project, University of Saskatchewan, 2009), ii.
64 Compton, *Performance Bond*, 10.
65 Compton, "Seven Routes," 112, 113.
66 Leow, "Mis-mappings," n.p.
67 Compton, *Performance Bond*, 113. *Blight* refers to any "baleful influence of atmospheric or invisible origin, that suddenly blasts, nips, or destroys plants," as well as any "malignant influence of obscure or mysterious origin" that causes destruction. *Oxford English Dictionary Online*, s.v. "blight," accessed May 28, 2021, https://www.oed.com.
68 Compton, 113.
69 *Oxford English Dictionary Online*, s.v. "cloze," accessed May 28, 2021, https://www.oed.com.
70 Compton, *Performance Bond*, 113, 114.
71 Quoted in Willard Bohn, *Modern Visual Poetry* (Newark: University of Delaware Press, 2001), 20.
72 Compton, "Seven Routes," 117.
73 The Poetry Foundation defines "concrete poetry" as verse "that emphasizes nonlinguistic elements in its meaning, such as a typeface that creates a visual image of the topic." "Glossary of Poetic Terms," Poetry Foundation, s.v. "concrete poetry," accessed May 28, 2021, https://www.poetryfoundation.org/learn/glossary-terms/concrete-poetry.
74 Compton, *Performance Bond*, 103.
75 Compton, "Forme and Chase," in *Performance Bond*, 144.
76 Compton, *Performance Bond*, 150–1.
77 Kary Taylor, quoted in Compton, *Performance Bond*, 150.
78 Percy Bysshe Shelley, "Ozymandias," Poetry Foundation, accessed May 28, 2021, https://www.poetryfoundation.org/poems/46565/ozymandias.
79 Compton, *Performance Bond*, 156.

80 It might surprise some to learn that there are more Black people in BC than in Nova Scotia. See data from Statistics Canada, "Canada [Country] and Canada [Country]" (table), *Census Profile*, 2016 Census, Catalogue no. 98-316-X2016001, released November 29, 2017.
81 Compton, "Seven Routes," 105.
82 Compton, 108, 112.
83 Wayde Compton, "Black History in Vancouver Recognized at Last: Hogan's Alley Memorial Project," Rabble.ca, February 25, 2013, http://rabble.ca/news/2013/02/black-history-vancouver-recognized-last-hogans-alley-memorial-project.
84 Wayde Compton, quoted in "Black History Month Stamp Celebrates Vancouver's Hogan's Alley," CBC News, January 20, 2014, http://www.cbc.ca/news/canada/british-columbia/black-history-month-stamp-celebrates-vancouver-s-hogan-s-alley-1.2516741.
85 Amy Smart, "Society Pitches New Life for Hogan's Alley after Vancouver Viaducts Come Down," CBC News, February 9, 2021, https://www.cbc.ca/news/canada/british-columbia/hogans-alley-vancouver-revitalization-1.5906747; Anna Dimoff, "Vancouver to Revive Hogan's Alley Community with Help of American Architect," CBC News, May 21, 2017, http://www.cbc.ca/news/canada/british-columbia/hogans-alley-community-plan-1.4124018.
86 Amiri Baraka, "Jazzmen: Diz & Sun Ra," *African American Review* 29, no. 2 (1995): 255.
87 "A revolution is first and foremost a movement from the old to the new, and needs above all new words, new verse, new passwords – all the symbols in which ideas and feelings are made tangible." C.L.R. James quoted in Barbara Ransby, *Ella Baker and the Black Freedom Movement: A Radical Democratic Vision* (Chapel Hill: University of North Carolina Press, 2003), 374.
88 In Haitian Vodou, Papa Legba is the loa (spirit) of the crossroads who serves as the intermediary between the loa and humanity. Guarding the spiritual crossroads, Legba permits or denies passage and is thus a messenger god – an opener and closer of gateways – whom we can think of as a West African/African American equivalent of Hermes/Mercury or perhaps the Hindu lord Ganesh (a remover of obstacles). Furthermore, Papa Legba is a trickster figure who not only creates chaos but escapes the codes of the world. Like Eshu (the Yoruba name of Legba), who, as Henry Louis Gates Jr. argues, "serves as a figure for the nature and function of interpretation and double-voiced utterance," Papa Legba embodies a complex metaphysics of change and communication at the crossroads. Gates, *The Signifying Monkey: A Theory of Afro-American Literary Criticism* (New York: Oxford University Press, 1988), xxi.

89 Edward Kamau Brathwaite, *The Arrivants: A New World Trilogy* (Oxford: Oxford University Press, 1973), 265.
90 Compton, "Vévé," in *Performance Bond*, 119, 121.
91 Haudenosaunee writer Alicia Elliott has described the current state of CanLit as a dumpster fire that perpetuates Canadian national myths, leaves little space for marginalized writers, and needs to do more to combat systemic discrimination. Elliott, "CanLit Is a Raging Dumpster Fire," *Open Book*, September 7, 2017, http://open-book.ca/Columnists/CanLit-is-a-Raging-Dumpster-Fire.
92 Linda Hutcheon, *Other Solitudes: Canadian Multicultural Fictions* (Toronto: Oxford University Press, 1990), 10.
93 Compton, *Performance Bond*, 15. Compton is riffing upon Countee Cullen's poem "Heritage" (written in 1925), which asks, "What is Africa to me?"
94 See Charmaine A. Nelson, *Representing the Black Female Subject in Western Art* (New York: Routledge, 2010).
95 Canadian novelist David Gilmour incited incendiary debate in Canadian literature when he made the statement that he does not teach works by women, gay individuals, or those of Chinese ethnicity. In an interview with *Hazlitt* magazine (owned by Random House), Gilmour stated, "What I teach is guys. Serious heterosexual guys." Emily M. Keeler, "Interview: David Gilmour on Building Strong Stomachs," Shelf Esteem, *Hazlitt*, September, 25, 2013, https://hazlitt.net/blog/david-gilmour-building-strong-stomachs. Gilmour's comments led to several editorial pieces, with some defending his comments, such as conservative thinker Margaret Wente.
96 Smaro Kamboureli and Roy Miki, eds., *Trans.Can.Lit: Resituating the Study of Canadian Literature* (Waterloo, ON: Wilfrid Laurier University Press, 2007), xv.
97 Shadd quoted in Myriam Chancy, *Searching for Safe Spaces: Afro-Caribbean Women Writers in Exile* (Philadelphia: Temple University Press, 1997), 80.
98 Darcy Ballantyne, Paul Barrett, Camille Isaacs, and Kris Singh. "The Unbearable Whiteness of CanLit," *The Walrus*, July 26, 2017, https://thewalrus.ca/the-unbearable-whiteness-of-canlit/. It is worth noting that Austin Clarke is one of the few Black writers included in any of the major overviews of CanLit, such as Margaret Atwood's *Survival* (Toronto: House of Anansi, 1972) and Nick Mount's *Arrival* (Toronto: House of Anansi, 2017); both books depict a literary Canada that is largely anglophone and almost entirely White.
99 Walcott quoted in Ballantyne et al., "Unbearable Whiteness." Back in 2007 Walcott raised similar concerns about CanLit: "Can CanLit read me? That is, Black faggot, dual citizen, sociologist, cultural critic? How would CanLit read me if it could? As exceptional? Who wants to be that? I take everything 'trans' seriously, and therefore I understand that much is at stake when

trans is invoked – the very foundation of the human becomes at stake, in my view." Rindaldo Walcott, "Against Institution Established Law, Custom, or Purpose," in Kamboureli and Miki, *Trans.Can.Lit*, 23.
100 Ballantyne et al., "Unbearable Whiteness."
101 Compton, *Performance Bond*, 31.
102 Compton, 15.

18
Jazz, Diaspora, and the History and Writing of Black Anglophone Montreal

WINFRIED SIEMERLING

On 30 June 2009 Montreal jazz pianist Oliver Jones and singer Ranee Lee opened the thirtieth Montreal Jazz Festival in its new venue, L'Astral. After a hiatus, Jones was returning to a festival that his presence had graced since its second year, 1981. Two years earlier, in April 2007, he had headlined a benefit concert attended by Daisy Peterson, his former piano teacher. Her brother Oscar, that other Montreal jazz legend, was represented by a large photograph on stage. That concert had been a fundraiser to help reopen the former Negro Community Centre (NCC), founded in 1927, whose mission had been to "alleviate social and economic conditions among Blacks in Montreal."[1] Jones had spent much of his time there as a child. Now he was back for a benefit that served as a vivid reminder of the strong, ongoing presence of one of Montreal's oldest Black communities; this Black anglophone community dates back to the late nineteenth century. It was preceded by the "oldtimers" of the Underground Railroad and, even before them, the Black enslaved captives of Montreal.[2]

The evening's celebration of Black musical traditions, institutions, and community history evoked cultural geographies that are rarely present in a wider public imaginary. In her 1984 memoir *Growing Up Black in Canada*, Carol Talbot uses the term "folk geography" when writing about "the 'felt' geography of a particular group [that] can indicate significant factors which will not be revealed by an orthodox scientific approach."[3] Cultural geographers such as Joyce Davidson and Christine Milligan have explored such "emotional geographies" in their field, and Canadian postcolonial scholar Katherine McKittrick has used the same approach to discuss Marie-Joseph Angélique, the Montreal enslaved captive accused of having started a fire that burned down most of Montreal in 1734.[4] There are now many Black communities in Montreal; the city's Haitian diaspora in particular has found literary expression and, in some cases, significant francophone reception – the most notable exception, with English translations and anglophone attention as well, is perhaps the work of Dany Laferrière. Yet, the pre-1960s Black geographies of Quebec have rarely been imagined so as to narrate their emotional contours. Canadian classics set in this space and time either elide Black emotional geographies or treat them problematically. Pierre Nepveu's comment in *Lecture des lieux* remains pertinent: "Lire Montréal, ce pourrait être, par exemple, raconter son histoire et réinventer en particulier son commencement" ("To read Montreal could mean, for instance, to tell its history and reinvent in particular its beginning").[5] Or perhaps one could say that it is time to "wake up," not so much from the dream of the nineteenth century (as in Walter Benjamin's *Arcades Project*) but from the images of Montreal that were part of the dream to finally put Canada and Quebec on the map against European and US culture. This dream was partly realized by some of the most important novels of the mid-twentieth century, but the priorities and perhaps necessities of that dream and "the hoary battles of the national epic" have eclipsed more complex realities that come to the fore retrospectively in more recent texts that afford other perspectives.[6]

While I will briefly examine earlier moments, this chapter focuses on the period from the 1920s to the 1950s that includes Montreal's jazz age. This era in the city's history was heavily marked by Black cultural contributions that appear non-existent or problematic at best in geographies offered by literary texts about the period. Consider, for example, three of the canonical novels about 1940s and 1950s Montreal: Hugh MacLennan's *Two Solitudes* (1945), Gabrielle Roy's *Bonheur d'occasion* (1945; translated as *The Tin Flute* [1947]), and Morley Callaghan's *The Loved and the Lost* (1951). MacLennan's *Two Solitudes* is a sweeping portrait of interwar Quebec that also claims to reimagine Canadian national space. Montreal, which was Canada's most important city at the time, serves MacLennan in the first pages as a metonymic microcosm of modern industrial Canada, with its social and ideological practices governed by linguistic difference. In that city, MacLennan writes, "two old races" meet; he is using an older nomenclature still evident in later documents (such as the Royal Commission on Bilingualism and Biculturalism in the 1960s)[7] in which the term refers to the anglophone and francophone White settlers of Canada: "Two old races and religions meet here and live their separate legends, side by side. If this sprawling half-continent has a heart here it is. Its pulse throbs out along the rivers and railroads; slow, reluctant and rarely simple, a double beat, a self-moved reciprocation."[8] The Quebec countryside of *Two Solitudes* is home to francophone agricultural labourers working the fields for the inheritors of the seigneurial regime under the ultramontane Catholic clergy; Montreal is the site of the francophone working poor and an anglophone capital that reaches deeply and aggressively into the surrounding countryside for ever more resources of capital accumulation. But while the "two races" in Quebec, and specifically in Montreal, are charted in the Canadian national space that MacLennan weaves out of personal and "emotional geographies," non-White characters remain invisible.[9]

This is also the case in another "classic" portrait of Montreal that appeared in 1945, the same year as MacLennan's novel: Roy's *Bonheur d'occasion*. The absence here is particularly striking given that Roy's setting is working-class Saint-Henri in southwest Montreal, which had been the home of a small but growing Black community since the end of the nineteenth century. After arriving in Montreal from Manitoba (via Europe) in 1939, Roy had taken a deep interest in Montreal as a meeting place of diasporas. For *Le Bulletin des agriculteurs*, she wrote a series of reportages titled "Tout Montréal" that took note of the city's cosmopolitan population. Yet when she wrote her fictional account of francophone working-class life in Saint-Henri, she expunged almost all indications of a multiracial Montreal.[10] True, when her protagonist, Florentine, is invited to a party in a house on Place George-Étienne Cartier, in one of the quarter's "better" neighbourhoods, a turn of the radio knob fills the room with "un air de jazz, furieux, à grands éclats de saxophone"(136; "a savage blast of music, with saxophones blaring," 88).[11] The younger generation opts to dance, embracing the swing music that so many White bands also played at the time. The originators of this music, however, are identified here only when Létourneau, a member of the parents' generation and a "marchand d'objets de piété, d'ornements et de vin eucharistique" (133; "a dealer in religious objects, ornaments and church wines," 86), inquires pejoratively, "Qu'est-ce que c'est que cette danse de nègres?" (137; "Is that some new Negro dance?," 89).

Roy focuses her novel on the francophone Montreal working class, especially its women; even so, it is striking how she renders invisible another universe that existed at the same time in the same neighbourhood. Oscar Peterson grew up a very short distance from Place George-Étienne Cartier and had begun attracting attention in 1942 as a Black musician in one of Montreal's popular White swing bands. Place Saint-Henri, at the very centre of the universe Roy describes, served as inspiration for the eponymous composition that became part of Peterson's 1964 album *Canadiana Suite*. The trains that continually crossed Saint-Henri loom large in Roy's novel. But she is more preoccupied with their noise and with the coal dust they shower on the neighbourhood than with their travellers and destinations – or with the Black porters and redcaps whose lives were interwoven with the railway's North American networks as much as they were a part of Saint-Henri. In 1955, in *Rue Deschambault* (published in English as *Street of Riches* [1957]), her book of vaguely autobiographical stories about her childhood in Saint-Boniface, Manitoba, Roy would write about the Black porters who boarded at her parents' and neighbours' houses. In "Les deux nègres," she emphasizes their love of music, and one of the Black boarders is assigned to the Montreal–Halifax run, thus fleetingly evoking the city and the neighbourhood she had portrayed a few years earlier in so much detail but without Black residents.

Black Montreal features prominently in Callaghan's *The Loved and the Lost*. The novel contrasts the rich Westmount district with the rest of Montreal, describing the former as "a rock of riches with poverty sprawling around the rock."[12] Within this particular geography, the Black jazz milieu of the St-Antoine district appears as the other, dark side – and ultimately the downfall – of the White hero's quest for wealth and social standing.[13] Black jazz, although an important theme here, ultimately serves as the background for a White character's unsuccessful search for meaning. Black Montreal and its music hold an ambivalent place in this novel: they are threats to the social order, yet they also hint at a utopian chronotope of interracial possibility. In any case, the perceptions of Callaghan's protagonist remain caught in primitivist stereotypes:

> Music came from the ground-floor open window, the music of a cello and a piano, and he could see three figures, one a Negro at a piano, another, who looked like a French Canadian, at the cello, and the third figure, the face hidden, was bending over the piano. The piano and the cello achieved an hypnotic effect in primitive counterpoint, repeating a simple theme over and over with curious discords; but it was the posture, the attitudes of the musicians as they played their solitary theme that held him spellbound: the cello twanged, the piano repeated the minor chords with a little variation, the musicians were held in their strange rapture, and there was nothing in the world for them but the lonely little theme and that one room in the cold night and their own intensity. (57)

Perhaps the third figure with the hidden face is the placeholder for a position that Callaghan's protagonist considers for himself. The image conveys social intimacy even while withholding the readability of the face. The protagonist remains an observer. Jim McAlpine's assertion of himself as an Emersonian "independent man" and his quest for innocence – which in the novel is connoted repeatedly by the colour white – use Black St-Antoine as background. Callaghan is "playing in the dark"; the neighbourhood, with its Blackness, becomes here a space for what Toni Morrison calls the "projection of the not-me" and a "playground for the imagination" containing "a fabricated brew of darkness, otherness, alarm, and desire" that *pace* Morrison is *not* "uniquely American."[14] In *The Loved and the Lost*, Blackness is construed through stereotypical significations, portrayed as exotic and ultimately potentially murderous and destructive otherness.[15] The novel can therefore hardly convey a sense of Montreal and the St-Antoine district as the home of everyday Black lives that have long been part and parcel of the city and its history. One must look elsewhere for perspectives that bring Black geographies and lives to the fore, and heed Nepveu's injunction that "to read Montreal could mean ... to tell its history and reinvent in particular its beginning."

II

Although its numbers were very small in the beginning, the Black diaspora has always been integral to the history and settlement of what is now Quebec. Canada's first documented Black enslaved individual, Olivier Le Jeune, lived in the first half of the seventeenth century in Quebec City. In the *Jesuit Relations*, Father Le Jeune even gave him a voice: "You say that by baptism I shall be like you: I am black and you are white, I must have my skin taken off then in order to be like you."[16] While Le Jeune presented this remark as a child's naïveté, and historian Marcel Trudel reproduces the passage without further comment, Robin Winks gives a certain ontological weight to the utterance.[17] Most remarkable, however, is the very fact that a Black voice was transcribed at all in the first person – a rare exception. About a century later, in 1734, when there were perhaps between forty and fifty Black enslaved individuals in Quebec, one of them, Angélique, was tried and hanged for allegedly burning down the better part of Montreal.[18] Her responses to interrogation – as rendered in the third person in court documents – were her only words transmitted.[19] In recent decades, however, a heterotopic Montreal of the eighteenth century has emerged in neo-slave dramas and narratives around the case of Angélique, in plays by Lorris Elliott (1985) and Lorena Gale (2000) and in novels by Paul Fehmiu Brown (1998) and Micheline Bail (1999).[20] As George Elliott Clarke points out, Angélique is also the subject of a song and a movie (*Raising*), and in 2006 Afua Cooper dedicated a monograph and Katherine McKittrick devoted an important book chapter to the topic, as mentioned above.[21]

In 1760, a few decades after Angélique was hanged, England and France signed a peace treaty that confirmed the continuation of slavery in Quebec under the English. The number of enslaved individuals rose in 1783, when United Empire Loyalists arrived with them; however, slavery ended in Quebec early in the nineteenth century, well before it was abolished throughout the British Empire in 1834.[22] Trudel found 1,443 documented Black enslaved individuals overall in Quebec, in addition to 2,683 Indigenous captives, or *panis*.[23]

Black slavery in Quebec is generally perceived by historians to have been less brutal than elsewhere. In part, this is because most Black captives here were house slaves (rather than field slaves) and considerably more valuable than Indigenous captives.[24] This difference hardly prevented them from seeking freedom, however, or from attempting to flee in considerable numbers. In the *Quebec Gazette* between 1769 and 1794, "advertisements for runaway slaves were more frequent ... than were those for the sale of slaves."[25] While Black captives were less significant in number than elsewhere, they certainly contributed to the building of Quebec. The clergy and the military, as well as notaries, doctors, and printers, employed slave labour.[26] Consider, for instance, William Brown, who with Thomas Gilmore founded the first newspaper in Quebec in 1764, the bilingual *Quebec Gazette/Gazette de Quebec*.[27] After 1773, Brown remained sole owner of the paper and its enslaved captives. One of them, Joe, fled at least six times between 1777 and 1789, once by escaping from prison. "Wanted" ads for Joe must have been printed in the very paper he normally helped produce. Having been trained as a printer, he was obviously valuable enough, despite all his resistance, for his master to have incurred considerable expenses to maintain his services.[28] François-Xavier Garneau, the most important nineteenth-century historian of French Canada, omitted the fact that slavery existed in Quebec in his 1846 volume *Histoire du Canada* (however, the fourth edition, issued by his son in 1882, ended this denial).[29] Documentary evidence and the work of other historians shed at least some light on this chapter of Black French-Canadian history.

On 1 August 1834, Black Montrealers congregated in a hall at St. Ann's Market to celebrate the abolition of slavery in the British Empire.[30] French Canada (and Montreal in particular) was an Underground Railroad destination, although the numbers who arrived were much smaller than in Upper Canada. The slave narrative of Lavina Wormeny was reported in the Montreal *Gazette*. A child of free parents in Washington, Wormeny had been abducted and enslaved; after multiple attempts, she escaped to Montreal in January 1861.[31] Gary Collison minutely reconstructs the earlier case of an enslaved individual, Shadrach Minkins, using census records, city directories, newspaper accounts, and other sources to document his escape from Norfolk, Virginia, to Montreal in February 1851. Despite spotty documentary evidence, Collison offers interesting conjectures about the size of Montreal's Black community at the time: "But just how many African-Americans joined Shadrach Minkins in Montreal, or where they came from, is unclear. Although the *Gazette* argued that there were more than four hundred, the published census of 1861 indicated only 46 Black residents. Manuscript census slips, however, show 228, and since this figure almost certainly represents an undercounting, the actual numbers may have been fairly close to the *Gazette* estimate."[32] Interestingly, by 1860 Minkins had moved from the old city to what was then – and remained, in Callaghan's novel – the St-Antoine district in southwest Montreal.[33] At the end of the nineteenth century, a larger Black community began to develop there. From the 1920s on, the area became a crucial site for the development of Montreal jazz.

By the second half of the nineteenth century the Lachine Canal, just to the south, had emerged as Canada's industrial heartland, featuring "iron works, flour mills, the Chemical and India Rubber Works, the Oil and Colour Works, the Candle Works, and the Canada Marine Work, among others."[34] This canal, opened in 1825 (the same year as its competitor, the Erie Canal in New York), was the realization of a dream of opening up the Great Lakes hinterland to trade. It had been dug to circumvent the Lachine Rapids, which since Jacques Cartier and the search for Cathay had prevented ships from entering the Great Lakes.[35] In many ways, the rapids and the efforts to circumvent them "explain[ed] Montreal."[36] Part of a century-long international "canal craze," the Lachine Canal allowed the more rapid transportation of goods. After 1846, it provided hydraulic power for flour and saw mills, grain elevators, foundries, nail factories, and other industries; after 1893, it also provided electricity.[37] The canal attracted numerous industries that together would turn Montreal into the industrial and commercial heart of Canada.

Yet, soon after they were built, canals had to compete with railways as the most effective conveyors of goods and people. A few years after the Champlain and St. Lawrence (Canada's first railway) was completed in 1836, the Montreal and Lachine Railroad was inaugurated in 1847 to bypass the Lachine Rapids, although it could not compete with the lower freight rates on the Lachine Canal. The twelve-kilometre track was soon incorporated into a network of lines connecting Montreal to the western hinterland and the Atlantic seaboard.[38] A generation later, after the railways began hiring Black men as redcaps and porters – one of the few reliable livelihoods for Black Montrealers – a larger Black community began to develop in the St-Antoine district. By the late 1850s, the Grand Trunk Railway connected Montreal with Toronto and Chicago; by the 1880s, the American Pullman Palace Car Company, the Grand Trunk Railway, and the Canadian Pacific Railway were employing Black sleeping car porters, with the latter company doing so directly out of Montreal.[39] At first, many of these porters used Montreal as only a temporary home because of immigration restrictions.[40] After this, the "period between 1897 and 1930 marked the beginning of a genuine black community in Montreal. Major institutions such as the Union United Church (Union) in 1907, the Universal Negro Improvement Association (UNIA) in 1919, and the Negro Community Centre (NCC) in 1927 were established."[41] These landmark institutions, which were so crucial for the development of Montreal's Black community, are often overlooked in the city's history.

The Black community contributed in various ways to another important chapter of Montreal history, the development of jazz – although the acceptance of that musical genre by the community was hardly smooth. Many parents preferred that their children learn classical music. Some aspects of jazz were met with suspicion and rejection by respectable members of the community, in large part because the genre was associated with alcohol. The Prohibition era in the United States lasted from 1920 to 1933. Nancy Marrelli notes that "Quebec was the last Canadian province to get prohibition in 1918 and it was the first to repeal it, in 1919."[42] This made Montreal attractive to many; as Dorothy Williams remarks, "as a result of Prohibition, Montreal was *the* place to be."[43] Prohibition favoured the development of jazz in Montreal: "From the 1920s until the early 1950s Montreal had an international reputation as a glamorous wide open city with a lively nightlife."[44] In his history of Montreal jazz, John Gilmore notes that "work for musicians was plentiful."[45] Many of the bands and venues were exclusively White. Marrelli offers the following racial geography of Montreal jazz from the 1920s to the early 1950s:

> The Montreal club scene was one of complex race, class, and language relations, as well as territorial boundaries. The "downtown" clubs were on St. Antoine Street, where many blacks lived because it was close to the railways where many of the men worked as porters. There was an active music scene in the black community, although there was a long history of discrimination in the unions until the early 1940s, and mixed black and white bands were not common. At various times it was trendy to have black musicians and black shows, particularly in east-end clubs, but all-white policies were the rule in hotels and were common for uptown clubs in the early years. The downtown clubs usually had black musicians and entertainers and their patron policies were wide open. That's where you could almost always find great music, and it was where other musicians went to "jam" after their shows in theaters or clubs in other parts of town.[46]

Gilmore also chronicles, after some earlier Black entertainers, a "second wave of black musicians who had heard tales about the exciting city and ventured north ... By the end of the decade [the 1920s], it had drenched

Montreal with talent and with the sounds of the latest black music."[47] Together with these musicians from elsewhere, home-grown talents like the pianists Steep Wade, Oscar Peterson, Oliver Jones, Joe Sealy, and Milt Sealey – all sons of railway employees – became part of Montreal jazz history.[48]

III

Particularly fascinating and influential – if historically elusive – was Steep Wade, although there are no recordings of his saxophone playing and very few of him on piano.[49] But his influence on pianists including Peterson, Sealey, and Jones is a matter of record. Born in Montreal in 1918, Wade began as an alto saxophonist and played with the Canadian Ambassadors, the "most successful of Canada's few black jazz bands active during the 1930s."[50] While Wade's lifestyle brought him notoriety, he gained musical fame as the pianist for the mixed-race International Band from 1947 to 1949. This formation was led by Louis Metcalf, a trumpeter who had played with Duke Ellington, Jelly Roll Morton, and King Oliver in New York. They became the first band to try bebop on Montreal audiences. This incursion took place during their 1947–50 residency at the Café St-Michel.[51] This club and Rockhead's Paradise across the street became "The Corner," the internationally known headquarters of Black Montreal jazz.[52]

This is where Oscar Peterson fell under the spell of Steep Wade. From 1942 onwards, Peterson played with the orchestra of Johnny Holmes, a White trumpeter whose swing band regularly packed eight hundred dancers into Montreal's Victoria Hall[53] – an episode to which I will return below. While still a teenager, Peterson also listened at Rockhead's to Wade, among other musicians, and was occasionally asked by him to fill in: "They used to sneak me in because I was under age at the time. Steep used to call me 'kid.' On different nights when he used to go for a walk or listen to someone else's music, he'd say 'Okay, kid, go on and play the show for me. I'll be back.' That's where I really served my jazz apprenticeship – in that environment."[54] At the Café St-Michel as well, late at night after performing with his own trio at the Alberta Lounge between 1948 and 1950, Peterson listened to Wade and sat in with the Metcalf International Band to familiarize himself with bebop; later he would identify Wade as "my favourite pianist."[55] According to legend, Peterson's engagement at the Alberta Lounge near the CPR Windsor station led to his appearance at Carnegie Hall and his subsequent international career.[56]

Peterson's career is part of jazz history. But his life, like Steep Wade's and Oliver Jones's, was also closely linked to the Black anglophone community in southwest Montreal, including institutions like the Union United Congregational Church, the NCC, and the UNIA with its (often moved) Liberty Hall. Peterson was born in 1925 next to Union United Church on Delisle Street and later would be married there.[57] Oliver Jones played his first public boogie-woogie at one of the church's events when he was five years old.[58] One day, across Atwater Avenue in Little Burgundy, Jones heard beautiful music through an open window and knocked at a door, which happened to be Peterson's. That is how, at the NCC, Jones became a student of Daisy Peterson, who also taught her brother as well as Joe Sealy. In 1954, that centre would move to Coursol Street, where Jones had been born before growing up on intersecting Fulford (now called Georges-Vanier), where the UNIA's Liberty Hall was located. While these locations are in what is now called Little Burgundy, for Jones they were all part of Saint-Henri. "I grew up in Saint-Henri," he confirmed during the intermission of a concert by Keith Jarrett at the 2007 Montreal Jazz Festival (a few days later, Jones would play the festival's closing concert). Jones's personal geography thus united under the name of Saint-Henri the experiences of his childhood and a network of connections and lives that were part of Montreal's oldest Black community. The area roughly coincided with what had earlier been called the St-Antoine district; as historian Dorothy Williams writes, it was "synonymous with the growth of the black community in the southwest core of the city of Montreal."[59]

We are fortunate to have Williams's history and other accounts of wider segments of that community.[60] Jazz historians like John Gilmore, Mark Miller, and Nancy Marrelli, as well as a number of documentaries, have delineated aspects of the more public, visible, and audible side of Black Montreal represented by jazz. Examples of such documentary films include *In the Key of Oscar*, *Oliver Jones in Africa*, *Crossroads: Three Jazz Pianists*, and *Show Girls*. Recordings of Oscar Peterson, Oliver Jones, singer Ranee Lee, bassist Charlie Biddle, guitarist Nelson Symonds, and others form part of the unique musical and cultural contributions of that community. But strangely enough, as noted above, its presence has remained all but unheralded in literary portraits of Montreal.

IV

One text that focuses on the Black community of southwest Montreal in that era is Mairuth Sarsfield's historical novel *No Crystal Stair* (1997).[61] It opens in the spring of 1942 and, like Roy's *Bonheur d'occasion* and parts of MacLennan's *Two Solitudes*, it has World War II as a background. Like Callaghan's *The Loved and the Lost*, it utilizes not just the city but often the very streets where Black Montreal jazz was born. But Callaghan treats Black Montreal as a backdrop against which White trajectories play out; Sarsfield, by contrast, places that culture at the novel's centre, shows its inner workings and contradictions, and explores how it relates to other cultural groups. Musical and (to some extent) literary traditions are key to Sarsfield's project.

In Sarsfield's Montreal, multiple diasporas and cultures meet, and Black Montreal is shown to be itself international and heterogeneous.[62] The novel's cast includes Black characters from the Caribbean and the United States and features fictive and historical participants in the Harlem Renaissance and famous Black exiles in Europe between the wars. Earlier Black history in Quebec is evoked with slavery in Quebec City and the events surrounding the hanging of Angélique in Montreal, while Nova Scotian history surfaces briefly with the Jamaican Maroons shipped to Nova Scotia and the exodus of Black settlers from there to Sierra Leone. A number of diasporic connections appear through the protagonist's work environment as part of the Westmount YMCA staff, yet at the centre is the Black community of the St. Antoine district and its institutions, including the Union United Congregational Church, a focal point of the community since its founding in 1907 by railway porters, and the Marcus Garvey Debating Society and Garvey's Universal Negro Improvement Association. In Williams's words, in "the heyday of the UNIA in Montreal (1919–1928), people attended Union Church in the morning and UNIA social activities at Liberty Hall in the afternoon" that often featured a "focus on Pan-Africanism."[63] Sarsfield also refers variously to the Coloured Ladies Club, Asa Philip Randolph's Brotherhood of Sleeping Car Porters, the importance of the railways as purveyor of employers, and Montreal jazz.[64]

Directly or indirectly, the railway influences most of Sarsfield's Black characters, connected as they are with work- and community-related aspects of Black Montreal such as unions and (in particular) Garveyism. Marion Willow, the novel's protagonist, is the widow of a railway redcap who is a McGill dentistry student. At "a Back to Africa rally in the old UNIA hall on Fulford Street" (24), she meets Edmond Thompson, a Guyanese chemist turned railway porter. Like him, Marion participates in the Marcus Garvey Debating Society. Edmond's attitudes reflect a dual strategy that was the choice of many Montreal porters at the time. In Marion's thinking, "above all, he was a true Garveyite. He believed, like she did, in the need for self-sufficiency for Black folks" (146). At the same time, however, this very Garveyite porter urges "his cricket-playing teammates ... to join the American J. Phillip [*sic*] Randolph Movement to form a Pullman porters' union" (22). In reality,

A. Philip Randolph's racial integrationism stood in stark contrast to the self-segregation advocated by Garvey.[65] As Williams points out, Garvey's anti-union message – strengthened by union racism and the very slow acceptance of Blacks by many unions – did not convince Blacks in Montreal: "By the mid-thirties, Randolph was embraced and honoured by all but the staunchest Garveyites in Montreal."[66] Sarsfield thus accurately evokes the contradictions but also the productive transfigurations of Garveyism in Montreal.

A comparable double strategy of Black self-reliance and integration is adumbrated in Sarsfield's portrayal of jazz and the role of Oscar Peterson within it. *No Crystal Stair* features the legendary Rockhead's Paradise and Café St-Michel at "The Corner," a location that is glossed in the novel as the centre of "the nightlife around Montreal's Mountain Street, with its Jazz entertainers and brown-skinned chorus girls imported from New York's Harlem. Both clubs were owned by former railway porters who – gossip contended – had made their initial nest eggs rum-running in the decade when Prohibition in the United States made smuggling liquor across the border profitable" (58). Besides writers and entertainers from the United States (such as Langston Hughes and Sammy Davis Jr.), the novel mentions a number of Montreal musicians, including Steep Wade (73, 142), Lou Hooper (137), Maynard Ferguson (136), Paul de Marky (137), and Johnny Holmes (135–6). What these musicians have in common is their connection with the Peterson family, and Daisy Peterson Sweeney and Oscar Peterson both appear briefly in the story. Given Sarsfield's dual strategy of emphasizing both Black strength and lively interaction across racial boundaries, it is not coincidental that a longer passage staging a discussion of tradition and influence in terms of Black cultural specificity turns around Oscar Peterson.

Peterson was trained in both classical and jazz piano. One of his important early solo concerts, at age twenty at the Majesty's Theatre in Montreal in 1946, featured both classical and jazz pieces.[67] From 1942 onward, as we have noted, Peterson played with the Johnny Holmes Orchestra, usually as its only Black musician, and this led to a few racist incidents.[68] Peterson continued to play in mixed bands throughout his career. At the same time, he was an icon of Black Montreal's culture and community, which he credited with his success; at one point in his autobiography, *A Jazz Odyssey* (2002), he even emphasizes the formative role of the UNIA and of Marcus Garvey's visit to Montreal.[69] This endorsement of a Black cultural leader who was mostly associated with Black nationalism might be surprising, but it hardly minimizes Peterson's integrationist stance, illuminated strikingly by the dedication of one of his best-known compositions, "Hymn to Freedom," to Martin Luther King Jr.

In *No Crystal Stair*, an early Oscar Peterson concert with the Johnny Holmes Orchestra – probably in the fall of 1942 – gives rise to a heated post-concert discussion among a racially mixed group (135–9, 141–2). The debate mostly concerns influences on Peterson's style and pitches his right-hand arpeggios against his left-hand bass. Affinities with Liszt and Rubinstein strike a White commentator as significant; a Black observer, however, sees Peterson as more "influenced by Duke Ellington's mastery of harmonic chords" and insists, "It's a soul thing" (141). This insistence rejects recognition on the basis of Whiteness as a norm. Emphasizing aspects of Peterson's technique that appear comparable to those of famous White musicians prevents a re-cognition of artistic possibility and excellence, eclipsing the specificity that makes Peterson's style different.[70] Whiteness here "constitutes itself as a universal set of norms by which to make sense of the world."[71] In the words of Sarsfield's character, "Here we go again: Ole Whitey's discovered him, so he must be for real" (142).

In this musicological debate staged by Sarsfield, the denial of difference is thus met by an insistence on Peterson's music as expressive of "race spirituality," which in turn is countered by a two-step protest: "You can't deny the European influence. Music doesn't have boundaries." The first statement is accurate in Peterson's case. The second seems a simple reiteration, yet in fact it denies difference and any kind of social aesthetics. Another character objects: "Yes, it does, and until Europe acknowledges the influence of jazz on its culture, there's no dialogue" (142).[72]

Significantly, this protest is voiced not by a Black participant in the debate but by a White Jewish woman. The discussion here switches to the issue of "passing," another important issue in the novel.[73] Of the two women present, one is of mixed Russian and Black Caribbean descent and passes as White, while the other is Jewish Canadian. Both women feel constrained to pass by dissimulating their "ethnic" names at work to fit in socially and professionally – Marushka and Sarita becoming Maria and Sara (142–3). The novel thus connects prejudicial pressures on racial and ethnic identities that lead to passing with the "Whitening" of Black jazz through forms of re/cognition that reaffirm Eurocentric vantage points. The insistence on Black jazz as a constitutive element in North American culture and on a "dialogue," by contrast, implies multiple vantage points and traditions.

Yet the novel indeed goes out of its way to emphasize *as well* the influence of European music on Peterson's style, and it certainly does not deny cross-cultural influence. Similar issues are raised by some of the novel's intertextualities as well as its theme of reading. Beginning with the title, which cites Langston Hughes's poem "Mother to Son" and its call for perseverance against harsh odds, the novel references a "Who's Who" of Black culture; in addition to those already named, it includes not only musicians and entertainers such as the Fisk Jubilee Singers, Bessie Smith, Cab Calloway, Duke Ellington, Sammy Davis Jr., Josephine Baker, and Paul Robeson but also writers like Frederick Douglass, W.E.B. Du Bois, Claude McKay, and Frantz Fanon. Some of the writers' names appear in an impassioned discussion about education, during which Marion Willow realizes that her bookish daughter's voracious reading of British literature should be balanced by readings from the Black tradition. *Anne of Green Gables*, however, also holds a special place in the novel; the daughter blasts an unfortunate playmate with "There's no poetry in your soul" (16), worries about the absence of "a kindred soul" (17), emphasizes her plight as a demi-orphan (21), and reads *Rilla of Ingleside* (30). Sarsfield's text emphasizes the wealth of Black geographies and traditions in Montreal, while relying at the same time on intertextualities that are at least "double-voiced,"[74] as demonstrated by repeated references to the Black tradition and the Harlem Renaissance but also to Lucy Maud Montgomery. A related strategy pertains, as we have seen, to the novel's discussion of jazz.

V

In Sarsfield's portrait of Black Montreal culture of the 1940s, jazz is only one element, albeit a highly visible one. It constitutes a specific and remarkable contribution (among many) to the city's history and culture. The debate about different cultural specificities and their dialogues takes on a wider meaning in that context. Evoking Black jazz as a community-specific and culturally rooted yet cross-culturally receptive and influential matrix, Sarsfield's novel is relevant for its reimagining of the multiple emotional and imaginary geographies that constitute Montreal's history. This is underscored by the historical depth of the community it portrays. Jazz is a visible and audible sign of that community, whose rooted history is intertwined with the founding of modern Montreal in the nineteenth century and its earlier Black history, which the novel cites back to Angélique and slavery in Montreal (86).

The role of Black performers – and here, particularly, of Oscar Peterson in Montreal jazz – serves Sarsfield in her portrayal of Black diasporic geographies as integral to Montreal and to Canadian culture. The novel stages an interculturally active version of multiculturalism, although Black self-reliance and Garveyism play at least equally important roles. *No Crystal Stair* thus outlines a dual strategy. Instead of playing opposite options against each other by insisting on *either* Black nationalism *or* integration, it pursues multiple possibilities by emphasizing both Black culture and its intercultural or transcultural options. The novel thus stages a "rooted cosmopolitanism" that rests on a culturally specific, grounded openness.[75]

No Crystal Stair is part of a wider group of texts that make anglophone Black Montreal come alive in literature. Also set in Little Burgundy is Ernest Tucker's 2006 crime novel *Lost Boundaries*, in which a Black lawyer crosses racial boundaries in the name of justice, while his mother, an anglophone worried about the announcement of a referendum, seeks to solve the same murder case in her own ways. H. Nigel Thomas's *Behind the Face of Winter* (2001), a Caribbean immigrant's coming-of-age story, is set in 1980s Montreal outside of Little Burgundy but references its division through highway construction and as the place of his mother's congregation, which had "come to Canada looking for green pastures beside still waters; the Lachine Canal bordering their warehouse church was still enough."[76] Cecil Foster dedicated a chapter of his *A Place Called Heaven: The Meaning of Being Black in Canada* to Black suburban Parc Agrignon in Montreal.[77] And George Elliott Clarke – whose 2003 jazz opera *Québécité* is provocatively set in Quebec City, one of the Whitest cities in Canada, and whose Trudeau in the eponymous 2007 jazz opera is a regular at bassist Charlie Biddle's nightclub in Montreal – features plenty of jazz in his novel *George and Rue*. In it, Montreal appears as both the "fabulous Montreal" that is Cynthy's Black Nova Scotian dream getaway and the site of George's wartime enlistment and eventual jailing and is thus remembered as "a burgh of cops and jail."[78] Among the more recent contributions to this field, the work of Kaie Kellough has added exciting new elements.[79] These often jazz-inflected Black anglophone Montreals are joined, of course, by a much larger corpus in French, produced by writers mostly from Haiti, who include Dany Laferrière, Émile Ollivier, Gérard Étienne, Anthony Phelps, Max Dorsinville, Jean Jonassaint, Joël Des Rosiers, Edgard Gousse, and Marie-Célie Agnant.[80] Their heterogeneous Black diasporic Montreals make for multiple rereadings of the city, a project that texts such as Pierre Nepveu and Gilles Marcotte's *Montréal imaginaire*, Nepveu's *Lecture des lieux*, and Sherry Simon's *Translating Montreal* have advanced so much in other ways. Together with Sarsfield's *No Crystal Stair*, which reminds us of Black Montreal historical continuities that are also evoked in Oliver Jones's musical interventions and his championing of community renewal, they invite us to see Black diasporas and their cultures as integral to a social and cultural architecture that, like the Arcades for Benjamin's Paris, make up and help explain Montreal.

NOTES

This chapter was originally published as Winfried Siemerling, "Jazz, Diaspora, and the History and Writing of Black Anglophone Montreal," in *Critical Collaborations: Indigeneity, Diaspora, and Ecology in Canadian Literary Studies*, edited by Smaro Kamboureli and Christl Verduyn (Waterloo: Wilfrid Laurier University Press, 2014, pp. 199–214) and is reprinted here by permission of the publisher. I would like to acknowledge support in the preparation of this chapter from a Standard Research Grant of the Social Sciences and Humanities Research Council of Canada. I would also like to thank my research assistant Jay Rawding for editorial assistance.

1 "Our History," NCC/Charles H. Este Cultural Centre, accessed December 28, 2009, http://www.nccmontreal.org/ncc-enghistory (site discontinued). The centre was closed in 1989 owing to a lack of funding. Before moving to its later location on Coursol Street in what is now Little Burgundy, the NCC – later renamed the NCC/Charles H. Este Cultural Centre in honour of its long-time minister – was located in the basement of Union United Congregational Church, a black Montreal landmark institution founded by railroad porters in 1907. See Leo W. Bertley, *Montreal's Oldest Black Congregation: Union Church, 3007 Delisle Street* (Pierrefonds: Bilongo, 1976). The NCC building was demolished in November 2014. "Montreal's Negro Community Centre Demolished," CBC News, November 20, 2014, https://www.cbc.ca/news/canada/montreal/montreal-s-negro-community-centre-demolished-1.2844166.
2 As Marcel Trudel's *Deux siecles d'esclavage au Canada* and other sources on the subject make clear, only about one-third of the enslaved individuals in New France were Black; the majority were Indigenous, or *panis*.
3 Carol Talbot, *Growing Up Black in Canada* (Toronto: Williams-Wallace, 1984), 19.
4 Joyce Davidson and Christine Milligan, "Embodying Emotion Sensing Space: Introducing Emotional Geographies," editorial, *Social and Cultural Geography* 5, no. 4 (2004): 523–32; Katherine McKittrick, *Demonic Grounds: Black Women and the Cartographies of Struggle* (Minneapolis: University of Minnesota Press, 2006).
5 Pierre Nepveu, *Lecture des lieux* (Montreal: Boréal, 2004), 49.
6 Sherry Simon, *Translating Montreal: Episodes in the Life of a Divided City* (Montreal and Kingston: McGill-Queen's University Press, 2006), 7.
7 Volume 4 of the Commission on Bilingualism and Biculturalism's final report reiterates its mandate to "recommend what steps should be taken to develop the Canadian confederation on the basis of an equal partnership between the two founding races, taking into account the contribution

made by the other ethnic groups" (3). But it also states, "We repeat that we accept the words 'race' and 'people' only in their traditional sense – meaning a national group, with no biological significance – and we prefer to emphasize the facts of language and culture rather than the concepts of 'race,' 'people,' or even 'ethnic group'" (7). Royal Commission on Bilingualism and Biculturalism, *Final Report of the Royal Commission on Bilingualism and Biculturalism*, vol. 4 (Ottawa: Queen's Printer, 1969).
8 Hugh MacLennan, *Two Solitudes* (1945; Toronto: Stoddart, 1993), 2.
9 Davidson and Milligan, "Embodying Emotion Sensing Space," 523.
10 See, especially, Gabrielle Roy, "Tout Montréal 1: Les deux Saint-Laurent," *Le Bulletin des agriculteurs* 37, no. 6 (1941): 8–9, 37, 40. Mary Jean Green observes, "In *Bonheur d'occasion* ... the multiethnic city she described in 1941 has disappeared, replaced by a bipolar city divided between rich and poor anglophone and francophone, where the only 'immigrants' are Roy's impoverished French-Canadian characters, who have migrated into the city from nearby farms. Although *Bonheur d'occasion* broke new literary ground by placing its French-Canadian characters in an urban setting, it did not go so far as to integrate Roy's early vision of the city as a place of hybridity." Green, "Transcultural Identities: Many Ways of Being Québécois," in *Textualizing the Immigrant Experience in Contemporary Quebec*, ed. Susan Ireland and Patrice J. Proulx (Westport, CT: Praeger, 2004), 13.
11 Quotations in French are from Gabrielle Roy, *Bonheur d'occasion* (1945; Montreal: Boréal, 1993). All English translations are taken from Hannah Josephson's translation of the novel: *The Tin Flute* (Toronto: McClelland and Stewart, 1969).
12 Callaghan, *The Loved and the Lost* (1951; Toronto: Macmillan, 1983), 166. Subsequent quotations are taken from this edition and cited directly in the text.
13 Sherry Simon points out that *The Loved and the Lost* and *Bonheur d'occasion* are among the few novels that "have used the vertical drop between mountain and river as dramatic material to be exploited"; many other works have concentrated instead on the east-west linguistic split. Simon, "The Post-Industrial Southwest," in *USED/Goods*, ed. Gisele Amantea, Lorraine Oades and Kim Sawchuk (Montreal: Conseil des Arts/Cut Rate Collective, 2009), 4.
14 Toni Morrison, *Playing in the Dark: Whiteness and the Literary Imagination* (New York: Vintage, 1990), 38.
15 David Leahy has argued that "given the semiotic field of blacks in the novel it is difficult to imagine that predominantly white readerships in the early 1950s would not have presumed Peggy's murderer was black." Leahy, "Race, Gender and Class Enigmas in *The Loved and the Lost* and *Au milieu, la montagne*," *Textual Studies in Canada* 5 (1994): 37.
16 Quoted in Robin W. Winks, *The Blacks in Canada: A History*, 2nd ed. (Montreal and Kingston: McGill-Queen's University Press, 1997), 1.

17 Marcel Trudel, with Micheline d'Allaire, *Deux Siècles d'esclavage au Québec; suivi du Dictionnaire des esclaves et de leurs propriétaires au Canada français sur CD-ROM* (Montreal: Hurtubise HMH, 2004), 14; Winks, *Blacks in Canada*, 1.
18 Daniel Gay, *Les noirs du Québec, 1629–1900*, Cahiers des Amériques (Sillery, QC: Septentrion, 2004), 29; Trudel, 86. Slavery in New France was authorized by Louis XIV in 1689 – four years after the *Code Noir* regulated slavery in the West Indies – but the decision had no direct impact because of intervening wars and perhaps for reasons of insufficient capital. See Trudel, 34–48; and Winks, *Blacks in Canada*, 5–23.
19 George Elliott Clarke has suggested that such transmissions should also be read as slave narratives. Clarke, "'This Is No Hearsay': Reading the Canadian Slave Narratives," *Papers of the Bibliographical Society of Canada* 43, no. 1 (2005): 17–18.
20 See Lorris Elliott, ed. *Other Voices: Writing by Blacks in Canada* (Toronto: Williams-Wallace, 1985); Lorena Gale, *Angélique* (Toronto: Playwrights Canada Press, 2000); Paul Fehmiu Brown, *Marie-Josèphe Angélique* (Saint-Léonard: Éditions 5 continents, 1998); and Micheline Bail, *L'Esclave* (Montréal: Éditions Libre Expression, 1999).
21 Afua Cooper, *The Hanging of Angélique: The Untold Story of Canadian Slavery and the Burning of Old Montréal* (Toronto: Harper Perennial, 2006); McKittrick, *Demonic Grounds*.
22 Blacks had standing in courts, which often ruled in their favour (Winks, *Blacks in Canada*, 11), and this rendered slavery impracticable; see Frank Mackey, "Charlotte, She Got the Ball Rolling," in *Black Then: Blacks and Montreal, 1780s–1880s* (Montreal and Kingston: McGill-Queen's University Press, 2004), 25–32.
23 Trudel, 69–99.
24 Winks, *Blacks in Canada*, 10–11, 15; Jane Rhodes, *Mary Ann Shadd Cary: The Black Press and Protest in the Nineteenth Century* (Bloomington: Indiana University Press, 1998), 29.
25 Winks, *Blacks in Canada*, 15. In 1799 and again in 1800, the "owners" of enslaved captives petitioned for legislative support to quell the increasing numbers of absconding self-liberating individuals, after several of them had secured their freedom through the courts. Mackey, *Black Then*, 4; Trudel, 304–12.
26 Trudel, 123–42.
27 See Francis-J. Audet, "William Brown (1737–1789), premier imprimeur, journaliste et libraire de Québec; sa vie et ses oeuvres," *Mémoires de la Société Royale du Canada*, 3rd ser., 26, sec. 1 (1932): 97–112.
28 Trudel, 161, 205–7.
29 Winks, *Blacks in Canada*, 19.
30 Mackey, *Black Then*, 92–6.

31 The account appeared in the *Gazette* on 31 January 1861; it is reprinted in Mackey, *Black Then*, 162–6.
32 Gary Collison, *Shadrach Minkins: From Fugitive Slave to Citizen* (Cambridge, MA: Harvard University Press, 1997), 206.
33 As Dorothy Williams specifies in her history of Montreal's Black community, "The current dimensions of section [*sic*] that was the St. Antoine district includes Little Burgundy and St. Henri. Little Burgundy runs from Atwater avenue east to Peel street, from the Lachine Canal north to the Ville Marie expressway. St. Henri extends along St. Antoine, from Atwater west to Glen Road." Williams, *Road to Now*, 36–7.
34 Collison, *Shadrach Minkins*, 205. As Collison remarks, "By moving to Mountain Street Shadrach Minkins put himself in the center of the most dynamic area of the city" (p. 204). Gerald J.J. Tulchinsky and Samuel Phillips Day both illustrate this claim: Tulchinsky, *The River Barons: Montreal Businessmen and the Growth of Industry and Transportation, 1837–53* (Toronto: University of Toronto Press, 1977); Day, *English America, or, Pictures of Canadian Places and People* (London: T. Cauthley Newby, 1864). For a history of Saint-Henri, see Société Historique de Saint-Henri, "Histoire de Saint-Henri: Saint-Henri, Avant, Pendant et Apres le Canal," accessed February 27, 2010, http://www.saint-henri.com.
35 Hence the name of the Lachine Canal: "Upon arriving in New France, Cavalier de LaSalle ... dreamed of discovering this very route [to China]. Later, his seigneury [*sic*] located near the rapids was mockingly dubbed La Chine – the name in French for China." Yves Desloges and Alain Gelly, *The Lachine Canal: Riding the Waves of Industrial and Urban Development, 1860–1950*, trans. Donald Kellough (Sillery, QC: Septentrion, 2002), 9.
36 Desloges and Gelly, 9.
37 Desloges and Gelly, 9, 129.
38 Tulchinsky, *River Barons*.
39 Agnes Calliste, "Sleeping Car Porters in Canada: An Ethnically Submerged Split Labour Market," *Canadian Ethnic Studies/Etudes Ethniques au Canada* 19, no. 1 (1987): 2; Dorothy Williams, *The Road to Now: A History of Blacks in Montreal* (Montreal: Véhicule, 1997), 32–3.
40 Williams, *Road to Now*, 33.
41 Williams, 38.
42 Nancy Marrelli, *Stepping Out: The Golden Age of Montreal Night Clubs, 1925–1955* (Montreal: Véhicule, 2004), 14.
43 Williams, *Road to Now*, 44.
44 Marrelli, *Stepping Out*, 9.
45 John Gilmore, *Swinging in Paradise: The Story of Jazz in Montreal* (Montreal: Véhicule, 1988), 43.
46 Marrelli, *Stepping Out*, 10–11.

47 Gilmore, *Swinging in Paradise*, 43.
48 Joe Sealy won a Juno award in 2000 for *Africville Suite*, an album partially inspired by his Africville-born father. Sealy co-founded the jazz record label Triplet Records in 1989 and still performs actively. He received the Order of Canada in 2010. Mark Miller, *The Miller Companion to Jazz in Canada and Canadians in Jazz* (Toronto: Mercury, 2001), 178–9.
49 Mark Miller notes, "His only recorded solo of any consequence, an 84-bar improvisation on *Now's the Time*, was made at Parker's side and issued 40 years later on the CD *Charlie Parker, Montreal, 1953* (Uptown)." Miller, *Miller Companion*, 207.
50 Miller, 37.
51 See Gilmore, *Swinging in Paradise*, chaps. 6 and 5; Miller, *Miller Companion*, 207, 136.
52 Marrelli points out that "The Corner" was "close to where the black community lived, and to the trains where many blacks worked as porters. At 'The Corner' black entertainment was the drawing card, but both black and white audiences were welcome." Marrelli, *Stepping Out*, 100.
53 Gilmore, *Swinging in Paradise*, 99.
54 Quoted in Gene Lees, *Oscar Peterson: The Will to Swing* (Toronto: Lester & Orpen Dennys, 1988), 42.
55 Mark Miller, *Jazz in Canada: Fourteen Lives* (Toronto: University of Toronto Press, 1982), 127.
56 Gilmore, *Swinging in Paradise*, 109–10.
57 Lees, *Oscar Peterson*, 22.
58 Marthe Sansregret, *Oliver Jones, le musicien et l'homme* (Outremont, QC: Stanke, 2005), 30.
59 Williams, *Road to Now*, 36–7.
60 Examples include Bertley, *Montreal's Oldest Black Congregation*; and Hostesses of Union United Church, *Memory Book: Union United Church, 75th Anniversary, 1907–1982* (Montreal: The Church, 1982).
61 Sarsfield's text was a finalist in the 2005 edition of CBC's Canada Reads. All subsequent quotations in the text are from Sarsfield, *No Crystal Stair* (Toronto: Moulin, 1997).
62 The novel brings up, for instance, the predicaments of French Canadian women during that period and features characters from Italian, Russian, and other backgrounds, as well as a fully multicultural wedding that combines a Russian Orthodox ceremony with the temptations of Creole cooking.
63 Williams, *Road to Now*, 61. On the UNIA in Montreal and in Canada, see Bertley, *Montreal's Oldest Black Congregation*; and Carla Marano, "'Rising Strongly and Rapidly': The Universal Negro Improvement Association in Canada, 1919–1940," *Canadian Historical Review* 91, no. 2 (2010): 233–59.

64 "The Coloured Ladies Club" in the novel corresponds to the Coloured Women's Club of Montreal, which was founded in 1902. Initially, it was "an exclusive club of only fifteen women – all wives of American porters," who assisted the Black community and its newly arrived immigrants (Williams, *Road to Now*, 50–1). On the important role of women in the UNIA, see Williams, 60–1.

65 Randolph "advocated a grand alliance between blacks and the trade union movement ... Many blacks regarded organized labor as an enemy of racial integration, because blacks were barred from most of labor's craft unions. Randolph relentlessly attacked unions that excluded black workers." "A. Philip Randolph, 1889–1979, Trade Union Leader," George Meany Memorial Archives, accessed 25 October 2007, http://www.georgemeany.org/archives/leader.html (site discontinued).

66 Williams, *Road to Now*, 59. On unions and racism in Canada, see Calliste, "Sleeping Car Porters"; and Calliste, "Blacks on Canadian Railways," *Canadian Ethnic Studies* 20, no. 2 (1988): 36–52.

67 Gilmore, *Swinging in Paradise*, 107.

68 On at least one known occasion, Holmes had to fend off racist exclusionary tactics by a ballroom when Peterson became one of the first Black musicians to play with the Holmes Orchestra at the Montreal Ritz-Carlton. See Marrelli, *Stepping Out*, 86; Gilmore, *Swinging in Paradise*, 103–5; and Lees, *Oscar Peterson*, 51–2, 59.

69 As a child, Peterson was expected to perform on the piano during Marcus Garvey's visit to Montreal; he described his impressions of Garvey and the UNIA: "He drove home that it would only be with the courage and determination to create and sustain our very own black industries, grocery stores, taxis, airlines, and even shipping lines that we would at last be truly free from the economic bondage that we endured. Intriguingly, if *we* thrust that form of thinking forward to today's world, Marcus Garvey was dead on the mark. When I think back to those countless Sunday afternoons, I realize that I got more from those [UNIA] meetings than I was aware of at the time. Not only did the repeated public performances in the hall increase my musical confidence, but – more importantly – I learned from Marcus Garvey and others the need for dedication and devotion to any cause that one sincerely believes in. Many of the young Montreal blacks of today may not even have heard of the UNIA; nevertheless, it served their forebears as a place of spiritual sustenance and personal reconstruction." Peterson, *A Jazz Odyssey: The Life of Oscar Peterson*, ed. Richard Palmer (London: Continuum, 2002), 28–9.

70 I have used the notational form of "re/cognition" elsewhere to emphasize the ambivalent and often contradictory duality by which cognitive change

("re-cognition") draws on available categories in a process of pattern matching ("recognition") that often produces identification as acceptance under dominant standards. In this sense, "recognition" limits "re-cognition" because the former assimilates potential difference to what is already known or accepted. I have developed this problem of re/cognition in the context of "New" World paradigms and of W.E.B. Du Bois's elaboration of "double consciousness," as a framework to study North American cultures comparatively and as the ongoing results of conflicted complex processes and articulations of cultural emergence. See Winfried Siemerling, *The New North American Studies: Culture, Writing and the Politics of Re/Cognition* (New York: Routledge, 2005).

71 For John Fiske, Whiteness exercises power through "exnomination" as "the means by which whiteness avoids being named and thus keeps itself out of the field of interrogation and therefore off the agenda for change." Quoted in George Lewis, "Improvised Music after 1950: Afrological and Eurological Perspectives," in *The Other Side of Nowhere: Jazz, Improvisation, and Communities in Dialogue*, ed. Daniel Fischlin and Ajay Heble (Middletown, CT: Wesleyan University Press, 2004), 140.

72 In an influential discussion of "Afrological" and "Eurological" perspectives, the trombonist and music scholar George Lewis draws on Fiske and other commentators on Whiteness to highlight, for example, the paradoxical status of boundaries in John Cage's statements about experimental music, which turn on notions of "indeterminacy" and "chance operations" but entirely dismiss jazz. This is all the more surprising given the influence of bebop on the New York school of which Cage was a member. With respect to Cage's elision of Black traditions, Lewis writes that "despite such declarations as 'the world is one world now' … it is clear that Cage has drawn very specific boundaries, not only as to which musics are relevant to his own musicality but as to which musics suit his own taste." Lewis, "Improvised Music," 136–7, 138.

73 See Jessica Wegmann-Sánchez, "Rewriting Race and Ethnicity across the Border: Mairuth Sarsfield's *No Crystal Stair* and Nella Larsen's *Quicksand* and *Passing*," *Essays on Canadian Writing* 74 (2001): 147–54.

74 Henry Louis Gates Jr., *The Signifying Monkey: A Theory of Afro-American Literary Criticism* (New York: Oxford University Press, 1988), xxiii.

75 Kwame Anthony Appiah, *The Ethics of Identity* (Princeton: Princeton University Press, 2005), 213–72.

76 H. Nigel Thomas, *Behind the Face of Winter* (Toronto: TSAR, 2001), 124.

77 Cecil Foster, *A Place Called Heaven: The Meaning of Being Black in Canada* (Toronto: HarperCollins, 1996).

78 George Elliott Clarke, *George and Rue* (Toronto: HarperCollins, 2005), 18, 84.

79 See especially his prose texts *Accordéon* (Winnipeg: ARP Books, 2016) and *Dominoes at the Crossroads* (Montreal: Esplanade, 2020); Kellough is also a poet and spoken word performer.
80 See Winfried Siemerling, "Ethics as Re/Cognition in the Novels of Marie-Célie Agnant: Oral Knowledge, Cognitive Change, and Social Justice," *University of Toronto Quarterly* 76, no. 3 (2007): 838–60.

SECTION EIGHT

Black Women's Orality and Knowings

19
"I don't know if I should say this": Black Women, Oral History, and Contesting the Great White North

FUNKÉ ALADEJEBI

> Well, I had an incident there with a female principal. It was ... *I don't know if I should say this*. She didn't have the same values I had, let me put it that way. Her values were far different from mine. I thought that we were there for the kids and obviously she was there for herself ... Because she had a tendency to treat some ... how do I put this ... if you were of colour, I felt. You didn't have to be Black.
>
> Cassandra Banks

When discussing her early teaching experiences in the 1970s, Cassandra Banks struggled to disclose what she perceived to be incidents of racial discrimination enacted by her school's White female principal.[1] Unable to articulate her concerns about the poor treatment that racialized students and teachers experienced, Banks instead attributed this mistreatment to personal values and selfishness. Despite expressing some uneasiness in her recollection of her former principal, Banks went on to explain that her experience was so bad that she eventually had to leave her position at the school. Soon after these statements, Banks quickly shifted the focus of her interview to describe more positive teaching experiences after she left the school. Yet, her tone, pauses, and hesitation to recall specific incidences with her principal may have been indicative of the ways in which racial prejudice created discriminatory practices and workplace hierarchies within Canadian schools.

Banks was one of a group of Black women teachers who recounted stories of communal and individual choice in the creation of their oral history narratives. Their accounts were not only shaped by broader social, political, and economic changes of the twentieth century but also characterized by the interview process itself. Banks's account, and the lived experiences of other women featured in this chapter, tells us of the challenges and triumphs of conducting historical research on and in living communities.² Examining the oral histories of ten Black female educators who taught in Ontario from the 1940s to the 1980s, this chapter reveals the ways Black women's stories can tell us not only of a collective Black Canadian experience marked by sexism, separation, and racial discrimination but also of individual actions and affirmations of professionalism and resistive pedagogical approaches that challenged assumptions about Black existences in Canada. Situating the uses and approaches of oral history to highlight Black women's individual and collective choices, I argue that the process of telling *her*stories can be understood as a Black feminist practice that is both political and restorative in nature.

From a methodological standpoint, the recording, writing, and interpretation of Black women's stories disrupts historical erasures that constructed a Canadian national identity through the lens of the Great White North and gives way to a greater understanding of the richness and multiplicity of Black life in twentieth-century Canada. By situating Black women as active and conscious participants both in Canada's nation-building project and in the fight and contestation of settler colonialism and its project to erase Indigenous and Black presence from the land, oral history can be a counterhegemonic practice that is both political and transformative in nature. In particular, the oral stories of Black women teachers offer a lens into understanding the intersections of their professional and personal lives, as well as racial and gendered hierarchies that structured Ontario schooling institutions in the twentieth century. These oral histories help us to locate Black women as producers of knowledge and reveal the everyday experiences of Black women often left out of historical writing.

In "Diasporic Memories: Community, Individuality, and Creativity – A Life Stories Perspective," Mary Chamberlain discusses Caribbean migrant workers' stories in creating alternative models of nationhood to account for the emotional rather than geographic borders that characterized African Caribbean migration and identities. She encourages us read oral stories for symbolic meanings in order to explore choices of language and repetition, and to examine how frameworks of family and belonging are remembered. According to Chamberlain, Black diasporic memory is necessarily layered, linking "the Black experience and provid[ing] a cultural continuity with those back home and overseas."³ Black women educators' recollections of their professional lives in the mid-to-late twentieth century gave me an opportunity not only to examine the stories women chose to discuss but also to interpret the tones, silences, pauses, laughter, and body language of interview participants to reveal the diverse possibilities of their memories, narratives, and identities. As such, I contend that the practice of oral history in Black communities considers research participants not as mere subjects of historical analysis but rather as engaged knowledge producers who made deliberate and conscious choices about the stories they described during the interview process.

Since the publication of seminal works such as *The Black Woman in Canada* (1976), *Silenced* (1983), and *No Burden to Carry* (1991), scholars of Black Canada have featured the oral histories of Black women to challenge historical erasure and illuminate the long-standing presence of persons of African descent in Canada.[4] These works recognized that the erasure of persons of African descent within the Canadian historical narrative was "the result of a society which uses power and powerlessness as weapons to exclude non-white and poor people from any real decision-making and participation."[5] By centring the life stories of Black women, these scholars challenged gender- and class-based assumptions about the place of (re)productive labour within the writing of Black Canada and posed a series of interpretative questions to offer critiques that confronted the gaps in historical literature and writing. By its very nature, the place of Black women's oral history within the writing of Black Canada addresses the fragmented and liminal representations of Blackness in the broader historical canon.

Conversely, while the stories that Black women chose to tell revealed much about Black life in twentieth-century Canada, a richness of analysis is also available in the method of archiving and presenting oral herstories. In the analysis that follows, I argue that oral history can provide a variety of methodological and pedagogical tools for "knowing" Black women and cast a new light into underexplored areas of writing Black Canadian history. Through an examination of oral interviews and the relationships that evolve from the interview process, we can interpret the silence of Black women and the traumatic hesitations of our interview participants differently.[6] This ultimately engages in a feminist practice that gives space for the individuality of each narrator and "value[s] silences, nonverbal communication, communal methods of interviewing, and gentle probing when the narrator circumvents topics she perceives as insignificant or uncomfortable."[7] By focusing on the lived experiences of Black women as a legitimate source of information in historical practice, oral history as a methodology helps to situate their stories within a larger context of settler colonialism in order to understand how their lives were characterized by and stood in response to experiences of enslavement, racism, and systematic discrimination.

Oral History as Historical Practice

Oral history became an important component in the study of marginalized communities as the new social history rose in popularity within academic disciplines in the 1960s and 1970s. According to Joan Sangster, labour and women's historians used oral history to uncover the hidden history and everyday experiences of working people.[8] Oral history helped to locate "ordinary" people as agents of social change within dominant narratives that purported a universal (White) Canadian experience. As the field continued to evolve, so too did debates about the (ab)uses of oral history and its usefulness for historical analysis. One such debate was around the place of shared authority and the growing recognition of the role of the interviewer in the research process. Valerie Yow, Pamela Sugiman, Joan Sangster, and others acknowledge that the historian is not an objective observer in the oral history process, but rather a participant in a collaborative relationship that strongly influences the interview process. These scholars argue that a complex and shifting relationship exists between interviewer and narrator that shapes the nature and kinds of stories collected. In her analysis of the relationship between the interviewer and interviewee in the oral history process, Yow contends that transference influences the interview process in critical ways. She reveals that interview processes can be influenced by a variety of factors including age, discomfort with interview questions, and rapport established during the interview. According to Yow, "Transference usually operates on an unconscious level, but it does not have to remain an unconscious influence."[9] As a result, power dynamics of the past, which include feelings, emotions, education level, age, and gender, can be transferred onto a person in present contexts and can influence shared authority within interview processes. Yow calls on oral historians to include reflexivity in their writing to discuss the ways subjectivity influences research and interpretation, instead of viewing the interview process as a purely objective encounter.

In my research within Black Canadian communities, shared authority and transference were demonstrated in complex and contradictory ways despite my insider-outsider status. Insider-outsider status considers the ways in which individual social locations shape interviewee/interviewer relationships and can function as a shifting category that is constructed through interactions between the researcher and participant.[10] A researcher can be considered an "insider" if they share similar characteristics or experiences such as gender, race, sexual orientation, or socioeconomic standing. At the same time, an "outsider" can be someone who does not belong to these characteristic groupings or a member who is not part of the immediate community and the participant's social circle. Although the status of the "insider-outsider" is constructed as an oppositional category, oral historian Alan Wieder makes the case that the insider-outsider position within oral history should be understood not as a binary but "rather a complex process that is nurtured by political, cultural, and personal contexts." Wieder argues, as do I, that as oral history projects grow, the role of the oral historian shifts along a continuum of both insider and outsider status based the ways the researcher connects with narrators.[11] In essence, while my positionality as a Black woman educator allowed for some commonalities in discussing similar gendered and racial experiences with interviewees, who were also Black women teachers, my status as researcher, place of birth (particularly when interviewing Canadian-born Black women), and age (the age gap between myself and the average participant was approximately forty years) meant that some discussions, particularly around sexuality and intimate partnerships, were virtually excluded from our discussions. Differing social and cultural spaces meant that considerations about shared knowledge were not assumed but rather cultivated through interview responses and relationship building happening before, during, and after the formal interview. Therefore, my placement as insider-outsider within Black Canadian communities shifted based on the ways interview participants valued and prioritized race, social status, age, place of birth, and professional training, as well as the sampling process used to locate participants, who were largely informed of my study by other community and kin relationships. The majority of my research participants described themselves as having a variety of ethnocultural roots but identified as Canadian, Caribbean, or American-born. The majority of these women came from working-class and middle-class backgrounds where their families struggled to find steady employment and economic stability. As a result, the families of the women featured in this chapter viewed education as a way to access better social and economic mobility.

As a result, the kinds of information women chose to disclose during the interview process reflected a series of complex decisions that included not only Black women's past experiences as educators but also contemporary interpretations of their past lives as retired workers and community activists. Fundamentally, their oral histories were also about how Black women teachers made sense of their professional and personal lives. Such was the case of Nydia Manning, who, after describing teaching junior programs at her school in Windsor, asked me if I was a teacher. Only after I confirmed my educational training did Manning proceed to give me details about her pedagogical approach within the classroom. My status as a teacher meant Manning assumed that I had shared knowledge of the teaching profession, that I understood the technical terms she used, and that there was some commonalty in our teaching experiences.[12]

However, simply using these assumptions about "insiderness" can obscure the ways in which power could be articulated and demonstrated throughout the interview process. Given my age and professional training, Manning and other educators extended their support during the interview process as part of a broader sense of care for Black women. They often recalled stories of the past as part of a larger practice of community mentorship and support. This was the experience of Belinda Soto, who had lived in her community for over thirty years; she taught at one school in the community for twenty-five years and "started getting the children of the children [she had taught]." In her interview, Soto recalled the significance of teaching and remaining in the community in that "it was very important to me to do the things we did. It was quite different then." While Soto also cited her children and marriage as reasons for remaining in her community, her sense of responsibility and commitment to the students she taught rooted her sense of belonging. Soto clarified that she did all her work in her community because "if you belong to something, and you are committed to it, you work at it. Simple as that."[13] During the interview process, educators like Soto often merged stories of self and community-based practices in ways that gave them the space to occupy various sites of consciousness; this included their roles as mothers, community leaders, and teachers of Black and racialized students.[14]

In some cases, women adopted these community-based practices and modelled ethics of care that emerged during the interview process. This was often displayed by an insistence on feeding me or requests that I stay for dinner, spend extended periods of time meeting community members and kin, or invitations to come back to visit after the interview was over. Soto, for example, took me on bike tour of her community and, when she was ready to conclude our interview, told me, "Anyway, I think that's probably enough, and we are gonna eat some supper."[15] That she did not ask whether or not I had the time to stay for dinner not only reflected assumptions about the level of comfort between interviewee and researcher but also highlighted the ways communal bonds of support became reinforced during our interview. That Soto and I bonded over conversations during and after our interview called for a level of reflexivity to review the research process itself and what happens when relationships evolve, infuence, and *turn into* oral history.[16] That is, our interactions asked me to consider the ways researchers unconsciously become part of the very process they are trying to analyse. In this case, my interactions with these Black women educators prioritized their roles as teachers, as they often spoke as if they were training and preparing me for my professional career as a teacher and took on this role as part of their political and social duty. This was demonstrated through Tammy Okafor's reflections about generational differences between educators in the late 1980s. Okafor explained,

> In the teaching profession, a lot of us older folks have been through things that a lot of the younger ones will never have to go through. And the younger ones have to realize that there is a lot to learn from us and they should really take that as a guide, it's not a blueprint, but they should take it as a guide and say you know what, maybe what some of the old folks are saying makes sense and I can learn from it and use it to help me in terms of what I want to do in my profession.[17]

Okafor reflected on the ways intergenerational alliances could be built to help educators deal with the challenges of teaching in Ontario schools. Scholar Andrea O'Reilly argues that this form of mentorship could be understood as community mothering, or othermothering, which "emerged in response to Black mothers' needs and serves to empower Black women and enrich their lives."[18] As such, some women recounted their stories in ways that considered their lives as educators as a continuous and communal role. This meant that generational differences led to a level of transference during the interviews and created "established roles" where some narrators took on mentorship personas in the interview.[19]

In other instances, insiderness allowed for an amalgamation of professional and community relationships that could be difficult to interpret. After describing her pedagogical approach when teaching Black students, Manning asked me if I found that Black community members thought I was better than others because I had graduated with a degree and continued with graduate studies. Using shared knowledge of our education and middle-class identities, Manning described "paying her dues" to allude to broader socioeconomic tensions within Black Canadian communities. She recalled, "When I moved here in this house, twelve years ago, it was the same thing. [Community members would say,] 'Oh, well, she thinks she's better.' You know, I paid my dues."[20] Manning revealed that this disconnect happened as she gained economic independence and greater social mobility. That she situated this discussion in relation to my education and career choices indicated a desire to root her story in a broader collective experience between Black professional women. Grace Mullings would echo these sentiments and situate my education to launch into a broader critique about professional mobility and oppression within Black communities. Mullings explained that the challenges she faced within the teaching profession came not only from members outside of her community, but also from Black Canadian community members. She grounded her example by connecting this tension to my own educational pursuits when she divulged that "sometimes it's what you can get from Black people ourselves. You're [researcher] going through getting a PhD, I'm sure you will encounter statements that are made towards you by your own. You will also encounter that some of the biggest mentors and helpers have been your non-Black people."[21]

Both Mullings and Manning grounded their discussion of fractured community relationships as the result of economic mobility largely through their desire to receive corroboration from me, someone who they believed reflected similar experiences of professional training, race, and gender. Oral historian Kristina Minister argues that this style of intersupport between women reflects a recognition of conversational processes specific to their gender and feminist oral history practice. Minister contends that verbal reinforcement is common during interviews between researcher and narrator. In fact, this kind of reinforcement serves as a way to support narrators as they describe their stories.[22] Merging the researcher-interviewee relationship to articulate a broader collective experience of professional women, Mullings and Manning reflected common practices within female-led professional networks that used shared knowledge and communication to gain information about professional training opportunities, learn about potential job openings, and cultivate relationships with other teachers in the field. Creating a sense of gender solidarity on the basis of shared professional careers, Manning and Mullings gave weight to the importance of female spheres of influence and support networks that were a necessary part of Black women's economic and social mobility.

In other instances, gendered frameworks helped me to not only interpret the ways Black women constructed their self-identity but also understand how they negotiated power within their own intimate partnerships. One particularly interesting relationship dynamic that emerged through my research involved the personal narrative of American-born educator Miriam Chambers and her husband, Earl. Within Miriam Chambers's account, marriage, family, and kin relationships became central components of her life story as an educator. Throughout the interview, she often merged stories of her teaching career with that of her husband, who also became an educator later in his career. Miriam Chambers often described experiences of gender-based discrimination as one of the few female educators working in the secondary school sector in her district. However, she often buttressed these stories by drawing references back to her husband, who quickly became part of the interview process. In her account of pay equity in the late 1970s, Miriam explained,

> It's like when [Earl] and I got married, they [male friends] heard he was marrying a teacher so they assumed that I was an elementary teacher. I don't know why they assumed that. Finally, I figured out that in Canada at the time, public school teachers did not need a degree. They only needed one year after grade 13 to teach. They assumed that being a woman, I would be a public school teacher and I wouldn't have gone on for a degree. So, because the men represented the majority in the secondary school [sector], they commanded more money. They did at the time. Considerably more. But in teaching, we didn't have to worry about, you know ... we got the same pay.[23]

Chambers had an illustrious career, having completed her degree at the University of Michigan in 1962 and working as a biology teacher in Michigan before moving to Canada with her Canadian-born husband. Her description indicated workplace hierarchies fractured by gender, teaching designation, and pay. While teaching became one of the earliest professional occupations open to Canadian women, the feminization of elementary education brought thousands of women into the teaching sector while also creating a sex-segregated labour market that kept male educators in place as principals, school trustees, and administrative heads. In addition, the legacies of nineteenth-century gender roles and divisions of labour further institutionalized the idea that women were better suited to train young children. In some instances, women were barred from taking entrance examinations that would make them eligible for employment in the secondary school sector. Such was the case in Nova Scotia, where women were barred from taking first-class licences until 1869; even then, they were ineligible to teach in provincial secondary schools because the highest designation needed for this position was an academic licence, granted after training in a normal school.[24] As a result of this gender discrimination, the secondary school sector was dominated by male teachers believed to have specialized training and expertise as "functional and public actors for intelligent citizenship."[25] Elementary teachers, by contrast, were perceived to have lower credentials and broad skills based on their gendered disposition as "natural nurturers" to help students socialize in the world.[26]

Although Chambers recognized these gendered assumptions about female employability and training in the twentieth century, her comments on equal pay may have been influenced more by the presence of her husband than by the reality of wage earning by male and female educators of the period. For instance, although the federal Female Employees Equal Pay Act, meant to ensure that men and women were paid the same salary for equal work, was passed in 1956, income discrepancies continued to exist between the wages of male and female educators. In 1976, the annual salary for female elementary school teachers was approximately $15,165, while male elementary teachers earned $19,337 annually.[27] Furthermore, this income discrepancy could not always be explained by levels of education and years of service, which also influenced the varying salaries of educators in the late twentieth century.

Despite her comment about wage parity between male and female secondary educators, Miriam Chambers clearly recognized the societal assumptions that viewed women as less qualified than their male counterparts. In fact, Kristina Llewellyn's analysis of women teachers in postwar Canada corroborates this notion that although female secondary school teachers could distance themselves from female stereotypes in the profession on account of their university credentials, they were still viewed with suspicion and seen as "more under-qualified than their male counterparts."[28] A similar circumstance may have also been present in Chambers's recollection of her work experiences in Canada; although she recognized gendered stereotypes that viewed women as less than capable of holding upper administrative positions, she described these experiences as separate from her own life. And yet, racism and sexism influenced the methods by which Chambers sought employment in Canadian schools. For example, she described the ways her husband helped her through job interview processes by calling school boards to ensure that they would hire a Black woman. This approach proved effective and she was able to gain a position at one of the schools her husband screened. Having a clear understanding of the unwritten, yet widely known, discriminatory practices that discouraged the hiring of Black teachers in various Ontario schools, Earl Chambers's position and status as a male figure – with some authority, even if it was muted by his race – gave him some leverage when approaching school administrators about their hiring practices.

While Miriam Chambers's story described the ways gender and race were interpreted by Black women teachers, the impact of gender during the interview process became another significant means of understanding oral history practice. As Earl Chambers became part of the interview process, he articulated a set of gendered interview practices that were different from those of his wife. Minister explains that female oral historians must acquire adaptive interviewing techniques that allow them to hear varying communication styles between men and women. In her analysis of the place of feminist frameworks in oral interviews, Minister explains that male interview participants tend to discuss acts and events that situate their power and reflect what they do. Conversely, women tend to refer to their personal relationships and reflect on who they are.[29] Minister contends that in order to hear what women deem essential to their lives, feminist oral historians need to learn how to watch and remain in tune with the ways in which women speak privately about each other. More importantly, Minister identifies different gendered interview scripts to which feminist researchers can be attuned during the interview process – for example, the ways in which "women use questions to maintain and enhance conversation, [while] men interpret questions as requests for information."[30]

These gendered scripts were evident in the varying examples and communication styles that Earl Chambers used during our collective interview. On Miriam Chambers's insistence, I began a separate interview with her husband, who started our interview by listing his credentials and explained, "I had a degree. I got my teaching credentials, got my masters and my supervisory credentials and went up that route without having been a principal."[31] Although racial discrimination in Canada's labour market largely limited Black men to precarious labour and seasonal work positions – including bellhops in local hotels, general labourers and porters on the railroads, and employment in auto plants – Earl Chambers's university degree and steady employment at a local gas company situated his entrance into the teaching profession as different from some Black men during this period.[32]

Earl Chambers's recollections also demonstrated how Black women's realities were systemically different from those of men. In fact, he articulated an employment trajectory uncommon for most women educators in the twentieth century. Black women teachers discussed difficulties gaining positions of responsibility and described constantly having their credentials questioned as they moved up the professional ladder.[33] Some Black women interviewed for this project explained that despite having adequate training and qualifications, they constantly had to explain their expertise to White administrators and other teachers. At least five interview participants explicitly indicated that the questioning of their qualifications was a negative part of their professional careers and they believed the perception of their lack of training limited the acknowledgement of positive work they were doing within schools. All of this was in spite of the fact that the Federation of Women Teachers' Associations of Ontario actively lobbied the Ministry of Education to recruit women into positions of responsibility throughout the province's schools. By 1979, the ministry had established an employment equity unit that worked to address issues facing all women in education but focused specifically on women in administration. Larger social conventions that viewed women teachers as less qualified and less capable than their male counterparts continued to inform twentieth-century workplace hierarchies and led to a disproportionate number of men in positions of responsibility and training at the secondary level in Ontario schools.[34]

Gender not only situated Earl Chambers's position in the teaching profession but also influenced the way he remembered and articulated his life story during the interview process. Sangster contends that oral historians must consider the ways gender, race, and class, as structural and ideological relations, shape the ways people remember their stories. She argues, "The exploration of oral history must incorporate gender as a defining category of analysis, for women often remember the past in different ways in comparison with men."[35] Citing the ways women's narratives could be characterized by avoidance and understatements, while men placed themselves at the centre of their accounts of public events, Sangster asks oral historians to consider the ways gender creates significant differences in the construction of memory.

As such, although Earl Chambers's experience acknowledged the racial challenges that he and other Black educators faced moving up the professional ladder, these experiences were different on account of Black residual patriarchy.[36] Instead, he describes his career as having "good challenges"; he explained, "Because you're a person of colour, you're noticed. That's a positive, rather than a negative. We were taught as a family ... you've got one strike against you but you've got two other strikes. It's a baseball analogy but, use them and use them well."[37] While Earl Chambers's account also alludes to similar notions of Black self-pride and awareness evident in many oral stories of Black Canadians, the fact that he positioned his credentials and ability to withstand the racial barriers placed before him as central to his narrative indicated both how he was a beneficiary of societal assumptions that privileged patriarchal power and that he was connected to a family culture that believed in pushing past forms of racial discrimination. His story also demonstrated the ways that interview processes can help researchers situate the material realities of Black Canadian life as marked by categories of race and gender. In other words, the interview process was not (or could not) be gender neutral, because it included recollections of the economic, social, and political conditions in which Black men and women operated. As oral historian Caroline Daley contends, "the content of oral history is often gendered because experiences were gendered."[38] While Miriam and Earl Chambers's interconnected interview experiences highlighted the ways in which gender-specific value systems shape and structure interview processes, these experiences also stood in conjunction with other social categories of identity that included race, place of birth, and class.

Remembering the gendered context that influenced Black Canadian women's lives can be understood as one of many ways interviewees complicated shared authority during the oral interview process. Black women teachers remained active agents in their life stories and asserted their authority and power throughout the interview process by not answering my questions or by choosing the time and pace at which they responded to my inquiries. One consistent area of tension in multiple interviews was around the disclosure of age. Several of my participants refused to tell me their age on tape, despite having filled out forms that included their date of birth. Such was the case of Canadian-born educator Cassandra Banks, who, after being asked to describe her early educational experiences, informed me, "Oh we [Black women] don't go there with age. [laughter] I am 20 now."[39] In another incident, Caribbean-born Halle Willis forcefully reacted to my questions about her age by responding, "I am not saying no date of birth" and promptly shifting our conversation to her life growing up in Trinidad.[40] At other moments, women rejected my questions by offering me advice instead. For example, even after sharing intimate stories about her difficult divorce, Edie Frazier advised me to be careful about asking women their date of birth. She informed me, "You don't ask people their date of birth or their religion, or their politics."[41] Although several Black women teachers disclosed intimate stories of love, hurt, rejection, and triumph, they maintained control over what parts of these stories were important to tell and, at times, separated discussions of their personal lives from those that shaped their careers as educators. Sometimes these assertions were peppered with laughter to shift the focus away from inquiries about their personal lives; at other times, they reflected Black women's desire and authority in dictating the ways they were presented in the research project. All of these choices grounded Black women as producers of knowledge and active agents in the stories of their own lives.

Oral History as a Gendered Form

While oral history can lend insight into the personal and individual experiences of Black women teachers, it can also reveal collective understandings that inform us about Black life in Canada. While Black women's narratives in my research were often multilayered and simultaneously reflective of positive and negative experiences, their reflections were also shaped by economic, social, and political conditions of the time. In the case of Black women teachers, these experiences were informed by sex-segregated labour markets, heteronormative assumptions about women's domestic duties, and (in)formal practices of racial discrimination. These barriers often impacted women's employment concurrently and educators mitigated these experiences by emphasizing their professionalism. When Joy Lyons described her teaching career after coming to Canada via the West Indian Domestic Scheme in 1968, she recalled that although she was aware of discrimination happening to other Black Canadians, she tried to focus on respecting people. Immediately after describing herself as a "top-notch" teacher, Lyons claimed there were multiple factors to consider when thinking about inequalities that existed within Canadian education systems. She later revealed, "Often times I was never too sure what was at work. Whether it was my immigrant status, my being a woman, [or] my being Black."[42] In Lyons's case, all three factors affected how she experienced her workplace despite her emphasis on professionalism and a strong work ethic in the retelling of her life story. Instead, the intersectional challenges she faced as a Black immigrant woman also spoke back to broader racial and gendered stereotypes that could not be separated as a singular, monolithic experience.

Although Black women's presence in early Canada was characterized by their labour in the domestic service field, by the twentieth century, Canada's labour market had opened up to allow Black women limited access to fields outside of domestic labour. However, stereotypes based on race, class, and gender continued to structure systemic patterns of discrimination in the twentieth century. As a result, Black women were believed to be "naturally" suited for specific types of work. It was not until World War II, as Dionne Brand argues, that Black women could enter employment fields that had once been unattainable.[43] At the same time, Black women continued to be limited to employment that was either within their own communities, through government agencies that assisted their communities, or in limited positions in the public sector.[44] Lyons's stories acknowledged the multiple forms of discrimination that she faced but rejected presentations of a narrative of victimization as a result of these systemic challenges. Her emphasis on doing a good job despite the complex barriers placed before her affirmed her knowledge and expertise within the professional teaching space and her advancement despite racial and gender discrimination. Lyons's deliberate choice of words reflected an emphasis to push away from a narrative that situated her as a victim of racism in her career and, instead, revealed that she did not *focus* on racism – "because you can focus on racist actions of people, but I tried not to focus on racist actions. I also believe in the whole issue of respecting people. So when things happened that I thought was racist, or someone would say something – *not about me* [emphasis added], but about others – I always challenged them. And show them that they made big generalizations about people. So I was always known as someone who would challenge notions about race, colour, and religion."[45] In essence, Lyons was telling her story to serve multiple purposes, the first of which considered the ways that wider audiences might perceive and interpret her stories of discrimination as narrations of victimization. Instead, she rejected this kind of interpretation and articulated anecdotes to disrupt broader assumptions that Black women were passive participants in Canadian schooling institutions. Offering an alternative narrative of Black female professionalism, and her long-standing career in public service as an example, Lyons reclaimed her power and legitimacy through this memory while also acknowledging the existence of racism within schooling systems.

Pamela Sugiman documents a similar practice with the men and women she interviewed as part of her analysis of Japanese Canadians and their experiences of internment in the 1940s. She argues that despite detailing experiences of vulnerability during internment, many Japanese Canadians often punctuated their stories with positive memories, "thereby restoring dignity and reinforcing the conclusion of ultimate integration into Canadian society."[46] According to Sugiman, while it is important to situate narrators within their cultural and historical contexts, scholars must consider how self-selected stories can contain messages that the narrator wants to communicate to a wider audience. Lyons's choice to distance herself from the more vivid descriptions and examples of discrimination that some of her peers may have experienced indicated a similar reclamation of dignity, one that shifted away from victimization to emphasize professionalism and resilience.

In other instances, the oral histories of Black women educators were deeply connected stories of physical and psychological violence that were not only difficult to tell but challenging to interpret. This often called for a form of "historical listening" that was attuned to the legacies of settler-colonial violence that extended into the twentieth century and is often silenced or erased from the Canadian historical narrative.[47] Indicating a longer and more systemic history of racial and gendered violence as experienced within schooling institutions, some educators labelled violent actions they encountered as minor and a part of the everyday school experience. When Nydia Manning recalled her childhood experiences in Windsor in the 1950s, her description of her school principal, whom she described as "old school," indicated an environment where racist beliefs and actions could be concealed as traditional practices of discipline in the school. Manning reluctantly described how her school principal often strapped Black students and distinctly situated the place of racialized violence within her early school experiences. She revealed, "When you [Black students] were in trouble and you went to the office, he'd have you tell right hand [or] left hand and pull out a card. So, you if you said right hand and he'd pull out the ace of spades, you'd get the strap. If you said left hand, he pulled out the queen of hearts or something then you didn't get the strap. Well the Black kids were all getting strapped ... So I saw a lot of Black kids getting the strap. I saw a lot of Black kids getting put into special classes."[48] Although physical punishment was used throughout Ontario schools until 2004, when it was federally prohibited in all Canadian schools, Manning remembered this as the first moment when she realized the differential treatment of Black students and said that this was one of the many "little things happening" to Black students.[49] She indicated that this kind of punishment happened more frequently to Black students because the school principal was prejudiced.

In his analysis of corporal punishment in Toronto schools, educational historian Paul Axelrod argues that the degree of strapping in individual schools often changed depending on when a new principal was appointed. He contends, "As the school's dominant authority figure, the principal, normally administered the strap, always in the presence of an adult witness, usually a teacher, or sometimes an office assistant."[50] In addition, Axelrod reveals that because corporal punishment was also viewed as a mechanism to secure (moral) order, social and gendered expectations often informed how the strap was meted out within schools. Given the history of separate schooling practices and twentieth-century justifications for the streaming of poor and racialized students in Ontario, Manning's story indicated the ways broader assumptions about Black student inferiority and deviance might have been interpreted through school disciplinary practices.[51] That Manning connected physical punishment and the streaming of Black students as among many occurrences of aggression and violence that Black students experienced in Ontario schools suggested a more pervasive and entrenched form of racial separation and discrimination not often highlighted in historical documentation about schooling practices in the province. Ontario moved toward more child-centred approaches to teaching and learning in the 1930s, yet Manning's story helps to contextualize the broader collective histories of Black Canadian educational experiences that were often fraught with violence, separation, and streaming practices.

Moreover, Black women teachers also recounted their own violent experiences within school systems as adults. Some spoke of how their workplaces became spaces where they experienced the most overt forms of prejudice, including verbal and written threats. When Caribbean-born educator Naomi Wise described her transition from teaching in Barbados to Ontario, she recalled a difficult time she had while teaching at a Toronto school in the 1970s. She received an ominous note from a White male colleague who described pouring acid on her. "It was one of those challenges," Wise explained. "Every morning you walked into that school not looking over your shoulder because you thought, you were working with people who were all there for the common good. You didn't think that someone there would be wanting to, you know … [pause] it was not a nice note."[52] Even several years after the incident, Wise had difficulty recounting the details of the threatening note. Her need to compose herself and her hesitation as she recalled traumatic incidents in her professional life spoke to the ways oral historians are called to listen to the silence of others differently. Similar to Manning's account, Wise also highlighted how school spaces could be transformed into dangerous locales for Black Canadians. Wise's experiences can be situated as part of a broader culture of race-based violence and discrimination within Canadian institutions, in which everyday insults and indignities often took a substantial emotional toll on racialized communities.[53] In Wise's case, the threat she described emphasized racial prejudice that her colleague held privately and only manifested violently once his authority and control were threatened.[54] At the time of her interview, the negative impact of this experience on Wise, almost four decades later, was reflected in her shifting body positioning, pausing, incomplete sentences, and uneasy retelling of her "not nice" experience.

The oral narratives of Black women teachers ask historians to conduct simultaneous interpretations about gender and professionalism, as well as to decipher community relationships and diversity within Black Canadian communities. Indeed, the contradictions and tensions that exist between and within these spaces challenge dominant notions carried by discourses of the Great White North, which often structure diverse Black Canadian communities as unchanging and unified monoliths. I argue that, instead, an examination of Black women's narratives allows for the multiplicity of Black Canadian experiences that includes their conflicts, divisions, commonalities, and desires for collective advocacy. By their very nature, these tensions gave space to complex negotiations as Black Canadians responded to broader social systems of discrimination, racial separation, and exclusion. At times, the narratives of Black women teachers gave way to contradictory accounts not openly discussed within Black Canadian communities and articulated complicated encounters that framed the women's expressions of Blackness within the Canadian landscape.

While contested negotiations of belonging and displacement marked many interviewees' accounts of their professional careers, these women also discussed the impact that broader social limitations and discrimination had on their social relationships. Their stories tell not of a singular identity in navigating life as Black women in Canada but of family (re)unification, fractured friendships, and reclaimed identities. Some Black women teachers told of the ways their lives were structured based on gendered experiences and transitions marked by life in Canada. Take, for example, my exchange with Edie Frazier and her hesitation to discuss her hypothesis around the challenges facing Black families as a result of migration to Canada.

> Q: So in your faculty, were there a lot of Black women?
> A: There were other Black women from, and this is 1970, there were other Black women from the Caribbean.
> Q: And then what happened?
> A: Then what happened was that, a lot of us ended up divorced.
> Q: A lot of you?
> A: Yeah.
> Q: So some of your friends were also divorced?
> A: Yeah.
> Q: Is there a reason? Is there something in your mind that makes you think this?
> A: It's not for me to say. [pause] I think the changes that were in Canada, presented challenges, which the women were more apt to overcome than the men were. And that caused a lot of friction in the family.[55]

After Frazier emigrated from Jamaica to Alberta, and then settled in Ontario, her marriage ended and she became a single parent raising four children alone. Having come from a middle-class financial and educational background in Jamaica, Frazier's ex-husband refused to accept his limited and lowered status once he arrived in Canada and ultimately left his family. Believing that she was more prepared to deal with the challenges that her family faced in Canada than her husband was, Frazier's experience mirrored a common immigrant experience: that of family displacement, economic disruption, and spousal separation.[56]

For immigrants who came from relatively high socioeconomic backgrounds in their birth homes, the movement from being members of a racial majority, the transition of becoming "Black" in White Canada, and their experiences of racial discrimination and prejudice placed heavy strains on familial relationships and, at times, disrupted these family structures. It also meant that these challenges, which Frazier recollected as being gendered in nature, informed her approaches within the classroom in the 1970s.[57] This fear about "not wanting to say" may have also alluded to gender-based and cultural assumptions about privacy within Black Canadian and other Black diasporic communities.

However, if we were to take notice of the pauses and hesitation in Frazier's response, there remains a place to interpret how women communicate stories about one another. Situating non-verbal cues and silence as equally important to the interview process, it is possible that Frazier was referencing close friends and therefore believed this commentary on their divorces was not hers to divulge. However, her later critique about broader gendered challenges that faced Black Caribbean families upon settlement in Canada indicated a deliberate attempt to situate the multiple subjectivities of Black womanhood. Frazier explained, "So when Black women educators came here from the Caribbean for instance to teach or to do university courses, that part of it wasn't difficult for us. It was the challenges that had to do with family, that had to do with the weather, that had to do with our training not being accepted and getting a good evaluation."[58] It is within this hesitation in telling Black women's stories that Frazier's Black feminism becomes more pronounced; she outlines the multiple ways that Black women both challenged and disrupted cultural expectations around racial and gender discrimination. Connecting the stories of other Black Caribbean women to broader conversations about migration, settlement, and discrimination, Frazier's description of her life in relationship to other women she knew demonstrated that some Black women did not neatly categorize community relationships in easily discernable ways.

Conclusion

Oral history offers a variety of methodological and political approaches to understanding the plurality of Black identities in Canada. While Black women's stories can tell us about the complex and contradictory circumstances that informed their professional and personal lives, *doing* oral history can be understood as a process of Black knowledge production and reclamation of Black female selfhood. Oral history calls on scholars of Black Canada not only to listen critically to the narratives articulated by our participants but to also interpret the silences, pauses, and non-verbal communication that participants demonstrate during the interview process. These choices can tell us much about the dynamics of race, gender, and power as experienced by Black Canadian women, as well as about communal methods of relationship building and support that become part of the oral history experience. This chapter emphasizes a probing of the lives of Black women teachers to understand their choices in knowledge production. These Black women teachers made conscious and deliberate choices in the information and narratives they shared. At times, those narratives were punctuated by moments of hesitation, pausing, or silence. Such moments became equally important to the interview process for representing not only the gendered forms of oral history but the ways in which Black women's material realities shaped their oral narratives. I have situated these choices within a broader historical context of Black life in twentieth-century Canada. At some moments, a participant's choice to tell me stories stood as a deliberate attempt to reframe her life as a professional working woman. Some took on positions as mentors during the interview process and recalled stories of their working lives as part of a larger practice of community mentorship and support. In other instances, these Black women teachers maintained authority and power by merging their priorities around age, class, professional training, and cultural expectations into their storytelling. Ultimately, they dictated the pace and tone of the interview process in ways that (re)asserted their dignity and their position as knowledge producers.

Often layered and complex, Black women's stories help situate the cultural and historical context in which Black Canadians navigated through processes of racialization and othering in the "Great White North." Although Black women's lives were marked by varying degrees of physical and psychological violence, they made conscious choices to reflect Black collective histories and the significance of Black professionalism in twentieth-century Canada.

NOTES

1 Cassandra Banks, interview by the author, Windsor, ON, 16 July 2011, audio recording. All interviewees have been provided with pseudonyms.
2 Pamela Sugiman, "I Can Hear Lois Now: Corrections to My Story of the Internment of Japanese Canadians," in *The Canadian Oral History Reader*, ed. Kristina R. Llewellyn, Alexander Freund, and Nolan Reilly (Montreal and Kingston: McGill-Queen's University Press, 2015), 298.
3 Mary Chamberlain, "Diasporic Memories: Community, Individuality, and Creativity – A Life Stories Perspective," *Oral History Review* 36, no. 2 (2009): 186.
4 Rella Braithwaite, *The Black Woman in Canada: A Book of Profiles on Black Women* (Toronto: Sister Vision, 1976); Makeda Silvera, *Silenced: Talks with Working Class West Indian Women about Their Lives and Struggles as Domestic Workers in Canada* (Toronto: Sister Vision, 1983); Dionne Brand, *No Burden to Carry: Narratives of Black Working Women in Ontario, 1920s to 1950s* (Toronto: University of Toronto Press, 1991). Also see: Peggy Bristow et al., *We're Rooted Here and They Can't Pull Us Up: African Canadian Women's History*

(Toronto: Toronto University Press, 1994); Carol B. Duncan, *This Spot of Ground: Spiritual Baptists in Toronto* (Waterloo: Wilfrid Laurier University Press, 2008); Karen Flynn, *Moving beyond Borders: A History of Black Canadian and Caribbean Women in the Diaspora* (Toronto: University of Toronto Press, 2011); Lawrence Hill, *Women of Vision: The Story of the Canadian Negro Women's Association, 1951–1976* (Toronto: Umbrella Press, 1996); and Nina Reid-Maroney, Wanda Thomas Bernard, and Boulou Ébanda de B'béri, *Women in the "Promised Land": Essays in African Canadian History* (Toronto: Women's Press, 2018).

5 Silvera, *Silenced*, 12.
6 Nicholas Ng-A-Fook and Bryan Smith, "Doing Oral History Education toward Reconciliation," in *Oral History and Education: Theories, Dilemmas, and Practices*, ed. Kristina R. Llewellyn and Nicholas Ng-A-Fook (New York: Palgrave Macmillan, 2017), 76.
7 Frances Davey, Kris De Welde, and Nicola Foote, "Feminist Pedagogies and Histories of Choice: Using Student-Led Oral Histories to Engage Reproductive Rights," in Llewellyn and Ng-A-Fook, *Oral History and Education*, 112. See also Kristina Minister, "A Feminist Frame for the Oral History Interview," in *Women's Words: The Feminist Practice of Oral History*, ed. Sherna Berger Gluck and Daphne Patai (New York: Routledge, 1991), 27–41.
8 Joan Sangster, "Reflections on the Politics and Praxis of Working-Class Oral Histories," in Llewellyn, Freund, and Reilly, *Canadian Oral History Reader*, 122.
9 Valerie Yow, "'Do I Like Them Too Much?': Effects of the Oral History Interview on the Interviewer and Vice-Versa," *Oral History Review* 24, no. 1 (1997): 75.
10 Cynthia Edmonds-Cady, "A View from the Bridge: Insider/Outsider Perspective in a Study of the Welfare Rights Movement," *Qualitative Social Work* 11, no. 2 (2012): 180.
11 Alan Wieder, "Testimony as Oral History: Lessons from South Africa," *Educational Researcher* 33, no. 6 (2004): 25.
12 Nydia Manning, interview by the author, Chatham, ON, 19 August 2011, audio recording.
13 Belinda Soto, interview by the author, Buxton, ON, 4 June 2011, audio recording.
14 Dolana Mogadime, "Black Girls/Black Women-Centred Texts and Black Teachers as Othermothers," *Journal of the Association for Research on Mothering* 2, no. 2 (2000): 230.
15 Soto interview.
16 Heather E. McGregor and Catherine A. McGregor, "When Oral History Calls on You: Stories from Nunavut," in Llewellyn and Ng-A-Fook, *Oral History and Education*, 89.

17 Tammy Okafor, interview by the author, Markham, ON, 15 April 2011, audio recording.
18 Andrea O'Reilly, introduction to *From Motherhood to Mothering: The Legacy of Adrienne Rich's Of Woman Born*, ed. Andrea O'Reilly (Albany: State University of New York Press, 2004), 11.
19 Yow, "'Do I Like Them,'" 76.
20 Manning interview.
21 Grace Mullings, interview by the author, Toronto, 22 July 2010, audio recording.
22 Minister, "Feminist Frame," 38.
23 Miriam Chambers, interview by the author, Toronto, 12 September 2011, audio recording.
24 Janet Guildford, "'Separate Spheres': The Feminization of Public School Teaching in Nova Scotia, 1838–1880," *Acadiensis* 22, no. 1 (1992): 60.
25 Kristina Llewellyn, *Democracy's Angels: The Work of Women Teachers* (Montreal and Kingston: McGill-Queen's University Press, 2012), 62.
26 Llewellyn, 62.
27 Federation of Women Teachers' Associations of Ontario, *Dear Teacher* (Toronto, 1978).
28 Llewellyn, *Democracy's Angels*, 64.
29 Minister, "Feminist Frame," 31.
30 Minister, 38.
31 Earl Chambers, interview by the author, Toronto, 12 September 2011, audio recording.
32 Dionne Brand, "Working Paper on Black Women in Toronto," in *Returning the Gaze: Essays on Racism, Feminism and Politics*, ed. Himani Bannerji (Toronto: Sister Vision, 1993), 232; Pamela Sugiman, "Privilege and Oppression: The Configuration of Race, Gender and Class in Southern Ontario Auto Plants, 1939 to 1949," in *Home, Work, and Play: Situating Canadian Social History, 1840–1980*, ed. James Opp (Don Mills, ON: Oxford University Press, 2005), 220; Judith Fingard, "From Sea to Rail: Black Transportation Workers and Their Families in Halifax, 1870–1916," *Acadiensis* 24, no. 2 (1995): 49–64; Elizabeth Beaton, "An African-American Community in Cape Breton, 1901–1904," *Acadiensis* 24, no. 2 (1995): 67–97; Agnes Calliste, "Sleeping Car Porters in Canada: An Ethnically Submerged Split Labour Market," *Canadian Ethnic Studies* 19, no. 1 (1987): 1–20.
33 R.D. Gidney, *From Hope to Harris: The Reshaping of Ontario's Schools* (Toronto: University of Toronto Press, 1999), 162; Alison Taylor, "Employment Equity for Women: Toward a Revolution from the Ground Up," in *Women and Leadership in Canadian Education*, ed. Cecilia Reynolds and Beth Young (Calgary: Detselig, 1995), 83.
34 Llewellyn, *Democracy's Angels*, 52.

35 Joan Sangster, "Telling Our Stories: Feminist Debates and the Use of Oral History," *Women's History Review* 3, no. 1 (1994): 7.
36 In his review of court cases involving family violence and spousal murder and rape, historian Barrington Walker considers Black patriarchy to describe the ways male power was perpetuated and reproduced in nineteenth-century Ontario. He argues that "Black men enjoyed a residual but fragile form of patriarchal power bestowed upon them by the dominant culture." Walker, *Race on Trial: Black Defendants in Ontario's Criminal Courts, 1858–1958* (Toronto: University of Toronto Press, 2010), 89–90.
37 Earl Chambers interview.
38 Caroline Daley, "'He would know, but I just have a feeling': Gender and Oral History," *Women's History Review* 7, no. 3 (1998): 345.
39 Banks interview.
40 Halle Willis, interview by the author, Toronto, 11 July 2011, audio recording.
41 Edie Frazier, interview by the author, Toronto, 5 August 2011, audio recording.
42 Joy Lyons, interview by the author, Toronto, 6 July 2011, audio recording.
43 Brand, *No Burden to Carry*, 181; Agnes Calliste, "Race, Gender and Canadian Immigration Policy: Blacks from the Caribbean, 1900–1932," *Journal of Canadian Studies* 28, no. 4 (1993–4): 132.
44 Statistical data and scholarship concerning Black participation in the Canadian labour market from the 1920s to the 1980s is limited; however, we can assume that Black people were often overrepresented in low-level jobs or semi-skilled manual labour despite high education and official language ability. Joseph Mensah's analysis of Black populations in Canada reveals that as late as 1996, despite having similar education and official language abilities to all Canadian women, Black women earned less and had fewer options for employment. Black women often had higher labour force participation rates yet experienced higher unemployment rates. Mensah's analysis draws directly from the 1996 census to reveal that Black women had an unemployment rate of 19.8 per cent, nearly double the unemployment rate for the average (White) Canadian woman. Furthermore, only 0.19 per cent of Black women held senior management employment positions, compared with 0.44 per cent of Canadian women on average. Mensah, *Black Canadians: History, Experience, Social Conditions* (Halifax: Fernwood, 2002), 150–3.
45 Lyons interview.
46 Pamela Sugiman, "'Life Is Sweet': Vulnerability and Composure in the Wartime Narratives of Japanese Canadians," *Journal of Canadian Studies* 43, no. 1 (2009): 199.
47 Ng-A-Fook and Smith, "Doing Oral History Education," 77.
48 Manning interview.
49 According to Paul Axelrod, the Board of Education of the City of Toronto in 1971 became the first school board in the province of Ontario to prohibit

the use of the strap. However, physical discipline was not officially abolished from all Canadian schools until 2004, following a ruling of the Supreme Court of Canada. The strappings that Manning mentioned were therefore not in violation of provincial laws but indicate how racial bias may have led to a disproportionate number of Black students getting strapped. Axelrod, "No Longer a 'Last Resort': The End of Corporal Punishment in the Schools of Toronto," *Canadian Historical Review* 91, no. 2 (2010): 262.

50 Axelrod, 268.

51 Kristin McLaren, "'We Had No Desire to Be Set Apart': Forced Segregation of Black Students in Canada West and Myths of British Egalitarianism," in *The History of Immigration and Racism in Canada Essential Readings*, ed. Barrington Walker (Toronto: Canadian Scholars, 2008), 33. "Streaming," as defined by Cheng, Wright, and Larter, is the "placement of pupils in groupings according to a criterion such as ability, achievement, interest, need or a combination of these factors for the purposes of providing instruction so that pupils can proceed towards appropriate educational goals at an appropriate rate." In elementary schools, students were grouped based on physical, intellectual, communicative, social, or emotional development. According to Harry Smaller, there was a disproportionate number of racial minorities in basic-level programming in Toronto schools. This was so prevalent that, in 1983, the Toronto Board of Education reported that 30 per cent of Black students who entered their schools in Grade 9 were funnelled into basic-level courses while only 17 per cent of White students were placed in these programs. The overrepresentation of Black students within basic-level programs was further compounded by the fact that these students often did not continue on to postsecondary studies and had limited opportunities and access to employment. Maisy Cheng, Edgar Wright, and Sylvia Larter, *Streaming in Toronto and Other Ontario Schools* (Toronto: Board of Education for the City of Toronto. Research Department, 1980), 2; Harry Smaller, "Vocational Education in Ontario's Secondary Schools: Past, Present – and Future?" (Training Matters: Works in Progress No. 2000-04, Labour Education and Training Research Network, York University, n.d.), accessed 16 March 2015, http://www.yorku.ca/crws/network/english/Smaller.pdf.

52 Naomi Wise, interview by the author, Toronto, 1 April 2012, audio recording.

53 Chavella T. Pittman, "Racial Microaggressions: The Narratives of African American Faculty at a Predominantly White University," *Journal of Negro Education* 81, no. 1 (2012): 83.

54 Sue et al. define "microassaults" as an extension of overt acts of racism. They are considered micro in nature because these racist beliefs are often concealed and only displayed publicly when a person has lost control or feels relatively safe enough to engage in this behaviour. Derald Wing Sue, Christina M. Capodilupo, Gina C. Torino, Jennifer M. Bucceri, Aisha M.B. Holder,

Kevin L. Nadal, and Marta Esquilin, "Racial Microaggressions in Everyday Life: Implications for Clinical Practise," *American Psychologist* 62, no. 4 (2007): 274.
55 Frazier interview.
56 Immigration scholars chart a number of challenges facing immigrant families, including levels of integration, socioeconomic achievement levels, the socialization of immigrant children, intergenerational difference and conflict, and union formation and dissolution. Family structures are linked to wider external social and economic forces, which affect marriage and kinship behaviours. Christine G.T. Ho argues that the greatest toll exacted by Caribbean transnationalism is marriage and relationship breakdown. Ho contends that Caribbean marriages often collapse under the weight of new pressures they encounter in new host countries. According to Ho, gender ideologies (which are strongly connected to economics and access to employment) in a new society often contribute to friction between spouses. Ho, "Transnationalism as a Gendered Process," *Latin American Perspectives* 26, no. 5 (1999): 49. For more on challenges facing Black immigrant populations in Canada, see Mensah, *Black Canadians*; Walker, *History of Immigration*; Carl E. James and Andrea Davis, eds., *Jamaica in the Canadian Experience: A Multiculturalizing Presence* (Halifax: Fernwood, 2012); Babacar M'Baye, Amoaba Gooden, and Wendy Wilson-Fall, "A History of Black Immigration into the United States and Canada with Culture and Policy Implications," in *African Cultures and Policy Studies: Scholarship and the Transformation of Public Policy*, ed. Zachery Williams (New York: Palgrave MacMillan, 2009), 219–46; and Amoaba Gooden, "Community Organizing by African Caribbean People in Toronto, Ontario," *Journal of Black Studies* 38, no. 3 (2008): 413–26.
57 Edie Frazier explained that although she was a trained educator, upon migrating to Canada she was given a lower professional designation and had to teach with a letter of permission. She stated that her husband refused to accept a lower economic and professional status in Canada, which later led to friction in the family: "he was irate because of the life we had in Jamaica, we had a good life in Jamaica and then to come here and he had to do a lesser job than what he used to do in Jamaica." Early Canadian immigration policies (such as the West Indian Domestic Scheme and Live-In Caregiver Program) limited the entry of Caribbean migrants, and ultimately access to employment, primarily favouring Black women and disproportionally restricting Black men. As a result, Black immigrant men who did enter Canada were often concentrated in skilled or semi-skilled blue-collar work, which saw limited mobility, contributed to lower socioeconomic statuses, and created a gender imbalance between Black Caribbean male and female migrants. Frazier interview; Joe T. Darden, "The Impact of Canadian Immigration Policy on the Structure of the Black Family in Toronto," in *Inside the Mosaic*, ed. Eric Fong (Toronto: University of Toronto Press, 2006), 151–5.
58 Frazier interview.

20
Re-thinking and Re-framing *RDS*: A Black Woman's Perspective

ESMERALDA M.A. THORNHILL

Author's Note, 2021

I originally wrote this essay, "Re-thinking and Re-framing RDS: *A Black Woman's Perspective," to commemorate the Twentieth Anniversary of the Supreme Court of Canada's 1997 landmark decision,* R. v. S. (R.D.).

Publication of this essay has been so unduly delayed that the year 2021 is already beginning to wind down. In the time elapsed since 2017, "race," racism, and racial reckoning have moved to the forefront of public consciousness. A number of significantly relevant events have stunned us all, including, notably, the very public and publicized spectacle of numerous Black, Aboriginal, and other racialized people being killed during police intervention both in Canada and in the United States.

For example, on 25 May 2020, forty-six-year-old George Floyd, a Black man, was killed in Minneapolis, Minnesota, when White police officer Derek Chauvin knelt on his neck and resolutely kept his knee on Mr. Floyd's neck for nine minutes and twenty-nine seconds. During all this time, Floyd, handcuffed and lying face down on the pavement, was repeatedly begging for his life and calling out in desperation for his mother. Police body cam footage showed that while he was thus restrained, Mr. Floyd gasped again and again – more than twenty times – **"I can't breathe."**

Those dying words, **"I can't breathe,"** *ushered in a* tsunami *of public outcry and outrage that triggered an eye-opening awareness about the lack of value placed on Black lives, and the ensuing fragility of those lives all too often snuffed out in cavalier fashion during police interaction. Black lives deemed expendable and devoid of worth as if they do not matter! George*

*Floyd's moribund words, **"I can't breathe,"** also grabbed American and Canadian collective attention and focused public scrutiny on the deadliness of the lethal chokehold – falsely touted as a* bona fide *police restraint tactic. Indeed, at the April 2021 trial of Derek Chauvin both police-led and expert evidence showed the chokehold in question to be excessive, inappropriate, and deadly. And as a consequence, the jury found Derek Chauvin guilty of the asphyxiation murder of George Floyd. He was sentenced to twenty-two years and six months.*

In hindsight, this newly awakened collective and global awareness about Black lives and the police use of chokeholds constitutes a fresh lens to help us filter and read anew the case of RDS. *This new prism now helps us to re-frame, contextualize, and put into proper perspective that fateful 17 October 1993 encounter between Officer Donald Stienburg and the adolescent RD.*

*I submit that this additional insight generated by **"I can't breathe"** better equips informed readers to appreciate more fully the Haligonian trial judge's familiarity with and first-hand knowledge of Halifax, as well as her accurate reading and understanding of the highly racially charged social context of the case before her.*

I further posit that this new awareness should now enable readers to more deftly grasp and comprehend RDS *and the far-reaching significance of Officer Stienburg's decision **to restrain both youths – RD and his cousin – with a chokehold.***

The facts could not be more clear. **Police Officer Stienburg's failure to disclose to the Court his chokehold on two minors was doubly determinant.** *Stienburg's non-disclosure while under sworn oath incontrovertibly undermined his own credibility, and then, more importantly, it raised doubts in Trial Judge Corrine Sparks's mind – leaving her no other option but to acquit young RD, based on the body of evidence adduced before her.*

The clarity of our "post-George Floyd hindsight" confirms that the charge of judicial bias brought against Judge Sparks was baseless. There was no justification for the far-reaching negative fallout, with its adverse impact, triggered by the exonerating Supreme Court of Canada majority decision. The ultimate effect was to sideline and bury the **RDS** *case and its landmark precedent-setting significance for Canada, even as it short-changed and pilloried the Trial Judge, Corrine Sparks.* **All completely unwarranted!**

> My Lord and my Ladies, we cannot ignore the fact that for centuries people of colour have made claims about bias in the courts, and the courts have been deaf to those claims, but yet, as soon as one [B]lack judge even raises the issue of race, suddenly claims for an apprehension of bias in the judiciary seemed to be well grounded.
>
> Burnley Rocky Jones, Statement to the Supreme Court of Canada, *RDS* (1997)

Introduction

Often under-examined in legal scholarship, the notion of "race" and the "*material reality*" of racism insidiously script outcomes and spawn legacies that continue to shore up Law as buttress, mediator, and regulator of the *Great White North!*[1] Compelled to chart and pilot our lives in the ever-shifting interstices between "race" and gender, Black Women in North America are intimately familiar with being perceived and treated as *disruptors* and interlopers who are "out of place." We Black Women remain acutely mindful that African-descended persons in Canada traditionally have been and are being construed **still** as *disruptive* of the country's touted founding image: "a White man's country"[2] – that is, a nation based on British and French European-ness. Similarly, Black bodies in Canadian courtrooms continue to be viewed as *disruptors* who undermine and threaten Law's conventional function of policing and regulating the *Great White North*. Black Women's cognition[3] of racism and racial discrimination in their multiple manifestations is so deeply scored into our daily reality[4] that the 1997 Supreme Court of Canada landmark case *R. v. S. (R.D.)* (hereafter referred to as *RDS*)[5] resonates with us on many levels in familiar – albeit disconcerting – ways, unrelentingly pounding home the message that when it comes to Blackness, implicit bias and institutionalized prejudice combine to make Law in Canada much more prone to **create** rather than to **correct** deficits.[6]

The twentieth anniversary of the Supreme Court of Canada's groundbreaking *RDS* ruling on "race" and racism, reinforced by decades of hindsight and a lifetime of experiential insight, makes it especially timely and fitting to *re-visit, re-read,* and *re-think RDS,* using an Afrocentric[7] critical race approach, refracted by the lens of my own Black Woman's perspective. Starting out as the criminal trial in Youth Court of an African Nova Scotian teenager on a bicycle, *RDS* quickly transmogrified into the presiding Black female trial judge herself being "indicted," "tried," "condemned," and yes, "punished" by the country's legal, political, and social systems.

I posit that the passage of time should reflect signs of continuity in the onward march of progress, such as new levels of social awareness, increasing and shifting expectations, and ever-rising baselines. I also believe that it is time to ensure that legitimate discursive space make appropriate room for much-needed *Black contextualization* and *Black counter-narrative* – more specifically, a coign of vantage, rooted in Black day-to-day existence that will appropriately foreground the under-examined palpable *material reality* of the everyday racism that runs rife throughout *RDS*.

The historical and legal significances of *RDS* are undeniable. *RDS* is one of those landmark trials determinant in constructing Canada's national narrative that presents itself as an agreed-upon public truth wherein, because of prevailing negative tropes, Blackness is by and large **still** automatically equated with danger, criminality, deviance, and incompetence. For many persons, *RDS* remains unsettling.[8] But more important than the actual court case or judicial ruling itself are its aftermath and its ongoing adverse fallout, replete with egregious acts of omission and commission, all stoked by a deep-seated racial animus. This essay critically examines *RDS* within the particular context of "race" – a seemingly elusive contextualizing factor that nevertheless in reality remains very present. The contextualizing factor of "race" should inform the case's adjudication process because it is so integral to a full understanding of the case.

For example, commenting on the impact of *RDS*'s elusive "race" factor, author Sherene Razack has candidly admitted, "I repeatedly sought, and failed, to find a way to describe the subject position from which I experienced R.D.S. The personal knowledge I felt I brought to the case, my everyday life as a woman of colour, could not be translated into the language this comment required. It seemed to have no place in academic argument." Indeed, as Razack argues, "something makes it difficult for the fully contextualized, historical meaning of these features of life in a racist community to enter the courtroom as things we know to be relevant to the case."[9]

The sobering reality of this dilemma impels me to assert forcefully in this essay our Black Women's positionality.[10] The insights and knowings of Black Women stem from our singular life experience, positioned as we are, notably, at the intersections of "race," gender, and often class, where we are forced to pilot our lives, navigating in and out of those small, narrow confines and treacherously shifting interstitial spaces, caught in the crosshairs of power and privilege – effectively contained and marginalized. In the words of philosopher bell hooks, this relegation to the margins gives us Black Women an "insider" qualification: "To be in the margin is to be part of the whole but outside the main body ... This sense of wholeness, impressed upon our consciousness by the structure of our daily lives, provide[s] us with an oppositional world-view – a mode of seeing, unknown to most of our oppressors, that sustain[s] us, aid[s] us in our struggle to transcend poverty and despair, strengthen[s] our sense of self and our solidarity."[11] Culled from an outsider location, our Black Women's personal knowings, knowledge, and frontline experience about the *material reality* of life in a racist society all constitute valuable "insider insight," an asset of incalculable worth not to be automatically disqualified or voided as illegitimate scholarship. For our complementary knowledge should also inform and enrich doctrinal writings, thereby enabling everyone to better read and more fully comprehend a case like *RDS* where "race" is an undeniable and intractable factor.

A time-honoured Zimbabwean proverb teaches us that "Until the lion tells his side of the story, the tale of the hunt will always glorify the hunter." Like lions, we African-descended Peoples need to wrest the telling of our story away from the hunters. For we have a duty to refute the hunters' historiography and recount our own narrative, in our own voices. It is time to present *RDS* in a new light, and from a different angle. Using an Afrocentric Critical Race approach, I place Black *realities, perspectives, experiences,* and *concerns* at the centre of my analysis, while I foreground our Black Women's vantage point as an important way of contextualizing these experiences. Invoking our unique insights as a particularized prism to refract and filter *RDS* anew, I articulate a counter-narrative that more accurately mirrors and authenticates the daily lived reality of Black Collectivity in Canada.

Grounded in my own Black Woman's individual, communal, and professional unvarnished experience, this essay contests **in my own "Voice of Authenticity"** the pervasive dominant historical narrative that marginalizes and excludes Black reality and denies Black Humanity. The essay targets certain goals geared to collective Black empowerment, notably,

i) to shed light on the obfuscated historical role of complicity and duplicity that Law and Canadian Legal Culture have played – and continue to play – in the lives of Black people living in Canada,

ii) to articulate, validate in Law, and entrench in legal discourse "Black culture, reality, perspectives, experiences and concerns,"[12]

iii) to affirm the vital political act of Black people moving from "object-hood" to "subject-hood,"[13] breaking silence and verbalizing **in our own voices** the physical and psychological *material reality* of everyday racism, and

iv) to identify, uncover, and spell out some of the multiple ways in which the factor of "race" and racism contextualize the *material reality* of everyday life for Black people in Canada.

Parameters

This essay uses *RDS* with a special emphasis and very deliberate focus on the original Youth Court criminal trial as the evidentiary base to show why so many Black Women (and Black men) in Canada believe that *when it comes to "race" and Law, everything has changed, but nothing has really changed.*

This essay is divided into four distinctive parts: Part I of the essay brushes in broad strokes the legal, historical, and political significance of *RDS*. Focusing on the Youth Court criminal trial, Part II presents the case itself by tracking the strands of its factual, legal, judicial, and "race" narratives. Then, using four concrete illustrative examples, Part III identifies the types of adverse direct fallout and aftermath ironically generated by *RDS*. Part IV concludes by critically interrogating the lessons and legacy of *RDS*.

PART I: THE SIGNIFICANCE OF RDS

Essentially typifying what I will term "a challenge to Authority vested in Black skin," *RDS* is in very many ways unprecedented. Not unlike what the 1954 United States Supreme Court ruling in *Brown v. the Board of Education*[14] symbolized for African Americans, the Supreme Court of Canada's *RDS* judgment appeared to African-descended peoples in Canada like a bright beacon of hope – simultaneously representing both a seismic shift in the evolution of Canadian Law and a watershed moment in the development of our country's coming to consciousness about "race." The *RDS* verdict fanned Black Community optimism, buoyed our collective hopes, and stoked Black dreams of old and young alike that racial equality and fair treatment might finally be firmly planted on a straight road to fulfilment.

The case of *RDS* turned out to be the first time the Supreme Court of Canada found itself *compelled* to break silence and openly address "race" directly, put as it was squarely on the table before our highest court.[15] And for the first time in Canada, "centre-stage space" was allocated for Black experiences and perspectives to be addressed in Court **with legitimacy**. In addition, this was the first case dealing explicitly with "race" to be argued under Section 15 of the 1982 *Constitutional Charter* before the Supreme Court of Canada.[16] A landmark case establishing groundbreaking authority in the matter of "race," *RDS* set new benchmarks for the factor of "race" and concomitant racism.

RDS comes fraught with added significance because it emerged as the leading Canadian authority in the area of *bias*. But what makes *RDS* even more outstanding is that this case represents the first time in Canada that the very highly unusual step was taken to charge **actual bias** against a judge. It was unheard of in Canadian legal history for a sitting judge to be accused specifically of racial bias! Doubly ironic is the fact that *RDS* was also the first case where the indicted judge happened to be a Black female judge – and the first Black judge ever to be appointed in Nova Scotia. Even more bizarre was the fact that Judge Corrine Sparks was at that time the only judicial appointee in the entire province of Nova Scotia who was not White.[17] Finally, she was also the first African Canadian woman judge ever appointed in Canada! While in some sectors the case approximated "a national crisis,"[18] receiving widespread coverage in newspapers, on the radio, and on television, the unprecedented significance of *RDS* was not lost on Canada's African-descended community. The stakes were very high because *Authority vested in Black skin*, at one of the most elevated levels of power in the country, was under attack. And so, many stakeholders, supporters, and ordinary citizens rallied around. Not surprisingly, *RDS* mobilized the largest number of African-descended lawyers in any single case and a remarkable number of NGOs petitioned the Court and were granted intervenor status,[19] thereby gaining standing, or the right to participate in the trial and adduce before the Supreme Court of Canada evidence related to "race" and racism.

RDS also proved to be noteworthy because the lawyer of record who represented the accused youth and piloted the case all the way up to the Supreme Court of Canada was the late Burnley Rocky Jones, a then newly minted African Nova Scotian lawyer and himself a product of the fledgling Indigenous Black and Mi'kmaq Initiative (IB&M)[20] – an access initiative to study law that he had helped to pioneer. Despite being an attorney with merely two years' practice experience under his belt, Jones nevertheless was a seasoned community organizer and activist committed to racial equality.[21] Throughout the trial and various appeals, Jones studiously kept "race" on the front burner before Canada's highest Bench.

It is additionally worthy of note that in this case we see the convergence of institutionalized racism, unfettered individual anti-Black racism, everyday racism, and normalized, "common sense" racism.[22] In *RDS*, the pervasive existence of racism in Canadian society was confirmed by the Supreme Court of Canada, which took judicial notice of anti-Black Racism, or *negrophobia*,[23] being a fact of life within communities in Canada: "anti-Black racism [is] a part of our nation's psyche."[24]

Raising the bar, *RDS* forever changed public expectations for legal decision-makers such as judges, adjudicators, assessors, and arbitrators. Setting new standards, *RDS* ushered in *social context education*, namely, programs of social context sensitization and awareness training for members of the Judiciary so as to awaken and raise their levels of consciousness.[25]

In addition to all the foregoing, *RDS* represents an attempt at *"reparative history,"*[26] which is concerned with the complex interconnections between the past and the present, all within the context of contemporary resistances to racism and the legacies of colonialism. Put another way, from a Black perspective, just like *"reparative history,"* *RDS* is also about reframing the radical histories of resistance to ongoing White supremacy – whether it be on the streets of a historically Black Community or in a trial courtroom of Nova Scotia.

From my own Black Woman's location, *RDS* stands out in importance because it constitutes a multipronged frontal assault on *Authority vested in Black female skin*. We witness the trial judge herself, Corrine Sparks, being accused of "racial bias" and being "tried" by the legal, political, and social systems of our country – all because her ruling to acquit teenage RD deviated from the traditionally accepted legal narrative. The idea that a judge would believe a Black male youth to be more credible than a White police officer[27] seriously disrupted conventional legal discourse, turning Canada's national "White Man's country" narrative topsy-turvy.

While *RDS* in essence plays out as a challenge to *Black Authority*, it also epitomizes Canada's difficulty, reluctance, and resistance to respond appropriately to "race" and deploy Law as an effective corrective to counter and eradicate racism. The case further reveals how in Canadian law, "race" is **still** denied and racism is **still** artful and opportunely camouflaged behind a purported "colour-blind" objectivity that places a premium on "White Innocence." But above all, for me, the importance of *RDS* ultimately lies in its potential as a catalyst to facilitate "courageous conversations" about "the elephant in the room," about "race" erasure in Law and the individual and institutional denial of persistent and ongoing racism.

PART II: FACTUAL, LEGAL, JUDICIAL, AND "RACE" NARRATIVES OF RDS

Narrative Strands of the Arrest

The narrative of every legal case comports at least a factual, legal, and judicial strand.[28] Interweaving and complementary, these basic strands are often completed by other, more context-specific narrative(s) depending on the particular area(s) of law targeted, such as immigration law, international law, family law, or administrative law. The narratives of *RDS* are punctuated by an ever-present, palpable "race" strand that adds depth, lends texture, and brings context to the case. The ability to discern and grasp this "race" strand is an essential and indispensable prerequisite – a *sine qua non* – for any accurate reading and clear understanding of the case.

On 17 October 1993, while biking his way back home in Halifax's "North End"[29] after an afternoon visit to his grandmother's residence, fifteen-year old RD,[30] an African Nova Scotian youth "of slight and slender build,"[31] was told that the police were holding his minor cousin, NR: "They got N down!"[32] Whereupon, RD quickly rode over, wending his way to the spot where a crowd of spectators – mostly young children averaging seven to eight years old – had congregated around a police car.

Immediately upon arrival at the scene, RD saw a White police officer, Constable Donald Stienburg, holding his cousin NR in handcuffs. At once, RD called out to NR, peppering his cousin with questions, inquiring as to whether he should call NR's mother to inform her: "What's wrong with you NR? What happened? What happened? I'll go tell your mother!" The police officer warned RD: "Shut up! Shut up! Or you'll be under arrest too!" Despite this warning, RD stubbornly persisted with his questions to NR: "What, what do you want me to go tell your mother?" Whereupon, according to RD's testimony, Constable Stienburg grabbed him, put him in such a chokehold that a woman bystander felt impelled to shout out to the police officer: "Let that kid go! Let that kid go! What's your phone number? What's your phone number?" And it was actually NR who yelled out to the bystander the grandmother's telephone number, since RD, still astraddle his bike, was immobilized in a chokehold and was experiencing difficulty breathing. RD testified, **"I couldn't do nothing. I couldn't breathe and my face was like – I was almost knocked out. He had me right under the chin ... I couldn't move. I was almost – I was dizzy ... I was like flaking out."**[33]

Constable Stienburg called for backup and two more police officers arrived on the scene. The two minor boys were arrested and taken to the police station, NR on suspicion of automobile theft,[34] and despite having been informed at the scene of arrest that he would be charged with "obstruction," RD discovered at the police station that in actuality he was being triply charged under the *Criminal Code*,[35] with

i) unlawfully assaulting a peace officer contrary to s. 270(1)(a);
ii) unlawfully assaulting a peace officer with intent to prevent the arrest of another person contrary to s. 270(1)(b); and
iii) unlawfully resisting a peace officer in the lawful execution of his duty, contrary to s. 129(a).

Then, after running a police check on RD and finding no record of "priors," the police telephoned the minor youth's mother to come and take him home.

Narrative Strands of the Youth Court Criminal Trial

One year and six and one half weeks later, on 2 December 1994 – after "weathering" four court appearances, which were all adjourned at the request of the Crown – RD appeared in Youth Court before Family Court Judge Corrine Sparks for his *in camera* trial on the three criminal charges cited above.[36] Like any other trial judge, Judge Sparks had the task to review and evaluate the evidence, as well as to interpret and apply the relevant law. She had the additional responsibility of assessing the credibility of the sole two witnesses: the arresting White police officer, Donald Stienburg, and the accused African Nova Scotian youth, RD. As trier of fact, it was also Judge Sparks's duty to make findings of fact from the body of evidence adduced before her. In the eyes of the Law, both the officer and the accused entered Judge Sparks's courtroom on an equal footing. Each witness was entitled to be believed, and each witness had to establish his respective credibility.[37]

There was no evidence other than their two testimonies, which diverged greatly from each other on many key aspects. The six-foot, two-hundred-pound Constable Stienburg testified that on a fall day in 1993 while on patrol he, along with another officer, Constable Attwell, and a third party "ride along," received a call that other officers were in pursuit of a stolen van whose occupants were described as "non-white" males.[38] Arriving at the designated area, which happened to be in the "North End," a Halifax Black neighbourhood, the two officers saw two Black youths running across the street and one officer, Constable Stienburg, decided to detain and arrest one of the running youths, NR, on suspicion of theft.[39]

According to the accused youth RD's account, he was riding his bike on his way back home from a visit to his grandmother, who lived in the area. Seeing the crowd, he approached out of curiosity and was told that the police had his cousin. On drawing nearer and seeing that a police officer did indeed have his cousin NR in handcuffs, RD called out, asking what was going on and whether he should call his cousin's mother. The officer told him to "Shut up! Shut up or you'll be under arrest too." When RD persisted in asking his cousin if he should call NR's mother, and in asking for the telephone number, Constable Stienburg arrested him. He put both youths in a chokehold, and RD had difficulty breathing and speaking.

Then Constable Stienburg further testified that RD had "hit him in the legs with the mountain bike," had yelled at him, and had pushed him.[40] The officer also did eventually admit to placing both teenagers "in a neck restraint." According to Stienburg, "I was holding both of the accused at the time trying to control both of them, because there was [*sic*] two people there and I was by myself. I believe I had them in a neck restraint, both of them at that time."[41]

RD denied the officer's allegations that he had "run into him with his bike," had "yelled at him," or had pushed him. According to RD, "No ... the police officer wasn't even in the conversation. I was talking to NR."[42] The Crown Prosecutor, Richard Miller, did not call any rebuttal evidence to counter RD's testimony.[43]

Judge Sparks evaluated the divergent testimonies of both witnesses and determined that, overall, the accused youth presented himself to the Court as a more credible witness than the police officer because RD appeared truthful. For example, when questioned, RD had candidly admitted to the Court that when he rode his bike over to the gathering crowd, "I was like being nosey. I wanted to know what was going on."[44] In addition, the youth was quite precise in his description of the time of day and the visibility ("overcast and misty"), while the police officer had failed to disclose to the Court that he had held both youths immobilized in a chokehold.[45]

The trial judge clarified the rationale for her decision in her statement that the police officer, a full-bodied man, "gave the Court the distinct impression that he had a rather difficult job in trying to restrain NR. But I really query in my own mind if this young boy was handcuffed what was the big ordeal about."[46] For Judge Sparks, RD's account that his cousin was already in handcuffs held "a ring of truth, and it certainly provides some detail with respect to the actual incident."[47] Taking care to point out that she did not accept everything RD had said, the trial judge stated that his testimony nonetheless raised for her certain doubts about the actual events of the day:

> He seemed to be a rather honest young boy. He said quite openly on cross-examination, he was being nosey. He wanted to go down to the street corner to see what was going on. He seemed to have been struck by the hostility which greeted him by the police officer [*sic*].
>
> I don't say that I accept everything that Mr. S [RD] has said in Court today, but certainly he has raised a doubt in my mind and, therefore, based upon the evidentiary burden, which is squarely placed upon the Crown, that they must prove all the elements of the offence beyond a reasonable doubt, and I have queries in my mind with respect to what actually transpired on the afternoon of October the 17th.[48]

For all the foregoing reasons, and finding that the Crown had not proved its case beyond a reasonable doubt as required by law,[49] and having accepted his version of the events, Judge Sparks decided that the accused teenager should be acquitted of all three charges.

She immediately delivered her verdict orally, and "at the end of her oral decision,"[50] Crown Prosecutor Miller interjected and directly confronted Judge Sparks by challenging, "Why would a police officer lie?" While Judge Sparks was under no obligation to answer this unseemly question,[51] she nevertheless chose **not** to censure the prosecutor's intemperate outburst but instead to respond carefully to this improper interpellation in the following manner:

> The Crown says, well, why would the officer say that events occurred the way in which he has relayed them to the Court this morning. I'm not saying that the constable has misled the Court, although police officers have been known to do that in the past. And I'm not saying that the officer overreacted, but certainly police officers do overreact, particularly when they're dealing with non-white groups. That, to me, indicates a state of mind right there that is questionable.
>
> I believe that probably the situation in this particular case is the case of a young police officer who overreacted. And I do accept the evidence of Mr. S. [RD] that he was told to shut up or he would be under arrest. That seems to be in keeping with the prevalent attitude of the day.
>
> At any rate, based upon my comments and based upon all of the evidence before the Court I have no other choice but to acquit.[52]

It was these very remarks "at the end of her oral decision"[53] – in response, actually, to his intemperate challenge to the Bench – that Crown Prosecutor Miller decided to invoke, "weaponize," and deploy as the basis for the charge of alleged racial bias that was brought against Judge Sparks.

Judge Sparks had found the accused youth to be more credible than the police officer, and both Crown Prosecutor Richard Miller and Constable Donald Stienburg were **not** pleased with this verdict to acquit RD. Confident of unfaltering institutional support and backup, they launched a full offensive on multiple fronts. Constable Stienburg complained formally both to his Chief of Police and to his union, suggesting that Judge Sparks "had acted with racial prejudice against a white police officer." The Police Chief took immediate action that quickly escalated. He "publicly expressed his concern about the 'racial bias'" of Judge Sparks and, in his capacity as Chief of the Halifax Regional Municipality Police, he wrote both to the Chief Justice of the Nova Scotia Family Court and to the Judicial Council, asking that action be taken against Judge Sparks.[54] State power was quickly and effortlessly leveraged, as Sherene Razack affirms: "The machinery that swung into action against Judge Sparks for calling attention to the operation of racism – the media, the judiciary, the civil service – is also all too familiar."[55]

An "anonymous informant" apprised the Halifax *Chronicle Herald*, and this newspaper, in conjunction with the Canadian Broadcasting Corporation (CBC), sought access to a taped recording of the *in camera* trial of RD. It was Judge Sparks who heard this *Chronicle Herald*–CBC application and she delivered a decision denying access to the requested taped recording since, in her judgment, that *in camera* trial now constituted "part of the record" and under the *Young Offenders Act*[56] a youth's record could not be "released to the public."[57] Judge Sparks ruled that "if this Court is to be scrutinized for the decision, then there is a procedure in place for such scrutinization [*sic*]. Consequently, the record of the Youth Court will be fully disclosed in due course, without any harm to the accused."[58]

Crown Prosecutor Miller then proceeded to file two notices of appeal. The first notice of appeal to the Nova Scotia Supreme Court contested the acquittal of RD, contending that

i) the trial judge had made findings not based on evidence, and
ii) owing to her own racial identity, the trial judge had manifested bias in favour of the Black accused and against the White police officer.

The second appeal challenged Judge Sparks's refusal to grant the Press access to the Youth Court trial transcript.[59]

Narrative Strands at the Nova Scotia Supreme Court (Trial Division)

The Crown Prosecutor and the police officer's appeal to the Nova Scotia Supreme Court, Trial Division, contended that Judge Sparks had made a biased decision that favoured the Black teenager because she herself was Black. The Crown further argued that the judge had manifested bias against the White police officer and had made findings not based on evidence.

Sitting as a summary conviction appeal judge, Nova Scotia Supreme Court Chief Justice, the late Constance Glube, heard the Crown's appeal on 18 April 1995. The new Crown Prosecutor, in this case, Adrian Reid, argued that Judge Sparks's remarks exhibited *not just an apprehension of bias but in actual fact "real bias* [emphasis added]."[60] After sternly warning that "judges must be extremely careful to avoid expressing views which do not form part of the evidence," Chief Justice Glube stated that the test for bias or reasonable apprehension of bias was an objective one before delivering her decision orally. Then reviewing the impugned remarks of Judge Sparks in the two paragraphs "at the end of the decision," Glube C.J. concluded: "In my respectful opinion, in spite of the thorough review of the facts and the finding on credibility, the two paragraphs *at the end of the decision* [emphasis added] lead to the conclusion that a reasonable apprehension of bias exists."[61]

Since she had found in the evidence no basis to substantiate Judge Sparks's "gratuitous" remarks regarding the "prevalent attitude of the day" or the observations pertaining to the police, Chief Justice Glube allowed the appeal and ordered "a new trial" in front of "a different judge" – which ironically, in the province of Nova Scotia would and could only mean a retrial in front of a *White* judge ... for whom, presumably, "race" (and gender?) would *not* be a factor. The irony of this systemic conundrum was not lost on African-descended people across Canada!

Narrative Strands at the Nova Scotia Court of Appeal

The defence lawyer for RD, Burnley Rocky Jones, appealed Chief Justice Glube's decision and on 13 October 1995, two years after his young client's arrest in Halifax's "North End," the Nova Scotia Court of Appeal determined in a 2–1 split decision that the trial judge's "unfortunate generalizations" about the police officer overreacting would make a reasonable person, fully informed of the facts, conclude bias on the part of the Bench.[62] Writing in quite a defensive manner, the majority of the Bench stated that Chief Justice Glube's decision "was not based upon a re-examination, and determination, of issues of credibility. Her decision was based solely on the issue of apprehension of bias."[63] Dismissing the defence's *Charter* arguments,[64] which had forcefully emphasized the need to adopt a substantive equality approach that would address "race" rather than taking a colour-blind formal equality stance that erases "race," this Court of Appeal majority ruling confirmed Chief Justice Glube's supposedly racially neutral and colour-blind order for "a new trial" before "a different judge" and dismissed the appeal of RD.

However, the third member of the Court of Appeal Bench, Freeman J.A. wrote a very strong dissent because he felt that the test for reasonable apprehension of bias had not been met in this case. According to Justice Freeman, there was no bias at all because "it was perfectly proper for the Trial judge, in weighing the evidence before her, to consider the racial perspective. I am not satisfied that in doing so she gave the appearance of being biased herself."[65] Justice Freeman continued in no uncertain terms: "The case was racially charged, a classic confrontation between a [W]hite police officer representing the power of the state and a [B]lack youth charged with an offence. Judge Sparks was under a duty to be sensitive to the nuances and implications, and to rely *on her own common sense which is necessarily informed by her own experience and understanding* [emphasis added]."[66]

Justice Freeman further took the time to make an important clarification that contextualized and put back into proper perspective Judge Sparks's comment about police officers "misleading" the Court and at times "overreacting." The acuity of this correction effectively voided the misinterpretation adopted by the Crown Prosecutor and Constable Stienburg. Justice Freeman's message was clear: Judge Sparks was **not** stereotyping all police officers as liars. He continued,

> It is unfortunately true and within the scope of general knowledge of any individual that police officers have been known to mislead the Court and overreact in dealing with non-white groups. That is a far cry from stating that Constable Stienburg did either. Such a statement could only be made on the evidence, and Judge Sparks was careful to make it clear, initially, that she was not saying he did. It was in that way she introduced the two concepts into her analysis as possible explanations for the conflict in the testimony, and she appeared to reject the first, that there was any attempt to mislead. That left overreaction.[67]

Recalling the role, mandate and authority of Trial Judges, Justice Freeman made the point of underscoring the deference that Courts of Appeal owe to these triers of fact. He concluded that Judge Sparks's original acquittal should be restored: "Trial judges have to incorporate their 'wisdom and experience' to assess the credibility of witnesses, and appeal courts must defer to a trial judge in determining what evidence to believe. Judge Sparks' remarks were consistent with a fair inquiry ... and her original acquittal should be restored."[68] In the face of losing this appeal and the planning of a new trial in front of a White judge, the defence team's resolve to petition the Supreme Court of Canada for the case to be heard was significantly strengthened by the force of Justice Freeman's dissent.

Narrative Strands at the Supreme Court of Canada

Refusing to give up, Burnley Rocky Jones, RD's defence counsel, then petitioned[69] for leave to appeal this Court of Appeal ruling to the Supreme Court of Canada, which in September 1997 ultimately restored Judge Sparks's original verdict to acquit RD – four long years after the minor youth's arrest.[70] On 10 March 1997 the case was heard by all nine Supreme Court Justices sitting as a full Court and they affirmed that Judge Sparks had done nothing wrong; nor had she come "close to the line," as some had contended along the way. She had merely taken into consideration – as she should – and factored into her judging the Halifax social context of the case before her.

Per La Forest, L'Heureux-Dubé, Gonthier and McLachlin JJ.: The oral reasons at issue should be read in their entirety, and the impugned passages should be construed in light of the whole of the trial proceedings and in light of all other portions of the judgment. They indicated that the Youth Court Judge approached the case with an open mind, used her experience and knowledge of the community to achieve an understanding of the reality of the case, and applied the fundamental principle of proof beyond a reasonable doubt. Her comments were based entirely on the case before her, were made after a consideration of the conflicting testimony of the two witnesses and in response to the Crown's submissions, and were entirely supported by the evidence. In alerting herself to the racial dynamic in the case, she was simply engaging in the process of contextualized judging which was entirely proper and conducive to a fair and just resolution of the case before her. Although the Judge did not make a finding of racism, there was evidence on which such a finding could be made.

The impugned comments were not unfortunate, unnecessary, or close to the line. They reflected an entirely appropriate recognition of the facts in evidence and of the context within which this case arose – a context known to the judge and to any well-informed member of the community.[71]

By a majority of six Justices concurring, with three dissenting,[72] the Supreme Court of Canada ruled that the charge of alleged apprehension of bias against Judge Sparks was both unwarranted and unfounded. A clear and convincing majority found that the impugned comments of Judge Sparks did **not** give rise to a reasonable apprehension of bias on her part. Accordingly, her original ruling to acquit the youth, RD, was confirmed and upheld, and the lower court decisions of both the Nova Scotia Supreme Court, Trial Division, and the Nova Scotia Court of Appeal were overturned.

My own Black Woman's knowings force me to ask: In light of the preceding attack, to what extent did this Supreme Court of Canada's clear confirmation of Judge Sparks's decision to acquit – itself an official "win"[73] – in turn translate into the legitimately expected validation and career enhancement of the judge herself?

Social Context and the "Race" Narrative: A Palpable Undercurrent

How did a Black youth's bike ride home from his grandmother's abode escalate so rapidly to the point where the Supreme Court of Canada had to intervene and sit as a full Bench? Indeed, how did it come to pass that the arrest of one Black youth – RD's cousin NR, himself a victim of racial profiling[74] – lead to the arrest, overcharging, criminal indictment, and trial of another young Black onlooker on a bicycle, RD? And then, how did this incident somehow manage to morph into what clearly became an *indictment, trial, public condemnation,* and *punishment* of the presiding Black female judge herself – all triggered by an outright intemperate question from Crown Prosecutor Miller "at the end of her decision"? This out-of-line interpellation by the Crown unleashed the onslaught that directly impugned Judge Sparks's credibility, ethics, and competence and ultimately challenged her very right to exercise fully her Judicial Authority.

To begin to untangle the answers to these and other puzzling questions, context and contextualization are critical, particularly when it comes to Black people living in Canada, where the history of "race," racism, and law has been obfuscated and is **still** being denied. The history and culture of racial oppression, transmitted through legally anonymous generations, cannot be sanitized, sterilized, or, in Professor Joanne St. Lewis's words, "made antiseptic with each individual being treated as a separate being, totally disconnected from history."[75] In other words, *RDS* does not exist *in vacuo*, devoid of context. *RDS* comes fraught with Canada's obscured racial history. It is therefore instructive to start with a "race" scan or "audit" of *RDS*, scouring like sleuths the various venues or spatial realities so as to figure out and identify the telltale markers that speak to, help pinpoint, and articulate the latent "race" narrative – the obfuscated yet indispensable backdrop that contextualizes this case.

Even though by long-established consensus the International Community has agreed that the concept of "race" has no scientific foundation,[76] yet the idea or notion of "race" remains an abiding and enduring psychosocial reality. For example, in Canada and elsewhere in the so-called "Western World" dominant groups typically **still** apply the notion of "race" selectively – that is, "race" is applied exclusively to those not perceived as "White." This is wrong because in truth, **we are all racialized. The blatant difference is that some of us are routinely racialized for disadvantage, discrimination, inequality, and injustice, while others among us are explicitly, implicitly, and by tacit default consistently racialized for privilege, entitlement, and dominance, all often aided and abetted by Law.**

From my own Black Woman's vantage point, I discern a clearly identifiable "race" narrative that courses through *RDS*, unrelentingly pulsing out all-too-familiar recurring situational dynamics of domination *versus* subordination ... of entitled, privileged insider *versus* disenfranchised, marginalized outsider ... of White Innocence *versus* Black "deviance" or "transgression." A number of "race" red flags embedded in its backstory punctuate the trajectory of *RDS*, constituting the elusive "race" social context of the case. By way of illustration, let us consider three distinct spatial realities:

i) the "North End" Black neighbourhood, home to RD and his grandmother,
ii) the neighbourhood street arrest scene of RD, and
iii) the Nova Scotia Youth Court trial courtroom where RD's criminal trial played out.

A close examination of the "race" narrative undergirding these three spaces instructively reveals the "North End," the neighbourhood street arrest scene, and the trial courtroom as spatial realities that are **not** racially neutral.

"RACE" IN THE BLACK NEIGHBOURHOOD

So enduring is the racial history of Halifax and Nova Scotia that contemporary configurations of residential housing **still** continue to reflect old historic patterns of "Jim Crow" racial segregation, sustained and informed mainly by stereotypical tropes of Black people as "criminal" and "dangerous."[77] Consequently, certain Haligonian districts or neighbourhoods are today **still** readily identifiable as "Black areas." As critical legal scholar Patricia Williams points out, "white people have always felt free to cruise through Black communities and to treat them possessively. Most Black neighbourhoods have existed only as long as whites have permitted them to exist."[78]

Historically, Black areas have been treated by the White Establishment as places of exile to which Black residents are banished, marginalized, and left to their own devices. Over the years, these Black neighbourhoods have learned and managed to "weather" their collective plight and build "Community" through self-sufficiency and collective care-taking. In such *everybody-knows-everybody* Communities as these, there prevails both an inherent suspicion and pervasive general collective distrust by residents of any police intervention or "outsider" intrusion that trenches on their "Home place" or "Collective space." Consequently, when police officers do make an appearance in their "Community," far from surprising, it is **inevitable and normal** for groups of residents to materialize instantaneously and gather around to watch the goings-on and monitor what "goes down." It is also not astonishing for the numbers of onlookers and bystanders to quickly multiply exponentially as the news of police presence rapidly spreads throughout the heart of the Community. This social reality gives rise to a number of instructive questions. For example, under the glare of multiple pairs of vigilant eyes,[79] to what extent might individual White police officers succumb – *or not* – to emotions of fear, panic, vulnerability, and being threatened? Faced with the situational stress of the moment and with being the focus of such close scrutiny, how might overwhelmed White police officers be prompted – *or not* – to make impetuous, injudicious decisions? Or, again, how might such White officers impulsively or unconsciously undertake – *or not* – actions that in hindsight could be considered excessive within the actual situational context and circumstances?[80]

The "North End" of Halifax is one such "Community Home Space" that **still** remains clearly identifiable as a "Black area," insidiously camouflaged by *facially* neutral descriptors. Geographic euphemisms like "North End," "Uniacke Square," "Gottingen Street" – all of which serve as signifiers for this Halifax Black Community – are artful, colour-blind camouflages, dog whistles that aid and abet, allowing "race" to be effectively rendered less visible and even made to disappear – cosmetically[81] – from what in reality remains a highly racialized space.[82] Nevertheless, this type of superficial erasure by racially neutral nomenclature fails to cancel out either the ever-present racial dynamics or the ongoing *material reality* of racism that is lived and experienced by the area's residents on a daily basis. **All of this forms part of the "race" narrative that runs rife through *RDS* and constitutes a key identifiable component of the case's social context.**

"RACE" AT THE NEIGHBOURHOOD ARREST SCENE

In order to cope with and survive the historical legacy of North American White racism,[83] Black Communities have innovated, creatively adopting and fostering particular traditions tailored to our imposed living circumstances. These collective practices form a bedrock part of our culture of survival and represent an integral component of the social context or fabric of Black Community life. For example, living in alienating, hostile White societies that render us invisible, Black individuals who are total strangers to each other – whether pedestrians on the street or bystanders in a public space – will automatically connect to and greet each other, communicating either with a magnetic-interlocking look or by a barely perceptible nod of respect. These **gestures of recognition** and acknowledgement convey unspoken greetings, salutations that self-affirm and validate our respective humanity: *"I see you. You exist."*[84]

Black parenting survival skills comprise yet another example of particularized Black tradition. Black parenting in historically White uncaring *milieus* has always included raising our children to make them understand that in a society permeated by *negrophobia* or *anti-Black racism*, they are each one by necessity responsible for every other member of the family – be that family biological, nuclear, extended, or Community.⁸⁵ A full understanding of this foundational element of the warp and weft of Black Communities would bring nuance, lend texture, clarify our reading, and thereby deepen our understanding of the street arrest scenario of RD. And then, it would come as no great surprise whatsoever for us to find young RD

  i) being informed by someone that the police "have your cousin";
  ii) calling out, repeatedly and with increasing insistence, to ask his cousin whether he, RD, should call NR's mother and notify her of the police intervention; and
  iii) ignoring a police officer's threatening orders to "*Shut up!*" and instead doggedly persisting in asking for his cousin's mother's telephone number.

When most Black youths, products of Black parenting, become caught up like RD in circumstances such as those with Officer Stienburg, the teachings and expectations of parental authority and Community tradition will frequently override, cancel, and void a police officer's peremptory ultimatum to "*Shut up! Shut up or I'll arrest you too!*" **All of this also forms part of the "race" narrative of *RDS* and constitutes a key identifiable component of the case's social context.**

"RACE" IN THE TRIAL COURTROOM OF THE YOUTH COURT

In addition to Trial Judge Corrine Sparks's own pointed observation, Court of Appeal Justice Freeman's dissent did indeed note with perspicacity that the case was "racially charged." Unfortunately, this insightful observation was not picked up by the Court of Appeal majority decision; neither was it examined **in depth** by the Supreme Court of Canada Justices, since for them it did not register any noteworthy significance. To these two higher Courts, the unprecedented racial configuration of Judge Sparks's courtroom on that day of RD's 1995 trial was not a critically important or relevant issue. However, for those observers alert to "race," the courtroom's atypical racial makeup⁸⁶ and its ensuing impact cannot and should not be dismissed or passed over in silence. Present on that portentous day in the trial courtroom were the following:

- the presiding Judge, the Honourable Corrine Sparks, *who was Black*;
- the young accused, RD, *who was Black*;
- the Defence Counsel, Burnley Rocky Jones, *who was Black*;

- the court clerk, *who was Black*;
- the arresting police officer, Constable Donald Stienburg, *who was White*;
- the Crown Prosecutor, Richard Miller, *who was White*.

In addition to the Black female clerk, the authority figure in the courtroom empowered to mete out justice was a Black woman who would decide the fate of the litigants before her: one Black youth, a minor; and one White man, a police officer. What perceptions, speculations, or conclusions did the foregoing unusual racial (and gendered) optics and dynamics generate for both White and Black participants? How did such a blatant departure from the habitual racial norm derail, challenge, or threaten entrenched, unspoken White expectations for routine courtroom "business as usual"? How might such White expectations have challenged, skewed, or even undermined *Authority vested in Black skin*? What unvoiced deep-buried sense of White entitlement might have surfaced bruised, thwarted, or unfulfilled?

Members of the legal profession well know that Professional Codes of Ethics, customary rules of practice, and procedural law together have established and set out prescribed courtroom protocol. One abiding rule undergirds all others: As "officers of the Court," all Counsel – whether Defence Lawyer or Crown Prosecutor – have a deontological or ethical and professional obligation to always show courtesy, respect, and deference to the Court, and to the Judge.[87]

The stipulation is clear. Officers of the Court must respect not only the courtroom space but, more concretely, the Authority of Law as personified by the person(s) sitting on the Bench, be that judge(s), adjudicator(s), or arbitrator(s). The formality of courtroom etiquette is strict and serious. The *gravitas* of courtroom protocol borders on the intimidating, bolstered as it is by a scaffolding of rigorous enforcement mechanisms, such as fixed formal titles of salutation or address for the Judge,[88] the presence of bailiffs, and detailed fines, along with charges and penalties on the books for contempt of court. The message is unmistakable: courtroom etiquette is not to be taken lightly. Moreover, the Authority in the courtroom **is** the presiding judge, and the courtroom space **is** the judge's to administer and govern – absolutely – because no one is above the Law and the judge embodies the law. Indeed, as Judge Whealy stated in another case relevant to the Black community, "A presiding judge not only has the authority but also the duty to oversee the demeanour, solemnity and dignity which must prevail in a superior court of law."[89]

When Counsel or parties do not agree with an oral or written ruling from the Bench, the appropriate and open course of action, according to accepted convention and prescribed legal procedure, is to contest the decision by registering a formal objection and/or by initiating appeal proceedings. It is **never** an available option to disparage, disrespect, or show contempt for the Court, or to confront directly the sitting Judge or adjudicator, including a Black Woman Judge. All lawyers and all counsel have an ethical and professional duty to show curial deference and respect, always. To challenge judicial authority head on, face to face, in the courtroom space constitutes a serious breach of etiquette that violates decorum and crosses the threshold to professional misconduct. Provocative questioning directed to the sitting judge should never be used or launched either to vent or to manifest Counsel's displeasure with a ruling from the Bench. There are prescribed procedures and avenues to contest such decisions. **All of this also forms part of the "race" narrative of *RDS* and constitutes a key identifiable component of the case's social context.**

From my own Black Woman's perspective, it is clear that Crown Prosecutor Miller's intemperate question – **mislabelled and unquestioningly accepted by many as a "rhetorical question"** – breached the prescribed curial deference that should have prevailed. Far from being a simple or disingenuous "rhetorical" question, his interpellation of Judge Sparks was ethically and professionally improper and disrespectful.[90] And yet, this egregious professional breach has been generally glossed over in silence or dismissed with such inaccurate slippery semantics as "rhetorical question"; the clear professional transgression has been allowed to stand unchecked and unchallenged. As a consequence, the response of Judge Sparks, which was made in good faith – and which, as she herself pointed out, had nothing to do with her ruling – was nonetheless misperceived and misconstrued by a disgruntled Crown Counsel and police officer to be evidence manifest of her racial bias against Constable Stienburg. Incredible as it is, thanks to their apparent effortless leveraging of State machinery, this distorted interpretation of theirs quickly gained unwarranted traction that in turn grounded the baseless claim of bias and paved the way forward for the series of ensuing contestations, appeals, and conclusions that combined to unleash far-reaching adverse fallout and aftermath.

PART III: ADVERSE FALLOUT AND AFTERMATH

The following examples illustrate in concrete ways just how far-reaching and adverse the fallout and aftermath of *RDS* proved to be.

Chilling Shutdown of Black Community

First and foremost, **within the African-descended Community**, *RDS*'s overall impact and effect was prompt and palpable. In Nova Scotia's

African-descended Community, for example, the Supreme Court of Canada victory generated an immediate air of jubilation, celebration, and optimism, because the *RDS* ruling held forth for members the promise of change for the better. However, when subsequent events and successive actions in the legal Community failed to validate Judge Sparks and her ruling, this initial euphoria became short lived, quickly fading away to be replaced by a lasting chilling effect that "shut down" the Black Community, shrouding reactions in a deafening silence.[91]

Questionable Acceptance of the Supreme Court of Canada's Verdict

In Canada's Legal Community, for example, the unprecedented *RDS* decision generated a veritable tsunami of short-term flurried attention.[92] Any trial decided by a Bench of multiple judges can generate multiple opinions of either concurrence or dissent, with any configuration of individual substantiating reasons. However, while there may be multiple sitting judges, with as many opinions as there are judges, **there will always be only a single verdict, decided by a simple majority**. The Supreme Court *RDS* ruling, and by implication Judge Sparks's decision to acquit, proved to be the disruptive catalyst that spurred many scholars to put ink to paper, weigh in, and comment on the verdict. Normally speaking, the clear and convincing majority high court ruling (6–3) should count as "a win" and, *ipso facto*, should confirm and validate the trial judge's decision to acquit the accused youth. However, numerous academics, researchers, and legal scholars alike elected to "splinter" the *RDS* judgment. They stubbornly probed the majority decision, isolating and dissecting various aspects of the individual separate reasons provided by the different members of the sitting Bench – all as if the final majority verdict itself carried no weight and should not count as the victory it was. From my own Black Woman's standpoint, such commentaries and writings ended up kindling doubts about the trial judge's decision to acquit the youth. More significantly, such second-guessing and lingering doubts gnawed away at any validation of Judge Sparks herself by the Legal Community – a normally anticipated outcome and legitimate expectation for any judge who has witnessed her contested ruling confirmed by the highest Court in the land.

Resistance to a Motion to Commend RDS Lawyer

Within the Dalhousie University Legal Academic Community, the ripple effect of adverse aftermath also reared its ugly head. The 26 September 1997 monthly meeting of the university's Law School Faculty Council took place on the very day the Supreme Court of Canada issued its judgment in *RDS*. In my capacity then as the first holder of the James Robinson Johnston Endowed Chair in Black Canadian Studies,[93] mandated "to bring Black culture, reality, perspectives, experiences and concerns into the Academy," I put forward a formal motion of commendation to recognize and formally record both the success of the *RDS* undertaking and the considerable investment and valuable assistance of Dalhousie's Faculty of Law, which was later renamed Schulich School of Law, and its Legal Aid Clinic. Importantly, in addition, the motion went on to underscore the outstanding contribution of the *RDS* lawyer of record: recent Dalhousie graduate, Law School alumnus, and product of the IB&M Initiative, Burnley Rocky Jones.[94] Moved by myself, then holder of Dalhousie University's Johnston Chair, the following motion was presented to members of the Law Faculty Council for approval:

> In light of today's Supreme Court of Canada's judgement in the landmark RDS case, we, the Faculty Council of Dalhousie Law School, do hereby formally and publicly acknowledge and affirm the contributions made and the role played by Dalhousie Law School Graduates, Faculty members, students, and staff in this case development. *We are particularly proud of the achievement of Burnley Rocky Jones, not only for his successful representation at trial and right up to the Supreme Court of Canada, but more importantly, for the proficiency with which his litigation clarified for the Court the factor of "Race" and helped to move law forward* [emphasis added].[95]

The above motion proved to be startlingly disruptive. Once it was read aloud to Faculty Council, the proposed motion unleashed a lengthy discussion wherein a significant number of Law Faculty colleagues objected to and/or opposed specifically the latter part of the motion that pointedly singled out for commendation the *RDS* lawyer of record, Burnley Rocky Jones. This unexpected wall of resistance sprang up like a well-rehearsed Greek choir that chorused over and over their objections to the proposed motion, verbalized in expressions such as: "He was **not** the only one! ... There were others! ... I too also worked on that! ... The motion should at least include the name of Professor Dianne Pothier!"[96] Quite noteworthy and much to her credit, the late Professor Pothier herself intervened during this heated discussion to state clearly to Faculty Council members that "it was not necessary" for her name to specifically appear in this motion alongside that of Jones.

It was ironic and unfathomable to me that my Law Faculty colleagues would be so fixated on disciplining and silencing "race" by invoking procedural blockage to minimize and exclude! My Black Woman's knowings and way of thinking make me remain mindful of how, like clockwork, the dynamics of "race" tend to play out, over and over again, marking and distinguishing those who are entitled ... those who, unquestioned and unchallenged, feel they have an exclusive right to occupy and hold centre stage – **always**. After listening for a length of time, I exercised my prerogative as Mover of the Motion to call for the vote, and this motion of commendation that at heart clearly unsettled so many was eventually "passed unanimously" by Faculty Council – ironically, with not a single objection or abstention whatsoever being formally registered for the record![97]

Exclusion of Judge Sparks from Nova Scotia's New Unified Family Court

In the eye of the Public, adverse aftermath also surfaced. The year 1998 saw Nova Scotia reorganize its Family Court as the new Unified Family Court,[98] with judges then to be appointed federally. An insufficiency of placements for all existing members led to a number of judges retiring or accepting early retirement packages. Ominously, Judge Sparks's name **did not figure** among the pool of judges selected for a federal appointment in the new Unified Family Court.

For many reasons, this exclusion of Judge Sparks from the new Unified Family Court of Nova Scotia was met with widespread disbelief and shock throughout Black Communities both in Nova Scotia and across Canada, as well as in certain sectors of the public. Firstly, since her appointment in 1987, Judge Sparks was **still** the only judge who was not White on the Family Court of Nova Scotia, a province that is home to two historically under-served racialized communities: Black and Aboriginal people. Moreover, Judge Sparks was at that time the female judge holding the highest seniority and the only Black judge sitting on the province's Family Court. Indeed, until 1996 when Judge Castor Williams was appointed to the Nova Scotia Court of Appeal, **Judge Sparks was the only Black judicial appointee in the entire province of Nova Scotia**.[99] Moreover, her ruling in *RDS* had just recently been confirmed and validated by the Supreme Court of Canada. Normally speaking, all of the foregoing should have brought her (or any other similarly situated judge) showers of accolades and should have conferred upon her considerable added value as a much admired, esteemed, and treasured member of the Judiciary and of the legal profession – unless some other factor interfered! From my Black Woman's vantage point, absence becomes as important as presence in understanding and evaluating symbolic action. In other words, the foregoing facts raise the question: Why did the normally anticipated course of events, accolades, and career-enhancing benefits routinely generated by this type of situation[100] not automatically flow and accrue to Judge Sparks?

In reaction to this pointed exclusion of Judge Sparks, again in my capacity then as the first Johnston Chair, I promptly penned a *Message from the Chair and Call to Action* in the form of an open letter of protest addressed to the then Minister of Justice, the Honourable Ann McLellan,[101] demanding that this anomaly be rectified before the fast approaching swearing-in day of the new appointees. The *Message from the Chair and Call to Action* open letter – with copies sent to then Prime Minister Jean Chrétien, Senators, House of Commons members, NGOs, and Media across the country – was geared first to bringing public awareness to this anomalous situation, and secondly, to informing, sensitizing, incentivizing, and mobilizing mass response and collective action to rectify the oversight.

This communiqué brought public transparency to the adverse impact and fallout of *RDS* by describing in detail the anomalous exclusion of Judge Sparks and issuing a *Call to Action* to all and sundry. Dispatched and posted online, the *Message from the Chair and Call to Action* generated a notable number of responses. However, it is instructive to note that this open letter addressed to Minister McLellan has to date never been the object of even a perfunctory acknowledgement of receipt on the Justice Minister's part. Nonetheless, many others did respond. *The Chronicle Herald* of Halifax both published an editorial and printed the actual *Message from the Chair and Call to Action* open letter as an op-ed piece. These were complemented by various community, collective, and individual initiatives such as an African United Baptist Association press conference as well as Statements and Questions raised in the Senate of Canada, from the floor of the House of Commons, and in the Nova Scotia Legislative Assembly.[102] But all these initiatives proved to no avail, for no corrective action was taken to rectify Judge Sparks's exclusion. I cannot help but wonder: Was this exclusion perhaps punishment for a verdict that, even though ultimately confirmed by the Supreme Court of Canada, nevertheless proved just too disruptive because it undermined the legal discourse of the *Great White North*?

Exclusion of RDS from The Women's Court

Within the Legal Feminist Community, the March 2008 launching of the *Women's Court of Canada* commemorated, with marked fanfare, the innovative rewriting of six key Supreme Court of Canada equality-related decisions from a feminist perspective. This was truly a watershed moment for all equality, especially for women's equality![103] Much to the astonishment of many women – especially Black Women like myself – the ensemble of selected judgments failed to include any key case addressing Black Women's racialized and gendered inequality. Conspicuously absent, for example, was the landmark case of *RDS*, or even that of *Baker v. Minister of Immigration (Canada)*,[104] two Supreme Court of Canada cases that have directly contributed in very significant ways to the evolution and transformation of Law and Equality in this country.

During the Conference's Closing Plenary Session, which allowed for questions from the floor, the only African-descended Woman jurist present – I myself – questioned organizers pointedly about the omission of these two key cases. The Women's Court organizers had no explanation to offer and no answer to provide. Instead, they mused aloud about a projected forthcoming "next phase" and the possibility of addressing these flagged exclusions and concerns "in the next round."[105]

PART IV: CRITICAL CONCLUSION

Having pondered the lessons and legacy offered by *RDS*, I realize that the parameters of this essay have not allowed me to really plumb the depths of this unique case. I have barely scratched the surface, leaving unaddressed quite a number of unexplored areas and under-examined key issues that still await scholarly attention and critical analysis, notably:

- the central role played by assumptions and presumptions, generated by stereotypes spawned during slavery, and sustained throughout Canada's racial history by ever-present tropes of negativity,
- the degree to which, at the intersection of "race" and gender, Judge Sparks is caught in the crosshairs of gendered racism[106] that undermines her Judicial Authority,
- the importance, identification, and critical analysis of contextualizing "race" narratives in curial spatial realities such as the Supreme Court of Nova Scotia, the Nova Scotia Court of Appeal, and the Supreme Court of Canada,
- law enforcement and the problematic issues of racial profiling, police identification of racialized individuals, and default police (over)reactions that kick in when Blacks are involved,
- the role and impact of "colour-blindness," its presumptive adoption in principle, and its wholesale acceptance as practice by Canada's legal profession, especially by the Courts, and
- Canadian Courts' pre-emptive dismissal of *Charter* equality arguments that directly address the issues of "race" and racial inequality within the context of Canadian Constitutional guarantees.

All of the above areas are worthy of rigorous, scholarly examination and critical scrutiny.

In addition to the foregoing, I am struck by certain elements at the crux of *RDS* that serve as keys to unlock the complexity and dynamics of the case. I see as determinant the interconnectedness and interplay of both **history** – that meta lens that filters our reality while providing much-needed depth, perspective, and context; and **power** – with its hidden freight of White privilege, White entitlement, and White comfort level that combine to generate both implicit and explicit presumptions.[107]

History

With incisive insight, the late historian John Henrik Clarke underscored for us the importance of History: "History is a clock that people use to tell their political and cultural time of day. It is a compass they use to find themselves on the map of human geography. It tells them where they are but, more importantly, what they must be."[108] Despite being undeniably important, the little known history of "race" and Law in Canada is an obfuscated one that **still** does not form an integral part of the national narrative. Our country's past is so riddled with all sorts of racial inequities that "race" has become that unmarked fault line, starkly present but unacknowledged, much like the proverbial elephant in the room. And yet, "race" literacy and knowledge of "race" in Canadian legal history should duly inform the even-handed application of law and the equitable dispensation of Justice. More specifically, in cases such as *RDS* where "race" **is** a central factor, cognition of the past and present history of Canadian Black Communities, for example, becomes an indispensable and relevant prerequisite to be demanded of every and any sitting adjudicator. For if Justice is to be served, we cannot – because of professed ignorance – afford to "gut" cases like *RDS* of the sociohistorical racial context that brings them texture, depth, and clarity.

Power

Since "race" and racism have been so obscured in Canadian legal history, Blacks and Whites are today **still** living in completely different universes where our respective perceived realities are widely divergent and Truth itself depends entirely on those who hold **Power**. As Russell Ferguson argues, "The place from which power is exercised is often a hidden place. When we try to pin it down, the centre always seems to be somewhere else. Yet we know that this phantom centre, elusive as it is, exerts a real, undeniable power over the entire framework of our culture, and over the ways we think about it."[109] Judge Sparks's verdict to acquit the Black youth disrupted the **Power** that habitually holds sway in the Canadian courtroom.[110]

When groups are unequal in access to power, they are likewise unequal in access to the resources necessary to implement their own voices. These unequal power relations are readily revealed in who gets to dictate and determine the rules; are visible in whose Agency, Autonomy, and Authority can be exercised unfettered; are evident in whose perspective is adopted; and can be seen in whose narrative gets to be accepted as reality and validated as Truth. For example, in the realm of the *Great White North*, the prevailing idea of what constitutes science, scholarship, and judging **still** remains the exclusive and unquestionable property of "Whiteness." And in this Eurocentric order, the White legal conceptual world **does not** – indeed it **cannot** – allow Judge Sparks's verdict to stand and thereby constitute credible science because an acquittal ruling like hers disputes the official narrative. In this way, *RDS* typifies for me an attempt to colonize knowledge by discrediting the Black female judge's judicial knowledge, legal know-how, and competence.

RDS plays out in a White conceptual world of epistemic domination where the trial courtroom constitutes a White discursive space. More specifically, from my Black Woman's location, I see the trial courtroom revealed as a colonized space of White privilege, White entitlement, and above all, White comfort. Through my Black Woman's knowings, I discern in *RDS* the past made present and the present reverting to the past. *RDS* resurrects for me what Portuguese writer Grada Kilomba has termed "plantation memories."[111] I watch the case play out not only to expose the continuum of endless colonial **White control** over Black bodies and Black subjects' voices but also to lay bare that seemingly insatiable desire of the White dominant group[112] to commandeer and dictate how we African-descended peoples and other peoples of colour approach, interpret, and articulate reality – especially our very own lived reality.

More concretely, in a number of ways, for me *RDS* resonates with, replicates, and re-inscribes the old familiar colonial order of **dominance** and **subjugation***:* of Master *vs.* Slave, of Superior *vs.* Inferior, of Dominant *vs.* Subaltern. From my own Black Woman's coign of vantage, I watch *RDS* play out as if restaged in a colonial past where the sitting Black female judge is suddenly catapulted back through time onto the stage of a plantation scenario. Rendered a subordinate in her very own courtroom, the trial judge's knowledge, perspective, conclusions, and ultimately her decision to acquit the accused Black youth collide head on with the prevailing Eurocentric concept of knowledge, scholarship, and science, **a concept that is itself intrinsically linked to Power as racialized White Authority**. This collision takes place on a highly contested terrain – the trial courtroom, a discursive space regulated by a colonial script potent enough to conjure up and bring Old Empire back to life. Here, the Black female body is stripped of Authority and deemed unfit for Power – the Power to speak and use her voice; the Power to adjudicate, to interpret and apply law *reparatively as a corrective* where the factor of "race" is involved; and especially the Judicial Power to also help develop and impact the evolution of Law, from her own Black Woman's perspective. Both the Crown Prosecutor and the police officer accuse Judge Sparks of racial bias and they proceed to leverage with effortless ease their own White privilege in order to activate and set in motion State-sponsored "bull-dozing machinery," geared to divesting her of Power. Why? Because her verdict to acquit the accused Black youth inexcusably breaks with established tradition, even as it thwarts and frustrates unspoken White expectations, and undermines conventional legal discourse. The ruling threatens and disrupts Canada's national narrative. In short, both the Black female judge and her verdict to acquit unsettle the Eurocentric order of the *Great White North*.

From my Black Woman's vantage point, *RDS* typifies yet another attempt to colonize knowledge and reinstall a *status quo* of domination wherein Blackness must be silenced. Any talk adverting to or taking into account the *material reality* of "race" and racism must be shut down. Hence the illegitimate charge of bias lodged against Judge Sparks and the orchestrated offensive launched by media, the judiciary, the legal profession, and the civil service. The message is clear. **Danger stalks the Black person – female Judge or other – who, hailing from the periphery would dare to speak Truth in her own voice from a location at the privileged Centre.** For, bringing sidelined insights and marginalized realities to centre stage for authentication and institutional validation is, in Razack's words, to "bring down the full wrath of the justice system, to define who is reasonable and who is not, who is a good judge and who is not, and who belongs and who does not."[113]

Needless to say, the price to be paid is high.[114] And so, the Black female trial judge is swiftly recast as the "Oppressor" who has wrongly accused "White Innocence" in the person of the White police officer. According to their distorted interpretation, Judge Sparks has injudiciously branded as racist not only Constable Stienburg but **all police officers.** Consequently, in their eyes, her judgment becomes sullied with the taint of bias, and she herself is construed, constructed, and recast as improper for the Bench ... out of place ... not belonging! At the same time, the White police officer is re-installed as the "Innocent White Victim."[115]

This inexorable pursuit of *White Innocence* compels the question: To what extent does the vilification of the Black body in the authority figure of the Black female trial judge satisfy this apparent need for White comfort to be assured of its sense of **Power** and **Authority** over a group of persons that Whites themselves have historically mislabelled as "less knowledgeable," "incapable," "incompetent," and "unfit"? My critical re-read of *RDS* has underscored for me the singular importance of *White comfort*. It has taught me – yet again – the lesson that Black voices are listened to **only** if we frame our ideas in language that is familiar and soothing to the comfort level of the White dominant group. Through *RDS*, I have also come to understand how glimpses of the *material reality* of racism tend to become visible in public and academic spaces

1) **only** when the normality of Whiteness, or the White *status quo*, is suddenly disturbed or disrupted, and
2) **only** when our own verbalized Black experiences with racism are (mis)perceived to endanger or threaten the comfort level of White society.

The way I see it, *White comfort level* operates as a way of regulating outsider voices by muting marginalized discourse and nullifying counter-narrative. More to the point, in *RDS* it is essentially a sorely disturbed collective *White comfort level* that dictated Judge Sparks be punished and "pilloried" for not delivering and sustaining a discourse palatable[116] to the tradition of the *Great White North*.

As a Black Woman jurist and legal academic, I am acutely aware of how *RDS* disrupts the White conceptual world in which I and others like myself are called upon to function professionally, on a daily basis. And, as I continue to explore and further deepen my reading of *RDS* from my own Black Woman's location, I do realize that like the trial judge's verdict to acquit RD, my own reading is **not** a scholarship that necessarily affirms the Eurocentric order of knowledge, or of legal knowledge. On the contrary, this essay will perhaps be received by some more as an act of transgression because in attempting to deterritorialize and expose for examination the territory of Whiteness as manifested in *RDS*, the essay does indeed subvert and disrupt conventional legal discourse.

Grounded in the reality of my Black Woman's experience, I perceive in *RDS* attempts to assert an epistemology that continues to re-inscribe **only** the specific, narrow, political views and interests of dominant White society. Fixated in colour-blind denial about "race," this type of theorization tends to allow no valid space for any outsider perspective or alternative narrative.

When very low importance is given to the phenomenon of "race" and racism, this dismissive "race" erasure exposes the commonplace societal disregard for those persons who themselves experience and are experiencing racism first-hand. Such neglect truly reflects the institutionalized unimportance of Blackness and Black people. To brush off as non-existent or irrelevant the manifest daily *material reality* of racism constitutes a significant theoretical problem that **still** prevails in academic and feminist discourse. For, indeed, it is real flesh-and-blood persons of African descent who **still** must confront, each day, multiple experiences that stun, stunt, and deflate. It is African-descended, living and breathing individuals and Communities who are **still** called upon to engage in unrelenting struggles to assert our humanity in the face of stereotypical onslaughts that would nullify and cancel our Black people's knowledge, knowings, understandings, and feelings *vis-à-vis* racism. In Canada, all of these, as well as countless psychic scars, have been tagged irrelevant by Law and have been largely denied, neglected, and/or dismissed by scholars, including by feminist scholars.[117]

Throughout History, bearers of bad tidings have often met with blame, punishment, and even death. So much so that the commonplace warning *Don't shoot the messenger!* cautions us not to be angry with the person who delivers unpleasant news. Has this admonition been heeded in *RDS*? Or does *RDS* constitute yet another poignant illustration of *punishing the messenger* – the Black female trial judge – because her verdict to acquit the accused Black youth discomforted and unsettled the discourse of the *Great White North*?

NOTES

1 As the African Canadian Legal Clinic argued in August 2002 before the United Nations Committee on the Elimination of Racial Discrimination (CERD) in Geneva, "Over the course of its history, Canada has consistently ignored, diminished or denied the experiences of Peoples of African Descent who have lived in various regions of this country from its early settler days up until the present time. The history has included: enforced enslavement; *de jure* segregation in educational opportunities; *de facto* segregation in residential settings; blatant discrimination in employment and wage earnings; over-policing and criminalization in the criminal justice system; insensitive and biased detention, searching and questioning of immigrants and refugees; and subjugation to media and cultural stereotypes based on hegemonic Eurocentric notions of white superiority and inferiority of African and African descendant peoples." African Canadian Legal Clinic, *Anti-Black Racism in Canada: A Report on the Canadian Government's Compliance with ICERD*, Geneva, July 2002.

2 Ted Ferguson, *A White Man's Country: An Exercise in Canadian Prejudice* (Garden City, NY: Doubleday, 1975).

3 In addressing the particularity of Black Women's location, "It is the many streams of consciousness passed on to me by foremothers and forefathers that focus my insight and filter my thoughts and conclusions. But more importantly, it is my day-to-day, particularized experience as a Black Woman societally marked and identified, first and foremost by 'race' and colour, that refracts my vision, hones my critical consciousness, and determines both my legal perspective and how I read reality. And lastly, my perspective is critically coloured and textured by the palpable and very enduring 'material reality' of racism and racial discrimination *à la canadienne* ... that is, Canadian style. This material reality, far from being a joyful Kodak moment, is a palpable reality wherein members of the vast and ethnically varied Community of African Descent – men, women, and children – are called upon, day in and day out, to overcome hurdles, navigate straits, weather assaults, mediate confrontations, and survive a relentless onslaught of micro and macro-aggressions that are all triggered by individual, institutional and societal reactions to our melanin-pigmented skin." Esmeralda M.A. Thornhill, "Deficits Corrected ... or Created? 'Race' and the Use, Misuse, and Abuse of Multicultural Policy and Practice in Canada" (unpublished keynote public lecture, David Lam Chair in Multicultural Education 2004 Lecture Series, Faculty of Education, University of British Columbia, Vancouver, March 2004, on file with author).

4 Esmeralda M.A. Thornhill, *Focus on Racism: Legal Perspectives from a Black Experience*, is in large part the author's oral deposition before the Royal Commission of Inquiry into the Prosecution of Donald Marshall Jr., vol. 7, edited transcript of *Proceedings of Consultative Conference on the Impact of the Administration of Criminal Justice on Aboriginal and Black Communities*, Halifax, November 24–6, 1988; also available in *Judicial Awareness: Race, Culture and the Courts, Volume of Reference Materials* (Ottawa: National Judicial Institute, March 1995), 91. English translation is from original French: "Regard sur le racisme: perspectives juridiques à partir d'un vécu noir," in *La sensibilisation de la magistrature aux problèmes raciaux et culturels auxquels font face les tribunaux*, Volume des textes de référence, l'Institut national de la magistrature, March 1995; originally published as the flagship article in "Racism ... Talking Out/Le racisme ... si nous vous en parlions," special issue, *Revue femmes et droit/Canadian Journal of Women and the Law* 6 (1993): 1. See also Thornhill, "So Seldom for Us, So Often against Us: Blacks and Law in Canada," in "Blacks in Canada: Retrospects, Introspects, Prospects," ed. Esmeralda M.A. Thornhill, special issue, *Journal of Black Studies* 38, no. 3 (2008): 321–37.

5 R. v. S. (R.D.), [1997] 3 S.C.R. 484, 1997 CanLII 324 (SCC) judgment of the Nova Scotia Court of Appeal, (1995), 145 N.S.R. (2d) 284, 418 A.P.R. 284, 102 C.C.C. (3d) 233, 45 C.R. (4th) 361, dismissing an appeal from a judgment of the Nova Scotia Supreme Court (Trial Division), [1995] N.S.J.

No. 184 (QL), allowing an appeal from acquittal by Sparks F.C.J. with oral reasons December 2, 1994, with supplementary written reasons, [1994] N.S.J. No. 629 (QL). Appeal allowed, Lamer C.J. and Sopinka and Major JJ. dissenting.

6 Thornhill, "Deficits Corrected ... or Created?"

7 Afrocentric theory places African ideals and values at the centre of inquiry. It is rooted in the centrality of African peoples as subjects. Afrocentric theory has much to do with location, place, and stance – in other words, the perspective from which the person approaches and examines data. Without repudiating the right of Europe to view the world from its own cultural centre, however, Afrocentric philosophy maintains that this view is not to be imposed as universal. In the words of its founder, Molefi Kete Asante, "The crystallization of this critical perspective I have named Afrocentricity which means, literally, placing African ideals at the centre of any analysis that involves African culture and behaviour ... To be Afrocentric is to place Africans and the interest of Africa at the centre of our approach to problem-solving." Asante, *Afrocentricity: A Theory of Social Change*, 2nd ed. (Trenton, NJ: Africa World Press, 1988), 2. For additional information on Afrocentric theory, see also Asante, *The Afrocentric Idea*, rev. and exp. ed. (Philadelphia: Temple University Press, 1998), 2; Asante, *Kemmet, Afrocentricity and Knowledge* (Trenton, NJ: Africa World Press, 1982); and Asa G. Hilliard III, *The Maroon within Us: Selected Essays on African American Community Socialization* (Baltimore: Black Classic Press, 1995).

8 In the words of scholar Sherene Razack, "My unease with the decision in RDS stems from the powerful lessons this case (the processes leading up to the trials as well as the trials themselves) offers to people of colour about 'the line.' This is the line we must not cross ... This line separates those who think race always matters from those who think it only matters, if at all, under highly limited circumstances involving specific individuals." Razack, "*R.D.S. v. Her Majesty the Queen*: A Case about Home," *Forum Constitutionel* 9, no. 3 (1998): 60.

9 Razack, 64, 65.

10 According to Renato Rosaldo, "The notion of position refers to how life experiences both enable and inhibit particular kinds of insight; in short, position can serve simultaneously as barrier and bridge." Rosaldo, *Culture and Truth: The Remaking and Social Analysis* (Boston: Beacon, 1989), quoted in Thomas K. Nakayama and Robert L. Krizek, "Whiteness: A Strategic Rhetoric," *Quarterly Journal of Speech* 81, no. 3 (1995): 291.

11 bell hooks expresses these thoughts on marginality in the preface to *Feminist Theory: From Margin to Center*, reproduced in "Choosing the Margin as a Space of Radical Openness," *Yearnings: Race, Gender and Cultural Politics* (Boston: South End Press, 1989), 149.

12 The avowed mission statement of the James Robinson Johnston Endowed Chair in Black Canadian Studies is "to bring Black culture, reality, perspectives and concerns into the Academy." James Robinson Johnston was the first African Nova Scotian to graduate from a university and to practise law in Canada. The Johnston Chair was established in 1996 at Dalhousie University to honour his memory and legacy. From 1996 to 2002, the author served as the first holder appointed to anchor the Johnston Chair. See "First James Robinson Johnston Endowed Chair in Black Canadian Studies – 1996–2002 Archives," on Esmeralda M.A. Thornhill's website, accessed February 20, 2018, http://ethornhill.ca/first-james-robinson-johnston-endowed-chair-in-the-black-canadian-studies-1996-2002-archives.

13 For more information, see Grada Kilomba, *Plantation Memories: Episodes of Everyday Racism*, 2nd ed. (Münster: Unrast, 2008).

14 Brown v. Board of Education of Topeka, 347 U.S. 483 (1954).

15 Many of these "firsts" are also set out in James W. St. G. Walker, "A Black Day in Court," in *The African Canadian Legal Odyssey: Historical Essays*, ed. Barrington Walker (Toronto: University of Toronto Press, 2012), 437–80.

16 Canadian Charter of Rights and Freedoms, Part I of The Constitution Act, 1982, being Schedule B to the Canada Act 1982 (UK), 1982, c 11.

17 Appointed in 1987, Judge Corrine Sparks was the only Black judicial appointee in the entire province of Nova Scotia until 1996, when Judge Castor Williams was appointed to the Nova Scotia Court of Appeal.

18 Jon Tattrie, "How a 'National Crisis' Showed the Value of Black Judges," CBC News, February 5, 2017, https://www.cbc.ca/news/canada/nova-scotia/nova-scotia-robert-wright-judicial-equity-1.3963884.

19 Intervenors in *RDS* included the Women's Legal Education and Action Fund in coalition with the National Organization of Immigrant and Visible Minority Women of Canada, the African Canadian Legal Clinic, the Afro-Canadian Caucus of Nova Scotia, and the Congress of Black Women of Canada.

20 The Indigenous Blacks & Mi'kmaq (IB&M) Initiative at Dalhousie University's Schulich School of Law was established in 1989 to increase representation of Mi'kmaw and African Nova Scotian students, and other Aboriginal and Black students, in the school and consequently the legal profession in order to reduce discrimination. Targeting Aboriginal and Black students and facilitating their access to the study of law, the initiative involves community outreach and recruiting as well as providing students with financial and other support, developing scholarships in the areas of Aboriginal law and African Canadian legal perspectives, and promoting the hiring and retention of graduates.

21 Burnley Rocky Jones's depth of political insight had been shaped and honed in the crucible of North America's struggle for Black empowerment

in the 1960s and 1970s. For example, Rocky Jones was among the many influential delegates – including, notably, Stokely Carmichael, Walter Rodney, and James Foreman – who attended the McGill University Black Student Association's unprecedented international **Congress of Black Writers**, convened in the fall of 1968. This watershed congress dramatically raised the level of critical "race" awareness in Montreal and in large measure contributed to the many subsequent challenges to entrenched institutional racism, such as the Sir George Williams University Affair of 11 February 1969.

22 "Common sense racism" is seen as so normal that it is neither examined nor analysed. Taken for granted and perceived as unchangeable, common sense racism is deemed to be perfectly ordinary and acceptable.

23 "Negrophobia" is alternatively referred to as "Afrophobia": a pervasive and ubiquitous animus of hostility toward African-descended peoples.

24 R. v. S. (R.D.), [1997] 3 S.C.R. 484, 1997 CanLII 324, at para. 46: "These are matters of which judicial notice may be taken." In R. v. Parks (1993), 15 O.R. (3d) 324, 342, Doherty J.A. did just this, stating, "Racism, and in particular anti-black racism, is a part of our community's psyche. A significant segment of our community holds overtly racist views. A much larger segment subconsciously operates on the basis of negative racial stereotypes. Furthermore, our institutions, including the criminal justice system, reflect and perpetuate those negative stereotypes."

25 *Social context education:* The landmark *RDS* case gave a much needed boost to the growing interest in social context, which since then has been fostered by a number of training initiatives undertaken by certain legal institutions geared to the Canadian judiciary such as the National Judicial Institute (NJI), Western Judicial Education Centre (WJEC), and Canadian Institute for the Advancement of Justice (CIAJ). For example, the Social Context Education Project (SCEP) was a special two-phase project of the NJI between 1996 and 2003. Phase one concentrated on full-court education seminars in every province of Canada with a view to creating a common base of information and understanding of the relevance and applicability of social context among all judges in Canada. Phase two focused on developing skilled judicial education leaders in this area through an intensive program of judicial faculty development, with curriculum development also included as a focus. Since 2003, social context has been integrated as a regular component of NJI work. It is now recognized that equality and contextual judicial inquiry are not optional but mandated by law in Canada through our Constitution and accession to relevant international conventions. It is an explicit ethical obligation of Canadian judges to "conduct themselves and proceedings before them so as to assure equality according to law"; see Canadian Judicial Council, *Ethical Principles for Judges* (Ottawa: CJC, 1998),

23. Increased judicial awareness of social context, then, is not only essential to good judging but required by law.
26 Colin Prescod, "Archives, Race, Class and Rage," *Race & Class* 58, no. 4 (2017), 76–84.
27 According to social worker Robert Wright, "It was a national story: a judge said that a young black person has a story that might be credible and that a white police officer may have a story that is not. The idea that a judge could judge that way, for a moment, was a national crisis." Quoted in Tattrie, "National Crisis."
28 The following description of the *RDS* case and the *verbatim* Youth Court trial dialogue reported here are based largely on testimonies culled both from the various court records (noted above) and from Walker, "Black Day."
29 "North End" is a euphemistic term used commonly in Halifax to designate a historically well-known and readily identifiable "Black neighbourhood." The "North End" is a neighbourhood occupying the northern part of Halifax Peninsula immediately north of Downtown Halifax. The Community of Africville was considered a separate community until the 1960s, when, in the name of urban renewal and integration, it was forcefully demolished by city authorities and its residents were forcibly relocated to the North End, many to public housing projects such as Uniacke Square off Gottingen Street. See also Shelagh Mackenzie, dir., *Remember Africville* (National Film Board of Canada, 1991), https://www.nfb.ca/film/remember-africville/.
30 In this essay I employ the first name initials "RD" to designate the accused youth, "S" being the first letter of his last name. In this way, I distinguish him clearly from the case itself, which I refer to as "*RDS.*"
31 *"Of slight and slender build ... "* in *R. v. R.D.S.*, [1994] N.S.J. No. 629.
32 Walker, "Black Day," 439.
33 Walker, 439.
34 Constable Stienburg and his partner had been alerted by a radio call about an abandoned stolen van and five "non-white" young males who had fled the scene. This charge against NR was eventually dropped. Detailed in Walker, "Black Day," 473n7.
35 Criminal Code, R.S.C. 1985, c. C-46.
36 Case No. Y0093168, Her Majesty the Queen v. R.D.S., Young Offender, 2 Dec. 1994. Copies of the trial transcript archived in the Library and Archives Canada (LAC), RG 124, vol. 5231. As cited in Walker, "Black Day," 473n7.
37 *R. v. R.D.S.*, [1994] N.S.J. No. 629, at para 15; *R. v. R.D.S.*, 1995 CanLII 7526 (NS CA), 12.
38 *R. v. R.D.S.*, [1994] N.S.J. No. 629, at para 5.
39 The case remains silent both on what the other officer did and on what happened to the other youth.
40 *R. v. R.D.S.*, [1994] N.S.J. No. 629, at para 5.

41 Testimony of Constable Donald Stienburg in Direct Examination, as reported in Walker, "A Black Day," 443; in *R. v. R.D.S.*, [1994] N.S.J. No. 629, at para 9.
42 Walker, "Black Day," 444; in *R. v. R.D.S.*, [1994] N.S.J. No. 629, at para 7.
43 *R. v. R.D.S.*, [1994] N.S.J. No. 629, at para 11.
44 Walker, "Black Day," 444.
45 *R. v. R.D.S.*, [1994] N.S.J. No. 629, at para 9.
46 Walker, "Black Day," 444; *R. v. R.D.S.*, [1994] N.S.J. No. 629, at para 10.
47 Walker, "Black Day," 444; in *R. v. R.D.S.*, [1994] N.S.J. No. 629, at para 9.
48 Walker, "Black Day," 444; also in *R. v. R.D.S.*, 1995 CanLII 7526 (NS CA), 3.
49 *R. v. R.D.S.*, [1994] N.S.J. No. 629, at para 13.
50 "At the end of her oral decision": see *R. v. R.D.S.*, CanLll 9321 (NS SC), p. 8. See also Richard Devlin and Diane Pothier, "Redressing the Imbalances: Rethinking the Judicial Role after R. v. R.D.S," *Ottawa Law Review* 31, no. 1 (1999): 4: "the case emerged from obscurity however because of the following remarks **at the end of Judge Sparks' oral judgment** [emphasis added]."
51 Judge Sparks admittedly proved to be a far cry from the likes of "Judge Judy," the well-known, irascible reality TV judge notorious for her caustic tongue and acerbic wit. Judge Judy's no-nonsense, impatient attitude would never have tolerated in her courtroom space such a question from the Crown Prosecutor or anyone else for that matter. Instead of dignifying the question with a response, more likely, without missing a beat, Judge Judy would have retorted, *"This is **my** playpen! **I** ask the questions here – **not you**!"*
52 Walker, "A Black Day,"445; in *R. v. R.D.S.*, 1995 CanLII 7526 (NS CA), at paras 3–4; *R. v. S. (R.D.)*, [1997] 3 S.C.R. 484, 1997, CanLII 324 (SCC) at para 4.
53 See note 49 *supra*.
54 Walker, "A Black Day," 446. In addition, although it was subsequently withdrawn, a formal complaint was also lodged with the Nova Scotia Police Commission.
55 Razack, "Case about Home," 65. Walker also notes that "the lines were drawn, with the police, the media, and soon the justice system itself aligned against Rocky Jones, and Connie Sparks on behalf of the youth RDS." Walker, "Black Day," 448.
56 Young Offenders Act, R.S.C. 1985, c. Y-1.
57 Walker, "Black Day," 446–7.
58 *R. v. S. (R.D.)*, 1994 Carswell NS 445, para 34; also in Walker, "Black Day," 447.
59 A hearing date for both appeals was set for April 1995.
60 Crown Prosecutor Adrian Reid argued that "the remarks (made in the course of her decision) show clearly the Trial Judge's conclusions on credibility flow from a racially based bias against police, and not from the

evidence ... this creates an appearance of unfairness ... the remarks exhibit real bias." Quoted in Walker, "Black Day," 448.
61 *R. v. R.D.S.*, 1995 CanLII 9321 (NS SC) p. 8; also in Walker, "Black Day," 449–50.
62 The appeal was heard by Justices Flinn, Pugsley, and Freeman and the judgment was delivered on 15 October 1995.
63 Walker, "A Black Day," 451.
64 The Charter arguments were presented to the Supreme Court of Canada by the late Professor Dianne Pothier.
65 *R. v. R.D.S.*, 1995 CanLII 7526 (NS CA), 11; Walker, "A Black Day," 452.
66 *R. v. R.D.S.*, 1995 CanLII 7526 (NS CA), 12; see also Justice Freeman's dissenting reasons in *R. v. R.D.S.* (1995) 145 NSR (2d) 284 [*RDS*] at paras 54, 62, 68–69: and Walker, "A Black Day," 452.
67 *R. v. R.D.S.*, 1995 CanLII 7526 (NS CA) at p. 12; see also Walker, "A Black Day," 452–3.
68 Walker, "Black Day," 453.
69 The Supreme Court of Canada Docket No. 25063, R.D.S. v. Her Majesty the Queen, records that after Application for leave to appeal was completed with service on 22 December 1995, Notice of Appeal was then completed on 4 June 1996, and the Appeal Hearing itself was scheduled for 10 March 1997.
70 The judgment was issued on 26 September 1997.
71 *R. v. S. (R.D.)*, [1997] 3 S.C.R. 484, 1997 CanLII 324 (SCC), p. 5.
72 Concurring in the majority decision were La Forest, L'Heureux-Dubé, Gonthier, McLachlin, Cory, and Iacobucci JJ., with Lamer C.J., Sopinka and Major JJ. dissenting.
73 Razack, "Case about Home," 65.
74 An under-examined but relevant aspect of this case is the issue of "racial profiling," which lies well beyond the fixed parameters of this essay.
75 See also Joanne St. Lewis, "Racism and the Judicial Decision-Making Process," *Currents* 8, no. 2 (1994): 16.
76 Ashley Montagu, *Statement on Race: An Annotated Elaboration and Exposition of the Four Statements on Race issued by UNESCO*, 3rd ed. (London: Oxford University Press, 1972).
77 According to Patricia Williams, "The national repetition that whiter neighbourhoods are safe and blacks bring sorrow is an incantation of powerlessness." Williams, "Spirit-Murdering the Messenger: The Discourse of Fingerpointing and the Law's Response to Racism," *University of Miami Law Review* 42, no. 127 (1987): 137.
78 Williams, 148.
79 For example, as I have argued elsewhere, "The Black High School male teacher and published writer who, happening upon two Metro constables manhandling a Black youth and former pupil, decides, as a precautionary

measure, to stop and observe the incident and is threateningly ordered to: 'Move on!' ... Racism is his reality." Thornhill, "Focus on Racism" (1995), 84–5.
80 The viral video of George Floyd's 2020 killing brought many of these elements to life, played out in real time for millions of viewers.
81 Despite these types of cosmetic attempts at camouflage, Society's collective consciousness continues to associate and identify these neighbourhoods as Black areas.
82 See, for example, Jackie Barkley, "Racism and Gentrification in Halifax's North End," *Halifax Media Co-op*, April 20, 2015, http://halifax.mediacoop.ca/blog/evancoole/33436.
83 See Thornhill, "Focus on Racism."
84 E.M.A. Thornhill, "Acercamiento a la presencia del negro dentro del teatro clásico español del Siglo de Oro: ¡El resplandor de la sombra!" (MA thesis, Université de Montréal, 1990).
85 Razack refers to this collective survival skill as "communal solidarity." For her, "the youth's story about trying to get a message home is entirely familiar. This act of communal solidarity underscores that people of colour must look out for each other in a racially hostile world and it specifically recalls the need to have community strategies for dealing with racist police who are so often beyond accountability." Razack, "Case about Home," 65.
86 *R. v. R.D.S.*, [1994] N.S.J. No. 629, par. 6.
87 For example, the Nova Scotia Barristers' Society Code of Professional Conduct stipulates, notably, both the lawyer's duty as prosecutor and the ethical obligation of respect and courtesy to the Court:

> 1-3 When acting as a prosecutor, a lawyer must act for the public and the administration of justice resolutely and honourably within the limits of the law while treating the tribunal with candour, fairness, courtesy and respect.
> 5.1-5 A lawyer must be courteous and civil and act in good faith to the tribunal and all persons with whom the lawyer has dealings.
> *Commentary*
> [1] Legal contempt of court and the professional obligation outlined here are not identical, and a *consistent pattern of rude, provocative or disruptive conduct by a lawyer, even though unpunished as contempt, may constitute professional misconduct* [emphasis added]."

See Nova Scotia Barristers' Society Code of Professional Conduct Approved by Council September 23, 2011 effective January 1, 2012 as amended January 20, 2012; July 20, 2012; February 22, 2013; September 19, 2014; January 23, 2015; May 22, 2015; February 266, 2016; April 22, 2016; May 27, 2016; May 26, 2017.

88 In Nova Scotia, Judges preside in the Family Court and in the Provincial Court, including the Youth Justice Court. When talking or writing to or about a specific judge sitting on the Provincial Court or the Family Court, s/he is referred to as "*Judge Jane/John Doe, My Lady, or Your Honour.*"

89 Formal ruling by Judge Whealy, a White, male trial judge hearing the case of Dudley Laws and Lawrence Motley, both Black men accused of transporting illegal migrants across the Canadian-US border. *R. v. Laws*, [1993] O.J. No. 2844 (22 Nov. 1993) at para. 10, quoted in Razack, "Case about Home," 63.

90 It is noteworthy that Walker also adverts in passing (in a footnote) to the Crown Prosecutor's anomalous interpellation of Judge Sparks: "Although the atmosphere of Youth Court is relatively informal, it is quite unusual to have a judicial decision interrupted in this way by the Prosecution or the Defence. Mr. Miller may not have intended any disrespect towards Judge Sparks with his interjection, but it could be interpreted as such." Walker, "A Black Day," 474n14.

91 According to the then active BLANS (Black Lawyers Association of Nova Scotia), "It took us over 100 years to get someone appointed to the Bench, and in just one stroke of the pen the individual is removed." Quoted in Cecil Foster, "An Uncertain Future for a Black Role Model," Opinion, *Toronto Star*, April 5, 1999.

92 The following list is non-exhaustive. Some scholarly journals published thematic issues based on *RDS*, including *Dalhousie Law Journal* 21, no. 1 (1998); and *Canadian Journal of Women and the Law* 10 (1998). In addition, quite a body of articles was generated commenting on *RDS*, notably Carol Aylward, "Take the Long Way Home: *R.D.S v. R.* – The Journey," *University of New Brunswick Law Journal* 47 (1998): 249–310; April Burey, "No Dichotomies: Reflections on Equality for African Canadians in R. v. R.D.S.," *Dalhousie Law Journal* 21, no. 1 (1998): 199–218; Razack, "Case about Home"; Devlin and Pothier, "Redressing the Imbalances"; Allan C. Hutchinson and Kathleen Strachan, "What's the Difference? Interpretation, Identity and R. v. R.D.S.," *Dalhousie Law Journal* 21, no.1 (1998): 219–35; Bruce Archibald, "The Lessons of the Sphinx: Avoiding Apprehensions of Judicial Bias in a Multi-racial, Multi-cultural Society" (5th) *Criminal Reports* 10 (1997): 54–64; and Jennifer Smith, "*R v. RDS*: A Political Science Perspective," *Dalhousie Law Journal* 21, no. 1 (1998): 236–48.

93 The first James Robinson Johnston Endowed Chair in Black Canadian Studies, inaugurated and held by Dr. Esmeralda M.A. Thornhill, Full Professor of Law, from 1996 to 2002, was "homed" in Dalhousie's Faculty of Law.

94 This motion was crafted with the initial intent that the then Dean of Law, the highest authority in the Faculty of Law, would present the Motion

and the Johnston Chair would second it. However, after reading the Draft Motion just before the meeting began, the Dean declined, stating that Jones was not the only one who had worked on the case and that, in any case, she fully intended to make mention of the Supreme Court of Canada ruling at the beginning of the Faculty Council Meeting.

95 Original motion presented to Faculty Council, formally recorded in the Law Faculty Council Meeting Minutes and on file with author.

96 It was the late Professor Dianne Pothier who, as co-Counsel with Jones, had argued the constitutional aspects of *RDS* before the Supreme Court of Canada.

97 A second complementary Motion was also unanimously ratified. This secondary Motion provided that the original ratified Motion of commendation be promptly disseminated by publicly posting it on the Electronic Bulletin Board at the Law School's Main Entrance. However, the following day I and other viewers were greeted by a unilaterally modified version of the formally ratified Motion: the name of Professor Dianne Pothier had been inserted alongside that of Burnley Rocky Jones.

98 "Expansion of the Unified Family Court System in Nova Scotia," May 2010, http://www.cbans.ca/getattachment/Publications-Resources/Resources/2010/Expansion-of-the-Unified-Family-Court-System-in-No/background FamilyCourt.pdf.

99 In 2017, the following judicial appointments of African Nova Scotians were made: Ronda Van Der Hoek, Rickcola Brinton, and Samuel Moreau.

100 "Normally, such affirmation by the Supreme Court should have been career-enhancing for Judge Sparks." Foster, "Uncertain Future."

101 Esmeralda M.A. Thornhill, "Exclusion of Her Honour, Corrine Sparks from the Unified Family Court of Nova Scotia," *Message from the Chair and Call to Action*, an open letter dated March 27, 1999 addressed to The Honorable Anne McLellan, Minister of Justice, with copies to Prime Minister Jean Chretien and Members of Parliament, NGOs, and Media. Document on file with author.

102 Robert Chisholm, Leader of the Opposition, *Letter of Support* addressed to Dr. E. Thornhill, First Johnston Chair, dated April 6, 1999 with enclosed documents: (1) copy of Letter of Concern signed by all members of the NDP Caucus and addressed to Minister of Justice and Attorney General of Canada, The Honourable Anne McLellan, dated March 30, 1999; and (2) *Resolution No. 2440 Notice of Motion*, by Leader of the Opposition (New Democratic Party), Nova Scotia House of Assembly Debates and Proceedings, March 30,1999. Kevin Deveaux, MLA for Cole Harbor-Eastern Passage, Questions raised during Question Period by MLA Deveaux: (1) *Justice- Supreme Court (N.S.) Family Division: Judge Sparks – Non-Selection*, House of Assembly Debates and Proceedings, March 30, 1999,

p. 5241; and (2) *Justice – Supreme Court (N.S.) Family Division: Appointments – Factors*, House of Assembly Debates and Proceedings, April 1, 1999.

103 According to Diane Peters of the Women's Court, "The goal of these parallel judgments is to see what equality – as defined under Section 15 of the charter, enacted into law in 1982 – could look like if it took priority in these decisions ... And while these shadow judgments have no legal standing, they've been almost universally well received as an exercise that embodies democratic and critical thinking and moves forward the fuzzy notion of true equality." Peters, "The Women's Court of Canada," *University Affairs*, September 12, 2011, https://www.universityaffairs.ca/features/feature-article/the-womens-court-of-canada/.

104 Baker v. Canada (Minister of Citizenship and Immigration), [1999] 2 SCR 817.

105 A most frustrating déjà vu! This was but a repeat scenario of an occurrence that had transpired twenty years previously, in September 1989, at the Charter Challenges Programme launch of the book *Canadian Charter Equality Rights for Women: One Step Forward or Two Steps Back* by Gwen Brodsky and Shelagh Day (Ottawa: Canadian Advisory Council on the Status of Women, 1989). This publication, which purported to analyse equality rights litigation during the first three years that Section 15 of the *Canadian Charter of Rights and Freedoms* actually was in effect, remained totally mute on the issue of "race." It failed to address the reality of Black and other racialized women and did not even mention us. When called to account by Black Women Conference participants who were then present, one co-author proceeded disingenuously to canvass and solicit one-on-one from these same Black women possible suggestions for solutions that they, the authors, might employ to address the "omission" during their imminent planned nation-wide book tour!

106 According to scholar Grada Kilomba, Black women occupy a very critical place in theory: "Black Women have ... been positioned within several discourses that misrepresent our own reality: a debate on racism where the subject is Black male; a gendered discourse where the subject is *white* female; and a discourse on class where 'race' has no place at all." Kilomba is a Portuguese-born interdisciplinary artist and writer with origins in the West African islands of Sao Tomé; she lives in Berlin. Her work draws on memory, trauma, race, gender, and the decolonization of knowledge and narrative: *Who can speak? What can we speak about?* and *What happens when we speak?* These are three constant questions in Kilomba's body of work. See Kilomba, *Plantation Memories*.

107 Take, for instance, the "presumptions" of **Black criminality, Black dangerousness, and Black incompetence**, which all derive from the purported savage, evil, and deviant nature of Black people. Our

supposed proclivity to crime, and savagery, as well as the inferiority and baseness imputed to us as a group, were used to justify our aptness for enslavement ... for Jim Crow segregation ... and for ongoing domination by White people.

108 "John Henrik Clarke Bibliography: Home," Cornell University Library, accessed June 28, 2021, https://guides.library.cornell.edu/clarke.
109 Russell Ferguson, "Introduction: Invisible Center," in *Out There: Marginalization and Contemporary Cultures*, ed. Russell Ferguson, Martha Gever, Trinh T. Minh-ha, and Cornell West (New York: New Museum of Contemporary Art; Cambridge, MA: MIT Press, 1990), 9, quoted in Nakayama and Krizek, "Whiteness," 291.
110 Nakayama and Krizek, "Whiteness," 292.
111 Kilomba, *Plantation Memories*.
112 Nakayama and Krizek, "Whiteness," 298.
113 Razack, "Case about Home," 60.
114 According to Razack, "Anyone of colour who is in a public role (and I count myself in this group), those few of us who are judges, lawyers, professors, teachers, politicians, in short anyone of us working in the corporate, educational, judicial or political elite, knows about the consequences of disputing the official story. We know now, if we didn't before, what happens when we dare to say that race matters. We have been warned. And this, no matter what the outcome of the decision itself, remains the enduring lesson of R.D.S." Razack, "Case about Home," 60.
115 Razack, 60.
116 Many Black people have observed how the requirement for discourses tailored to suit or soothe White comfort level often changes the meaning of our own dialogue and ends up working subversively instead to elevate and insidiously reinforce the ideas of the White dominant group.
117 When it comes to "race," two other presumptions are deeply ingrained in Canadian social convention and, as a rule, enjoy wide acceptance: (1) **"race" is** *not* **a relevant factor; it is, rather, a non-issue**; and (2) **racism – if shown to exist – is really nothing more than an annoying aberration, a mere exception.**

BOOKEND II

The Past Has a Future: Critical Intellectual Histories of Blackness

21
Wrestling with Multicultural Snake Oil: A Newcomer's Introduction to Black Canada

DANIEL McNEIL

As part of the process of applying to become a permanent resident of Canada, I was exposed to a variety of documents that pontificated about Canadian customs and beliefs. *A Newcomer's Introduction to Canada*, published by the Ministry of Public Works and Government Services, was probably the most memorable. I can vividly recall its rather cartoonish depictions of a country in which Canadian men "may formally embrace old friends or family [with a handshake] but almost never kiss other men in public" and "passionate kissing or touching are considered impolite and offensive in public."[1] I remember wondering how it justified such calls for Canadian immigrants to regulate their public displays of affection while advising them to perform public displays of deference when interacting with Canadian police officers. Most of all, however, I cannot forget how its section on acceptance, tolerance, and respect compressed its commitment to addressing racism in Canada into six short sentences: "Some people may tell you that there is no racism in Canada. Others may say that racism is a very serious problem. The truth lies somewhere between. Some Canadians may make you feel unwelcome. However, the majority of Canadians are fair-minded. They will accept and respect anyone who accepts and respects them."[2]

The 1997 edition of *A Newcomer's Introduction to Canada* does not, in short, encourage critical reflection about performativity, heteronormativity, and governmentality. Nor does it demonstrate any self-deprecating irony about its desire to capture a diverse array of happy, smiling subjects and portray Canada as a benevolent and open-minded country.[3] It does, however, provide us with a range of material and symbolic resources to perceive how the Canadian state sought to portray Canadians as fair-minded people who value tolerance and acceptance. It reminds us that representatives of the middle and upper levels of Canadian institutional society in the 1990s did not necessarily consider it "truthful" to claim that racism is a *very* serious problem in Canada when faced with evidence of, and protests against, systemic racism (including, but not limited to, Phil Fontaine's testimony about the history of residential schools; the military scandal that has come to be known as the "Somalia Affair"; and a Yonge Street Uprising led by the Black Action Defence Committee against the acquittal of the LAPD officers who beat the African American Rodney King, the acquittal of two Peel Region police officers charged with second-degree murder in the shooting death of Black teenager Michael Wade Lawson, and the killing of a twenty-two-year-old Black man, Raymond Lawrence, by an undercover Toronto police officer). It offers us one avenue to explore how anti-racist inititatives were grafted onto multiculturalism policies and discourses that had, in the 1970s, been designed to integrate cultural and linguistic groups into the Canadian nation-state.[4]

When I first read *A Newcomer's Introduction to Canada* while working through the mounds of material needed to complete my application for permanent residence, I filed its short, staccato sentences away as an unfortunate by-product of bureaucratic writing by committee. However, after discovering that many contributions to a Canadian public sphere used similar clichés to appeal to an imaginary audience with a sixth-grade reading level, I began to consider more disconcerting possibilities. What if the system of privilege and awards in Canada – the importance attached to grants awarded by a federal government, the belief that bestowing prestigious awards on members of racialized and ethnic communities would advance "harmonious race relations," and so on[5] – meant that the assumptions of *A Newcomer's Introduction to Canada* framed the questions and approaches developed by Canadian researchers? What if the assumptions and approaches of Canadian public servants had seeped into writing by and about Black Canadians as well as the grammar of Black Canada? What if they overdetermined the journalistic commentary and scholarly research about race in Canada that supports an establishment in which appointed figures are acclaimed for translating the experiences of "visible minorities" into "accessible," oversimplified language rather than creatively and critically conveying how Black identities, like all identities in modern societies, are necessarily complex, contradictory, and subject to contestation?[6]

This chapter reflects on such questions to provide some formative context for definitions of Black Canadian thought that contend that very few Black Canadian writers wish to transcend borders,[7] presume that all African Canadian intellectuals must carry a Canadian passport,[8] and attach significance to recognition and authenticity within a Canadian multicultural state (i.e., the attempts to appeal to a fair-minded spirit of Canadians as well as evidence-based interventions that wish to puncture this rather self-congratulatory image to prove that racism is, indeed, a very serious problem in Canada).[9] The first section addresses an article by Peter James Hudson and Aaron Kamugisha that demarcates Black Canadian thought into two heuristic categories: a Black liberal tradition and a Black radical tradition. While sympathetic to the attempts of Hudson and Kamugisha to move discussions about Black Canadian thought beyond hackneyed and clichéd polarities such as African Canadians versus Caribbean immigrants, I point out some of the potential pitfalls involved in the division of Black Canadian thought into liberal and radical camps. In doing so, I also reflect on their selection of George Elliott Clarke as perhaps the key representative of the Black liberal tradition in Canada and their description of Rinaldo Walcott as one of the leading figures of a Black radical tradition in Canada that has been informed by Black British intellectuals such as Paul Gilroy. The second section discusses the shape and contours of Gilroy's *The Black Atlantic*, a much-cited and debated text that has been praised for its ambition and criticized for its limitations of breadth (e.g., failing to substantively address the movement of people and ideas in contexts such as Canada and the African continent) and depth (e.g., not providing material about the specific histories and politics of socialist and feminist movements in the United States and the Caribbean). In revisiting this seminal text published in 1993, I clarify key features of Gilroy's discussion of a network of cultures spanning Africa, North and South America, the Caribbean, and Europe. I also set the stage for the third section, which connects disagreements between Clarke and Walcott to their divergent readings of Gilroy's work and other prominent contributions to postcolonial studies in the 1990s.

The fourth section suggests future directions for Black Canadian thought that complicate and exemplify the translocal approach of Richard Iton's *In Search of the Black Fantastic: Politics and Popular Culture in the Post–Civil Rights Era*. First published in 2008, this book by a Montreal-born professor of political science and African American studies has been hailed as one of the most important contributions to the Black diaspora, internationalism, and transnational Black identities since *The Black Atlantic*.[10] I draw on its key arguments about the anti-Blackness of the nation-state and the perils of liberal governmentality that celebrate "false happy endings" in which slavery gives way to emancipation, colonialism to postcolonial independence, racism to colour-blindness, and so on. I engage with its rich articulation of a Black fantastic in which intellectuals recognize how anti-Black racism and Black resistance in cities such as Charleston, Halifax, Accra, Marseilles, and Liverpool articulate with one another. I also pay close attention to Iton's argument that the recognition of these translocal connections is necessary if we are to unsettle, recognize, contest, and profane those marginalizations and theographies that lead to the tendency to represent "coloniality in the United States in the grammars of race, Jim Crow, segregation, racism and 'race relations' ... in the United Kingdom and France as a matter of a colonial past ... and in Canada as those things that only happen elsewhere."[11]

On Black Canadian Thought

In their introduction to a special issue of the *C.L.R. James Journal* on Black Canadian thought, Hudson and Kamugisha deploy Bernard Boxill's demarcation of African American political thought into Black liberal and Black radical traditions.[12] They consider the Black liberal tradition to be "arguably the dominant mode of thinking about Blacks in Canada ... a default setting whose contours elide with that of a normative liberalism within contemporary Canadian thought and consciousness, although a number of thinkers have attempted to elaborate it in a more deliberate and systematic fashion."[13] They see writers working in this tradition foregrounding the nation, expressing faith in the redemptive possibilities of the Canadian state and the rewards of Canadian multiculturalism, and using history to prioritize Black representation within Canadian society. To go further, they argue that a liberal tradition "has a reformist posture regarding capitalism, believing, to varying degrees, in the possibilities of the free market for racial justice. It has a limited engagement with the Black World and the history of Pan-African thought beyond Canada and is largely mute on the question of Canadian imperialism. Often, this work is engaged with the writings of white Canadian liberal philosophers including Will [Kymlicka], John Ralston Saul, and Charles Taylor and their assertions of Canadian tolerance and inclusivity and their ultimate belief in the benevolence of the Canadian state when it comes to protecting group rights."[14] In short, Hudson and Kamugisha write against the grain of ahistorical and schematic approaches to Black Canadian studies that are recognized and rewarded within the Canadian public sphere even though (or, more damningly, because) they do not move beyond a superficial engagement with a radical tradition that develops an anticapitalist political stance constructed from "a politics around work and its overcoming, a politics around law and its disassociation from racial domination, and a folk historicism that sets special store by the recovery of historical sensibility."[15] The authors are also sensitive to what they perceive as the "persistent problem of the institutionalization of Black Studies within the Canadian university" and Black Canadian studies that is often subsumed within such fields as Canadian studies or diaspora studies. Although they allude to writers such as Cecil Foster and Donna

Bailey Nurse who may be connected to this Black liberal tradition, they identify George Elliott Clarke as "perhaps the best known scholar" working within the Black liberal tradition while claiming that his work often "traverses into a more conservative field."[16]

To illustrate a Black radical tradition, Hudson and Kamugisha draw attention to David Austin, Katherine McKittrick, and other writers who emerged within "a sort of existential moment in the history of Black Canada: in a moment when, after the heyday of the identity politics of the eighties and nineties, a reactionary anti-Blackness has erased many cultural gains, and when the hegemony of neoliberal multiculturalism has compressed the possibilities and shrunken the terrain of Black freedom and the imagination of radical modes of Black liberation."[17] They connect Austin, McKittrick, and other members of a Black radical tradition in Canada to "intellectual foundations established ... in Toronto, [which] while being deeply influenced by British Cultural Studies (especially via the work of Black British intellectuals including Stuart Hall, Paul Gilroy and Hazel Carby) ... [drew] on a diverse set of intellectual traditions including the political economy of the New World Group, African American literary theory, strands of European poststructuralism, Queer Theory, and the Africana philosophy of Sylvia Wynter and others."[18] Hudson and Kamugisha also describe Rinaldo Walcott as a key representative of the Black radical tradition and "the leading Black Canadian cultural theorist who in the last two decades has done more than any other figure to create a field of Black Canadian studies and has mentored countless students."[19]

The co-editors of the special issue on Black Canadian thought hope that the categories of Black liberal and Black radical traditions may offer us "a way of thinking about Black Canadian thought that moves beyond the ... recourse to the exhausted and clichéd – and often times fictional – polarities of Native versus Immigrant, African Canadian versus West Indian, etc."[20] This aspiration can be unpacked in multiple ways. Much more can be said, for example, about the use of contested terms such as "Native Black Canadians" and the need for greater dialogue between the distinct and related interdisciplinary fields of Black studies and Indigenous studies.[21] For analytic focus, I limit my discussion to the spectre of the acrimonious debates between Clarke and Walcott in the 1990s that haunts the attempts of Hudson and Kamugisha to treat them as exemplars of Black liberal and radical traditions. Although Hudson and Kamugisha frame Walcott's *Black Like Who? Writing Black Canada* as a "pioneering critical treatment of African Canadian literature and culture," it is difficult to overlook Clarke's denunciation of *Black Like Who?* as a "slipshod ... superficial ... atrocious" book and Walcott's attempt to characterize Clarke's work as nativist, regressive, and melancholic.[22] The debates between Clarke and Walcott in the 1990s have been deemed "crucial to the emerging field of Black Canadian Studies" by writers who do not seem to appreciate the irony of using two Black Canadian feminists in a manner that evokes narrow, masculinist conceptions of gladiatorial combats and battles between the "father figures" of African American studies (in which we are asked to declare our preference for Booker T. Washington or W.E.B. Du Bois, Malcolm X or Martin Luther King Jr., Cornel West or Ta-Nehisi Coates).[23] In a playful and ironic essay for *Transition* in 2008, Hudson even suggests that George Elliott Clarke, "the Scotian," "sees Walcott [as] a representative of a Toronto-centred West Indian literary mafia that aims to control black Canada's literary future by turning it into an 'immigrant literature.'"[24]

When addressing Clarke's work for the special issue on Black Canadian thought in 2014, Hudson and Kamugisha place it within liberal *and* conservative traditions. This recognizes Clarke's self-fashioning as a writer who "critically admires Pierre Eliot [*sic*] Trudeau, is a proud Canadian nationalist (as well as a defiant 'Africadian' regionalist), ... [and] bristles against writers and texts that he perceives to stray into the more radical provinces of Black Nationalism and Pan-Africanism."[25] It may also invite us to connect their notes and comments to essays and dissertations in which Clarke expresses his ambivalence toward a liberal ideology that "exalts 'liberty,' the freedom of the individual, of market equality, small-is-good government, experimentation, and the erosion of prejudice" and thinks through the connections between English Canadian and African American literature in relation to classical conservative collectivism, which stresses communitarian values and respect for tradition to inform its "dissident or dissenting relationship with mainstream American – essentially liberal – culture."[26] Lest we forget, Clarke has not hidden the significance of George Grant and other Canadian conservatives who inform his sorties against the "small-*l* liberal, American bias" of Robin Winks's *The Blacks in Canada: A History*.[27] With that said, Hudson and Kamugisha's notes on Black Canadian thought do not mention that Clarke's critique of mainstream liberal (Euro)American culture might find a home in the political thought of African Canadian liberals, conservatives, *and* radicals. If Clarke is to be aligned with conservatism, it is as someone whose thinking about cultural particularity is informed by *Red* Toryism, the critical questions of *maîtres à penser* such as Frantz Fanon and other anti-colonial thinkers, and his self-fashioning as a "Leftist, African-Canadian intellectual of African-American and West Indian heritage" whose "'Baptist Marxist' commitment to a sassy, Malcolm-X style blackness was complicated by ... equally strong indulgence in the muscular intellectualism of the liberal Canadian prime minister Pierre *Elliott* [emphasis added] Trudeau."[28] Acknowledging such influences from across the political spectrum ("Grant, Trudeau, Fanon, *and* Malcolm X"[29]) means that Clarke's *Odysseys Home* does not critique *Black Like Who?* merely because he believes it strays too far down the path of radicalism and pan-Africanism; rather, he finds fault with Walcott's "shouting down of history" by connecting it to the "*liberal* [emphasis added] lies" of the "Jamaican-American scholar Orlando Patterson" that assume Black survival in the modern world must mean the abandonment of any search for a past through "myth making and historical reconstruction."[30]

The Black Atlantic: Modernity and Double Consciousness

Hudson and Kamugisha's discussion of Black intellectual traditions in Canada in the special issue of the official journal of the Caribbean Philosophical Association (CPA) does not mention the work of Lewis Gordon, the first president of the CPA, who developed more expansive genealogies of distinctive liberal, radical, conservative, feminist, existentialist, postmodernist, and other Black intellectual traditions.[31] In his summary of Black intellectual traditions, Gordon describes the "extraordinary influence" of Paul Gilroy's *The Black Atlantic* and connects the book to postmodernist, poststructuralist, postcolonial, cultural, and queer studies movements in the 1980s and '90s. The seminal text documents the lives and circumstances of Black Atlantic thinkers who, often from positions outside of academia, disrupt narrow and sclerotic definitions of "the West."[32] Put slightly differently, Gilroy develops close readings of a select group of African American intellectuals who traversed and transcended national and professional boundaries in the hopes of clarifying abstract and theoretical accounts of modernity and double consciousness.

Despite Gilroy's wilful idiosyncrasy and frustration with the "parasitic and mannered outpourings" of bourgeois writers and "merely scholastic contributions to the intellectual history of the West,"[33] critics have associated the "huge international acclaim" accorded to *The Black Atlantic* to its ability to reflect and appeal to a "metropolitan academic climate" in the mid-1990s that popularized concepts of "fusion, hybridity and syncretism as explanatory tools for the analysis of cultural formation."[34] To situate it within a *metropolitan* climate in the "First World," Laura Chrisman describes *The Black Atlantic* as an "anti-national" text that expresses intolerance toward all nationalisms.[35] To foreground its appeal to an *academic* audience, she notes its reliance on a particular perspective that considered the affirmation of Black debts to European philosophy as a means to provide a countermodel of social emancipation. Such readings reflect the "neurotic energy" of a text that Gilroy hoped would address the "insinuating rhythms of everyday life," "read the signs in the street in defiance of contemporary pressures to retreat into a contemplative state," and secure him a "proper job" as a "scholar."[36] Linking *The Black Atlantic* to a *cultural* turn in the academy, Chrisman's article portrays it as an "anti-economistic" text that reduces Black social movement to Black art and reduces Black art to suffering and a death drive rather than the positive, resistive elements in Black political history.[37] Her reading provides us with important insights about a text that often frames labour and liberation, labour and art, socialist and Black value systems, and national and international impulses as antinomies rather than mutually enabling categories. It provides significant material for other critical readings of *The Black Atlantic* that bristle at its limited attention to comparative histories of labour movements, its academic idioms and locutions (such as "it bears repetition"),[38] and its focus on North America and western Europe (a "New York–London nexus").[39] It also prompts us to examine whether *The Black Atlantic*'s focus on the Global North means that it promotes an anti-national agenda, or whether it is more accurate to consider it a carefully constructed critique of methodological nationalism.

There are certainly moments in *The Black Atlantic* in which Gilroy specifies that his critique is centred on a "dogmatic focus on discrete national dynamics" and that his goal is to subvert the dominant mode of work that is written on an "*exclusively* [emphasis added] national basis."[40] Such qualifiers, used in conjunction with judiciously chosen examples of progressive nationalism, may offer a bulwark against the charge of anti-nationalism. However, the text overwhelmingly links nationalism to pathological forms of ethnic absolutism and defensive and aggressive forms of behaviour. The primary targets of Gilroy's critique include "morbid celebration of England and Englishness" by little Englanders who succumb to "narrow nationalism," and Black nationalists hamstrung by parochial tastes.[41] On the one hand, he frames nationalism and ethnic absolutism as alien threats to a project that maps unity *and* differentiation in the African diaspora. On the other, he defends the authority of a "more difficult option: the theorisation of creolisation, metissage, mestizaje, and hybridity" for students of resistance and accommodation intrinsic to modern Black political culture.[42] While the text considers cultural and political historians who focus on the nation and the defence of their disciplinary boundaries to be "squeamish," it valorizes outernational perspectives and considers the concept of diaspora indispensable to the study of "the political and ethical dynamics of the unfinished history of blacks in the modern world."[43] As a theorist who suggests that claiming a diasporic connection to Africa – without making the continent one's home – expresses a "more difficult cosmopolitan commitment,"[44] Gilroy can frustrate readers who believe that the study of multicultural national histories, or projects of national liberation and transnational cultural formations within one continent, may be as difficult and complex as mapping translocal connections across the Atlantic Ocean.

Gilroy's justification of diasporic research against "those who are content to produce *merely* [emphasis added] national histories" is a useful illustration of how he situates his work vis-à-vis debates about the decline of public spheres (particularly radical, countercultural ones) and the rise of public intellectuals (particularly those who were tasked with interpreting and translating the desires of subaltern groups) in the early 1990s.[45] It evokes, for example, Edward Said's 1993 Reith lectures for the BBC, which esteem intellectuals who "transform the *merely* [emphasis added] professional routine most of us go through into something much more lively and radical; instead of doing what one is supposed to do one can ask why one does it, who benefits from it, how can it reconnect with a personal project and original thoughts."[46] Although the index of *The Black Atlantic* does not mention Said, and includes only three references to his work in its endnotes, Gilroy has acknowledged that the book was modelled on Said's *Orientalism*.[47] In the same year that he published *The Black Atlantic*, Gilroy published a review of Said's *Culture and Imperialism* that connects the work of the Palestinian American public intellectual to the "struggles of diverse postcolonial peoples for democracy and liberation" who do not find their dreams of another world crushed by the fall of actually existing Communism in Eastern Europe and the Soviet Union. His review expresses admiration for Said's "resolutely principled" work and its exploration of "representations of western supremacy that have been gored by cultural historians and literary critics to whom empire was a non-event or sideshow." In addition, it appreciates Said's ability to draw insights from the "great critic" Raymond Williams while simultaneously critiquing Williams's failure to develop a sustained, contrapuntal reading of Western and non-Western texts and experiences as belonging together because imperialism connects them.[48]

In a conversation with Williams about media, the margins, and modernity, Said expressed his belief that "in the relationships between the ruler and the ruled in the imperial or colonial or racial sense, race takes precedence over both class and gender."[49] Gilroy's engagement with Williams, Said, and other cultural theorists in *The Black Atlantic* repeatedly encourages more critical reflection about the intersection of race, class, and gender. However, critical commentary on *The Black Atlantic* tends to focus on the the relative absence of case studies about the life and work of Black women in the book rather than his desire to translate Stuart Hall's famous line about race being the modality in which class is lived to consider gender the modality in which race is lived.[50]

Toni Morrison is one of the few female authors whom Gilroy discusses at any length in *The Black Atlantic*. In a text that is interested in the life and work of activist-intellectuals who crisscrossed the Atlantic, it is significant that Gilroy engages with Morrison's work but not her life inside or outside of the United States. While challenging the overvaluation of Black male pain in such areas, *The Black Atlantic* does not address how its conception of modernity and double consciousness may be transformed by a deeper engagement with the theorization of home in African American and African Canadian feminist literature that addresses roots, soil, and land.[51] The book's determination to claim that Morrison, and other African American writers he admires, have consistently refused to identify themselves as Americans (without noting that Morrison had consistently asserted her desire to write for African Americans) is particularly striking when read in dialogue with its portrayal of Spike Lee, and other African American filmmakers Gilroy casts in a less sanguine light. That is to say, Gilroy connects Lee to an assertive form of American cultural nationalism and insiderism (while noting that Lee had consistently asserted his desire to direct films for African Americans). In the midst of debates about Black public intellectuals in the mid-1990s, Gilroy wished to intervene in a context in which it was a filmmaker in Hollywood who was becoming the archetypal model of Black creativity rather than a writer, musician, singer, or preacher.[52] His critique of this visual turn, and what he considers the de-skilling and debasement of Black music in the age of "digital simulation," is linked to his careful analysis of the overemphasis on the body and skin in commodified cultures.[53] It is also aligned with his critique of Lee as a cultural protectionist who associates racial mixing and hybridity with the "dilution" and regression of Black music, and develops a conservative politics of family that presents pathological family forms being ruled by women and healthy Black families being headed by a patriarch.[54]

When invited to reflect on his selection of African American men to explicate Black Atlantic cultures, Gilroy acknowledges that the life, work, and political culture of Ida B. Wells-Barnett is appropriate to the heuristic project of mapping a Black Atlantic (one thinks, for example, of her lectures and talks in the United Kingdom against the barbarity of lynching in America). He also notes that if he were to begin the project in the twenty-first century, he would include a case study on the life and work of Anna Julia Cooper, a distinguished scholar and educator who attended the first Pan-African Conference in 1900 and received her PhD from the University of Paris-Sorbonne in 1925.[55] Somewhat surprisingly, Gilroy does not explicitly mention the theoretical insights of Caribbean women such as the abolitionist and autobiographer Mary Prince, the activist and journalist Claudia Jones, or the writer and cultural theorist Sylvia Wynter.

Although *The Black Atlantic* does not develop case studies of male thinkers from the Caribbean either, it acknowledges the Caribbean intellectuals C.L.R. James and Frantz Fanon as perhaps the two most important Black Atlantic thinkers of the twentieth century. James's conversations with Richard Wright about the ability of Blacks in the modern world to grapple with existential questions, and his insistence that ordinary people do not need an intellectual vanguard to help them to speak or tell them what to say, inform Gilroy's critique of scholars who presume that they need to shepherd Black folk into respectable, national limits and shield them from the complexity of work that transcends national boundaries. Similarly, Fanon's warning about the messianic urges to promote heroes who act as another form of leader, as well as his rigorous critique of the essentialist and bourgeois dimensions of the Negritude movement, add content and cutting edge to Gilroy's discussion of Afrocentricity in *The Black Atlantic*.[56] Fanon famously noted the pitfalls of political and poetic work that sought to return to a culturalist subconscious of an Africanist life philosophy by proposing a unified and undifferentiated Black subject. He was wary of work that uncritically celebrated cultural traits such as irrationality, rhythm, animism, oneness with nature, and sensuality as empirically verifiable elements of precolonial African societies (rather than concepts and behaviours that may be critically analysed as products of racist stereotyping disseminated through colonial discourse). He expressed skepticism about forms of Negritude that focused on re-evaluating historical achievements of colonized cultures and societies without transforming subjectivity under the ossified structure of bourgeois colonial society so that history and memory would not be sites of shamefulness.

In *The Black Atlantic* and other venues, Gilroy depicts Afrocentricity as an essentialist movement that reflects the discourse of nineteenth-century European colonialists and presents a vision of Black masculine heroes in which audiences might recite a roll call of male role models along the lines of "Marcus, Malcolm, Martin, Marley, Mandela and *Me!*"[57] According to Gilroy, such forms of Black nationalism might be of use in galvanizing communities against the encroachments of crack cocaine but provide a poor basis for the writing of cultural history and the calculation of political choices.[58] Such caustic remarks may have been calculated to provoke plural reading publics "fractured along the experiential fault lines of gender, race, and class" in the United States and the United Kingdom.[59] The next section reads them out of the context of this "special relationship" between the United States and United Kingdom to consider how they have also been appropriated and misappropriated by scholars determined to advance critical inquiry about nation, diaspora, and the politics of recognition in Canada.

What Is Canada to the Black Atlantic?

Gilroy's work is not imbued by a Canadian structure of feeling – the less tangible and delicate parts of life and experience that come into awareness when we "notice the contrasts between generations, who never talk quite 'the same language,' or when we read an account of our lives by someone from outside the community, or watch the small differences in style, of speech or behaviour in someone who has learned our ways yet was not bred in them."[60] In his contribution to a seminal cultural studies conference in 1990, Gilroy spoke of a place in the nineteenth century called "Western Canada" rather than "Canada West," and *The Black Atlantic* only references Canada on two occasions.[61] One reference takes the reader to an extended quotation about Donald Byrd's youth in Detroit, when he stared across the river and imagined Canada as a foreign, exotic land that represented Europe. The other leads us to Martin Delany's time in Canada, in which Gilroy describes Canada as the site from which Delany wrote his novel *Blake* and planned his trip to Africa and Europe.[62] Such comments reflect a tendency to treat Canada as a resting area for great artists before they go across the Atlantic to find the *real* drama, action, and history. As Richard Wright wrote from Quebec in July 1945, "because of the war, this is the closest I can get to Paris," and Canada is noticeably absent in the chapter that Gilroy devotes to Wright's life and work.[63] Gilroy is concerned with how the creative development of Wright was "boosted and transformed by the decision to relocate himself *far away* [emphasis added] from the United States" and only notes the time he spent in Africa, Spain, Asia, and Central and South America before his premature death in Paris in 1960.[64]

In mapping African Canadian literature, George Elliott Clarke wrote against the grain of gestures of diasporic inclusiveness that treat Canada as a "blunt irrelevance."[65] Instead of accepting erasure or marginalization, Clarke proposes that Canada-centric research is necessary "because the expansive cosmopolitanism of the African diaspora cannot be understood without taking into account the creative ways in which blackness has managed to thrive in this predominantly white settler-state."[66] To go further, he claims that Canada is the "perfect space" to study an African diaspora because African Canadian identity borrows unapologetically from Caribbean and American source cultures as well as British, French, and African ones.⁶⁷ Seeking to address this excellent diversity, *Odysseys Home* reflects the dominant impact of African American and Caribbean influences on African Canadian culture in the body of the text and alludes to British, French, and African influences on African Canada (often in footnotes and asides).⁶⁸ Read in conjunction with Clarke's desideratum for scholars to mine the footnotes of texts – as well as federal, provincial, municipal, and university archives that store personal and public histories, fiction, autobiography, ethnography, and poetry – to amend false precepts about African Canadian culture, such comments may be considered a clarion call for scholars to raid the archives to unlearn the dominative mode.⁶⁹ Read in isolation, they may appear to marginalize British, French, and African influences on African Canadian culture and mirror the marginalization of African Canadians from *The Black Atlantic* that he is determined to contest.

Critics of Clarke's essays, including Lucy Evans, have suggested that he makes sense of *The Black Atlantic* by "simplifying it."⁷⁰ Although Evans does not provide extensive substantiation for her claim, one may note Clarke's decision to describe Gilroy's project as anti-essentialist even though *The Black Atlantic* critiqued anti-essentialism as a "libertarian … cultural saturnalia which attends the end of innocent notions of the essential black subject, which is insufficiently alive to the lingering power of specifically racialized forms of power and subordination."⁷¹ *Odysseys Home* also seems to misappropriate postcolonial theory when it suggests that African Canadians "enact a version of Edward Said's Orientalism" because Black America is, for Black Canada, "an exotic *Other*."⁷² Clarke's analysis of how African America acts as a "privileged *Other* for African Canada," and how American conception of Blackness is made to dominate the entire Occident, may have been more conducive to the adaptation of Said's discussion of the aesthetic representations of a homogenized and exotic Orient and the material exploitations of European and American colonial enterprise.⁷³

Rinaldo Walcott contends that Clarke's domestication or misappropriation of diasporic and postcolonial theorists for Canada-centric ends may reflect a fear that he will be abandoned by the nation. Such comments underscore Walcott's critical questions about the desire to produce a comprehensive account of Black Canada that, inevitably, marginalizes certain voices and perspectives.⁷⁴ His intellectual projects question the presumption that the revelation of Black heritage and genealogy to a broader audience will both install and correct a lack of knowledge. They strive to unsettle our understanding of what counts as the archive and complicate celebratory narratives that emphasize how migrants and diasporic groups enrich Canada. They draw on diasporic thought that dares to denounce bourgeois barbarism while vandalizing Eurocentric norms about what counts as knowledge and intellectual value.[75] Without ignoring critical interventions regarding Gilroy's tendency in *The Black Atlantic* to use the life and work of African American men to illuminate his discussion of modernity and double consciousness, Walcott adapts Gilroy's theorization of diaspora to analyse cultural forms that cannot be contained within the nation-state.[76] Whereas Clarke contests the lack of recognition granted to Canadian history and culture in Gilroy's text, Walcott's *Black Like Who?* draws on Gilroy's insistence on reading and adding Europe and Black Britain into the texture of arguments and debates concerning intellectual property and ethnic absolutism to meditate "on the place of black Canadas in *contemporary* [emphasis added] discourses of ... the black Atlantic."[77]

In Search of the Black Fantastic

If one were to construct a Venn diagram that connected readers of Gilroy's *Black Atlantic*, of Clarke's *Odysseys Home*, and of Walcott's *Black Like Who?*, Richard Iton's *In Search of the Black Fantastic* would feature prominently in the middle. The professor of political science at the University of Toronto between 1994 and 1999 bore witness to the feuding between Clarke and Walcott as well as the attempts of the Canadian state to define the "Canadian way of life" for recent immigrants. Rather than reopen any old wounds, the author of *In Search of the Black Fantastic* expresses appreciation for Clarke *and* Walcott in his acknowledgments, while the body of the text published in 2008 examines the appeal of cultural nationalism as part of its exploration of time, space, and belonging in the African diaspora. Gilroy's work – from *"There Ain't No Black in the Union Jack"* (1987) to *The Black Atlantic* (1993) and *Postcolonial Melancholia* (2005) – is also a major influence on Iton's analysis of Black politics and popular culture, and the back cover of *In Search of the Black Fantastic* features Gilroy's endorsement of Iton's "deep and stimulating exploration of [Black Atlantic people and] their political aspirations and achievements."

Iton's acclaimed book examines the relationship between aesthetics, politics, nation, and diaspora after landmark legislation such as the Civil Rights Act (1964) and Voting Rights Act (1965) that provided African Americans with increased opportunities to access the political realm through elected office. While acknowledging that a culturalist approach may result in facile commodification, accommodation, and incorporation – and that cultural resistance does not always engender transformation of the status quo – *In Search of the Black Fantastic* charts a path distinct to works that only associate politics with elected officials and groups concerned with or licensed by the state.[78] It confronts the assumption that art and culture have no place in real politics and that entertainers have no business speaking about politics (or might limit their discussions of politics to manhood politics that violently attacks the Black poor, rejects public displays of introspection, and expresses unambiguous misogyny and homophobia).[79] Rather than limit the notion of politics to the formal realm, it takes seriously the political aspirations and achievements of Black Atlantic cultures in popular cultural forms, protests, riots, and rebellions. In doing so, it participates in an ongoing conversation with Gilroy's early work about politically infused acts of pleasure in joyfully disorganic and "mongrel cultures" in the United Kingdom.[80]

In Search of the Black Fantastic conjoins rhetorical questions about the sources of political legitimacy in the post-civil rights era (Are political scientists, for example, willing and able to consider the politics of the concert stage and the dance floor as well as the polling booth and the protest march?) into nuanced schemas for understanding the changes wrought by technology. It acknowledges those technological innovations of the late twentieth century – synthesizers, programmers, drum machines, samplers – that inform popular music but added qualifying phrases so that gentle readers may reflect on how "the skill barrier – traditionally defined – was lowered" in "*many* [emphasis added] respects." Similarly, it describes "*certain* [emphasis added] forms of sociality that were lost as a result of technological changes and different skill levels of performers" (such as the experiences of musicians playing together in the studio and the expectation and desire to see live and spontaneous performances).[81] Responding to the accelerated rhythms and the visual surplus of the post–post–civil rights generation, but writing before the attention granted to Black Twitter and syllabi created to address state violence against Black citizens in cities such as Ferguson and Baltimore, it acknowledges the status and privilege granted to Black cultural forms that were deemed most immediate (with live comedy and music at the summit, followed by recorded forms of comedy and music, music videos, vernacular theatre, television, film, literature, and dance).[82]

Although Iton's monograph focuses on Black cultural politics in the United States, it is consistently alive to the generative possibilities of diasporic analysis. While providing caveats that diasporic politics were not inherently progressive, *In Search of the Black Fantastic* extensively explores the progressive possibilities of diasporic thought that inspire Black "space traitors" – women and men who pursue activities that overflow, undermine, and dislocate national boundaries. Iton explicates how transnational movements and actors committed to the non-existence or perpetual instability and vulnerability of liberation movements in Haiti,

Liberia, and Ethiopia have made the nation-state as an organizational mechanism appear "intrinsically anti-black." He not only demonstrates how bourgeois subjects in the overdeveloped world come to consider White nationalisms natural and unremarkable (at least when they are, in our contemporary conjuncture, glossed with multicultural sheen) – he also reveals how such ideologies and discourses result in Black nationalisms appearing "egregious, schizophrenic, constitutively absurd, tragic, territorialized, and to some extent performative, given the real impossibility of black autonomous states along the classical lines of the modern projects that were unveiled in the eighteenth and nineteenth centuries."[83] In short, Iton invites conversation between studies of diaspora, Indigeneity, coloniality, and Afropessimism. He demonstrates how diasporic cultural politics can make legible, audible, and visible a range of discourses and experiences that, when separated from one another, disarticulated, and read and struggled against in isolation, may not be recognized.

Coda: Structures of Feeling in the Black Atlantic

The coda to this chapter considers how we might use Iton's interest in the specific dimensions of nostalgia for the post–civil rights period to articulate points of comparison between Clarke and Gilroy. Just as earlier sections worked to outline the connections between Clarke and Walcott, which unsettle the emphasis placed on their points of contention, I end by connecting Clarke (b. 1960) and Gilroy (b. 1956) to the structures of feeling of a diasporic generation that came of age carefully listening to Black musicians who crisscrossed the Atlantic in the late 1960s and the early 1970s. Although Raymond Williams initially used the term "structure of feeling" to describe nascent or ephemeral thoughts and feelings within a British context (in contradistinction to a more formal concept of ideology that is used to describe a more fixed and fully articulated way of looking at the world), it has acquired quite discrepant and even contrary meanings over time and across space. For example, Gilroy uses "structures of feeling" and "zones of feeling" to describe the "inner dialectics of diaspora identification," and Jonathan Flatley uses the concept to refer to a mediating structure "that facilitates and shapes our affective attachment to different objects in the social order" and is as durable and permanent as ideology, perhaps even more so.[84]

One of the key motifs of *The Black Atlantic* is its interest in the deliberative democracy of oral cultures that place a premium on call and response or the ethics of antiphony.[85] Such an emphasis on cultural and political exchange that enlarges our understanding of public spheres may be connected to Gilroy's structures of feeling as a music critic and "young soul rebel" writing about African American and Caribbean expressive cultures for radical magazines and journals in London during the 1980s. It also speaks to his zones of feeling as a Black Atlantic intellectual in the 1990s and 2000s who began to perceive his generational identity as a "curse" and an "affliction" and, after fruitless quests to find Black record stores close to Yale University, pronounced the death of the transatlantic musical culture that had brought him to America.[86] Since leaving his full-time position as professor of African American studies at Yale in 2005, he has mourned the de-skilling and debasement of Black music and come to believe that he has been "identified as an outsider and shut out from African American political thought and culture."[87] He is not particularly melancholic about this expulsion, since he has entered into a structure of relation in Europe in which he is hailed as the most influential intellectual writing in the United Kingdom and regularly invited to contribute to the opinion pages of liberal newspapers, join panel discussions on the BBC, and serve as a consultant to British museums and art galleries.[88] In a panel discussion at the Convention on Modern Liberty in London in 2009, Gilroy was asked to consider what works of art have moved our rights and liberties forward. He responded by reciting the poetry of Shelley, and recalling a treasured memory of listening to Bob Marley singing "Get Up, Stand Up" in a pub on Fulham Road. Marley's ability to misappropriate the UN Declaration of Human Rights, and to put it in the hands of ordinary people, made him an exemplary figure for Gilroy's ideas about vernacular intellectuals and responsible troubadours. The act of listening to Marley in a communal setting is also important to an intellectual who fashions himself as a member of a "diasporic generation" that came of age in a "rare period" in which they carefully listened to a "glorious parade of black Atlantic performers" in live concerts – as well as at underground raves, in record stores, and on pirate radio stations – who conquered commodified cultures with their "rebel spirit."[89]

Clarke may have found it more difficult to access funk and reggae concerts in Nova Scotia than Gilroy did in London, but his search for a Black fantastic was also inspired by African American musicians like George Clinton and visits to Montreal to see James Brown perform live.[90] Clarke also shares Gilroy's respect for scholars like Lawrence Levine, who took the value of Black vernacular culture seriously without taking the words of Black creative artists too seriously or literally,[91] and confesses that his time at Duke University in the 1990s helped him to discover that African America is more or less as "self-absorbed" as the American mainstream (even though he has also defined African American Blackness as internationalist).[92] Such reflections remind us that neither Clarke nor Gilroy can be easily slotted into discussions that describe a "post–civil rights generation" as the "children of Harold Cruse" without mentioning the xenophobia and anti-Caribbean rhetoric that Cruse demonstrated in *The Crisis of the Negro Intellectual*.[93] Clarke's vision of globally informed, Canada-centric research and Gilroy's commitment to planetary humanism are both informed by a "Bandung generation" of anti-colonial activist-intellectuals from African and Asian nations. Their work also endeavours to say something of value to "post-Bandung" generations that must battle historical amnesia, culturally produced ignorance, and American cultural imperialism.[94]

Many readers of Gilroy's work will not need reminding that his general or abstract comments about overdevelopment and liberal governmentality can productively be applied to the Canadian state. Nor that the attempts to elaborate specific descriptions of Black Canada – in which scholars speak of a society where the dominant European identity "lives with the insecurity of being the child of a once powerful empire and the cousin to the existing superpower, but it is also related to being squeezed between Caribbean and African American intellectual traditions" – are not unique to Canada and may also be applied to Black British cultures.[95] Nevertheless, his suggestive, provocative, and explorative remarks about Canadians selling "multicultural snake oil" to the world, in a panel discussion that reflected on Tate Britain's "Artist and Empire" exhibition in November 2015, may be helpful for more literal-minded readers who wish to translate the work of British or American theorists to address a Canadian context.[96] They were delivered a few weeks after Justin Trudeau's well-known quip that gender parity in his cabinet was the right and obvious thing to do "because it's 2015" and provide a pointed rejoinder to teleological comments from the newly appointed Liberal prime minister about historical progress bending toward justice.[97] That is to say, Gilroy's evocative metaphor reminds us to attend to the radical imaginations of anti-colonial intellectuals and troubadours who shaped the 1960s and continue to unsettle our understanding of linear progress. Reminding readers about a "changing same" of racism and racial hierarchy in an age of digital reproduction, Gilroy invites us to consider Fanon and other anti-colonial theorists in the twentieth century as contemporaries for activist-intellectuals seeking to provide some content and cutting edge to resistance to ongoing struggles against forms of "progressive neoliberalism" that merge entrepreneurial fantasy and managerial technique, identity politics and market-driven policies, and the mystique of meritocracy and the allure of technocratic expertise.[98] Rather than offer journalists oversimplified material with which to pontificate about globalized "anywheres" against localized "somewheres," or limit their discussions of diversity and intersectionality to non-White individuals who are invited to enter into privileged elites in North America or Europe, Gilroy's unabashed utopianism and planetary humanism draw attention to the universality and legitimacy accorded to subjects who are framed as multicultural *national* citizens in the Global North in relation to both multicultural world citizens and purportedly "monocultural" Others (in, for example, stereotypical representations of Arab terrorists, Muslim extremists, or Indigenous radicals).[99]

Writers who draw on Gilroy and other diasporic thinkers to address the political, intellectual, aesthetic, and activist work done within, across, and outside the Canadian state unsettle the idea that the nation is the only frame of meaning.[100] They suggest the possibilities of a mode of Black Canadian thought that "resists provincialism and parochialism" and the state of closure and security accorded to national citizenship, to the passport, and to the social insurance card.[101] They communicate the political and moral intelligence of sojourners, residents, and citizens of Canada who examine connections between slavery, racial violence, and Black creativity in, say, Montreal, Boston, and Bristol (rather than speak in an oversimplified manner about Canada, the United States, and the United Kingdom). They invite us to scrutinize the mutually enabling categories of nation and diaspora with deep thought and feeling. If we read and reread them with care, we may have more powerful tools to contest the rather unconvincing depictions of healthy, self-regulating Canadian citizens that veil the violence of settler colonialism.

NOTES

This chapter benefited from the generous and insightful comments of colleagues in Indigenous and Canadian studies at Carleton University, the Harriet Tubman Institute for Research on Africa and Its Diasporas at York University, and beyond. I'd particularly like to thank Funké Aladejebi, Henry Daniel, Rebecca Dolgoy, Jurek Elzanowski, William Felepchuk, Michele A Johnson, Ajay Parasram, and Peter Thompson for reading and commenting on drafts of this chapter; they should not necessarily be associated with its arguments and certainly not with its faults.

1 *A Newcomer's Introduction to Canada* (Ottawa: Minister of Public Works and Government Services Canada, 1997), 67, 69.
2 *Newcomer's Introduction*, 10.
3 In a critical discourse analysis of the 2002 edition of the *Newcomer's Introduction to Canada*, researchers interpreted over half of the images in the text as representing non-White individuals. These depictions included representations of Black women in professional positions as doctors and teachers, although the images associated with law and the state tended to be White (e.g., police officers and customs and immigration officials). Shauna

Wilton, "Official Literature for New Canadians: Images and Perceptions of Canada," in *Canada from the Outside In: New Trends in Canadian Studies*, ed. P. Anctil & Z. Bernd (Brussels: Peter Lang, 2006), 233–46.

4 Daniel McNeil, "Even Canadians Find It a Bit Boring: A Report on the Banality of Multiculturalism," *Canadian Journal of Communication* 46, no. 3 (2021): 403–29.

5 Canada, Department of Supply and Services, *Equality Now! Report of the Special Committee on Visible Minorities in Canadian Society* (Ottawa: Minister of Supply and Services, 1984).

6 On elitism in Canada, see, for example, George Elliott Clarke, "An Anatomy of the Originality of African-Canadian Thought," *C.L.R. James Journal* 20, no. 1–2 (2014): 74; Peter James Hudson and David Austin, "Research, Repression, and Revolution – On Montreal and the Black Radical Tradition: An Interview with David Austin," *C.L.R. James Journal* 20, no. 1–2 (2014): 202; and McNeil, "Even Canadians Find." Much more can be said about how this elitism is manifested in the Canadian public sphere and in articles that introduce evidence from an "acclaimed" or "award-winning" author, or a professor from an elite university, as trusted and beyond reproach, rather than something to be debated by ordinary people who do not need an intellectual vanguard to tell them what to do or how to think. For more on the perils of Black intellectuals who seek to harmonize "the interests of the black poor and working class with those of the black professional-managerial class," see Kenneth Warren, Adolph Reed Jr., Cedric Johnson, Touré F. Reed, Preston Smith II, and Willie Legette, "On the End(s) of Black Politics," nonsite.org, September 16, 2016, n.p., https://nonsite.org/on-the-ends-of-black-politics/.

7 Donna Bailey Nurse, introduction to *Revival: An Anthology of Black Canadian Writing*, ed. Donna Bailey Nurse (Toronto: McLelland & Stewart, 2006), xviii.

8 George Elliott Clarke defines the African-Canadian activist, artist, and intellectual as "a citizen of the African Diaspora, *with a Canadian passport* [emphasis added] and a polyphonous consciousness, and a multicultural, multiracial set of global affiliations." Clarke, "Anatomy," 77. Clarke's earlier definitions of "African Canadian" claimed sojourners and residents "located in or derived from Canada." Clarke, *Odysseys Home: Mapping African-Canadian Literature* (Toronto: University of Toronto Press, 2002), 17n1.

9 Hudson and Austin, "Research, Repression, and Revolution," 228. For more on Canadian multiculturalism and recognition, see, for example, Richard Day, *Multiculturalism and the History of Canadian Diversity* (Toronto: University of Toronto Press, 1999); Himani Bannerji, *The Dark Side of the Nation: Essays on Multiculturalism, Nationalism and Gender* (Toronto: Canadian Scholars, 2000); Eva Mackey, *The House of Difference: Cultural Politics and*

National Identity in Canada (Toronto: University of Toronto Press, 2002); Sunera Thobani, *Exalted Subjects: Studies in the Making of Race and Nation in Canada* (Toronto: University of Toronto Press, 2007); May Chazan, Lisa Helps, Anna Stanley, and Sonali Thakkar, eds., *Home and Native Land: Unsettling Multiculturalism in Canada* (Toronto: Between the Lines, 2011); and Glen Sean Coulthard, *Red Skin, White Masks: Rejecting the Colonial Politics of Recognition* (Minneapolis: University of Minnesota Press, 2014).

10 David Austin, *Fear of a Black Nation: Race, Sex, and Security in Sixties Montreal* (Toronto: Between the Lines, 2013), 36.

11 Richard Iton, *In Search of the Black Fantastic: Politics and Popular Culture in the Post–Civil Rights Era* (Oxford: Oxford University Press, 2008), 201–2.

12 Bernard Boxill, "Two Traditions in African American Political Philosophy," *Philosophical Forum* 24, no. 1–3 (1992–3): 119–35.

13 Peter James Hudson and Aaron Kamugisha, "On Black Canadian Thought," *C.L.R. James Journal* 20, no. 1–2 (2014): 8.

14 Hudson and Kamugisha, 8.

15 Paul Gilroy, *The Black Atlantic: Modernity and Double Consciousness* (London: Verso, 1993), 248n30.

16 Hudson and Kamugisha, "On Black Canadian Thought," 4, 8.

17 Hudson and Kamugisha, 10.

18 Hudson and Kamugisha, 7, 11. See also Sylvia Wynter, "On Disenchanting Discourse: 'Minority' Literary Criticism and Beyond," *Cultural Critique* 7 (1987): 207n3; and Katherine McKittrick, ed., *Sylvia Wynter: On Being Human as Praxis* (Durham: Duke University Press, 2014).

19 Hudson and Kamugisha, "On Black Canadian Thought," 10.

20 Hudson and Kamugisha, 7.

21 Clarke and Walcott have both discussed intersections between Black and Indigenous communities that may feel alienated from the Canadian nation in their scholarship. In *Odysseys Home: Mapping African-Canadian literature*, Clarke reflects on his Mi'kmaq ancestry and the significance of the Charter of Rights and Freedoms in making Canada the first nation to constitutionally recognize racially mixed people (the Métis people of Canada), albeit within the category of Aboriginal peoples. Walcott discusses Black "out of placeness" in relation to Indigeneity and settler colonialism in, for example, "The Problem of the Human: Black Ontologies and 'the Coloniality of Our Being,'" in *Postcoloniality-Decoloniality-Black Critique: Joints and Fissures*, ed. Sabine Broeck and Carsten Junker (Frankfurt: Campus, 2014), 93–105.

22 George Elliott Clarke, review of *Black Like Who? Writing Black Canada*, by Rinaldo Walcott, *University of Toronto Quarterly* 68, no. 1 (1998): 401–2; Clarke, *Odysseys Home*, 202; Rinaldo Walcott, "Rhetorics of Blackness,

Rhetorics of Belonging: The Politics of Representation in Black Canadian Expressive Culture," *Canadian Review of American Studies* 29, no. 2 (1999): 1–24; Walcott, "Introduction to the Second Edition," in *Black Like Who?*, 11–23.

23 Richard Almonte, "Must a Black Text Always Be Written by a Black Author? Race, Authorship, Ethics, and the Plays of Andrew Moodie and George F. Walker," *Essays on Canadian Writing* 75 (2002): 142.

24 Peter Hudson, "Honkey Night in Canada," *Transition*, no. 96 (2008): 78.

25 Hudson and Kamugisha, "On Black Canadian Thought," 8.

26 Clarke, *Odysseys Home*, 21n12, 13, 230; George Elliott Clarke, "A Comparative Study of the Development of English Canadian and African American Poetry and Poetics" (PhD diss., Queen's University, 1993), ii.

27 Clarke, *Odysseys Home*, 64.

28 George Elliott Clarke, "Cool Politics: Styles in Honour of Malcolm X and Miles Davis," *Jouvert* 2, no. 1 (1998), https://legacy.chass.ncsu.edu/jouvert/v2i1/CLARKE.HTM; Clarke, *Odysseys Home*, 27.

29 Clarke, *Odysseys Home*, 14.

30 Clarke, 13, 201–2.

31 Lewis Gordon, "Black Intellectual Tradition," in *Encyclopedia of American Studies*, ed. Simon J. Bronner (Baltimore: Johns Hopkins University Press, 2018), http://eas-ref.press.jhu.edu/view?aid=780.

32 Gilroy, *Black Atlantic*, 47.

33 Gilroy, 168, 42. For further examples of Gilroy's critical opposition to "timid academics" and "scholasticism," see Paul Gilroy, *Darker Than Blue: On the Moral Economies of Black Atlantic Culture* (Cambridge, MA: Harvard University Press, 2010), 73, 162; and Gilroy, "Fanon and Amery: Theory, Torture and the Prospect of Humanism," *Theory, Culture & Society* 27, no. 7–8 (2010): 17.

34 Laura Chrisman, "Journeying to Death: Gilroy's Black Atlantic," *Race & Class* 39, no. 2 (1997): 51.

35 Chrisman, 55.

36 Gilroy, *Black Atlantic*, 47; Gilroy in "A Dialogue on the Human: An Interview with Paul Gilroy," ed. Rebecka Rutledge Fisher and Jay Garcia, in *Retrieving the Human: Reading Paul Gilroy*, ed. Fisher and Garcia (New York: SUNY Press, 2014), 207–8.

37 Chrisman, "Journeying to Death," 54.

38 "It bears repetition" is frequently used as a signpost in *The Black Atlantic* (see, for example, pp. 105, 155, 172, and 218). The text also uses similar phrases such as "as we have already seen" (169), "it merits repeating" (223) and "it is worth emphasising that part of the overall argument of the book" (197) to signpost its argument to an academic audience. For other examples of this academic "tic," see Paul Gilroy, "Exer(or)cising Power: Black Bodies in the Black Public Sphere," in *Dance in the*

City, ed. Helen Thomas (London: Palgrave Macmillan, 1997), 24, 32; *Against Race: Imagining Political Culture beyond the Color Line* (Cambridge, MA: Harvard University Press, 2000) 59, 165, 196, 237; "After the Great White Error ... the Great Black Mirage," in *Race, Nature, and the Politics of Difference*, ed. Donald S. Moore, Jake Kosek and Anand Pandian (Durham: Duke University Press, 2003), 90; *Darker Than Blue*, 30, 33, 71, 77, 82, 137; "Shameful History: The Social Life of Races and the Postcolonial Archive," *Moving Worlds: A Journal of Transcultural Writing* 11, no. 2 (2011): 25, 30; and "'My Britain Is Fuck All': Zombie Multiculturalism and the Race Politics of Citizenship," *Identities* 19, no. 4 (2012): 384.
39 Lucy Evans, "The Black Atlantic: Exploring Gilroy's Legacy," *Atlantic Studies* 6, no. 2 (2009): 251.
40 Gilroy, *Black Atlantic*, 33. See also Paul Gilroy, "Nationalism, History and Ethnic Absolutism," in *History Workshop Journal* 30, no. 1 (1990): 114–20; "Diaspora," *Paragraph* 17, no. 3 (1994): 207–12; and "Diaspora and the Detours of Identity," in *Identity and Difference*, ed. Kath Woodward (London: SAGE, 1997), 301–46.
41 Gilroy, *Black Atlantic*, 10, 12, 120, 188. See also Paul Gilroy, *Small Acts: Thoughts on the Politics of Black Cultures* (London: Serpent's Tail, 1993), 191.
42 Gilroy, *Black Atlantic*, 2, 29.
43 Gilroy, 80, 211.
44 Gilroy, *Against Race*, 131.
45 Gilroy, "Nationalism," 118–19.
46 Edward Said, *Representations of the Intellectual* (New York: Vintage, 1996), 83.
47 Gilroy, *Black Atlantic*, 230n1, 230n3, 236n27. See also Gilroy in "Dialogue on the Human," 209.
48 Paul Gilroy, "Travelling Theorist," *New Statesman & Society*, 12 February 1993.
49 Raymond Williams and Edward Said, "Media, Margins and Modernity," in *The Politics of Modernism: Against the New Conformists*, by Raymond Williams (London: Verso, 1989): 196–7.
50 Gilroy, *Black Atlantic*, 85
51 See, for example, Peggy Bristow, coord., *"We're Rooted Here and They Can't Pull Us Up": Essays in African Canadian Women's History* (Toronto: University of Toronto Press, 1994); Charmaine Nelson, ed., *Ebony Roots, Northern Soil: Perspectives on Blackness in Canada* (Newcastle upon Tyne: Cambridge Scholars Press, 2010); and Nina Reid-Maroney, Boulou Ebanda de B'béri, and Wanda Thomas Bernard, eds., *Women in the "Promised Land": Essays in African Canadian History* (Toronto: Women's Press, 2018).
52 Gilroy, *Small Acts*, 234.
53 Gilroy, *Black Atlantic*, 103; *Against Race*, 3. 188, 205; *Darker Than Blue*, 128.
54 Gilroy, *Small Acts*, 190–1; *Black Atlantic*, 96.
55 Gilroy in "Dialogue on the Human," 208.

56 Gilroy, *Black Atlantic*, 34, 79.
57 Gilroy, *Small Acts*, 196, 208–36; see also *Black Atlantic*, 194.
58 Gilroy, *Black Atlantic*, 10, 12, 120, 188; see also *Small Acts*, 191.
59 Gilroy, *Black Atlantic*, 164–5; "Dialogue on the Human," 211, 214.
60 Raymond Williams, *The Long Revolution* (London: Chatto & Windus, 1961), 64.
61 Paul Gilroy, "Cultural Studies and Ethnic Absolutism," in *Cultural Studies*, ed. Lawrence Grossberg, Cary Nelson, and Paula A. Treichler (London: Routledge, 1992), 195; Gilroy, *Black Atlantic*, 256. There is also one reference to Chatham, Ontario, and one to Windsor, Ontario.
62 Gilroy, *Black Atlantic*, 23.
63 Richard Wright to Carl Van Vechten, letter, June 21, 1945, and postcard, n.d. [summer 1945], Carl Van Vechten papers, Beinecke Library, Yale University; Robin W. Winks, *The Blacks in Canada: A History*, 2nd ed. (Montreal and Kingston: McGill-Queen's University Press, 1997), 462–3.
64 Gilroy, *Black Atlantic*, 151, 154.
65 Clarke, *Odysseys Home*, 8.
66 Clarke, 10.
67 Clarke, 12.
68 Clarke, 62–3n2.
69 Clarke, 64n3. In *Odysseys Home*, Clarke deploys "sic" – to denote a word that appears odd or erroneous but is being quoted exactly as it stands in the original – on over sixty occasions.
70 Evans, "Exploring Gilroy's Legacy," 263.
71 Clarke, *Odysseys Home*, 49; Gilroy, *Black Atlantic*, 32.
72 Clarke, *Odysseys Home*, 39.
73 Clarke, 69n38, 82.
74 Rinaldo Walcott, *Black Like Who? Writing Black Canada* (Toronto: Insomniac, 2003), 19, 26.
75 Aimé Césaire, *Discourse on Colonialism* (New York: Monthly Review Press, 1955).
76 Walcott, *Black Like Who?*, 158n2, 23.
77 Walcott, 31.
78 Iton, *Black Fantastic*, 11.
79 Iton, 104, 110, 175, 203.
80 Paul Gilroy, "There's a Riot Going On," *Emergency* 1, no. 2 (1983–4): 56–60; Gilroy, *"There Ain't No Black in the Union Jack": The Cultural Politics of Race and Nation* (London: Unwin Hyman, 1987); Gilroy, *Black Atlantic*, 3.
81 Iton, *Black Fantastic*, 119.
82 Iton, 121.
83 Iton, 196–7.

84 Gilroy, *Black Atlantic*, 3, 23, 77; Jonathan Flatley, *Affective Mapping: Melancholia and the Politics of Modernism* (Cambridge, MA: Harvard University Press, 2009), 25–6.
85 Gilroy, *Black Atlantic*, 69.
86 Paul Gilroy, "Analogs of Mourning, Mourning the Analog," in *Stars Don't Stand Still in the Sky: Music and Myth*, ed. Karen Kelly and Evelyn McDonnell (New York: Press, 1999) 262; Gilroy, *Against Race*, 2; *Black Atlantic*, 109.
87 Gilroy in "Dialogue on the Human," 210.
88 Colin MacCabe, "Paul Gilroy: Against the Grain," *openDemocracy*, 19 April 2006, https://www.opendemocracy.net/en/gilroy_3465jsp/.
89 Gilroy, *Darker Than Blue*, 122; Gilroy, *Black Britain: A Photographic History* (London: Saqi, 2007), 236, 248; Gilroy, *"There Ain't No Black,"* 199.
90 Clarke, *Odysseys Home*, 266; George Elliott Clarke, afterword to *Burnley "Rocky" Jones: Revolutionary: An Autobiography*, by Burnley "Rocky" Jones and James W. St. G. Walker (Halifax: Roseway, 2016).
91 Gilroy, "After the Love Has Gone," 68; Clarke, *Odysseys Home*, 11–13, 19n7; Lawrence Levine, *Black Culture and Black Consciousness: Afro-American Folk Thought from Slavery to Freedom* (New York: Oxford University Press, 1978).
92 Clarke, *Odysseys Home*, 5, 50, 266.
93 Cruse is claimed as the intellectual father for a post–civil rights generation in Mark Anthony Neal, *Soul Babies: Black Popular Culture and the Post-Soul Aesthetic* (London: Routledge, 2002). Some implications of this US-centric approach are evident in Neal's analysis of R Kelly, which liberally borrows from the insights on biopolitics in Gilroy's *Against Race* but chooses to only cite a Chicago-born informant – rather than acknowledge Gilroy's planetary humanism – in its endnotes (pp. 17, 197n43). Revealingly, Neal's *Looking for Leroy* also reveals the pitfalls of national consciousness as it seeks to map the diverse and cosmopolitan roles chosen by African American musicians, directors, and actors without a concomitant interest in the creative artistry of non-American members of the African diaspora. The text devotes a chapter to the career of the African American actor Avery Brooks, for example, but does not mention the non-American work of the Black British actor Idris Elba in a chapter that focuses exclusively on the fictional African American character Elba portrayed on HBO's *The Wire*. Mark Anthony Neal, *Looking for Leroy: Illegible Black Masculinities* (New York: New York University Press, 2013). On Cruse's xenophobia, see Winston James, *Holding Aloft the Banner of Ethiopia* (New York: Verso, 1998), 262–91.
94 Gilroy, *Black Atlantic*, 101; Clarke, *Odysseys Home*, 7, 184.
95 Hudson and Austin, "Research, Repression, and Revolution," 228.
96 Annie Coombs (chair), Paul Gilroy, Zareer Masani, and Ruth Phillips, "Plenary Panel: Reflection," Artist and Empire: The Long Nineteenth

Century, Tate Britain and the School of Arts at Birkbeck University of London, November 25, 2015. An audio recording of the panel is available at https://backdoorbroadcasting.net/2015/11/artist-and-empire-the-long-nineteenth-century/.
97 Fred Chartrand, "Trudeau's 'Because It's 2015' Retort Draws International Attention," *Globe and Mail*, November 5, 2015.
98 Jackson Lears, "One Hundred Seconds," *Raritan* 40, no. 1 (2020): ii–v.
99 Jodi Melamed, "The Spirit of Neoliberalism: From Racial Liberalism to Neoliberal Multiculturalism," *Social Text* 24, no. 4 (89) (2006): 18.
100 Iton, *Black Fantastic*, 198.
101 Iton, 198; Hudson and Kamugisha, "On Black Canadian Thought," 11.

Contributors

Wendell Nii Laryea Adjetey is an assistant professor of post-Reconstruction US history at McGill University. Broadly, his research and writing excavate freedom linkages among the United States, Canada, and the African diaspora. Adjetey earned an MA, MPhil, and PhD from Yale University.

Anna Ainsworth is a professor at Seneca College in the School of English and Liberal Studies. Her work has been in the fields of critical race studies, migration studies, gender and politics, and Canadian multiculturalism. She has published work in the collections *Africa in the Age of Globalisation* (2015) and *Today's Youth and Mental Health* (2018).

Funké Aladejebi is an assistant professor of history at the University of Toronto. She is the author of *Schooling the System: A History of Black Women Teachers* (2021), which explores the intersections of race, gender, and access in Canadian educational institutions. Her research interests are in oral history, the history of education in Canada, Black feminist thought, and transnationalism. Her current research projects can be found at www.funkealadejebi.com.

Adam Arenson is a professor of history and director of the urban studies program at Manhattan College. His work considers the importance of regional identity and borders in North American politics and culture. He is the author of *The Great Heart of the Republic: St. Louis and the Cultural Civil War* (2011) and co-editor of *Civil War Wests: Testing the Limits of the United States* (2015) and *Frontier Cities: Encounters at the Crossroads of Empire* (2013). For more about his past works and current projects, see adamarenson.com.

Jenna Bailey is an adjunct assistant professor in the Department of History at the University of Lethbridge and a senior research fellow at the Centre for Oral History and Tradition (COHT) at the University of Lethbridge. She is an oral historian and documentary filmmaker who has worked on numerous community oral history projects including the multi-award-winning Shiloh Centre for Multicultural Roots Project and the Coyote Flats Pioneer Village project, both of which won the Governor General's History Award for Excellence in Community Programming (2015, 2018). Jenna is also the author of the bestselling book *Can Any Mother Help Me?* (2007).

Claudine Bonner is a scholar of African diaspora history and education and a member of the Department of Sociology and the Women's and Gender Studies Program at Acadia University in Nova Scotia. Her research is grounded in history and broadly applied in analyses of race, gender, education, and identity in contemporary Canada. Her scholarship bridges the gap between studies of the Black Canadian experience and the broader African diaspora. Bonner's current research explores early twentieth-century Caribbean migration to eastern Canada, and the pan-Africanist connections between communities.

Gillian Creese is Associate Dean of Arts, Faculty, and a professor in the Department of Sociology and the Institute for Gender, Race, Sexuality and Social Justice at the University of British Columbia. Her research interests include migration, racialization, and gender; equity issues in work and trade unions; and feminist research methods. Her most recent book is *Where Are You From? Growing Up African-Canadian in Vancouver* (2020).

Julie Crooks is curator, Arts of Global Africa and the Diaspora, at the Art Gallery of Ontario, where she has curated the exhibitions "Mickalene Thomas: Femmes Noires" (2018), "*Free* Black North" (2017), and "Women in Focus Collection Rotations" (2017–ongoing). Prior to joining the AGO in 2017, Crooks curated exhibitions for many organizations including BAND (Black Artists Networks in Dialogue) and the Royal Ontario Museum's *Of Africa* project. She holds a PhD from the Department of History of Art and Archaeology at the School of Oriental and African Studies (SOAS), University of London. Crooks's area of specialty is art of Africa and the diaspora.

David Este is a professor in the Faculty of Social Work at the University of Calgary. He specializes in the areas of health and well-being of people of African descent, the settlement of immigrants and refugees, and mental health. He has published in journals such as *International Journal of Culture and Mental Health*, *Ethnicity and Health*, *Journal of Black Studies*, and *Canadian Social Work Review*. He is co-author of *Race and Well-Being: The Lives, Hopes, and Activism of African Canadians* (2010) and lead editor of *Race and Anti-Racism in Canada* (2018).

Amoaba Gooden is an associate professor of Pan-African studies at Kent State University. Her ongoing research includes the study of African Canadian organizing, leadership, and community building. She is the editor of "Constructing Black Canada: Becoming Canadian," a special edition of the *Southern Journal of Canadian Studies*. Her publications can be found in *African Canadian Leadership: Perspectives on Continuity, Transition and Transformation*, *S'TENISTOLW: Moving Forward in Indigenous Higher Education*, *Journal of Black Studies*, *Journal of Pan-African Studies*, *Wagadu: Journal of Transnational Women's and Gender Studies*, and *Canadian Woman Studies*.

Sylvia D. Hamilton is a Nova Scotian writer, filmmaker, and artist whose recognitions include a Gemini Award, the Portia White Prize, and honorary degrees. Her films include *Black Mother Black Daughter*, *Portia White: Think on Me*, and *The Little Black School House*, among others. Her poetry collection, *And I Alone Escaped to Tell You* (2014), was shortlisted for several major awards. Her multimedia installation, "Here We Are Here," has shown at galleries and museums in Nova Scotia, New Brunswick, Ontario, and Quebec. She is the recipient of the 2019 Governor General's Award in History (Popular Media) and is an Inglis Professor at the University of King's College in Halifax.

Natasha Henry is a PhD candidate in the Department of History at York University. The 2018 Vanier Scholar is researching the enslavement of African people in early Ontario. Natasha is the president of the Ontario Black History Society. Her publications include *Emancipation Day: Celebrating Freedom in Canada* (2010), *Talking about Freedom: Celebrating Freedom in Canada* (2012), and several entries on African Canadian history in the *Canadian Encyclopedia*. Through her various professional, academic, and community roles, Natasha's work is grounded in her commitment to research, collect, preserve, and disseminate the histories of Black Canadians.

Carl E. James holds the Jean Augustine Chair in Education, Community and Diaspora at York University, Toronto, where he teaches in the Faculty of Education and in the graduate programs in Sociology, and Social and Political Thought. His research interests include examinations of the schooling experiences, educational performance, employment opportunities, career trajectories, and social achievements of Black youth. His recent publications include *Colour Matters: Essays on the Experiences, Education and Pursuits of Black Youth* (2021).

Michele A. Johnson is a professor in the Department of History, York University, and teaches a variety of courses at both the undergraduate and graduate levels that focus on Black people in the Americas. Johnson's research interests focus on issues of race/racialization, gender relations, labour, and cultural productions/performances and have resulted in a variety of publications in areas of Caribbean cultural and social history as well as domestic service in Jamaica and Canada.

Deirdre McCorkindale is a PhD candidate in history at Queen's University. Her area of study is the history of race in North America, specializing in African American and African Canadian history. Her current research concerns the nature of education and intelligence testing in southwestern Ontario.

Daniel McNeil is a professor and Queen's National Scholar Chair in Black Studies at Queen's University. His teaching and scholarship bring together history, diaspora studies, cultural studies, and cognate fields of inquiry to explore the complexities of global Black communities in the twentieth and twenty-first centuries. He is the author of *Sex and Race in the Black Atlantic* (2010) and co-editor of *Migration and Stereotypes in Performance and Culture* (2020). *Thinking While Black*, his book about the political aspirations and cultural achievements of soul rebels, Black Atlantic intellectuals, and planetary humanists over the past fifty years, will be published in 2022.

Sean Mills is a professor and Canada Research Chair in Canadian and Transnational History at the University of Toronto. He is the author of two prize-winning books, *The Empire Within: Postcolonial Thought and Political Activism in Sixties Montreal* (2010) and *A Place in the Sun: Haiti, Haitians, and the Remaking of Quebec* (2016). Mills is also co-editor of *New World Coming: The Sixties and the Shaping of Global Consciousness* (2009) and *Canada and the Third World: Overlapping Histories* (2016).

Winfried Siemerling is University Research Chair and professor of English at the University of Waterloo and an associate of the W.E.B. Du Bois Institute at Harvard. He won the Gabrielle Roy Prize for *The*

Black Atlantic Reconsidered (2015; companion website blackatlantic.ca). Earlier books include *Canada and Its Americas* (2010; co-edited) and *The New North American Studies* (2005). He has contributed to *The Oxford Handbook of the African American Slave Narrative* (2014), *The Cambridge History of Postcolonial Literature* (2012), and *African American Literature in Transition 1750–2015* (2021). He was elected to the Royal Society of Canada in 2019.

Karolyn Smardz Frost is an archaeologist and historian specializing in African Canadian and African American transnationalism. An adjunct professor at Acadia and Dalhousie Universities, Karolyn is a former Harriet Tubman Institute Senior Research Fellow, York University, and in 2012–13 served as Bicentennial Visiting Professor at Yale. Her 2007 volume *I've Got a Home in Glory Land: A Lost Tale of the Underground Railroad* won the Governor General's Award for Non-fiction; she is co-author of *The Underground Railroad: Next Stop, Toronto!* (2002) and co-editor of *The Archaeology Education Handbook* (2000), *Ontario's African-Canadian Past* (2008), and *A Fluid Frontier: Slavery, Resistance and the Underground Railroad in the Detroit River Borderland* (2016). Her most recent volume, *Steal Away Home* (2017), tells the story of fifteen-year-old Cecelia Jane Reynolds, who arranged her own flight to freedom in 1846.

Cheryl Thompson is an assistant professor in the School of Creative Industries at Ryerson University. Her research focuses on histories of racial performance, the critical study of media and advertising, and the intersections of gender, class, and power. Her work has appeared in *Emergent Feminisms: Challenging a Post-Feminist Media Culture* (2018), *Journal of Canadian Studies*, *Canadian Journal of History/Annales canadiennes d'histoire*, *Feminist Media Studies*, and *Fashion Studies*. Her books include *Beauty in a Box: Detangling the Roots of Canada's Black Beauty Culture* (2019) and *Uncle: Race, Nostalgia and the Politics of Loyalty* (2021).

Now retired, **Esmeralda M.A. Thornhill** is a Simone de Beauvoir Institute research associate. Lawyer, linguist, and pedagogue *by training*, lecturer, researcher, anti-racism trainer, and writer *by experience*, long-time social justice advocate and community organizer *by conviction*, she is a founding member of the Congress of Black Women of Canada. In 1983 she conceptualized and taught the first ever university-accredited course on Black Women's Studies offered in Canada (Concordia). When Dalhousie University selected her to inaugurate the James Robinson Johnston Endowed Chair in Black Canadian Studies (1996–2002), she became the first African Canadian woman to hold a tenured full professorship of law in Canada (1996–2016). Author of multiple reports, briefs, depositions, essays, and articles, her edited volumes include *Blacks in Canada: Retrospects, Introspects, Prospects* (2008), and *Racism ... Talking Out* (1993). Her writings appear in, notably, *Canadian Bar Review, Canadian Journal of Women and Law, Alberta Law Review, Revue québécoise de droit international, Le Devoir*, the *Chronicle Herald* (Nova Scotia), *Journal of Intergroup Relations*, and *US Congressional Record*.

Barrington Walker is associate vice president, Equity, Diversity and Inclusion, and professor, Department of History, at Wilfrid Laurier University. He is the author and editor of several books, including *Race On Trial: Black Defendants in Ontario Criminal Courts 1858–1958* (2010). He also the author of one forthcoming book.

Paul Watkins is a professor of English at Vancouver Island University (VIU). He is also a research team member with the International Institute for Critical Studies in Improvisation (IICSI). At VIU, he is the artistic director of the "Writers on Campus" (Nanaimo) series. He has published widely on multiculturalism, hip-hop, sound studies, Canadian poetry, jazz, and DJ culture, and he co-edited a special issue of *Critical Studies in Improvisation* focused on improvisation and hip-hop. He is currently working on a book manuscript that explores sound and music in Black Canadian poetics. See pauldbwatkins.com.

www.ingramcontent.com/pod-product-compliance
Lightning Source LLC
Chambersburg PA
CBHW052005070526
44584CB00016B/1624